The Economic and Social History of Brazil since 1889

FRANCISCO VIDAL LUNA
Universidade de São Paulo

HERBERT S. KLEIN
Columbia University and Stanford University

CAMBRIDGE
UNIVERSITY PRESS

CAMBRIDGE
UNIVERSITY PRESS

32 Avenue of the Americas, New York, NY 10013-2473, USA

Cambridge University Press is part of the University of Cambridge.

It furthers the University's mission by disseminating knowledge in the pursuit of education, learning, and research at the highest international levels of excellence.

www.cambridge.org
Information on this title: www.cambridge.org/9781107616585

© Francisco Vidal Luna and Herbert S. Klein 2014

This publication is in copyright. Subject to statutory exception and to the provisions of relevant collective licensing agreements, no reproduction of any part may take place without the written permission of Cambridge University Press.

First published 2014

A catalog record for this publication is available from the British Library.

Library of Congress Cataloging in Publication Data
Luna, Francisco Vidal, author.
The economic and social history of Brazil since 1889 / Francisco Vidal Luna, Herbert S. Klein.
  pages cm
Includes bibliographical references and index.
ISBN 978-1-107-04250-6 (hardback)
1. Brazil – Economic conditions – 1918– 2. Brazil – Economic policy.
3. Brazil – Social conditions – 1889– 4. Brazil – Social policy.
5. Brazil – Politics and government – 1889– I. Klein, Herbert S., author.
II. Title.
HC187.L836 2014
330.981–dc23   2013028539

ISBN 978-1-107-04250-6 Hardback
ISBN 978-1-107-61658-5 Paperback

Cambridge University Press has no responsibility for the persistence or accuracy of URLs for external or third-party Internet Web sites referred to in this publication and does not guarantee that any content on such Web sites is, or will remain, accurate or appropriate.

The Economic and Social History of Brazil since 1889

This is the first complete economic and social history of Brazil in the modern period in any language. It provides a detailed analysis of the evolution of the Brazilian society and economy from the end of the empire in 1889 to the present day. The authors elucidate the basic trends that have defined modern Brazilian society and economy. In this period Brazil moved from being a mostly rural traditional agriculture society with only light industry and low levels of human capital to a modern literate and industrial nation. It has also transformed itself into one of the world's most important agricultural exporters. How and why this occurred is explained in this important survey.

Francisco Vidal Luna received his PhD in Economics in 1980 from the Universidade de São Paulo in São Paulo, Brazil, where he also was Professor of Economics until 2002. Author of some 50 articles and papers and 11 books on Brazilian economic history and the Brazilian economy, he has been an academic, a government administrator, and a banker.

Herbert S. Klein received his PhD from the University of Chicago in 1963 and is Gouveneur Morris Professor Emeritus of History at Columbia University. Author of some 25 books and 165 articles in several languages on Latin America and on comparative themes in social and economic history, he is currently a Research Fellow and Latin American Curator at Stanford University's Hoover Institution.

To Adela Luna Campuzano de Vidal and Bernette Rudolph

Contents

List of Graphs, Tables, and Maps	*page* vi
Introduction	xv
1 The Old Republic, 1889–1930	1
2 The Vargas Period, 1930–1945	82
3 Formative Democracies and the Military Interregnum, 1945–1985	143
4 Consolidation of Democracy since 1985	246
Appendix	355
Bibliography	391
Index	421

List of Graphs, Tables, and Maps

Graphs

1.1. Population of Latin American Countries in 1850 (000) *page* 3
1.2. Population of Latin American Countries in 1900 (000) 4
1.3. World and Brazilian Coffee Production, 1852–1991 7
1.4. Importance of São Paulo and Rio de Janeiro in Brazilian Coffee Production, 1884–1939 14
1.5. Coffee-Producing Regions of São Paulo, 1836–1935 (in arrobas) 15
1.6a. Coffee: Prices and the Value of Exports of Brazil, 1857–1906 17
1.6b. Coffee Prices and Production in Brazil, 1857–1906 18
1.7. Growth of per Capita Income, 1800/1989 22
1.8. Total Fertility Rate, 1903–1988 23
1.9. Crude Death Rates for Brazil, 1900–1995 23
1.10. Net Primary School Enrollments by State, 1889–1933 28
1.11. Population of the Principal Capitals of Brazil, 1872–1920 (000) 29
1.12. Percentage of Population by Region, 1872–1920 31
1.13. Estimates of the Balance of Payments, 1886/1897 38
1.14. Exchange Rate and Accumulated Cost-of-Living Index, 1887–1906 39
1.15a. Index of Exchange, Prices, and Coffee Exports, 1898–1920 43
1.15b. Index Coffee: Plantings, Production, and Stocks in Brazil, 1898–1920 43
1.15c. Percentage of Brazilian Production and Exports to World Production and Exports, 1898–1920 43

vi

List of Graphs, Tables and Maps   vii

1.15d. Coffee: World Stocks, World Consumption, and Stocks, Brazil/Exports Brazil, 1898–1920 — 43
1.16a. Percentage of Brazilian Production and Exportation of Coffee, 1920–1940 — 50
1.16b. Percentage of World Consumption and Brazilian Exports, 1920–1940 — 50
1.16c. Index of Plantings and Production and Total Stocks of Coffee, 1920–1940 — 50
1.16d. Index of Exchange Rate, Coffee Price, and Exports, 1920–1939 — 50
1.17. Participation of Principal Exports in Total Exports, 1821/1939 — 51
1.18a. Production and Exports of Sugar, 1858–1927 — 54
1.18b. Average Price of Sugar Exports, 1857–1937 — 54
1.18c. World Cane Production as Percentage of Total World Cane and Beet Sugar Production, 1839–1939 — 54
1.18d. Brazilian Sugar Production and Exports by World Totals, 1853–1937 — 54
1.19. Index of the Quantity, Value, and Price of Rubber Exports, 1880–1929 — 56
1.20. Cacao, Production, Value, and Quantity Exported, 1890–1938 — 57
1.21a. Crops as Percentage of Total Value of Production, 1920 — 58
1.21b. Crops as Percentage of Total Value of Production, 1930 — 58
1.22. Brazilian Products as a Share of World Production, 1920 — 59
1.23. Expansion of Railroad System, 1854–1938 — 61
1.24a. Machines and Equipment Exported to Brazil, 1875–1938 — 64
1.24b. Investment Indicators, 1902–1939 — 64
1.24c. Composition of Imports, 1901–1938 — 64
1.24d. Production and Importation of Cotton Textiles, 1901–1938 — 64
1.25a. Industrial Production and Workers by States – Census 1907 — 66
1.25b. Textile Industry – Census 1907 — 67
1.25c. Participation in the Importation of Consumer Goods – Census 1907 — 67
1.25d. Participation in the Production of Consumer Goods, 1907 — 67

1.26. Percentage and Number of Principal Industries and
Average Workers per Unit – Census 1920 68
1.27. Evolution of the Real Value of Industrial Production
and the Participation of São Paulo, 1907–1938 69
1.28. Participation in GDP, 1929 74
1.29. Rate of Annual Variation in GDP, Population, Total
Exports, and Coffee Production, 1850–1929 75
2.1. Prices, Production, and Destruction of Coffee and
Brazilian Participation in World Market, 1924–1952 91
2.2. Exports, Imports, and Terms of Trade, 1926–1950 94
2.3. Variation in Real GDP by Economic Sectors,
1926–1947 106
2.4a. Growth of Industry, 1920, 1940, and 1950 108
2.4b. Participation of São Paulo in Industry, 1920, 1940,
and 1950 108
2.5. Participation of Regions and Principal States in
Industry – Census 1940 109
2.6. Industrial Indicators by Sector, 1940 111
2.7a. Establishments by Number of Workers, 1940 111
2.7b. Percentage of All Workers by Size of Establishment,
1940 112
2.8. Participation of Manufacturing Industry in GDP, by
State, 1948 113
2.9. Economically Active Population by Sectors,
1920–1950 115
2.10. Participation in Exports of Principal Agricultural
Products, 1920–1950 116
2.11. Production of Principal Agricultural Products,
1920–1950 117
2.12. Percentage of Value of Production by Major Crops,
1920–1950 118
2.13a. Principal Agricultural Products, Productivity by Area,
1933–1950 119
2.13b. Principal Agricultural Products, Productivity by Area,
1933–1950 119
2.14. Percentage Cultivated Area by State, 1938 and 1947 . . . 122
2.15. Agricultural Indicators, 1940 122
2.16. Gini Index of Landownership – Brazil and Principal
States, 1920–1950 123
2.17. Distribution of Agricultural Indicators by Region and
State, 1940 124
2.18. Foreign Immigration to Brazil by Year, 1884–1945 127

List of Graphs, Tables and Maps

2.19. Relative Importance of Regions in Total Population, 1920, 1940, and 1950 — 128
2.20. Students Matriculated by Course, 1932, 1945 — 129
2.21. Literate Adults 18 Years and Older by Regions – Census of 1920 and 1940 — 131
2.22. Literacy Rate by Sex and Color of the Population Five Years of Age and Older, 1940 — 131
2.23. Literacy by Age Cohort and Sex in the Census of 1940 — 134
2.24. Percentage of Workers Who Were Managers, Employees, and Self-Employed by Color, 1940 ($n = 7.4$ million) — 135
2.25. Distribution of the Population by Color by Region, 1872 — 135
2.26. Distribution of the Population by Color by Region, 1940 — 136
2.27. Infant Mortality by Region, 1930–1940 — 137
2.28. Average Life Expectancy by Sex, 1949/1951 — 138
2.29. Crude Birth Rate for Selected Latin American Countries, 1930 — 139
2.30. Birth Rate by Age of Mother, Brazil, England, and the United States, 1939–1940 — 140
2.31. Birth Rate by Age and Color of the Mother, Brazil, 1940 — 140
3.1. Price of Coffee and Its Role in Exports, 1945–1955 — 148
3.2. Annual Change in GDP, Monetary Base, and Inflation, 1945–1955 — 150
3.3. Investments in the Plano de Metas, 1957/1961 — 161
3.4. Plano de Metas – Forecasted Resources — 165
3.5. Annual Change in Fiscal Deficit, M1, and Inflation, 1950–1964 — 167
3.6. Target Plan – Investments and Foreign Financing — 168
3.7. Industrial Establishments and Employees, 1939–1959 (1939 = 100) (establishments in 1939 = 43,250; workers in 1939 = 851,755) — 170
3.8. Participation in the Value of Industrial Production of the Principal Sectors, 1939–1959 — 171
3.9. Participation in the Total Value of Production, 1920–1960 — 173
3.10. World Production, Consumption, and the Price of Coffee, 1940–1966 — 175
3.11. Brazilian Coffee Production by State and Percent in Exports, 1940–1966 — 175
3.12a. Participation in Exports, 1947 and 1960 — 177

3.12b.	Participation in Imports, 1947 and 1960	177
3.13.	Composition of the Economically Active Population by Sector of Activity, 1920–1960	178
3.14a.	Index of Change in GDP by Sector, 1950–1964 (1957 = 100)	179
3.14b.	Annual Change in GDP and GDP per Capita, 1950–1964	179
3.15a.	Income per Capita – Brazil, Regions, and States, 1960	180
3.15b.	Percentage of GDP by Regions and States, 1960	180
3.16.	Index of Minimum Real Salary, 1960–1977	193
3.17.	Variation in GDP, 1958–1983	197
3.18.	Balance of Trade of Brazil, 1964–1983	200
3.19.	Foreign Debt of Brazil, 1964–1983	201
3.20.	Grain Production in Brazil, 1961–2003 (wheat, cotton, peanuts, rice, beans, corn, and soybeans)	206
3.21.	Annual Variation in the Cost of Living in the City of São Paulo, 1960–1984	208
3.22.	Illiterates by Age and Sex in 1970	225
3.23.	Illiterates by Color and Sex in 1982	226
3.24.	Major States Experiencing Internal Migration by Decade, 1950–1980	227
3.25.	Size of Urban and Rural Populations in Brazil, 1940–1980	228
3.26.	Growth of Population of the Cities of Rio de Janeiro and São Paulo, 1872–1980	229
3.27.	Distribution of Births by Age of Mothers in 1903, 1963, and 1988	233
3.28.	Total Fertility Rate by Region, 1940–1980	234
3.29.	Age Pyramid of the Population of Brazil in 1980	235
3.30.	Age Pyramid of the Population in 1991	235
3.31.	Relative Share of Various Age Categories, Brazil, 1940–1980	236
3.32.	Components of Growth of the Brazilian Population, 1940–1980	237
3.33.	Infant Mortality 1950/1955 to 1980/1985	238
3.34.	Share of Total Mortality by Age Group, 1950/1955 to 1980/1985	239
3.35.	Infant Mortality by Region, 1950–1980	240
3.36.	Life Expectancy at Birth in Brazil, 1950/1955 to 1980/1985	241
3.37.	Life Expectancy at Birth by Region and Sex in 1980	242
3.38.	Annual Geometric Growth Rate of the Population, 1872–2010	242

4.1.	Sarney Government – Average Change in the Monthly Cost of Living, IPCA, 1985–1990	258
4.2.	Variation of Average GDP per Decade, 1960–2000	260
4.3.	Evolution of Rural Credit in Constant Prices, 1969–2010	261
4.4.	Estimates of Government Agricultural Subsidies, 1986–1989	266
4.5a.	Government Storage Loans as Percentage of Production of Major Crops, 1975–1992	267
4.5b.	Government Stock Purchase as Percentage of Production of Major Crops, 1975–1992	267
4.6.	Commercial and Current Transactions Balance of Brazil, 1990–2011	278
4.7.	Monthly Variation in General Price Index (FGV), 1944–2012	280
4.8.	Industrial Source of Funds Collected for Privatization	282
4.9a.	Brazilian Dollar Reserves by Month, 1994–2004	284
4.9b.	Brazilian Dollar Reserves, Annual, 1994–2011	284
4.10a.	Annual Variation in GDP, 1995–2011	291
4.10b.	Growth of BRICs (Brazil, Russian, India, and China), 1995–2011	291
4.11.	Government Revenues (federal and local) as a Percentage of GDP, 1990–2009	293
4.12.	Public-Sector Borrowing Requirements (PSBR), Primary Surplus and Interest Payments, as a Percentage of GDP, 2000–2009	293
4.13.	Exchange Rate, and Effective Exchange, 2000–2012 (effective rate and effective exchange rate)	295
4.14.	Participation in Brazilian Exports, 2000–2011	296
4.15.	Participation of Manufacturing in the GDP, 1995–2011	300
4.16.	Agriculture: Index of Production, Inputs, and Total Factor Productivity, 1970–2006	301
4.17.	Index of Agro-Pastoral Commodity Prices – IC-Br, 2005–2012	303
4.18.	Rate of Investment and Variation in the GDP, 1965–2010	304
4.19.	Rate of Unemployment and Minimum Real Wage, 1994–2012	307
4.20.	Economically Active Population in Metropolitan Regions, 2002–2012	308
4.21.	Birth Rates by Age of Mother, 1980–2000	312

4.22.	Percentage of Economically Active Population by Sex, 1992–2007	313
4.23.	Percentage Distribution of Children Born in 2001 and 2011 by Age of Mothers (PNAD 2001, 2011)	315
4.24.	Total Fertility Rate by Region, 1940–2010	316
4.25.	Projected Growth of the Brazilian Population, 1980–2050 (based on 2008 IBGE projections)	317
4.26.	Crude Birth and Death Rates in Brazil, 1881–2007	318
4.27a.	Infant Mortality Rates by Region, 1997–2008	320
4.27b.	Child Mortality Rates by Region, 2000–2008	320
4.28.	Relative Share of Youths and Aged in Total Population, 1872–2010	324
4.29.	Age Pyramid of the Brazilian Population in 2010	325
4.30.	Evolution of the Percentage of Extremely Poor Households in the States in 1981 with Rates over 30 Percent	331
4.31.	Percentage of Indigent and Poor Families in Brazil, 1977–2004	333
4.32.	Reduction of Poverty for Brazilian Families, 2004 and 2009	334
4.33.	Literacy Rate of Brazilian Population 15 Years of Age and Older, 1900–2010	341
4.34.	Percentage Illiterates by Age by Color/Race, 2010 (15 years of age and older)	342
4.35.	Marriages by Type, 1960–2010	344
4.36.	Heads of Families by Type, 1992–2009	345
4.37.	Gini Index of Inequality in Brazil, 1981–2009	348
4.38.	Average Years of Schooling by Color for Persons 25 Years of Age and Older, 1992–2009	351

Tables

2.1	Agro-Pastoral Establishments, Total Area, and Utilization, 1920–1950	120
2.2	Persons 10 Years of Age and Older Who Have Completed a Course of Studies by Sex and Color, 1940	132
2.3	Students (5 to 39 years of age) Matriculated by Level of Course, Sex, and Color, 1940	133
3.1	Plano de Metas – Sectors, Goals, and Level of Attainment	162
3.2	Productivity of the Principal Agricultural Crops, 1931–1962	172

3.3	Crop Areas, Personnel, Tractors, and Plows Employed by State, 1950–1960	173
3.4	Principal States for Coffee Production, with Area Planted and Output, 1956–1962	176
4.1	Annual Change in GDP of the Principal Latin American Countries, 1980–1989 (%)	260
4.2	Indicators of External Debt, 2007–2011 (U.S. $ million)	297
4.3	Principal Characteristics of Agriculture in the Agropastoral Census of 2006	302
A.1	Basic Data on the Coffee Economy of Brazil, 1870–1990	355
A.2	Economic Indicators for the External Sector, 1870–2011	360
A.3	Economic Indicators for the Internal Sector, 1870–2011	366
A.4	Principal Agricultural Exports, 1821–1939 (in £000)	371
A.5	Principal Agricultural Exports, 1953–2010 (in U.S.$000)	376
A.6	Brazilian Exports by Type of Product, 1964–2011 (in U.S.$ millions FOB)	378
A.7	Value of Industrial Production by States, 1907–1938 (in *contos de réis*)	379
A.8	Annual Indices of Industrial Production by Class and Type of Product, 1971–2000 (1991 = 100)	380
A.9	Distribution of the Population by State and Region in the Demographic Censuses of Brazil, 1872–2010	383
A.10	Origin of Brazilian Transoceanic Immigrants, 1820–1972	384
A.11	Estimate of Brazilian Population Change, 1980–2050, IBGE Projections of 2008	388
A.12	Religion of the Brazilian Population, 1872–2010	390
A.13	Number of Students Enrolled in Higher Education by Type of Institution, 1960–2010	390

Maps

1.1.	Regions of São Paulo, 1900, by Sequence of Settlement	15
1.2.	Regional Distribution of the Brazilian Population in 1872 ($n = 9.9$ million)	30
1.3.	Regional Distribution of the Population in 1920 ($n = 30.6$ million)	31
4.1.	Population by State, 1950	328
4.2.	Population by State, 2010	329

Introduction

Our object in writing this general economic and social history of Brazil since the founding of the republic in 1889 is to provide the reader with the basic trends that have defined modern Brazilian society and economy. There have been previous surveys in Portuguese and other languages covering many aspects of the economic evolution of this major world economy, but there have been few works that have covered this entire period or have surveyed the social transformations that accompanied these major economic changes.

As we will see in this volume, Brazil has had an uneven march toward modernization, often falling behind many of its peer nations and then engaging in protracted periods of growth that suddenly moved the country more in step with international trends. These spurts have left sectors behind in their traditional forms, while revolutionizing other parts of the economy and society in impressive ways. Overall Brazil has moved from a significantly underdeveloped society with a majority rural and illiterate population at the beginning of this period to a modern literate and urbanized society that is a world competitor in the one area in which it was most backward in 1889, that is, in agricultural production.

Not only is Brazil now a literate society where the majority live in modern urban centers, but it is among the half-dozen leading nations in terms of production of science and in providing the best in tertiary education. It has also become a serious industrial nation, though with only modest technical advancement compared to its Asian peers. Finally, it is a model developing society in terms of integrating its population into a national health and pension system through the progressive integration of the national labor force into the formal labor market, the expansion of basic services, and income transfers on a massive scale to its unincorporated population.

There had also been steady improvement in poverty reduction in general and extreme poverty in particular, both of which have been reduced to historic lows. Although Brazil remains one of the world's more unequal societies in terms of income distribution, in the past two decades there has been a massive increase in the share of the working and middle classes within the total population with a resulting historic decline in inequality.

It is our aim to show how the economy and society of one of the world's largest countries has evolved and the causes and consequences of these changes over time. Given the differing pace of economic and social changes, we have found that a division of chapters that parallels long-term political changes is the most adequate way to divide this study. Finally, given that the state has been such an important actor in all of these social and economic institutions and their evolution, we have also provided a basic political history to orient the reader in the role that the state has played in these developments.

In writing this work we have tried to explain any special terminology to the reader the first time we use it. We have also translated the names of most institutions into English, although we have retained the Portuguese initials used to name these organizations. At the same time we have provided a full citation to the Portuguese title the first time it was used. We have also used "external" interchangeably here as a synonym for "international" when referring to economic conditions.

This book is based on a collaboration of the two authors over many years of joint research and publications, and we would both like to thank Matiko Kume Vidal and Judith C. Schiffner for their encouragement and support throughout these many years.

1

The Old Republic, 1889–1930

Brazil was first visited by the Portuguese in 1500 and initially attracted temporary traders who exchanged European goods with the Indians for Brazil wood, which was used as a dye in Europe. This symmetrical relation changed when the Portuguese decided to permanently settle this American territory. This decision, unusual in the evolution of Portuguese imperial expansion, was based on the need to defend itself against European rivals. Portugal's undeveloped American possession had become a base for North European attacks on its Asian trade routes, which passed through the South Atlantic. Having a small population in relation to its overseas imperial obligations Portugal preferred to establish small commercial settlements, or factories, and accompanying forts in order to dominate international trade, rather than relying on settler colonies to sustain its imperial system. But in the case of Brazil it had to opt for the second alternative, and using a feudal mechanism left over from the wars with Moslem Spain, it initially divided up its American colony in captaincies that were given to private entrepreneurs. But this system eventually failed and the government was forced to transform Brazil into a settler colony.

Like all the European colonizers of the New World who followed the Spanish, the Portuguese had to obtain a product that was exportable to Europe in order to sustain the colonial enterprise. Without precious metals, the Portuguese only had access to Indian slave labor and had to develop new products acceptable to the European market. The solution was the establishment of a slave-based plantation economy producing cane sugar, a product that the Portuguese had already developed in their Atlantic islands in the fifteenth century. First using captured Indian slave labor, by 1600 the plantations of Brazil were already being manned by African slave labor brought by Portuguese slavers from West Africa. By the middle of the sixteenth century, Brazil had become the world's largest producer of cane sugar, and the industry provided the funds necessary for the Portuguese to maintain their continental possession in the New World.

The settlement of Brazil occurred in distinct phases. In the first phase the economy and population were concentrated on the northeastern coast. It was here that the sugar plantation economy was first developed on a major scale, and this region continued to dominate the colonial economy and the world sugar market for more than a century. A second center of settlement quickly developed in the southeastern region around the port of Rio de Janeiro and its hinterland and at the coastal ports to the south and in the interior zone around what would become the current city of São Paulo. Here a frontier culture developed with whites, mestizos (*caboclos*), and Indians; and this population sustained the raiding expeditions carried out in the unexplored western and southern interior. It was these raiders known as *bandeirantes*, who in the late seventeenth and early eighteenth centuries discovered gold and diamonds in this hinterland. Brazil then entered an intensive mining phase in areas now belonging to the states of Goiás, Mato Grosso, and Minas Gerais. In the latter region the wealth of the alluvial gold deposits drew Africans and Portuguese in large numbers, and there rapidly evolved a mosaic of major interior urban centers, among them such mining cities as Ouro Preto, Mariana, and Diamantina. The mining activity peaked in the mid-eighteenth century, which led to a long-term decline in what had now become the most populous region of the colony.

But the growth of sugar in the hinterland of Rio de Janeiro and in the highlands near São Paulo counterbalanced the decline of mining and also helped to shift the center of population and economic activity to the southeastern region. This shift was recognized by the Crown, which moved the viceregal capital from Salvador de Bahia to Rio de Janeiro in 1763. It was further enhanced with the royal support of a military expansion to the borders of the Rio de la Plata by the end of the eighteenth century.

But with the growth of the French and English Caribbean plantation economies in the eighteenth century, the relative importance of Brazilian sugar declined on the international market. Nevertheless, Brazil was still a major exporter to southern Europe and the sugar economy sustained the growth of the southeastern as well as northeastern regions. The arrival of

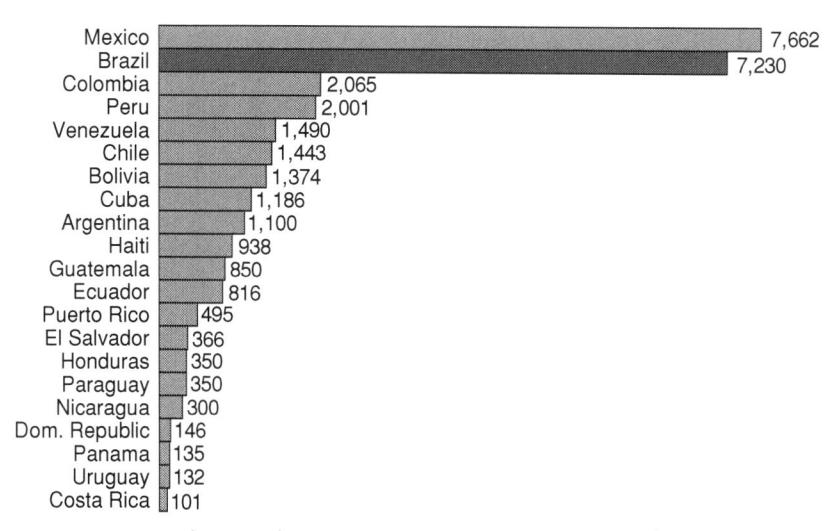

Country	Population
Mexico	7,662
Brazil	7,230
Colombia	2,065
Peru	2,001
Venezuela	1,490
Chile	1,443
Bolivia	1,374
Cuba	1,186
Argentina	1,100
Haiti	938
Guatemala	850
Ecuador	816
Puerto Rico	495
El Salvador	366
Honduras	350
Paraguay	350
Nicaragua	300
Dom. Republic	146
Panama	135
Uruguay	132
Costa Rica	101

GRAPH 1.1. Population of Latin American Countries in 1850 (000). *Source*: Sánchez-Albornoz 1986

coffee as a new slave plantation crop began in earnest in the late colonial and early imperial period. Moreover, it was in the southeastern region where this slave plantation economy would be centered, and it was to this region that several million African slaves arrived in the period up to 1850.

The continued dynamism of Brazil from sugar and gold cycles through the coffee boom led to the massive introduction of African slaves over the three centuries of colonial settlement. At the same time there was the steady migration of Portuguese immigrants, and in turn there developed a large and racially complex free class of ex-slaves, their descendants, and mixed populations of Indian ancestry. Given the land resources and benign climate, mortality remained stable while fertility in and outside of marriage was high by European standards. Given these fairly high rates of immigration and natural increase, the Brazilian population grew at significant rates by the nineteenth century, and by the second half of the nineteenth century Brazil had replaced Mexico as the largest nation in Latin America (see Graphs 1.1 and 1.2). Its urban centers were growing rapidly, population was increasing at unprecedented rates, and people were settling its open frontier in all parts of the nation. It had already absorbed more African slaves than any other single region in the Americas to 1850, and with the end of slavery in 1888 it was able to attract a comparable number of free European immigrants. It was one of the few

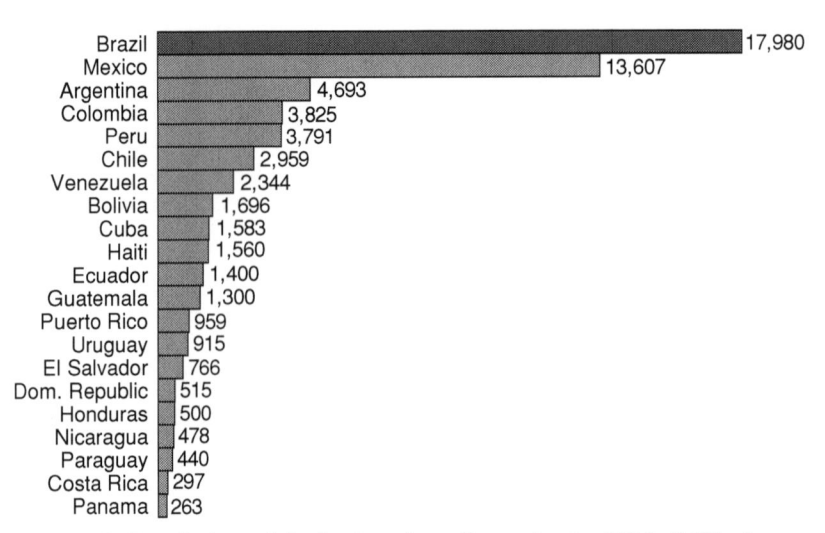

Country	Population
Brazil	17,980
Mexico	13,607
Argentina	4,693
Colombia	3,825
Peru	3,791
Chile	2,959
Venezuela	2,344
Bolivia	1,696
Cuba	1,583
Haiti	1,560
Ecuador	1,400
Guatemala	1,300
Puerto Rico	959
Uruguay	915
El Salvador	766
Dom. Republic	515
Honduras	500
Nicaragua	478
Paraguay	440
Costa Rica	297
Panama	263

GRAPH 1.2. Population of Latin American Countries in 1900 (000). *Source*: Sánchez-Albornoz 1986

Latin American states able to compete with the North American countries in taking a share of the great European transatlantic migration of the late nineteenth and early twentieth centuries.

But in many other ways, Brazil was like the less dynamic societies of the region, primarily in terms of the quality of life and the human capital of its population. Its people lived predominantly in the rural areas until the last quarter of the nineteenth century, and they were overwhelmingly illiterate. Even compared to some of the poorer South American countries, Brazil educated a surprisingly small percentage of its citizens. In terms of mortality, Brazilians experienced more deaths per resident population than the Rio de la Plata countries, and in this was more like the less advanced states of the region. Because of these high death rates, Brazilians had an extremely low life expectancy at birth only comparable to the poorest regions of Europe and the Americas, and again well behind its neighbors to the south. It was only in its especially high fertility that it was comparable to all the other nations of the region. Given its traditions of slavery and large land grants in the colonial period, it was a highly stratified society and in this differed little from the other nations of the continent. There were the usual sharp differences between urban and rural; more advanced and less advanced regions; and the wealthy and the poor. But because of the massive forced immigration of Africans there were also social divisions based on race that were typical of the United

States and the more Amerindian societies of the continent. Brazil thus entered the republican period as an expanding but highly stratified and still fairly backward nation in terms of its sociodemographic indices.

The two most negative of such indices were those of mortality and literacy. The high levels of poverty and lack of infrastructure in the areas of health and sanitation meant that in 1872 an estimated 39 percent of those born alive died before their fifth birthday and the average life expectancy at birth was only in the upper twenties for males and females. This was probably still the average life expectancy in 1900 when 37 percent of newborns died before their fifth birthday.[1] It took another two decades for the infant and child deaths to fall to 33 percent of all live births and life expectancy at birth to finally reach the lower thirties for men and women, a figure long passed by the most advanced states in the hemisphere.[2] It has been estimated that the crude death rate was 31 to 32 deaths per thousand resident population in the late nineteenth century, and still an estimated 29 deaths per thousand residents in 1900.[3]

Along with this high mortality Brazil was experiencing very high levels of fertility, which fueled its high rate of natural growth. It has been estimated that in 1903 the average number of children being born for women in the cohort 14 to 49 years of age was seven children.[4] This meant that the crude birth rate was something like 46 to 47 births per thousand resident population, which was well above the crude death rate.[5] This difference guaranteed that the population was growing at a very impressive 2.3 percent in the last quarter of the nineteenth century and

---

[1] In contrast, it has been estimated that in 1905, life expectancy in Argentina, probably the best in Latin America, already reached 39.4 for men and 40.7 years for women – a good 10 to 15 years more than in Brazil at this time. Zulma Recchini de Lattes and Alfredo E. Lattes, eds., *La Población de Argentina* (Buenos Aires: C.I.C.R.E.D. Series, 1974), 49 CUADRO 2.7.

[2] Eduardo E. Arriaga, *New Life Tables for Latin American Populations in the Nineteenth and Twentieth Centuries*, Population Monograph Series, No. 3 (Berkeley: University of California, 1968), 29–35, Tables III-3–III-6.

[3] The first estimate comes from Giorgio Mortara, "The Development and Structure of Brazil's Population," *Population Studies* 8,2 (November 1954), 122, and the second from Elza Berquó, "Demographic Evolution of the Brazilian Population during the Twentieth Century," in *Population Change in Brazil: Contemporary Perspectives*, ed. David Joseph Hogan (Campinas: UNICAMP, 2001), 15, Table 2. Mortara estimated the crude death rate at 31 to 32 per thousand resident population.

[4] Cláudia Júlia Guimarães Horta, José Alberto Magno de Carvalho, and Luís Armando de Medeiros Frias, "Recomposição da fecundidade por geração para Brasil e regiões: atualização e revisão." Paper presented at Anais do ABEP 2000, Table 6.

[5] Mortara, "The Development and Structure of Brazil's Population," 122.

up to 2.9 percent per annum by the period 1900–1910.[6] Few countries in the world in the nineteenth century grew as rapidly as did Brazil. On average Brazil was growing at 2.3 percent per annum for the century after 1870, which meant that the population was doubling every thirty years.[7]

Despite the never-ending expansion into the western and southern frontiers, the population of Brazil was still highly concentrated even into the nineteenth century. The majority of the people lived along the Atlantic coastline, with most of the interior space being lightly populated and consisting primarily of forest and grasslands. But much of this would change in the last quarter of the nineteenth century as the railroads and the coffee plantations moved westward to open the interior to settlement. The expansion of coffee production in the second quarter of the nineteenth century provided Brazil with a new international export whose demand systematically grew through increasing adoption of coffee drinking by a growing and ever more urban and richer population in the advanced countries of the world. Given Brazil's exceptional physical conditions for coffee cultivation, the country quickly assumed the position of world leader in the supply of this product, and was easily capable of increasing production adequately to respond to changing demand conditions. For more than sixty years coffee was produced with slave labor, but at the end of the nineteenth century there occurred a transition to free wage labor based on the participation of European and Asian immigrants. The concentration of coffee production in the axis formed by the states of Rio de Janeiro, São Paulo, and Minas Gerais gave to this region an economic and political supremacy within the nation that was unquestionably maintained until 1930.

Along with the substitution of slaves by free wage workers in 1888, the monarchy was replaced by a republic a year later and the São Paulo state emerged as the leading economic center of the country. As coffee production moved west from the Paraíba Valley, which spanned the two states of Rio de Janeiro and São Paulo, to the interior of the state of São Paulo, this movement finally pushed São Paulo into a leadership position within the national economy. Finally, the emergence of the republic, although a peaceful transition, represented a fundamental reorganization of the locus of national power that shifted from a centralized state to

---

[6] Mortara, "The Development and Structure of Brazil's Population," 122; and Berquó, "Demographic Evolution of the Brazilian Population," 13, Table 1.

[7] Thomas W. Merrick and Douglas H Graham, *Population and Economic Development in Brazil: 1800 to the Present* (Baltimore, MD: Johns Hopkins University Press, 1979), 30–31.

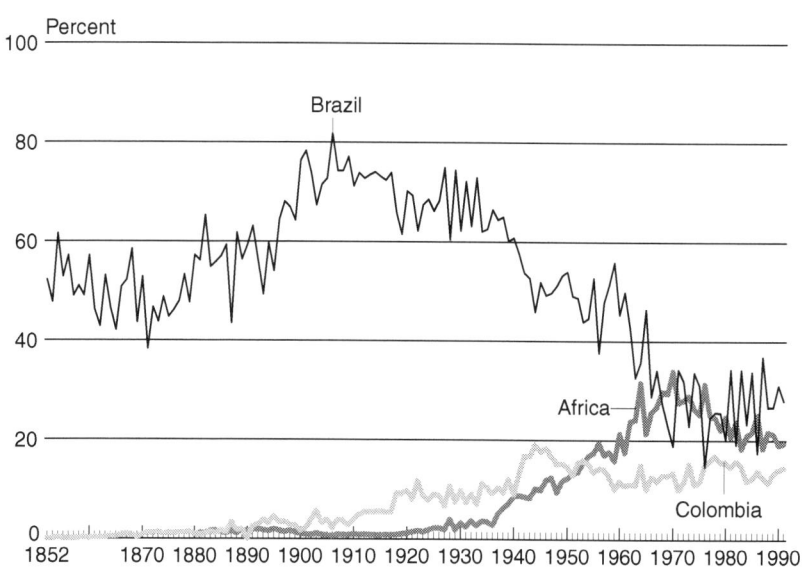

GRAPH 1.3. World and Brazilian Coffee Production, 1852–1991. *Source*: Bacha 1992

a more federal one and the emergence of new regional political actors who would consolidate their position throughout the period of the Old Republic.

Many of these changes accompanied the evolution of coffee production. Initial expansion had occurred in the Paraíba Valley, first in the part pertaining to Rio de Janeiro in the region of Vassouras.[8] Coffee plantations then moved north and west into the region called the *zona de mata* in the southwestern part of the province of Minas Gerais and the areas around the counties (or *municípios*) of Areias and Bananal in the northeastern part of the province of São Paulo. In this first period of coffee expansion, the Paraíba Valley was the world's single-largest producer of coffee. By 1850 Brazil accounted for half of world production, and coffee in turn accounted for half the value of national exports. Moreover, as world demand increased Brazilian coffee production expanded at an even faster pace, and in the last five years of the century Brazil accounted for 70 percent of world production (see Graph 1.3 and Appendix Table A.1).

Labor was the principal factor limiting the expansion of coffee given the availability of land in the Paraiba Valley and later in the interior of São

---

[8] On the history of coffee in Vassouras and its region see Stanley J. Stein, *Vassouras, a Brazilian Coffee County, 1850–1900* (Cambridge, MA: Harvard University Press, 1957).

Paulo in what is called the Old or Traditional West region.[9] Thus the end of the slave trade in 1850 put at risk the expansion of coffee. Given this scarcity of labor there was a natural movement of slaves drawn toward the most economically productive economic cultivation. The result was that the coffee regions steadily increased their share of slaves after 1850. The steady flow of northern and northeastern slaves to the southern region reached such a dimension, particularly for new areas of production in São Paulo, that the state put a tax on slaves entering the state. It was feared that the concentration of slaves in only some states would reduce political support in favor of slavery in the nation as a whole.[10]

Planters as early as the 1850s began to experiment with using salaried European workers in the coffee fields. The new coffee plantations of the western zone were the most threatened by the scarcity of labor, and it was in this very region that the first tentative uses of European immigrant labor were tried. But these initial attempts failed as free workers did not accept the wages provided and were not willing to work alongside slaves.[11] But slowly the São Paulo government sought a permanent solution to the labor problem as it was evident that slavery would soon be abolished. This would mean some form of government subsidization was needed to attract free laborers. In 1871 the state passed a law that

[9] The traditional West Paulista region encompasses the municipalities of Campinas, Jundiaí, Piracicaba, Itu, Mogi Guaçu, and Mogi Mirim, which in the second quarter of the nineteenth century contained São Paulo's sugar industry.
[10] The northeastern region, the traditional sugar-producing center, had a significant slave population allocated in economic activities of low economic value, compared with coffee. On the interregional flow of slaves, see José Flávio Motta, "Escravos daqui, dali e de mais além: o tráfico interno de escravos em Constituição (Piracicaba), 1861–1880," *Revista Brasileira de História* 26,52 (2006), 15–47; José Flávio Motta and Renato L. Marcondes, "O comércio de escravos no Vale do Paraíba paulista: Guaratinguetá e Silveiras na década de 1870," *Estudos Econômicos* 30,2 (Abril–Junho 2000), 267–299; Ana Rosa Cloclet da Silva, "Tráfico interprovincial de escravos e seus impactos na concentração da população da província de São Paulo: século XIX" (VIII Encontro da ABEP, Associação Nacional de Estudos Populacionais, 1992).
[11] In 1852 Senador Vergueiro, a planter from West Paulista, brought a group of immigrants to his Fazenda Ibicaba; the conflicts that occurred with the immigrants ended the initiative. On the theme of immigration, see Pierre Monbeig, *Pioneiros e Fazendeiros de São Paulo* (São Paulo: Hucitec-Polis, 1984); Thomas H. Holloway, *Immigrants on the Land: Coffee and Society in São Paulo, 1886–1934* (Chapel Hill: University of North Carolina Press, 1980); Thomaz Davatz, *Memórias de um colono no Brasil (1850)* (Belo Horizonte: Itatiaia; São Paulo: Ed. Universidade de São Paulo, 1980); Warren Dean, *Rio Claro: A Brazilian Plantation System, 1820–1920* (Stanford, CA: Stanford University Press, 1976); Pedro Carvalho de Mello, "The Economics of Labor in Brazilian Coffee Plantations, 1850–1888 (PhD thesis, Department of Economics, University of Chicago, 1977).

authorized the emission of bonds to help planters finance the bringing to Brazil of European agricultural immigrant workers.[12] In that same year a group of paulista entrepreneurs formed the Association to Aid Colonization and Immigration (*Associação Auxiliadora de Colonização e Imigração*), with the object of bringing in immigrants to work in the coffee estates. It was also in 1871 that the Law of Free Birth was enacted, which signaled the future demise of slave labor since it declared all children born to slave mothers would be free as of 1872. Until the 1880s most of these efforts at supplanting slave workers with immigrants were quite limited, but a new phase began with the establishment of the *Hospedaria dos Imigrantes* in the city of São Paulo in 1881, which was a government-sponsored residence and labor exchange that funneled immigrants into interior plantations. The law that created this important institution stipulated that immigrants would be reimbursed for their rail transport from the port of Santos to the capital, as well as the difference in the cost of a passage between Europe and Brazil and Europe and the United States.[13] The need to resolve the labor question became acute as the slave labor system began to fall apart in the decade of the 1880s with the increasing volume of runaway slaves and local communities declaring themselves havens for escaped slaves. In 1884, under pressure from the coffee growers, the government of the state of São Paulo assumed the entire cost of the travel of all immigrants from Europe to the farms of São Paulo. This financial reimbursement was made directly to the head of the immigrant family.[14] It was this law that definitely established the basis for a massive introduction of European immigrants to São Paulo. The formal abolition of slavery in 1888 removed the last obstacle. Until the late 1880s, the very survival of slavery limited the intensification of European immigration. The coexistence of the two labor systems was conflictive and some countries banned the immigration of their nationals to Brazil, a ban that would last as long as slavery. With the abolition of slavery, and the creation of a legal and institutional structure in São Paulo to support

---

[12] Law 42 of 30 March 1871 authorized the provincial government to issue bonds to "help the farmers of the Province that wanted to have settlers come to their farms, as colonos...." The aid would be granted "for the payment of travel and other expenses which each colono had until they arrived at the establishment of the rural farmer that had solicited them." The aid would be repaid in eleven years. Available at http://www.al.sp.gov.br/portal/site/Internet/.

[13] Law 123 of 16 July 1881. The law permitted the immigrants to remain in the *Hospedaria* for a maximum of eight days. Available at http://www.al.sp.gov.br/portal/site/Internet/.

[14] Law 28 of 29 March 1884. Available at http://www.al.sp.gov.br/portal/site/Internet/.

immigration, and with state financial support, there now occurred a massive flow of European immigration to the state. Between 1827 and 1884, only 37,000 foreign immigrants had arrived in São Paulo, but in the decade after 1884 half a million immigrants reached the state. Of the 2.3 million immigrants who came to São Paulo between 1887 and 1928, half were subsidized by the government. Although other states received immigrants in this same period, the majority went to São Paulo.[15] Thus despite the progressive dismantling and final abolition of slavery in the decade of the 1880s, there was no discontinuity in the production of coffee.

In this new free labor era, the West Paulista region became the hegemonic producer of coffee within Brazil. The movement of coffee toward the West Paulista plains was initiated in the 1870s as a result of land exhaustion and limitation in the Paraiba Valley. The paulista western zone and other newly evolving areas of the state were developed on virgin lands with high soil productivity and local planters were more open to experimenting with new labor regimes. In contrast, the lower productivity coffee plantations of the Paraiba Valley went into decline and were no longer competitive without slave labor.

Free labor required a new labor organization in coffee. The immigrants – usually called *"colonos"* – were not involved in the planting of new coffee trees, which was normally done by contractors. In turn, these contractors were partially paid by allowing them to produce other crops among the newly planted coffee trees while they were maturing.[16] In the case of the *colonos*, their remuneration was either as sharecroppers or salaried workers paid to care for a fixed number of trees. In the first case, the plantation owners and the *colonos* assumed the risks associated with the production and sale of coffee. In the second case, the *colono* had a part of his remuneration fixed, depending on the quantity of coffee trees under his responsibility and another parcel that varied with the size of the plantation. Normally *colonos* also had the right to plant subsistence crops among the coffee trees or in open fields. This right to produce subsistence crops was essential to attract immigrant labor. In the West Paulista and other new plantation regions, this was the predominant

---

[15] *Anuário Estatístico do Brasil* (hereafter cited as AEB) (1939–1940): 1307. In São Paulo, in 1890, there were 57 foreign born for every 1,000 inhabitants; the average for Brazil was only 25. In 1920 this difference was repeated. In São Paulo there were 259 foreign born to 1,000 residents, compared to only 73 per 1,000 average for Brazil (AEB, 1939–1940, 1302).
[16] Rogério Naques Faleiros, *Fronteiras do Café* (São Paulo: Fapesp-Edusc, 2010).

form of remuneration for these farmworkers involving salaries and land to plant their own crops. In the older coffee zones such as the Paraiba Valley, sharecropping was the norm since it required less capital from the owner and lowered his risks.

Along with labor, the other obstacle to the expansion of coffee production was transport. From the middle of the nineteenth century the necessity of creating an efficient rail transportation system to ship coffee to the coast was recognized as a fundamental necessity. The traditional system of transporting the crop by mules created high costs and limited the potential expansion of the system.[17] The first attempts to construct a railroad system in Brazil preceded the development of the coffee industry. In 1835 a government attempt to link a railroad from the capital of Rio de Janeiro south to the state of Rio Grande do Sul was a failure because of a lack of private capital. A second major project in 1838 to link the port of Santos with the sugar regions of Campinas and Piracicaba also failed.[18] These first frustrated projects involved government concessions of zones of exclusion along the railroad lines. But this exclusivity was not sufficient to guarantee the economic viability of the enterprises. The solution came in 1853 when the government guaranteed interest on the funds invested in railroad construction.[19] The *Estrada de Ferro D. Pedro II*, which went from Rio de Janeiro to Cachoeira in the state of São Paulo, was the first railroad to be successfully built. Along with granting an exclusive control over the length of the railroad line, the state guaranteed a return of 7 percent to investors, of which 2 percent came from the provincial

---

[17] On the mule transport system see Herbert S. Klein, "The Supply of Mules to Central Brazil: The Sorocaba Market, 1825–1880," *Agricultural History* 64,4 (Fall 1990), 1–25.

[18] The port of Santos is located approximately 60 kilometers (km) from São Paulo. Thus the routes between the city of São Paulo – which is 700 meters above sea level – and the port of Santos had to overcome a steep obstacle between the plateau and the coast. The railroad from Santos to São Paulo, which would be essential for the economic expansion of the state of São Paulo, represented a complex and expensive engineering project.

[19] Subsidies were essential since private financiers feared that their profits would prove insufficient. William R. Summerhill, *Order against Progress: Government, Foreign Investment, and Railroads in Brazil, 1854–1913* (Stanford, CA: Stanford University Press, 2003), 40. According to Anne Hanley, "Railroads and utilities followed a second route for attracting investors: government guarantees. These companies benefited from explicit or implicit government backing against failure. The railroads built during the 1870–1890s all received profit guarantees from the government for the explicit purpose of attracting investors." Anne G. Hanley, *Native Capital: Financial Institutions and Economic Development in São Paulo, Brazil, 1850–1920* (Stanford, CA: Stanford University Press, 2005), 74.

government of Rio de Janeiro. By 1865 the line reached Vassouras, but only arrived in Cachoeira ten years later.[20] The railroad served the coffee region of the Paraiba Valley, permitting the export of coffee to the port of Rio de Janeiro.[21]

The São Paulo coffee zones continued to rely on mule transport to reach their natural export port of Santos until the 1860s. But in 1867 the São Paulo Railway was inaugurated which connected Santos to the city of Jundiaí. This was the traditional entrance to the West Paulista region. The English company that built the railroad had the same guarantee of 7 percent return on its investment.[22] Now the pace increased everywhere in Brazil with the most concentration of railroad lines occurring in the province of São Paulo. Using local planter and foreign capital, a complex railroad network was created that spread through the interior of the province and even reached the unexplored backlands.[23] The railroads permitted the exploitation of lands of exceptional quality, particularly apt for coffee cultivation. Thus the second half of the century resolved the two crucial blockages that limited the expansion of coffee: the insufficiency of labor and the lack of a cheap transport system.[24]

The rail network that was being gradually deployed concentrated mainly in the coffee-producing region of São Paulo, Rio de Janeiro,

---

[20] Adolpho Augusto Pinto, *História da viação pública de São Paulo* (São Paulo: Governo do Estado de São Paulo, 1977), 21–31. The route between Rio de Janeiro and Vassouras was 122 km; between Rio de Janeiro and the paulista city of Cachoeira it was 265 km.

[21] According to Summerhill there was an essential difference in the policy of subsidies in Brazil and the United States. In Brazil the majority of subsidies were provided by the central government, while in the United States it was the states who offered these subsidies. Summerhill, *Order against Progress*, 39.

[22] With the establishment of the republic, the former provinces were transformed into states.

[23] On the railroads, see Flávio A. M. Saes, *As ferrovias de São Paulo, 1870–1940* (São Paulo: Hucitec-INL-MEC, 1981); Monbeig, *Pioneiros e Fazendeiros de São Paulo*; Célia Regina Baider Stefani, *O sistema ferroviário paulista: um estudo sobre a evolução do transporte de transporte de passageiros sobre trilhos* (MA thesis, FFLCH-USP, São Paulo, 2007); Odilon Nogueira de Matos, *Café e ferrovias: a evolução ferroviária de São Paulo e o desenvolvimento da cultura cafeeira* (São Paulo: Alfa-Omega, 1974); Summerhill, *Order against Progress*; Robert H. Mattoon Jr., "Railroads, Coffee, and the Growth of Big Business in Sao Paulo, Brazil," *The Hispanic American Historical Review* 57,2 (May 1977), 273–295; Pinto, *História da viação pública de São Paulo*.

[24] Despite the importance of railroads for coffee and a significant network deployed to move its production, the Brazilian railway system had expanded timidly during the empire when compared to the United States. There, in 1893, a railroad network reached 176,000 km; in Brazil only some 11,000 km. AEB (1939–1940), 1336; and *Statistics of Railways in the United States* (Washington, DC: Government Printing Office, 1894).

The Old Republic, 1889–1930

and Minas Gerais, which was also the richest area of the country.[25] Although the logic of its implementation sought to reduce the transport costs of coffee, the railway moved other types of goods between ports and between different regions, creating more integrated regional markets, for domestic production and for imports.[26] The railroads began to play an essential role also in the movement of passengers. Previously, goods and passengers had been transported by an extremely precarious transport system, thus the emergence of the railroads had an important modernizing social as well as economic impact. But, unlike other countries that established their railroads in more advanced stages of industrialization, the "backward linkage" of railroad construction was reduced in Brazil, since most inputs for the construction and operation of the railroads were imported.[27] Moreover, although most of the capital invested was private, the state guarantees on dividends represented an important subsidy to the rail system. Since the railroads were in constant deficit and the government was obliged to honor its obligations on these dividends, over time the government began to take control over the companies.

Given its extensive agricultural frontier and virgin lands, Brazil could now meet the increasing world demand for coffee. Between 1852 and 1900 the annual rate of the growth of world coffee consumption was 2.5 percent per annum. In this period world consumption went from 4.6 million sacks of coffee to 18.1 million sacks, of which 73 percent was produced by Brazil.[28] There were also important changes in the regional base of coffee production in this period. The state of São Paulo was transformed into the nation's and the world's greatest coffee producer, surpassing Rio de Janeiro in the decade of the 1890s. This growth continued into the next century, and by the 1910s São Paulo accounted for 70 percent of total Brazilian production (sees Graph 1.4 and Appendix Table A.1).

There was also a steady migration within state borders of coffee production. Coffee was initially concentrated in the northeast part of

---

[25] Moreover, although the majority of the capital was private, the guarantee of interest payments represented an important subsidy to the rail system. Since part of the railroads was in deficit and the government was obliged to honor its obligations and pay out minimum dividends, over time it began to take control of the companies.
[26] When the embryonic industry arises, the formation of a wider range of markets enables larger-scale production, but at the same time the inefficiencies of the transport system prevent the small interior manufacturers from benefiting from this market growth.
[27] On this theme, see Summerhill, *Order against Progress*, Chapter 6.
[28] Edmar L. Bacha and Robert Greenhill, *150 anos de café*, 2nd ed., rev. ed. (Rio de Janeiro: Marcelino Martins & E. Johnston Exportadores, 1993), Tables 1.1 and 1.2.

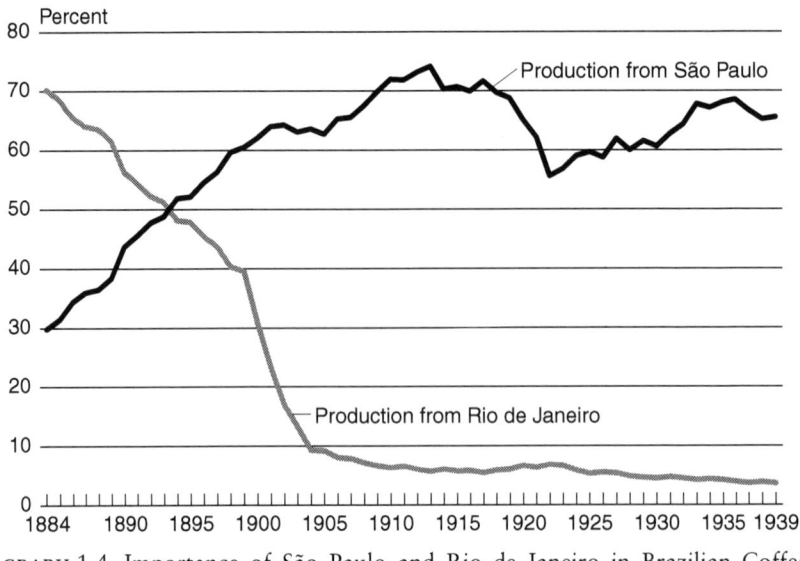

GRAPH 1.4. Importance of São Paulo and Rio de Janeiro in Brazilian Coffee Production, 1884–1939. *Source*: Bacha 1992

São Paulo; it then moved to the center of the state. From this traditional West Paulista zone the coffee migration reached Mogiana in the north of the state and finally moved to the northwest region of the state (see Graph 1.5 and Map 1.1). This was the area that was still unclaimed forest backlands at the beginning of the century. A complex and ample system of rail transport permitted this movement of coffee to ever newer virgin lands that offered exceptional conditions for the cultivation of coffee. This movement of coffee production westward toward the interior of the state of São Paulo was of fundamental importance in the history of Brazil. The coffee penetrated into regions where the topography and climate were highly favorable to coffee production. Better farming techniques and level and extensive planes guaranteed that soil erosion would not be as crucial an issue as it had been in the Paraíba Valley. For all of these reasons this far western part of São Paulo would become the largest coffee-producing center in the world in the late nineteenth and early twentieth centuries and thus the country's main wealth-producing region (see Map 1.1).

But the special characteristics of supply and demand for coffee created an unstable market with great fluctuations in price. World demand grew steadily due to the growth of population, urbanization, and income in the consuming countries, but at the same time was seriously affected

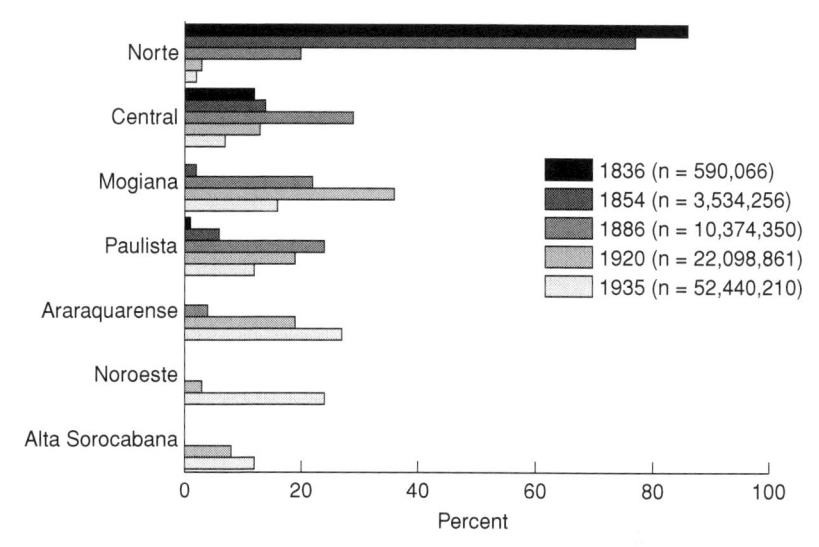

GRAPH 1.5. Coffee-Producing Regions of São Paulo, 1836–1935 (in arrobas). *Source*: Milliet 1982

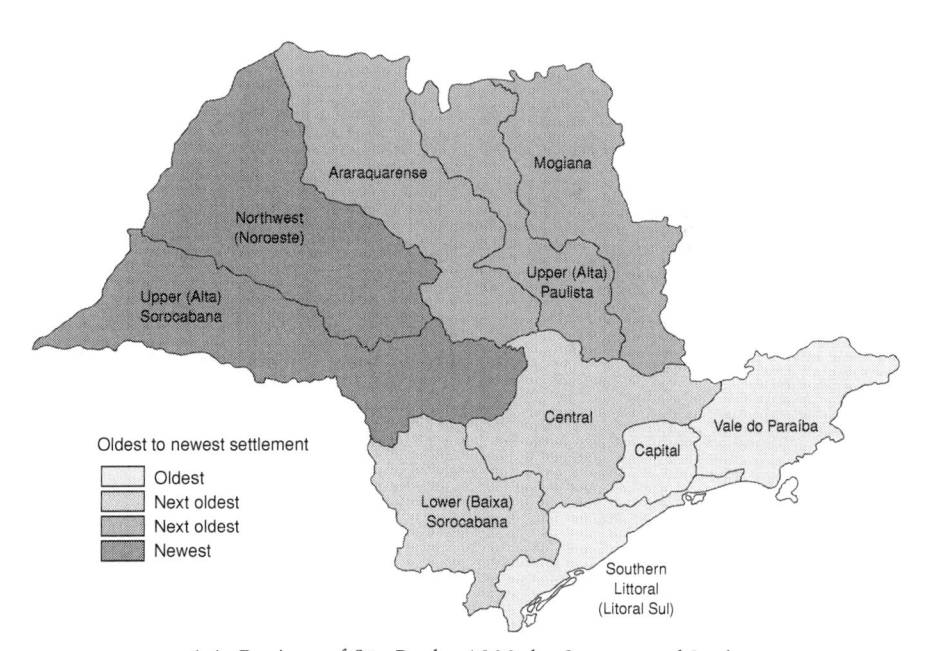

MAP 1.1. Regions of São Paulo, 1900, by Sequence of Settlement

by periodic crises in the economies of Europe and the United States. These crises temporarily reduced the income and consumption of consumers and thus affected the behavior of market players.[29] Although plantings were influenced by prices, other exogenous factors sometimes delayed this price influence for several years. Coffee trees, for example, only began to produce at four years of age and continued to produce for some 20 to 30 years, and sometimes even as much as 50 years. Equally, climate changes, especially severe winters and ice conditions, influenced production, which meant that harvests varied by year and in turn would influence subsequent year sales and production. Severe ice storms could even destroy trees and require new plantings. Finally, a factor of major importance was the exchange rate. Prices were quoted in English pounds, but the relevant price for the producer was in national currency. Thus fluctuations in the exchange rate influenced the decisions of producers as much as changing international prices. All of these factors led to delayed responses to changes in supply and demand along with occasional dramatic price fluctuations in the coffee market.[30]

There were three cycles in coffee prices between 1857 and 1906 with no secular trends in these prices in this period.[31] The causes for these booms and busts were similar. The cycle began with a rise in consumer income or a fall in world production and ended with an economic crisis in Europe or the United States, the principal consumer markets. In the three cases, as a consequence of the external crisis there occurred a devaluation in the exchange rate that compensated in national currency for part of the losses suffered by producers. Depending on the intensity of the crisis, coffee merchants took advantage of the fall in prices to recompose their stocks of coffee. In spite of the crisis, there could actually be an increase in the quantities of coffee exported, thus reducing the impact on the

---

[29] The formation of consumer prices was influenced not only by the international price of coffee, but also by the market conditions specific to each country, which included the exchange rate, the processing of the product, profit margins, and taxes. Usually the consumer prices were more stable than prices in the international market.

[30] On this theme see the seminal work of Antonio Delfim Netto, *O problema do café no Brasil* (São Paulo: IPE-USP, 1981).

[31] Delfim Netto, *O problema do café no Brasil*, Chapter 1. Bacha disagrees with Delfim Netto on the nonexistence of a secular trend in coffee prices. Working with a price in cents per pound of coffee, deflated by the wholesale price index in the United States in the period from 1821 to 1901, Bacha concludes that a rising tendency in the price of coffee did exist in this period. Edmar Lisboa Bacha, "Política Brasileira do Café. Uma avaliação centenária," in Bacha and Greenhill, *150 anos de café*, 15–121.

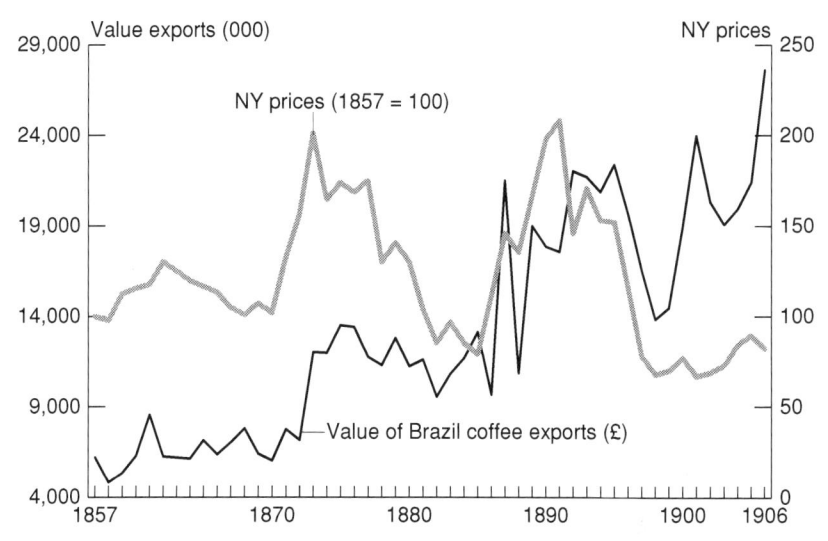

GRAPH 1.6a. Coffee: Prices and the Value of Exports of Brazil, 1857–1906.
Source: Bacha 1992, Delfim Netto 1981, and Ipeadata

value of Brazilian exports. If the devaluation of Brazilian currency helped the producers, it badly affected national consumers who depended on imports. These exchange-rate fluctuations were generally provoked by problems in the balance of payments and were reflected in changes in internal prices, the level of economic activity, and the distribution of income.[32] As we will see, the process functioned relatively well until the end of the decade of the 1880s, but could not avoid the crisis of overproduction that occurred in the first years of the twentieth century (see Graphs 1.6a and 1.6b and Appendix Table A.1).

The introduction of wage labor in the late 1880s profoundly transformed the Brazilian economy, affecting as it did internal demand, monetary policy, and even the balance of payments. Substituting slave labor for salaried labor changed the structure of demand of the working-class population and the flow of income within the economy. Salaried workers directly accessed the market, in contrast to slaves, whose consumption was determined by their masters. Moreover, the immigrants introduced new habits of consumption, expanding the variety of goods needed to

[32] Celso Furtado analyzes in detail this process, which he calls the "socialization of losses" in *Formação Econômica do Brasil* (São Paulo: Cia Editora Nacional, 1968a), Chapters 18–19.

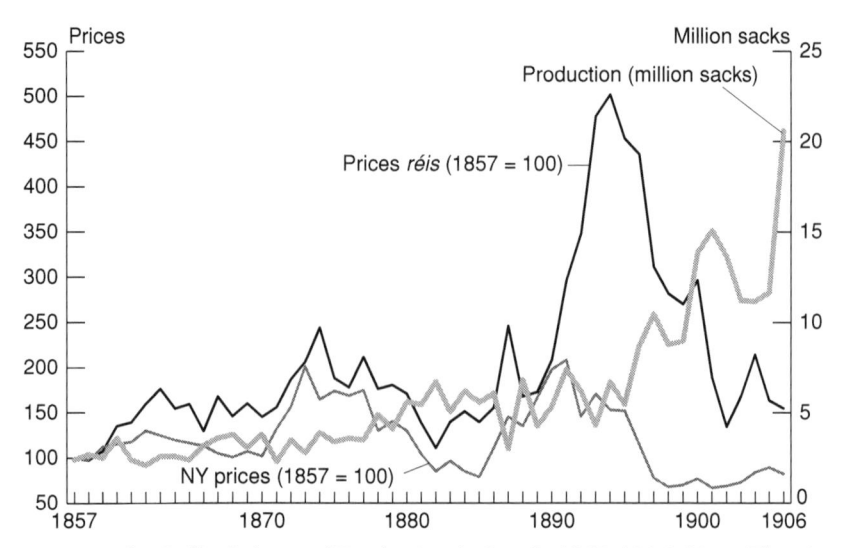

GRAPH 1.6b. Coffee Prices and Production in Brazil, 1857–1906. *Note*: The *réis* was money in circulation in Brazil and had an average value of 27 pence per 1,000 *réis* (*mil réis*) in 1857. *Source*: Bacha 1992, Delfim Netto 1981, and Ipeadata

be produced to meet their demands either through internal production or importations. This transition to wage labor gave particular impulse to manufacturing and service activities in the national economy. The gestation of Brazilian manufacturing occurred as a result of this fundamental transformation in the organization of national labor.[33]

This new labor system also had other impacts on the Brazilian economy, primarily in the form of increased demand for credit. In terms of monetary and foreign exchange policies, the empire consistently followed the gold standard seeking to reach parity of 27 pence per *mil réis* (or 1,000 *réis*), which was established in 1846. Occasional variations from this standard, usually provoked by crises in the balance of payments, were seen with great preoccupation by the government. For this reason, the authorities maintained a rigid control over the supply of money, which they understood to be the principal cause for the devaluation of the national currency, the *mil réis*.

By the decade of the 1880s, although the abolition of slavery was seen as inevitable, there persisted doubts as to the speed of the emancipation process. The Law of Free Birth gave added life to slavery, since the masters had the right to opt between either retaining the children of their slaves

---

[33] Furtado, *Formação Econômica do Brasil*, Chapters 16–17.

The Old Republic, 1889–1930

until the age of 21 or receiving indemnification from the state for immediate emancipation.[34] The law gave support to the two principal concerns of the slaveholding interests that were a slow and programmed transition to emancipation and an option for indemnification, thus postponing immediate emancipation to the disgust of the abolitionists. Even as late as the second half of the decade of the 1880s there emerged proposals to retain slaves as apprentices for even more years and for commitment by the state for compensation for any slaves emancipated. But the continued delay of abolition weakened the stance of the master class, intensified social pressure, and further encouraged slave rebellions. The number of fugitive slaves increased and the police and military refused to stop or recapture them. The final abolition decree – the Lei Áurea had only two articles. Article 1 declared the absolute and unqualified extinction of slavery in Brazil and article 2 revoked any other laws that were contrary to this position. There was neither transition to semiservile labor apprenticeships nor indemnification for the slave owners. The political climate permitted no concessions to the slave owners. The opportunity had been lost to them. As the Baron of Cotegipe declared, "the extinction of slavery which came with this law is nothing more than the recognition of the de facto situation."[35] Soon thereafter the monarchy itself came to an end.[36]

---

[34] Paragraph 1 of Law 2040 stipulated that: "The said minor children shall be kept by and under the authority of the masters of their mothers, who will be required to raise them and care for them until the age of eight full years. When the son of a slave arrives to this age, the master of the mother will have the option of either receiving state indemnification of $600,000 for the child's freedom, or of utilizing the services of the minor until the age of 21 years. In the first case, the Government will receive the least and give the destination according to the present law."

[35] "[T]he extinction of slavery, which now comes in this project, is no more than the de facto recognition of the current situation. It has the great advantage that with its passage, it will end this anarchy, with no more excuses for such movements, and attacks against property and against public policy. Here is what I think are the advantages of the project...." Senado Federal, *A Abolição no Parlamento: 65 anos de luta, 1823–1888*, 2 vols. (Brasília: Subsecretaria de Arquivo, 1988), II:487. The Barron of Cotegipe was President of the Council of Ministers in the empire, in the period from 1885 to 1888.

[36] On the political structure of the empire, see Sérgio Buarque de Holanda, ed., "O Brasil Monárquico," in *História Geral da Civilização Brasileira*, II:5 (Rio de Janeiro: Bertrand Brasil, 1997); Richard Graham, *Patronage and Politics in Nineteenth-Century Brazil* (Stanford, CA: Stanford University Press, 1990); Raymundo Faoro, *Os donos do Poder. Formação do Patronato político brasileiro*, 2 vols. (Porto Alegre: Ed. Globo; São Paulo: Ed. Universidade São Paulo, 1975), Chapters IX–XII; José Murilo de Carvalho, *A construção da Ordem: a elite política imperial; Teatro das sombras: a política imperial* (Rio de Janeiro: Civilização Brasileira, 2003).

Emancipation angered the most conservative groups that had supported slavery and the monarchy.[37] But there were also other issues, going back to the 1870s, which weakened the imperial government. There was the rise of a powerful republican movement and a series of conflicts between the monarch with the army and the Roman Catholic Church. The republican movement grew out of the demands of the urban middle classes for greater political representation and was also closely associated with the abolitionist movement.[38] But the republican movement even gained support among some conservative groups, as was indicated by the creation of the Republican Party of São Paulo (*Partido Republicano Paulista*), which had the participation of members of the coffee elite. Although these planters remained aloof from the abolitionist discussion, they were deeply committed to autonomy for the provinces through the creation of a federalist system.[39] The conflict with the Church had its origin in the new policies enunciated by the Vatican in the papal bulls of Pious IX. These policies sought to reenforce the authority of the Church in relation to civil society and also condemned the Masonry, which was an institution with enormous prestige in Brazil. The spark for the conflict was the order of the bishop of Olinda prohibiting masons from participating in religious brotherhoods. As the constitution gave the state the right to validate ecclesiastical decrees, the Cabinet ordered the revocation of the measure. The bishop objected and was imprisoned. In turn, the military question came with the strengthening of the army after the end of the Paraguayan War in 1870. From the period of the war onward the army increased its participation in politics through the direct involvement of high-ranking officers in the political parties. The influence of positivism among the officers also fortified the republican ideal. But in the 1880s the military came into conflict with the monarch and its power

---

[37] In 1808 the Portuguese royal family relocated to Brazil escaping Napoleon's invasion of Portugal. In 1821, the court returned to Portugal, but left the royal heir Pedro I, as Prince Regent of Brazil. In 1822, Brazil won its independence under the monarchy, and Dom Pedro I was its first emperor. In 1831 Pedro I returned to Portugal to protect the throne and abdicated on behalf of his son, Dom Pedro II, who ruled Brazil until 1888, when he was deposed by the proclamation of the republic.

[38] According to Cardoso, "[T]he last three decades that preceded the Republic of '89 marked major changes in the bases of the Brazilian economy: with the expansion of coffee plantations in South-Central region, and more specifically, in the northeast of São Paulo, as the decade 1870/1880 was characterized as a period of intense commercial/financial activity allowing a urban-industrial boom." Fernando Henrique Cardoso, "Dos Governos Militares a Prudente – Campos Sales," in *História Geral da Civilização Brasileira*, III:1, ed. Boris Fausto (Rio de Janeiro: Ed. Bertrand Brasil, 1989), 17.

[39] Faoro, *Os donos do Poder*, Vol. 2, Chapter 12.

was curtailed. Its representation in the most important monarchic institutions, the Senate and the Council of State, was decreased. The army felt marginalized and unappreciated as a result of these conflicts. In 1887 officers created the *Clube Militar*, which was presided over by Deodoro da Fonseca, who would later become the first republican president. The club saw itself as a defender of the interests of the officer class and as a nucleus of opposition to the regime.[40] While D. Pedro II lived, the empire could be maintained. But as one historian noted, "no one seemed willing to sacrifice themselves in defense of the regime. The majority expected the natural death of the second reign with the natural death of the emperor, and prepared themselves for the inevitable change."[41] Thus the power vacuum that occurred after 1888 reflected a lack of political support for the monarchy. Although there was no effective opposition to the overthrow of the monarchy, the act was greeted with surprise by the population. Even Deodoro, who led the overthrow of the monarchy and was the first republican president, had always been loyal to the emperor and onetime critic of the republican movement.[42] But the deterioration of the political situation led even traditional monarchists to participate in the overthrow of the monarchy, as was the case with Deodoro.

In evaluating the monarchical regime in Brazil, it is evident that its major accomplishment was in giving political and territorial stability to the country. But it was stifled by its centralization, immobilization, and incapacity to evolve along with the necessities and changes in the Brazilian economy and society. In spite of the expansion of coffee in the second half of the nineteenth century, a product highly valued in the international market, the country presented low levels of per capita growth throughout the century, but especially in the post-1850 period. In 1800 Brazil had a per capita income of 91 percent of that of the United States; by 1913 its per capita income had fallen to just 14 percent of the American rate. This result reflected the evolution of the per capita income of the Brazilians, which had increased by only 0.4 percent in the first half of the nineteenth century and experienced a negative decline of −0.4 percent between 1850 and 1913. In short, per capita income in Brazil in this period was stagnant, while in the United States it grew on average

---

[40] On this theme, see Buarque de Holanda, "O Brasil Monárquico," 306–360.
[41] Buarque de Holanda, "O Brasil Monárquico," 354. On the Second Empire, see Lilia Moritz Schwarcz, *As Barbas do Imperador. D. Pedro II, um monarca nos trópicos* (São Paulo: Cia. das Letras, 1999).
[42] On this theme, see Buarque de Holanda, "O Brasil Monárquico," 306–360; and Faoro, *Os donos do Poder*, Chapters 11–12.

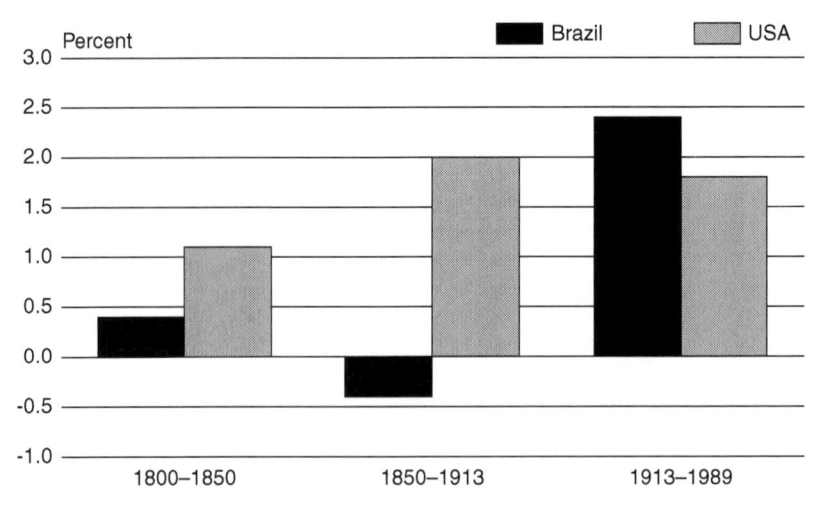

GRAPH 1.7. Growth of per Capita Income, 1800/1989. *Source*: Kalmanovitz 2012

between 1.1 percent in the first half of the century to 2 percent per annum in 1850–1913 period (see Graph 1.7).[43] These numbers show that the origin of the economic backwardness of Brazil in the nineteenth century occurred despite the expansion of coffee. The conservative policies of the empire, including its long defense of slavery, did not permit the dynamism of the coffee industry to spread to the rest of the national economy.

The relative stagnation of per capita income not only reflected the slow growth of national income, but also was influenced by the high rate of natural population growth and international migration at the end of the nineteenth and the beginning of the twentieth centuries. This natural population growth was influenced by continuing high fertility and slowly declining mortality. Although fertility also began to decline after 1900, it remained quite high until well into the twentieth century (see Graph 1.8). Mortality actually declined much faster than fertility, which had the effect of increasing natural population growth (see Graph 1.9). This was primarily due to the vaccination and sanitation movements of the 1890s to the 1910s, which were particularly important in affecting mortality levels in the expanding urban areas. The campaigns of vaccination, the slow provision of clean water, and the beginnings of modern urban sanitation for the leading urban centers, along with the introduction of

---

[43] Salomón Kalmanovitz, "Las conseqüências econômicas de la Independencia en América Latina," in *Institucionalidade y desarrollo econômico en América Latina*, ed. Luis Bértola and Pablo Gerchunoff (Santiago de Chile: Cepal, 2012), 62–63.

GRAPH 1.8. Total Fertility Rate, 1903–1988. *Source*: Horta, Carvalho, and Frias 2000, Table 6

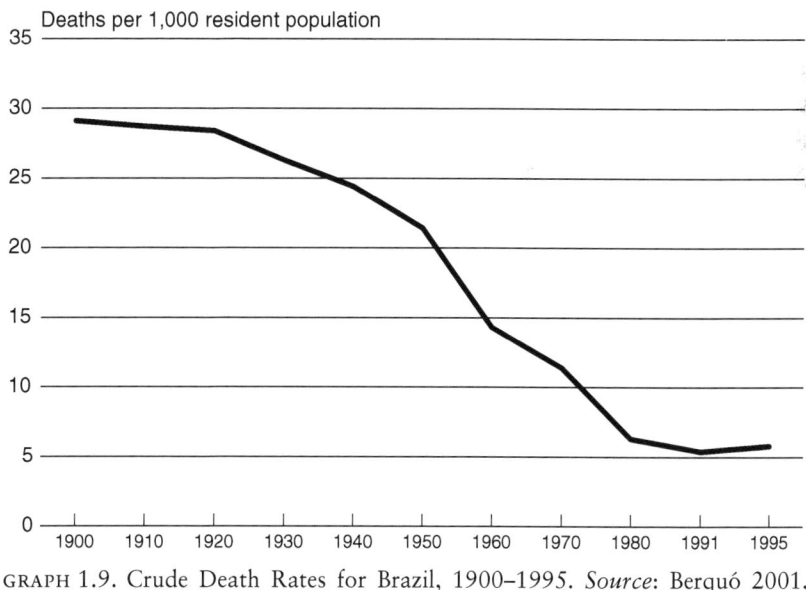

GRAPH 1.9. Crude Death Rates for Brazil, 1900–1995. *Source*: Berquó 2001, Table 3

pasteurization, were the causes for this declining mortality. This was the cause for the mortality decline in all of Latin America, though rates in the richer countries declined much faster than the poorer ones prior to 1930.[44]

Despite massive immigration, which brought in primarily working-age adults in the era of the slave trade and after 1888, Brazil had an extremely young population due to the very high levels of natural increase. Thus in the census of 1890 those under 19 years of age represented 51 percent of the total population, and their share rose to 55 percent of the national population in 1900 and 57 percent by the census of 1920.[45] All this meant that the average age of Brazilians was under 20 years for the entire period of the Old Republic. Because of this high native fertility, European immigration, though impressive, had only a moderate impact on national population growth as compared to its impact in Canada and Argentina in the same period. It was estimated that immigrants accounted for 14 percent of total growth of the national population between 1872 and 1890, some 30 percent in the peak decade of 1890 to 1900 and just 7 to 8 percent in the following four decades.[46] Brazil was more like the United States in this respect, since immigration accounted for less than 10 percent of the total growth in both countries in the century from 1841 to 1940.[47]

But immigration did have a big impact on the color composition of the population. Before the abolition of slavery it seemed that Brazil would be a predominantly Afro-American–based population. Brazil was the largest recipient of African slaves of any country in the Americas, with some 4.9 million arriving to its shores between the early 1500s and 1850.[48] Thus it is no surprise that in the census of 1872, some 58 percent of the population of some 10 million persons were blacks (*pretos*) and mulattos (*pardos*), while the foreign born represented just 3 percent of the imperial population. This was still before the abolition of slavery and the massive shift to European workers. In this pre-1880 era Brazil only attracted a small migration of farmers going to agricultural colonies mostly in the

---

[44] Eduardo E. Arriaga and Kingsley Davis, "The Pattern of Mortality Change in Latin America," *Demography* 6,3 (1969), 226.
[45] Calculated from IBGE, *Estatísticas históricas do Brasil*, Vol. 3, "Séries Econômicas, Demográficas e Sociais de 1550 a 1988" (2 edição revista e atualizada), 31, Table 1.6 "População presente. segundo o sexo e os grupos de idade – 1872–1920." All figures are only for the population whose age is known.
[46] Merrick and Graham, *Population and Economic Development*, 37.
[47] Merrick and Graham, *Population and Economic Development*, 38–39.
[48] Herbert S. Klein, *The Atlantic Slave Trade*, 2nd ed., rev. ed. (New York and Cambridge: Cambridge University Press, 2010), Appendix Table A.2.

far southern states.⁴⁹ This would change dramatically after 1888 with the massive arrival of free European and Asian immigrants coming to replace the former slaves on the coffee plantations of the center southern region. Between 1880 and 1930 some 4.1 million European and Asian immigrants arrived in Brazil.⁵⁰ By the census of 1900 the white and Asian foreign-born population had increased to 7 percent of the national total and because of their concentration in the coffee producing regions, they made up an impressive 23 percent of the population in the state of São Paulo and 25 percent of the old Federal District residents, which at that time was the city of Rio de Janeiro.⁵¹ These immigrants had an impact in slowly but steadily changing the color composition of the national population. From the late nineteenth century there was a steady growth in the white population of the country, which increased its share of total population from 38 percent to 44 percent between the census of 1872 and 1890. But in 1940 the white share of the population peaked at 64 percent and has been steadily declining ever since.⁵²

Although the majority of immigrants were literate, overall the literacy rate in the late-nineteenth- and early-twentieth-century Brazilian censuses was very low. This was because Brazil for most of its imperial and early republican history was a relatively backward nation in terms of providing public education for its population even by Latin American standards. In the census of 1890 only 14.8 percent of persons over the age of four could read and write,⁵³ which was almost identical to the figure in the first imperial census of 1872. This level put it among the poorest nations of

---

[49] *CENSO 1872:* Quadros do Império, Quadro 2 (população presente em relação à idade sexo, condição, cor, idades) as reproduced and recalculated by NEPO/UNICAMP.

[50] Maria Stella Ferreira Levy, "O Papel da Migração Internacional na evolução da população brasileira (1872 a 1972)," *Revista de Saúde Pública* 8 (Suppl.) (1974), 71–73, Table 1.

[51] *Recenseamento do... 1920.* IV, Part 1 (população), lxiii, Table 1 "População brasileira e estrangeira dos estados, 1872, 1890, 1900, 1920." It should be noted that the Federal District, the capital of the country, was transferred in 1960 from Rio de Janeiro to Brasília.

[52] IBGE, POP106, "População presente e residente, por cor ou raça (dados do universo e dados da amostra) Decenal 1872–2000," and IBGE, PD336, "População residente, por cor ou raça Anual 2001–2009," both available at http://seriesestatisticas.ibge.gov.br/lista_tema.aspx?op=0&no=10. But color definitions are notoriously fluid in Brazil, especially when the usual manner of counting is by self-definition. It is interesting to note that by 2005 whites had fallen to less than half the total Brazilian population and have steadily declined through the census of 2010 in which they were only 47 percent of the national population, though still being the largest color group in Brazil.

[53] Directoria Geral de Estatística, *Sexo, raça e estado civil, nacionalidade, filiação culto e analfabetismo da população recenseada em 31 em Dezembro de 1890* (Rio de Janeiro:

the hemisphere. But the shift of education to state responsibility after 1899 meant that there was a major investment in schools on a systematic basis. Brazil between 1899 and 1933 experienced the most rapid change in its literacy rates of any Latin American country.[54] By the census of 1920 the national literacy rate had doubled to 28.8 percent.[55] All this change was due to the investments of the states in public education, with the states with the largest export economies investing the most sums.[56] Nevertheless, despite this impressive growth, the literacy rate was still well below the rates in the Rio de la Plata nations and even several other South American nations.[57]

Though the goals of a free primary education had been enunciated as early as the 1820s, the government made little effort to carry out this fundamental task. There was an ongoing debate about whether the central government or the state and municipal regimes were primarily responsible for providing education, which resulted in few governments spending significant sums on education. Also the independent empire of Brazil inherited a colonial tradition that was antithetical to higher education and even the printing of books. In the Spanish American colonial empire local universities were created in all the major capitals, and the printing of religious works, Indian grammars, and government documents was the norm from Mexico City to Lima from the sixteenth century onward. In contrast, the Portuguese colonial administration rejected the idea of creating local universities in its American colony and did not even permit a colonial printing industry to develop. The Portuguese crown primarily encouraged religious primary and secondary education in the colonial

Officina da Estatística, 1898), 373, Quadro "População recenseada na República dos Estados Unidos do Brasil quanto ao analfabetismo."

[54] André Martínez Fritscher, Aldo Musacchio, and Martina Viareng, "The Great Leap Forward: The Political Economy of Education in Brazil, 1889–1930," Working Papers No. 10–075 (Cambridge, MA: Harvard Business School, 2010), 2, available at http://www.hbs.edu/research/pdf/10-075.pdf.

[55] Alceu Ravanello Ferraro, "Analfabetismo e níveis de letramento no Brasil: o que dizem os censos?" *Revista Educação & Sociedade* (Campinas) 23,81 (Dezembro 2002), 34, Table 1.

[56] All this was due to the increase of state investments in education, which went from an average of 0.7 *mil réis* per student in 1900 to 1.2 *mil réis* (both in 1913 *mil réis*) in 1925. In the period 1899 to 1933 the number of primary schools went from 8,157 to 28,707 and total primary school enrollments from 258,804 to 2,218,569. Martinez Fritscher et al., "The Great Leap Forward," 48, 52, Tables 2 and 8.

[57] In the Argentine census of 1914, some 49 percent of the native born and 43 percent of the immigrants were literate. Noam Lupu and Susan C. Stokes, "The Social Bases of Political Parties in Argentina, 1912–2003," *Latin American Research Review* 44,1 (2009), 71n14.

period and forced the elite to return to Europe to get a higher degree at the major Portuguese universities.

With the creation of an independent nation in 1822, this hostility toward public education began to change. Many of the local state and municipal governments now began to promote primary public education. In the 1830s and 1840s came the first few teacher-training schools, and by mid-century a few selected public secondary schools were added to the expanding number of public primary schools. The elite, of course, continued to send their children to the small number of select private religious schools that traditionally provided primary and secondary education.[58] The imperial government also recognized the need to create advanced professional schools, and by the middle of the nineteenth century it had established engineering and medical academies.[59]

But at the time of the creation of the republic at the end of the nineteenth century, the educational situation was still rather precarious. The majority of the population was not enrolled in schools, the illiteracy rate was among the highest in the Americas, and there still existed no universities in the country. But slowly this pattern began to change, and there was a quantitative increase in the number of children attending school. As late as 1871, there were 134,000 students, only 7 percent of whom were in secondary schools, and only 28 percent of whom were women, for a population of more than 10.1 million. This represented barely 13 children matriculated in schools for every 1,000 inhabitations.[60] By 1889 the ratio was 18 children per thousand residents, by 1907 it was 29 children, and by 1920 it was 41 children per thousand resident population. Although the most economically dynamic states advanced the most, all states increased their share of net enrollment rates for the primary grades (see Graph 1.10). Clearly, while total enrollments of primary school children was increasing by 1930, there still was a deficit of children at the primary grades, and secondary education, both public and private, was available only for the elite.

Urban growth was also slow. As late as the 1890s only three cities had more than 100,000 population: the Federal District of Rio de Janeiro

---

[58] Manoel Bergström Lourenço Filho, *Tendências da educação brasileira*, 2nd ed. (Brasília: Inep/MEC, 2002), 17–19.
[59] Simon Schwartzman, *A Space for Science – The Development of the Scientific Community in Brazil* (College Station: Pennsylvania State University Press, 1991), Chapter 3.
[60] Data from *Relatório do Ministério dos Negócios do Império 1871 Apresentado Em Maio De 1872*, 27–36.

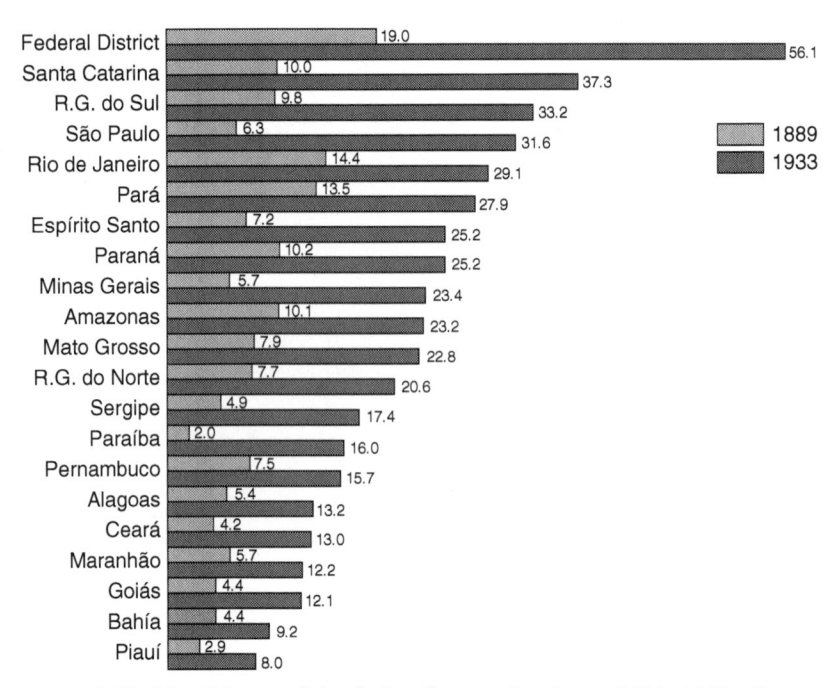

28   The Economic and Social History of Brazil since 1889

State	1889	1933
Federal District	19.0	56.1
Santa Catarina	10.0	37.3
R.G. do Sul	9.8	33.2
São Paulo	6.3	31.6
Rio de Janeiro	14.4	29.1
Pará	13.5	27.9
Espírito Santo	7.2	25.2
Paraná	10.2	25.2
Minas Gerais	5.7	23.4
Amazonas	10.1	23.2
Mato Grosso	7.9	22.8
R.G. do Norte	7.7	20.6
Sergipe	4.9	17.4
Paraíba	2.0	16.0
Pernambuco	7.5	15.7
Alagoas	5.4	13.2
Ceará	4.2	13.0
Maranhão	5.7	12.2
Goiás	4.4	12.1
Bahía	4.4	9.2
Piauí	2.9	8.0

GRAPH 1.10. Net Primary School Enrollments by State, 1889–1933. *Source*: Fritscher, Musacchio, and Viareng 2010, "The Great Leap," Table 3, p. 49

with a half million, Salvador with 174,000, and Recife with 111,000 persons. At that point in time the city of São Paulo only had a population of 65,000. Clearly the overwhelming majority of the Brazilians lived in the rural area. But in the new century urban population began growing at an ever-expanding rate. As early as 1910 the principal towns were doubling their populations every ten years. It was estimated that São Paulo now held 346,000, the Federal District some 870,000, and Belém and Porto Alegre now joined the over 100,000 population level (see Graph 1.11).[61] By 1920 two cities had outdistanced all the others. Rio de Janeiro now held 1.1 million persons and the fast-growing city of São Paulo now contained 579,000. There were also three cities with more than 200,000 (Belém, Recife, and Salvador), with Porto Alegre reaching 179,000, and the new city of Belo Horizonte growing at the extraordinary rate of 7 percent per annum. A few urban centers thus grew quite rapidly and continued their extraordinary growth for the rest of the century. But by the standards of other Latin American nations Brazil was still only

[61] AEB Anno 1 (1908–1912), 256, "População das Capitaes dos Estados do Brazil (1872, 1890, 1900, and 1910)."

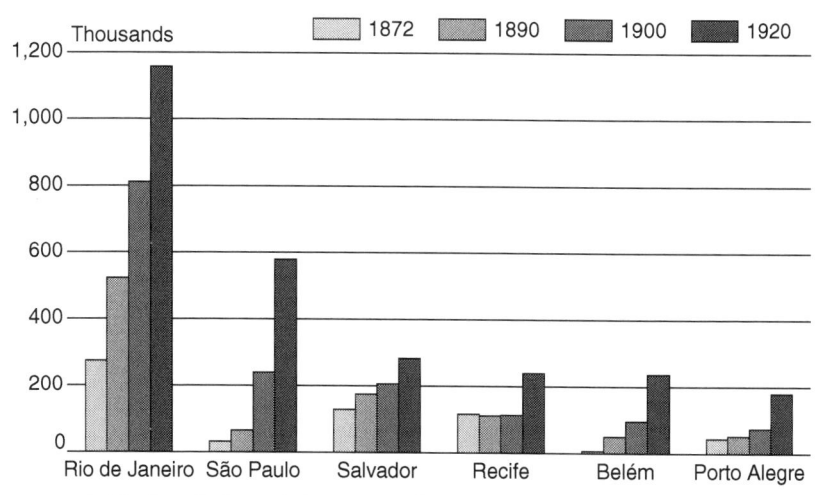

GRAPH 1.11. Population of the Principal Capitals of Brazil, 1872–1920 (000). Source: IBGE

moderately urbanized. In 1900 only 10 percent of the population lived in cities of more than 20,000 persons. This compared to 24 percent in Argentina and 19 percent in Chile. By 1920 the figure was just 13 percent, and by then Argentina had 37 percent of its population living in these cities and Chile had 28 percent living in these towns. In this respect Brazil was still more like Mexico, Peru, Colombia, and Venezuela, than like its southern neighbors.[62] Even as late as 1970, only 39 percent of the national population were living in cities of 20,000 persons or more.[63]

But if cities were growing in this period, it was rural to rural migration that was probably the most important internal population movement within the new republic. A vast internal frontier existed to the West and most of the states had many regions that were not settled until the end of the twentieth century. This meant that there was a constant stream of farmers and workers moving toward the open frontiers as the Indians were progressively pushed back, and the railroads penetrated the interior regions. At the same time there was a major internal migration between regions, and the relative share of population residing in given regions

---

[62] Merrick and Graham, *Population and Economic Development*, 186, Table VIII-1.
[63] Merrick and Graham, *Population and Economic Development*, 188, Table VIII-2. The official IBGE figure for that year was much higher. Unfortunately the government's definition of *urban* is based mainly on administrative status and not necessarily related to population size. See Committee on Population and Demography, *Levels and Recent Trends in Fertility and Mortality in Brazil*, Report No. 21 (Washington, DC: National Academy Press, 1983), 15.

30   *The Economic and Social History of Brazil since 1889*

MAP 1.2. Regional Distribution of the Brazilian Population in 1872 ($n = 9.9$ million)

systematically changed over time. Whereas the traditional provinces of the northeast held the majority of the population in the early eighteenth century, by the end of the colonial period the south central provinces of Espírito Santo, Rio de Janeiro, Minas Gerais, and São Paulo began to challenge that dominance, especially after the migration of the viceregal capital to Rio de Janeiro in 1763. By the first imperial census of 1872, these two zones between them contained 87 percent of the national population. While that share dropped to 81 percent by 1920, there also was a major shift between the two regions. The old northeastern states progressively lost their share to the southeastern states. By 1890 the southeastern region became the largest region in terms of population, and by 1900 that share of national population increased to 44 percent while the northeast fell to 39 percent and these trends continued into the 1920 census when the southeast attained 45 percent of the population to just 37 percent for the northeast (Maps 1.2 and 1.3 and Graph 1.12).

The Old Republic, 1889–1930 31

MAP 1.3. Regional Distribution of the Population in 1920 ($n = 30.6$ million)

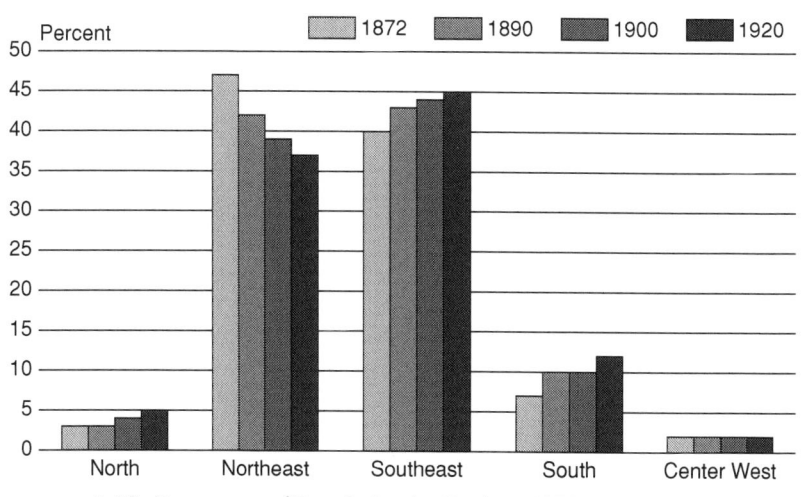

GRAPH 1.12. Percentage of Population by Region, 1872–1920. Source: IBGE

These changes in population structure and distribution help explain some of the factors that led to federalist and republican movements. Although there was a peaceful transition from empire to republic, the republican regime would carry out profound changes in the structure of the central government and the organization of its powers. The republican constitution of 1891 replaced the old imperial centralism with a federalist regime with ample autonomy given to the states. Despite the oligarchic power and electoral manipulations, there were regular elections and successive presidents elected for more than thirty years. This federalist ideology had its origins in the 1870s, with the rise of the republican movement, and appealed to the regional oligarchic groups, who even if they lost control over the central government still had space for maneuvering within their states. The constitution of 1891 provided a classic liberal federalist model that expanded state powers, even to the extent of the states being able to undertake loans.[64] This state right to borrow in the local and international markets would be crucial to the São Paulo effort to maintain coffee prices from 1906 on. Nevertheless, the federal government still retained ample powers in terms of monetary policy and the armed forces. The central government also preserved the power to tax imports, which represented the principal source of income for the nation, while allowing the states the right to tax their exports. In other respects the 1891 constitution established the classic federal republic, with the division of powers among an executive, a legislature, and a judiciary. There were of course, special features of this constitution. Although election was now direct and universal, illiterates were denied the vote, which apparently reduced the voting population quite considerably. Freedom of religion was guaranteed and the Catholic Church was denied official status as the country was declared a secular state, a revolutionary act by the standards of most of the other Latin American republics.

The first provisional government of the republic was led by Marshal Deodoro da Fonseca, who quickly moved to eliminate the provincial governors, the municipal councilmen, and the Council of State. Given their

[64] During the discussion of the constitution, there appeared two conflicting positions. One preaching the liberal democratic regime, with separation of powers, and the other, led by the positivists and with the support of the army, wanting a strong executive. The liberal democratic current won, thus the Constitution of 1891 defined the country as a federal republic, under the representative regime, consisting of three branches: executive, legislative, and judiciary. The vote would be direct and universal, but excluded the illiterate, who represented during that period the majority of the population. Though not mentioned in the constitution, women were denied the right to vote.

new political power under the republic, it is not surprising that the first election brought two military men to power. Marshal Teodoro da Fonseca was elected president of the republic and Marshal Floriano Peixoto as vice president.[65] This first period of republican government was marked by political turbulence and numerous military conflicts. Deodoro from his inauguration on November 15, 1889 entered into conflict with liberal groups and parliamentary delegates, which led him to close Congress and declare a state of siege. The issue was his desire to increase the powers of the federal executive and limit the autonomy of the states. The opposition finally erupted in an armed rebellion led by Admiral Custódio de Melo, and Deodoro, having lost political support of the elite, handed in his resignation in November 1891. Vice President Floriano Peixoto assumed the presidency, and though a centralist, the regional oligarchies supported him in order to consolidate the republican regime. In 1894, Prudente de Morais, representative of the São Paulo coffee bourgeoisie was elected the first civilian president of the republic, though he too faced innumerable regional conflicts.[66] His successor, the civilian Campos Sales, also from São Paulo, was finally able to consolidate the power of the largest states and create a system of harmonious coexistence between the central government and the regional oligarchies. This was a tacit agreement known as the Politics of the Governors, and involved the central government supporting the state oligarchies in exchange for receiving their support at the federal level. Given that the elections were marked by fraud, the power of the center government could be used to recognize the candidate who best represented the local elites. This agreement permitted a relative political stability that lasted through the whole period of the Old Republic.[67]

The early years of the republic were also marked by turbulence in the economic area. Under the empire there was a preoccupation with the

---

[65] Although the constitution consecrated the direct vote, the first president and vice president were elected by indirect voting. There was a dispute over the presidency, and Marechal Deodoro beat the paulista candidate Prudente de Morais by a small margin of 129 against 97.
[66] His government was marked by numerous uprisings, including the Federalist Revolt in Rio Grande do Sul, which turned into a civil war. The main cause of the conflict related to the extreme positions concerning the level of autonomy of the states. During his tenure there was also the Canudos conflict. A local religious dispute without larger importance was transformed into the symbol of monarchical reaction, which had to be fought at any cost. After several defeats of the government forces, Canudos was destroyed along with the death of most of the followers of Antonio Counselor.
[67] On the political structure of the Old Republic, see Faoro, *Os donos do poder*, Chapter XIV.

convertibility of the money, which created a permanent scarcity of money supply. The limited extension of the banking system and its concentration in Rio de Janeiro amplified the monetary problem in areas distant from this city, especially in the northeast. But the problem also occurred in the capital, since the currency sent to other areas to attend to the high demand during the harvest period delayed their return to Rio de Janeiro; and thus created a scarcity of money to attend the business needs in the capital, the principal urban center of the country and its largest commercial center.[68] The problem of monetary scarcity became more acute with the extension of wage labor, the expansion of economic activities, and the elevated surpluses in the balance of payments that occurred in the last years of the empire.[69]

These considerations led to the beginnings of a discussion on monetary reform. The debate put to the fore two distinct proposals to reform the monetary system. One group could be classified as "metalist," meaning that the current exchange rate should be maintained at the 1846 parity,[70] and if it was possible, transform the *mil réis* into a money that could be fully convertible into gold. They claimed that the fluctuations in the established parity were essentially provoked by excesses in monetary emissions, without taking into account the problems created by the frequent crisis in the balance of payments.[71] The other group emphasized the periodic crises provoked by the scarcity in the money supply. They wanted

---

[68] This process of lack of money had already occurred since the 1860s, which according to Calógeras was due to "crops requiring periodic remittances of money, which impoverished the places where the currency was exported, and these funds only returned slowly given the difficulty of communications. Rio de Janeiro, mainly a political and economic capital, at the time of harvests of the North, saw the drainage of its cash to the places of that region and suffered the consequences: increased discount rate, higher interest rates, and difficulties in conducting business for lack of money...." João Pandiá Calógeras, *A política monetária do Brasil* (São Paulo: Cia Editora Nacional, 1960), 161.

[69] "Liberation, however, meant not only the loss of slave labor, but also the need to carry out massive investments in building new houses for the settlers, accustomed as they were to a standard of living higher than the black, but also a great need of capital to pay wages." Delfim Netto, *O problema do café no Brasil*, 23.

[70] Parity was 27 pences per *mil réis*.

[71] Franco, in an excellent work on the subject, built a series of the balance of payments for the period and argues that the fluctuation in the exchange rate "was due, undoubtedly, to the instability of Brazil's balance of payments." The poor trade balance, variations in the inflow of foreign investments, and occasional foreign financing obtained by the government were the main causes of instability in the balance of payments, and therefore the fluctuations in the exchange. Moreover, the foreign exchange market, although of free access, was extremely concentrated and speculative, increasing the effects of external shocks. Gustavo H. B. Franco, "Reforma Monetária e instabilidade durante a transição republicana" (MA thesis, Economics, Rio de Janeiro: PUC/Rio, 1982), 32.

greater stability and expansion in the monetary supply, and for this reason defended the extension of the banking system into the provinces. In 1885 the government was authorized to issue money. It would be a temporary emission meant to resolve the extreme scarcity of money. But in 1887, in dealing with a new crisis of liquidity, there was proposed and approved a monetary reform that permitted the emission of currency backed by bonds and metallic money.[72] Aside from creating a new banking law,[73] the last cabinet of the empire approved an ample program of credit for agriculture, seen as a type of payment to former slave owners who had not received any compensation for their freed slaves.[74] Moreover, since the credit was arranged by the banking system there was a process of natural selection that benefited the agriculturalists of the most productive regions and penalized the planters in difficulties, particularly the coffee growers of the Paraíba Valley who were the ones most affected by emancipation.[75] Although the region had lost its competitiveness, it survived because of its extensive slave labor force. Emancipation was a double blow for that region, with the planters losing an important part of their patrimony, which had been composed of slaves, while their low productivity prevented them from adopting free wage labor.

[72] The law was legislated in January 1889, but there were no expressions of interest from any bank, by mid-year, when changes occurred in the regulation of the law.
[73] The cabinet of the Viscount of Ouro Preto, a liberal, assumed office in June 1889 in an attempt to promote reforms and political agreements that could preserve the monarchy.
[74] The replacement of slave labor, free labor needed increased working capital in the coffee sector, usually funded by internal resources of the sector provided by the coffee export commission merchants. With higher working capital requirements, this traditional credit proved insufficient and the actual export houses, usually agents of large international companies, entered the scene. These export houses acquired greater bargaining power in the purchase of production because growers and commissaries were unable to hold their stocks for better prices. Delfim Netto, *O Problema do café no Brasil*, 23. On the credit system used by coffee producers also see Renato Leite Marcondes, "O Financiamento Hipotecário da Cafeicultura no Vale do Paraíba Paulista (1865–87)," *Revista Brasileira de Economia* 56,1 (Janeiro–Março 2002), 147–170; Rodrigo Fontanari, "O problema do financiamento: uma análise histórica sobre o crédito no complexo cafeeiro paulista. Casa Branca (1874–1914)" (MA thesis, Franca, UNESP, 2011); Rodrigo da Silva Teodoro, "O crédito no mundo dos senhores do café. Franca 1885–1914" (MA thesis, Campinas, Instituto de Economia, UNICAMP, 2006); and Joseph Earl Sweigart, "Financing and Marketing Brazilian Export Agriculture: The Coffee Factors of Rio De Janeiro, 1850–1888" (PhD thesis, University of Texas at Austin, 1980). This increase in the power of export houses led to an increase in the power of British capital, which was already well placed in Brazilian shipping and insurance in general, including coffee exported. See Richard Graham, *Britain and the Onset of Modernization in Brazil 1850–1914* (London: Cambridge University Press, 1968).
[75] On the financial crisis that resulted from the abolition of slavery, see John Schulz, *The Financial Crisis of Abolition* (New Haven, CT, and London: Yale University Press, 2008), Chapter 5.

When Rui Barbosa assumed the post of Minister of Finance in the provisional republican government, the monetary question would be at the center of his preoccupations.[76] In spite of the relatively peaceful political transition, the new government faced international concerns about its economic viability since the monarchy and slavery disappeared at almost the same time. Although at the end of 1888 there was external stability that permitted the government to maintain the desired parity in the exchange and support convertible money, future uncertainty generated a flight of capital, problems in the balance of payments, and a resulting monetary depreciation. There was a run on the banks to exchange convertible money, thus reducing the money in circulation and weakening the banking system.[77] The resolution of this crisis was the issuance of a new monetary reform in January 1890, which resulted in a system of plurality in emission of nonconvertible currency, backed by government securities.[78] Needs of commerce and the expansion of the salaried labor force were the reasons used to justify the rapid expansion of the money supply.[79] In 1892 the plural currency printing system was

---

[76] Barbosa was a jurist and intellectual of great prestige from the end of the empire until well into the republican era. He was a senator, minister, and twice a candidate for the presidency of the republic. He adamantly opposed the metalists' ideas and so acted on his beliefs when he assumed the Ministry of Finance.

[77] On this period, see Franco, "Reforma Monetária"; Gail D. Triner, *Banking and Economic Development: Brazil, 1889–1930* (New York: Palgrave, 2000); Annibal Villanova Villela and Wilson Suzigan, *Política do Governo e crescimento da economia brasileira* (Brasília: IPEA, 2001); Gustavo H. B. Franco, "A primeira década republicana," in *A ordem do Progresso*, ed. Marcelo de Paiva Abreu (Rio de Janeiro: Editora Campus, 1992); Raymond W. Goldsmith, *Brasil 1850–1984. Desenvolvimento Financeiro Sob um Século de Inflação* (São Paulo: Editora Harper & Row do Brasil, 1986), Chapters 2–3; John Schulz, *A crise financeira da abolição* (São Paulo: Ed. Universidade de São Paulo, Instituto Fernando Braudel, 1966); Dorival Teixeira Vieira, *Evolução do Sistema Monetário Brasileira* (São Paulo: IPE-USP, 1981), Parts 2–3.

[78] They created three currency-issuing banks regionally distributed. Such banks were allowed to perform a wide range of activities, including free transfer of lands to settlers and the establishment of industrial enterprises; they also had preference in public tenders for the construction of railways, docks, ports, etc.

[79] According to Rui Barbosa, "[G]old immobilized in a country where the circulation suffers from lack of it, was to bring another element to the pathogenic organism already impoverished and sickly.... The circulating medium of a people is not evaluated by the quantity, considered absolutely, but on the one side by its power of movement, that is by the greater or lesser ease with which it circulates in the country... on the other hand, by the economy which makes the direct use by the commercial devices designed to represent it and dispense it." Rui Barbosa, *Finanças e política da República. Discursos e escritos* (Rio de Janeiro: Cia. Impressora, 1892), 73.

replaced by the creation of a major bank with a monopoly over monetary issue.[80]

It was this banking reform, the cheap credit for agriculture and the legal changes that made it easier to form corporations, which promoted the rapid growth of the money supply in this period.[81] All these changes and reforms created a climate of euphoria in the first years of the republic, generating a process of intense speculation in the stock exchange, which resulted in the creation of dozens of new companies that used the market to issue new stocks to finance their operations. These new companies were often founded with modest resources, but then raised large amounts of capital in the market from other investors. As these stocks rapidly increased in value, there was created a market bubble, which has been called the "Encilhamento."

Accompanying the process of monetary expansion and speculation were new ideas emerging about the importance of industry for the development of the nation.[82] It was thought that this essentially agricultural country should transform itself following the U.S. model and this was promoted by Finance Minister Rui Barbosa.[83] But the market euphoria

---

[80] Vieira, *Evolução do Sistema Monetário Brasileira*, 189. In 1896 the Treasury stripped the monopoly of issue, which then belonged to the Bank of the Republic of Brazil, and assumed this role directly.

[81] A law passed in 1860 imposed a rigid state control over the anonymous societies. To constitute a corporation, authorization was required from the executive branch of government, after prior approval of the State Council. The review of the request to form a limited liability company required analyzing the social ends of the companies, their convenience, assessing their property, and asking whether they aimed to monopolize staples. The law of 1882, considered liberal, limited legislative authorization to banks, and for some specific business sectors and foreign companies. The law imposed obligations and responsibility for managers. Moreover, it prohibited the releasing of shares to the public before the integration of the capital. There was also the requirement for the company to start its operations and trade its shares on the secondary market. However, it allowed the company's indebtedness to the extent of their capital. Despite these changes, the private equity market did not develop. The new Corporation Law of 1890 had a completely liberal character. Furthermore, it only required deposit of 10 percent of authorized capital for the company to be incorporated, considered to be constituted, and its shares traded. Maria Bábara Levy, *A indústria do Rio de Janeiro através de suas sociedades anônimas* (Rio de Janeiro: Prefeitura do Município do Rio de Janeiro, 1994), 127. On the public and private interests involved in the monetary question, see Triner, *Banking and Economic Development: Brazil, 1889–1930*, Chapter 3. On banking reform also see Hanley, *Native Capital*.

[82] On this theme see Nícia Vilela Luz, *A luta pela industrialização do Brasil* (São Paulo: Editora Alfa Omega, 1978).

[83] Quoted in Luz, *A luta pela industrialização do Brasil*, 113. See also Gisele Silva Araújo, "Tradição Liberal, positivismo e pedagogia. A síntese derrotada de Rui Barbosa," *Perspectivas* (São Paulo) 37 (Janeiro–Junho 2010), 113–144. The devaluation of the national

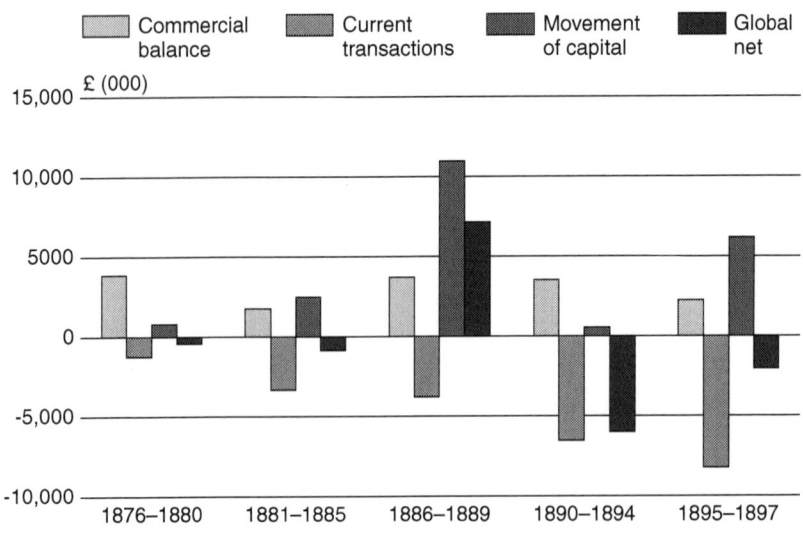

GRAPH 1.13. Estimates of the Balance of Payments, 1886/1897. *Source*: Franco 1982

in which these ideas were stated lasted only a short time. First there was an end to foreign loans and foreign investments. Then there was a severe problem in the balance of payments. While in the period 1886–1889 there was a positive trade balance of £7.1 million, in the following five-year period there occurred a deficit of £6 million despite elevated exports. Various factors can explain this retraction of the international financial markets in relation to Brazil. First of all there were doubts about the political process and how it would affect the economy. Then there was the bankruptcy of the Baring Brothers Bank in Argentina, which agitated the English financial market and fatally affected Brazil (see Graph 1.13).[84]

    currency protected determined productive sectors. Some of the new companies, created during the period of the Encilhamento, became permanent parts of the manufacturing sector. According to the pioneering work of Stanley Stein, the Encilhamento deserves greater attention for its importance in the genesis of Brazilian industry. Referring to the textile industry, Stein noted that "by liberalizing the chartering of joint-stock companies, by widening the bank's range of economic activity, and by increased note issue, the republican government accelerated the process of capital formation. In effect, the paper money inflation supplied the textile industry with liquid capital that otherwise would probably have taken a longer period of time to accumulate." Stanley J. Stein, *The Brazilian Cotton Manufacture: Textile Enterprise in an Underdeveloped Area, 1850–1950* (Cambridge, MA: Harvard University Press, 1957), 96.

[84] In the 1880s Argentina went through a process similar to the speculation that occurred in Brazil culminating with the collapse of several banks and companies in early 1890, including the traditional Baring Brothers Bank. Breaking the bank caused uproar in the Argentine financial market, with serious repercussions on the London market. Felipe

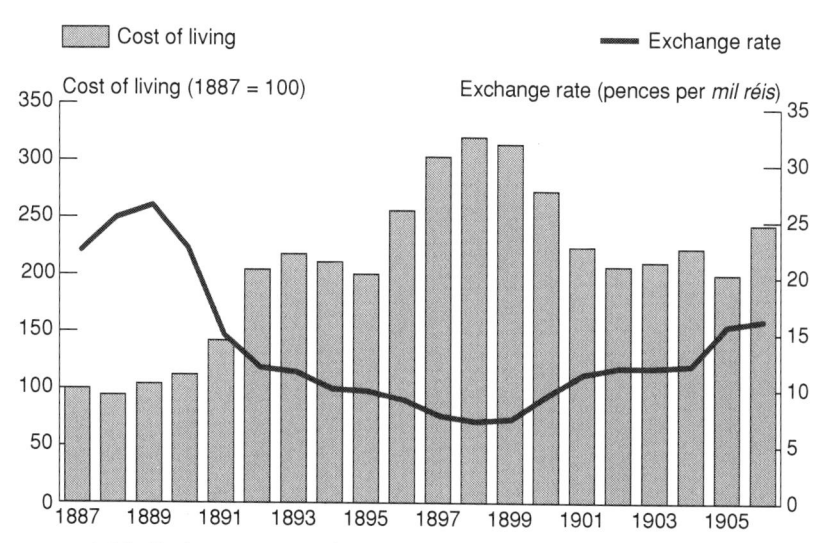

GRAPH 1.14. Exchange Rate and Accumulated Cost-of-Living Index, 1887–1906.
Source: Ipeadata

The exchange rate, which had been maintained at parity until the last year of the monarchy, systematically declined after 1890 in a trend that would only be reversed at the end of the decade. Prices in general, which had been falling in the last two years of the monarchy, began to rise in 1889 and increased by 240 percent in the decade of 1890 (see Graph 1.14). With the coming of President Prudente de Morais to office a policy of retrenchment was initiated. As the emission of money was seen as the principal cause of the extraordinary devaluation of the exchange rate, the government tried to control the money supply. In 1896 it finally took over direct control of the monopoly of printing money that had previously been conceded to the banking system. It was less successful in controlling its budget deficits. Not only was it forced to meet expenses of unusual events, such as the revolt of the navy and the struggles in Rio Grande do Sul,[85] but also there was an extraordinary pressure to service the public debt, a large part of which consisted of foreign loans. The

Amin Filomeno, "A crise Baring e a crise do Encilhamento nos quadros da economia-mundo capitalista," *Economia e Sociedade* 19,1 (Abril 2010), 135–171; Kris James Mitchener and Marc D. Weidnmier, "The Baring Crises and the Great Latin American Meltdowns of the 1890s," available at http://emlab.berkeley.edu/~webfac/eichengreen/e211_fa06/Mitchener.pdf; and Gail Triner and K. Wandschneider, "The Baring Crisis and the Brazilian Encilhamento, 1889–1891: An Early Example of Contagion among Emerging Capital Markets," *Financial History Review* 12,2 (2005), 199–225.

[85] The most recent study of the naval revolt is Joseph Love, *The Revolt of the Whip* (Stanford, CA: Stanford University Press, 2012).

imperial government, to balance the external and public accounts, had taken numerous foreign loans whose servicing was a heavy burden on the new republic's public budget.[86] As the basic federal income depended on import taxes, crises in the value of exports reduced government revenues. If at the same time there occurred a depreciation of the *mil réis*, the effect was multiplied because the export tax incomes were received in national currency and the servicing of the foreign debt required the government to purchase foreign currency.[87] The government had to pay its debts in British pounds sterling, thus the decline of the exchange rate was a factor in generating instability in the public finances. This fiscal deterioration, the inflation of prices and the depreciation of the Brazilian currency internationally, made the foreign bankers unwilling to provide new credit to Brazil. To add to Brazil's problem there was a major expansion of the coffee harvest, which in 1897 led to a reduction in world prices for coffee, and in turn lowered the value of Brazilian exports. Given this dramatic crisis, the government was obliged to negotiate a refinancing of its external debt. The government of Campos Salles in 1898 was forced to obtain a "funding loan" that allowed the government to make no payment on this external debt for 13 years. In exchange, the government promised to eliminate the budget deficit and retire from circulation an amount of money equivalent to the value of the funding loan.[88] The revenues of its customs houses were used to serve as a guarantee of these loans. In order to obtain income to honor its external obligations, the government also instituted a gold charge on its custom duties, which meant that it did not need to compete in the exchange market to acquire the currency

---

[86] In 1889 the debt of the federal government was £30 million, the equivalent of 276 *contos de réis*. In 1898, when the funding loan was made, the external debt increased to £36 million, but this was now equivalent to 1,193 *contos de réis* due to the revaluation of the national currency. AEB (1939–1949), 1424.

[87] As Celso Furtado noted, increasing the relative importance of external debt service in the public budget made it increasingly difficult for the government to finance its expenditures with current revenues in periods of depression. Thus a correlation was established between the foreign loans, budget deficits, emissions of paper currency imbalances, and current account balance of payments. Furtado, *Formação Econômica do Brasil*, 171.

[88] According to Marcelo de Paiva Abreu, Brazil under the empire was an excellent debtor, always paying on its external debt. It was the only Latin American economy to not suspend the servicing of its external debt from the first external loan of 1824 to the first funding loan of 1898. Marcelo de Paiva Abreu, "Os Funding Loans Brasileiros – 1898–1931," *Pesquisa e Planejamento Econômico* 32,3 (Dezembro 2002), 515–540; Veja-se também Marcelo de Paiva Abreu, "A dívida externa do Brasil, 1824–1931," *Estudos Econômicos* 15,2 (1985), 168–189. On the financial policies of the empire, also see Paulo Roberto de Almeida, *Formação da diplomacia econômica no Brasil: as relações econômicas internacionais do Império* (São Paulo: Editora Senac-Funag, 2001).

needed to service the foreign debt. The objectives of the government were achieved, the budget deficits were reduced, prices fell, and the value of Brazilian money increased internationally (see Graph 1.14 and Appendix Table A.3). But these policies led to the bankruptcy of numerous banks and companies that had been created in this decade.[89]

This monetary and exchange turbulence had a direct impact on the coffee market. That market had natural fluctuations that over the long period led to a balance between supply and demand, without any clear tendency in coffee prices in the second half of the nineteenth century.[90] These crises in the coffee market caused sharp declines in coffee prices and devaluation of the Brazilian currency through its impact on the balance of payments. Although the devaluation represented a partial compensation to the grower, who received his income in *mil réis*, the net effect was a fall in the profitability of the coffee industry, discouraging new plantings. As demand revived, the market responded with increases in international prices and higher returns to producers and a return to new plantings of coffee.

But this natural pattern changed in the decade of the 1890s. In 1892 the international price of coffee began a long-term secular decline, but its impact was muted given the strong devaluation of local currency that maintained the profits of local planters and in turn stimulated new plantings. Moreover, as the remuneration of the producers was in the national currency, they could accept lower prices in the international market and still maintain profitability if there was – at the same time – a strong devaluation of the national currency. As Brazil was the major producer in the world, this behavior of national producers tended to further erode coffee prices in the international market. Lower international prices combined with the falling value of the national currency may have still been remunerative to producers, but it led to less revenue for Brazil's exports, worsening the external sector of the economy. Moreover, in these conditions, falling international prices did not lead to a decline in national production or new plantings. This created a structural excess of supply that was evident by the middle of the following decade, all of which led to a further decline in international prices which fell by 60 percent between 1891 and 1898. The success of the stabilization policy carried out by Campos Salles, which resulted in the recuperation of the exchange

---

[89] On this theme, see Hanley, *Native Capital*, Chapter 6. She shows that the crisis provoked a consolidation and expansion of the foreign presence in the paulista banking sector.
[90] As in studies of Delfim Netto, *O problema do café no Brasil*.

rate, dramatically reduced the income of planters, who were paid in *mil réis*. But despite this drop in coffee profitability, which led to the discouragement of new planting, production actually increased each year. This paradox of continued expansion and falling prices and profitability was the result of earlier coffee plantings gradually entering into production at this time thus leading to overproduction (Graphs 1.15a to 1.15d and Appendix Table A.1).

From the end of the 1890s there was growing the idea that the government should intervene in the market, especially given the coffee overproduction crisis characterized by low coffee prices and the accumulation of stocks of coffee. But the government of Campos Salles, which had promoted economic stability and which believed in the regenerative forces of the market, was against any type of governmental intervention. As then Minister of Finance Joaquim Murtinho put it: "The government is convinced that official intervention could only increase our ills, we should let coffee production be reduced through natural selection, liquidating those who could not survive and leaving the strongest and best organized to continue the struggle."[91] But the crisis became ever more acute, with world stocks reaching dramatic levels, thus increasing pressure on the government to intervene. Coffee now entered the market from the trees planted in the decade of the 1890s and by 1902 the state of São Paulo was forced to prohibit the planting of new trees for a five-year period. Given the importance of the coffee economy for São Paulo,[92] it was the most active state seeking a solution to the crisis of overproduction.[93]

Although the coffee economy continued in crisis, the relative stability of production in the years 1904 to 1905 reduced the pressure for intervention. The policy of intervention was discussed in Congress with no

---

[91] Joaquim Murtinho was Minister of the Treasury in the government of Campos Salles, and principal director of the policy of stabilization of the Campos Salles government. *Relatório apresentado ao Presidente dos Estados Unidos do Brazil pelo Ministério de Estado dos Negocios da no anno de 1900* (Rio de Janeiro: Imprensa Nacional), iv.

[92] The importance of coffee in the São Paulo economy is evident in a number of areas. E.g., in the decade of the 1900s more than half the income of the state railroads came from the transporting of coffee (Saes, *As ferrovias de São Paulo*, 92–93); in 1905 coffee represented 64 percent of the total agricultural production of the states. Maria Sílvia C. Beozzo Bassanezi and Priscila M. S. Bergamo Francisco, eds., *Estado de São Paulo: estatística agrícola e zootécnica, 1904–1905* (Campinas: NEPO/UNICAMP, 2003), CD-ROM; in 1905 as well some 60 percent of export taxes collected by the paulista government came from coffee exports. *Anuário Estatístico de São Paulo 1905*, 148–153, 190.

[93] Delfim Netto affirms that the regime of exploitation in São Paulo, based on the colonato regime, makes the crisis more acute in São Paulo, in relation to other producing states. Delfim Netto, *O problema do café no Brasil*, 44–45.

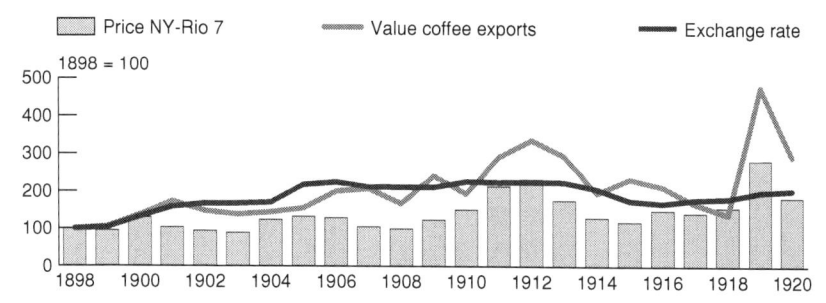

GRAPH 1.15a. Index of Exchange, Prices, and Coffee Exports, 1898–1920. *Source*: Bacha 1992 and Ipeadata

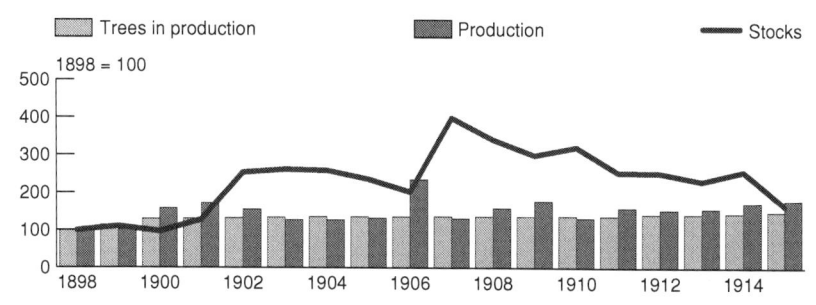

GRAPH 1.15b. Index Coffee: Plantings, Production, and Stocks in Brazil, 1898–1920. *Source*: Bacha 1992 and Ipeadata

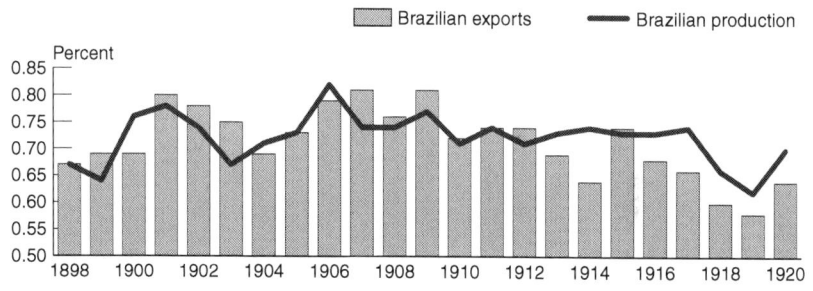

GRAPH 1.15c. Percentage of Brazilian Production and Exports to World Production and Exports, 1898–1920. *Source*: Bacha 1992 and Ipeadata

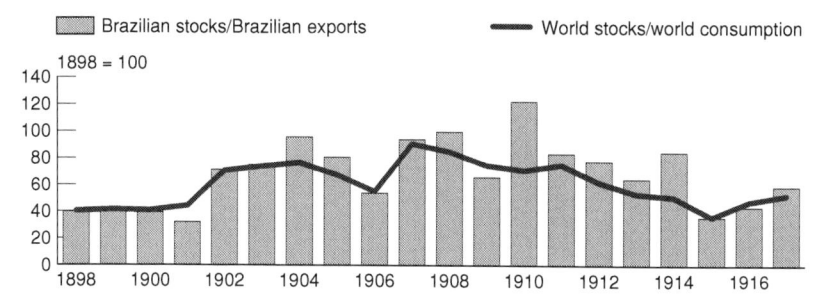

GRAPH 1.15d. Coffee: World Stocks, World Consumption, and Stocks, Brazil/Exports Brazil, 1898–1920. *Source*: Bacha 1992 and Ipeadata

success, since the opponents to intervention would not accept a policy of government price supports (called "valorization") just for coffee. Nevertheless, the second semester of 1906 saw an even more serious crisis as stocks reached very high levels and as estimates for the harvest of 1906/1907 suggested there would be an abundant crop.[94] By now Brazil alone in one year produced more than the world consumed in that year. At a meeting of the producers in 1906 there was signed the Taubaté Convention in which it was proposed that the government should buy the excess coffee production at a minimum preestablished price; and that it also should restrict the production of low-quality coffee, stimulate internal consumption, and promote the product abroad.[95]

Although the government believed in a free market, it was obliged to carry out its first intervention at the time of the exceptional harvest of 1906.[96] Coffee was crucial for Brazil, since it represented the principal economic activity of the nation and accounted for more than half of Brazilian exports. The support of the coffee economy began when the

[94] The stockpile of coffee bags was 11 million bags for a consumption of 16 million. And the initial estimate of the harvest of 1906/1907 was 16 million, but production reached 20 million bags. There was no place to offer a crop of this magnitude. As previously noted, coffee trees began to produce only at four years of age and continued to produce for some 20 to 30 years, and sometimes even as much as 50 years. Thus, although the crisis was evident, the production did not depend on current decisions, but plantings made at least five years earlier.

[95] Delfim Netto, O problema do café no Brasil, Chapters 2–3. In various parts of this section devoted to interventions in the coffee market, we have used the work of Delfim Netto.

[96] In an important study of the First Republic, Steven Topik argues that despite the liberal ideas that dominate the political and economic environment, there was a high participation of the state in the economy. He suggests that this intervention went beyond what leaders may have wanted but was deemed essential in order to promote Brazilian exports. Steven Topik, *The Political Economy of the Brazilian State, 1889–1930* (Austin: University of Texas Press, 1987). The author goes on to affirm that "The Brazilian Government participated in the economy because of the strength of foreign capitalists as well as the weakness of the domestic bourgeoisie. To compensate for the lack of Brazilian capital, the State had to create inviting conditions for foreign capital to expand the agricultural economy through duty exemptions, guaranty profits, subsidies, direct investments in private companies, and monopoly concessions." Steven Topik, "The Evolution of the Economy Role of the Brazilian State, 1889–1930," *Latin American Studies* 11,2 (November 1979), 329. In an interesting article Marichal and Topik show that although guided by the theory of liberalism, Brazil and Mexico are closely linked to the international economy and were forced to adopt interventionist policies in the commodities market, tariffs, and the railroads. Carlos Marichal and Steven Topik, "The State and Economic Growth in Latin America: Brazil and Mexico, Nineteenth and Early Twentieth Centuries," in *Nation, State and the Economy in History*, ed. Alice Teichova and Herbert Matis (Cambridge: Cambridge University Press, 2003), 349–372.

federal government created a Currency Board, which would buy foreign currency at 15 pence per *mil réis* and would issue convertible currency. In the case that there was an abundance of foreign currency, since it operated at a fixed rate, the Currency Board could limit the increase in value of the *mil réis*. But there was a potential serious risk should there be a shortage of foreign currency in the market. This could occur either because of an international crisis or one in the coffee market. The tendency would then be to devalue the *mil réis*. As the Currency Board bought *mil réis* at a fixed rate, there would be a run on the Currency Board to exchange *mil réis* for English pounds, depleting the accumulated reserves.[97] Congress also authorized the president to establish negotiations with the states to regularize the commerce of coffee and stabilize its price, being able to endorse credit operations needed to accomplish this.

Because of the gravity of the situation and both the inertia of the federal government and the relative indifference of other coffee-producing states, the government of São Paulo initiated its own program.[98] It was able to raise the funds overseas to purchase just under two million sacks of coffee. But this policy could not continue at only the level of São Paulo when it was known that the 1906/1907 harvest was going to produce 20 million sacks of coffee. To guarantee the service of its debt the state instituted a tax of 3 francs per sack exported, in accordance with the previous Taubaté Convention, which had producers and the government agreeing to act together in a coordinated manner to tax coffee exports. At the end of the 1906/1907 harvest the world stocks of coffee was 16.4 million tons, half of which pertained to the state of São Paulo.[99] In 1907 the federal government obtained new external loans and passed the funds on to São Paulo; in 1908 it made a similar operation, but in this case far more money was obtained, on the order of £15 million. This particular operation signaled to the market the viability of the operation headed by São Paulo state. This government now had the financial ability to retain the coffee stocks for the time needed to balance the market. These loan arrangements

---

[97] Vieira, *Evolução do Sistema Monetário Brasileiro*, 238–274.
[98] According to Sérgio Silva, there was a hesitation on the part of the federal government, largely explained by the position of Lord Rothschild, who publicly came out against its application, since he feared that it would compromise the operation and the obligations assumed in the funding loan of 1898. Sérgio Silva, *Expansão cafeeira e origens da indústria no Brasil* (São Paulo: Editora Alfa-Omega, 1995), 60.
[99] Given the large stock of coffee purchased, financed largely by short-term funding, the state government of São Paulo was forced to rent Sorocabana Railway Co. Ltd. to secure new loans.

also involved agents who operated in the international coffee market who had an interest in the success of the operation. Moreover, these retained stocks remained deposited overseas, with full market visibility.[100] After falling to its lowest price in more than fifty years, coffee prices recuperated on the international market. The smaller harvests in the following years allowed for the gradual sale of the stockpiled coffee in the market.

The results of this first valorization, or price-support scheme, were impressive. In the first place, the restriction on planting established in 1902 maintained production at a relative stable level in the following years, much below the exceptional production of the harvest of 1906/1907 and prices continued to rise until 1912. With rising coffee prices and rising exports, along with income generated from foreign loans, there was a great inflow of foreign exchange in this period. The result would have been for the *mil réis* to rise in value, but the Currency Board bought foreign exchange at a fixed price, and this led to stability in the exchange. In turn, the stability of the exchange rate benefited exporters, who otherwise would have been prejudiced by a change in the value of the *mil réis*. The limitation on new plantings and the gradual sale from the stockpiled coffee guaranteed the stability of the market and of international prices. By 1915 the stocks of Brazil were in correct proportion to exportations, reaching the level that existed at the beginning of the century before the period of the Encilhamento. Despite these positive aspects in stockpiling and producing coffee, Brazil lost part of its share in the international market. In the world coffee market, Brazil production dropped from 74.2 percent in the mid-1900s to 71.1 percent in the 1910s; in terms of exports the drop was more dramatic going from 76.2 percent to 67.7 percent of total world exports of coffee. This relative decline occurred because Brazil retained part of its production in stocks, giving an opportunity for other producers to sell their product. In the average of the 10 years after the intervention carried out by São Paulo, the country stockpiled 80 percent of the world's coffee stocks (see Graph 1.15d and Appendix Table A.1).

It should be recalled that the intervention represented a reaction to the conditions of overproduction. Restricting plantings, taking the excess production off the market, creating a tax on exports to support the

---

[100] The majority of coffee purchased was sent to the great importing ports of the United States and Europe, consigned to the largest merchants in the market, who, in turn, provided the funds to finance the operation. Delfim Netto, *O problema do café no Brasil*, 72.

servicing of the debt assumed to pay for the stockpiling operation, and creating a Currency Board, all functioned adequately to protect the coffee market until World War I. Despite the excellent performance of coffee exports and the consequent positive balance of payments, the operations of the Currency Board avoided the valorization of the *mil réis*, thus benefiting exporters. But in 1913 the conflict in Europe that would lead to World War I began. This created international instability, with a consequent drop in coffee prices and capital flight, leading to a run on the Currency Board as it tried to defend the *mil réis*. By August 1914 the Currency Board was forced to close. The flight from *mil réis* to gold dramatically reduced the money supply, thus negatively affecting business. The international crisis also led to a major decline of coffee prices in the international market (see Graph 1.15a). When unsold coffee stocks increased there was even further pressure exerted on international prices, and planters soon demanded a new intervention of the government in the market. The state of São Paulo, successful in the first operation, received federal funds and promised to buy and retain coffee. The low coffee harvests of 1918 and 1919, and the end of World War I brought a new equilibrium to the market. Prices rose and stocks were reduced.

But this new normality lasted only a short time. The harvest of 1920 produced a bumper crop just as there was an economic crisis in the consumer markets, especially the United States. Credit was restricted in the international financial market and there was a repatriation of capital to the central countries, a typical response to international crises and one of the principal causes for the periodic economic disequilibrium in the peripheral countries such as Brazil. In the coffee market consumption declined along with prices and stocks increased. This formed the background for a new third state intervention in the coffee industry. In contrast to the two previous interventions, which were made by the state of São Paulo, this one was undertaken by the federal government. The success of the two previous programs facilitated the decision. The federal government bought four million sacks of coffee and regulated the access of coffee arriving at the ports. This third plan of valorization was a success and, combined with a low harvest in 1922/1923 and the end of the acute crisis in the central economies, led to a rapid recovery of the market.

It should be recalled that the three interventions were quite temporary, relating to short market crises and an annual overproduction. Part of the inventory was taken off the market. There were also temporary controls of planting and natural fluctuations in coffee production that led to a rebalance in the coffee market. The government was then able to sell its accumulated coffee stocks. Despite the government's intervention in these three schemes, there was no permanent structure to keep prices high. Once a crisis had passed, the market was allowed to function freely. But in all three cases these policies helped Brazil's competitors, who benefited from the greater stability of international prices without the onus of stockpiling their own coffee.

The success of these intervention schemes promoted the idea of establishing a permanent defense of coffee. The idea first appeared in 1921 when Congress approved the creation of the Permanent Defense of National Production, which involved all products, not just coffee. But the federal government decided not to establish this institute or remain in the coffee market. When stocks of the third recovery operation were sold, the federal government transferred operation of the defense of coffee to the state of São Paulo that created the Institute for the Permanent Defense of Coffee, which subsequently became the Coffee Institute of São Paulo.

The aim of the institute was to regularize the flow of coffee to the embarkation ports. Keeping coffee in the interior warehouses reduced the pressure on the market. The aim was to supply the market but avoid excess supplies. To make this operation viable it was necessary to finance the state purchase of coffee stocks. This system reduced the importance of coffee merchants (called *comissários*), particularly in their role of providing credit to the producers. Equally the speculation that went on at the ports now ceased to exist. To finance this operation the state of São Paulo took out a loan of £10 million, whose servicing would be paid with a tax on each sack of coffee that circulated in the state. In 1927 the other producer states adhered to the program, establishing unique criteria to control the ports of embarkation, stipulating a daily movement to the ports of 1/25 of the quantity exported in the previous month. As in the earlier plans there was established a Currency Board (*Caixa de Estabilização*), which functioned like the old *Caixa de Conversão*. From 1924 to 1928 there was a major growth in the money supply, but inflation was controlled and the exchange rate remained stable all due to the work of the Currency Board.

From a short-term perspective, the permanent defense plan could be considered a success.[101] Coffee prices rose, the quantity exported

---

[101] Topik discusses the overall results of the coffee valuation program, including the permanent defense phase. He finds that all these programs were successful in the sense of

increased, and income from coffee exports grew by 60 percent. However the long-term consequences were disastrous. In the first place, the permanent defense program reduced the risk to the Brazilian producer, and their production and price was maintained at too high a level. This gave a stimulus to new plantings, with a new rhythm of production peaks occurring every four to five years and with harvests now reaching more than 30 million sacks. This pattern intensified to just a two-year cycle in the years after 1929. The average harvest in the four years preceding the initiation of the permanent defense of coffee was hardly 15 million sacks. This program was even more negative in its impact when we consider Brazil's competitors. Brazil offered the coffee needed to balance the international market. That is, Brazil entered the market as a residual supplier, allowing competitors to put all their products on the market. It guaranteed these competitors a market at extremely high prices, which permitted these less productive competitors to enter the market. As a result these competitors increased their production and export of coffee at the expense of Brazil (Graphs 1.16a to 1.16d and Appendix Table A.1).

The crisis of 1929 hit the coffee market in a moment of local overproduction, a natural result of the policies of long-term protection that had been adopted. Even before the crisis of 1929 the coffee market experienced a delicate moment given the exceptional 1927 Brazilian harvest of some 30 million sacks of coffee, which added to a total world production of 40 million coffee sacks, when consumption at this time barely reached 23 million sacks of coffee. But high international prices in the late 1920s stimulated new coffee tree plantings that then increased output. Maintaining the policy of regulating total shipments of coffee to the ports, the exceptional harvest created ever-increasing stocks in the warehouses, and also increased demand for credit to purchase the stocks and finance the time they remained warehoused. Given the system of convertibility then in place, the increase in credit would depend on the reserves of gold in the financial system. But as soon as signs of an international crisis appeared, there was an immediate restriction of credit in the international market. As in all such crises, there was also a flight of capital to the central countries. This crisis of confidence thus stimulated the demand for foreign

---

appreciation of the price of coffee and the major beneficiaries were effectively growers, particularly in the period of permanent defense. Topik, *The Political Economy of the Brazilian State, 1889–1930*, Chapter 3.

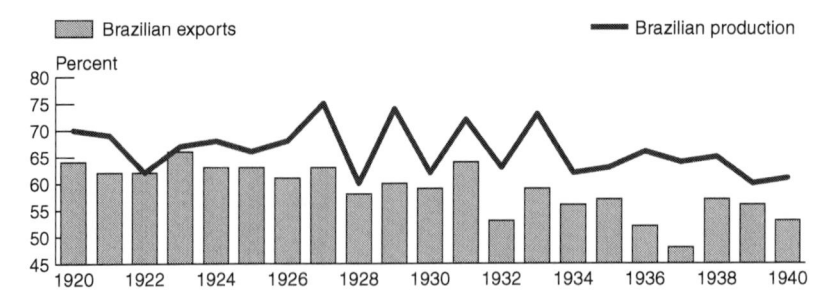

GRAPH 1.16a. Percentage of Brazilian Production and Exportation of Coffee, 1920–1940. *Source*: Ipeadata

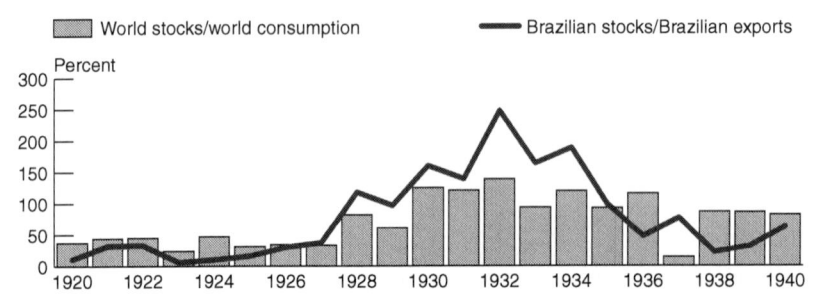

GRAPH 1.16b. Percentage of World Consumption and Brazilian Exports, 1920–1940. *Source*: Ipeadata

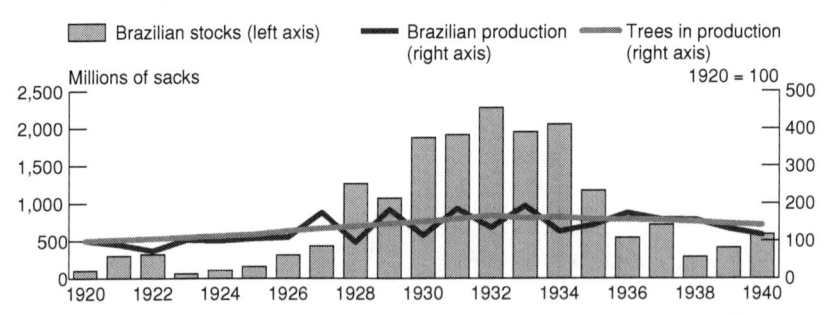

GRAPH 1.16c. Index of Plantings and Production and Total Stocks of Coffee, 1920–1940. *Source*: Ipeadata

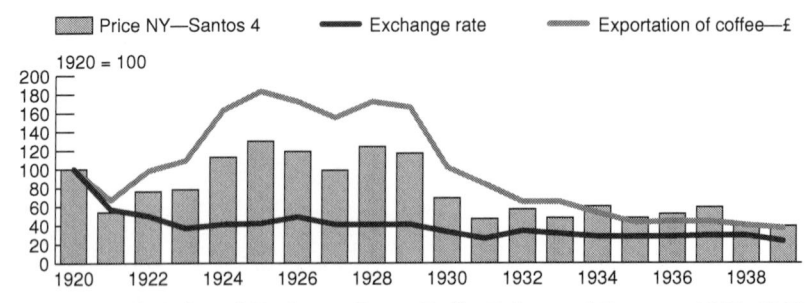

GRAPH 1.16d. Index of Exchange Rate, Coffee Price, and Exports, 1920–1939. *Source*: Ipeadata

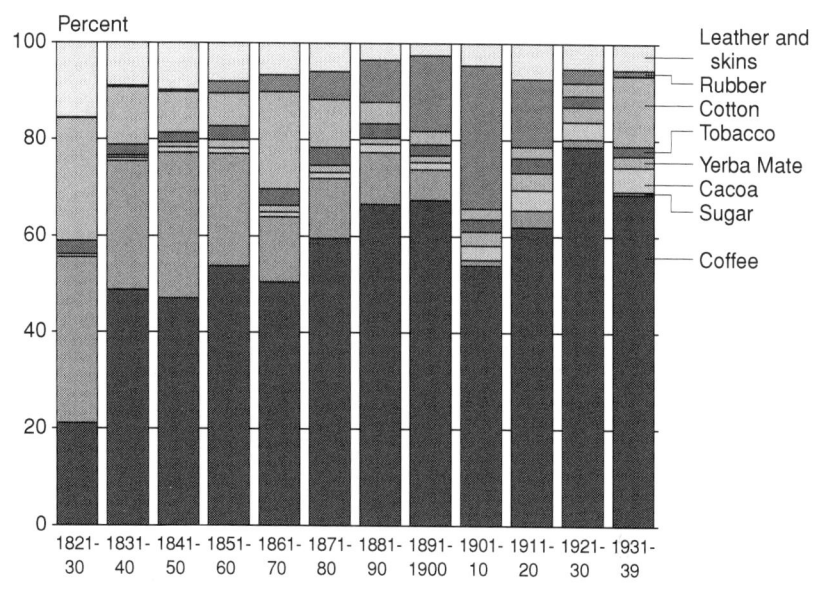

GRAPH 1.17. Participation of Principal Exports in Total Exports, 1821/1939.
Source: *Anuário Estatístico do Brasil* (1939–1940)

currency and simultaneously reduced the gold reserves at the Currency Board and in the banking system, and therefore dramatically decreased the money supply. In this situation it was practically impossible to expand credit and to maintain convertibility of the national currency. This not only caused insufficient resources to be available to maintain funding for the continuation of the policy of permanent defense of coffee, but also led to the paralyses of the Currency Board.

In spite of the importance of coffee production to the national economy throughout the period of the Old Republic, other goods were produced throughout Brazil that entered the international and internal markets. In the export market sugar was the leading crop after coffee. After the decline of gold and diamond exports in the late eighteenth century, sugar once again dominated Brazilian exports as it had in the sixteenth and seventeenth centuries. As late as the 1820s, sugar accounted for a third of the value of Brazilian exports, as compared to a fourth of the value obtained by cotton and just a fifth for coffee exports. But coffee soon expanded and progressively dominated mid- and late-nineteenth-century imperial exports, and throughout the period of the Old Republic it accounted for an average of some 65 percent of the value of exports (see Graph 1.17 and Appendix Table A.4).

Although sugar lost its supremacy in the decade of the 1830s, it maintained its importance as the second most important export crop until the 1890s, only being temporarily displaced by cotton during the period of the U.S. Civil War. Brazilian sugar had been produced in traditional mills until the 1870s. As other competitors introduced new milling technology with the so-called central mills, Brazilian influence in the world market declined, even though local production increased. From the decade of the 1880s Brazil's sugar exports declined systematically with only a temporary short recovery in the 1920s. But in general, Brazilian sugar was of little importance in the international market during the period of the Old Republic (see Graphs 1.18a to 1.18d).[102] The key factor here was the late development of a modern sugar milling industry in Brazil, compared to the earlier adoption of such technology by its competitors.[103]

From the 1870s the Brazilian government attempted to modernize the sugar industry through the introduction of these central mills. Traditionally producers cultivated the cane and milled it. In contrast, the steam-driven central mills were so large and productive that they needed to consume cane produced by outside farmers. The normal pattern was for traditional mills to go out of production as planters concentrated on just harvesting cane, thus creating two distinct entities: millers who also planted some cane, and full-time cane producers who sent their cane to be milled at the central mills. But despite numerous government efforts, the central milling system could not be firmly established. The reasons for this early failure were due to several factors. First, the most modern and expensive milling equipment was not used in many cases, even when established with foreign capital, and so capacity was limited. Second, there was no coherent development of suppliers to these mills given the high cost of transport and the fact that many of the traditional "*senhores de engenho*" (mill owners and planters) refused to abandon their mills

---

[102] Noel Deerr, *The History of Sugar* (London: Chapman and Hall, 1949).
[103] Peter Eisenberg examined the technological backwardness of production in Pernambuco. He affirms that "The combination of cheap land and cheap uneducated labor produced a conservative attitude of 'routinism' toward technological innovation.... Capital costs and market insecurity also affected the rate of innovation. The slow accumulation of retained earnings in the traditional engenho, in comparison with the cost of acquiring modern machinery, prevented the average senhor de engenho from adopting modern technology." Peter Eisenberg, *The Sugar Industry in Pernambuco: Modernization without Change, 1840–1910* (Berkeley: University of California Press, 1974), 42–43.

since they represented their local political power.[104] It was not until the first years of the twentieth century that, with government support, the first *usinas* (or sugar factories) were established. These were modern milling operations with their own vast fields of cane production.[105] Once transformation of the industry began, change was rapid. In 1917 there already existed 215 *usinas* and they now produced half of the national sugar output.[106] In that year Pernambuco accounted for 40 percent of national production, Rio de Janeiro for 20 percent, and Alagoas for 10 percent. São Paulo, with just 8 percent of national output could only supply 40 percent of its own sugar needs and had to import the rest from other parts of Brazil.[107] As of 1939 there were 345 *usinas* and 18,000 *engenhos*, with the *usinas* now producing 70 percent of the sugar. The survival of the old mills despite the rapid growth of the modern mills shows how delayed the transition to the new technology was, especially compared with Cuba and other international producers that had all made a complete transition to the new system by this time. But the rise of the *usinas* did have an impact on national production as older zones declined in importance and new zones, which were using the new mills, rose in importance. By the end of the Old Republic, the northeastern share of output had declined significantly and the southeastern states had increased their importance, with São Paulo (at 15 percent), Minas Gerais (at 13 percent), and Rio de Janeiro (at 13 percent) catching up to Pernambuco, which now accounted for only 28 percent of sugar (Graphs 1.18a to 1.18d).[108]

Cotton had two periods of major importance in the history of Brazilian exports. The first occurred at the beginning of the nineteenth century when European wars favored exports, and the second during the "cotton famine" of the U.S. Civil war period when U.S. cotton exports were drastically reduced giving a new space for Brazilian production.

---

[104] On this theme, see Gileno de Carli, *O açúcar na formação econômica do Brasil* (Rio de Janeiro: Annuário Açucareiro, 1937); Eisenberg, *The Sugar Industry in Pernambuco*; Alice P. Canabrava, "A grande Lavoura," in *História da civilização brasileira*, II:4, ed. Sérgio Buarque de Holanda (São Paulo: Difusão Europeia do Livro, 1971), 85–140.
[105] Eisenberg, *The Sugar Industry in Pernambuco*, Chapter 5.
[106] Carli, *O açúcar na formação econômica do Brasil*, 32–33.
[107] Ministério da Agricultura, Indústria e Comércio, *Indústria assucareira no Brazil* (Rio de Janeiro: Directoria Geral de Estatística, 1919), 44, 68.
[108] AEB (1939–1940), 198–203. This activity employed 134,000 persons: 98,000 in agriculture, 25,000 in factories, 3,000 in specialized work, and 8,000 in the railroads.

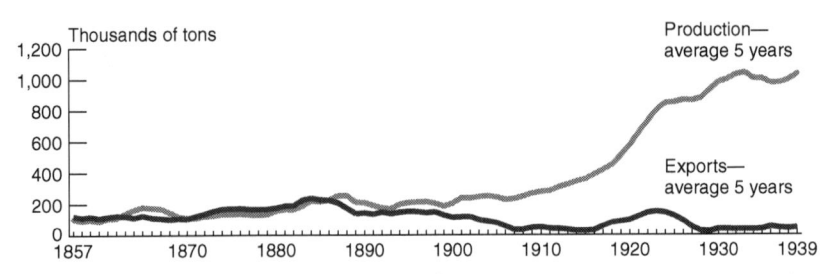

54   The Economic and Social History of Brazil since 1889

GRAPH 1.18a. Production and Exports of Sugar, 1858–1927. *Source: Anuário Estatístico do Brasil* (1939–1940) and Deerr 1949

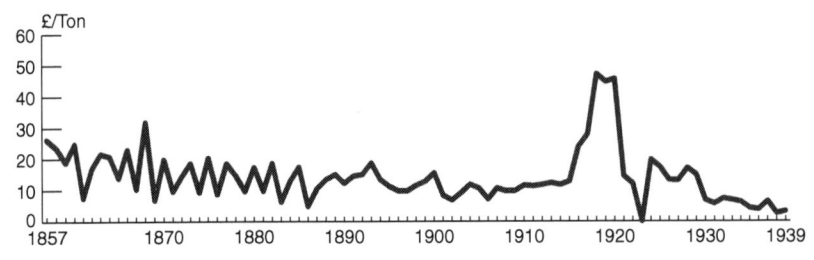

GRAPH 1.18b. Average Price of Sugar Exports, 1857–1937. *Source: Anuário Estatístico do Brasil* (1939–1940)

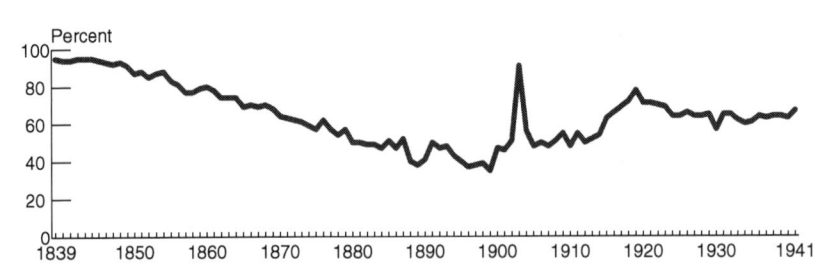

GRAPH 1.18c. World Cane Production as Percentage of Total World Cane and Beet Sugar Production, 1839–1939. *Source:* Deerr 1949

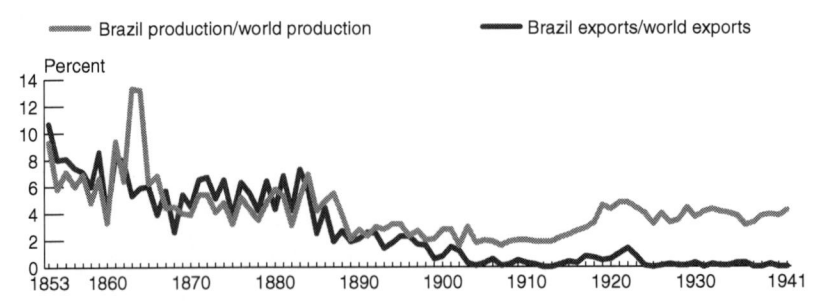

GRAPH 1.18d. Brazilian Sugar Production and Exports by World Totals, 1853–1937. *Source:* Deerr 1949

But once these wars were resolved, international sales were reduced and during the Old Republic period cotton was a relatively minor Brazilian export.[109]

But rubber became an important product, especially in the period just before and during the Old Republic. Native to the Amazonian region, rubber gained major importance in the world economy in the second half of the nineteenth century as methods were developed to process rubber and use it in industrial activities. But the major growth came with the use of rubber for tires in the new automobile industry at the end of the nineteenth century. With the expansion of auto production, the demand for rubber grew exponentially. The problem was that rubber trees grew naturally and so the production was artisanal. As it developed in Brazil, rubber collecting required a large quantity of workers given the dispersed nature of the rubber trees in the forest. These rubber collectors worked in terrible environmental and working conditions and their productivity was quite low. Moreover, these workers had to be imported from other regions. It is estimated that the Amazon rubber zones received around 260,000 laborers from the northeastern states. These workers arrived already in debt and were subject to a brutal labor system.[110]

The government stimulated production in the Amazon and for a short period Brazil held a monopoly on world production, including rubber shipped from other Amazonian regions such as Bolivia. But the development of new rubber tree varieties in the 1910s allowed Asian producers to develop major plantations of the rubber trees and compete successfully with Brazilian production.[111] By the late 1910s the East Asian producers were beginning to export and quickly surpassed Brazilian production. As prices fell on the international market, the higher-cost nonplantation-produced rubber of Brazil lost market share to its rubber

---

[109] On this theme see Alice P. Canabrava, *O algodão no Brasil, 1861–1875* (São Paulo: T. A. Queiróz Editor, 1984).

[110] Furtado, *Formação Econômica do Brasil*, Chapter 23. In this chapter the author offers a magisterial analysis that he called the "Transumância Amazônica." On this theme, also see Barbara Weinstein, *The Amazon Rubber Boom, 1850–1920* (Stanford, CA: Stanford University Press, 1983); Maria Lígia Prado and Maria Helena Rolim Capelato, "A borracha na economia brasileira na primeira república," in *História geral da civilização brasileira*, III:1, ed. Boris Fausto (Rio de Janeiro: Bertran Brasil, 1989), 285–307; Zephyr Frank and Aldo Musacchio, "Overview of the Rubber Market, 1870–1930," available at http://eh.net/encyclopedia/article/frank.international.rubber.market.

[111] Although synthetic rubber was developed outside of Brazil, it was initially not an adequate substitute for the natural product.

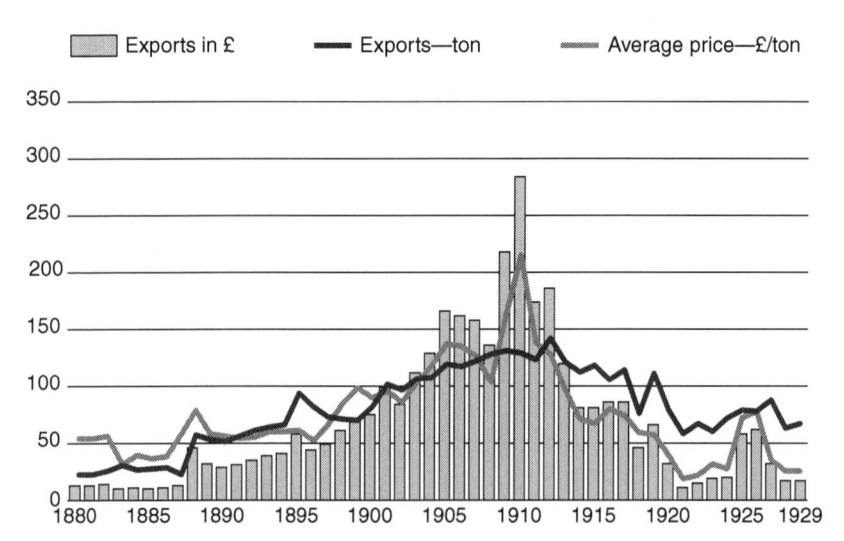

56 The Economic and Social History of Brazil since 1889

GRAPH 1.19. Index of the Quantity, Value, and Price of Rubber Exports, 1880–1929 (mean 1900/1904 = 100). *Source*: IBGE Séries Históricas 1990

plantation–producing rivals in East Asia. In the 1920s Henry Ford, wishing to free himself from what was now the British colonial Asian monopoly of rubber production, tried to establish rubber plantations in the Amazon.[112] But the project was a failure despite the enormous amounts spent on the project, since Brazilian rubber trees were destroyed by parasites as soon as they were planted close together. The result was that, by the end of the twentieth century, Brazil was an importer of natural rubber (Graph 1.19).

Another product of importance in this period that was native to Brazil was cacao, which was also a product native to the Amazon. Like rubber, it was initially gathered naturally and with low productivity due to the forest environment in which it was produced. Brought from the Amazon to southern Bahia in the second half of the twentieth century, it was then more systematically organized and harvested allowing Brazil to become a major participant in the world market. This development of the cacao industry in southern Bahia produced a major social transformation in the region as well as major conflicts over land between local landlords (the so-called *coronéis*, or colonels) and peasants as was depicted in the

[112] See Greg Grandin, *Fordlandia: The Rise and Fall of Henry Ford's Forgotten Jungle City* (New York: Metropolitan Books, 2009).

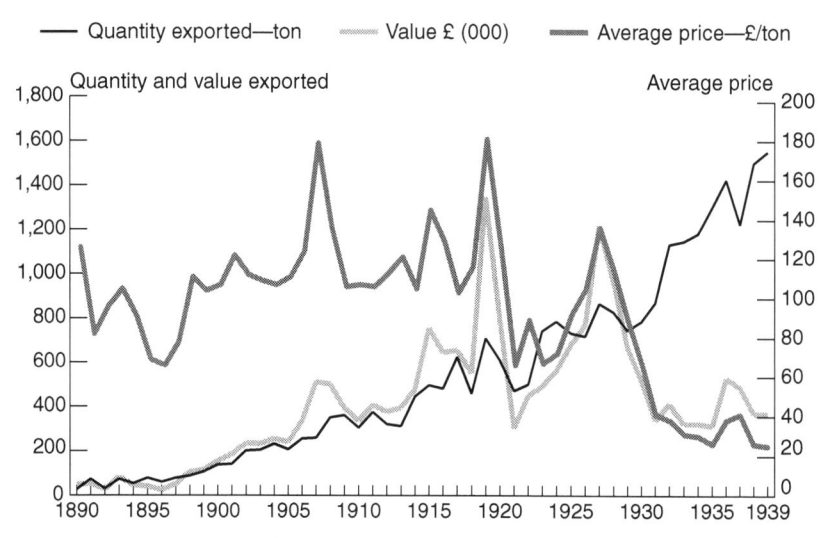

GRAPH 1.20. Cacao, Production, Value, and Quantity Exported, 1890–1938. Source: IBGE Séries Históricas 1990

novels of Jorge Amado. During the period from 1890 to 1930 cacao production grew at an annual rate of more than 6 percent. In turn, prices remained stable until 1929 when they began to fall, declining by 75 percent by 1939 (see Graph 1.20), thus creating a profound crisis in this sector.[113]

There were also other primary products that were significant in the local, regional, and national markets. In 1920 and 1930 corn was the second most important agricultural product in terms of value, only surpassed by coffee. Given its importance in human and animal consumption, it is no surprise that in the census of 1920 some 2.4 million hectares were planted in corn, which was greater than the 2.2 million hectares planted in coffee. Other products with significant internal markets included rice, beans, manioc, and sugar. Moreover, the cattle industry now accounted for 47 percent of agricultural output. But cotton, however important in the nascent textile industry, did not appear in the list of the 12 most

---

[113] To create instruments of market intervention in 1931 the Cacao Institute of Bahia was created. Later, in 1957, the Executive Commission for Rural Economic-Recovery of Cocoa Farming (CEPLAC) was established. The emergence of a plant plague in the 1980s devastated production in the south of Bahia, and the country changed from being an exporter to an importer of cacao.

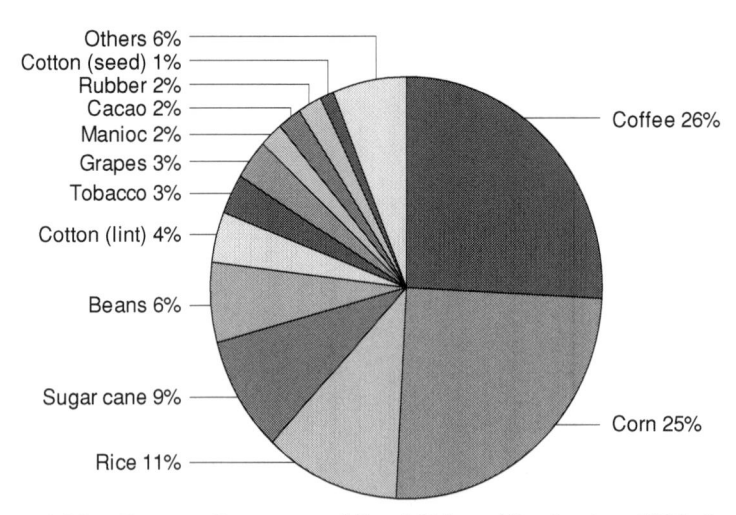

58   The Economic and Social History of Brazil since 1889

GRAPH 1.21a. Crops as Percentage of Total Value of Production, 1920. *Source*: Recenseamento Geral 1920

important agricultural products (see Graphs 1.21a and 1.21b). In contrast to coffee and to a lesser extent with sugar, which was produced on large plantation units with salaried workers, most of these major products destined for the internal market were produced on family farms based on family labor and sometimes a few hired hands. Moreover, this

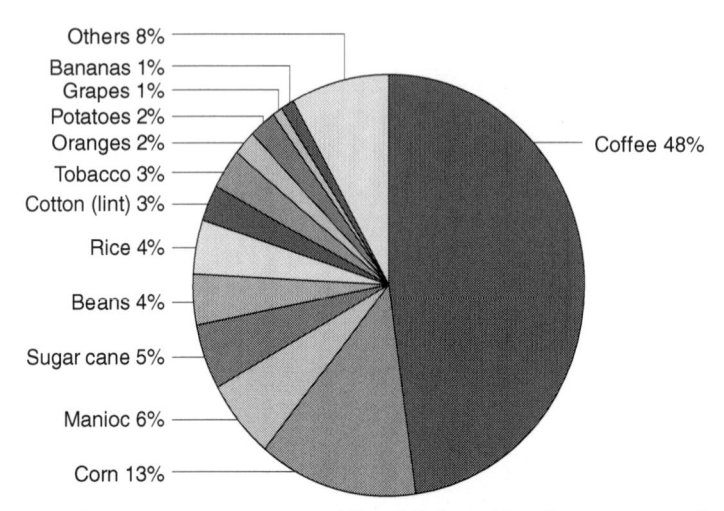

GRAPH 1.21b. Crops as Percentage of Total Value of Production, 1930. *Source*: Recenseamento Geral 1930

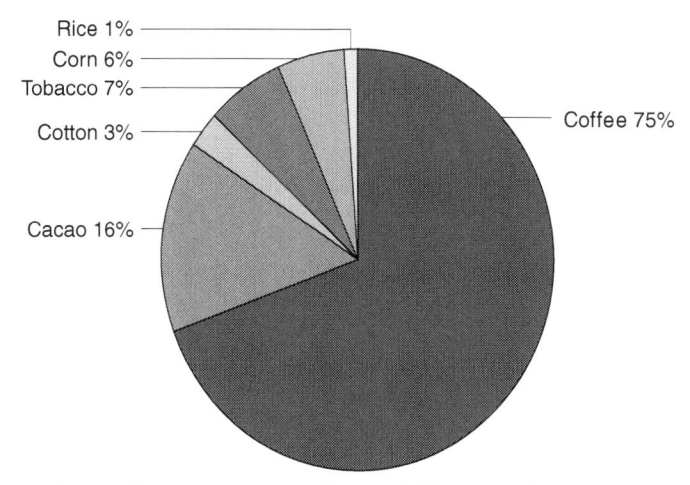

GRAPH 1.22. Brazilian Products as a Share of World Production, 1920. *Source*: Recenseamento Geral 1920

production had less of a multiplying effect on the economy, in contrast to coffee.[114]

By 1920 then, Brazil was still a minor player in the world agricultural market except for coffee. It was the leader in coffee production, accounting for 75 percent of world output, and was second in the production of cacao – but accounted for only 16 percent of world production. In other crops it had little impact in total world production despite its vast farmlands. It produced only 6 percent of world corn output, 7 percent of its tobacco, and just 3 percent of the world's cotton. In all other products such as rice, potatoes, and wheat it was a distinctly modest producer (see Graph 1.22). This low output by world standards was due to the still poor application of even minimum technology to Brazilian agriculture in this period. In 1920, of the 224,000 rural establishments that were listed in the census, only 1,652 even possessed plows.[115] This low

[114] In a study that we did of the agricultural census of São Paulo state in 1905, we found a large part of the cereal production occurred on coffee fazendas, showing that these coffee estates were not mono-production units. For this reason, contrary to what was usual in Brazil in other regions and periods, a significant proportion of cereal production occurred in median and large units that intensively used salaried workers (or *colonos*). See Francisco Vidal Luna, Herbert S. Klein, and William R. Summerhill, "A agricultura paulista em 1905," *Revista Estudos Econômicos* (São Paulo), forthcoming.

[115] *Recenseamento Geral do Brasil, 1920*. IBGE, Vol. 3, Part 3, vii, xiv; and the *Censo Agrícola de 1905*, available in digital format from the Núcleo de Estudos de População (NEPO), of the Universidade de Campinas.

usage explains the very low proportion of 3 percent that machines and agricultural equipment accounted for in the total value of these rural establishments in 1920. Even in São Paulo, the value of machines was only 4 percent, while lands represented 79 percent and other improvements another 18 percent.[116] Thus little had changed since the São Paulo agricultural census of 1905, which listed an equally low usage of plows even in regions dedicated to coffee.[117]

Brazil did have a significant livestock industry, with some 70 million animals, the majority being cows and pigs. Minas Gerais and Rio Grande do Sul possessed the largest flocks of animals. This latter state had been the traditional provider of jerked beef in the late colonial and imperial periods, primary for slave consumers. But this ended with slavery and by the last part of the nineteenth and beginning of the twentieth centuries the region established modern slaughterhouses and produced refrigerated beef and other meats, but mostly for the local market.

Whatever the weakness of the Brazilian agricultural sector, there is little question that the expansion of agriculture in the nineteenth century had a major impact on the internal economy and was crucial in modernizing ample sectors of the economy. The intensification of the agro-exporting sector required investments in machines and equipment, as well as the expansion and modernization of the transport system. The last quarter of the nineteenth and beginning of the twentieth centuries saw the full elaboration of an extensive railroad system with national and foreign capital that facilitated production of coffee and other products by connecting the ports with the areas of production.[118] As can be seen in Graph 1.23, there were two great periods of investments in railroads, the decade of the 1880s and the period from 1908 to 1914. Some 40 percent of the railroad network that existed in 1938 in the state of São Paulo, for example, had been constructed in this latter seven-year period. Moreover, traffic data from the São Paulo railroads shows an accelerated secular growth in the years 1916 to 1938, with only a short

---

[116] *Recenseamento Geral do Brasil, 1920.* IBGE, Vol. 3, Part 3, lx.
[117] For an analysis of the 1905 agricultural census of São Paulo, see Vidal Luna, Klein, and Summerhill, "A agricultura paulista em 1905."
[118] In this period the majority of foreign investments went into railroads, particularly English capital. "In the context of the relatively thin finance and segmented Brazilian capital market, access to both debt and equity finance in Britain proved in the long term to be indispensable to the expansion of Brazil's railroad sector." Summerhill, *Order against Progress*, 44.

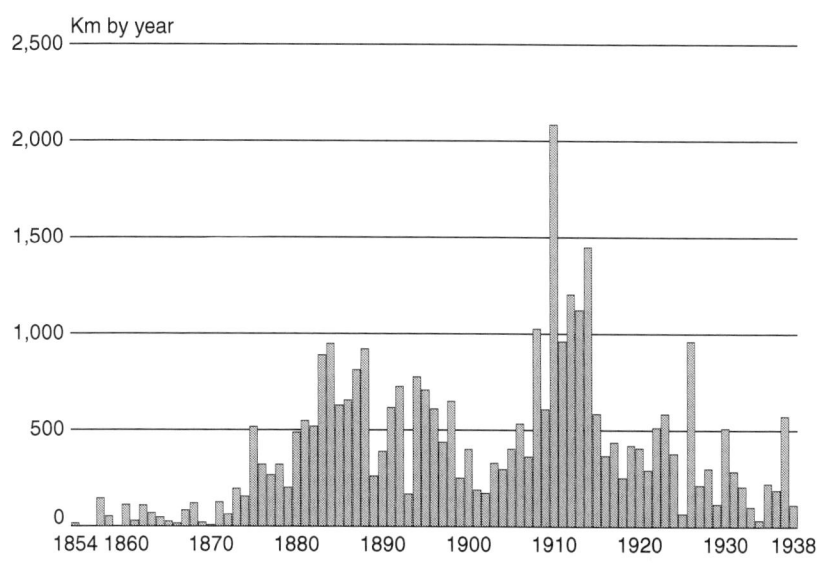

GRAPH 1.23. Expansion of Railroad System, 1854–1938. *Source*: Pinto 1977 and *Anuário Estatistico de São Paulo*

decline in the period from 1930 to 1934. The movement of freight and passengers had increased by a factor of three in this thirty-three-year period.

But agriculture was not the only market sector to expand in this period. There would also be the beginnings of an industrial economy in Brazil. Given the revolution in transport, which reduced the costs of moving goods throughout the country and opened up new territories for agricultual expansion, the transition to a salaried rural workforce throughout much of the country was another factor that promoted the growth of an internal market.[119] The expansion of wage labor increased dramatically with the abolition of slavery and the introduction of millions of immigrants, and it had multiple effects. It increased the size and diversified the consumer market, encouraged an increase in monetary circulation, and created a modern labor market. It was this growth of a wage labor force that set the stage for the industrial transformation of Brazil.

---

[119] As Celso Furtado argued in his classic work economic history, "[T]he factor of major importance which occurred in the Brazilian economy in the last quarter of the 19th century was, without doubt, the increase in importance of the wage labor sector." Furtado, *Formação Econômica do Brasil*, Chapter XXVII, 159.

Industrial development was started with the earnings generated by the coffee export sector and was promoted by the major expansion of the salaried workforce.[120] The agro-exporting sector, though not as modernized as other late-nineteenth- and early-twentieth-century agricultural societies, nevertheless generated the resources needed to invest in infrastructure, and to extend and modernize the internal productive structure.[121]

That the agro-export sector was fundamental in intiating industrial activity can be seen in the first products produced by Brazilian factories and by the association of industrial activity with cycles in the export economy. Before the crisis of 1929, industrial expansion corresponded to the most dynamic periods of the agro-export economy. Thus a cotton textiles industry emerged to provide clothing for slaves or provide bags to hold materials being exported.

Unfortunately data on early industrial activity is limited for Brazil. However, the economic historian Wilson Suzigan in an original study was able to calculate the amount of machinery and equipment exported

---

[120] Although linked to the ideas of CEPAL, Furtado has developed his own innovative ideas about industrialization. The CEPAL model argued that the root of underdevelopment was in the foreign trade between the core and peripheral countries, whose international division of labor delegated to the peripheral countries specializing in primary products, while manufacturing was in the central countries. The growth pattern of the peripheral countries was "facing out," and the decision center of the economy of developing countries was abroad. The economy of the peripheral countries was "reflexive and dependent." Breaking the pattern of growth would be possible only with industrialization, which could occur with the imbalances caused by external shocks from World War I, the Crisis of 1929, and World War II. In this new pattern of development, industrial investment replaced the external demand as the dynamic factor in the economy. This position of CEPAL stimulated the so-called theory of adverse shocks in the interpretation of Brazilian industrialization, which represents an extreme form of interpreting the thought of CEPAL. The position of CEPAL, launched by Raul Prebisch, represented a revolution in economic thinking in Latin America and launched the idea of industrialization by import substitution, which several Latin American countries were to adopt. Raúl Prebisch, "O desenvolvimento econômico da América Latina e seus principais problemas," *Revista Brasileira de Economia* 3 (1949), 49–111.

[121] There is an interesting insight developed by Nicol, who sought to analyze the relationship between the agricultural revolution and the process of industrialization in developed countries, believing that the path of industrialization is the technological revolution in agriculture. When he studies Brazil, he also identifies agriculture in the nineteenth century as the dynamic factor in industry. But although there was a large agricultural growth in that century, there was no agricultural revolution by the European or Japanese standards. Brazilian agriculture had evolved little technologically. That conditioned the pattern of development of our industry. Robert N. V. C. Nicol, "A agricultura e a Industrialização no Brasil (1850/1930)" (PhD thesis, Economics, Universidade de São Paulo, FFLCH-USP, 1974).

to Brazil in this early period.[122] The growth in investment in industry first occurred in the period from 1890 to 1896, which corresponded to the period of Encilhamento, which clearly had real consequences in the economy. Besides promoting a major growth in the money supply, the period also saw a high and stable level of exports. There was also a major expansion in the cotton industrial sector, and many of Brazil's largest firms were founded in this period of easy credit and abundant capital.[123]

The level of exports reached in 1896 was only surpassed in 1906, and from then until 1913 there was an accelerated expansion of industrial investments that corresponded to a new cycle of high exports of coffee generated by the first valorization scheme. There was an abrupt decline in such investments during World War I, but there was a recuperation in the early 1920s aided by elevated coffee exports and sales. With the crisis of 1929 occurred an abrupt retraction (see Graphs 1.24a to 1.24d). That Suzigan's figures well track the changes in industrial development can be seen in the correspondence between imports of machines and equipment in general and that of imports of machines and equipment for the textile industry.[124] The movement of the apparent consumption of cement and steel, as well as the importation of capital goods is highly correlated, showing as we have noted, these two cycles of investment during the Old Republic – that of 1901 through 1913 and 1921 through 1929 (see Graphs 1.24a to 1.24d).

Although there appears to exist a correlation between the cycle of exports and factory investments, actual production seemed to move in

---

[122] The study covers exports from the United Kingdom, the United States, Germany, and France in the period 1855–1939. Wilson Suzigan, *Indústria Brasileira. Origens e Desenvolvimento* (São Paulo: Brasiliense, 1986).
[123] Stein, *The Brazilian Cotton Manufacture*, 88. As Stein noted, "...mills already in existence expanded capital stock, although part of the new capitalization took the form of stock dividends. The nominal capitalization of textile mills listed on the Rio de Janeiro stock exchange swelled from 13,500 contos ($7,290,000) in 1889, to 54,100 eighteen months later; to 72,550 in August of 1891, and to 84,210 contos ($25,263,000) on January 1, 1892. Furthermore, cotton mill proprietors (and the entrepreneurs of other industries) placed orders abroad for new machinery in 1889, 1890 and early in 1891." Also see Albert Fishlow, "Origens e conseqüências da substituição de importações no Brasil," in *Formação Econômica do Brasil. A experiência da industrialização*, ed. Flávio Rabelo Versiani and José Roberto Mendonça de Barros (São Paulo: Saraiva, 1977), 7–41.
[124] In the data of imports of machinery and equipment for the textile industry we added sewing machines, revising the part of the series produced by Suzigan.

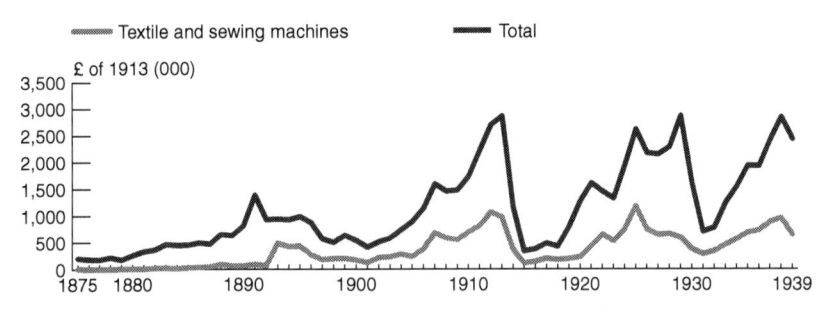

GRAPH 1.24a. Machines and Equipment Exported to Brazil, 1875–1938. *Source*: Suzigan 1986

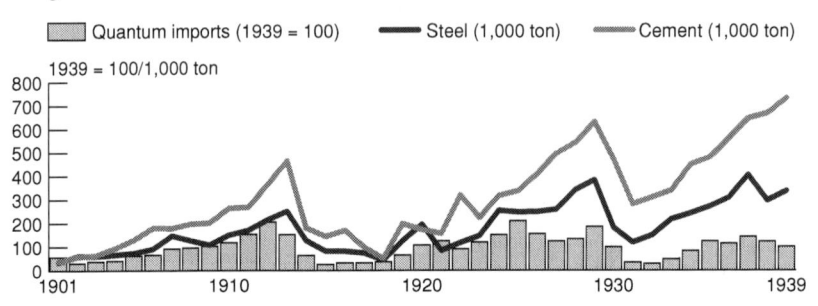

GRAPH 1.24b. Investment Indicators, 1902–1939. *Source*: Suzigan 1986

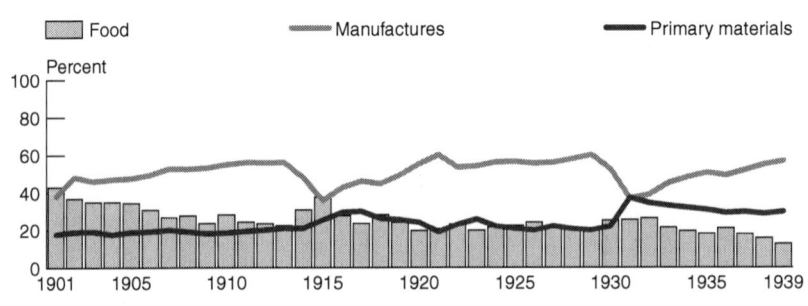

GRAPH 1.24c. Composition of Imports, 1901–1938. *Source*: *Anuário Estatístico do Brasil* (1939–1940)

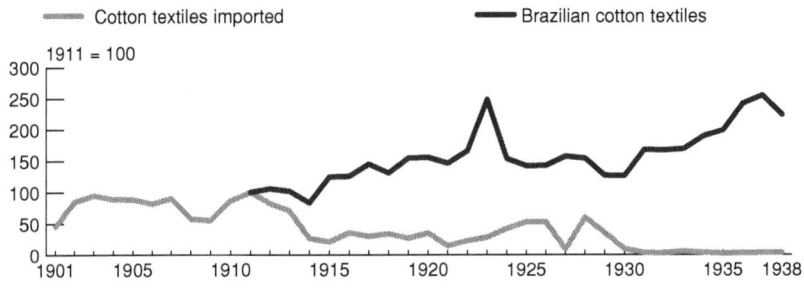

GRAPH 1.24d. Production and Importation of Cotton Textiles, 1901–1938 *Source*: Stein 1979, Annex III

the opposite direction. Brazilian industrial textiles production grew systematically from the late nineteenth century until 1923, and then fell for the rest of the 1920s. Thus, contrary to investments, production moved countercyclically to coffee exports. Textile output increased when exports fell and rose when there were adverse shocks to the export sector (see Graph 1.23).[125] Imported textiles that had always represented an important part of Brazilian imports (representing 29.2 percent of all imports in the period from 1870 to 1875), slowly declined from 1910 onward as imported cloths were replaced by national production. Textile imports accounted for only 18 percent of all imports in 1911, and dropped to 7 percent in 1914, a level that was maintained until the 1929 crisis. In periods of crisis for the export economy, the composition of imports by type showed an increase in the raw material imports and a decline in manufactured products. This shift showed that there was an acceleration in industrial capacity during periods of coffee export crises, as seen in the experience of national textile manufactures (see Graphs 1.24a to 1.24d).[126]

In 1906 the first general census of industry occurred in Brazil. By this time, the Federal District (the city of Rio de Janeiro) was the most important manufacturing zone in the republic and contained between 25 percent and 30 percent of all national factories in terms of capital, value of production, and number of workers; São Paulo was second, at half the percentages in all areas. Other important zones included Rio Grande do Sul, the state of Rio de Janeiro, and Pernambuco. Minas Gerais, though it had a significant number of factories, had little influence in terms of national production.

In this year there were some 150,000 factory workers, of whom 52,000 were employed in the 194 textile factories. Moreover, the average number of workers in these textile works were considerably above the average in all factories in general. In textiles, as in all manufacturing, the

---

[125] When discussing the impact of adverse shocks on industrialization, Versiani and Versiani demonstrated that investments increased in periods of high coffee exports; the adverse shocks reduced the rate of investment, but increased the utilization of the productive capacity. Flávio Rabelo Versiani and Maria Tereza R. O. Versiani, "A industrialização brasileira antes de 1930: uma contribuição," in *Formação Econômica do Brasil*, ed. Flávio Rabelo Versiani and José Roberto Mendonça de Barros (São Paulo: Saraiva, 1977), 121–142.

[126] Imported textiles had always represented an import part of Brazilian imports (representing 29.2 percent of all imports in the period from 1870 to 1875), but slowly declined from 1910 onward as imported cloths were replaced by national production. Villela and Suzigan, *Política do Governo e Crescimento da Economia Brasileira*, 441.

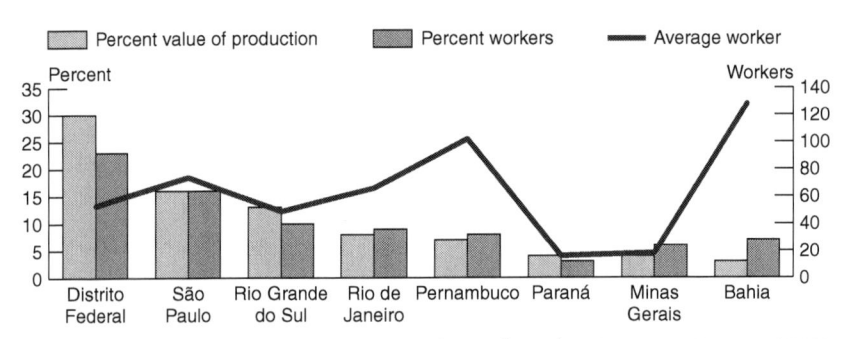

GRAPH 1.25a. Industrial Production and Workers by States – Census 1907.
Source: IBGE, Estatísticas Retrospectivas 1990

Federal District was the leader in the average output per mill, and average numbers of workers, and was far superior to any other zone (see Graphs 1.25a to 1.25d). Brazil by this period had become self-sufficient in the production of shoes, hats, beer, pasta, furniture, and all tobacco products. While textiles were the largest part of the Brazilian industrial sector, there were still imports of cotton, silk, and woolen cloths. These still represented the most important imported products, and they accounted for a third of the consumer market for these cloths.

Much of this industrial base had changed significantly by the census of 1920. By that year there existed 13,336 industrial firms: 30 percent in the food sector, 15 percent in clothing, 12 percent in ceramics, and the rest primarily in wood and textiles. Broken down by value, firms producing food products made up 41 percent of the total value of industrial production and textiles 27 percent. In contrast, the largest employee of industrial workers and use of motor force was the textile industry (41 percent) followed by food and clothing. In terms of size, the preponderance of textiles was evident, averaging 93 workers per plant compared to an average of 21 workers per factory in all industries. Interestingly, although there was a sharp increase in the total number of employees in industry in general, there was a reduction in the average number of workers by industry, probably as a consequence of the increasing diversity of the industry in general.[127]

---

[127] The census of 1907 and 1920 are not totally comparable, since the first is incomplete. They serve more to provide an understanding of productive structures in each year than for a direct comparison between the two censuses. On this theme, see Silva, *Expansão cafeeira e origens da indústria no Brasil*, Chapter IV.

The Old Republic, 1889–1930 67

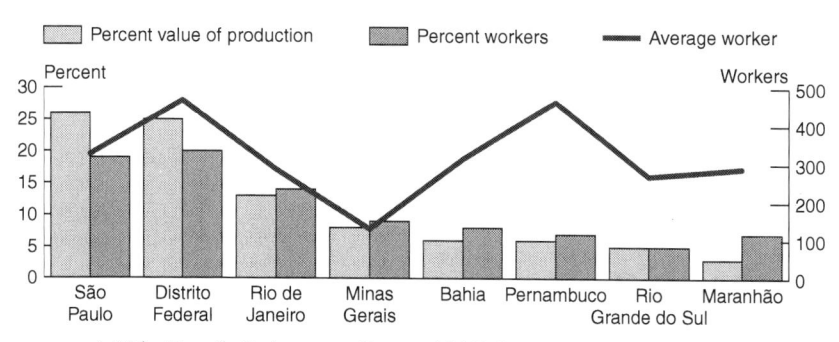

GRAPH 1.25b. Textile Industry – Census 1907. *Source*: IBGE, Estatísticas Retrospectivas 1990

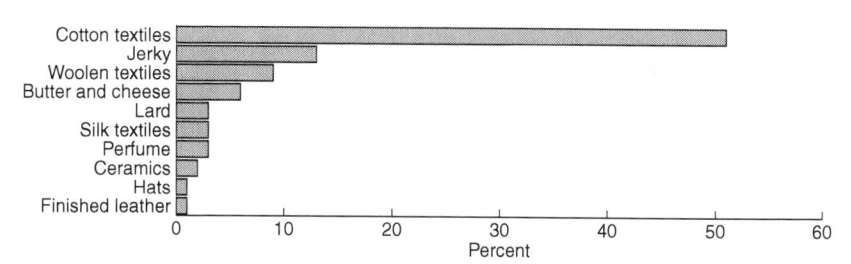

GRAPH 1.25c. Participation in the Importation of Consumer Goods – Census 1907. *Source*: IBGE, Estatísticas Retrospectivas 1990

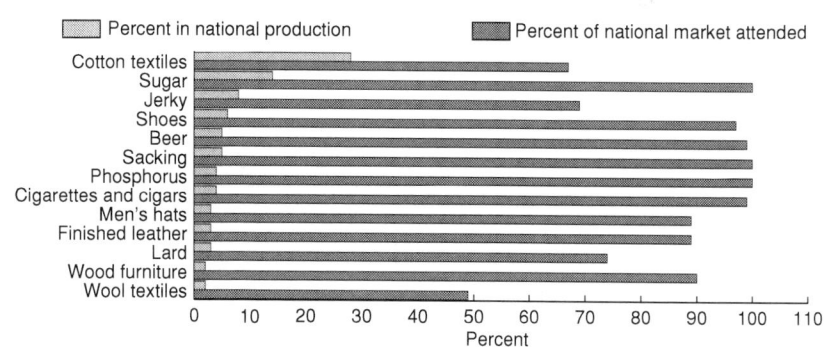

GRAPH 1.25d. Participation in the Production of Consumer Goods, 1907. *Source*: IBGE, Estatísticas Retrospectivas 1990

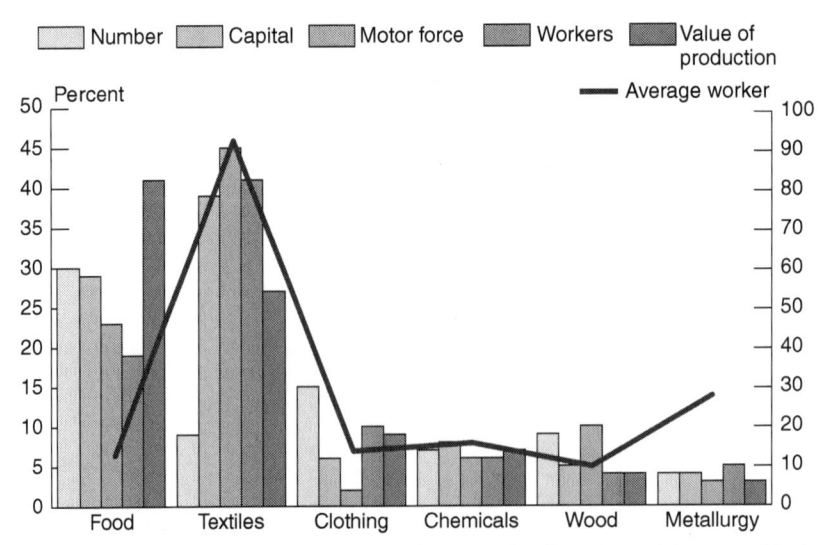

GRAPH 1.26. Percentage and Number of Principal Industries and Average Workers per Unit – Census 1920. Source: IBGE, Séries Históricas Retrospectivas 1990

Despite the existence of large factories, national industry was defined by numerous small enterprises. In 1920, of the 9,450 enterprises subject to the "consumption tax,"[128] the majority of factories (89 percent) employed just nine workers or less, but accounted for only 15 percent of all workers. At the other extreme were 61 companies with more than 500 workers, which represented less than 1 percent of all enterprises, but accounted for 42 percent of the industrial workers. On average these companies had a thousand workers per unit. Although this indicates a relative concentration within the industrial sector, the few factories of this large size indicated the relative modest nature of Brazilian industry. Industry until the 1920s essentially produced mass-consumption articles of low aggregated value, but also produced high-volume products, difficult to import (see Graph 1.26).[129]

This growth of industry between 1907 and 1920 was matched by a spectacular rise of São Paulo, which in this period finally surpassed the

---

[128] The consumption tax was established in November 1899 (Lei 641). It was initially charged on tobacco products, drinks, matches, salt, shoes, candles, perfumes, pharmaceutical products, vinegar, canned fruit, playing cards, hats, canes, and cotton and linen fabrics consumed in the country. Later it was enlarged beyond the original list of products. The tax was levied in the form of a stamp.

[129] Warren Dean, *The Industrialization of São Paulo* (Austin: University of Texas Press, 1969), 9.

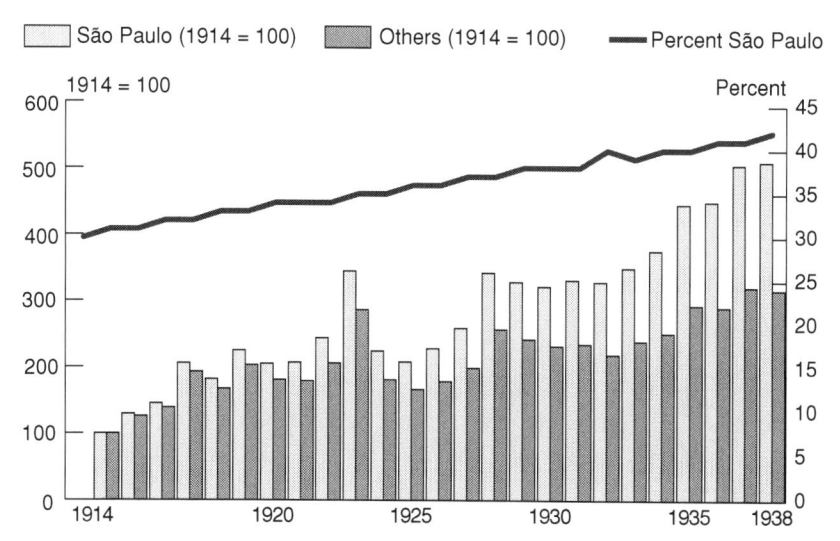

GRAPH 1.27. Evolution of the Real Value of Industrial Production and the Participation of São Paulo, 1907-1938. Source: IBGE, Anuário Estatistico do Brasil (1939-1940)

Rio de Janeiro Federal District and the state of Rio de Janeiro as the premier manufacturing leader of the nation. São Paulo grew faster in terms of manufacturing than any other state.[130] By 1928 São Paulo alone accounted for 38 percent of all industrial companies and this dominance would increase in the 1930s (see Graph 1.27 and Appendix Table A.8).

The reasons for the emergence of the supremacy of São Paulo have been well studied and are essentially related to the rise of the coffee economy and of the new coffee bourgeoisie. The dramatic growth of coffee led to important backward links to everything from transport, manufacturing, imports, and exports, to the development of a service sector. Moreover, the income from coffee exports provided the funds needed to develop the necessary infrastructure to promote this industry and its exports.[131]

---

[130] Just as an indicator of this, we can cite the census of 1920, which shows that the installed power in São Paulo already represented 43 percent of installed electricity in the country. *Recenseamento de 1920*, Vol. 5, Part 1, p. lxxxix.

[131] For other fundamental studies, see Dean, *The Industrialization of São Paulo*; Wilson Cano, *Raízes da Concentração Industrial em São Paulo* (São Paulo: Difel, 1977); Silva, *Expansão cafeeira e origens da indústria no Brasil*; Joseph Love, *São Paulo in the Brazilian Federation, 1889-1937* (Stanford, CA: Stanford University Press, 1980); Flávio A. M. Saes, *A grande empresa de serviços públicos* (São Paulo: Hucitec, 1986); Fernando Henrique Cardoso, *Mudanças Sociais na América Latina* (São Paulo: Difusão Européia do Livro, 1969), Chapter 8; Renato Monseff Perissinotto, *Estado e Capital Cafeeiro em São Paulo (1889-1930)* (São Paulo: Fapesp; Campinas: UNICAMP, 1999). In addition

It was the successful creation of a wage labor force in coffee after the abolition of slavery that enabled São Paulo to become the premier coffee-producing state. Its growth was spectacular after this. Between 1880 and 1929 São Paulo coffee production went from one million sacks of coffee to 20 million, which then represented two-thirds of Brazilian production. Production of this magnitude was due to the planting of 824 million coffee trees on more than a million hectares. To plant, process, and transport this extraordinary harvest required a major labor force, transport structure, energy, and commercial and banking infrastructure.[132] São Paulo had Brazil's most complete railroad network, which connected the producing areas to the port of Santos. This railroad network had 7,000 kilometers, which was approximately a fifth of the entire Brazilian rail network. As of 1920, the paulista railroads alone employed 47,473 persons.[133] A third of the income of the paulista railroad came from shipping coffee.[134] As for labor, the state attracted both natives and foreigners to work in the coffee industry. Between 1897 and 1939 some 800,000 Brazilians from other states and 2.3 million from overseas arrived in the state. São Paulo received 55 percent of all foreign-born immigrants who arrived in Brazil.

These wage workers were employed in the most dynamic sector of the national economy. In turn, the wealthiest coffee planters became entrepreneurs in a wide variety of businesses, especially those derived from or dependent on coffee. These businesses included railroads, the generation of electricity, importing merchant houses, financial services, coffee brokers, and the new industries supplying the expanding internal market. Thus the income generated in the coffee economy and allied activities permitted the construction of an internal market far greater than had existed under slavery.[135] There was a generalized expansion of

---

to the private capital invested in national infrastructure, foreign capital, particularly English, also played a key role in the sector, either through direct investments or financing of projects controlled by national capitals. Richard Graham, *Britain and the Onset of Modernization in Brazil 1850–1914* (London: Cambridge University Press, 1968) and Hanley, *Native Capital*.

[132] On the public services in São Paulo, see Flávio A. M. Saes, *A grande empresa de serviços públicos* (São Paulo: Hucitec, 1986).

[133] In 1920, with 6,937 km extension of tracks, São Paulo railroads employed 47,473 people. The rail network had 693 stations, 507 warehouses, 759 locomotives, and 10,435 wagons. *Anuário do Estado de São Paulo*, 1920, Vol. 2, 88.

[134] Saes, *As ferrovias de São Paulo, 1870–1940*, 92–93. According to the author, "the fundamental concern of the railway administration is the volume of coffee shipped, this variable defines the very profitability of the company" (86).

[135] As the sociologist and former president of Brazil Fernando Henrique Cardoso noted: "The means by which the coffee economy prospered amplifying the flow of exchanges,

the mercantile economy. For the *colonos* who could not gain access to land, most moved to other activities as workers or even entrepreneurs. Moreover, even as *colonos* they had the right to produce their own crops on the coffee *fazendas*, which also permitted them to initiate the process of accumulation along with their wages.[136]

Various studies show that the origin of many of the factories came from capital generated in the coffee sector. In fact, the paulista coffee barons could be characterized as significant capitalist entrepreneurs, who participated in a very wide number of major enterprises, often in the form of stock ownership of these corporations. Two of the principal railroads, the Mogiana and the Paulista, had their origin in coffee capital and had shareholders who were coffee planters.[137] Warren Dean, in a classic work on the pioneers of industrialization in São Paulo, stressed the existence of three different groups of entrepreneurs. The first were the importers, who supplied the local market with imported goods that were not produced locally.[138] These importers had multiple operations in the country, including even assembling and maintaining imported machines and equipment. Some imported products that still needed finishing, or even incorporated parts not imported that had to be produced in the local market, and this led to the creation of local factories. Moreover, these importers knew the internal producers and were also furnishers of raw materials and manufactured parts and equipment for these new factories and had access to foreign capital. In many cases this permitted them to shift from being distributors of a given product to national manufacturers of that product. Thus at the margin of the importation process there developed a segment of the industrial plant in Brazil headed by these importers.

The coffee planters represented another important group who promoted Brazilian industrialization. Earlier sugar producers had promoted

---

was due to the increase in the capacity of consumption of farmers and, to a lesser extent, of *colonos*. The capacity of these later, even for those whose chances were limited to escape the condition of colons, could not be compared to the habits of consumption of slaves." Cardoso, *Mudanças Sociais na América Latina*, 192–193. The author also emphasizes the impact occurred primarily in the city of São Paulo, the natural route between the port and the producing regions and the center of the market for immigrant labor. This contributed to its geographical location and its status as political and administrative capital.

[136] On the possibilities of *colonos* accumulating savings see the study of Zuleika Alvim, *Brava Gente! Os Italianos em São Paulo 1870–1920* (São Paulo: Brasiliense, 1986).

[137] Silva, *Expansão cafeeira e origens da indústria no Brasil*; Saes, *A grande empresa de serviços públicos*; João Manoel Cardoso de Mello, *O capitalismo tardio* (São Paulo: Brasiliense, 1982); Perissinotto, *Estado e Capital Cafeeiro em São Paulo (1889-1930)*.

[138] Dean, *The Industrialization of São Paulo*, 19.

agro-industries and this occurred in coffee as well. Equipment and agricultural machines needed by growers, initially imported, were then assembled, adjusted, repaired, and finally constructed in part in Brazil. Thus coffee planters participated in innumerable manufacturing activities in all sectors, including in textiles, as well as being major investors in the railroad companies and even administered them.[139]

The third important initiators of early industrialization in São Paulo were the immigrants. In this case we can divide the immigrants into two large groups. Those who came to work in the countryside, beginning as *colonos* on the coffee *fazendas*, and through their own efforts were capable of becoming small, medium, and large farmers or factory owners. Another group, emphasized by Dean, were foreigners who had relatively high-status positions in Europe and arrived in Brazil as specialized workers or with the capital needed to establish themselves in Brazil. These elite immigrants established an important share of the early great factories. According to Dean, these entrepreneurial immigrants and the big importers took advantage "of the ready-made market that the rural and urban European-born masses provided for those who were familiar with their tastes and habits."[140]

The 1920 census shows that foreign owners in industry were almost of equal importance to that of the national entrepreneurs. Brazilian-born manufacturers employed 28,466 workers, compared to 25,071 employed in factories owned by foreigners. The two groups had roughly similar amounts of usage of motor power, the value of production, and the amount of capital employed.[141] Among the foreign-born factory owners, it was the Italians who predominated. They controlled 40 percent of the capital, workers, motor force, and value produced by these factories.

---

[139] Dean, *The Industrialization of São Paulo*; Saes, *A grande empresa de serviços públicos*; Perissinotto, *Estado e Capital Cafeeiro em São Paulo*. Antonio da Silva Prado is seen as an example of this type of entrepreneurial planter, since he took part in many manufacturing companies and utilities. He was, e.g., a shareholder and president of Cia. Paulista.

[140] Dean, *The Industrialization of São Paulo*, 52. Among the foreigners who came with resources, Dean highlights the case of Francisco Matarazzo, who would become the largest Brazilian industrialist. Among the big businessmen who originally came to work in the field, the author cites two cases: Dante Ramenzoni, manufacturer of hats, and Nicholas Scarpa, owner of mills and textile factories.

[141] "[E]ither with regard to motive force (33,774 HP. Against 30,201 HP., respectively), and also regards the value of annual production (278,394,598$000 against 251,479,256$000), the largest foreign industrial capital compared to the largest of the Brazilians (126,858. 497$000 versus 123,385,437$000)." *Recenseamento Geral do Brasil, 1920*, Vol. V, Part 1a, Indústria, Rio de Janeiro, Typ. Da Estatística, 1927, p. LXI.

Most of these foreign industrialists were concentrated in São Paulo. In this state were the majority of the Italian, Spanish, and Syrian industrialists, while the Portuguese factory owners were most likely to be in the Federal District and German ones in Rio Grande do Sul.[142]

Finally, it is worth stressing that São Paulo was home to a coherent and powerful group of coffee planters. From the beginnings of the coffee economy in the state, a group of truly modern entrepreneurs emerged who were willing to take on business risks and defend their interests, including using the state to defend them.[143] They were absentee landowners who resided in the city, where they could act more fully, either individually or as a group, in favor of their interests. They were involved in party politics and exercised public office. They were preoccupied with the questions of the needs for modern transport and the labor question from the middle of the nineteenth century and were the first to experiment with free labor in coffee and to mobilize the machinery of the state to finance immigration. The establishment of the republic favored them, since they were able to exercise a greater influence over national politics and could also force the state government to favor their interests. The republican push toward decentralization favored their interests, since states gained fiscal autonomy and the ability to make loans, which were fundamental in the policy of defense of coffee.[144]

Despite the importance of industry, commerce, and transports, it should be stressed that agriculture was the predominant activity in São Paulo and the nation. As late as 1929 it still accounted for 37 percent of gross domestic product (GDP) as against only 20 percent for industry (see Graph 1.28). Even as late as the census of 1940, four-fifths of the population was rural. There was a debate even in the 1920s about the utility of providing protective tariffs to promote industry, which was held to be too costly for Brazilian consumers.[145]

---

[142] *Recenseamento Geral do Brasil, 1920.* IBGE, Vol. V, Part 1a, p. LXI–LXIV.
[143] Furtado, *Formação Econômica do Brasil*, Chapter XX.
[144] The republican constitution gave the central government the right to tax imports, but permitted the states to tax exports.
[145] Typical of this position was an editorial written in 1928 in a leading newspaper that held: "It's necessary to repeat a thousand times, Brazil is essentially an agricultural country. What is important is to develop agriculture, ranching and mining. The 8,500,000 km², that we possess some 80% to 90% is still undeveloped. It is just ridiculous to sacrifice the interest of this development for a half dozen industries in Rio and São Paulo. The 300,000 factory workers could be better employed in working the land, which is more important for our development. Our agricultural policy should be tied to our tariff policies. There is nothing more prejudice to agriculture than a tariff protectionist policy which increases the costs of goods consumed by agriculture." Diário

Government 7.9%

Agriculture 36.9%

Commerce 26.5%

Transport 8.4%

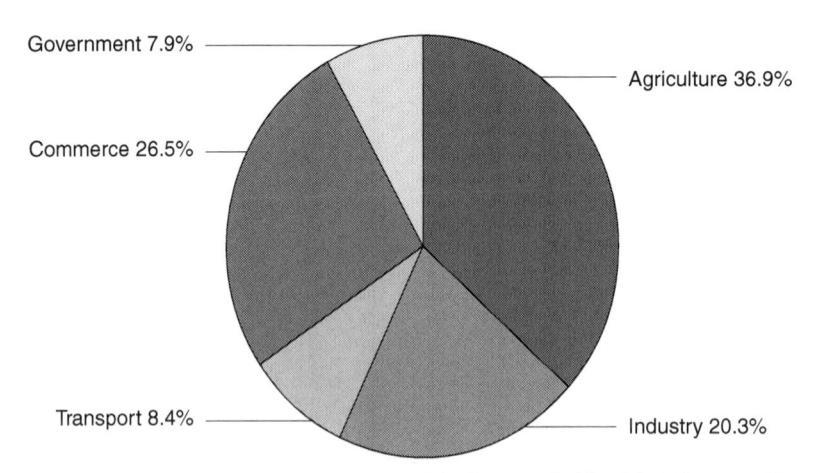

Industry 20.3%

GRAPH 1.28. Participation in GDP, 1929. *Source*: Goldsmith 1986, p. 148

Despite these attacks, agriculture and industry had a relatively calm relationship during the first republic, without extreme positions dominating the debate. Industry grew or contracted depending on the fluctuations in the coffee export economy. An abundance of overseas sales and an overvalued exchange permitted an expansion of investments. Tariffs on imports raised to increase state revenues represented an effective protection. Periods of declining exchange rates made imports more costly and stimulated local production of goods, agricultural and industrial. Besides this, capital from the coffee *fazendeiros* was allocated to industrial activity. Thus, in a general way, there was relative harmony between industry and agriculture. This relation only became conflictive when a specific company or industry sought tariff protection. Such protection of a local industry signified additional costs to the national consumers and to agriculture. According to Suzigan, in the period before World War I tariff protection was not very high.

... and considering the aggregate effect of the variations in the customs duties in the rate of exchange and in relative prices, it can be seen that protection did not increase due to the various compensatory factors of these variables. Moreover protection was unequal and unstable not only because of natural differences in the rights of importation, but also due to the different levels of dependence of each industry in relation to imported goods, upon which were also focused import duties.[146]

Nacional, 7-6-28, cited in Boris Fausto, *A revolução de 1930* (São Paulo: Brasiliense, 1975), 33.
[146] Suzigan, *Indústria Brasileira*, 349.

The Old Republic, 1889–1930

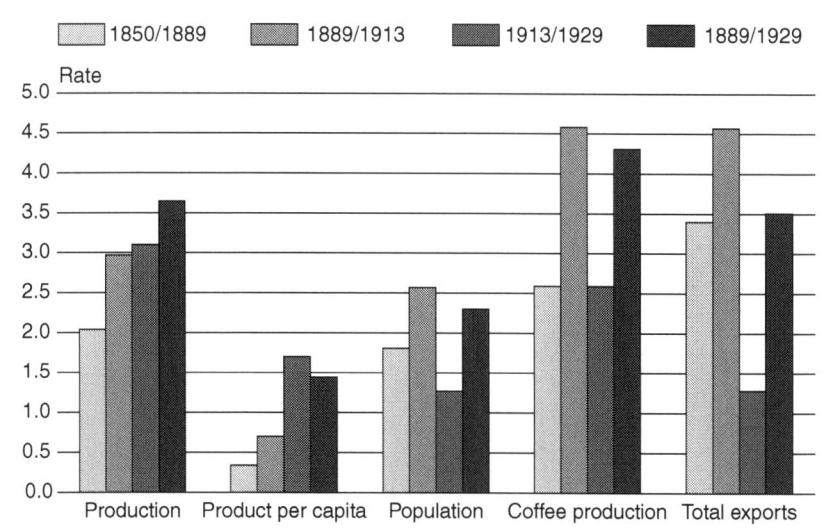

GRAPH 1.29. Rate of Annual Variation in GDP, Population, Total Exports, and Coffee Production, 1850–1929. *Source*: Ipeadata and Goldsmith 1986

It was only after 1914 according to Suzigan, that the government began to stimulate the development of individual industries, although it never practiced a systematic industrial policy. Thus the incentives and subsidies granted were haphazard and not always effective. If World War I was a stimulus to local production, the protection occurred for lack of imported products or their high cost. The postwar would be a period of major investments, stimulated by the great expansion of activities and with expanded resources coming from exports. Brazilian industry in this period directed itself toward the internal market and subordinated itself to the agro-exporting economy.

Throughout the Old Republic, GDP systematically increased, with an annual growth rate of 3.7 percent. But given the strong growth of population in this same period (at 2.3 percent), the growth of per capita income was only a timid 1.4 percent per year. But if we break down this growth of per capita GDP into shorter periods, some important differences emerge. In the final phase of the empire (1850–1889) per capita GDP grew at a mere 0.34 percent per annum. In the first years of the republic until the beginnings of World War I this annual percentage increased only to the relatively modest value of 0.7 percent per annum. In the second part of the Old Republic (between 1913 and 1929), however, the rate grew far more rapidly at a reasonable 2.6 percent per annum (see Graph 1.29). Nevertheless, Brazilian growth compared to the United States was modest even in this period. The differences between the wealth of these two countries was five times greater in 1929 in per capita terms compared to what it had been in 1820, then at less than one time greater.[147]

However slow the growth, there was profound change in this period of the Old Republic. With the massive arrival of European immigrant labor there came an influx of new ideas from Europe about the role of the working classes in the economy and polity of the nation. In all the American countries experiencing late-nineteenth- and early-twentieth-century growth of a wage labor market, there developed a modern labor movement, along with allied movements of anarchism, socialism, and communism. In Brazil this led to a new political activism of the working class with organized labor unions, local and general strikes, and political agitation in the urban and rural sectors. Especially with the resolution of the slavery question, the decades from the 1890s to the 1920s were filled with an ever-increasing confrontation between workers and management and between the elite and the working classes.

Initially, the major centers of strike activity were the cities with the largest industries, Rio de Janeiro and São Paulo, and the key port of Santos. From the beginning anarcho-syndicalist, socialist, and "bread and butter" unionism (variously referred to as *trabalhismo* or *sindicalismo reformista*) competed for control of the embryonic labor movement. The evolution of the Brazilian labor movement moved in the traditional trajectory from mutual aid societies and multioccupational and district associations to craft and then industrial unions and eventually to labor confederations, though the formation of a Brazilian confederation was slow compared to other labor movements in the Americas. Because of their higher ratio of native workers, the labor movement in the federal capitol (Rio de Janeiro) tended to be more ameliorative, while the more foreign immigrant dominant workforce in São Paulo tended toward more radical solutions. The demand for an eight-hour day was the basic issue from 1900 onward, along with wages, working conditions, and the right to strike were constant themes as these local unions became ever more powerful and allied themselves with middle-class intellectuals in the socialist, anarchist, and Catholic movements and eventually with the new communist movement after World War I. The boom period from 1905 to 1913 produced the first major wave of significant strikes throughout

---

[147] The difference between the two estimates for the GDP and per capita GDP occurs because we use two separate calculations. In the first case, when we analyzed only data from Brazil, the result was obtained from Goldsmith, *Brasil 1850–1984*, 82–83, 147. In the comparison of Brazil with the United States we used Angus Maddison, *The World Economy: A Millennial Perspective* (Geneva, Switzerland: OCDE, 2001), 74.

the country. The response of the government was a repressive law in January 1907 expelling foreigners who "compromised national security and public tranquility," which was modified in 1913 to give the government unrestrained power to expel foreign-born workers. An estimated 556 foreign born were expelled from 1907 to 1922.

The leaders of these early strikes were workers in the skilled trades, railway and port workers and typographic workers – the elite of the labor movement or those who worked in key transport infrastructures. After limited attempts in 1910 to control the labor movement in the administration of Marechal Hermes da Fonseca, the government resorted to repression and this, combined with the economic crisis of the middle years of the decade, greatly reduced strike activity. But this period of quiescence changed dramatically with a general strike in São Paulo in May 1917. The period from 1917 to 1920 would be a time of the first major industrial unions being formed, with a consequent increase in very large strikes. These strikes now involved the textile and metallurgical workers – the largest industrial labor force in the country. The assassination of a labor leader in July 1917 led to a general strike for all workers in the city of São Paulo. In this period, strikes and protests spread throughout the country. This was the most intense period of strike activity in the history of Brazil until the 1940s. This active period ended with a general strike in Rio de Janeiro in 1920 that led the government to incarcerate 2,000 strikers and take over many of the unions. The last decade of the Old Republic was a period of violent repression as the government desperately attempted to destroy the labor movement. During most of the decade the government operated in a state of siege, and the "social question" and the "dangerous classes" became a major theme among the political elite.[148]

In reviewing the evolution of the Old Republic and its economic and social development, it is evident that by the end of the 1920s the country had undergone major transformations since the early days of the republic. Although coffee predominated and the country was still essentially agrarian, the productive structure of the country had been amplified and diversified, especially in the industrial area, which now took a considerable part of national capital, productive capacity, and labor. There was

---

[148] For a chronology of this period, see Vito Giannotti, *Historia das lutas dos trabalhadores no Brasil* (Rio de Janeiro: Mauad X, 2007). The standard analyses of these movements is that of Boris Fausto, *Trabalho urbano e conflito social* (São Paulo: DIFEL, 1997) and Claudio Batalha, *O movimento Operário na Primeira República* (Rio de Janeiro: Jorge Zahar Editor, 2000).

also a growth of population in the state capital cities and along with the expansion of transport and services there had also slowly emerged a new urban middle class.

Nevertheless, coffee at the beginning and end of the republican period was still the motor that drove the economy, financed imports, and upon which most of the government depended to provide the foreign funds to service its external debt. Coffee production, in turn, was affected by climatic phenomenon and international conditions, which affected exportations and the movement of capital, thus generating instability in the balance of payments and limiting the conduct of the political economy of the state. Given the severe fluctuations in the early years of the republic and the impact of World War I, the government directed most of its concern to protecting this vital industry. In the first years of the new century the government tried to obtain economic stability at the cost of a strong recession, a financial crisis, and the overvaluation of the national currency. All this led to a reduction in the income for coffee producers. But by 1906 the extraordinary coffee harvests forced the first direct government intervention in the market. From 1908 to 1913 there was a growth in exports and the balance of payments was positive, all due to growing coffee exports now aided as well by rubber exports. In spite of the elevated surplus in the commercial balance, the Currency Board permitted a stable exchange rate, allowed an ample money supply, and stimulated economic activities. The internal product grew systematically as did industrial output, and between 1906 and 1913 imports of machinery to Brazil multiplied by three.[149]

The crisis of 1913 and the outbreak of war altered the economic landscape. War led to difficulties in the export of coffee and to importations in general.[150] There was a strong drop in coffee prices and deterioration in the terms of trade. Convertibility was broken and there was a strong expansion of money. It is now accepted by most economists and historians that the only positive development in this crisis was the stimulation given to national industry to supplement or replace the lack of imports. But even in industry there was a decline in investments that probably retarded the future expansion of this sector. Although by the postwar period Brazil had reached a new level of industrial activity, many

[149] Suzigan, *Indústria Brasileira*, 354–364.
[150] The situation became more acute with the intensification of submarine warfare, which practically prevented the international movement of goods. The situation led the government to carry out the second intervention in the coffee market by buying stocks that grew quickly.

of these war-induced industries did not survive the end of the conflict in Europe.

With the end of the war and the freeze of 1918, which sharply reduced coffee output, prices rose rapidly and the government could easily sell its stocks of accumulated coffee from the first intervention. But the crisis of 1920 created by the recession in the United States, again reduced coffee prices and led to a new government intervention in the market and the creation of a new Currency Board to control the exchange rate and avoid the valorization of national currency. Then from 1924 to the crisis of 1929, Brazil suffered from overproduction of coffee as new plantings came on line and output quickly exceeded world demand. This created a crisis that was exacerbated by the Great Depression of 1929. There was a flight of capital, the Currency Board was obliged to end its activities because of the loss of its gold reserves, and the result was a strong crisis in the balance of payments.

The transition to a republic after 1889 was in many ways a profound political moment of change. The traditional agricultural elite based on coffee production could now directly influence national policy without the intervention of an autonomous executive, as was the case under the empire. Moreover, their local interests were able to dominate state policies and through the importance of São Paulo, they could influence the national government. This power structure and the key economic importance of coffee in Brazil led to an economic policy that essentially gave economic and political power to a few powerful states and a central government totally dependent on these local oligarchies. The result was a major and continuous intervention of the state to guarantee the profitability of the coffee economy. At the same time, industry finally became a significant component of the national economy for the first time with a new textile industry partly based on national production of cotton. All these activities appeared to suggest that a new and more complex urban economy was emerging. It also more fully committed government to promoting local economic elites through a decentralization of the taxing and budgetary restraints that a powerful centralized state had exercised before the creation of the republics.

This transition in the political arena was accompanied by a fundamental transformation in the internal market and in class organization as the labor force changed from one based significantly on slavery to one based exclusively on free labor. The question of labor was a major concern of the economic elites of the empire, particularly the coffee planters even before final emancipation in 1888. With the end of the Atlantic slave trade in 1850 and the gradual reduction of the slave population in Brazil, the expansion of economic activities, particularly coffee production, required additional supplies of manpower, which had been temporarily resolved by the displacement of slaves to areas of higher economic productivity from the 1850s to 1888. But after emancipation and the transition to free labor, this could only be resolved with the turn toward mass European immigration. The introduction of free wage labor led to positive and negative impacts on the internal market. International prices for coffee now had more destabilizing influence on the national economy because of its impact on wage labor, which, in turn, had a multiplying impact on the rest of the economy. A decline in coffee prices led to a decline in wages, which, in turn, had an impact on internal consumption of numerous goods and services. However, the establishment of an economy based on wage labor and the arrival of mass immigration from Europe generated a stimulus to the expansion of domestic economic activities, particularly in such areas of high concentration of coffee production and immigrant settlement as São Paulo. Though this transition began in the last days of the empire, its greatest impact began with the republic and would continue to the present day as the internal economy expanded and became ever more complex. Moreover, it was these new wage workers and immigrants whose demands gave impetus to increased importations and to the evolution of national industries and services.

But for all these economic changes, social and political conditions for the mass of the Brazilian population under the new republican regimes initially differed little from the imperial period. There was the beginning of a decline in the very high levels of urban mortality through the slow introduction of pasteurization and modern sanitation improvements that began to provide filtered water supplies and sewage disposal. But birth rates remained among the highest in the hemisphere and the population remained predominantly rural. Improvements in public education were slowly reducing the illiteracy rates, but the nation remained one where only a minority could read and write. The regional oligarchies took advantage of these conditions to reduce the more democratic aspects of the old imperial regime, by denying the vote to illiterates, which thus reduced the electoral rolls and further guaranteed the predominance of the traditional oligarchies.[151]

---

[151] On the relatively high ratio of voters in the empire, see Herbert S. Klein, "A participação politíca no Brasil do século XIX: Os votantes de São Paulo em 1880," *Dados. Revista de Ciências Sociais* (Rio de Janeiro) 38,3 (1995), 527–544.

The Old Republic, 1889–1930

Finally, despite the impressive growth of coffee, which was now concentrated in the southeastern region there was very little change in agriculture. Landownership was highly concentrated, the poor farmers were primarily squatters, and the use of machinery and fertilizers was extremely limited. Traditional levels of agricultural productivity remained the norm, and Brazil could not even compare with such advanced agricultural regions as Argentina, Canada, or the United States in terms of productivity per crop. The beginnings of modern truck farming based on the new European immigration was beginning to emerge in the areas surrounding the major cities as immigrant *colonos* finished their labor contracts in coffee and began to purchase small farms that now supplied the cities. But for all intents and purposes, Brazilian agriculture in the new republic differed little from the imperial agriculture of the nineteenth century.

As we will see, the fall of the Old Republic would finally create the conditions for a new movement in all areas of the economy and lead to serious changes in social conditions within the country. It would take a political revolution and the impact of a major crisis in international trade, due to the world economic crisis of the Great Depression, to finally force more significant changes in Brazil.

2

The Vargas Period, 1930–1945

The issue that arose in the republican era and that would explain many of the developments in the post-1930 period was the social question. The slow emergence of an urban middle class and an industrial labor force created new social tensions that the old oligarchic government could not resolve with simple repression. It would take a political revolution and a completely new vision to begin to deal with the question of the incorporation of these new groups into national society in a coherent way.

Thus the Vargas revolution had as one of its core concerns the involvement of the state in dealing with the new social realities of an ever-more complex society. The Vargas period was one in which the state began to create a series of basic institutions to deal with labor relations, public health, pensions, and the economy, all designed to move the traditional oligarchic rural-based society into the modern era. This was done with a nondemocratic government that could forge new alliances with the growing industrial sector and harness the emerging urban middle class and the evolving labor movement into a permanent support of the regime in exchange for worker protections and the creation of a state-supported welfare regime. Its authoritarian nature allowed it to reduce the power of the old oligarchies and prevent them from successfully opposing these changes as it built up new alliances.

The Revolution of 1930 was initially a political revolution that led to the overthrow of the political system of the Old Republic. But the establishment of a new authoritarian regime that would last 15 years would have a fundamental impact on the economy and society of Brazil. The Old

Republic had been based on cooperation of the regional oligarchies in the respective states and the control of the central government by the coffee bourgeoisie. In the presidency of the republic, representatives of São Paulo and Minas Gerais succeeded each other respectively, these being the most populous states of Brazil. The electoral regime was totally corrupted, always validating the oligarchies in power. When necessary there were interventions in the states to resolve conflicts between the central power and the regional oligarchy. The new regime brought a return to the centralized state of the imperial period, with the local oligarchies losing a great deal of their power in the national government. At the same time the formal liberal political system would be replaced by an authoritarian interventionist regime that provided new services for large segments of the population as it denied them political autonomy.

But there was no social revolution during the Vargas period. There was no significant change in the distribution of income or in the economic domination of rural landed elite in agriculture. Given the preponderance of coffee in Brazilian exports, Vargas was forced to accept that the interests of the coffee producers predominated. Moreover, the incipient industrial sector depended in large part on the dynamics of the agro-exporters, thus producing little conflict with, or opposition to, the interests of the coffee sector. But over the years, there developed conflicts in some social sectors and schisms within the hegemonic coalition of oligarchies. The very dynamic of the agro-export economy amplified and diversified the internal market and created new social agents, particularly the urban middle classes with their own needs and aspirations, which were little attended to by the Old Republic regime.

Already in the 1920s the Old Republic was beginning to show serious signs of fracturing. The earliest of these oppositions to the oligarchic republic occurred within the army, with the so-called *tenentismo* movement, which was a rebellion led by junior officers against the policies of the Old Republic, especially after the election of Artur Bernardes, whom they attempted to overthrow in 1924.[1] Uprisings occurred in various regions of the country; especially important was the one in the city of São Paulo. When defeated these paulista rebels moved to the frontier

---

[1] Artur Bernardes represented Minas Gerais and counted with the support of São Paulo in his election, but Rio de Janeiro, Rio Grande do Sul, Bahia, and Pernambuco supported the opposition candidate, demonstrating the division of the regional oligarchies. In 1922, during the election the uprising at the Copacabana fort occurred, which marked the beginning of the *tenentismo* movement.

and eventually settled in the western region of Paraná. Another group of lieutenants who had rebelled in Rio Grande do Sul against loyalist troops eventually joined the paulista rebels. In April 1925 they decided to traverse all of Brazil in order to promote their ideas and generate popular protest against the central government and the oligarchies. The so-called Prestes column,[2] covered some 24,000 kilometers in the interior of the country, avoiding confrontations with loyalist troops. Eventually they disbanded in 1927 and the majority of its leaders went into exile in Bolivia and Paraguay. If the movement had little effect in mobilizing the population against the regime, it exercised an influence on the urban population, already discontented with the government. According to the historian Boris Fausto, the *tenentismo* movement represented a "diffuse political and ideological movement, with characteristics predominantly military, where the authoritarian reformist ideas appeared in embryo." Aside from having little identity with the civil society, the lieutenants "identified themselves as being responsible for the national salvation, guardians of republican institutional purity all in the name of an inert people."[3] They put themselves into direct confrontation with the oligarchies that fragmented the country and defended the authoritarian solution as a way to reform the country. It is important to stress that the *tenentista* movement reflected a split within the army, and represented a break in the hierarchy of that institution.

The decade of the 1920s showed other signs of the fragility of the Old Republic political elite. Aside from the *tenentista* rebellion, there occurred great popular protests, particularly in Rio de Janeiro. The Artur Bernardes government (1922–1926) was under a state of siege for most of the period. The strong devaluation of the currency, which was reflected in the increasing costs of imported products, partially explains this urban unrest.[4] In 1926 the Democratic Party of São Paulo (Partido Democrático de São Paulo) was established with liberal professionals and some representatives of the coffee bourgeoisie.[5] This party opposed the oligarchic

---

[2] The Prestes column was led by Luis Carlos Prestes, and had its origin in the *tenentista* movement. Prestes later affiliated with the Communist Party and was one of its maximum leaders until his death in 1990.
[3] Boris Fausto, *A Revolução de 1930* (São Paulo: Brasiliense, 1975), 57.
[4] This was a period of great popular discontent, particularly due to high inflation rates that reached more than 70 percent between 1922 and 1925.
[5] On this theme see Maria Ligia Coelho Prado, *A democracia ilustrada. O Partido Democrático de São Paulo, 1926–1934* (São Paulo: Ática, 1986).

The Vargas Period, 1930–1945

group that controlled paulista politics and proposed a secret obligatory voting system, with a control by the courts to prevent the manipulation of the results.[6]

The fracturing of the dominant political structure was made evident in the succession to the presidency of Washington Luís (1926–1930), who represented the paulista bourgeoisie. Traditionally there had occurred an alternation between the paulista and *mineiro* presidents. Thus to maintain the equilibrium that defined the regime, the candidate for the next presidency should have been indicated by the elite of Minas Gerais. However, Washington Luís insisted that the candidate be a paulista. This resulted in an alliance of opposition leaders lead by Minas Gerais and Rio Grande do Sul, with the support of the Partido Democrático of São Paulo, who launched Getúlio Vargas as their candidate for the presidency. During the electoral period there occurred the worst crisis ever experienced by the coffee market – a combination of the overproduction of the coffee harvest and the Great Depression of 1929. During this crisis, Julio Prestes, then governor of São Paulo, won the presidential election.

The electoral result seemed to suggest that the traditional oligarchic alliance would be maintained, and the regional schisms resolved within the dominant power structure. But new alliances had been formed between the old lieutenants and the younger elements of the oligarchies of Minas Gerais and Rio Grande do Sul, who had actively participated in the presidential campaign. Their object was to overthrow the traditional government. Probably this conspiracy would not have succeeded if there had not occurred the assassination of João Pessoa, the vice presidential candidate under Vargas. Although this was a crime of passion not related to politics, it served to give force to the conspirators who succeeded in overthrowing Presidente Washington Luís, and imposing Getúlio Vargas as president of the republic.[7]

---

[6] The mechanism to validate those elected was up to their own legislation, allowing the perpetuation of the majority.

[7] According to José Maria Bello, "The revolution of 1930 started from civil or political origins, but of course, its success, as all such movements, depended on the attitude of the armed forces. By direct interference of a small part of it, or through inaction or lack of ardor in the struggle of those loyal to legality. Among the soldiers of the revolutionary vanguard excelled the young group of officers, from the uprisings and previous pronouncements, almost all exiles or refugees in neighboring republics in the country." José Maria Bello, *História da República* (São Paulo: Cia Editora Nacional, 1976), 296–297. On the Vargas period, see Affonso Henriques, *Ascensão e queda de Getúlio Vargas*, 3 vols. (São Paulo: Record, 1966).

Whereas the Old Republic was based on an alliance of regional oligarchies and the coffee elite, the new government had a more complex and heterogeneous structure, and it was controlled by groups of military men, technicians, and young politicians.[8] Many of these men, like Vargas, had participated in the old regime.[9] Later the industrialists were incorporated into this new power structure. The old liberalism was replaced by an authoritarian, centralizing and modernizing regime. This type of transition was occurring in many Latin American countries as a result of the Great Depression. According to most scholars, this new authoritarianism signified the transition from an oligarchic state grounded on the landed elite to a new political structure based on compromise between competing groups. But initially none of the newer power groups provided the legitimacy and commitment to a state that was required: the middle class because it had no political autonomy from traditional interests, the coffee interests because they were displaced from political power, and the internal market participants because they were not linked to the basic centers of the economy. In none of these cases, the particular social and economic interests could be used as the basis for the political expression of general interest. As the political scientist Francisco Weffort noted, it was "under these conditions, that there appeared in Brazilian history a new character: the urban masses. It was the only possible source of legitimacy for the new Brazilian government." The political conditions that made this mechanism possible were already present in the institutional crisis that occurred in the 1930s.[10] The style of government inaugurated by Vargas, classified by some as populism, or by others as a regime of mass

---

[8] The lieutenants, who had a fundamental role in the armed movement that overthrew the established government, as a group have had great importance in political leadership and administration in the early years of the new governments. But little by little they were losing strength as an organized group because of their radicalism, their incapacity to question the government, or they were absorbed by the new oligarchic groups that rose to power. Some of the lieutenants individually maintained an essential role throughout the period Vargas. Fausto, *A Revolução de 1930*, 70–82.

[9] Vargas already had been Minister of the Treasury in the government of Washington Luís and governor of the state of Rio Grande do Sul. On Getúlio Vargas, see Richard Bourn, *Getúlio Vargas of Brazil, 1883–1954: Sphinx of the Pampas* (London: Knight, 1974); John W. F. Dulles, *Vargas of Brazil: A Political Biography* (Austin: University of Texas Press, 1967); Lira Neto, *Getúlio 1882–1830. Dos anos de formação à conquista do poder* (São Paulo: Cia. das Letras, 2012); Pedro Paulo Zahluth Bastos and Pedro Cezar Dutra, eds., *A Era Vargas. Desenvolvimento, economia e sociedade* (São Paulo: Editora UNESP, 2012).

[10] Francisco Weffort, *O populismo na política brasileira* (Rio de Janeiro: Paz e terra S/A, 1980), 49–50.

politics, sought to lead by manipulating popular aspirations that could only be understood in the context of the political and economic crisis that opened with the revolution of 1930. To establish this support from the urban working classes that were new to national politics, the leaders of the 1930s reform movements believed that only "institutional authoritarianism, or the paternalistic authoritarianism of charismatic leaders of the mass democracies" could undertake industrialization and modernization of their respective societies.[11]

On assuming the government, Vargas dissolved the national, state, and municipal legislatures and appointed interventors to replace the state governors. He also emphasized the power of the federal government and reduced the powers of the states.[12] After the approval of a new constitution in 1934, he was elected, using indirect elections, to his formal constitutional term of office that would last to 1938. Vargas's confrontation with new political movements such as the fascists (the so-called *integralistas*) and the communists was one of the factors used to justify its destruction of democratic government.[13] In 1935 the government approved a law of national security, which furthered the authoritarian

---

[11] Weffort, *O populismo na política brasileira*, 61. Populism in Brazil has been the object of innumerable studies since the 1960s. Critical studies on this theme recently appeared, among them: Jorge Ferreira, "O nome e as coisas: o populismo na política brasileira," in *O populismo e sua história*, ed. Jorge Ferreira (Rio de Janeiro: E. Civilização Brasileira, 2000); Angela de Castro Gomes, "O populismo e as ciências sociais no Brasil: notas sobre a trajetória de um conceito," in *O populismo e sua história*, ed. Jorge Ferreira (Rio de Janeiro: Civilização Brasileira, 2000); Angela de Castro Gomes, *A invenção do Trabalhismo* (São Paulo: Vértice, 1988); and Boris Fausto, "Populismo in the Past and Its Resurgence." Paper presented at the Conference in Honor of Boris Fausto, Stanford, CA, May 21, 2010.

[12] There was resistance in many states against the choice of interventors, many of who were outsiders. The most serious case occurred in São Paulo. The São Paulo society refused to accept the interventor indicated by the central government. In 1932, it led a movement for greater autonomy of the states and a return to the rule of law: "The movement that began ... has no other intention than to reintegrate the country's legal order and return to the Brazilians their enjoyment of rights and franchises that are the hallmark of our civilization." The movement should have counted with the participation of Minas Gerais and Rio Grande do Sul, but at the last minute these two states remained loyal to the central government and São Paulo faced federal troops with no other allies. Although defeated, the movement served as a warning to the federal government, which now appointed as interventor a representative of the bourgeoisie of São Paulo and started to respond with greater attention to the claims of the state. After the so-called Constitutionalist Revolution of 1932, there was also greater federal support for the paulista coffee growers. Edgard Carone, *A segunda República* (São Paulo: Difusão Européia do Livro, 1973), 53.

[13] Nationalism was a fundamental part of the first Vargas government. On this theme, see Robert M. Levine, *Father of the Poor? Vargas and His Era* (New York: Cambridge

aspects of the regime. In the same year, the Aliança Nacional Libertadora was created, which was a left coalition, with the participation of communists, some leaders of the *tenentista* movement, and such newer social groups as the labor unions. In November 1937, when the electoral process was in full swing, with Vargas competing as a presidential candidate, he decided to carry out a coup d'état, forcing Congress to impose another new constitution and abolish the elections.[14] Until his overthrow in 1945 Vargas governed by decree without a national legislature. If in its initial period the Vargas regime was authoritarian, with the creation of the Estado Novo in 1937 he moved toward a more repressive state, with the suspension of civil liberties, arbitrary imprisonment, total censorship of the press, and the establishment of an extensive propaganda machine.[15]

Despite its authoritarian and repressive actions, the Vargas regime from 1930 to 1945 was a progressive one in terms of its labor and welfare actions and its support for industrialization of the country. It would accomplish the latter objective through a process of import substitution and direct intervention of the state in the industrial sector. It also undertook a major political change in national politics, creating a powerful central government administration and giving the balance of power back to the federal government and taking it away from the states. It also brought new political groups into national politics. In turn, the

---

University Press, 1998); Thomas E. Skidmore, *Politics in Brazil, 1930–1964: An Experiment in Democracy* (New York: Oxford University Press, 1967), Chapter I; and John D. Wirth, *The Politics of Brazilian Development 1930–1954* (Stanford, CA: Stanford University Press, 1970).

[14] "The Constitution of 1937,... left nothing of the old constant of liberalism. It was complete political dictatorship of the president of the republic...." Bello, *História da República*, 315–317. On this theme, see Karl Loewenstein, *Brazil under Vargas* (New York: The Macmillian Company, 1942), Chapter II and Levine, *Father of the Poor? Vargas and His Era*.

[15] Although the regime then implanted resembled fascism, with several of its members showing great sympathy for that type of government, its political representation in Brazil, *integralismo*, was also placed outside the law in 1938, after the assault on the residence of the president, which was an attempt to overthrow him. The *integralistas*, who hoped to be incorporated into the government, were also eliminated from the political process of the Estado Novo. After closing Congress, dissolving political parties, and suppressing the Left, the government eliminated the fascist *integralistas*, the last organized force for political participation. On this theme, see Eli Diniz, "O Estado novo: estrutura de poder e relações de classe," in *História Geral da Civilização Brasileira*, ed. Boris Fausto (São Paulo: Difel, 1981. Tomo 3: O Brasil Republicano. Vol. 3: Sociedade e política [1930–1964]), 77–119; Lourdes Sola, "O golpe de 37 e o Estado Novo," in *Brasil em perspectiva*, ed. Carlos Guilherme Mota (São Paulo: Difusão Européia do Livro, 1969), 257–284; and Levine, *Father of the Poor? Vargas and His Era*.

urban working class and the urban middle class would henceforth become major political actors in national politics. But what the regime did not do was seriously challenge the economic power of the old elite.

Although the coffee bourgeoisie lost its political power with the rise of Vargas, the coffee economy could not be abandoned by Vargas given its fundamental importance in providing funds for imports. The crisis in this sector was profound, caused by overproduction that was allied to the general deterioration in the world market. The permanent defense of the coffee industry, as described earlier, generated an overproduction of coffee in the 1920s that the international market was incapable of absorbing. By the late 1920s the Brazilian harvest was up to 30 million sacks of coffee, while world consumption was only 23 million. São Paulo, which administered the permanent defense of coffee scheme, obtained a loan of £20 million to deal with its obligations in the short term and solicited support as well from the federal government, which was denied. Given the impossibility of obtaining foreign credit in the late 1920s, then President Washington Luís, refused the alternative solution, which was to aid the coffee industry through increases in the money supply since this would have destroyed the stability of the exchange rate. But the collapse of coffee exports led to a severe reduction in the value of exports, provoked the flight of capital, and led to the closing of the Currency Board, which thus ended in what he feared would happen if he helped the planters.

In turn, the new Vargas government faced the same crisis and was obliged to support the coffee sector in order to avoid a more profound crisis. In the first place, it created a mechanism that pardoned part of the debts of the coffee growers. Then it restricted production. The extraordinary large harvest of 1929 was repeated in the two following years, reaching maximum levels in 1933. Vargas faced two options. Let the coffee prices fall freely and thus force the abandonment of coffee fields until equilibrium was reached between supply and demand, or maintain prices at a profitable level for producers. This second option would be accomplished by destroying the stocks of reserve that existed which could not be sold, thus reducing the pressure on international prices. This later option was adopted to preserve the coffee industry and, more importantly, reduce the impact of the market crisis on the level of income of the producers, but it also had the effect of stimulating production.[16]

---

[16] Celso Furtado, who developed this argument, was criticized by revisionists such as Peláez, but later studies, like those of Silber, demonstrate the validity of his argument. Celso Furtado, *Formação Econômica do Brasil* (São Paulo: Cia Editora Nacional, 1968a), Capítulos XXXI, XXXII, and XXXIII; Carlos Manuel Peláez, *História da*

In order to develop this new aid program for coffee, the federal government assumed command of operations. Although there was a slight decline in output in 1931, it was clear that this was an exceptional harvest and that excess production would be the norm in the coming years. The federal government bought the stockpiled coffee from the state of São Paulo, and decreed two new taxes. One was charged for new tree plantings to prevent the expansion of production, and the other was a new tax on coffee exports to finance the defensive operations of purchasing and holding coffee off the market, which partially funded the operations for the defense of coffee.[17] Part of this state-purchased coffee would be destroyed. To carry out this program the Vargas regime created the National Coffee Council and later the National Department of Coffee,[18] which would carry out the federal government program. In 1933 the debts of the coffee growers were reduced by half and the remaining debt financed over a 10-year period.[19] In the same year the coffee crop

---

Industrialização Brasileira. Crítica à Teoria Estruturalista no Brasil (Rio de Janeiro: Apec, 1972); and Simão Silber, "Política econômica. Defesa no nivel de renda e industrialização no período 1929–1939" (MA thesis, São Paulo, FEAUSP, 1973). Moreover, as Fishlow, Villela, and Suzigan show that despite attempts to maintain monetary and budgetary orthodoxy, numerous events, such as external crises, droughts, internal revolts, led to expansionary though unwanted policies, aiding in recovery of domestic income. Albert Fishlow, "Origens e conseqüências da substituição de importações no Brasil," in *Formação Econômica do Brasil. A experiência da industrialização*, ed. Flavio Rabelo Versiani and José Roberto Mendonça de Barros (São Paulo: Saraiva, 1977); Annibal Villanova Villela and Wilson Suzigan, *Política do governo e crescimento da econômica brasileira – 1889–1945* (Brasília: IPEA, 2001), Chapter 6; Wilson Cano, "Crise de 1929, soberania na política econômica e industrialização," in Bastos and Dutra, *A Era Vargas. Desenvolvimento, economia e sociedade*, 121–158; and Flávio A. M. Saes, "A controvérsia sobre a Industrialização na Primeira República," *Estudos Avançados* 3,7 (Setembro–Dezembro 1989), 20–39.

[17] The tax on new plantings had little impact, because there was no incentive to start new plantings. The new tax on exports played an important role in financing the operation, but costs exceeded income and the defense of the coffee program needed supplementation through credits from the Bank of Brazil and the National Treasury. On the topic, see Silber, "Política econômica. Defesa no nivel de renda e industrialização no período 1929–1939," Chapter II. Moreover, according to Fishlow the export tax was not a simple internal arrangement of the coffee sector. In a way, it was generated by the foreign buyer and thus kept the income of the coffee sector at higher levels than those that would have occurred otherwise. There is an assumption that most of the tax was diverted from abroad due to inelastic demand resulting from the dominance of Brazil in the global market. Fishlow, "Origens e conseqüências da substituição de importações no Brasil," 28.

[18] Conselho Nacional de Café and Departamento Nacional do Café.

[19] This was an old paulista elite demand that was finally resolved after the Constitutionalist Revolution of 1932.

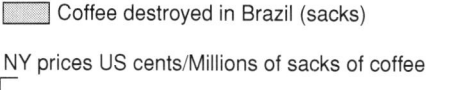

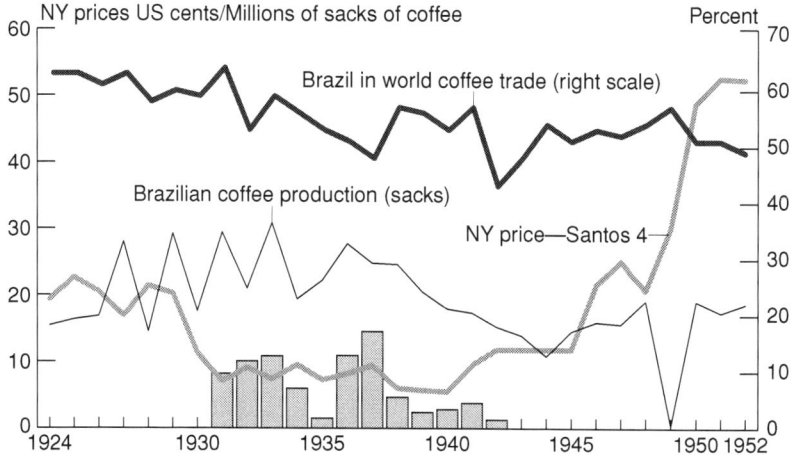

GRAPH 2.1. Prices, Production, and Destruction of Coffee and Brazilian Participation in World Market, 1924–1952. *Source*: Bacha et al. 1992

reached its historic maximum production, and the government was forced to carry out a new severe program of restrictions. It prohibited not only new plantings, but also replantings of old trees, and created a program that divided all the coffee being sent to the ports in three parts: 30 percent would be exported, 30 percent placed in stocks, and 40 percent would be destroyed.[20] With periodic adaptations, this system would be maintained until 1944, resulting in the burning of 78.2 million sacks of coffee, the equivalent of three times the annual world consumption.[21] This reduction program succeeded in gradually diminishing national production. World prices remained low until the end of the 1930s, only recuperating after the beginning of World War II. This control scheme also helped Brazil's competitors, who continued to export at even very low prices, and Brazil by the end of the decade lost 10 percent of its world market share (see Graph 2.1 and Appendix Table A.1).

As we have seen, there has been some debate among scholars about the effectiveness of the post-1930 coffee defense policy. The leading scholar on the coffee economy, Celso Furtado, stressed the countercyclical nature

---

[20] Antonio Delfim Netto, *O problema do café no Brasil* (São Paulo: IPE-USP, 1981), 142–157.
[21] Delfim Netto, *O problema do café no Brasil*, 151. On how the defense of coffee scheme worked, also see Peláez, *História da Industrialização Brasileira. Crítica à Teoria Estruturalista no Brasil*, Chapter 1.

of that policy, which allowed it to maintain the level of employment in the economy and had great influence on the relatively quick recovery of the Brazilian economy, even compared with developed economies: "By guaranteeing minimum purchase prices which was profitable to the vast majority of producers, the government policy was actually keeping up the level of employment in the export economy, and indirectly in sectors linked to domestic producers. When you avoid a major contraction in the monetary income of the export sector, one reduces in proportion the multiplier effect of unemployment on the other sectors of the economy."[22] Although disputed by some authors, this interpretation has prevailed as the most consistent interpretation of policy regarding the economy during the crisis period.[23]

Given the gravity of the international crisis, which directly affected the balance of payments, the government was obliged to exercise a permanent control over the foreign exchange market, and its activities in this area favored economic activities directed toward the internal market. The crisis drastically reduced Brazilian exports and the terms of trade and paralyzed the flow of foreign loans and capital, provoking a strong devaluation of Brazilian currency.[24] In 1931 the government negotiated a consolidation of its international debt and gave a monopoly over the foreign exchange market to the *Banco do Brasil* and established priorities for access to foreign currencies that were official purchases to pay for the public debt, purchases for the import of essential products for the domestic market and

---

[22] Furtado, *Formação Econômica do Brasil*, 200.
[23] "When the Great Depression occurred, the country already had a very broad internal market and an industrial structure that, although in its infancy, had a relative diversification, which exercised a powerful diffusion effect on the economic space in which the region was located. Thus, within the primary export model there took place a vigorous process of urbanization accompanied by the establishment of a framework of basic services and the development of a number of 'traditional' industries, such as food, beverage, furniture, and textiles. Even metallurgy, though still an artisanal activity, was quite well established in the country. It is understandable therefore that the protective action to resolve the external imbalance adopted by the Brazilian government also resulted in support of domestic demand, which resulted in a favorable stimulus to the partly underused productive capacity of the domestic economy. The external imbalance persisted for long periods and defending the income level of the class linked to the export sector, remained the stimulus for the diversification of domestic activity which were subsisting imports which were in demand from those classes." Maria da Conceição Tavares, "Auge e Declínio do processo de substituição de importações no Brasil," in *Da substituição de importações ao capitalismo financeiro*, ed. Maria da Conceição Tavares (Rio de Janeiro: Zahar, 1972), 59–60.
[24] Between 1930 and 1931 there occurred a devaluation of 55 percent between the *cruzeiro* and the dollar.

for the return to foreigners of interest and dividends on their Brazilian investments.[25] Despite this control, the external crisis remained quite severe for several years, especially as the decline in the terms of trade and the servicing of the debt accounted for an important share of the balance-of-payments surplus.[26] Although there occurred some modifications, and some segments of the economy were given free access due to external pressure, the structure of exchange controls was maintained unaltered until the end of the decade.

Although there had been a sharp devaluation of national currency, which benefited national producers and exporters, the government sought to avoid an even greater devaluation. As Brazil was the dominant producer in the international coffee market, the behavior of its producers directly influenced market behavior. And if there was an even more pronounced devaluation, coffee producers, who received their income in local currency, were willing to accept even lower international prices for their coffee, because the depreciation would be offset by the fall in international prices, reducing still more income from exports. But government costs increased with the continued fall in the exchange rate, since it obtained the majority of its revenues in local currency, but needed to service its foreign debts in foreign currency.[27] Finally, the depreciation of the currency had a serious impact on consumers of imported products (see Graph 2.2 and Appendix Table A.2).

Despite the gravity of the international economy and the crisis of coffee, which extended for the entire decade, the gross domestic product (GDP) declined only moderately in the first two years of the crisis and then maintained a consistent growth in the subsequent years.[28] This reflected

---

[25] According to a survey by Villela and Suzigan between 1931 and 1934, debt service pledged half of the trade balance of those years. On exchange-rate policy between 1889 and 1945, see Villela and Suzigan, *Política do governo e crescimento da economia brasileira – 1889–1945*, 317–339.

[26] Marcelo de Paiva Abreu, "Crise, crescimento e modernização autoritária: 1930–1945," in *A ordem do Progresso*, ed. Marcelo Paiva Abreu (Rio de Janeiro: Editora Campus, 1992), 73–104.

[27] As there was an oversupply of coffee, and its demand is inelastic to price, the government tried to maintain the *cruzeiro* at a relatively high rate of exchange, for if there was a further devaluation, this would give compensation to the coffee exporters who would be willing to sell their coffee to foreign markets at even lower prices, thus reducing the value of Brazilian exports, because there would be no compensation in the amount exported. On this theme see Abreu, "Crise, crescimento e modernização autoritária," 73–104.

[28] According to Werner Baer, the growth of industrial production in the first half of the decade of the 1930s was based on the more complete utilization of the existing capacity, in large part formed and underutilized in the previous decade. Werner Baer, *A economia*

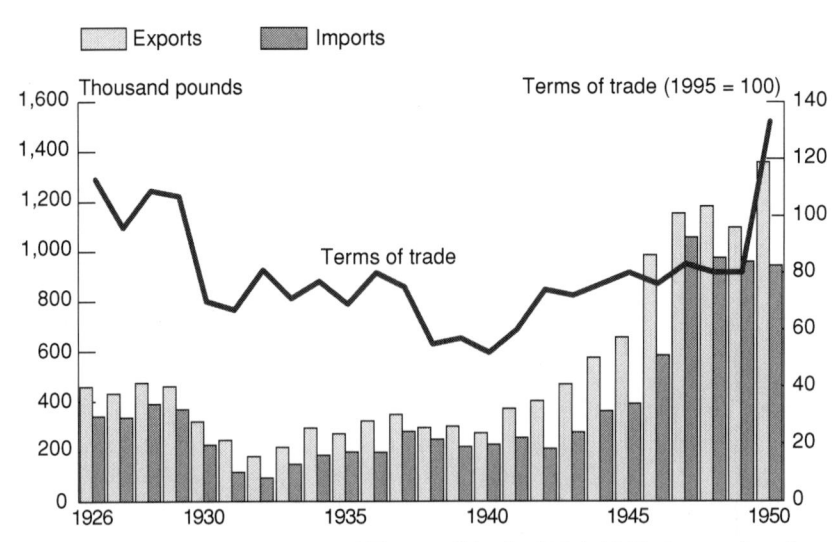

94   The Economic and Social History of Brazil since 1889

GRAPH 2.2. Exports, Imports, and Terms of Trade, 1926–1950. *Source*: Ipeadata

the fact that the agro-export economy that was the dynamic element of the Brazilian economy from the beginning of colonization was substituted by the internal market. Given the external constraints on trade and credit and the new orientation of the economy, there was a clear tendency to support industrialization, a policy that would be maintained throughout the period of the Vargas regime. The Vargas government also made profound changes in the structure of the state, modernizing it from a conservative and authoritarian perspective.

The pace of structural reform only increased with the *Estado Novo*. Given that Congress was closed and the opposition was muzzled, Vargas was able to make major changes unopposed. He abolished the federalist model and put far greater power into the hands of the central government. These reforms were consolidated by the early 1940s by which time he had created powerful institutions and developed a cadre of civil servants able to run them, all of which gave new power to the central state.[29] In these

---

brasileira (São Paulo: Nobel, 2002), 57. It is interesting to observe, according to Stephen Haber, that domestic production of textiles already showed a dynamism even before the crisis of 1929, and for that reason had been one of the industries that had the slowest recuperation in the 1930s. Stephen H. Haber, "Business Enterprise and the Great Depression in Brazil: A Study of Profits and Losses in Textile Manufacturing," *The Business History Review* 66,2 (Summer 1992), 335–363.

[29] Sola, "O Golpe de 37 e o Estado Novo," 269.

reforms the Department of Public Administration (DASP, or *Departamento Administrativo do Serviço Público*), created in 1938, was a fundamental institution that reorganized the structure of the state and helped form a technical and professional government bureaucracy.[30] It also elaborated and controlled the public budget and exercised an important role of generally advising the government. The DASP also had branches in the states, and together with the interventors, was responsible for the state administrations, thus contributing to the process of political and administrative centralization of the nation.[31]

At the same time the Vargas regime created numerous executive and advisory organizations to support the executive actions of the federal government. Aside from the creation of the National Department of Coffee, other areas that received support were federal institutes for the sugar, timber, salt, and cacao industries.[32] Along with this, the agricultural sector was supplied with essential credit and price support institutions such as the Agricultural and Industrial Credit Desk (*Carteira de Crédito Agrícola e Industrial*), a branch of the Banco do Brasil (1937) and the Finance Commission for Production (*Comissão de Financiamento da Produção*), which was charged with fixing minimum prices. In the area of mineral resources was created the National Department of Mineral Production, the National Council of Petroleum, the Council of Water & Electric Energy, and the National Council of Mines & Metallurgy.[33] In the industrial area were created commissions designed to promote industrialization such as the Executive Commission on Textiles, a National Commission of Combustibles and Lubricants, another national commission to promote an arms industry, and one to develop the important iron ore reserves called the Commission for Vale do Rio Doce.[34] There was even one created in 1937 to promote foreign trade, the Federal Foreign Trade Council" (CFCE), which played an important role in the preparation of plans and studies, not only in the area of foreign trade but also for

---

[30] In addition to creating the career civil service with recruitment rules, the DASP created standards to streamline the administrative process.
[31] On this theme, see Beatriz M. de Souza Wahrlich, *Reforma administrativa da era de Vargas* (Rio de Janeiro: Fundação Getúlio Vargas, 1983).
[32] These were called the Instituto do Açúcar e do Álcool, the Instituto do Mate, the Instituto do Pinho, the Instituto Nacional do Sal, and the Instituto do Cacau da Bahia.
[33] Departamento Nacional da Produção Mineral, the Conselho Nacional do Petróleo, the Conselho de Águas e Energia Elétrica, and the Conselho Nacional de Minas e Metalurgia.
[34] Comissão Executiva Têxtil, Comissão Nacional de Combustíveis e Lubrificantes, Comissão Nacional de Ferrovias, Comissão Vale do Rio Doce, and the Comissão Nacional do Material Bélico.

planning the economy as a whole.[35] There was also enacted new fundamental legislation to regularize economic, social, and political relations, such as the codes governing water, minerals, air, industries, and forests,[36] as well as a new corporations and commercial law.

It is worth stressing the essential role exercised by the Banco do Brasil in the economic area, which now controlled the exchange rate and played a primary role in credit operations in promoting agriculture and industry.[37] In 1945 the Banco do Brasil, gained additional power with the creation of the Superintendency of Money and Credit (*Superintendência da Moeda e do Crédito*).[38] This organization represented a major advance in the administration of national monetary policy, exercising in practice part of the functions of a classic central bank, which in the case of Brazil was only created in 1964.[39]

Until the beginning of World War II the international crisis required a rigid control of imports. As the economy recuperated relatively rapidly, internal demand – previously supplied by imports – could not be sustained because of these restrictions in the balance of payments. The government deliberately promoted a policy of import substitution by manipulating a complex system of tariffs, favoring the importation of essential goods, primary materials, and capital goods, and heavily taxing

---

[35] Sonia Miriam Draibe, *Rumos e Metamorfoses. Estado e Industrialização no Brasil: 1930–1960* (Rio de Janeiro: Paz e Terra, 1985), Chapter 1.
[36] The Código de Águas, Código de Minas, Código Brasileiro do Ar, Código de Propriedades Industriais, and Código de Florestas.
[37] The Bank of Brazil played a fundamental role in the economy as the principal commercial credit entity of the nation and as the Treasury Office, from which it also centralized the income and expenditure of the government apparatus. Draibe, *Rumos e Metamorfoses*. On the role played by the Bank of Brazil throughout the period of the Old Republic see Steven Topik, "State Enterprise in a Liberal Regime: The Banco do Brasil, 1905–1930," *Journal of Interamerican Studies and World Affairs* (Special Issue) 22,4 (November 1980), 401–422.
[38] The SUMOC section of the Bank of Brazil fixed the percentage of reserves the commercial banks were forced to keep, as well as the rediscount rates and liquidity of financial assistance, along with the interest charged on bank deposits. In addition, it oversaw the activities of commercial banks, guided exchange-rate policy, and represented the country at international bodies. Banco Central do Brasil, available at http://www.bcb.gov.br/?HISTORIABC.
[39] According to the Central Bank of Brazil, SUMOC was created for the purpose of exercising monetary control and preparing the organization of a central bank. It had the responsibility to determine the percentage of required reserves of commercial banks, discount rates, and financial assistance liquidity, as well as interest on bank deposits. In addition, it oversaw the activities of commercial banks, guided policy on the exchange rate, and represented the country before international organizations. Available at http://www.bcb.gov.br/?HISTORIABC.

finished products. These tariffs, plus an expensive and controlled access to foreign currency, created enough protection to make investments in national production advantageous, as much for agriculture as the industrial sector.[40] Although the second half of the 1930s saw an increase in Brazilian exports, there was no change in the exchange control system because of the strong pressure on the balance of payments needed to service the debt, the need to import such essentials as petroleum, and the need to attend to the demand for primary materials and machines and equipment for the new industrial sector. Despite pressure from the advanced economies, which wanted more flexible exchange control, the country maintained exchange controls during the entire period, with only moderate revisions.[41] World War II made this situation more complex. There was a strong external demand for some specific Brazilian products, with an increase in prices and quantities exported that led to an increase in the capacity to import. But the European and Asian wars also meant that there was a lack of goods to import, which further stimulated local industry. At the same time the import of machinery and equipment, various primary materials, and gasoline was restricted. Although some domestic industries had problems of supply of foreign parts, in general national production was stimulated by the war. Nevertheless, the lack of imported products and their substitution for national ones generated strong inflationary pressures.[42]

---

[40] "We can then conclude that the import substitution that occurred during the Great Depression, unlike what happened during World War I or after this period, gave an impetus to a more sophisticated production structure. Corresponding to this change, there was a change in the distribution of imports in favor of more specialized products, which Brazil was unable to replace quickly. Partly guided by politics, but also by price mechanism, essential and complementary imports could be obtained to reinforce the growth process." Fishlow, "Origens e conseqüências da substituição de importações no Brasil," 34. According to the same author, in the relative prices of 1920, the imported components within the total supply declined from 34 percent to 15 percent; and in the prices of 1939, from 50 percent to 25 percent.

[41] In 1935, because the freedom granted for the remittance of profits, there was a strong currency crisis, almost forcing the suspension of debt payments. There was constant pressure from the United States for the country to adopt a more flexible exchange control. Abreu, "Crise, crescimento e modernização autoritária," 83; also on this theme, see Maria Antonieta Parahyba Leopoldi, "A economia política do primeiro governo Vargas (1930–1945): a política econômica em tempos de turbulência," in *O tempo do nacional-estadismo: do iníco da década de 1930 ao apogeu do Estado Novo*, 2 vols., ed. Jorge Ferreira and Lucília de Almeida Neves (Rio de Janeiro: Civilização Brasileira, 2003), 2:241–285.

[42] "The movement of expansion and change in the production structure was accompanied with great entrepreneurial sensitivity by the coffee fazendeiros who also became

In acting to resolve specific blockages in the infrastructure and in the need to provide basic raw materials, the government seriously aided the industrial sector.[43] With the creation of the national manufacturing and infrastructural companies such as the National Steel Company, the Vale do Rio Doce Company for producing iron ore, the National Salt Company for salt and soda ash, the national factory to produce motors, and the Hydroelectric Company of São Francisco,[44] the federal government established a new form of direct intervention in the productive sphere of the economy acting where private initiative did not have the interest to mount the capital needed, either because of risk or low profitability. Such efforts demanded a great economic effort on the part of the Brazilian state, which utilized fiscal resources and external loans to finance these new industries and large amounts of its export income to import the goods needed to create these state industries.

The case of the National Steel Company deserves special mention. Until 1942 there was no large steel mill functioning in Brazil despite numerous proposals to create one.[45] The steel mill was seen as essential for the plan of industrial consolidation that was then being developed and had the strong support of the military that saw this as a question of

industrialists. This transference is but one aspect among many that supports the development of industrialization in Brazil and that it is somewhat unique in Latin America. We refer to the coincidence of the most dynamic sectors in both development models. This coincidence, which was due initially to the relative abundance of external economies in the Rio-Sao Paulo axis, transformed the center-south of the country into a region strongly polarized, through a mechanism that greatly facilitated the cumulative dynamics of import substitution, although this resulted in a dramatic increase in regional imbalances." Tavares, "Auge e Declínio do processo de substituição de importações no Brasil," 60.

[43] "1940 marks the beginning of the economic achievements properly innovative, planned as early as 1939, when Vargas and the Minister of Finance, Souza Costa, worked on developing a five-year plan, whose items included: a steel plant, aircraft factories, hydroelectric in Paulo Afonso, the San Francisco River drainage, railroads and the purchase of destroyers and aircraft as well as ships for Lloyd Brasileiro from Germany. Only part of this plan was carried out, but the importance for the national life of the innovations implemented, was not small." Sola, "O Golpe de 37 e o Estado Novo," 275.

[44] Companhia Siderúrgica Nacional, Companhia Vale do Rio Doce, Companhia Nacional de Álcalis, Fábrica Nacional de Motores, and Companhia Hidroelétrica de São Francisco.

[45] Although Brazil had plenty of iron ore, its coal was of poor quality, limiting the development of a steel industry. Moreover, there was great debate about the control of the company, given its strategic role. Many felt that the project could not be controlled by foreign capital. In the end, the project was implemented by the state and imported coal was used. On this subject, see Wirth, *The Politics of Brazilian Development 1930–1954*, Part 2. The smaller usinas that functioned in the period, like the Belgo Mineira, operated with vegetable fuel.

national security. Given Brazilian support for the allies in World War II, the U.S. government assisted this effort with financing from the Export – Import Bank. Initially proposed as a joint project with private partners and U.S. Steel, no accord was reached, and the government decided to go it alone and assumed complete responsibility for the enterprise.[46]

The government also spent considerable effort developing programs and new ministries to deal with education and health. As a government influenced by fascist ideology and the resurgent Catholic Church there was much concern with changing the orientation of public and private education. Though under the republic the Catholic Church was no longer an official state religion, it found support in the Vargas regime, which in 1931 decreed the introduction of religious education in public schools. During the term of one of the more profascist and pro-Catholic ideologues of the Estado Novo, Education Minister Gustavo Capanema, there was much discussion about the need for a new moral and civic culture, and there was also a major increase in private and church-controlled secondary education but only modest growth in primary education.

Moreover, various efforts to develop tertiary education amounted to little, largely for fear of a liberal opposition entrenching itself in such schools. The attempts to create a significant university in the Federal District of Rio de Janeiro in the early 1930s died under the control of Capanema, and in fact the first serious university created in Brazil developed out of largely private initiatives and local government support in the state of São Paulo. Although Brazil had medical, law, and engineering schools from as early as the nineteenth century, there was no single university established. But in 1933 leading political leaders and industrialists in São Paul succeeded in establishing the University of São Paulo by combining various institutes and a new faculty of science and letters. This was Brazil's first university. It was liberal, lay, and public and was initially modeled along the lines of a standard French university. France sent a mission of distinguished French academics to help establish the school,

---

[46] It is argued that Vargas would have negotiated the project simultaneously with the United States and Germany. The U.S. support would have been a compensation for the position of Brazil in favor of the Allies. It is known that various persons of the Vargas government showed sympathy for the Nazi regime. The geographical position of Brazil would have major strategic importance to the Allies. By contrast, the American market was the most important for Brazilian exports. On this theme, see Wirth, *The Politics of Brazilian Development*; Sérgio H. Abranches, "Governo, empresa estatal e política siderúrgica: 1930–1975," *As origens da crise: Estado autoritário e planejamento no Brasil*, ed. in Olavo Brasil de Lima Jr. and Sérgio H. Abranches (São Paulo: Vértice, Revista dos Tribunais, 1987), 155–213.

among whom were Claude Levi Straus and Fernand Braudel. In the first teaching year the central faculty of philosophy had only European scholars who came from France, Italy, and Germany teaching in all the sciences and social sciences. This was a revolutionary concept in Brazilian higher education, and it would take several years before this core faculty became a major part of the university and could finally establish its independence from the engineering, mining, law, and medical schools. But eventually this new *Universidade de São Paulo* and the *Instituto Osvaldo Cruz* of Rio de Janeiro developed as the true pioneers of modern Brazilian science.[47]

But initially Brazil's first major university remained a small center training only a limited number of students and for another several decades tertiary education was available to a distinct minority of the Brazilian elite and still was dominated by the professional schools that had little interest in science or research. If little was accomplished in tertiary education, the Vargas regime did initiate what would become a massive new development in education, and this, interestingly enough, came from the Ministry of Labor. Thus was the establishment of the first serious modern industrial and commercial education program. In 1939, when decreeing that large companies with 500 or more workers had to provide commissary facilities, the government also provided that such companies would also be required to maintain "courses of professional development" for its workers.[48] This idea of private industrial-sponsored education was being pushed by the new Ministry of Labor and the São Paulo industrial federation (*Federação das Indústrias do Estado de São Paulo*) under the leadership of Roberto Simonsen, largely against the wishes of the Education Ministry.[49] Influenced by the German ideas of a modern industrial apprenticeship, the industrialists pushed for control over an area totally neglected by the state until that time. The result was the creation in 1942 of what would become one of the world's largest modern privately run industrial education systems, first the *Serviço Nacional de Aprendizagem Industrial* (SENAI) for industry and then later in 1946 came the

---

[47] The standard source for this history is Simon Schwartzman, *A Space for Science – The Development of the Scientific Community in Brazil* (College Park: Pennsylvania State University Press, 1991), Chapter 5.

[48] Simon Schwartzman, Helena M. B. Bomeny, and Vanda M. R. Costa, *Nos tempo de Capanema* (São Paulo: Editora da Universidade de São Paulo and Ed. Paz e Terra, 1984), Chapter 8.

[49] Simonson had also been one of the key persons, along with Júlio de Mesquita Filho, owner of O Estado de São Paulo, and the political leader Armando de Sales Oliveira, behind the establishment of the University of São Paulo. Schwartzman, *A Space for Science*, Chapter 5.

Serviço Nacional de Aprendizagem Comercial (SENAC) for commerce. The industrialists convinced the federal government to create a payroll tax to develop a school system administered by the private industrial associations in each state. SENAI quickly established training courses and would enroll many thousands of students in short- and long-term programs and would even educate a future president of the republic.[50]

The success of SENAI is in many ways related to one of the more fundamental changes that were undertaken by the Vargas government. It was in the area of labor relations that the Vargas regime carried out the most profound changes in contrast to the ideology and activities of the governments of the Old Republic. Although it was consistent with previous regimes in violently suppressing movements on the Left, the government also carried out a new policy of co-opting urban workers through modern labor legislation. These codes involved the right to unionize, basic worker rights to bargaining, and social security. Although this legislation came from government initiative and not from the pressure of the working class, it did reflect the government's perception that urban workers and their organizations, especially in the industrial sector, had become an important part of the national scene. This was a fundamental change from the Old Republic.[51] While this co-optation diminished the autonomy of labor organization, leading to government-controlled unions and dependent union leaders, these organizations now became an important part of the Vargas political base.[52] The charismatic figure of Vargas derives in large part from his control and manipulation of the labor movement harnessed to the state.

---

[50] On the origins of SENAI see Barbara Weinstein, "The Industrialists, the State, and the Issues of Worker Training and Social Services in Brazil, 1930–50," *Hispanic American Historical Review* 70,3 (August 1990), 379–404; and her book-length study: *For Social Peace in Brazil: Industrialists and the Remaking of the Working Class in São Paulo, 1920–1964* (Chapel Hill: University of North Carolina Press, 1996).

[51] Washington Luís affirmed that "the social question is a case for the police." Although always cited, some authors have challenged the veracity of this phrase. See John D. French, "Proclamando leis, metendo o pau e lutando por direitos," in *Direitos e Justiças no Brasil, Ensaios de História Social*, ed. Silva Hunold Lara and Joseli M. N. Mendonça (Campinas: Ed. UNICAMP, 2006), 379–416.

[52] "The state that emerged from the Revolution of 1930 maintained the fundamental policy of politically weakening the working classes, harshly repressing their vanguard and their party organizations, but at the same time sought to establish with the whole working class a new relationship. Politics, pure and simple, carried out by the old ruling classes, no longer had the conditions to be able to sustain itself. In the platform of the Liberal Alliance were already traces of a greater interest in the so-called social problem, worker unrest of the early years of the 1930s ended up effectively 'sensitizing' the government to this question." Fausto, *A Revolução de 1930*, 107–108.

The labor legislation enacted by Vargas was comprehensive and represented an advance in Brazilian labor relations. With the creation of the Ministry of Labor in 1930, successive legal norms were developed that ordered relations between unions and management in cooperation with the government, and that were guaranteed by government approval. Moreover, the government adopted the policy of what is called *unicidade sindical*, which established one single union for each industry and municipality.[53] Such legislation limited the number of foreign workers per enterprise (the law of two-thirds national workers), regularized the work day, guaranteed holidays, and provided for controls of women and child labor. There were also collective work contracts and Boards of Labor Conciliation composed of representatives of workers and management to deal with labor contracts and disputes.[54] Labor Day (May 1) became a great public event and was called the "day of the worker." Finally, with much ceremony in the Vasco da Gama stadium in Rio de Janeiro, Vargas signed the first minimum wage decree in Brazilian history. In 1940 he created the union tax (paid by the workers but distributed by the government to the unions), which provided income to the unions and represented a fundamental instrument of co-optation between the state and the unions.[55] These union dues and the single union per industry model were used to cement labor support for the government. In 1941 the Labor Justice system was created to judge work-related disputes, and in 1943 there was the consolidation of all the union laws in one unified code that guaranteed the rights of workers.

Another major part of the Vargas social policy was the establishment of social welfare institutions. As was the norm in the majority of Western nations, the first formal retirement plans (the *caixas de pensões*) began with small groups of workers in well-defined sectors of the economy in the decades of the 1920s and 1930s. In the case of Brazil, as in most

---

[53] In 1939 the "uniqueness" or monopoly of labor association by territorial unit was established, which represents a ban on more than one union to represent the same job category. This rule, which in combination with the union tax represents the harnessing of the power of unions to the state, continues today, although the constitution set the freedom of association for workers. Even the Partido dos Trabalhadores (PT), which in the opposition attacked the trade union unity rule and the union tax, when it took office did not bother to amend the legislation.

[54] Convenções Coletivas de Trabalho and Juntas de Conciliação e Julgamento.

[55] The union tax represented a contribution in the amount of one workday for all workers, unionized or not. The funds raised were distributed to the unions, which lived on this discretionary contribution. The income of the unions depended on this tax, and so the unions were dependent on the state and not on the contributions from their union workers. This tax exists until today.

of Latin America, there had always been very limited retirement plans for public servants going back to the colonial period (when they were called *montepios*). But effective modern pension plans only began in the 1920s. The first of these private worker plans was created in 1923 when the railroad workers gained the right to medical assistance, retirement plans, and widows' pensions under the Elói Chaves law. In 1926 such rights were extended to port workers and in the following decades to ever more numerous groups of workers. In 1931 these pension funds, or so-called *Caixa de Aposentadoria e Pensões* (CAPs), were extended to public servants and in 1932 to mine workers. Each sector had its own CAP, and they were organized with tripartite financing of workers, employees, and government through obligatory contributions.[56] In turn, the government rationalized the system by integrating local CAPs into institutes (*Institutos de Aposentadoria e Pensões*, or IAP), which ensured pensions for entire sectors of the economy. As many have noted, the move to IAPs represented a significant shift in the social insurance system from essentially private to primarily public administration and from individual companies to whole classes of workers.[57] Moreover, as of 1936, the government took over the surplus funds collected by these CAPs and new IAPs and invested them in government securities of various kinds to create a capital patrimony for these pension programs.[58] Much of these securities involved investments in government-developed industries and in the construction of the new capital Brasilia. In this, Brazil was like many other states, in applying these surplus funds to national industrial activities.[59]

[56] James Malloy, *The Politics of Social Security in Brazil* (Pittsburgh, PA: University of Pittsburgh Press, 1979), 40–50; Celso Barroso Leite, "Da lei Elói Chaves ao Sinpas," in *Um século de previdência social: balanço e perspectivas no Brasil e no mundo*, ed. Celso Barroso Leite (Rio de Janeiro: Zahar, 1983), 39–44.
[57] Amélia Cohn, *Previdência social e processo político no Brasil* (São Paulo: Editora Moderna, 1981), 8.
[58] Eli Iôla Gurgel Andrade, "Estado e previdência no Brasil: uma breve história," in *A previdência social no Brasil*, ed. Rosa María Marques et al. (São Paulo: Editora Fundação Perseu Abramo, 2003), 71–74.
[59] Francisco Eduardo Barreto de Oliveira, Kaizô Iwakami Beltrão, and Antonio Carlos de Albuquerque David, *Dívida da União com a Previdência Social: uma perspectiva histórica*, Texto para Discussão No. 638 (Rio de Janeiro: IPEA, 1999). That such use of pension reserves to fund public projects or even private industries was not atypical behavior can be seen in the Mexican experience of establishing a welfare state under Aleman in the 1940s and of the fascist state under Mussolini during the 1930s. See Rose J. Spalding, "Welfare Policymaking: Theoretical Implications of a Mexican Case Study," *Comparative Politics* 12,4 (July 1980), 419–438; and Maria Sophia Quine, *Italy's Social Revolution: Charity and Welfare from Liberalism to Fascism* (New York: Palgrave, 2002), 115.

The first retirement institute was created for all maritime workers in 1934, and then for commercial and bank workers in 1936. In 1938 it was the turn of transport workers and by 1939 there were 98 CAPs and five IAPs insuring some 1.8 million workers, all under the control of the Ministry of Labor.

Finally, the government carried out a major initiative in health policies. In contrast to educational policy, which progressively moved from a decentralized toward a more centralized federal system in the course of the nineteenth and twentieth centuries, the history of public health in Brazil has moved in the opposite direction. From the beginnings public health was a central government concern, first with the ports and the imperial capital, then with the territories, and finally with the states and municipalities. The fact that the early leaders of the sanitation movement, which was concerned with sewage and clean water, were Brazil's leading scientists with close connections to the political elite helped in pushing public health issues to the forefront of concerns of the federal government. Brazil experienced a wave of epidemics that swept through the nation in the second half of the nineteenth century. The epidemics of yellow fever in 1849 and of cholera in 1855–1856 brought a willingness on the part of the imperial and republican governments to deal aggressively with public health and sanitation issues.

In 1851 the government created an Imperial Council of Public Hygiene, and in 1886 a more powerful General Inspectorship of Hygiene was established with control over port inspectors and state vital statistics. Even under the new republic, which devolved most central government functions to the states, the federal government strengthened the national public health institutions. In 1902 Oswaldo Cruz, the leading scientist of his day, organized a campaign against yellow fever in the state of Rio de Janeiro, and in 1904 he was made head of the national General Directorate of Public Health.[60] There soon followed national campaigns against yellow fever, bubonic plague, and smallpox, and a law forcing obligatory vaccination of the entire population against this classic disease. Then in the 1910s and 1920s the government supported a national registration of diseases along with a host of other public health measures. In 1923, another leading scientist, Carlos Chagas, helped found a new National Public Health Department (DNSP).[61] Under his direction the national government promoted maternal and infant health; began work

[60] Directoria Geral de Saúde Publica.
[61] Departamento Nacional de Saúde Pública.

on industrial accidents and rural health; and encouraged the registration of medicines and a host of other public health activities. Finally, with the creation of the first pension and retirement groups in the 1920s, there also developed a systematic movement for creating local clinics to practice preventive medicine that were tied to these new IAPs and CAPs. Many of these pension funds maintained hospitals and clinics and often provided better medical service for their members than was available from the local municipalities or other government agencies.

The overthrow of the Old Republic by Vargas only strengthened the public health groups in the central government. In 1930 a separate Ministry of Education and Health was organized, with a Department of Health attached to it. In 1934 this department was reorganized into a larger combined National Health and Social Medicine Assistance Department, which gathered under its aegis the various directories and services dealing with hospitals, ports, the Federal District, and the numerous formal campaigns against specific diseases in given areas. These campaigns, which seem to have been quiescent in the period from 1930 to 1934, took on a new life once again in the post-1935 period, often with the help of the Rockefeller Foundation. In 1937 the federal public health subministry department assumed the role of coordinator of all the state health departments, and a special fund for public health was created in all the municipalities under federal direction. There were also now the first systematic attempts to fund and develop rural health clinics.

The federal government under Vargas thus maintained its active role as the dominant player in national public health throughout the 1930s and 1940s, and in 1953 all of these efforts were finally coordinated into a separate Ministry of Health. The new ministry assumed control over everything from health statistics to education of health care workers, from creating nursing schools and funding research institutes, to evaluating the quality of medicines produced in the country.[62]

All these social and economic initiatives of the government created the basis for a modern social welfare state, though one still relatively restricted in coverage to a limited portion of the modern urban sector. Nevertheless,

---

[62] On the health reforms and initiative of this period see Cristina M. Oliveira Fonseca, *Saúde no Governo Vargas (1930–1945): dualidade institucional de um bem público* (Rio de Janeiro: Editora Fiocruz, 2007). For the very active international relations in health carried out by Vargas, see André Luiz Vieira de Campos, *Políticas internacionais de saúde na era Vargas: O Serviço Especial de Saúde Pública, 1942–1960* (Rio de Janeiro: Editora Fiocruz, 2006); and Lina Faria, *Saúde e Política: a Fundação Rcokefeller e seus parceiros em São Paulo* (Rio de Janeiro: Editora Fiocruz, 2007).

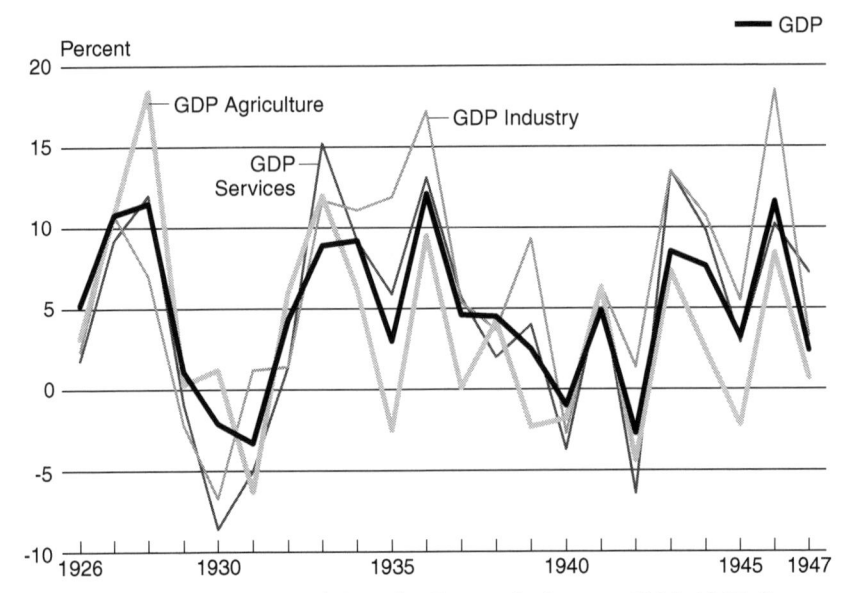

106   *The Economic and Social History of Brazil since 1889*

GRAPH 2.3. Variation in Real GDP by Economic Sectors, 1926–1947. *Source*: Ipeadata

this was a major change from the liberal ideology of the previous government and the ideas and institutions created by Vargas would profoundly influence the post-1950 development of a modern welfare state.

As for its economic reforms and initiatives, the Vargas regime also succeeded in stimulating the economy. Despite the slow recuperation of the international economy, Brazil grew at an impressive rate in the period from 1930 to 1945, with overall GDP growing at 4 percent per annum. While agriculture grew at 2.1 percent and services at 3.9 percent, industry grew at an impressive 6.2 percent per annum.[63] This meant that industry increased its relative participation in the national economy from 20.3 percent in 1929 to 28.6 percent in 1945. In turn, agriculture fell from a participation rate of 36.9 percent to 28.0 percent in the same period (see Graph 2.3 and Appendix Table A.3).[64]

This extraordinary industrial growth can be seen in the changes that occurred from the industrial census of 1920 to that of 1950: in that time the number of industrial establishments multiplied by seven, the number of workers by four, and the energy used (what was called the motor force

[63] Ipeadata: available at http://www.ipeadata.gov.br/.
[64] Raymond W. Goldsmith, *Brasil 1850–1984. Desenvolvimento Financeiro Sob um Século de Inflação* (São Paulo: Editora Harper & Row do Brasil, 1986), 148. In Brazil the series of GDP calculated from the national accounts began in 1947.

employed) by eight. Moreover, while all regions showed great growth, the leading zone was clearly the southeastern region. In this period the industrial leadership of the southeast region was solidified as this zone came to absorb two-thirds of the industrial workers and the motor force employed by industry. Within this region it was São Paulo that gained the most. It increased its share of industrial workers and motor force energy from 30 percent to 40 percent of the national total in both indices in this period. It was in the period from 1920 to 1940 that most of this growth in São Paulo industry occurred, which thus guaranteed its premier position within the Brazilian industrial structure. Although Minas Gerais and Rio Grande do Sul maintained their relative positions, the Federal District (that incorporated the city of Rio de Janeiro) grew at a much slower pace and thus lost its relative share of national production.[65] In São Paulo the number of workers increased by five times and the motor force used in industry by 11 times in this period, while in the Federal District, growth was only three times for workers and four times for motor force.

In the period from 1920 to 1940 the application of motor force to industry and the number of workers grew at the same rate. But in the period from 1940 to 1950 the motor force used in factories increased by 9.1 percent per annum and that of the workforce by 6.1 percent, which suggested that in this second period the use of motor power in industry grew more rapidly than the workforce, implying increasing labor productivity. This is also seen in the fall in the average number of workers per factory and the rise in the average use of motor power (see Graphs 2.4a and 2.4b).

Because of the extraordinary role of São Paulo, the southeast region as a whole by the census of 1940 was clearly the leader in Brazilian industry. The southeast accounted for close to three-quarters of the value of industrial goods produced, and of the total value of companies, machines, capital, and labor. In contrast the south and northeastern regions represented but 10 percent each of these factors. São Paulo alone had 45 percent of the total value of industrial production, some 54 percent of the value of machines and equipment and 39 percent of the value of industrial production. In contrast the Federal District accounted for 22 percent of goods produced, the state of Rio Grande do Sul just 9 percent, and 8 percent for the state of Minas Gerais (Graph 2.5).[66]

---

[65] In relation to industrial workers, the Federal District participation went from 19 percent to 13 percent, with the installed factory motors dropping even more, from 19 percent to 10 percent.

[66] On the participation of São Paulo in the industrial process, see Wilson Cano, *Raízes da Concentração industrial em São Paulo* (São Paulo: Difel, 1977).

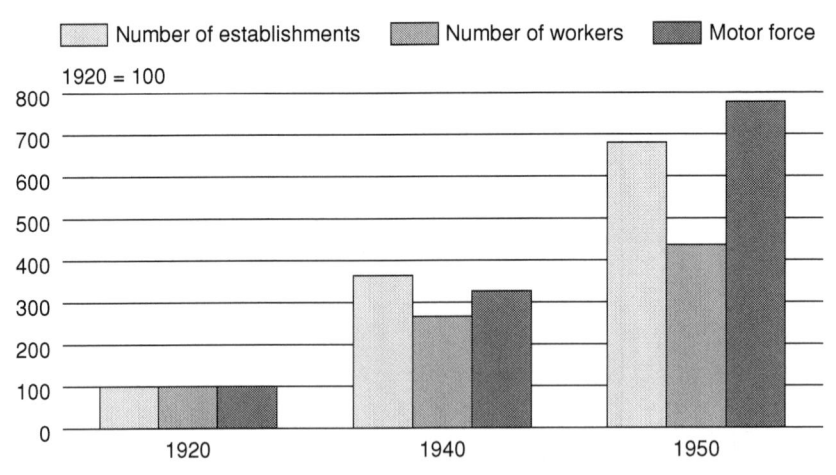

108   The Economic and Social History of Brazil since 1889

GRAPH 2.4a. Growth of Industry, 1920, 1940, and 1950. Source: Anuário Estatistico do Brasil (1957), Vol. 18

Another clear indicator of the importance of São Paulo in the industrial economy was the generation of energy that was a fundamental input into the manufacturing process. In 1947, the installed national hydroelectric power generated a potential of 1.5 million kilowatts of electricity, which, in turn, accounted for 84 percent of the national total production of electricity. Of this total of hydroelectric power, more than half was generated

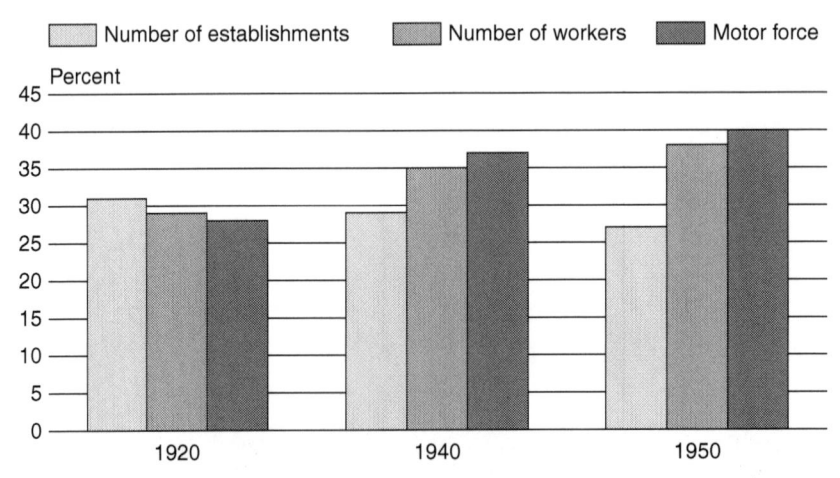

GRAPH 2.4b. Participation of São Paulo in Industry, 1920, 1940, and 1950. Source: Anuário Estatistico do Brasil (1957), Vol. 18

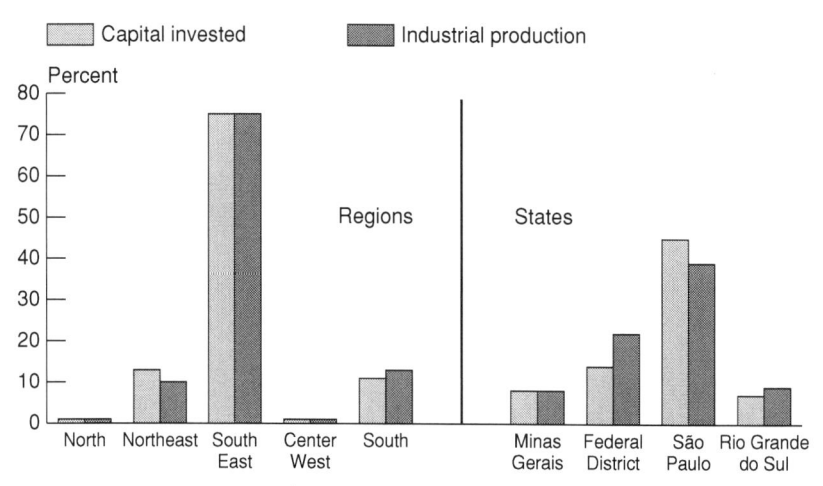

GRAPH 2.5. Participation of Regions and Principal States in Industry – Census 1940. Source: Recenseamento Geral de 1940, Vol. III

in São Paulo, and only a fourth came from the second-largest producer, the state of Rio de Janeiro.[67]

There was also a major difference in the role of domestic capital invested in industrial production in the different states and regions. Overall Brazilian capital accounted for 59 percent of industrial production. In the Federal District nationals had a minority ownership of industry, whereas in Minas Gerais and Rio Grande do Sul, Brazilians controlled about 85 percent of the factories. In São Paulo nationals owned 56 percent.[68] Even if ownership involved a large share of foreign capital, the raw materials used in the industrial process were primarily of Brazilian origin (some 80 percent of all products used), and the workforce was primarily (80 percent) male.

As of 1940 processed food accounted for the largest number of the 40,000 industrial companies (some 30 percent), followed by lumbering

[67] AEB (1948), Rio de Janeiro, IBGE, 1949, 157. On the history of the development of electric energy in Brazil, see José Luiz Lima, "Estado e desenvolvimento do setor elétrico no Brasil: das origens à criação da Eletrobrás" (MA thesis, São Paulo, Faculdade de Economia e Administração, USP, 1983).
[68] Data exclude anonymous society and only consider individual companies and partnerships. Of the foreign investors, the Portuguese were the leaders, accounting for 33 percent of all foreign industrial investment, followed in importance by the Italians at 28 percent, and then the Germans and Spaniards. To some extent this composition followed the patterns of the origin of immigrants arriving in Brazil, though with the Spaniards underrepresented and the Germans overrepresented.

and nonmetallic mining.[69] Food producers also had the largest share of total production (20 percent) followed by textiles (18 percent), chemicals and pharmaceuticals, and energy. The importance of food and textile companies is also reflected in the fact that they accounted for half of the capital, labor, salaries, and energy used by industry in Brazil. The electrical generating companies were the most intense users of capital, accounting for half the value of machines and equipment in the census of 1940. But textiles had the highest average employment per company – 145 workers versus an overall average of 24 workers per factory. As could be expected, the electrical generating sector had the highest rate of foreign owners (85 percent) whereas the textile industry saw only 26 percent of the companies owned by foreign capitalists.[70]

But overall industry was still quite traditional in Brazil in 1940, with only a small capital goods industry and the majority of factories producing consumption goods. The consumer goods industries accounted for half of the value of companies, employment, capital, and goods produced, whereas the capital goods industry (companies in metallurgy and machines) accounted for only 6 percent of these factors. This indicates that despite rapid growth the Brazilian industrial sector was still not very diversified and was most heavily centered in the traditional industries (see Graph 2.6).[71] That this industrial sector was still quite new can be seen in the fact that two-thirds of the companies listed in the 1940 census had been founded only after 1920.

Firm size was still modest in this period. More than half of the companies had fewer than five employees and 89 percent of the firms had 25 workers or less.[72] Those employing more than 250 workers accounted for just 1 percent of the establishments, though they controlled 40 percent of the workers (see Graphs 2.7a and 2.7b).

In terms of employment, the textile industry stands out as an unusual case. In this industry firms employing up to 25 workers accounted for 64 percent of all textile mills but only 11 percent of all workers. Given

---

[69] In the sector of processing nonmetallic minerals the extraction of salt and hydro sources and extraction of stones and building materials dominated.
[70] The mechanical industry had 57 percent foreign capital; in the processing of nonmetallic minerals, which included the cement and flat glass industries, the rate was 49 percent.
[71] Brazilians controlled approximated 75 percent of the paid up capital in the two groups.
[72] The census of 1940 distinguishes between an enterprise and establishment, which is a judicial unit. An establishment represents a unit of production and could have more than one enterprise in it.

The Vargas Period, 1930–1945 111

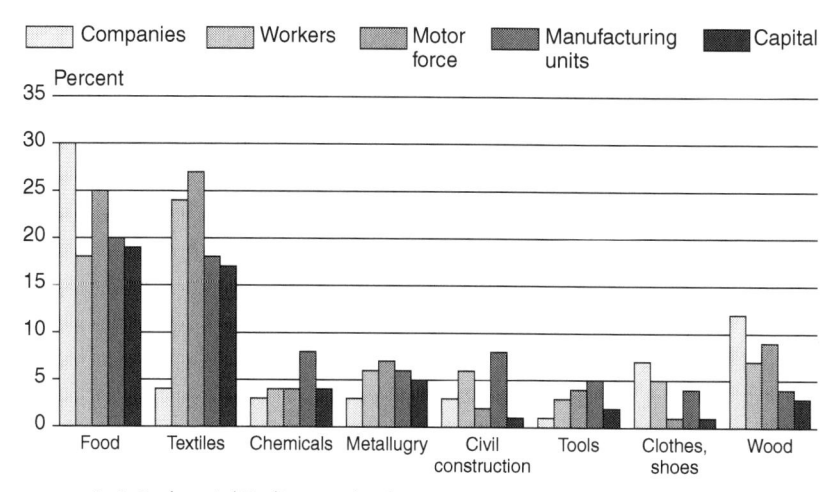

GRAPH 2.6. Industrial Indicators by Sector, 1940. *Source*: Recenseamento Geral de 1940, Vol. III

that the average worker per mill was very high – 106 workers per company – the highest of any industry, then one can see that large companies dominated the industry. Firms with 250 or more workers, numbering 218 companies (or 10 percent of all textile mills) accounted for three-quarters of all textile workers. Of the 85 industrial companies with more than 1,000 workers each, more than half (48 in number) were

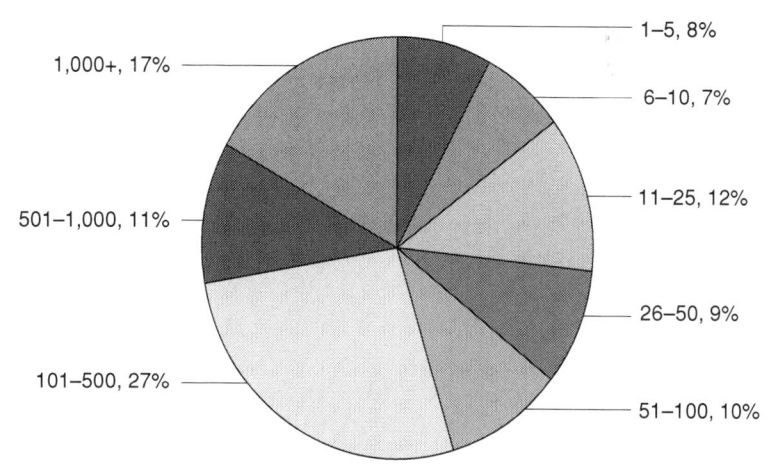

GRAPH 2.7a. Establishments by Number of Workers, 1940. *Source*: Recenseamento Geral de 1940

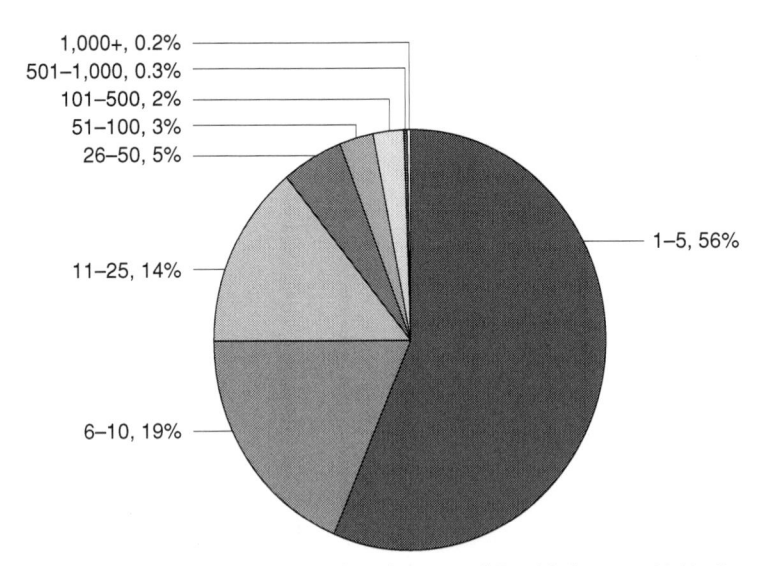

GRAPH 2.7b. Percentage of All Workers by Size of Establishment, 1940. *Source*: Recenseamento Geral de 1940

textile mills (see Graph 2.8). Moreover, it was the textile industry that was most heavily based on female workers (52 percent), compared to the capital good and other industries, where males predominated.

By 1948 manufacturing represented 21 percent of the GDP. Again, the states of São Paulo and Rio de Janeiro were above average and some of the northeastern states had relative high numbers because of their involvement in the sugar industry (see Graph 2.8).[73]

Agriculture, like industry, also expanded in this period of international crisis. This was a multifaceted industry producing for the internal market food and raw materials for industrial consumption as well as coffee and other agricultural products for the international market. Thus an increasing share of production was going into the market instead of subsistence. Agriculture played the role of generating exportable surpluses and providing the domestic market with food and raw materials that replaced

---

[73] These percentages were obtained from national accounts, whose series began in 1947 and represent the participation of industries of transformation. In that year, according to the national accounts, industry in general accounted for 24.5 percent of the national GDP. They may not be compatible with the earlier figures for the period before the national accounts and whose calculations were performed by Goldsmith, *Brasil 1850–1984*, 148. Also see IBGE, available at http://seriesestatisticas.ibge.gov.br/lista_tema.aspx?op=0&no=12, and Conjuntura Econômica, Setembro 1971, available at http://www.docpro.com.br/BibliotecaVirtual/Conjuntura/Pesquisalivre.html.

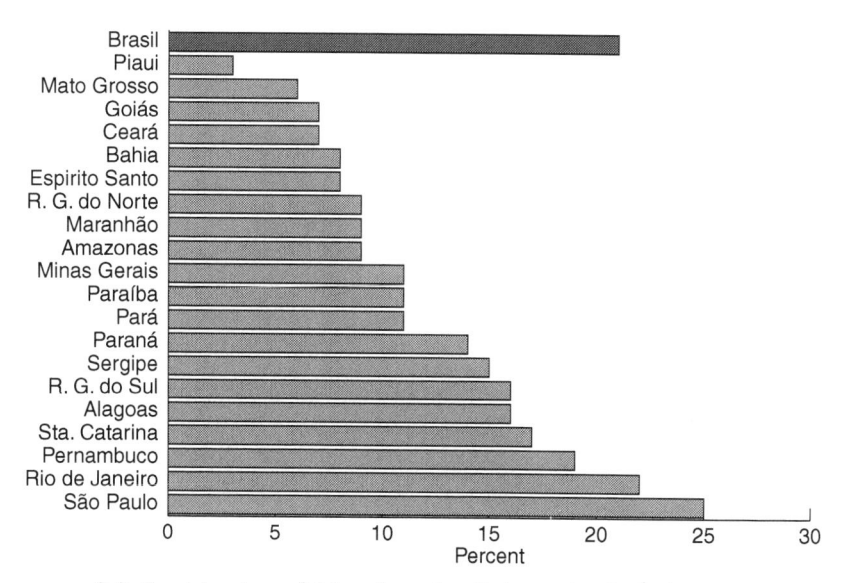

GRAPH 2.8. Participation of Manufacturing Industry in GDP, by State, 1948.
Source: FGV, Conjuntura Econômica, 25, 9 1971

imports.[74] For this reason state organizations were created to promote the production of many products, as was the Agricultural Portfolio Loan and Industrial Bank of Brazil in 1937, in which agriculture for the first time was provided with more adequate credit instruments.[75] This growth and diversification were the norms in this period from 1920 to 1950. These changes, moreover, were achieved with a declining workforce, as rural workers were attracted to urban centers and work in the expanding

---

[74] According to Pedro Fonseca, "The redirection of the economy towards the internal market, either by industry or by agriculture, it seems, was not a random act. Even without government planning in the strict sense of the term, modern proposals and actions of the government point to the existence of such a project. The discovery of the internal market, however, did not imply the abandonment on the part of economic policy of the external adjustment of the economy. Instead, substituting imports and diversifying exports were seen as measures capable of achieving surpluses in the balance of payments and ensuring the country's ability to honor its international commitments." Pedro Cezar Dutra Fonseca, *Vargas: o capitalismo em construção (1906–1954)* (São Paulo: Brasiliense, 1989), 219. Vargas affirmed in speeches the necessity of increasing agricultural production and exports and diversifying its products. Getúlio Vargas, *A Nova política do Brasil: O Estado Novo (10 de novembro de 1937 a 15 de julho de 1938)* (Rio de Janeiro: José Olympio, 1944), 305.

[75] Iliane Jesuina da Silva, "Estado e agricultura no primeiro governo Vargas (1930–1945)" (PhD thesis, Campinas, Universidade Estadual de Campinas, 2010), Chapter 4.

industrial sector.[76] But despite changes in this crucial transition period, agriculture nevertheless maintained its traditional productive structure with its high concentration of landownership.

Agriculture was still dominated by an historic landed elite and rural labor arrangements changed little in this period. None of the extensive labor legislation enacted by Vargas affected rural workers, who remained tied to the land in traditional labor arrangements. As late as the end of the 1940s in some areas, traditional landed colonels still predominated.[77] In other areas a slow modernization process was beginning, which would become more intense in the years from the 1970s onward and would be completed by the end of the twentieth century. Given his dependence on the traditional rural elite that supported his government and that enabled him to make advances in the urban areas, Vargas was prevented from making social transformations in the countryside.[78]

Although as late as 1950 agriculture still absorbed 60 percent of the national labor force, there was a gradual fall in this percentage in favor of industry and services after 1920. This freeing of the labor force from traditional agriculture was essential in order to consolidate the urban industrial sector. Although the rural population continued to grow, it grew at less of a rate than the urban population and the economically active population was now increasing rapidly in services in this period from 1920 and 1940 (see Graph 2.9).[79] This expansion of the relative importance of the industry significantly increased the overall productivity of the economy, due to the huge difference in these two sectors of the economy. By 1948 agriculture represented 28 percent of GDP nationally, but varied widely in importance among the states. In São Paulo it

---

[76] Between 1920 and 1950 the percentage of the economically active population in manufacturing increased from 5 percent to 8 percent. In this same period, the ratio in agriculture remained stable at 37 percent. Thomas Merrick and Douglas Graham, "População e desenvolvimento no Brasil: Uma perspectiva histórica," in *Economia Brasileira: Uma Visão Histórica*, ed. Paulo Nauhaus (Rio de Janeiro: Editora Campus, 1980), 200–201.

[77] Maria Isaura Pereira de Queiroz, *O mandonismo local na vida política brasileira* (São Paulo: Alfa-Omega, 1976), Parts 1–2. Overall, in 1940 the rural area was still dominated by large estates and labor relations with nonsalaried workers. Moreover, farmworkers did not have any kind of social protection. The changes occurring during the Vargas government in labor relations had not been extended to the countryside.

[78] It should be stressed that Vargas based his power in the industrial sector and urban workers, with the traditional rural elite, which did not accept any kind of transformation either in the agrarian structure or labor relations, prevailing in the rural area. The possibility of effecting a modernizing transformation in the urban and industrial areas demanded a conservative position in relation to the countryside.

[79] In the service sector the percentage was 134 percent, in industry 86 percent, and in agriculture 61 percent. Merrick and Graham, "População e desenvolvimento no Brasil: Uma perspectiva histórica," 45–88.

The Vargas Period, 1930–1945

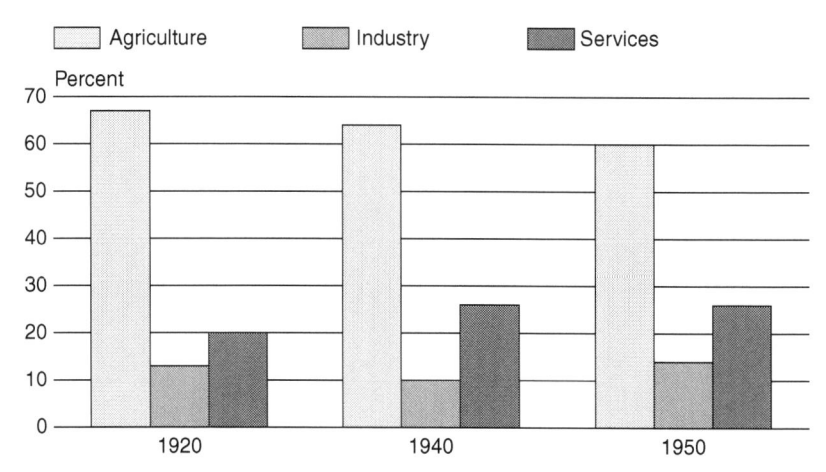

GRAPH 2.9. Economically Active Population by Sectors, 1920–1950. Source: Merrick and Graham 1980

represented about a third of the internal income, but in the majority of the states it was close to 50 percent. Given the importance of its service sector, Rio de Janeiro differed from the other states with a much lower rate for agriculture and higher one for services (see Graph 2.9).

But agriculture was still predominant in exports. In 1945, agricultural and ranching products accounted for 90 percent of Brazilian exports, with coffee alone representing a little more than two-thirds of the value of all exports. Along with coffee, cotton now emerged as an important crop supplying the internal market and the national textile industry as well as the international market. Some 11 percent of the value of exports was made up of raw cotton and 13 percent of the total value as finished textile products. Clearly textiles were the single most important manufactured goods exported in this period, and manufactured products represented only 5 percent of exports in 1945. Moreover, cotton growing expanded with national manufacturing and was able to satisfy the internal industrial market and even produced enough to sell overseas. There was even production of cotton seed oils, which became an important consumption item in the national market.[80] Cotton until the Vargas

---

[80] Historically, cotton had been produced for the external market and thus was much influenced by changes in the international market. When international demand increased, such as during the period of the U.S. Civil War, there was an increase in Brazilian production to attend the international market. Since Brazil was a low-quality high-cost producer and once international markets returned to normal, production and exports declined. This situation changed at the beginning of the twentieth century due to the establishment of a national textile industry that created a new and growing market

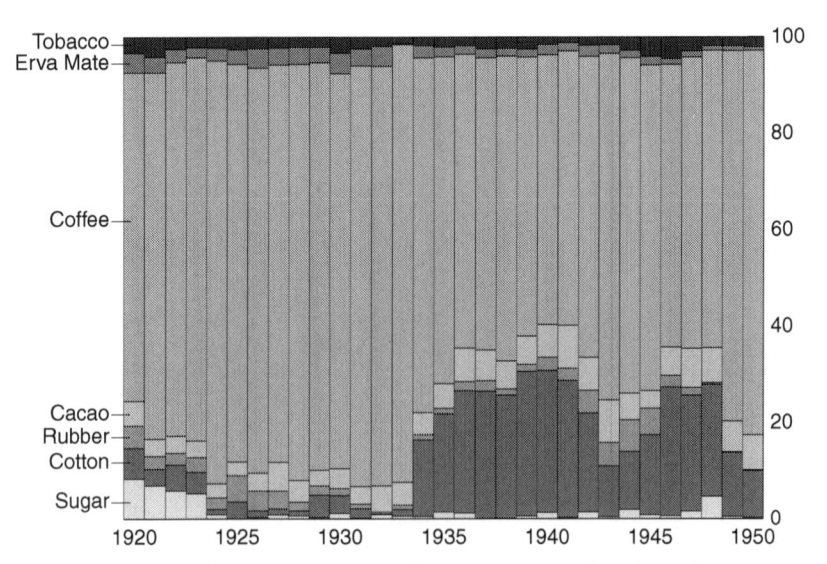

GRAPH 2.10. Participation in Exports of Principal Agricultural Products, 1920–1950. *Source*: IBGE Séries Históricas Retrospectivas

period was concentrated in the northeast region and was still produced by traditional methods. But in the decade of the 1940s São Paulo became a major producer and provided two-thirds of production, with the northeast (Ceará, Rio Grande do Norte, Pernambuco, and Paraíba being the largest regional producers) now accounting for only one-third of national cotton output. In contrast, the other traditional agricultural exports, such as sugar, rubber, cacao, yerba mate, and tobacco, had a modest role and only accounted for 8 percent of exports in 1945, the same level that they occupied in 1920 (see Graph 2.10 and Appendix Table A.4).

Although agriculture lost some share of the workforce and declined in relative share of GDP, actual production expanded dramatically in this period. This expansion of agricultural production was due to the growth of population and industry in this period, which increased demand. Between 1930 and 1945, agricultural output grew by 250 percent, for an annual rate of 9 percent. Besides cotton, which went to industry, rice and manioc, essential in the food consumption of the national population, also grew at the impressive rate of 6 percent per annum. But the production of sugar and beans grew at a much slower pace than manioc and rice,

for cotton. Alice P. Canabrava, *O algodão no Brasil, 1861–1875* (São Paulo: T. A. Queiróz Editor, 1984); Alexandre Bragança Coelho, "A cultura do Algodão e a questão da integração entre preços internos e externos" (MA thesis, Universidade de São Paulo, 2002).

The Vargas Period, 1930–1945 117

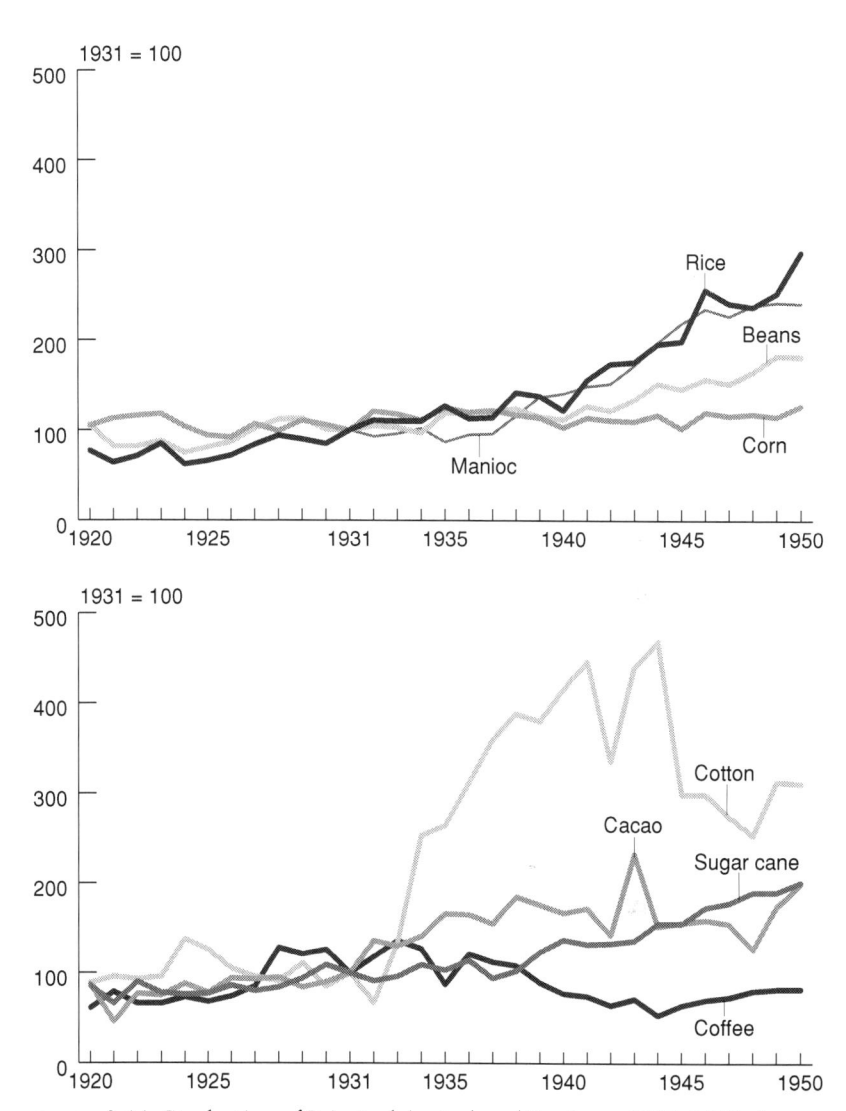

GRAPH 2.11. Production of Principal Agricultural Products, 1920–1950. *Source*: IBGE – Séries Históricas Retrospectivas

achieving only a 2.4 percent annual growth in this period. Corn, a basic food crop of animals and humans, had a stable production throughout this period. Coffee had gone through a severe crisis in the 1930s and 1940s but seemed to be increasing, especially in the 1950s (see Graph 2.11).

Of all the agricultural crops harvested in this period, seven products dominated. These were coffee, cotton, corn, rice, beans, manioc, and sugar – the seven accounting for 85 percent of the value of production

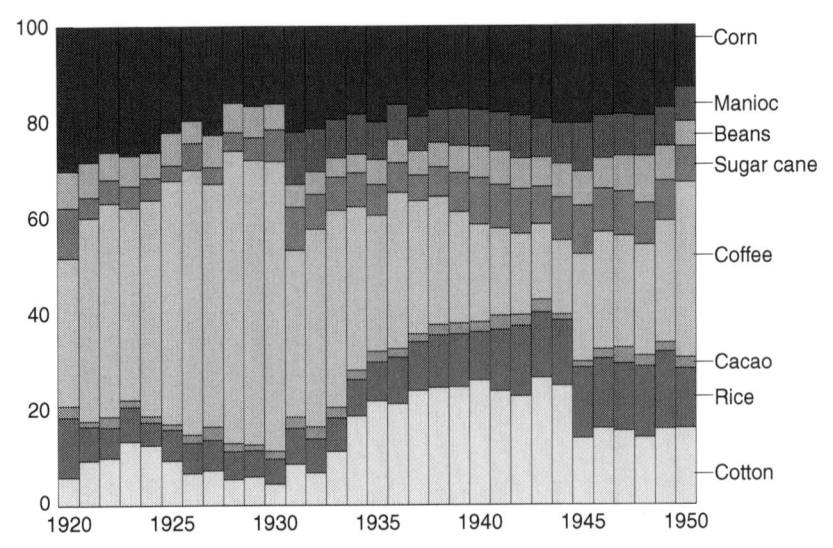

GRAPH 2.12. Percentage of Value of Production by Major Crops, 1920–1950.
Source: IBGE – Séries Históricas Retrospectivas

between 1938 and 1947. Coffee, cotton, corn, and rice were the most important. In terms of acreage, these three crops occupied more than 90 percent of the area cultivated in this period. Corn was the crop that had the largest amount of acreage, some one-third of the total area in crops, followed by coffee and cotton. Following its historical trajectory, corn saw the greatest expansion in hectares cultivated and thus saw a tremendous growth in output, which went from 330,000 tons to 1.1 million in the period from 1920 to 1950 (see Graph 2.12).

Regions planted in coffee also changed in this period as coffee moved north and south of São Paulo. Although São Paulo was still important, Paraná production increased enormously and was quickly catching up. Along with these two states there was also coffee produced in Minas Gerais, Espírito Santo, and Rio de Janeiro. In 1950, São Paulo had 137 million new coffee trees planted and a stock of 956 million trees in production. By this time Paraná had 118 million new trees and a total of 160 million trees in production and was in the process of overtaking the leader.[81]

---

[81] By the *quinquenieum* of 1956–1960 Paraná coffee production had already passed that of São Paulo. In the following five-year period, the Paranaense production was 85 percent above the production of São Paulo state.

The Vargas Period, 1930–1945   119

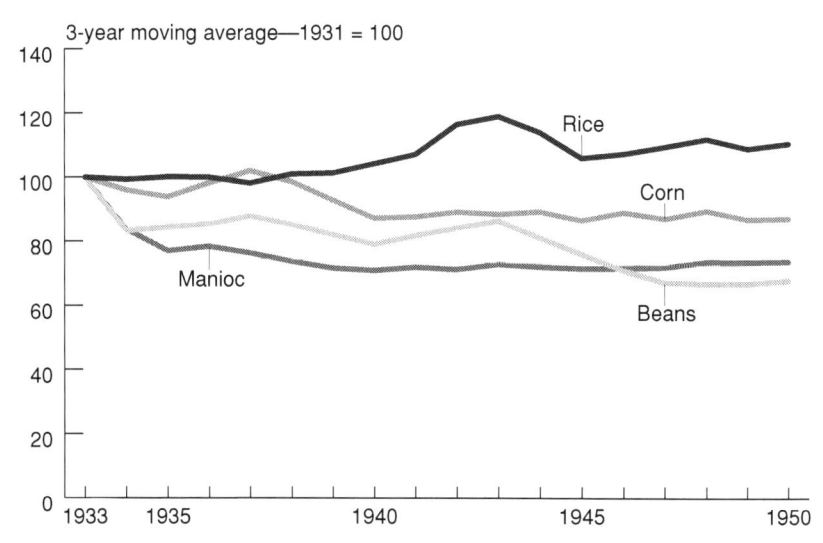

GRAPH 2.13a. Principal Agricultural Products, Productivity by Area, 1933–1950.
Source: IBGE – Séries Históricas Retrospectivas

Despite the growth in total output of most crops in the Vargas period, there was little change in productivity (see Graphs 2.13a and 2.13b). In fact, there was a decline in productivity in cotton in the late 1940s

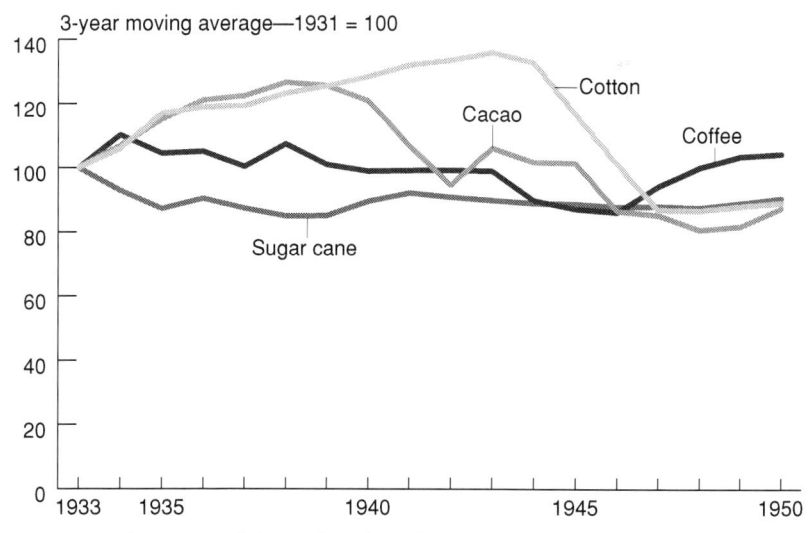

GRAPH 2.13b. Principal Agricultural Products, Productivity by Area, 1933–1950.
Source: IBGE – Séries Históricas Retrospectivas

120   The Economic and Social History of Brazil since 1889

TABLE 2.1. *Agro-Pastoral Establishments, Total Area, and Utilization, 1920–1950 (area in hectares)*

	1920	1940	1950
Establishments	648,153	1,904,589	2,064,642
Total Area	1 75,104,675	197,720,247	232,211,106
Crops			
permanent		5,961,770	4,402,426
temporary	6,642,057	1 2,873,660	14,692,631
Pasturage			
natural		83,068,814	92,659,363
planted		5,072,319	14,973,060
Matas and Forests			
natural	48,916,653	49,085,464	54,870,087
planted			1,128,994
Productive Lands Not Utilized	29,296,497	34,310,721	
Unusable Lands		12,361,127	15,173,204
Equipment			
tractors		1,706	3,380	8,372
plows	141,196	447,556	714,259

Source: IBGE, Séries Históricas Retrospectivas.

as output declined from the same area planted in the crop.[82] The same negative productivity occurred with cacao, whose production fell in the 1940s as the area planted to the crop remained the same. All this lack of productivity was due to the continued use of traditional agricultural techniques in most crops, along with the reduced use of machinery and very limited use of fertilizers and manure. Even plows were little used. In 1950 there was only 1 plow per 400 hectares of rural property, and just considering cultivated lands, the ratio was 1 per 28 hectares. Tractors were still not used. In 1940 only one-fourth of farms used some type of agricultural machinery. Moreover, what machinery was used was highly concentrated. The northeast and center west zones used practically no machinery – while they were used far more in Rio Grande do Sul where some 81 percent of farms had them and in São Paulo where 48 percent of the farms listed such machinery. Only after 1960 did machinery become widespread in Brazilian agriculture (see Table 2.1).[83]

There were also some changes in the number of farms and the area cultivated in this period. From 1920 to 1940 there was a major expansion

[82] In 1945, two-thirds of the total production of cotton was made up by herbaceous cotton and one-third came from cotton trees, which was a permanent crop. Between the peak of 1944 and 1950, e.g., the two types of cotton production decreased by one-third.
[83] The modernization of Brazilian agriculture began in the 1950s through imports, but it was in the 1960s that the process accelerated, with the establishment of a local industry

of farms, but this stopped in the decade of the 1940s. The farmlands used to produce annually planted crops (such as wheat, rice, and corn) doubled between 1920 and 1940 but grew little thereafter. On the other hand land dedicated to more permanent crops (such as coffee and oranges) declined in this period. Pastureland, mostly natural grazing lands, did not expand in the 1940s – though in size lands dedicated to grazing were five times greater than land dedicated to crops in 1950.[84] The cultivated area was concentrated in a few states, such as São Paulo, Minas Gerais, Rio Grande do Sul, and Rio de Janeiro, which already occupied a significant part of each state's territories. In contrast, other regions such as the *cerrado*,[85] which today is a great cereal-producing region, were largely abandoned or underutilized (see Graph 2.14).

According to the census of 1940, farms and ranches of 100 hectares or less controlled 18 percent of the farmlands, produced 55 percent of the total agricultural output, and contained 66 percent of the workers and owners involved in agriculture. The units containing 100 to 1,000 hectares held just a third of the total farms, had a third of the value of output, and had 28 percent of farmworkers. Finally, the great estates of more than 1,000 hectares – just 1 percent of all properties – had half the farmlands, 6 percent of the workers, and 10 percent of the value of total production. All this meant that in 1940 the great weight of production and employment was on farms and ranches of less than 100 hectares, and the great estates had little impact in either of these areas. This suggests that these very large estates had more political and social value than economic importance. At the other end, farms and ranches of 20 acres or less, while accounting for a third of property owners, held just 1 percent of the lands and 20 percent of the rural workers – essentially family members – and they accounted for a tenth of the total value of production. In contrast to

---

dedicated to the production of equipment and inputs for agriculture. Eduardo Fernandes, Bruna Almeida Guimarães, and Ramalho Romulo Matheus, *Principais Empresas e Grupos Brasileiros no Setor de Fertilizantes*, available at http://funcex.org.br/material/ redemercosul bibliografia/ biblioteca/ESTUDOS BRASIL/BRA 160.PDF.

[84] The temporary crops evolved from 6.6 million hectares in 1920 to 12.9 in 1940 and 14.7 in 1950. Permanent crops occupied 6.0 million hectares in 1940 and 4.4 million hectares in 1950 (there is no data in the 1920 census). In 1950, considering the temporary and permanent crops, they occupied only 8 percent of the total areas of the properties surveyed. The other areas were in pastures, woods, and forests and otherwise unusable.

[85] With an area of 2,036,448 km², the Cerrado covers 22 percent of the Brazilian territory, and includes the Federal District, Goiás, Tocantins, much of Maranhão, Mato Grosso do Sul, and Minas Gerais, in addition to covering smaller areas of six other states. The Cerrado is the source of three major river systems of South America (Amazon/Tocantins, San Francisco, and La Plata), which results in high potential aquifer and great biodiversity. Available at http://www.brasil.gov.br/sobre/meio-ambiente/geografia.

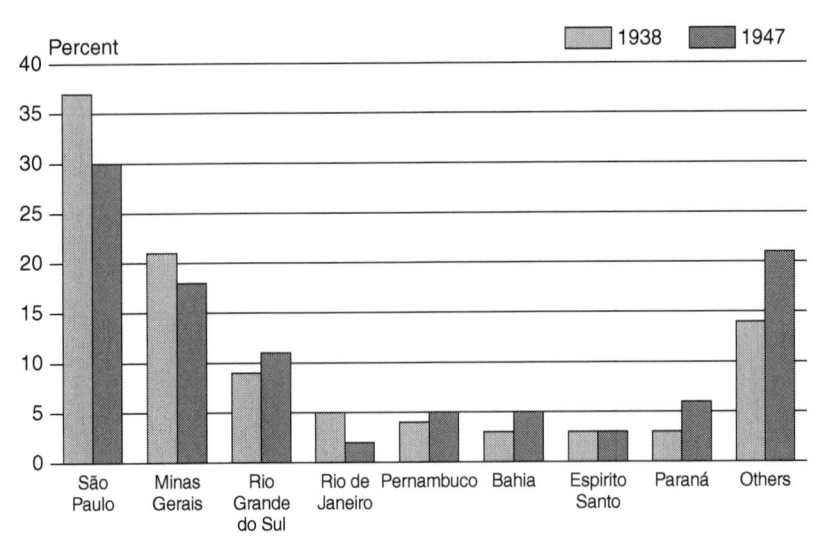

GRAPH 2.14. Percentage Cultivated Area by State, 1938 and 1947. *Source*: IBGE – *Anuário Estatístico do Brasil* (1948), p. 80

the latifundium, there was creation of value in these small farms, but at a low level of productivity for the two million people working on these small plots (see Graph 2.15). There was little difference in use of manure to fertilize the land by size of unit; in larger and smaller farms only 5 percent used this enrichment for crops.

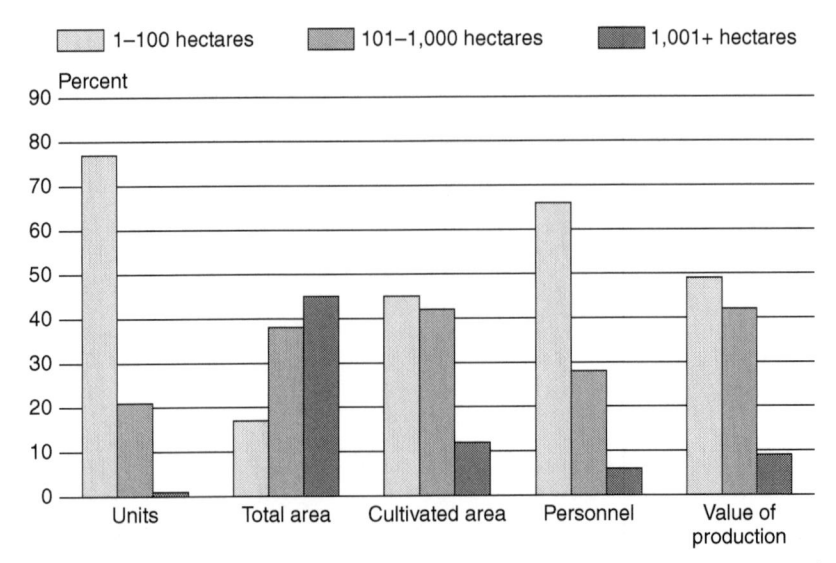

GRAPH 2.15. Agricultural Indicators, 1940. *Source*: IBGE – Recenseamento Geral de 1940

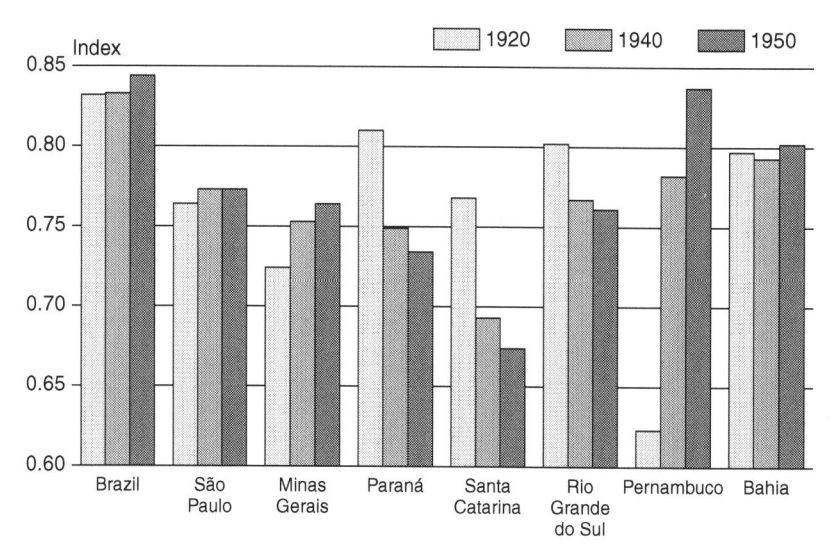

GRAPH 2.16. Gini Index of Landownership – Brazil and Principal States, 1920–1950. *Source*: Szmrecsányi 1995, p. 193

This unequal structure in the distribution of land and resources marked Brazilian society since the colonial period and was reflected in the high Gini indices of inequality, which remained at the same 0.83 level in all three censuses of 1920, 1940, and 1950. As could be expected, the most agriculturally productive states (São Paulo, Minas Gerais, Paraná, Santa Catarina, and Rio Grande do Sul) had the lowest index of inequality in the nation (see Graph 2.16).

There were also some interesting variations on crop types and farm families and their workers by region. In 1940 the southeast accounted for half the value of agricultural production (São Paulo alone accounted for a quarter of national output); and because of coffee this region had more permanent plants than other regions. In the south family members were the majority of rural workers. This explains why in the typical southeastern state of São Paulo the average farm had eight workers, and the number was half that in the typical southern state of Rio Grande do Sul.[86] At this time the center west was the only region that did not have

---

[86] The South of Brazil, particularly Santa Catarina and Rio Grande do Sul, received a different form of immigration not related to the export economy. These immigrants, mainly Germans and Italians, received land in small plots, and formed the nuclei of colonization whose production of goods was for the domestic market. These colonies were of fundamental importance in establishing the regime of small farms prevailing in the region and on modernization of agriculture, with greater use of fertilizers and equipment. On this theme, see Carlos H. Oberacker Jr., "A colonização baseada no

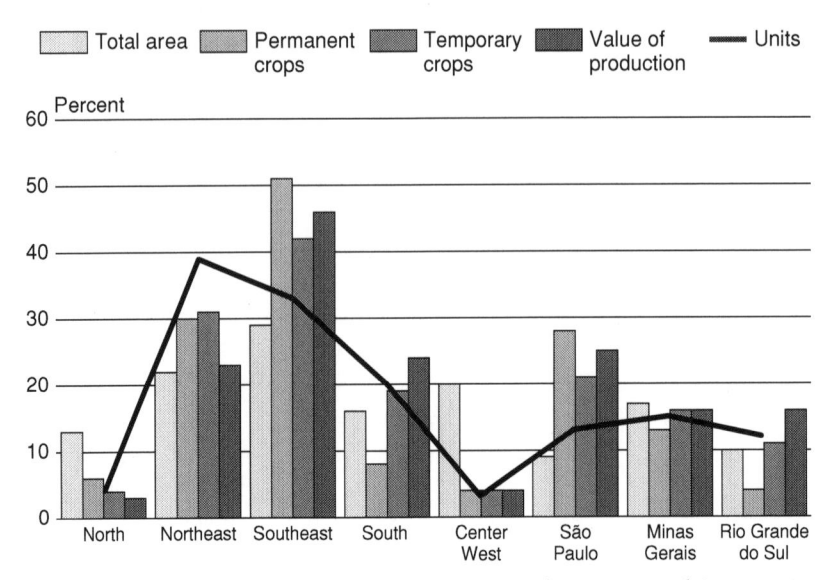

124 The Economic and Social History of Brazil since 1889

GRAPH 2.17. Distribution of Agricultural Indicators by Region and State, 1940.
Source: Recenseamento Geral de 1940

major agricultural activities (see Graph 2.17). Moreover, productivity and the use of machinery also varied sharply by region. In general the southern and southeastern states were double or triple the average crop productivity of the northeastern states.[87] This was clearly due to use of fertilizers, manure, and machinery. Only 4 percent of northeastern farms had machinery in contrast to 60 percent of farms using them in the south and 27 percent in the southeast. Here as well Rio Grande do Sul was the major state using such instruments on 81 percent of rural units, compared to only 48 percent in São Paulo. Looking at just the number of plows per unit, the states of São Paulo, Minas Gerais, and Rio Grande do Sul are basically similar having between 1.2 and 1.37 per unit and the northeastern region as a whole only 0.36 per establishment. In 1940 there

---

regime de pequena propriedade agrícola," in *História Geral da Civilização Brasileira*, II:3, ed. Sérgio Buarque de Holanda (São Paulo: Difusão Europeia do Livro, 1969), 220–245.

[87] In terms of the average output per establishment, using the 100 index for the northeast, we find output levels in the south of 197 and in the southeast of 232. As for individual states, the index is 177 in Minas Gerais, 220 in Rio Grande do Sul, and 317 in São Paulo. Likewise, if one considers the 100 index for the proportion of property value used in machinery and equipment, the result went from 313 in Minas Gerais, to 382 in Rio Grande do Sul and 495 for São Paulo.

were fewer than 3,000 tractors in Brazil and these too were concentrated in São Paulo and Rio Grande do Sul.

As this survey of agriculture and industry shows, the Vargas period was one of significant transformations in the economy of the country. Industry expanded significantly in this period. Externalities also aided the growth of the economy. Both the Great Depression and World War II stimulated the growth in manufacturers. All this was supported by government policy through exchange controls that benefited local production. The state even began investing in production, and this would become even more common a state activity in the second half of the twentieth century. Agriculture also was stimulated by international developments and became more diversified in terms of supplying food and raw materials for the internal market as well as fomenting exports. This was especially the case with cotton production, which became the supplier of the crucial textile industry, the largest of the manufacturing sectors.

Although the internal economy recuperated quickly after 1930, it was only in the decade of the 1940s that the export sector returned to 1920 levels. The overproduction of coffee would only be resolved by burning 78.2 million sacks of coffee and prohibiting new plantings, and these policies along with the outbreak of World War II led to coffee again achieving rising exports. World War II had a dual impact on the Brazilian economy. It stimulated production to satisfy increasing external demand and increased output to provide substitutes for the internal market for imported goods that were no longer available. Not everything was positive, of course. Primary materials, fuels, machines, and equipment became difficult to import and thus were unable to satisfy local demand and were obtained at higher prices. At the same time, increasing exports and declining imports in the war period created surpluses in the balance of trade and led to the accumulation of reserves. But most of these reserves could not be freely used to purchase goods since they were credits accumulated against Great Britain. During this war period there was an expansionist economic policy,[88] and a significant increase in prices occurred. Since the exchange rate was maintained at a stable level, the national currency was overvalued. The maintenance of the exchange rate, among other reasons, was tied to the necessity to buy foreign currencies on the part of the government to pay its debts in foreign exchange, and for the government to control internal inflation. At the end of the war there was a major

---

[88] The public deficit previously funded with the sale of securities went on to be financed with emissions. Abreu, "Crise, crescimento e modernização autoritária," 95.

increase in demand not only for consumer goods but also for restocking local industries.[89]

Clearly the economic and political reforms of the Vargas period had a major impact on expanding the industrial labor force and encouraged the steady expansion of the urban sectors of the country. There would also be important changes in social policy that for the first time systematically dealt with the problems of pensions and welfare, at least for the most advanced urban industrial working population. But in other social areas, change was slow. Fertility remained high and mortality, though declining, was still dominated by deaths caused by infectious diseases. Although life expectancy was slowly improving in the more advanced regions, such as São Paulo, levels of infant and maternal mortality remained quite high. The number of students enrolled at the primary and secondary levels steadily increased, but not at a rate to make a significant dent in the very high levels of illiteracy. Thus Brazilians in this era remained predominantly illiterate. There were of course, changes. The Vargas era marked the slow end of international migration and the ever-increasing movement of native-born populations across regions. This, in turn, led to an increase of population in the southeastern states and their relative decline in the northeastern ones. There was also a steady and significant growth of major metropolitan centers. Despite the growth of Rio de Janeiro and São Paulo, now with more than 1.5 million people, the majority of Brazilians remained overwhelmingly rural.

The decline of international migration, which had occurred in the late 1910s as a result of European wars, was quickly followed by impressive numbers of arrivals in the 1920s, especially of immigrants from Italy, Portugal, and Japan. There was another small movement of Eastern Europeans in the late 1930s and early 1940s, but renewed European war eventually brought this movement to an end, and it never fully recovered (see Graph 2.18). The Italians and the Spaniards no longer came in large numbers after 1920 and only the Portuguese and Japanese kept their steady pace until the years of the Great Depression of the early 1930s.

But a new migration soon took its place as the expanding urban and industrial economy of the southeastern states sought an ever-larger number of workers. Migrants from the northern and northeastern regions began appearing in the southeastern states as early as the 1920s and became an ever-increasing number in the following decades. Slowly but

---

[89] Carlos Lessa, *Quinze anos de política econômica* (São Paulo: Brasiliense/UNICAMP, 1975), 9.

The Vargas Period, 1930–1945

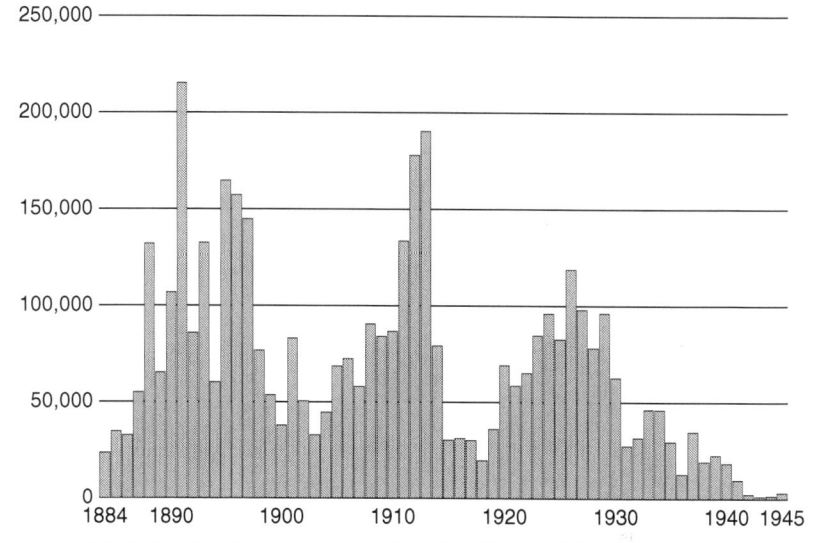

GRAPH 2.18. Foreign Immigration to Brazil by Year, 1884–1945. *Source*: IBGE, *Estatísticas do século XX*, Table "pop_1951aeb-033"

steadily the north and northeastern states lost population to all the other regions of the country (see Graph 2.19).[90]

These regional immigrants were joined as well by inter- and intrastate migrants who moved from the rural areas to the cities in ever-increasing numbers. Between 1890 and 1940 the population of the capital cities of the states rose from 1.3 million to close to 6 million persons.[91] Moreover, the two leading cities of the country grew rapidly in the period between 1920 and 1940. Rio de Janeiro, the federal capital, went from 1.1 to 1.5 million, but even more rapid was the expansion of the city of São Paulo, which went from half a million to 1.2 million in the same twenty year period.[92] But the country remained predominantly agricultural and rural for this entire period. The government estimated the urban population

---

[90] Here and elsewhere we are using the current definition of regions, which was adopted with the 1970 census. The major difference from earlier regional definitions is that Bahia and Sergipe are now part of the northeast region, and the new southeastern region now included the states of Rio de Janeiro, Espiritu Santo, Minas Gerais, and São Paulo. All the states included in each region can be seen in Maps 1.1 and 1.2 in the preceding text.

[91] IBGE, *Estatística do Seculo XX*, Table "pop_1976aeb-009."

[92] IBGE, Série: CD79 – População dos municípios das capitais (população presente e residente), available at http://seriesestatisticas.ibge.gov.br/series.aspx?vcodigo=CD79& sv=58&t=populacao-dos-municipios-das-capitais-populacao-presente-e-residente.

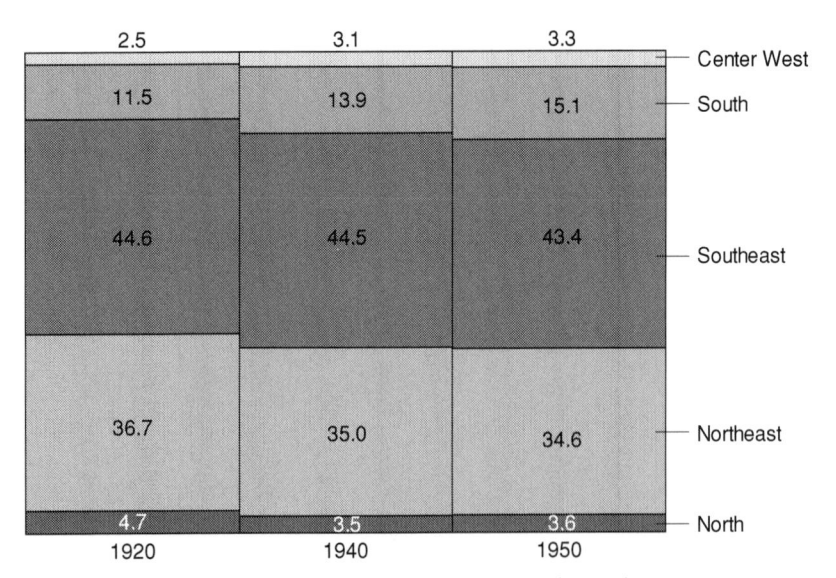

2.5	3.1	3.3	Center West
11.5	13.9	15.1	South
44.6	44.5	43.4	Southeast
36.7	35.0	34.6	Northeast
4.7	3.5	3.6	North
1920	1940	1950	

GRAPH 2.19. Relative Importance of Regions in Total Population, 1920, 1940, and 1950. *Source*: Recensamiento Geral do Brasil 1940, "Sinopse do Censo Demográfico, Dados Gerais"

of Brazil at 31 percent of the population in 1940, with only the southeastern region having a significant level of urbanization (39 percent of the population).[93] This vision of an overwhelmingly rural society is also shown in a census of occupations in 1937 that listed 75 percent of the 11.8 million workers in "agriculture, cattle ranching and rural industries."[94]

Just as there was only a modest increase in the urban population, in education there was also only modest change over this whole period. Despite all the ideological debates, discussions, and administrative reorganization, there were only limited actual advances. As of 1932, only 2.3 million students were attending school in the country, and this represented approximately a quarter of the population 20 years of age and under. Moreover, very few of the students who were matriculated were found in postprimary schools. Only 5 percent were enrolled in any form of secondary education, and only 2 percent in superior studies – which included normal schools producing primary and secondary school teachers. In the following 23 years change did occur, but only at a relatively slow

---

[93] IBGE, Série: POP122 – "Taxa de urbanização," available at http://seriesestatisticas.ibge. gov.br/series.aspx?vcodigo=POP122&sv=33&t=taxa-de-urbanizacao.
[94] IBGE, *Estatística do Século XX*, Table "trabalho1937aeb_17."

The Vargas Period, 1930–1945

1932
(n = 2,274,213)

Superior 2%
Secondary 5%
Primary 93%

1945
(n = 3,974,252)

Superior 1%
Secondary 10%
Primary 89%

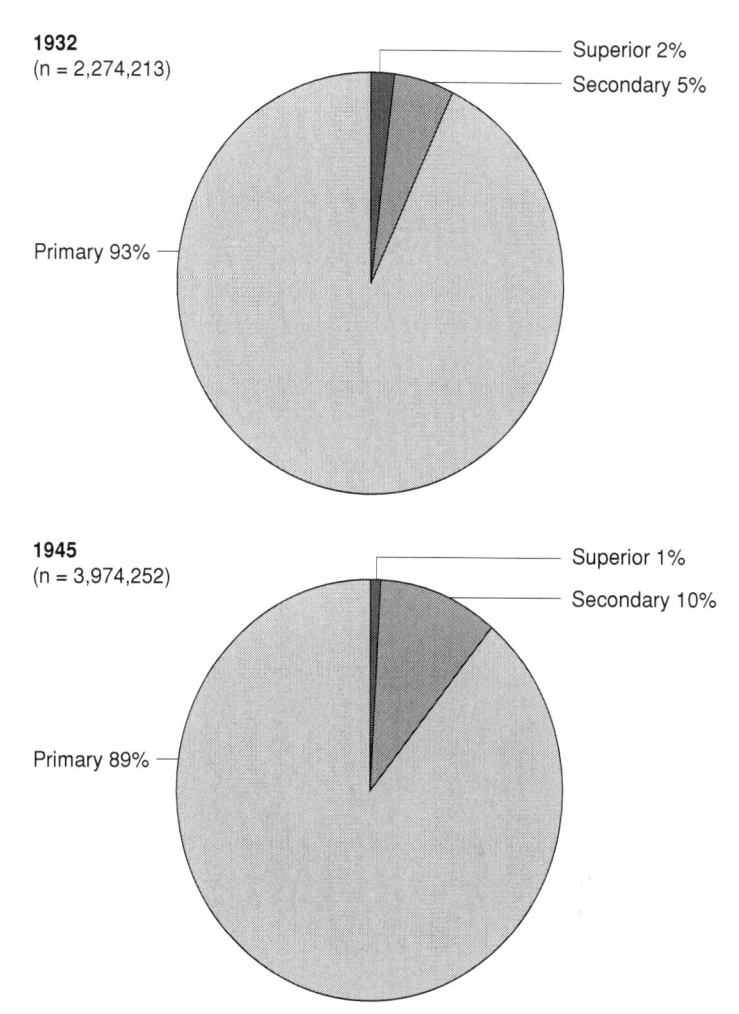

GRAPH 2.20. Students Matriculated by Course, 1932, 1945. *Source*: IBGE, *Estatísticas do século XX*, Table "Educação1947aeb-04"

pace. Primary education enrollment grew at only 2.1 percent per annum, slightly below the growth of the national population, and tertiary education at just 0.5 percent per annum. Only secondary education expanded faster than population growth reaching an impressive 5.3 percent per annum. These differential growth rates can be seen in the relative share of students matriculated in each of these differing levels (see Graph 2.20).[95]

[95] Data for these graphs comes from IBGE, *Estatística do Século XX*, Table "Educação1947aeb-04."

Even as late as 1940, the number of students matriculated by age cohort was extremely low. In the census of that year it was reported that only 26 percent of the boys aged 7 to 18 were enrolled in school and the figure for girls of this age was just 25 percent. When broken down by age and level of schooling, it is interesting to note that primary basic and precolegial (all together eight years of school) held about the same ratio of students out of the total population at risk, but that for the last four years of secondary school the drop-off was dramatic, those attending school accounting for just a tenth of boys and just 8 percent of the girls in this age group.

These numbers improved somewhat in the next decade, especially in terms of basic primary education. It is estimated that the number of students enrolled in primary school reached 5.2 million students in 1950 and thus increased two and a half times in the period since 1930. This growth was also reflected in the net matriculation rate, which climbed to 73 percent for five to nine year olds in primary grades in 1950. But almost all the effort was directed to these first four years of basic education. Overall only 32 percent of children and youths ages 5 to 19 were matriculated in school, which meant that only 8 percent of children ages 10 to 19 were enrolled in school.[96]

This low level of schooling meant that the illiteracy rate remained extraordinarily high. In the census of 1920 literates made up only 34.8 percent of the adult population 18 years and older, and in the census of 1940 this figure had only risen to 43.6 percent of adults. Moreover, the distribution of this minority of literate persons by region clearly correlated with regional differences in poverty and wealth. It was the southeast home to the booming industrial, coffee, and immigration population that had the highest literacy rates and the northeast the lowest (see Graph 2.21). Though all regions had increased their share of literates in these ten years, the gap between regions actually increased, with the northeast having just 52 percent of the number of literates in the southern region in 1920 and only 48 percent in 1940.

Not only was there an obvious distinction in education and literacy of rich and poor, as represented by regions, but there was also a sharp distinction in literacy and educational level by color. Thus for 1940 there is data based on color for the first time in the republican period, and it was evident that blacks and mulattoes were the least literate, and whites and Asians the most literate of the national population (see Graph 2.22).

---

[96] This data is taken from FVG, "A educação no seguno governo Vargas," available at http://cpdoc.fgv.br/producao/dossies/AEraVargas2/artigos/EleVoltou/Educacao.

The Vargas Period, 1930–1945　131

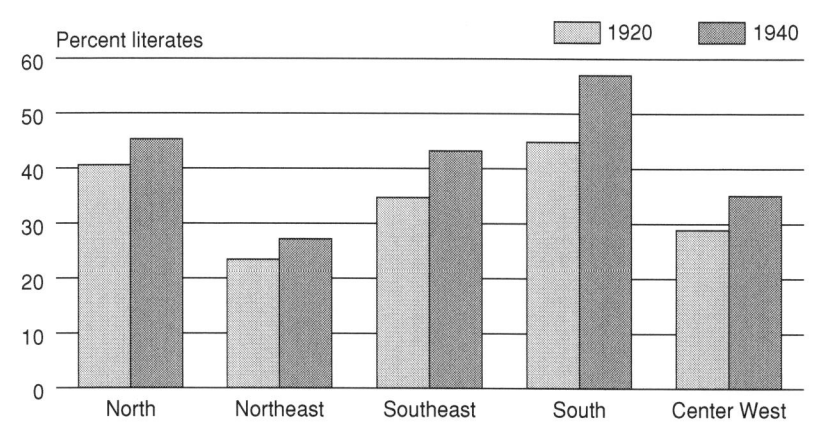

GRAPH 2.21. Literate Adults 18 Years and Older by Regions – Census of 1920 and 1940. *Source*: IBGE, *Estatísticas do século XX*, Table "pop_1941_45aeb_009"

While all groups were reaching fairly high levels of primary education at approximately equal rates by 1940, the discrimination by sex and race persisted at higher levels of the educational system (see Tables 2.2 and 2.3).

That these distinctions by sex and color would continue in the future as well as they had in the past are evident from the statistics available on rates of completion and current registration of students. In a survey of persons more than ten years of age, it was evident that *pretos* (blacks) and *pardos* (mulattoes) had far fewer diplomas from secondary and university courses than the other two groups. It was also evident that women received far

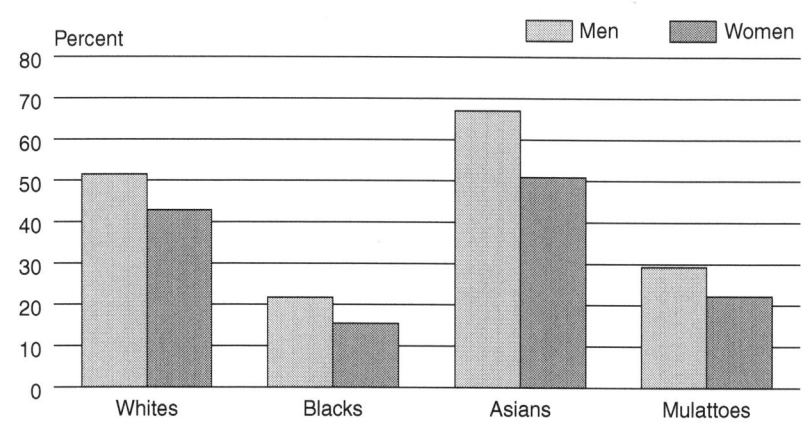

GRAPH 2.22. Literacy Rate by Sex and Color of the Population Five Years of Age and Older, 1940. *Source*: Recenseamento Geral de 1940, Série Nacional II, Quadro, p. 28

TABLE 2.2. *Persons 10 Years of Age and Older Who Have Completed a Course of Studies by Sex and Color, 1940*

Grade of Schooling	Whites Men	Whites Women	Blacks Men	Blacks Women	Asians Men	Asians Women	Mulattoes Men	Mulattoes Women	TOTAL Men	TOTAL Women
Elementary	71.4	79.6	94.1	95.5	79.2	88.2	86.6	89.8	73.5	81.0
Middle	18.7	19.3	4.5	4.3	16.3	11.5	10.0	9.8	17.5	18.0
Superior	10.0	1.1	1.3	0.2	4.5	0.3	3.4	0.4	9.1	1.0
	100.0	100.0	100.0	100.0	100.0	100.0	100.0	100.0	100.0	100.0
Grade known	932,383	840,651	33,225	30,063	10,014	6,993	90,797	82,566	1,066,419	960,273

Source: IBGE, Recenseamento Geral de 1940, Serie Nacional II, Quadro 25, p. 30.

TABLE 2.3. *Students (5 to 39 years of age) Matriculated by Level of Course, Sex, and Color, 1940*

Grade of School	Whites Men	Whites Women	Blacks Men	Blacks Women	Asians Men	Asians Women	Mulattoes Men	Mulattoes Women	TOTAL Men	TOTAL Women
Elementary	85.6	89.0	98.1	98.7	90.1	95.0	95.3	96.5	88.0	91.0
Middle	12.1	10.4	1.7	1.2	9.0	4.9	4.1	3.3	10.1	8.5
Superior	2.3	0.6	0.1	0.0	0.9	0.1	0.6	0.1	1.9	0.5
	100.0	100.0	100.0	100.0	100.0	100.0	100.0	100.0	100.0	100.0
Grade Known	1,332,922	1,180,434	133,052	132,306	13,973	11,423	260,351	252,452	1,740,298	1,576,615

Source: Recenseamento Geral de 1940, Série Nacional II, Quadro 21, p. 30.

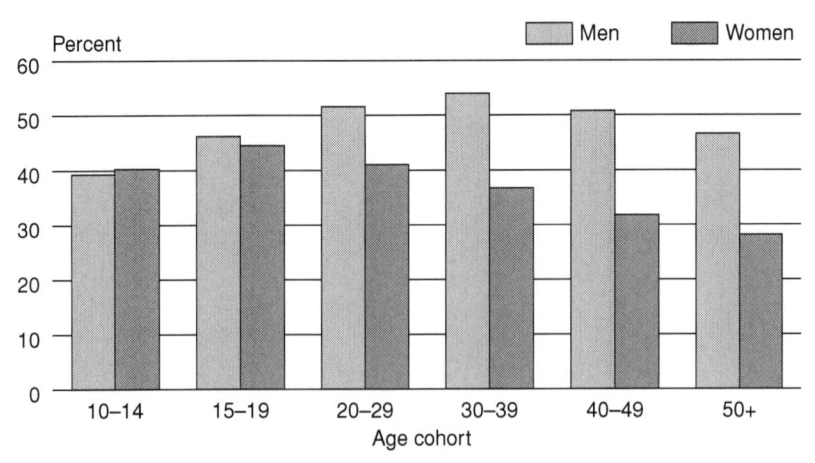

GRAPH 2.23. Literacy by Age Cohort and Sex in the Census of 1940. *Source*: IBGE, *Estatística do Século XX*, Table "pop_1965aeb-05.1"

fewer advanced degrees than men, though there appeared less distinction by sex in primary and secondary education. This reflected the fact that women only tended to drop out of the educational system after completing the secondary grades. In contrast to the experience of women, blacks and mulattoes tended to drop out after completing the primary grades. But literacy rates by age and sex in 1940 seem to indicate that the bias against women was slowly disappearing. For the youngest cohort, that of 10 to 14 years of age there was virtually no difference in rates of literacy, whereas the bias against women increased with each succeeding age cohort (see Graph 2.23).

As could be expected there were sharp differences in occupational level and in ratios of employment between men and women. But these same patterns of discrimination can be seen in terms of employment by race. While the data are grouped in very large categories, it is evident that blacks and mulattoes are to be found far less in the employer category than whites or Asians – with the Asians being essentially all Japanese in this period (see Graph 2.24).

There were also important distinctions by residence and race in Brazil in this period. Race was not evenly distributed across the nation. While most of Brazil had been predominantly Afro-Brazilian until the 1880s, the massive arrival of European immigrants primarily to the southeastern and southern states meant that these regions dramatically changed their color composition over time. Whereas the northern, northeastern, and southeastern states along the coast were quite similar in the census of 1872

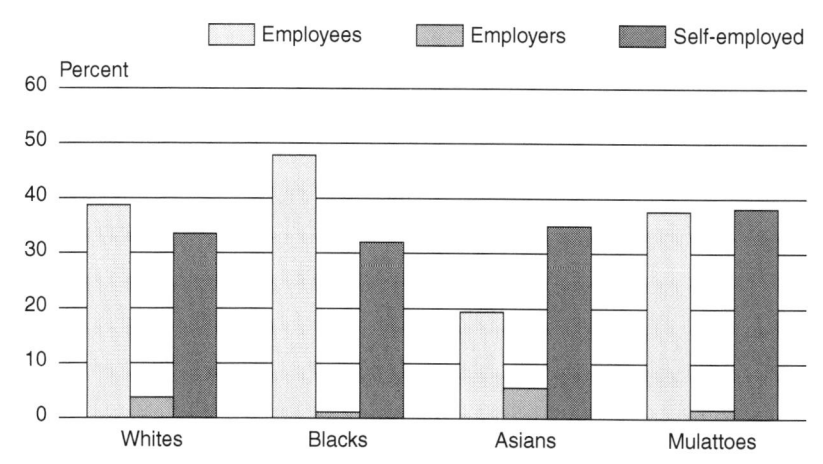

GRAPH 2.24. Percentage of Workers Who Were Managers, Employees, and Self-Employed by Color, 1940 ($n = 7.4$ million). *Source*: Recenseamento Geral de 1940, Série Nacional II, p. 36, Table 30

with a predominantly Afro-Brazilian population, by the census of 1940, when color again became a census category, there had occurred a quite dramatic change during these six decades. While the north retained its 1872 color ratios, all the other regions increased their share of white residents. Also the southeastern and central west region went from being predominantly Afro-Brazilian to predominantly white. Moreover, the southern states of Rio Grande do Sul, Paraná, and Santa Catarina increased their dominant white population, which went from having 75 percent of its population defined as white, to 90 percent categorized as being of this color (see Graphs 2.25 and 2.26). This was the maximum year for

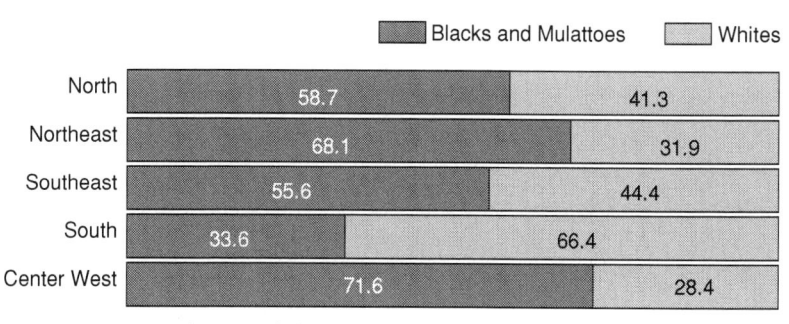

GRAPH 2.25. Distribution of the Population by Color by Region, 1872. *Source*: Censo de 1872

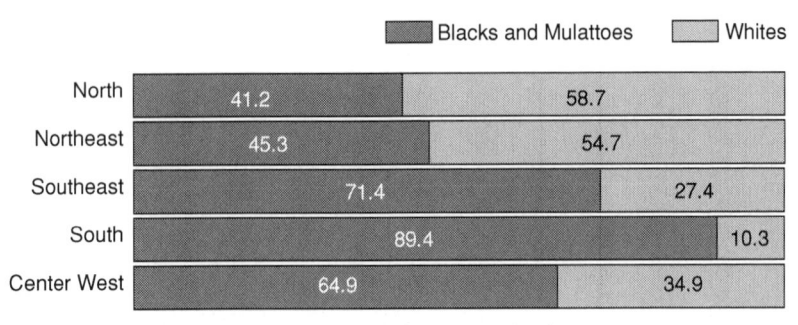

	Blacks and Mulattoes	Whites
North	41.2	58.7
Northeast	45.3	54.7
Southeast	71.4	27.4
South	89.4	10.3
Center West	64.9	34.9

GRAPH 2.26. Distribution of the Population by Color by Region, 1940. *Source*: IBGE, *Estatística do Século XX*, Table "pop_1953aeb-10"

"whites" in Brazil.[97] Thereafter, the end of major European immigration and the massive movement of populations across regions in the following decades, combined with lessening hostility toward self-definitions of nonwhite color, meant that the percentage of whites in the population would decline over time from census to census reaching just 48 percent in 2010.[98]

Although detailed data on health and life expectancy by race are unavailable on a national scale for this period, one indication of sharp class and race differences is the infant mortality, which varied sharply by region. Thus the north and northeast had rates above the national average of 162 infant deaths (under one year of age) per thousand live births, while the south and southeastern regions had rates below the national average. This same regional difference in infant mortality remained throughout the period even as the total national rate slowly dropped into the lower 150s deaths per thousand live births by 1940 (see Graph 2.27).

As in much of the rest of the world, this pattern of mortality would substantially change after 1945 with the progressive introduction of sulfur drugs and then of penicillin, the first of the major antibiotics. As late as 1939/1941, data available for 11 principal cities showed that deaths from infectious disease were double the importance of cancer deaths.[99] Although infectious diseases still remained the primary killers for most

---

[97] For the official breakdown of color by the census of 1872 to 2000, see IBGE "Série: POP106 – População presente e residente, por cor ou raça (dados do universo e dados da amostra)," available at http://seriesestatisticas.ibge.gov.br/series.aspx?vcodigo=POP60&sv=32&t=populacao-por-religiao-populacao-presente-e-residente.
[98] IBGE, Censo Demográfico 2010, Características Gerais da População, Table 2093, available at http://www.sidra.ibge.gov.br/cd/cd2010CGP.asp.
[99] IBGE, *Estatística do Século XX*, Table "pop_1941_45aeb_019."

The Vargas Period, 1930–1945 137

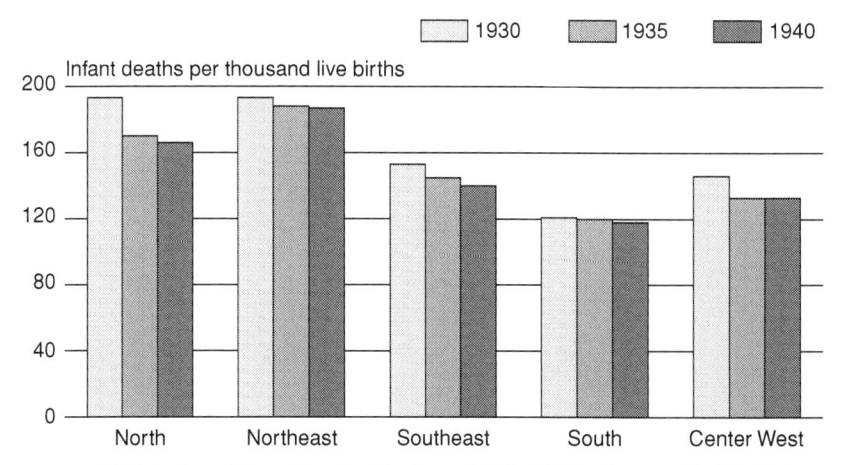

GRAPH 2.27. Infant Mortality by Region, 1930–1940. *Source*: IBGE Série – CD100 – Taxa de mortalidade infantil

of this period, their impact was slowly declining. This influence of the medical revolution brought about by general availability of antibiotics by the 1950s meant that average life expectancy increased impressively in this period. It was estimated that between 1939/1941 and 1949/1951 average life expectancy at birth rose an extraordinary 10 years for men and women, such that men born by the later period averaged 49.8 years and women 56.0 years.[100] This was really the first massive change in average life expectancy in the century since life expectancy before this had risen only slowly from the late nineteenth century until the 1940s. This increase in life expectancy was influenced by the continuing decline not only of adult mortality but even more importantly of infant mortality, which was as much influenced by increasing availability of sanitation and health care for mothers, as by the introduction of antibacterial medicines. By 1950 the infant mortality for the nation had dropped to 135 infant deaths, while the rate in the city of São Paulo had fallen to 86 deaths per thousand live births.[101] While this decline was impressive, it still meant that surviving the first year of life resulted in adding between four and five more years of life expectancy for those who reached their first birthday (see Graph 2.28).

While there exists few complete data giving regional breakdowns of life expectancy, data from the capital cities suggests that, like infant

[100] IBGE, *Estatística do Século XX*, Table "Saúde1952aeb-02."
[101] IBGE, *Estatística do Século XX*, Table "Saúde1959aeb-1."

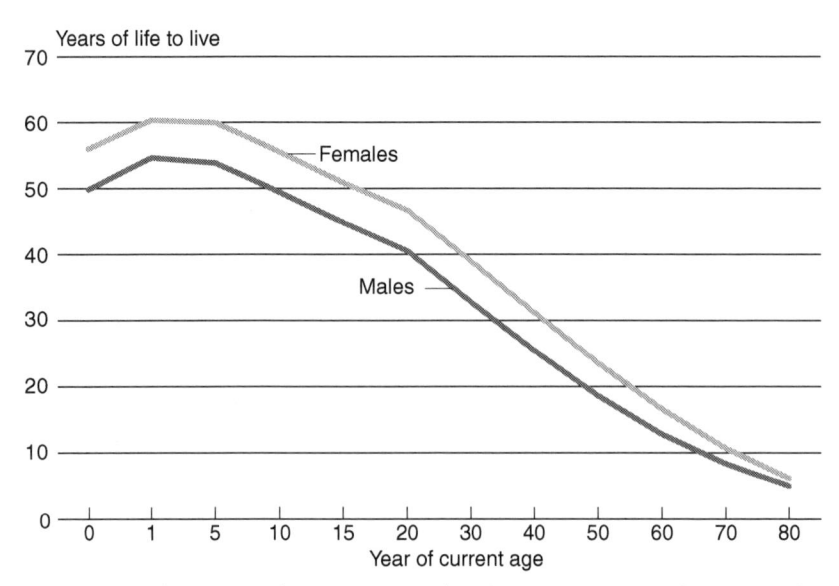

GRAPH 2.28. Average Life Expectancy by Sex, 1949/1951. Source: IBGE, Estatística do Século XX, Table "Saúde1952AEB-02"

mortality, there was a sharp regional difference, with the northern regions having considerably lower life expectancy than the southern regions. Thus the male residents of São Paulo in 1940 had a life expectancy of almost 47 years and close to 52 years for women. In contrast the life expectancy of the residents of the northeastern cities of Salvador de Bahia and Recife (Pernambuco) were 14 fewer years for men and 19 fewer years for women.[102]

In contrast to mortality and life expectancy, there was little change in fertility in the Vargas period. The crude birth rate remained in the mid-40s for this entire period. It has been estimated to be 46 births per thousand resident population in 1900 and again in 1930,[103] which placed it among the Latin American countries with the highest birth rates (see Graph 2.29). As late as the 1950s Brazil still had 43 births per thousand residents, with only the southeastern and southern states of São Paulo and Rio Grande do Sul falling below 40 births. These crude rates, in turn, were reflected in more refined total fertility rates, or the average number

[102] IBGE, Estatística do Século XX, Table "Saúde1959aeb-1."
[103] Alberto Palloni, "Fertility and Mortality Decline in Latin America," Annals of the American Academy of Political and Social Science 510 (July 1990), 136, Table 3.

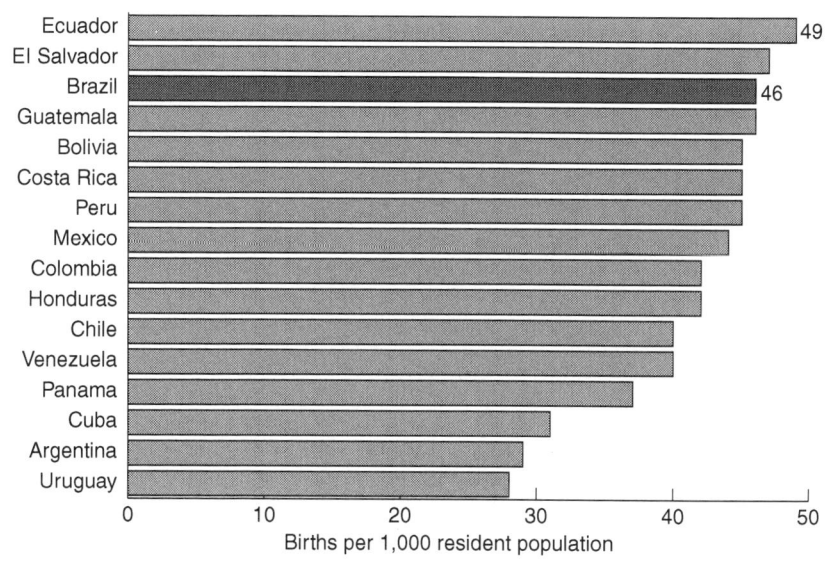

GRAPH 2.29. Crude Birth Rate for Selected Latin American Countries, 1930. Source: Palloni 1990, p. 136, Table 3

of children produced by women in all fertile years in a given time period. In 1940 Brazilian mothers produced more children at all ages compared to women in the advanced industrial nations, and not only continued with high birth rates to the end of their fertile years, but surprisingly, the peak age of reproduction was in the 25 to 29 age cohort, whereas in England and the United States this peak came in the previous 20 to 24 age group. The relative height of the curves seen in Graph 2.30 shows the great difference in total fertility rates, with the period rate for England below replacement of 1.8 children, the United States with 2.1 replacement level, and the Brazilian women aged 14 to 49 giving a total number of 6.5 children per mother. Surprisingly, in this area of fertility, there was very little difference by color, with all mothers having high fertility. The slightly lower fertility of *pretas* (blacks) and to a lesser extent of *pardas* (mulattos) can probably be explained by differing conditions of health and well-being (see Graph 2.31).

In assessing the Vargas regime, probably its most lasting impact included its new vision of the role of industry in the development of Brazil and its vision of the need to create heavy industry, which only the state could provide in this early period of industrialization. Steel and other

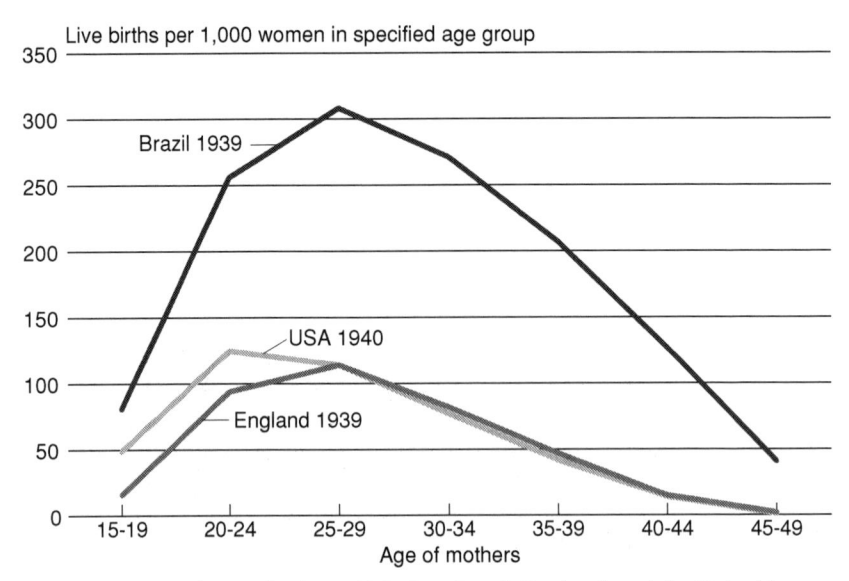

140   *The Economic and Social History of Brazil since 1889*

GRAPH 2.30. Birth Rate by Age of Mother, Brazil, England, and the United States, 1939–1940. *Source*: Mortara 1954, p. 130, Table 5

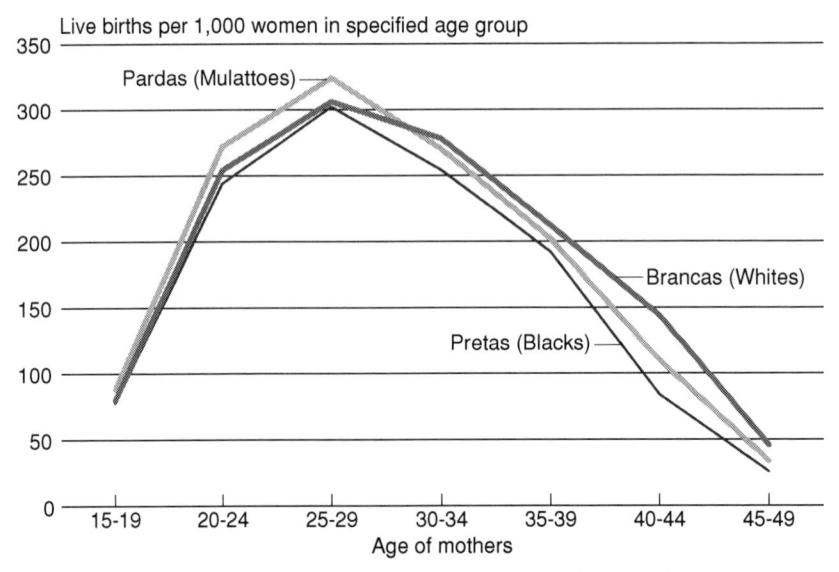

GRAPH 2.31. Birth Rate by Age and Color of the Mother, Brazil, 1940. *Source*: Mortara 1954, p. 130, Table 5

basic industries were fostered and developed by the state. Though the coffee elite was protected in its profitability, harsh government control now affected supply conditions in a systematic and long-term way. Though its economic plans did not add up to a coherent set of proindustrial policies, the impact of World War II on trade created the conditions to accelerate the process of import substitution, despite the difficulties in the importation of primary materials and capital goods. Thus the Vargas period, for its advances in import substitutions, combined with the growth of heavy industry was sufficient to finally propel Brazil into a modern industrial society of some significance.

In the social area there was also significant change under Vargas. Despite much discussion of education reform, the student population grew relatively slowly in this period. But there was the emergence of a very new and very important beginning of industrial education supported by the state and carried out by the associations of regional industrialists that would emerge by the 1950s as one of the world's largest such educational institutions. Even more significantly there was the beginning of a modern pension system and the emergence of technical administrators needed to run these institutions. Moreover, the number of persons receiving pensions, benefits, and health care through the new IAPs was increasing dramatically. Health care in general expanded under Vargas and the long-term trends of mortality decline continued from earlier periods, although infectious diseases still remained primary killers on the eve of the massive introduction of antibiotics in the 1950s. There were also some dramatic changes in population settlement in this period that coincided with the end of major international migrations and the systematic growth of massive internal migration within Brazil, which continues to the present day. This internal migration had the impact of slowly reducing the social and economic disparities between regions, which though still extreme by 1950, were declining. It also fueled the growth of major metropolitan centers throughout Brazil.

Thus it is no surprise that all governments that followed the Vargas era, whether military or democratic, would be profoundly influenced by all the changes effected by Vargas. These post-1950 governments no longer questioned their right to intervene in the economy, and their commitment to industrialization grew ever stronger over the following years. Nor were they any less concerned with the social question, as all new governments recognized the growing power of the working classes and the importance of the new middle classes in creating stability and support for any effective regime. Though not committed to redistribution of income, all the regimes following Vargas were committed to the expansion of the welfare state and its goal of universal access to health, education, and social security. In Brazil, the government was now seen as the major player in the economy and in society, and this belief had as its origin the ideas and practices that emerged in the two decades of the Vargas period.

3

Formative Democracies and the Military Interregnum, 1945–1985

The forty year period from the overthrow of Vargas's authoritarian state until the return to democratic rule was one in which many of the issues that brought Vargas to power would still be debated and discussed if not totally resolved: how to industrialize a late developing country, how to incorporate the new urban labor force, and how to resolve the growing tensions as Brazil changed from a rural to an urban dominated society. Both populist post-Vargas democrats and post-Vargas military officers faced these same issues. In each case their proposed solution for these problems would differ. But adopting a repressive system or an open democratic one, there was a surprising similarity of all regimes on what they expected the economy and society to look like after their proposed solutions. Whether it was a top-down military attempt to educate and modernize the society at the cost of workers' wages and rights, or whether it was a democratic regime that sought to provide a modern welfare state and a better distribution of income, all had to resolve the questions related to the transformation of Brazil from a predominately rural and highly stratified society to one that was primarily urban and industrialized.

One of the first issues facing the post–Estado Novo regimes was the innumerable economic and political consequences that World War II had for Brazil. War altered world commercial and financial flows. There was a strong demand for raw materials that aided Brazilian exports, but at the same time there was a lack of imports, principally fuel, manufactured products, and even raw materials and machines and equipment. As the maritime war intensified, there was a decline in international trade, which affected Brazilian exports despite high world demand. The scarcity of imported products, increased internal prices and stimulated local production of goods that substituted for the imports that were lacking. The traditional fall of export income in such a crisis of international trade was in this case replaced by an accumulation of reserves.

In the political area as well there were consequences from the war. Although ideologically the Brazilian government, or at least some of its principal leaders, had a great affinity for the Axis powers, circumstances forced Brazil to support the Allies. Its territory was used by American forces and the country sent troops to fight for the Allies in Italy. Brazil thus committed itself to the war effort, which was aimed at destroying the authoritarian forces of the Axis powers and restoring democracy. This was obviously in conflict with its internal political situation, where the Estado Novo was a dictatorship that eliminated democratic liberties, closed down Congress and parties, engaged in political persecutions, and censured the press.[1] In the course of the war there began to arise movements in favor of the liberalization of the regime, even involving some of the leaders who gave support to Vargas.[2] The process of questioning the legitimacy of the regime reached even the army, which overseas acted in favor of democracy and internally sustained an authoritarian regime with fascist characteristics. Feeling the pressure of this movement for change, Vargas called for elections for the presidency and for a constitutional assembly. These elections were called for December 1945. Moreover, Vargas declared that he would not be a candidate. To run for election three principal parties were now formed, and these parties would dominate national politics until 1964. From the liberal opposition forces was born the National Democratic Union (*União Democrática Nacional*, or

---

[1] "It seemed the most absurd of the indefinite continuation of a system of government inspired by the totalitarianism of the right, in a country that in the distant battlefield, contributed to its complete destruction. The reaction against the 'Estado Novo' became more lively. The opposition sought to coalesce, although secretly. The military, which had endorsed the non-violent coup of 1937, began to better judge their own responsibilities in the need to carry out a democratic restoration." José Maria Bello, *História da República* (São Paulo: Cia Editora Nacional, 1976), 332.

[2] In the famous manifesto of the Mineiros, published in 1943, leaders of the state, at the same time that they reinforced the position they had taken in the overthrow of the Old Republic, questioned Vargas's Estado Novo. "Commending the men of 1930, civilian and military, for their efforts in the destruction of the old electoral machines, based as it was on the employment of seduction and the use of public funds, we are confident that we will not see a repetition of those processes, even under the appearance of the testing of corporatism, they move away from historical spontaneity and become a simple lever on the governments of fascist character." Affonso Henriques, *Ascensão e Queda de Getúlio Vargas*, 2 vols. (Rio de Janeiro and São Paulo: Distribuidora Record, s/d), 2:157–159.

UDN). From the government side was organized the Social Democratic Party (*Partido Social Democrático*, or PSD). Finally, under the patronage of Vargas was created the Brazilian Labor Party (*Partido Trabalhista Brasileiro*, or PTB), which was based on the unions, an essential element in the mobilization of urban working-class masses.

The move toward a democratic system perhaps would have developed normally, but the opposition did not believe that Vargas would easily give up power. When there emerged a movement within the *trabalhista* party for a constitutional assembly with Vargas participating, the opposition liberal forces and the army understood this as a maneuver by Vargas to continue in power. The government rapidly lost political support. The army, which had carried Vargas to power, would be the principal agent for his removal.[3] But the election was carried out and the government candidate and former minister of war, General Gaspar Dutra, was elected. This electoral result showed the prestige of Vargas. Aside from electing his candidate president, Vargas was elected as a senator and deputy by several states.[4] The election could be considered the first truly effective democratic election in Brazil.[5]

The Constitutional Assembly that was elected now approved a new constitution that provided for a presidential and federal government. The legislative power would be exercised by a national Congress composed by a Senate and a Chamber of Deputies on the basis of proportional representation. Voting was obligatory, with men and women having the vote, but with illiterates excluded. Although going back to liberal principals of a divided executive, legislature, and judicial system with

---

[3] "Mr. Getúlio Vargas, seemed to rely not only on the old sympathies of the masses, including the Communist, but also on the armed forces. He insisted on continuing as head of the government. The appointment of his brother, accused of ill temper, to head the Police, replacing João Alberto, appeared suspicious, it seemed the ultimate provocation. It precipitated the final outcome. After several hours of dramatic confrontation, the troops of the garrison of Rio, with the motorized weapons of war, militarily occupied the city. Without any resistance, Getúlio Vargas renounced the government. For the first time, in the chronicle of revolutions and coups, so common in Latin America and the contemporary history of other nations, a head of government or a deposed head of state was not exiled, nor had his political rights revoked." Moreover, the deposed Vargas suffered no sanctions and retired to his farm in the south. Bello, *História da República*, 334. On this theme, see Thomas E. Skidmore, *Politics in Brazil, 1930–1964: An Experiment in Democracy* (New York: Oxford University Press, 1967), Chapter 2.

[4] The electoral law allowed a candidate to apply for more than one state at the same time and run for the Senate and the House of Representatives simultaneously.

[5] Jorge Ferreira, "1946–1964: A experiência democrática no Brasil," *Revista Tempo* 28 (Junho 2010), 11–18. Available at http://www.historia.uff.br/tempo/site/?cat=57.

strong property rights, the constitution maintained unaltered the bases that sustained the syndical structure and that permitted the manipulation of workers through union leaders who were beholden to the government – the so-called *pelegos*. Although federalism was reinstated, the central government was given significant powers and there was no return to the extensive decentralization of the Old Republic.[6]

The Dutra government tried to imprint a more liberal orientation on the government, including in the economic area, but was prevented from doing so by circumstances, especially by restrictions in the international area.[7] Perhaps the measure that had the greatest impact in the economic area was the decision to liberalize external economic relations. Believing in a rapid postwar reorganization of the world economy and in the favorable perspective in the coffee market, whose prices had been frozen in agreement with the United States during the war,[8] and given its abundant reserves, the government had eliminated exchange controls. There was a considerable improvement in the coffee market, with a major rise in prices, which led to a 50 percent increase in the value of coffee exports.[9]

However as soon as exchange controls were eliminated there was an explosion of imports, which had been repressed during the war. In the

---

[6] On the Constitution of 1945, see Aliomar Baleeiro and Barbosa Lima Sobrinho, *Constituições Brasileiras: 1946* (Brasília: Senado Federal e Ministério de Ciência e Tecnologia, 2001); and Marco Antonio Villa, *A História das Constituições Brasileiras* (São Paulo: Editora Leya, 2011).

[7] According to Carlos Lessa, between 1948 and 1950, economic policy was largely conditioned by the behavior of the external sector. "At this stage, although there were fundamental consequences for the subsequent process of industrialization, we do not see a definite and conscious concern with industrial development. The decisions were taken basically to resolve problems in the external sector and basically concerned were with the containment of internal and external imbalances. Industrialization in this step came as a result and not a main goal pursued intentionally, which is why we classify it as unintentional." Carlos Lessa, *Quinze anos de política econômica* (São Paulo: Brasiliense/UNICAMP, 1975), 6. Also see Fausto Saretta, "O Governo Dutra na Transição Capitalista no Brasil," in *História Econômica do Brasil Contemporâneo*, ed. Tamáz Szrecsányi and Wilson Suzigan (São Paulo: Edusp/Hucitec/Imprensa Oficial SP, 1996), 99–120.

[8] With the intensification of the war there was a sharp fall in coffee prices. Probably for political reasons, the United States signed the Inter-American Coffee Agreement, which established export quotas. Prices reacted strongly, but were frozen by the Price Administration of the United States in 1941. Price controls remained in force until the end of the war. Edmar Bacha and Robert Greenhill, *150 anos de café*, 2nd ed., rev. ed. (Rio de Janeiro: Marcelino Martins & Johnston Exportadores, 1992), 32–38.

[9] The United States, the main consumption market for Brazilian coffee, had a trajectory of strong growth in the early postwar years, while the European economies recovered slowly from the effects of war.

immediate postwar period there occurred two important alterations in Brazil's trade flows. There was a reduction in exports of primary materials and manufactures in general, particularly as concerns cotton. Imports expanded for items that were of the greatest scarcity during the war, such as machines and equipment. The worst part was that the accumulated reserves, which could have been used to balance the external accounts, were not composed of convertible reserves. These funds were formed mostly by rights in English pounds, which served for payments for exports to Great Britain during the war and whose utility was very limited. They could only be used in trade with Great Britain, which continued buying Brazilian products, while Brazil imported most of its goods from the United States, the only country with abundant supplies at the end of the war. Thus Brazil accumulated nonconvertible foreign-exchange reserves during the war and would continue to generate positive trade balances in such nonconvertible funds, but needed convertible currency for its purchases from the United States. Soon there was an exchange bottleneck and the exchange controls were renewed in July 1947, after which Brazil again began to accumulate convertible currency.[10]

The new fixed exchange rates would now be maintained despite the strong inflation that occurred in this period. The control of inflation and the fear of the reduction in the international price of coffee were the principal causes for the rigidity of the exchange rate, which overvalued the national currency in the second half of the 1940s.[11] Despite this overvalue of the local currency, there was a balance in the external accounts at the end of the Dutra period in large part due to the control over the external sector accounts as well as improved conditions in the international coffee market.[12] The recuperation of previous war-scarce supplies with the return of traditional suppliers to the market, and the increase in the value of Brazilian money, prejudiced the exportation of many products that

---

[10] "The economic policy of this period showed some discrepancy between the government's original ideas and the actual state of the economy. The most concrete expression of this lag was the dramatic changes that were made in economic policy from the early years of the government, when compared with its initial propositions." Saretta, "O Governo Dutra na Transição Capitalista no Brasil," 103.

[11] As has already been explained, as Brazil still maintained a leadership position in the international coffee market, local currency devaluations represented major income for the coffee producers and hence their willingness to reduce their offering price of the product for export. This exchange-rate policy was based on the understanding of the price inelasticity of demand for coffee.

[12] The prices remained fixed during the final years of the war, then slowly rose in the first years of the postwar period, but grew dramatically the period from 1949 to 1950. In cents per pound of coffee, the price rose from 22 to 26 cents a pound in 1946 and 1948 to 32 cents in 1949 and 50 cents in 1950.

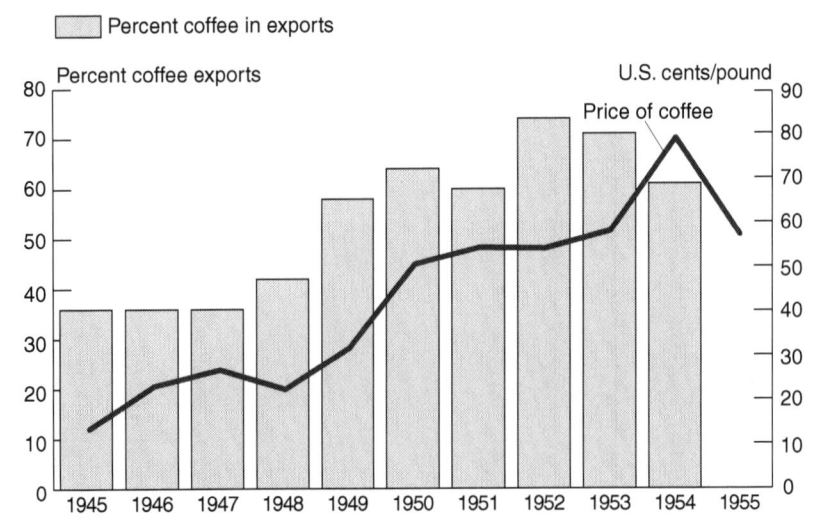

GRAPH 3.1. Price of Coffee and Its Role in Exports, 1945–1955. *Source:* Bacha 1992 t. 1.6 and Ipeadata

had been exported from the country during the war years. Coffee made the difference in favor of Brazil. At the beginning of the 1950s coffee returned to its old importance and accounted for two-thirds of the value of Brazilian exports (see Graph 3.1 and Appendix Table A.1).

The exchange control and the institution of licenses for imports represented a great stimulus for the industrial sector. Use of licenses for the right to import goods created difficulties for importers, and even when licenses were obtained importers were obliged to buy high-cost exchange. Moreover, there was a two-tier exchange rate. Those importing machines, equipment, fuel, and primary materials had a privileged channel to obtain licenses and could buy foreign currencies at a cheaper rate. To this was added an overvalued national currency that was an additional protection for local producers.

It should be recalled that the Dutra years also were the period of great international transformations, due to the political and economic reorganization of the world caused by the war. While Europe was destroyed by the war, the United States surged ahead to international leadership, with a modern, highly productive economy with unequalled competitive power. It was thanks to U.S. aid through the Marshall Plan that Europe could recover from the impact of the war. Moreover, the war had also destroyed the international monetary order, which needed new rules, and was discussed in the Bretton Woods conferences in 1944. It was also during the

Dutra period that the Cold War was initiated with the global division into two international political blocks due to a direct conflict between capitalism and communism. This resulted in the immediate alignment of Brazil with the block led by the United States.[13] In 1948 the report of the Abbink Mission suggested that a program of Brazilian development should be oriented toward generating capital internally, obtaining foreign capital, and improving productivity. But the economic conditions of the country did not permit the establishment of liberalization in the external area, with its free flow of capital, which would have been the necessary condition to attract foreign capital.[14]

Although the Dutra government was not a promoter of policies directly aimed at intensification of industrialization, the economic policies it did adopt served to continue the process of import substitution.[15] Exchange control with preferences for the imports of capital goods and the other consumption items necessary for local industry existed alongside limited and high-cost exchange for manufactured goods.[16] The Dutra government at the same time tried to promote an austere fiscal policy, which had few practical results, but also developed a policy of credit expansion that particularly benefited local industry, which grew during this period.[17] By the end of the Dutra period, inflationary pressures returned,

---

[13] Brazilian diplomacy believed that Brazil would have a more pronounced role in the discussions of the new international order and on the European question, and would obtain a permanent seat on the UN Security Council. But it has been frustrated over the political evolution of these issues. The automatic alignment to U.S. policy did not result in the expected diplomatic gains. On this issue, see Gerson Moura, *O alinhamento sem recompensa: a política externa do governo Dutra* (Rio de Janeiro: Fundação Getúlio Vargas. Centro de Documentação de História Contemporânea, 1990), available at http://bibliotecadigital.fgv.br/dspace/bitstream/handle/10438/6613/792.pdf?sequence=1.

[14] Sérgio Besserman Vianna, "Política econômica externa e industrialização: 1946–1951," in *A ordem do Progresso*, ed. Marcelo de Paiva Abreu (Rio de Janeiro: Editora Campus, 1992b), 105–122. Also see Maria Celina D'Araujo, *O segundo governo Vargas 1951–1954: democracia, partidos e crise política*, 2nd ed. (São Paulo: Ática, 1992), 156–167. Available at http://www.cpdoc.fgv.br.

[15] According to Werner Baer the impulse of industrialization occurred after World War II and was a result of measures taken to address the balance-of-payments difficulties. "Such measures only gradually became conscious instruments for the creation of an industrial complex, especially in the 1950s. The exchange control was one of the basic tools for the industrialization of the country." Werner Baer, *A economia brasileira* (São Paulo: Nobel, 2002), 72.

[16] Vianna, "Política econômica externa e industrialização," 105–122. Given the ample instruments available to the Bank of Brazil, there were always conflicts with the Minister of Finance when he wanted to carry out policies of contraction.

[17] "To the Orthodox thinkers would suppose perhaps that you yourself should have avoided the printing of paper money, but I assure you that these emissions have financed

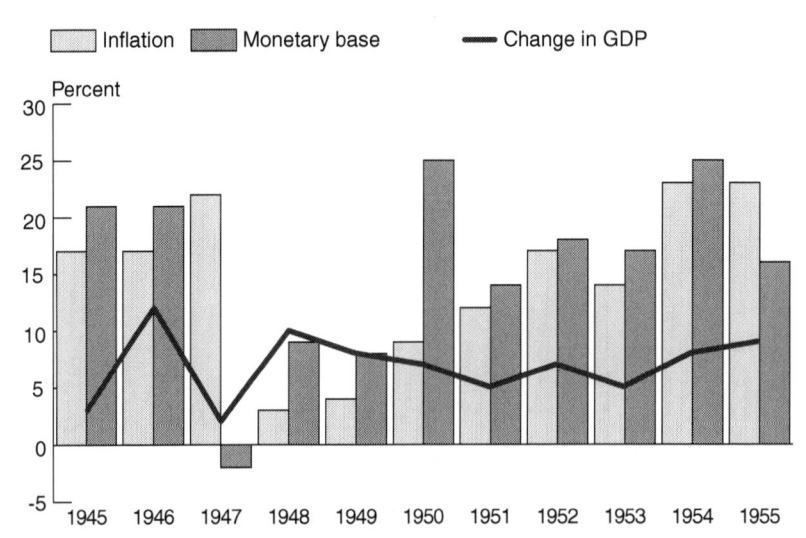

150   The Economic and Social History of Brazil since 1889

GRAPH 3.2. Annual Change in GDP, Monetary Base, and Inflation, 1945–1955.
Source: Abreu 1992a, Anexos, and Ipeadata

and there was fiscal imbalance and a strong foreign exchange constraint (Graph 3.2 and Appendix Table A.3).

In the political area the government maintained an extremely conservative position, though always within democratic politics. It was in constant friction with the working class, who had supported the government through the Vargas-created PTB. The fall in real wages in this period contributed to the further deterioration of this relationship between government and workers. The Communist Party, which had participated in the Constitutional Assembly, was declared illegal by the Dutra government. In international relations, the Dutra administration in contrast to his predecessor maintained an automatic alignment with the United States on all issues.

By the last years of the regime, the administration found itself politically worn out, while the prestige of Getúlio Vargas was growing.[18]

---

many investments essential to the economic development of the country.... Your Excellency could not allow the momentum of growth in the country to fall because of financial beliefs which in the rest of the world are being rejected." *Relatório do Ministério da Fazenda de 1949* (Rio de Janeiro: 1949), 21.

[18] As previously noted, Vargas was elected senator, but participated little in parliamentary life, devoting himself to developing political contacts for his return to power. On his farm in the south he received a pilgrimage of politicians, showing his position of national leadership.

Vargas launched himself as a candidate for the presidency and offered an electoral platform that proposed an intensification of industrialization and the extension of worker rights. Vargas won the election with massive support from the voters of São Paulo, despite the opposition of the Dutra regime.[19]

Although he was democratically elected, Vargas needed the support of the military, as was now typical of most Latin American governments in the Cold War period. The army exercised the role of arbiter in civilian conflicts, or assumed on its own the role of guardian of national values and of national development. In this period the army was divided between a strong nationalist current, which advocated an active role of the government in the industrialization of the country with restrictions on foreign capital, and a second group less nationalist, which sought an automatic alignment with the United States.[20] These conflicts had a marked impact on the conduct of the new Vargas government, and the intensification of the Cold War and the Korean War exacerbated these conflicts.

There is some debate about the scope of the economic policy of the second Vargas mandate. There was no doubt as to the administration's position, which was clearly in favor of industrialization, but the contingencies of managing the economy in the short term did not always allow the government to maintain a more coherent and comprehensive long-term policy.[21] But Vargas seemed to have a plan to promote several

---

[19] In São Paulo there was a new political leadership under Governor Ademar de Barros, who had great influence in the state, and controlled the PSP (Social Progressive Party). He gave powerful support for the candidacy of Vargas. The PSD, originally formed by Vargas, with strong penetration in the rural areas, although it launched its own candidate who was supported by Dutra, divided and a part of the leadership went to Vargas. The liberals, represented by the UDN, contested the result of Vargas's victory, alleging that he needed an absolute majority. They would do the same at the next election and called for a military intervention in support of their claims, but they never obtained any significant victory at the polls.

[20] The discussion and positioning in relation to communism exercised a key role in the conflicts with the military, as evidenced during the Dutra period, with the positioning on the Cold War, and reinforced by Korean War, that extended from 1950 to 1953.

[21] On this theme, see Carlos Lessa and José Luiz Fiori, "E houve uma política national-populista?," *Encontro Nacional da ANPEC* (São Paulo: ANPEC, 1984); Pedro Cezar Dutra, *Vargas: o Capitalismo em Construção* (São Paulo: Brasiliense, 1986); Sérgio Besserman Vianna, "Duas Tentativas de Estabilização: 1951–1954," in *A ordem do Progresso*, ed. Marcelo de Paiva Abreu (Rio de Janeiro: Editora Campus, 1992a), 123–150; Lessa, *Quinze anos de política econômica*, 10–14; Sonia Miriam Draibe, *Rumos e Metamorfoses. Estado e Industrialização no Brasil: 1930–1960* (Rio de Janeiro: Paz e Terra, 1985), 180–240.

changes in the economy and society of Brazil. He proposed that there be public and private investments in infrastructure and basic industries, reserving a sphere of activities for state enterprises. He wanted to see the capitalization of agriculture to modernize rural production through state investments in technical improvements, mechanization, credit, storage, and marketing. He also proposed bettering the condition of the life of the urban masses, through improving transports and food supplies. In the fiscal area he wanted to base the financial system on a central state and regional banks and to extend and rationalize government taxes in order to direct the flow of public and private investments. He accepted the entrance of foreign capital into priority areas of investment. However comprehensive these guidelines, they were not accompanied by an integrated plan with clearly defined aims and funding.[22]

But there was a new era in government-to-government loans that flourished in this period. Based on new ideas of the American government about foreign aid, and based on negotiations begun with the Dutra administration, a Mixed Brazil–United States Commission was established with the object of creating conditions for the increase in the flow of public and private national and foreign investments needed to accelerate Brazilian economic development.[23] The commission approved 41 projects, basically in the areas of energy and transport and were financed by funds from the federal and state governments and foreign sources that came to the equivalent of U.S.$387 millions, which would be obtained as loans from the U.S. government's Eximbank and the International Bank of Reconstruction and Development. As part of this development plan a new Economic Betterment Fund (*Fundo de Reaparelhamento Econômico*) and National Economic Development Bank (the *Banco Nacional de Desenvolvimento Econômico*, or BNDES) were created.[24] The diagnosis and

---

[22] Draibe, *Rumos e Metamorfose*, 183. Also see Pedro Paulo Zahluth Bastos and Pedro Cezar Dutra, "Desenvolvimento incoerente? Comentários sobre o projeto do segundo governo Vargas e as ideias econômicas de Horário Lafer (1948–1952)," *Economia* (Selecta, Brasíla) 6,3 (Dezembro 2005), 191–222. Available at http://www.anpec.org.br/revista/vol6/vol6n3p191_222.pdf.

[23] The U.S. participation in the Joint Brazil–United States was based in the Law on International Development, known as the Point Four Program. The Joint Commission had been used in previous studies produced by American missions: that of Cooke (1942) and of Abbink (1948), who had indicated the structural imbalances and the most important for investments.

[24] CPDOC/FGV, *Brasileiros e Americanos Estudam Problemas do Brasil. As soluções indicadas pela Comissão Mista Brasil-EEUU. Um capítulo da história econômica*

guidelines of the commission would later be utilized to develop the Target Plan (or *Plano de Metas*) of the Juscelino government.

Despite the preoccupations with long-term plans, the administration was forced to deal with short-term issues demanding immediate action. As we have seen throughout this work, the permanent foreign constraint made the exchange controls the main instrument of economic policy. The reserves accumulated during the war period had been spent at the beginnings of the Dutra government, in the short period of liberalization of exchange-rate policy, and already by 1946 there was a crisis in the balance of payments and exchange controls were resumed. The alternative of a devaluation of the local currency was ruled out since it would have prejudiced the commercial policy of coffee, reducing its prices on the international market and worsening the external question. The control of imports was reflected in inflationary pressures. Thus a fixed exchange rate was maintained and importations required a prior license granted in accordance with the priorities set, discriminating against nonessential imports.[25] The maintenance of a fixed exchange rate and the inflationary pressures affected exports in general. In 1952 coffee came to represent 74 percent of Brazilian exports. This percentage can be explained by the favorable performance of coffee, but also by the dramatic fall in exports of other products.[26]

In 1952 there was deterioration in the international accounts of the nation.[27] Although the government had increased control over import

---

do nosso país, 279–336. Available at http://www.centrocelsofurtado.org.br/arquivos/image/201109231638540.MD2_0_277_1.pdf.

[25] Antonio Claudio Sochaczewski, *O desenvolvimento econômico e financeiro do Brasil, 1952–1968* (São Paulo: Trajetória Cultural, 1993), Chapter 3.

[26] Exports of other products that reached U.S.$710 million, dropped to U.S.$373 million because many products were burdened by the exchange rate then in effect. Among others there was a significant decrease in the value of cotton exports, which accounted for the second item in the exports. The situation of this sector had become dramatic, forcing the government to buy the entire cotton crop through the Bank of Brazil in 1952. In the case of this product, there was also an external crisis in the sector, which hampered exports. Cotton exports fell from 143,000 tonnes to 26,000 tonnes between 1951 and 1952.

[27] According to Sérgio Besserman Vianna, by late 1951, despite the small trade surplus, foreign reserves in convertible currencies were negative U.S.$30 million. He affirms that the continued surge in imports and decrease in exports in 1952 "would not have caused the depletion of our foreign reserves and the accumulation of substantial trade arrears if other sources of input and output currencies had not acted in the same direction." Sérgio Besserman Vianna, "A Política Econômica no Segundo Governo Vargas (1951–1954)" (MA thesis, Rio de Janeiro: PUC/RJ, 1987), 61.

licenses, the Korean War prompted an anticipation of imports to avoid the types of shortages that had occurred in World War II.[28] The crisis became acute at the end of 1952, with the current account transactions highly negative, causing a big accumulation of delayed commercial transactions. The consequence was the change in exchange-rate policies at the beginning of 1953, and the fixed exchange rate eliminated, which was a policy that would now last for several years. The government created a free market in exchange rates for financial transactions, kept control of imports, and allowed part of the exchange generated by exports to be sold on the open market.

In October of that year came an alteration to this policy. The government would be the buyer of foreign exchange from exporters, paying the official rate plus a bonus, differentiated by product. This change represented an important stimulus for exports in general, which had lost their competitiveness due to the overvaluation of the local currency.[29] Imports were divided into categories and participated in specific auctions, with a limited supply of foreign exchange offered for each category and setting a minimum premium over the official rate in each auction. Thus the bureaucratic process of granting prior licenses for imports would be replaced by market rules. The difference between the value of purchases and sales of foreign exchange was appropriated by the government, and would henceforward be a significant portion of tax revenue. This change had enormous importance for industrialization, because it consolidated a reserve of the market for the production of import-substituted goods by raising the cost of imports. As industrialists had access to privileged categories of exchange, there was an implicit subsidy on imports of capital goods and inputs necessary for the industrialization process.[30] This system, with some modifications, lasted until 1957. The conditions regulating the flow of foreign capital were established in legislation in 1953,

---

[28] According to Vianna, in 1952 there was a tightening in the supply of licenses to import, but the gap between the grant date and the actual date of importing allowed imports to remain high throughout the year. The maintenance of high imports and contraction in exports, coupled with low flow of foreign capital caused a serious foreign exchange crisis that year. Vianna, "Duas Tentativas de Estabilização: 1951–1954," 127.

[29] Although the Resolution No. 70 of SUMOC benefited exporters in general, who received a bonus in addition to the official rate, which was still frozen, there was strong opposition from coffee growers, who received a smaller rebate. The measure became known as the "exchange confiscation." It represented a means of appropriating part of the revenue earned from exports of coffee and directing it to other productive sectors or to meet government commitments.

[30] Lessa, *Quinze anos de política econômica*, 11.

with some modifications made in 1954. Preference was given to foreign investments in areas considered priorities of the government. But the influx of foreign capital would only increase with the government of Juscelino Kubitschek.

The critical conditions continued in 1953 with high inflation and balance-of-payment difficulties that reduced the growth in output. Nevertheless, there were significant investments in industry. But at the same time there was a radical change in American politics and policies that directly affected the industrialization plans of the Vargas government. With the inauguration of President Eisenhower, the United States reduced international aid and instead encouraged private investment.[31] Moreover, most of U.S. development aid, which had concentrated on Europe in the immediate postwar era, shifted to the Middle East and Asia in the period from 1953 to 1961. Latin America now remained outside American preferential attention. The U.S. republican administrations in the 1950s decided that the only way to relieve the external restrictions facing the Latin American governments was to unify and liberalize their exchange-rate systems with the aim of creating a favorable environment for the flow of private capital.[32] Within this new foreign policy, they abandoned such programs as Point IV and paralyzed the financing of projects proposed by the Mixed Brazil-U.S. Commission. Even a loan negotiated with the U.S. Eximbank to pay for delayed commercial transactions was discontinued.

While the international situation became increasingly acute for Vargas, the regime also faced difficulties internally due to strong popular protest. From the beginning of its tenure, the new Vargas administration had tried to maintain its leadership in the labor movement, with new measures of support for the unions, including allowing access to leadership positions of more left-wing leaders. But the economic situation, particularly the rise in the cost of living, mobilized social forces leading to great public demonstrations. This unrest led to a general strike in São Paulo in 1953, which began as an industrial strike in the textile industry and then spread to other professional groups, involving 300,000 workers in a 24-day strike. Vargas lost control over the union movement, and the strike involved a major participation of the Communist Party. The next year there was a strike of maritime workers in which 100,000 workers participated and

---

[31] Vianna, "A Política Econômica no Segundo Governo Vargas," 83–100.
[32] Demosthenes Madureira de Pinho Neto, "A Estratégia brasileira em perspectiva internacional," in *O BNDES e o Plano de Metas* (Rio de Janeiro: BNDES, Junho 1996). Available at http://www.bndes.gov.br/SiteBNDES/export/sites/default/bndes_pt/ Galerias/Arquivos/conhecimento/livro/plametas.pdf.

that also had a strong political impact. It was in response to this growing labor unrest that Vargas, in a major ministerial reform, appointed João Goulart as Minister of Labor.[33]

After resolving the maritime strike by granting most of the concessions demanded by the unions, Goulart became an important intermediary between the government and the unions. He, in turn, became the lightening rod for the fierce right-wing opposition to the Vargas government that saw Goulart as a serious threat. At the same time there was unrest in the army, with demands for better salaries and equipment. But, in turn, they were opposed to increases in salaries of other government workers and were against Goulart's proposal to double the minimum wage. In 1954 in a ministerial reform, Goulart (known as Jango) was dismissed. At the same time the Vargas administration assumed a more nationalist position in an attempt to reduce conservative opposition to his regime. While this nationalist posture was supported by segments in the military, it angered the anticommunist groups that defended the automatic alignment with the U.S. interests. As part of this new posture, for example, he created Eletrobrás, a state enterprise in the area of energy, though it only went into operation several years later. On May 1 he announced an increase of 100 percent in the minimum wage, which not only represented an attack on the opposition, but also made his policy of stabilization more difficult.

This profound political crisis was probably one of the factors that led to his suicide. Carlos Lacerda, a deputy of the UDN party, represented the most aggressive opposition to his government. Assuming that his elimination would reduce the opposition to Vargas, a palace group, which included the head of the presidential guard, made an attempt on the life of Lacerda that failed and killed instead an army captain who was with him. When the origin of this conspiracy was revealed, Vargas lost political support, including from the military, which sent him an ultimatum demanding his resignation. Vargas's option was to commit suicide.[34] The suicide and the testament letter that he left had a great political impact and mobilized the masses against his elite opponents. Vargas would be remembered as the political leader who defended the poor and was the

---

[33] Maria Celina D'Araujo believes that the cabinet reform, which brought Goulart to the Ministry of Labour, should not be understood as marking two different stages of the government, but rather a new attempt to adjust the conservative leaders to new developments. According to the author, "[T]he government tried to circumvent not only economic hardship but also the opposition of the military, the political arena and the media." D'Araujo, *O segundo governo Vargas 1951–1954*, 127–128.

[34] See Skidmore, *Politics in Brazil, 1930–1964*, 167–180.

founder of the welfare state and prolabor legislation that persists to this day.[35]

But his legacy was also profound in terms of basic economic policies. He and subsequent presidents showed a permanent preoccupation with advancing the process of industrialization. This meant resolving bottlenecks in fundamental sectors such as transport and energy, along with creating a more efficient administrative and financial structure that could promote and administer a development program.[36] The BNDE, Petrobrás, Eletrobrás, the Economic Betterment Fund, the National Road Plan, the Federal Electricity Foundation, the Council of Industrial Development,[37] the modernization of financial instruments of the Bank of Brazil with the creation of the Superintendency of Money and Credit (SUMOC), and special sections in the bank for foreign trade and another for agricultural credit and industrialization[38] are examples of institutions created or modernized by the Vargas government with the specific object of promoting Brazilian development through industrialization. However incomplete and underfunded the effort of Vargas was in this area, there is no question that he left an important structure for the development plan that would be carried out in the Juscelino government.

Finally, the second Vargas government made a very significant investment in science and higher education. This program led to the creation of two fundamental institutions that survive to this day and have made a great impact on tertiary education and the development of modern research in science in Brazil. In 1951 he created the National Research Council (*Conselho Nacional de Pesquisa*, or CNPq) and the National

---

[35] The Testament Letter pointed to the alliance between the internal enemies and international groups and indicated to what an impasse the country had reached. It criticized such groups for standing against the rights of workers and their defense of national interests, embodied in Petrobrás and Eletrobrás and in the limitations imposed on foreign capital.

[36] In a message to Congress in 1951, he mentioned the inadequacy of the administrative structure: "The structure of the Federal Administration has not experienced any significant change since 1945.... Moreover, the reorganization ... that was carried out in the period 1936 to 1945, had to be experimental, by virtue of historic and social circumstances and the very essence of the art of organization.... Federal Administration duplication, parallels and conflicts of jurisdiction, are notorious in their frequencies, all requiring a general plan for their restructuring, which the government is already considering...." Draibe, *Rumos e Metamorfoses*, 214.

[37] The Fundo de Reaparelhamento Econômico, the Plano Nacional Rodoviário, the Fundo Federal de Eletrificação, and the Conselho de Desenvolvimento Industrial.

[38] The Carteira de Exportação e Importação and the Carteira de Crédito Agrícola e Industrial.

Campaign for Improving Personnel in Higher Education (*Campanha Nacional de Aperfeiçoamento de Pessoal de Nível Superior*, or CAPES), both of which have been crucial transformative institutions, in developing trained cadres of academics and scientists and in modernizing Brazil's tertiary education in the following decades.

The suicide of Vargas did not reduce political tension. Although the constitutional process was followed and the vice president assumed the presidency, in the eighteen months left of the Vargas term there followed two more presidents before the Minister of War was able to guarantee free elections. This resulted in the victory of Juscelino Kubitschek, who was elected by an alliance of the PSD-PTB, which constituted the political base of Vargas.[39] Juscelino had been governor of Minas Gerais and mounted a conservative government, the majority of his ministers coming from the PSD.[40] Nevertheless, he was able to obtain enough political support that his government represented a period of relative political tranquility.[41] There is little question that in the economic area the Juscelino government was basically a continuation of the fundamental ideas espoused in the last Vargas regime. The most important feature of the Juscelino administration would be his Target Plan, which laid the groundwork for a serious implantation of government-sponsored industrial development.

When the new Juscelino government took office in the mid-1950s it encountered a country facing serious structural difficulties and economic instability. The long process of import substitution, which permitted a

---

[39] The same opposition, concentrated in the UDN, again challenged the legitimacy of the election of Juscelino, claiming it had not obtained the absolute majority, which was not constitutionally required. Marshal Lott, who permitted Juscelino to take office, as Minister of War, was the guardian who was charged with maintaining the democratic regime in spite of several military uprisings.

[40] Upon assuming office, Juscelino sought to take a series of measures to reduce political tension, e.g., he raised the siege, suspended the censorship of the press and television, and approved an amnesty law to participants in several rebellions, excepting only the Communists. On Juscelino Kubitschek, also see Ronaldo Costa Couto, *Juscelino Kubitschek* (Brasília: Edições Senado: Camara Federal, 2011); Claudio Bojunga, *JK: o artista do impossível* (Rio de Janeiro: Objetiva, 2001); Juscelino Kubitschek de Oliveira, *Juscelino Kubitschek I (depoimento de 1974)* (DPDOC, 1979), 15 pages; and Juscelino Kubitschek de Oliveira, *Juscelino Kubitschek I (depoimento de 1976)* (DPDOC, 1979), 77 pages.

[41] The army was divided. The majority, joined by their anticommunist sentiments, tried to eliminate all remnants of the Vargas government that they held was populist and had intended to install a Syndicalist Republic in the country. But there was one important officer group that advocated the nationalist ideas of Vargas, which could be symbolized in Petrobrás. João Goulart, who represented the union strength and had been Vargas's Minister of Labor, was elected vice president of the republic, the target of distrust of the military.

significant extension of the Brazilian industrial park, had created rigidity in the structure of imports.[42] Nevertheless, the process of industrialization had advanced, above all in the production of consumer goods and to a lesser extent in heavy industry. But the country still faced serious economic blockages, especially in the areas of energy and transport. At the same time there were strong inflationary pressures, public deficits, and serious problems with the balance of payments.

In order to deal with these problems, the new government decided not to adopt the traditional policy of economic stability, and instead opted for an ambitious plan of investments. This Target Plan adopted by the Juscelino government constituted the most coherent and well-developed policy in support of industrialization in the history of Brazil. It gave absolute priority to construction of the upper levels of the industrial pyramid vertically integrated with the basic social capital to support this structure, continuing the process of import substitution developed over the previous twenty years.[43] Moreover, even if the government had wanted to carry out a stabilization policy, it would have encountered strong political opposition as demonstrated in previous attempts to implement adjustment programs. Sectional interests, business demands, political and social pressures, all made it difficult to apply restrictive policies that limited credit expansion, contained fiscal spending, reduced subsidies, or controlled salaries.[44] Opting for growth it co-opted ample social groups, including industrialists and workers. Even the opening up of the economy to foreign capital, one of the foundations of the Target Plan, although attacked by some groups as a government sellout, was accepted by the main political forces supporting the government, including the military.

The political stability of the Juscelino period essentially depended on the forces represented by the two political parties, the PSD and the PTB, and the army.[45] For this reason, the regime had not only to maintain

---

[42] Maria da Conceição Tavares, "Auge e Declínio do processo de substituição de importações no Brasil," in *Da substituição de importações ao capitalismo financeiro*, ed. Maria da Conceição Tavares (Rio de Janeiro: Zahar, 1972), 27–115.

[43] Lessa, *Quinze anos de política econômica*, 14.

[44] On this theme, see Carlos Manuel Peláez and Wilson Suzigan, *História Monetária do Brasil* (Brasília: Universidade de Brasília, 1981), 267–268; and Luiz Orenstein and Antonio Claudio Sochaczewski, "Democracia com Desenvolvimento: 1956–1961," in Abreu, *A ordem do Progresso*, 171–212.

[45] According to Benevides, from the beginning of the republic until 1964, relations between the civilian government and the military have been governed by the convention of what was called the "moderator power." Juscelino, despite the legitimacy he earned through the elections and the popular support he had from the majority in Congress, had realized

a strong military base, but also to co-opt the military as a corporation, meeting their specific demands, such as increased salaries and the modernization of their armaments. The military were also encouraged to support an aggressive economic policy that the administration claimed would be nationalist and progressive.[46] If the opening to foreign capital displeased the most nationalist officer groups, the preservation of the petroleum monopoly of the government was fundamental to preserve their support.

This period of building basic infrastructure with state funds would be crucial for the Brazilian economy. The industrial growth that occurred since the end of World War II had not been accompanied by a corresponding growth in infrastructure, thus creating inefficiencies and growing costs. In the energy sector, BNDES, the government's development bank had implemented an expansion plan, but its slow pace compromised continued growth. Equally, the stimulus provided by the exchange system allowed the consumer goods industries to expand, without a corresponding growth in the production of machines and equipment. Recognizing these problems, the Target Plan formulated by the government consisted of 31 objectives, divided into the areas of energy, transport, food, basic industry, education, and the construction of Brasilia, which was considered the culmination of the entire Target Plan (see Graph 3.3). Aside from the investments made in the construction of Brasília, electric energy, transport, and heavy industry received almost all of the investments.

In the area of energy, the plan aimed to increase significantly the production of electricity and refined petroleum.[47] All the investments primarily went to public corporations. In the area of transports, also dominated by the state, a program of modernization of rolling stock and permanent way of railroads was established, which allowed the rail system to increase loads by 21 percent, although there was no significant increase in the rail network. The plan also involved the ports, merchant marine, airports, and air transport. Meanwhile the construction and paving of highways

---

the need to maintain not only a support scheme for the military, but also to co-opt them to power. He was well aware of the successive military interventions in times of crisis of the political system, historically requested by members of the opposition as well as by the government. Maria Victoria de Mesquita Benevides, *O governo Kubitschek. Desenvolvimento Econômico e Estabilidade Política* (Rio de Janeiro: n.p., 1977), 151–154.

[46] Benevides, *O governo Kubitschek*, 170–177. On the role of the military in the political stability of the Kubitschek government, see Chapter IV.

[47] In 1961 Brazilian petroleum production reached 95,000 bb/d and refined petroleum 308,000 bb/d. The capacity of electric generation went from 3.5 million kilowatts (kw) to 4,770,000 kw.

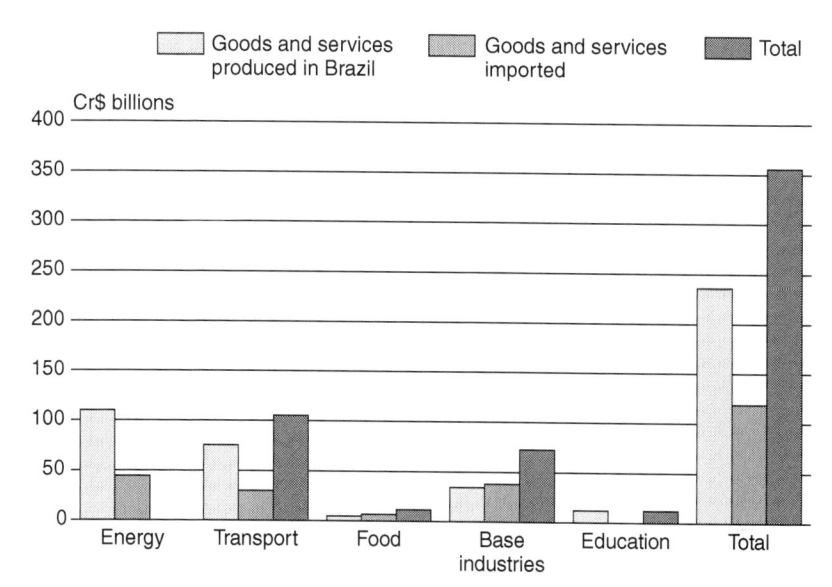

GRAPH 3.3. Investments in the Plano de Metas, 1957/1961. *Source:* Lessa 1975, p. 18

would be one of the most ambitious and most successful parts of the plan, increasing by 75 percent the federal road network and tripling the paved federal highways.[48] Under the Juscelino government there would be a reorientation of the transport system stressing the highway system and the establishment of a national automobile industry. The basic industries sector was also crucial for the acceleration of the industrial process as promised by Juscelino.

The goals of the plan were ambitious and contemplated various key sectors such as steel, cement, alkali, pulp and paper, aluminum, nonferrous metals, and rubber. The national automotive industry, which until then had only produced trucks and utility vehicles, was now geared to producing cars. Agriculture was also included in this ambitious plan, with goals of extending the use of tractors and fertilizers and expanding the storage network. Another goal was to increase the internal production of wheat, which weighed heavily on the balance of payments, but this effort met with little success. Finally, the plan contemplated the formation of technical personnel (see Table 3.1).

---

[48] Between 1956 and 1961 the federal road system went from 20,000 kilometers (km) to 35,000 km. The federal paved roads went from 2,800 km to 9,600 km. AEB (1957), 147; AEB (1962), 111.

TABLE 3.1. *Plano de Metas* – Sectors, Goals, and Level of Attainment

	Sector (% of Investments Envisioned)	Objective	Goal Level Attained
	ENERGY (43.4%)		
1	Electric energy	Increase installed capacity to 3,500,000 kw	High
2	Nuclear energy	Various, including installing a Research Reactorpesquisas	High
3	Coal	Increase production to 2,500,000 tons	Low
4	Petroleum – produced	Increase production to 90,000 bb/d	High
5	Petroleum – refined	Increase production to 175,000 bb/d	Surpassed
	Transports (29.6%)		
6	Railroads – refitting	Repair rolling stock and roadbed	High
7	Railroads – construction	Increase by 1,500 km	Par
8	Roads – paving	Pave some 3,000 km	Surpassed
9	Roads – expansion of routes	Construction of 10,000 km	Surpassed
10	Port service and drainage	No numeric goals	Par
11	Merchant Marine	Expand the tonnage	Surpassed
12	Air transport	Buy planes and improve airports	Reached
	FOOD (3.2%)		
13	Wheat	Increase production by 1,500,000 t	Low
14	Warehouses and silos	Increase capacity	Reached
15	Refrigerated storage	Increase capacity	Low
16	Industrial slaughterhouses	Increase capacity	Par
17	Mechanized agriculture	Increase number of tractors	Reached
18	Fertilizers	Increase use and distribution of fertilizers	Surpassed
	BASIC INDUSTRY (20.4%)		
19	Steel	Increase production to 2,300,000 t	Reached
20	Aluminum	Increase production to 25,000 t	Par
21	Nonferrous metals	Increase production of various products	Par
22	Cement	Increase production to 5,000,000 t	High
23	Alkalies	Increase production of various products	High
24	Cellulose and paper	Increase to 200,000 t of cellulose and 450,000 t of paper	Reached
25	Rubber	Expansion of natural and synthetic rubber	Partial[c]
26	Iron ore exports	Export of 8,000,000 t	Par
27	Automobile industry[a]	First Goal: 100,000 vehicles; revised goal: 347,000	92% achieved
28	Naval construction	Increase capacity to 160,000 dwt/a	Par[d]
29	Mechanical and heavy electric industry	No numeric goals	High[e]
	EDUCATION (3.4%)		
30	Formation of technical personnel	No numeric goals	High
	Goal Synthesis		
31	Construction of Brasília[b]	Construction of the capital in the center of the country	Surpassed

[a] There was the goal to achieve 90 to 95 percent national products, reached in 1962.
[b] There was no estimate of the initial investment for the construction of Brasília.
[c] Synthetic rubber reached its goal, natural rubber remained at pregoal levels.
[d] In 1960 there was a total of 58,000 dwt in projects approved.
[e] Production in the machine industry increased 100 percent in relation to 1955 and electrical industry grew by 200 percent.
Source: Celso Lafer, "O planejamento no Brasil: Observações sobre o Plano de Metas," 1973.

Perhaps the two most ambitious parts of the plan and those with the greatest repercussions in the future were the establishment of a viable automobile industry and the construction of Brasília. Automobile production is known to be one of the activities that have a significant impact on the industrial process, with important forward and backward lineages.[49] As the government required a minimum percentage of parts (of between 90 and 95 percent) to be nationally produced, an auto parts industry was quickly put together, involving the mechanical, electrical, plastic, and rubber sectors, while at the same time there was created a reseller, maintenance, and replacement network. The success of the automobile industry was made possible by the success of the government in meeting most of the goals of the plan in the fields of energy, transport, and basic industry. In turn, the growth of the automobile fleet had a strong effect on the expansion of the road network and represented the new dominance of the automobile and trucks in the movement of passengers and goods, to the detriment of the rail system.

The construction of Brasilia, the new national capital in central Brazil, was considered the major synthesis of all the plans of the government, and its construction also had strong impacts on the Brazilian economy.[50] On the one hand, the size of investments, and the location of the new capital, changed the spatial occupation of Brazil, stimulating its shift from the coast, where population and economic activities had been concentrated, toward the interior of the country. This shift also required highway infrastructure works, explaining part of the investments carried out in new roads. Brasilia, perhaps the greatest symbol of Juscelino, was inaugurated on April 21, 1960, during his term of government.

The financing of the program and the international constraints faced by Brazil constituted a great difficulty for implementing Juscelino's development plan. The exchange rate remained regulated by Instruction 70 of SUMOC, which, as we previously noted, controlled imports and promoted those that were essential to the national economy. On the other

---

[49] Luiz Bias Bahia and Edson Paulo Domingues, "Estrutura de inovações na indústria automobilística brasileira," Texto para Discussão No. 1472 (Brasília: IPEA, 2010), 9.
[50] The relocation of the capital to the center of the country appeared as a wish of the republican government as early as the first republican constitution in 1891. But it was only with the government of Juscelino that the decision was made to build Brasília. Construction began in 1956, and in 1960 came the formal change of the national capital from Rio de Janeiro to Brasilia, although the transfer of the central administration was not completed until 1970. The construction of Brasília was heavily criticized at the time because of its enormous costs.

hand, financial transactions and services operated in the free market. Also operating in the free market were amortizations and interest on loans, and remittances of profits and dividends of companies operating in priority sectors. In 1955, the Juscelino government introduced the possibility of imports without exchange coverage, which would have an important impact in the process of internationalization of the Brazilian economy.[51]

The great transformation promoted by the Juscelino regime was the opening up of Brazil to foreign capital. The first phase of Brazilian industrialization, based on the traditional sectors such as textiles, food, and drinks, had developed largely with national capital. After World War II it was foreign capital that became an important factor in the maturation of this sector. This new industrial expansion also permitted Brazilian insertion in the international market. An aggressive entrepreneurial state that invested heavily in infrastructure and basic or heavy industries became attractive to multinational companies. The government manipulated a set of instruments in the form of subsidies, credit, foreign exchange, tariff protection, and direct investments in infrastructure or sectors where the private sector, domestic or foreign, would find it unattractive to invest. Brazil's development bank, the BNDES, had a key role in defining the priority projects that would count with its essential support.[52] There were thus two basic sources of funding for this massive industrialization project of the government: foreign direct investment or international finance, and state fiscal resources. According to the government plan most of the resources would come from the public budget, and also by funding from the resources of its own public enterprises, particularly for investments in energy and transport, where public enterprises dominated (see Graph 3.4).

From the beginning of the 1950s, the public sector systematically expanded its participation in economic activity, with significant participation not only in infrastructural investments, particularly in transportation, but also in the production of basic inputs. The government

---

[51] On this theme, see Ana Cláudia Caputo and Hildete Pereira de Melo, "A industrialização brasileira nos anos de 1950: Uma análise da Instrução 113 da Sumoc," *Estudos Econômicos* 39,3 (Julho–Setembro 2009), 513–538. Caio Prado argued that it would not be "groundless baseless, so that the national industries rebelled against the measures adopted by Instruction no. 113 of SUMOC, even carrying out formal protests to the Brazilian government." But the instruction was maintained. Caio Prado Junior, *História Econômica do Brasil* (São Paulo: Brasiliense, 1972), 314.

[52] Rosane de Almeida Maia, "Estado e Industrialização no Brasil: Estudo dos Incentivos ao setor privado, nos quadros do Programa de Metas do Governo Kubitschek" (MA thesis, São Paulo, FEA-USP, 1986).

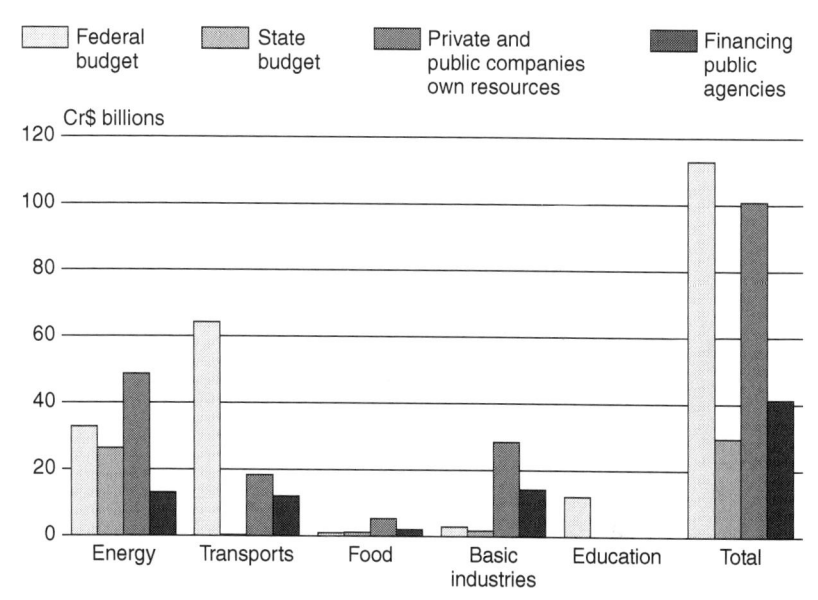

Formative Democracies and the Military Interregnum 165

GRAPH 3.4. Plano de Metas – Forecasted Resources. *Source:* Sochaczewski 1993, p. 101

dominated the steel industry through the *Companhia Siderúrgica Nacional* and participated through the BNDES state bank in two great steel mills then in construction: Usiminas (in Minas Gerais) and Cosipa (in São Paulo).[53] The limited production and refining of petroleum remained under the control of the state company *Petrobrás*;[54] the extraction and exportation of iron ore was dominated by the state-owned *Companhia Vale do Rio Doce*; the production of caustic soda was made by the state's *Companhia Nacional de Alcalis*; the *Companhia Hidroelétrica do São Francisco* and the hydroelectric one at Furnas, both state owned, extended the government's participation in the generation of energy; and the public sector had a major role in the transport sector through the Federal Railroad system (*Rede Ferroviária Federal*), the merchant marine with Lloyd

---

[53] On the establishment of the steel industry in Brazil, see Sérgio H. Abranches, "Governo, empresa estatal e política siderúrgica: 1930–1975," in *As origens da crise: Estado autoritário e planejamento no Brasil*, ed. Olavo Brasil de Lima Jr. and Sérgio H. Abranches (São Paulo: Vértice, Revista dos Tribunais, 1987).

[54] In 1960 national petroleum production was around 80,000 barrels a day. A major increase in Brazilian production began at the end of the 1960s with the beginnings of offshore drilling on the continental shelf, though it would not be until 2006 that Brazil reached self-sufficiency in oil production. Today national production of oil is at two million barrels per day and is obtained exclusively from the continental shelf.

Brasileiro, and road construction through the National Department of Roads (DNER), which administered a National Highway Fund.[55] Besides controlling the BNDES bank, the main source of funding for investments in the country and main financier of the Target Plan, the state-owned Bank of Brazil also played a key role in financing industry and agriculture. It was the public sector that performed a fundamental role in the implementation of the Target Plan, directly or through investment of public enterprises, or by manipulating a set of instruments – taxes, foreign exchange, and financial instruments – which gave it an overall control over the process of ongoing development. The public sector now accounted for between 17 percent and 18 percent of gross domestic product (GDP), and that did not count its activities through participation of public enterprises.

Given the ambitious nature of the Target Plan, there was tremendous demand for financial resources, without the capacity to expand revenues proportionately. This led to budget deficits. A large part of the deficit was financed by loans from the Bank of Brazil to the Treasury. Since the Bank of Brazil worked as a commercial bank and a central bank, its liabilities to the public were part of the monetary base. Issuing government bonds to finance all this was difficult, since the bond market was quite limited due in part to the mismatch between high inflation, on the order of 25 to 30 percent, and the usury law, which limited interest rates to 12 percent.[56] That meant that the financing of the Treasury's deficit was made through the expansion of the money supply, thus generating inflationary pressure. But the principal preoccupation of economic policy was with development and not with fiscal and monetary stability.[57] The SUMOC section of the Bank of Brazil exercised the functions of a central bank, controlling exchange policy, fixing discount rates, establishing the rules on the compulsory deposits of banks, and requiring the registration of foreign

---

[55] The *Fundo Rodoviário Nacional* (National Road Fund) was created in 1948 and its resources came from a tax on fuels and lubricants, which were used in the construction and maintenance of the road network. On the state's role in developing these industries, see Gail D. Triner, *Mining and the State in Brazilian Development* (London: Pickering & Chatto, 2011).

[56] The usury law (decree No. 22.626) was decreed on April 7, 1933.

[57] In October 1958 there was an attempt to implement a stabilization program, called the Monetary Stabilization Program (EMP), with strict monetary and fiscal targets. But the program experienced a fierce opposition. The lack of objective conditions for its implementation led to the resignation of the Finance Minister, who was replaced by the president of the Bank of Brazil. Moreover, the conflict between the president of the Bank of Brazil and the Minister of Finance is usually resolved by the fall of the minister and his replacement by the bank president.

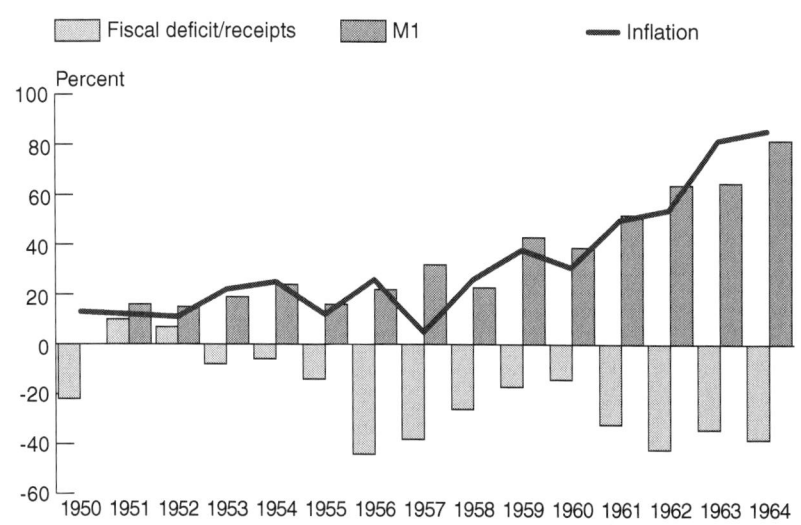

GRAPH 3.5. Annual Change in Fiscal Deficit, M1, and Inflation, 1950–1964. Source: Ipeadata

capital. The Bank of Brazil, besides being a commercial bank and the principal agricultural bank in the country, also operated a Rediscount Portfolio,[58] a Banking Mobilization Fund,[59] a Portfolio Exchange,[60] and a Foreign Trade Portfolio (Cacex). It also exercised the role of the Treasury Cashier, centralizing the income and payment for the Treasury and giving it credit when needed, and through the SUMOC, the Bank of Brazil administered the reserves of the commercial banks. As the Bank of Brazil was not subject to reserve requirements, in view of its multiple functions as executor of the financial and exchange-rate policy of the government, it exercised in practice the role of the monetary authority. To restrict its operations, limits were imposed in the active operations of the various portfolios. But this control was subject to numerous political pressures that effectively precluded effective control (see Graph 3.5 and Appendix Table A.3).[61]

[58] Carteira de Redescontos.
[59] *Caixa de Mobilização Bancária*. Though the Portfolio Rediscount of the Bank of Brazil performed discounts virtually for all types of active commercial banks, the Banking Cash Mobilization filled the role of loan of last resort, providing assistance to banks in distress.
[60] Carteira de Câmbio.
[61] This unusual role of the Bank of Brazil would only be solved with the creation of the Central Bank in 1964. According to Gentil Corazza, despite the division of functions between the Treasury, the Bank of Brazil, and SUMOC, this monetary system created a perverse process of money creation that was concentrated in the Bank of Brazil, mixing

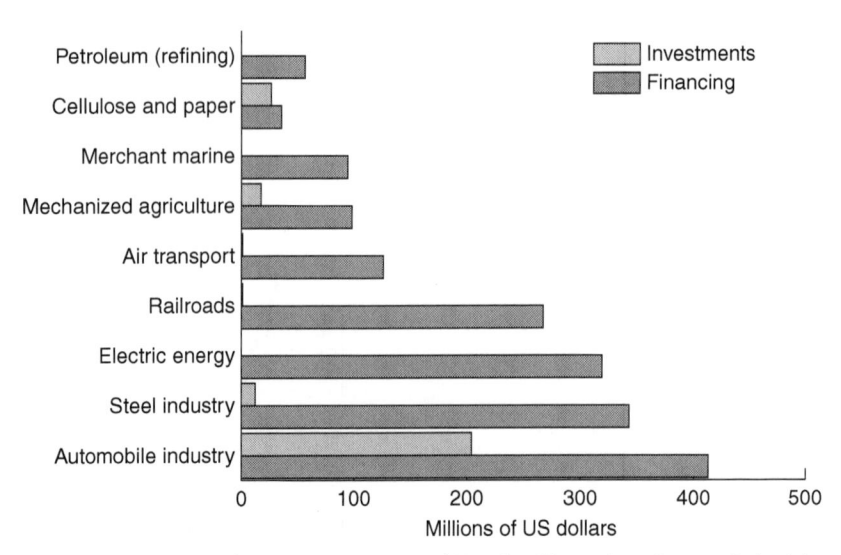

GRAPH 3.6. Target Plan – Investments and Foreign Financing. *Source:* Relatório SUMOC, in Lessa 1975, pp. 34–37

The international sector represented another important source of financing for the development plan, as much in loans as in direct investments. The relative aversion to foreign capital shown by the second Vargas government was replaced by a frankly favorable policy toward foreign investments under Juscelino, which attracted many multinational corporations in various sectors of activity. The majority of this foreign capital came in the form of loans, but close to a fifth of these resources came from direct investments. The main beneficiaries from these direct foreign investments were basic industries, particularly the automotive industry, and to a lesser extent pulp and paper, and steel. This foreign capital investment focused on the areas of electricity, railways, shipping, aviation, steel, and automobiles (see Graph 3.6).

Faced with the deficiencies of a public administration ill-equipped for carrying out the Target Plan, the Juscelino government chose to create

> multiple roles deemed incompatible with monetary policy. The Bank of Brazil was the financial agent of the Treasury licensed to conduct credit operations, the custodian of the voluntary reserves of the commercial banks, and the largest commercial bank in the country and the only rural bank. These multiple functions of the Bank of Brazil combined resulted in the bank derailing any control over the issuance of money supply. Gentil Corazza, *O Banco Central do Brasil – Evolução Histórica e Institucional.* Available at http://www.net.fee.com.br/sitefee/download/jornadas/1/s3a4.pdf.

a parallel structure instead of promoting the reform of the administration, which would have taken time, caused political friction, and required legislative approval. This parallel structure was based on already preexistent institutions such as the Bank of Brazil and the BNDES bank, and by new entities such as the Executives Group (*Grupos Executivos*). This later group basically operated in the private sector, coordinating all the institutions involved in sector policies. The BNDES, in turn, centralized the public activities, prioritizing projects, for funding and for granting guarantees for foreign loans.

The results achieved by these new administrative structures were exceptional in the area of transport, power generation, and industry in general, which reached new levels of production. The government was also successful in the consolidation of basic industries, and in the establishment of the automobile industry in Brazil. This later sector required the government not only to help establish automobile assembly plants, but given the demand that the cars have a high level of national input, it also helped create an auto parts industry. Given the limited consumer market in Brazil, the major American car companies were initially not interested in deploying production units in Brazil. The first to enter were the German automakers Volkswagen and DKW (Vemag Brazil), the French Simca, and the American Willys Overland.[62] The industrialization process under way played an important role in the expansion of income and the consumer market. But this would take time and would only occur in the decade of the 1970s.

By the census of 1960 there existed 110,000 industrial establishments in Brazil, employing 1.8 million workers, of whom almost 41 percent were employed in the areas of textiles, clothing, food, and drinks.[63] This sector of light industry, which represented half the value of industrial production in 1949, now accounted for only a third of the value of industrial production. In the same period, metallurgy, equipment manufacturers, the transport material industry, and the chemical industry increased their relative share, reaching about a third of the value of industrial production. From the point of view of the size of productive units, measured by the average number of workers employed, which was 16 workers per factory

---

[62] He personally convinced the American automobile companies to produce cars in Brazil, without results. But this situation did not last long. Flávio Limoncic, "The Brazilian Automotive Industry in International Context: From European to American Crisis" (Michigan, "New perspectives on Latin American and US Noon Lectures Series," January 2009), 8 pages.

[63] In 1939 and 1949 the same sectors employed 55 percent and 51 percent, respectively.

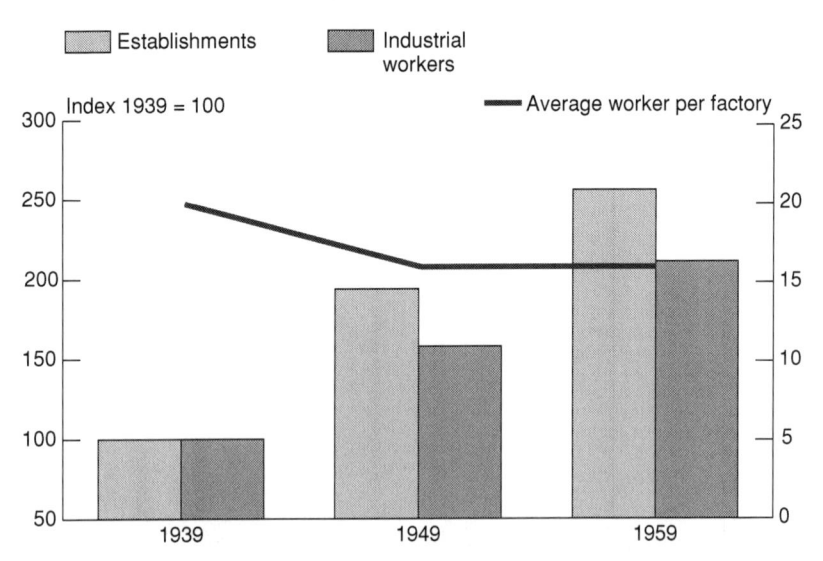

170   *The Economic and Social History of Brazil since 1889*

GRAPH 3.7. Industrial Establishments and Employees, 1939–1959 (1939 = 100) (establishments in 1939 = 43,250; workers in 1939 = 851,755). *Source:* IBGE – Séries Históricas Retrospectivas

overall, some sectors such as textiles, rubber, electrical and communications equipment, pharmaceuticals, and paper and cardboard employed on average more than 50 people. In terms of the average value of production, the rubber industry, pharmaceuticals, tobacco, and electrical and communications equipment stood out as above average industries (see Graphs 3.7 and 3.8).

Although agriculture represented one of the items in the Target Plan, it was not really a priority of the government. Thus little change occurred in agriculture in this period of massive government and private investments. But despite the relative backwardness of the Brazilian agriculture, the sector does not seem to have represented an obstacle to the development of industry since it was able to supply the basic food needs of an expanding population by increasing output through traditional means. Significant growth occurred in agriculture during the 1940s and 1950s, although it maintained the structure inherited from the colonial period, except in areas influenced by coffee, and did not show any gains in productivity from earlier periods. This growth in production came from the employment of new lands and more workers. This demand for food was driven by the postwar growth in urban population, which permitted

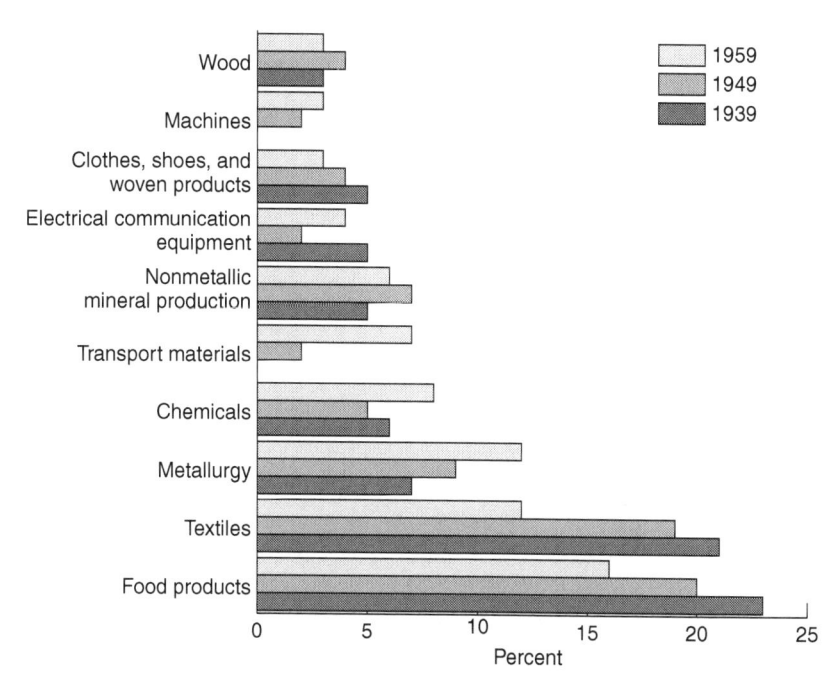

Formative Democracies and the Military Interregnum   171

GRAPH 3.8. Participation in the Value of Industrial Production of the Principal Sectors, 1939–1959. *Source:* IBGE – Séries Históricas Retrospectivas

agriculture to release more workers into the urban area at no cost to its own needs and created an increased demand for agricultural products in the expanding cities. This so-called labor reserve army permitted farmers and plantation owners to continue obtaining cheap laborers, thus reducing their interest in creating more efficient means of production. At the same time, the availability of new agricultural lands was also a disincentive to the more intensive use of capital in the form of plows, tractors, fertilizers, and pesticides. The beginnings of modernization in agriculture only occurred in the 1970s when agriculture became an important market for industry.

But beyond the economic issues, the maintenance of the rural infrastructure was supported by powerful political interests since the urban transformation and industrialization policies of the government depended on alliances with the PSD for support, and that party was strongly rooted in the countryside. This can be shown by the concentrated structure of ownership of land, which remained virtually unchanged between 1920 and 1970. During this period the Gini index for the distribution

TABLE 3.2. *Productivity of the Principal Agricultural Crops, 1931–1962 (tons/hectares)*

	Cotton	Rice	Cacao	Coffee	Sugar Cane	Beans	Manioc	Corn	Wheat	Soybeans
1931	0.51	1.50	0.50	0.36	46.63	1.32	22.94	1.50		
1940	0.65	1.51	0.56	0.40	39.44	0.79	12.55	1.25		
1950	0.43	1.64	0.55	0.40	39.45	0.69	13.09	1.29		
1960	0.55	1.62	0.35	0.94	42.48	0.68	13.12	1.30	0.63	1.20
1961	0.57	1.70	0.33	1.02	36.35	0.68	13.07	1.31	0.53	1.13
1962	0.56	1.66	0.85	0.98	42.64	0.63	13.44	1.30	0.92	1.10

Source: IBGE, Séries Históricas Retrospectivas.

of landownership from agricultural establishments remained virtually unchanged, rising from 0.83 to 0.84.[64]

Agricultural production in the 1960s was extremely concentrated in just ten crops that accounted for four-fifths of the value of production.[65] It is evident that coffee maintained its leadership throughout this period, with also a major production of corn, cotton, and rice. Meanwhile, soybean plantings were only just entering into production and had not become a significant part of the crop mix as it would in later decades. These ten crops in 1960 occupied an area of 25 million hectares, with corn occupying the most space (7.3 million hectares), followed by coffee, cotton, and rice. Although there was no change in basic productivity of these crops except in coffee between 1920 and 1960, there was now a greater presence of plows and tractors on Brazilian farms (see Table 3.2 and Graph 3.9).

In the 1950s some 10.6 million hectares were brought into production and 4.5 million farmworkers were added, a modest increase compared to previous years. But there was an increase in this decade of machines that finally began to appear on Brazilian farms in significant numbers. As was to be expected, most of these tractors and plows were concentrated in the south and southeast regions. In the northeast there was now 1 plow for each 310 hectares while in the southern region the ratio was

---

[64] Although the overall mean remained stable it decreased significantly in some states, such as Santa Catarina, Paraná, Acre, and Amazonas. In other states, such as Maranhão, Pernambuco, and Mato Grosso, concentrations increased. The index in São Paulo remained stable, around 0.77.

[65] In 1961, seven products (coffee, rice, cotton, corn, sugar cane, beans, and manioc) represented 75.9 percent of the value of production. AEB (1962), 53–55.

Formative Democracies and the Military Interregnum 173

TABLE 3.3. *Crop Areas, Personnel, Tractors, and Plows Employed by State, 1950–1960*

	Crop Areas 1950	Crop Areas 1960	Personnel Employed 1950	Personnel Employed 1960	Tractors 1950	Tractors 1960	Plows 1950	Plows 1960
North	234,512	458,490	326,502	536,619	61	266	381	306
Northeast	5,283,804	9,306,681	4,334,936	6,566,035	451	2,989	14,489	21,171
Southeast	8,447,903	10,297,939	3,999,860	4,465,344	5,155	35,215	318,863	394,696
Minas Gerais	2,937,126	3,673,466	1,868,657	2,076,829	763	5,024	79,968	93,040
São Paulo	4,257,633	4,973,300	1,531,664	1,683,038	3,819	28,101	224,947	286,580
South	4,530,566	8,279,870	1,949,923	3,174,233	2,566	22,720	383,435	604,050
Paraná	1,358,222	3,471,131	507,607	1,276,854	280	4,996	30,405	82,324
Rio Grande do Sul	2,502,691	3,795,840	1,071,404	1,277,390	2,245	16,675	312,001	440,467
Center West	608,272	1,416,805	385,613	678,623	139	2,303	3,091	11,797
TOTAL	19,095,057	29,759,785	10,996,834	15,521,701	8,372	63,493	714,259	1,031,930

Source: IBGE, Séries Históricas Retrospectivas.

1 plow for each 5 hectares in the south and 11 hectares in the southeast. As for tractors, there was 1 for every 3,114 hectares in the northeast and just 1 per 292 hectares in the southeast, with São Paulo as usual being the leading state with a ratio of 1 tractor for every 177 hectares (see Table 3.3).

During the Juscelino years, coffee continued to be an important part of Brazilian exports, but with new signs of overproduction. Output had

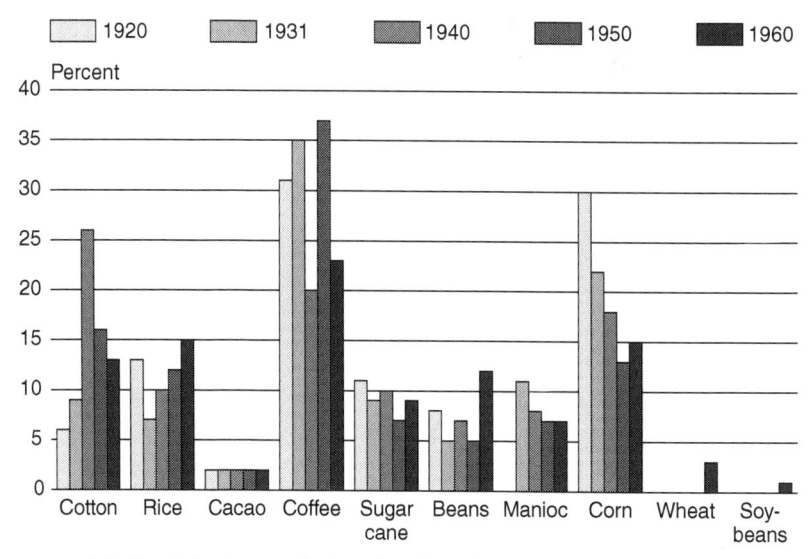

GRAPH 3.9. Participation in the Total Value of Production, 1920–1960. *Source:* IBGE – Séries Históricas Retrospectivas

been around 20 million sacks of coffee during the late 1940s but began to expand in the middle of the 1950s due to the increase in world prices during the Korean War. By 1959 production reached 44 million bags of coffee (out of total world production of 79 million bags), this at a time when world consumption was only 42 million bags. While this temporarily mid-1950s boom increased the importance of coffee in Brazil's export mix, it created the usual crisis conditions of overproduction. Coffee quickly began to be stockpiled, and by 1963 Brazil had 63 million bags warehoused, all of which put downward pressure on prices. The government of Juscelino thus faced the usual boom and bust period of coffee production – rising prices, increasing output, followed by falling prices and a systematic decline in the value of coffee exports. Until 1959 the government bought coffee to protect this sector, but the continued expansion of coffee production in Brazil and the world meant that this policy would have little effect on world prices. In 1959 an agreement was signed between the Latin American and African coffee producers giving each country a quota for exports. In 1962 came a new agreement, this time with all world producers and the United States. In that year the International Organization of Coffee was established, and the next year an international agreement led to an intense program of eradication of coffee plants worldwide. Between 1962 and 1967 half of the world's coffee trees were eradicated. It was nevertheless during this new period of expansion and contraction that the Brazilian coffee industry saw a major shift in production zones. The state of Paraná went from just 5 percent of national production in the 1940s to accounting for more than half of national production by the late 1950s (see Graphs 3.10 and 3.11, Table 3.4, and Appendix Table A.1).

But this boom and bust period marked the last high point in the role of coffee in Brazilian exports. As can be seen when we compare the mix of exports in 1947 with those in 1960, there was occurring a significant shift with a reduction in the importance of primary materials and the increase in foodstuffs. Even in primary materials exports there were changes, with an increase in wood exports (primarily pine) and minerals (basically iron ore) and with a major decline in cotton. In the food exports, there was an increase in sugar and cacao, with coffee now at 56 percent of the value of all exports and declining. As for imports, there was more stability among the major items, which were primary materials, food stocks, and manufactures. However, this latter category was changing due to the growth of national industries. Thus automobiles, for example, which represented 9 percent of imports in 1947, practically disappeared from

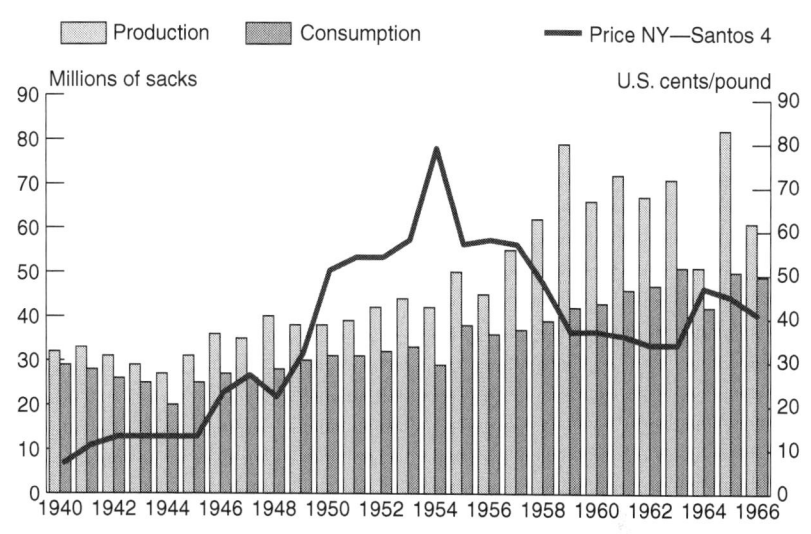

Formative Democracies and the Military Interregnum 175

GRAPH 3.10. World Production, Consumption, and the Price of Coffee, 1940–1966. *Source:* Bacha 1992, pp. 288–340

imports in 1960. Moreover, in foodstuffs some 80 percent of imports in this category were wheat and codfish (*bacalhau*), which shows that by this later date Brazil was basically self-sufficient in agricultural production (see Graphs 3.12a and 3.12b).

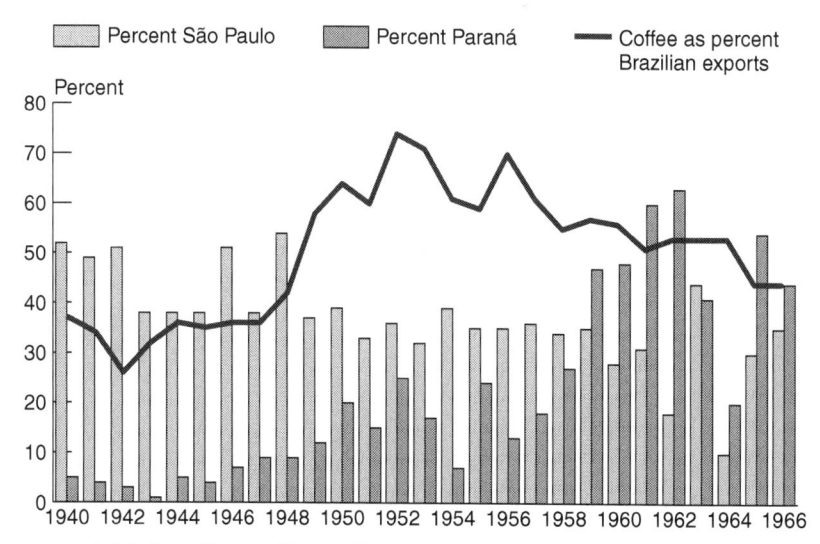

GRAPH 3.11. Brazilian Coffee Production by State and Percent in Exports, 1940–1966. *Source:* Bacha 1992, pp. 288–340

176   The Economic and Social History of Brazil since 1889

TABLE 3.4. *Principal States for Coffee Production, with Area Planted and Output, 1956–1962*

	1956	1957	1958	1959	1960	1961	1962
	Area Planted (in *alqueires*)						
Minas Gerais	686,686	711,510	781,738	790,623	798,967	802,364	812,380
Espirito Santo	271,925	281,670	321,697	299,550	306,372	287,977	306,553
São Paulo	1,556,846	1,593,226	1,619,520	1,647,034	1,635,187	1,521,588	1,365,136
Paraná	635,427	807,555	1,032,776	1,225,676	1,335,601	1,411,227	1,620,798
BRAZIL	3,411,651	3,672,325	4,077,920	4,296,645	4,419,537	4,383,820	4,462,657
	Production (in tons)						
Minas Gerais	204,912	262,341	280,218	543,502	496,276	542,270	492,301
Espirito Santo	97,813	130,309	151,633	287,571	204,730	256,283	293,037
São Paulo	434,946	602,879	620,399	1,462,133	1,157,989	1,269,699	752,495
Paraná	115,026	277,780	508,835	1,823,427	1,948,627	2,083,722	2,555,155
BRAZIL	979,278	1,409,304	1,695,855	4,396,844	4,169,584	4,457,408	4,380,607

Source: *Anuários Estatísticos do Brasil*, various years.

The changes that were occurring in the economy between 1930 and 1960 had an impact on the economically active population as well with major changes in their productive allocation. Employment in the agricultural sector grew less than employment in industry and services, thus reducing its relative importance. A large increase in employment occurred in the services sector, which now employed a third of the population economically active in 1960 compared to 13 percent in industry and 54 percent in agriculture. Although these changing indicators show the result of a process of rural exodus in search of opportunities in cities in the period from 1930 to 1960, the agricultural population was still growing in this period, at an annual rate of 1.6 percent (see Graph 3.13).

All the investments carried out under the Target Plan of the Juscelino government led to significant growth of the production, particularly in industry, which showed a mean variation of 11 percent growth in the period, to commerce, which also had an outstanding performance (8 percent), and even agriculture, which though less supported, still showed an increase in the five years of government, resulting in average percentage of almost 6 percent growth. But this growth was not evenly distributed. As of 1960, Brazil still exhibited strong regional disparities in GDP and per capita GDP. The GDP was U.S.$17 billion, with a per capita income of U.S.$244. The southeast accounted for 61 percent of

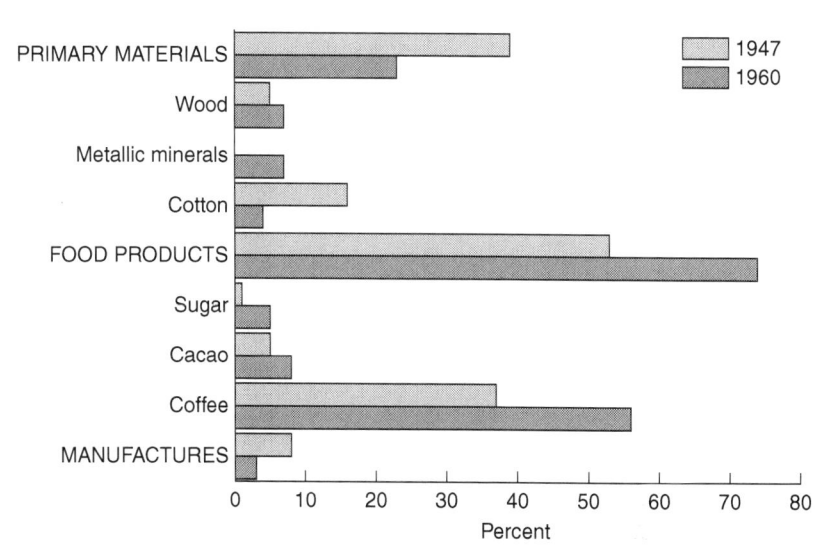

Formative Democracies and the Military Interregnum 177

GRAPH 3.12a. Participation in Exports, 1947 and 1960. Source: *Anuários Estatísticos do Brasil* (1948 and 1962)

domestic income, the south 18 percent, and the northeast just 16 percent. São Paulo alone generated 32 percent of the domestic income of the country. In terms of income per capita, while the national average was Cr$27,000, we find that two states had the highest income – that of Guanabara (which was the city of Rio de Janeiro), which was Cr$77,000, and São Paulo with an average of Cr$47,000, and typical ones of the northeast with the lowest ones: Piauí with Cr$8,000, Maranhão at Cr$9,000, and

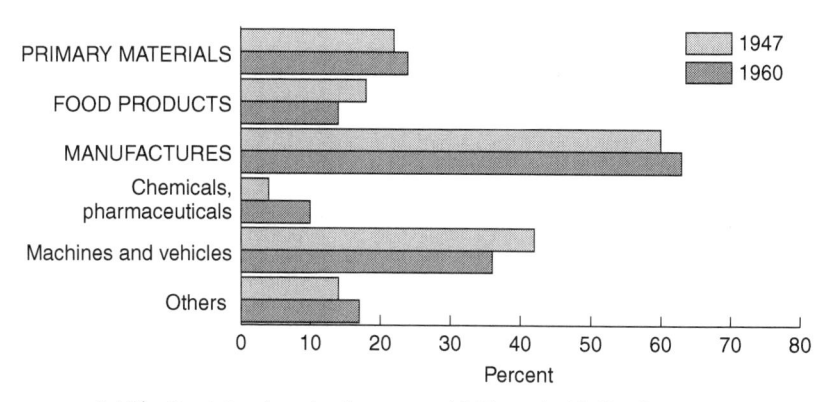

GRAPH 3.12b. Participation in Imports, 1947 and 1960. Source: *Anuários Estatísticos do Brasil* (1948 and 1962)

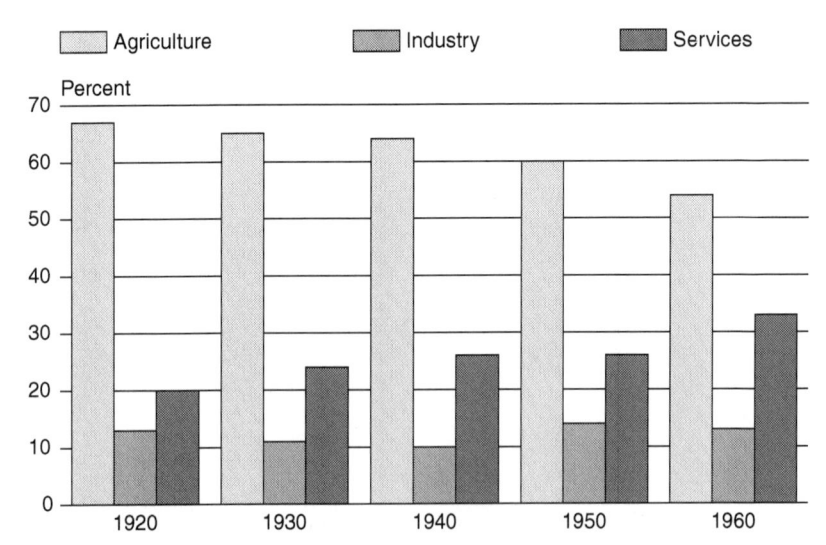

178   The Economic and Social History of Brazil since 1889

GRAPH 3.13. Composition of the Economically Active Population by Sector of Activity, 1920–1960. *Source:* Merrick and Graham 1980, pp. 64–65

Ceará with a per capita of Cr$12,000[66] (see Graphs 3.14a, 3.14b, 3.15a, and 3.15b).

By the end of his mandate, Juscelino had completed a large part of his Target Plan, seriously advancing Brazilian industrialization. He had greatly transformed the country that he had inherited from his predecessor, but left the nation with serious economic problems. Annual inflation had now reached 50 percent; also there was a major deficit in current accounts, a very high deficit in public accounts, a crisis in coffee production with low prices leading to large stockpiling, and an expanded capacity of production incompatible with the size of the internal market. There were also questions about the possible exhaustion of the process of import substitution.[67]

---

[66] To adapt the centesimal system, in 1942 the traditional *mil réis* was replaced by *cruzeiro*. Later the historic Brazilian inflation caused numerous changes in the Brazilian monetary standard. In 1967, the government created the *cruziero novo* or new *cruziero*, which was worth 1,000 old *cruzeiros*. The name *cruzeiro* returned in 1970. In 1986 the *cruzeiro* was replaced by the *cruzado*, which, in turn, was changed to *cruzado novo* in 1989. In 1990 the *cruzeiro* reappeared, which was substituted in 1993 by the *cruzeiro real*. Finally, in 1994 came the *real* currency that continues today, due to the successful monetary reform implemented by the Real Plan. Banco Central do Brasil, available at http://www.bcb.gov.br/?refsismon.

[67] Tavares, "Auge e Declínio do processo de substituição de importações no Brasil," 27–115.

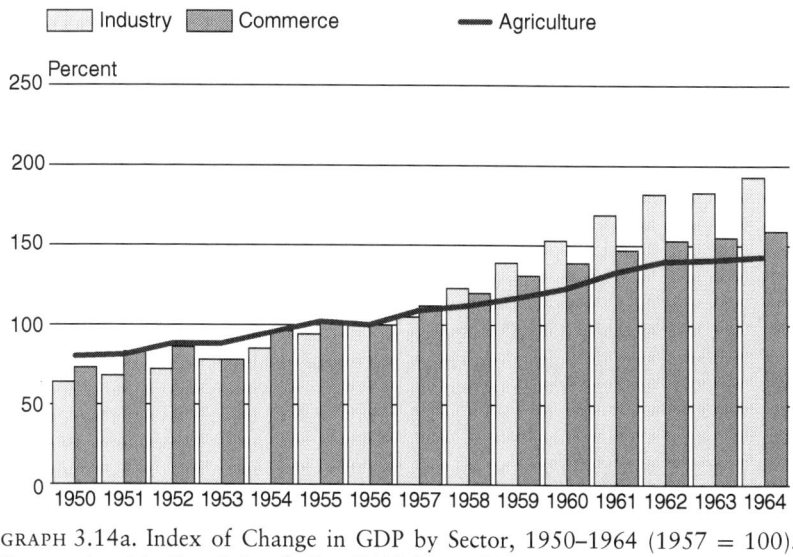

Formative Democracies and the Military Interregnum 179

GRAPH 3.14a. Index of Change in GDP by Sector, 1950–1964 (1957 = 100). Source: Anuário Estatístico do Brasil (1968), p. 414

The presidential elections of October 1960 resulted in the victory of Janio Quadros. He was a populist who had experienced a meteoric career in São Paulo with a quite local party. The UDN opposition to the old Vargas and Juscelino parties decided not to present a candidate and

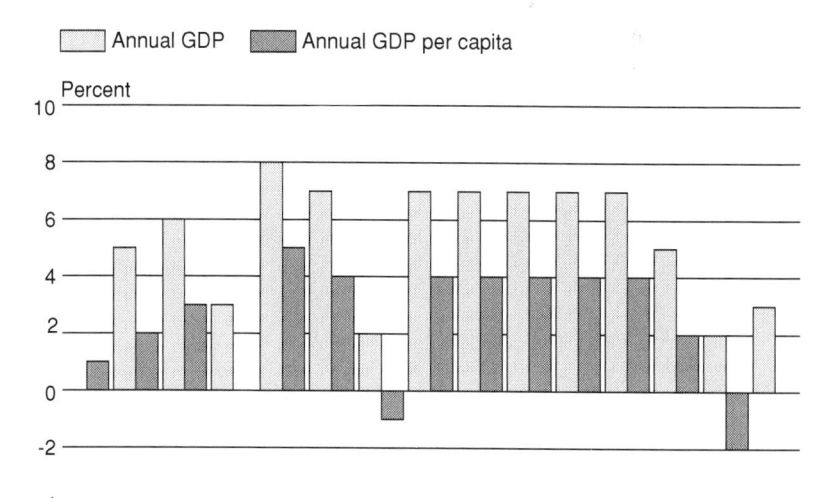

GRAPH 3.14b. Annual Change in GDP and GDP per Capita, 1950–1964. Source: Anuário Estatístico do Brasil (1968), p. 414

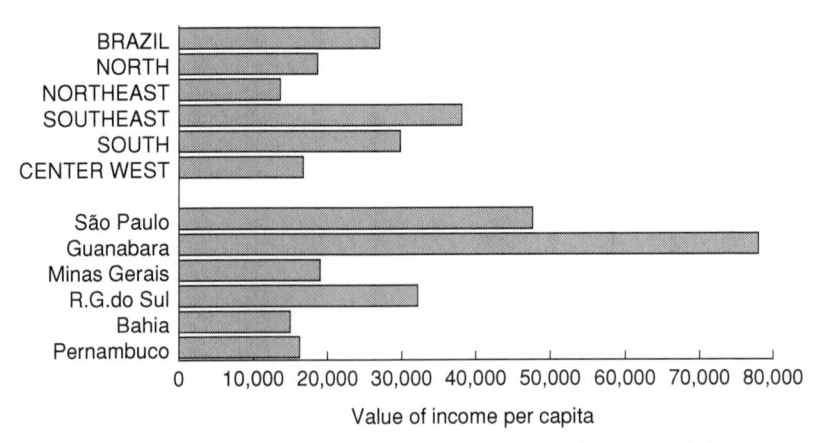

GRAPH 3.15a. Income per Capita – Brazil, Regions, and States, 1960. *Source: Anúario Estatístico Brasil* (1963)

supported Quadros instead, and he was able to defeat General Lott who was the candidate of the old Vargas alliance of the PSD and the PTB. As the election for vice president was made independently, João Goulart, the former Minister of Labor of Vargas and vice president to Juscelino, was elected vice president. Janio Quadros immediately undertook controversial measures in the internal area. Normally of a conservative position, he surprisingly gave a high government decoration to Che Guevara. He also proposed carrying out an international policy of greater independence from the United States and denounced the critical economic situation left

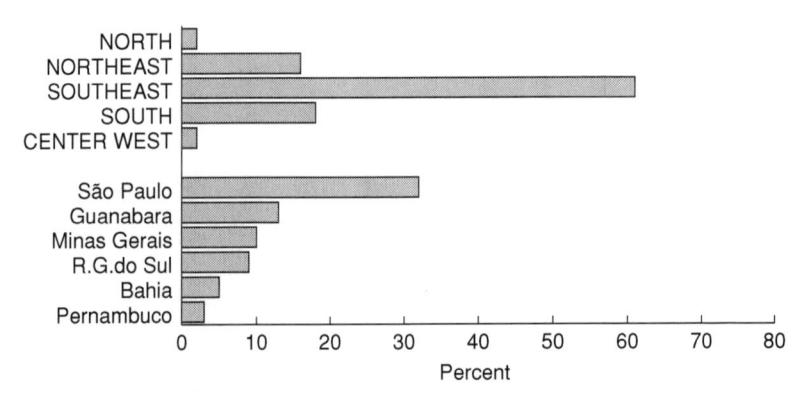

GRAPH 3.15b. Percentage of GDP by Regions and States, 1960. *Source: Anúario Estatístico Brasil* (1963)

by the previous government.[68] To deal with the grave economic situation Janio launched a stabilization program, devalued the national currency, and reduced public expenditures and the money supply.

Then just six months into his administration, Janio suddenly renounced his position. Though he never explained his resignation, it was clear that his administration did not have parliamentary support. The old PSD-PTB parties would not support him and the UDN quickly abandoned him after the presidential election. It is assumed that Janio made this dramatic resignation gesture hoping that there would be opposition to his move that would have permitted him to impose the conditions for his remaining in power. But this did not occur. His resignation letter was quickly read in Congress and this was sufficient to validate his act.[69]

Vice President João Goulart was to be his constitutionally defined successor. But the army opposed his assuming office, continuing to fear his leftist positions. Since Goulart was then on an official visit overseas, he postponed his return until a political and principally a military solution could be found so that he could assume the presidency. The solution came in the form of implementing a parliamentary system of government.[70] Nevertheless, despite these constraints, the Goulart period would be marked by growing mobilization of the unions, students, organized peasants in new peasant leagues, and the rise of new leftist groups within the Catholic Church. In a coalition between leftists and nationalists came ideas for comprehensive structural reforms, dealing with land,

---

[68] In his inaugural speech he made a scathing critique of his predecessor, denouncing the expansion of the currency, external debt, the anticipations of revenue made by the Portfolio Exchange of the Bank of Brazil, the commitments undertaken by BNDES, the debt of the Treasury with the Bank of Brazil, and the debt of the nation with the Social Security System. He worried about the situation of balance of payments, because commodity prices were down in the international market. In the coffee market prices continued to fall, and Brazil had already purchased to store 40 million bags. He indicated the budgetary difficulties, estimating a large deficit for the first year of his government and criticized the high inflation. He also stated that the government of Juscelino left the government with a series of delays in external payments, including the IMF and Eximbank. Discourse on assuming the presidency of Janio Quadros. Available at http://brasilrepublicano.com.br/fontes/30.pdf.

[69] On the government of Janio Quadros, see Maria Victoria de Mesquita Benevides, *O Governo Jânio Quadros*, 2nd ed. (São Paulo: Brasiliense, 1999).

[70] According to Skidmore, the popular forces that supported the possession of Jango were deceived into thinking that he now had the full support of the military. But this was only one group within the military that supported Jango, and the military ministers still exercised a veto. But it was the division among the military, combined with an ample broad-based support of the center and left parties, who were eager to ensure compliance with the constitutional process. Skidmore, *Politics in Brazil, 1930–1964*, 263.

education, urbanization and even for voting rights for illiterates.[71] Given his limited base of support in parliament and the limits to his power in the new parliamentary governmental structure, Goulart was able to mobilize society in favor of a plebiscite that resulted in a return to a presidential system in January 1963.

The Goulart government faced a severe crisis in the economy with inflation reaching more than 80 percent in the year. In an attempt to resolve this crisis he launched a so-called Triennial Plan with the aim of combating inflation and promoting growth.[72] The plan pointed out the structural imbalances of the process of import substitution as a major cause of inflation, and argued that this could not be corrected without a program to anticipate such imbalances. But the plan did not discuss the possible exhaustion of the import substitution model itself, which would be the center of debate in the following years. The government pointed to the international and public sectors as the main causes of inflation. So to relieve pressure from the public sector the government proposed increasing taxes, reducing public spending, raising funds from the private sector, and mobilizing financial resources. Although Goulart was determined to carry out the plan, there were no objective conditions for its success. In 1963 inflation rose to 82 percent and there was virtually no growth that year in the GDP.[73]

In April 1964, after a period of major political turbulence, the army carried out a military coup, overthrew the Goulart government, and established a military dictatorship that would remain in power for 21 years. On April 9 the recently installed military regime issued the first of a long

---

[71] According to Skidmore, although the reforms had objective reasons, they could be understood as an attempt by Goulart to change the structure of political power. A granting of the vote to illiterates or creating literacy programs for the masses could radically change the electoral equilibrium and open the road to other profound changes in the social structure. Skidmore, *Politics in Brazil, 1930–1964*, 289.

[72] The Plano de Metas was launched in December 1962 and was coordinated by the economist Celso Furtado.

[73] Roberto B. M. Macedo, "Plano Trienal de Desenvolvimento Econômico e Social," in *Planejamento no Brasil*, ed. Betty Mindlin (São Paulo: Perspectiva, 2001), 51–68; Lessa, *Quinze anos de política econômica*, 72–79; Marcelo de Paiva Abreu, "Inflação, estagnação e ruptura: 1961-1964," in *A ordem do Progresso*, ed. Marcelo de Paiva Abreu (Rio de Janeiro: Editora Campus, 1992a), 105–122, 197–212; Skidmore, *Politics in Brazil, 1930–1964*, 252–308; Lucila de Almeida Neves Delgado, "O governo João Goulart e o golpe de 1964: memória, história e historiografia," *Tempo* (Niterói) 14,18 (Junho 2010), available at http://www.scielo.br/scielo.php?pid=S1413-77042010000100006&script=sci_arttext; Sérgio Monteiro, "Política econômica e credibilidade: uma análise dos governos Jânio Quadros e João Goulart," available at http://www8.ufrgs.br/ppge/pcientifica/1999_13.pdf.

Formative Democracies and the Military Interregnum   183

list of institutional "acts" that would turn the democratic state into an authoritarian one. The so-called AI-1 decree gave Congress the power to elect a new president, and it indicated Marshal Castelo Branco, one of the main leaders of the coup. Rather than return to their civilian allies in the UDN, the military, for the first time, decided to develop its own political project under full military control, and it would remain in power for more than two decades. Political repression now became the norm, and the military arrested thousands of people, including dissident military officers. The government was especially hard on the leaders of the movements of urban and rural workers. During the military regime, censorship, repression, imprisonment, and torture became widespread.[74]

The military regimes that controlled the country in this authoritarian period exhibited unique characteristics. On the one hand, they were repressive, fiercely anticommunist, and engaged in the Cold War as staunch allies of the United States. On the other, they were determined to organize a powerful centralized state, dominated by the executive branch, limiting the other federal branches as well as the field of action of states and municipalities. They preserved elections and Congress remained in operation. But the powers of the legislature were greatly reduced, and its members were controlled by the purge of the legislators of the Left and center who opposed the guidelines issued by the executive branch or were critical of the regime. These politicians had their political rights annulled (cassados).

The military did not constitute a homogeneous group. There were internal divisions of power and different points of view about the level of centralization of the system, the length of time needed for military intervention, and the means used to carry out its program. For some,

---

[74] There exists an extensive bibliography on the military period. One can obtain a general vision from the following works: Thomas E. Skidmore, *The Politics of Military Rule in Brazil, 1964–85* (New York: Oxford University Press, 1988) and his essay "Politics and Economic Policy Making in Authoritarian Brazil, 1937–1971," in *Authoritarian Brazil*, ed. Alfred Stepan (New Haven, CT: Yale University Press, 1976), 3–46; Philippe C. Schmitter, "The 'Portugalization' of Brazil," in *Authoritarian Brazil*, ed. Alfred Stepan (New Haven, CT: Yale University Press, 1976), 179–232; Juan J. Linz, "The Future of an Authoritarian Situation or the Institutionalization of an Authoritarian Regime: The Case of Brazil," in *Authoritarian Brazil*, ed. Alfred Stepan (New Haven, CT: Yale University Press, 1976), 179–232; Bolivar Lamounier, "O 'Brasil autoritário' revisitado: o impacto das eleições sobre a ditadura," in *Democratizando o Brasil*, ed. Alfred Stepan (Rio de Janeiro: Paz e Terra, 1985), 83–134; Alfred Stepan, "As prerrogativas militares nos regimes pós-autoritários: Brasil, Argentina, Uruguai e Espanha," in *Democratizando o Brasil*, ed. Alfred Stepan (Rio de Janeiro: Paz e Terra, 1985), 521–572; Maria Helena Moreira Alves, *Estado e oposição no Brasil, 1964–1984* (Petrópolis: Vozes, 1984).

repression, censorship, and torture were extreme features that should only be employed in the last instance, for others, they were fundamental tools needed to destroy the Left. In spite of conflicting positions within the military government, repression and torture became a functioning part of the regime. The dispute between the military groups appeared to be critical in times of presidential succession – another peculiarity of the Brazilian dictatorship. Fearing the emergence of a personalist regime under the domination of some chieftain who might remain in power, the military establishment pledged itself to adopt fixed presidential terms and formal but not democratic "elections." Throughout the military period, Congress carried out a type of presidential election that essentially confirmed the previous selection made by the military. The internal conflicts in the choice of new presidents were kept under military control. This resulted in different military groups alternating in power, and despite these conflicts, the military was able to achieve consensus enabling it to maintain their government.

During the evolution of these military governments there was a clear increase in repression. In the first years, during the government of Castelo Branco, the army maintained relative democratic freedoms and the expectation was for a rapid return to civilian government. Castelo was one of the leaders of the moderate wing of the military who believed it would be possible to return power to civilians once the populist and subversive elements were expelled from the political scene. This was the same vision adopted by the civilian leaders of the conservative UDN, the party that played an active role in the military coup and that now constituted the regime's parliamentary base. Initially, Castelo assumed power for the remaining years of the Goulart presidency, which would terminate at the end of 1965. But under pressure from hard-line officers, he agreed to extend his mandate until March 1967.[75]

In November 1965 there occurred elections for state governors during which time the old party structure remained in place. In two important states, that of Minas Gerais and Guanabara,[76] the elected candidates were members of the hated PSD. The reaction of the regime was to issue another institutional act, which modified the party system and the

[75] Lira Neto, *Castelo: a marcha para a ditadura* (São Paulo: Contexto, 2004).
[76] With the move of the federal capital to Brasilia in 1960, the territory that had constituted the old Federal District (the city of Rio de Janeiro) became the state of Guanabara. Then in 1975 the former state of Rio de Janeiro and the Guanabara State were merged into a single state, with the name of Rio de Janeiro, whose state capital was the city of Rio de Janeiro.

entire electoral process. In the future elections for president and governors, the vote would be indirect. Moreover, all the old parties were abolished and a system of only two parties replaced them: one party would be pro government and the other a party of opposition. Thus for two decades traditional parties were eliminated and there was established just two groups, the Renovating National Alliance (*Aliança Renovadora Nacional*, or ARENA) and Democratic Brazilian Movement (*Movimento Democrático Brasileiro*, or MDB); the first congregating the members of the old UDN, giving support to the military government, and the second representing an opposition alliance.[77]

In March 1967, General Costa e Silva assumed the presidency. He was a member of the hard-line group, one of the leaders of the coup, and had been Minister of War in the Castelo Branco administration. His appointment represented a victory of the hard-liners in the military who wanted tougher repression. Under this new presidential mandate relations between the government and civil society grew ever tenser, with great popular protests carried out by students and workers. In its AI-5 act the regime grew ever more authoritarian, consolidating the dictatorship and initiating one of the most repressive and bitter periods in Brazilian history. The military now emphasized the "doctrine of national security," an ideology of the Cold War that Washington promoted throughout the Americas, but that evolved with some special Brazilian aspects as developed by the military's Superior War College (*Escola Superior de Guerra*). It was this doctrine that guided the activities of the National Information Service (*Serviço Nacional de Informações*, or SNI) and of the organs of state repression that were reinforced by military tribunals that now dealt with so-called political crimes. Congress was closed and a severe censorship was imposed even affecting artistic expression in all its forms. The political rights of politicians were annulled, civil servants were dismissed, and university professors expelled. Exile was the destination of thousands of Brazilians including the future president of Brazil Fernando Henrique Cardoso, who was then a professor at the University of São Paulo. The state of law was abolished and as a consequence of this repression there emerged urban terrorism and rural guerrillas, one of whom would become

---

[77] In 1966 there was a movement to group together the opposition to the military regime. A "Broad Front" was created that sought to unite such traditional enemies as Juscelino and Lacerda, who issued the so-called Lisbon Declaration. The following year there was also a meeting between Lacerda and former president Goulart, who was also in exile. Throughout 1967 and 1968 the Broad Front seemed to gain political support, but Lacerda was outlawed (*cassado*) in 1968 and the Broad Front was declared illegal.

another future president of Brazil, Dilma Rousseff, who was eventually imprisoned by the regime. Despite the low risk that this armed opposition represented for the regime, it served to justify even more the repressive acts carried out by the military in its campaign against "communism" and subversion.[78]

In 1969, President Costa e Silva suffered a heart attack. It was assumed that he would be replaced by his civilian vice president, but the military changed the rules and imposed General Emílio Garrastazu Médici as president with a mandate of five years. To give some legitimacy to the electoral process, Congress, which had been closed since the issuance of act AI-5, was reopened and it proceeded to elect the president indicated by the Junta Militar. Médici would create the most closed and repressive military regime in Brazilian history. He was president from October 1969 until March 1974. These would be years of great economic euphoria with high rates of growth. The rapid growth provided a better standard of living for the middle class, and job creation in the labor market incorporated large parts of the population. It was also a period of increasing concentration of income. These results gave the government relative popularity, despite its fierce censorship, repression, and constant violation of individual rights. In contrast to other military governments, that of Médici intensively used the media to sell the image that Brazil was a country that was progressing rapidly and would soon become a world power.

In spite of the relative success of the hard-line group, Médici was replaced by General Ernesto Geisel, who pertained to the moderate officer group led by Castelo Branco. Upon assuming power, Geisel promised to return the government to civilian rule. It is evident that this shift of elements of the Brazilian armed forces for a democratic solution was linked to several basic developments. The first was the growing corruption of the officers in government and the strong wage inequality that developed in favor of junior officers employed in the federal civilian agencies, which infuriated more traditional officers who saw the basic integrity of the armed forces and its hierarchical arrangements of power and prestige threatened. Second, there occurred a change in U.S. foreign policy that reduced Washington's support for military regimes. With the Vietnam War and the Watergate scandal in the Nixon administration, the ideology of the Cold War was slowly being challenged in the United States, and

---

[78] The journalist Elio Gaspari launched a series of books on the military period that represents an excellent general vision of those years. See Elio Gaspari, *A ditadura envergonhada* (São Paulo: Companhia da Letras, 2002a); *A ditadura escancarada* (São Paulo: Companhia das Letras, 2002b); *A ditadura encurralada* (São Paulo: Companhia das Letras, 2004); and *A ditadura derrotada* (São Paulo: Companhia das Letras, 2003).

now the leaders in Washington were less willing to support or tolerate the military regimes that, in previous decades, had been made with American support throughout Latin America. This change was made with the election of Jimmy Carter in 1976.

For the return to democracy, Geisel proposed a process of "opening" – called the *abertura*, which, however, would be slow, gradual, and secure. But the military hard-liners did not want any change toward liberalization, and the government lost control over the organs of repression. Despite the censorship, soon there were also discussed serious cases of corruption. Although Geisel wanted a gradual return to the barracks, he could not challenge the more radical officers for fear of losing control over the process. Moreover, in the economic area Geisel confronted a critical situation as a result of the first oil shock of 1973. Maintaining high indices of growth was essential for the viability of the policy of gradual democratization.

The Geisel administration would be marked by advances and setbacks. Some questioned the feasibility of implementing a true democracy with free elections and real democratic contests. Many believed that the regime would institutionalize a system with a strong authoritarian structure, like the one that still existed in Portugal.[79] There was a debate about the viability of a two-party or multiparty system and even the possibility of establishing a single-party state was proposed. For many, the strength of the official party, which included intimidation of voters, changes in electoral rules, and the muzzling of the opposition leaders indicated that the regime was headed for a one-party solution. The results of the elections of 1970 seemed to point to this outcome. In 1974, however, the situation changed when the opposition won the most significant federal and state legislative elections. It was a surprise because the government believed that the ARENA would win, but the election results showed the total public opposition to the regime.

Even when Geisel began the opening process it was difficult to predict the future of democracy in Brazil, since the transition that began in 1974 was only concluded in 1985. The frequent setbacks that occurred questioned the viability of the ongoing process. The outcome of the conflict between moderate and hard-line officers would become important to the process of the "*abertura*" and the final format that it would take. Despite the commitment by Geisel, torture continued and was clearly out

---

[79] There is an interesting debate on the regime and its institutionalization in Alfred Stepan, ed., *Authoritarian Brazil: Origins, Policies and Future* (New Haven, CT: Yale University Press, 1973).

of control, causing deaths that would have a strong negative impact on public opinion nationally and internationally. At one point he had to take the risk of firing the Minister of the Army to end the defiance of these antidemocratic military and paramilitary extremists. However, clashes with the hard-line officers and the need to maintain the electoral process led to delays in the process of redemocratization.

In 1976, there were municipal elections. The government consistently favored their own candidates, but the opposition was victorious in the major cities. Despite all the economic growth that occurred, the middle class was clearly against the regime, and even business leaders were beginning to express dissatisfaction. In 1977, the government responded to the opposition victory and increasing civilian pressure by adopting the so-called civil package in April. Congress was closed and new measures were introduced to prevent the opposition from gaining power in an arbitrary modification of the electoral rules. The new rules imposed were intended solely to secure the government party victory at the next election. The governors would continue to be elected indirectly, and a third of the Senate would be chosen the same way. These two steps ensured that the ARENA would have a majority in Congress and the election of governors would be controlled by the federal government. Moreover, the military changed the representation in the Chamber of Deputies, distorting the proportionality between the population of states and the number of deputies that they would be entitled to elect. It increased the minimum number of elected representatives of the smaller states and imposed a ceiling on the number of those elected from more populous states, reducing the representation of larger units of the federation. This created a regional distortion in the Chamber, which continues until today. The representation of the north-northeast is proportionally much greater than that of the more modern and richer south-southeast region. The new electoral law further restricted the access of the opposition to the media and extended the presidential term to six years.

But there were also positive developments. Before the completion of his mandate, Geisel repealed the AI-5 act that was one of the foundations of the authoritarian regime. He reinstated habeas corpus, removed prior press censorship, and returned to an independent judiciary. In addition, there were changes in the National Security Act, making it less comprehensive. Finally, Geisel returned political rights to most of the opposition figures who had suffered from those arbitrary measures.

The reawakening of an independent trade union movement was another important development that occurred in the period of the Geisel government. Since the early days of the authoritarian regime, the military had kept the urban and rural unions under strict government control, intervening in the majority of them and annulling the rights of most active union leaders. In cities, the union structure established by Vargas remained fairly stable, giving the state the power to manipulate unions through the appointment of *"pelegos"* or scab union leaders named by the state. In the rural area the active peasant leagues that existed before the military coup had been destroyed. With the Geisel government, however, appeared new union leadership in the urban and rural areas. In the latter were formed new peasants groups free from government intervention and closely linked to the Catholic Church. In the cities there arose a new, independent leadership, and a new wave of strikes occurred. Ten years after the violent repression of strikes of Osasco and Contagem (1968), the workers of the automobile factories in the ABC district in the greater São Paulo metropolitan area went on strike and stopped production.[80] The leader of the strike movement was Luiz Inacio da Silva, or Lula, then president of the Metalworkers Union of São Bernardo do Campo and Diadema who would later become president of the republic.[81] To avoid violent confrontations, workers adopted peaceful tactics and negotiated directly with employers. At the same time, the strike and its positive outcome were seen as an important step in a return to democracy and had the support of broad segments of civil society, especially the Church, which was very active throughout the process of democratization.

In 1978 Geisel succeeded in maintaining the power of the moderates by selecting General João Baptista Figueiredo (then chief of SNI) as his successor. This election represented the definitive overthrow of the

---

[80] The ABC district is the name given to the conglomerate of three municipalities (Santo André, São Bernardo, and São Caetano) in the greater São Paulo metropolitan region where the automobile industry was concentrated in its initial phase. It was here as well that the most active centers of unionism were created in Brazil. Lula was the president of the metal workers union of São Bernardo do Campo and Diadema. For a survey of these developments, see John D. French, *The Brazilian Workers' ABC: Class Conflict and Alliances in Modern São Paulo* (Chapel Hill: University of North Carolina Press, 1992).

[81] The metalworkers' strikes of Osasco and Contagem, both in 1968, were the last after the 1964 coup. Ten years later, the strike movement emerged in the industrial regions of São Paulo. On the history of this movement see Ricardo Antunes and Arnaldo Gonçalves, *Por um novo sindicalismo* (São Paulo: Editora Brasiliense, 1980); André Luis Corrêa da Silva, "'João Ferrador na República de São Bernardo': O impacto do 'novo' movimento sindical do ABC Paulista no processo de transição democrática (1977–1980)" (MA thesis, Porto Alegre, Universidade Federal do Rio Grande do Sul, 2006); and French, *The Brazilian Workers' ABC*.

hard-liners in the army. Figueiredo assumed office in March 1979 promising to continue the opening process. He was determined to transfer his position to a civilian successor, but that would take place in the context of complex political negotiations and in the midst of a serious economic crisis. Figueiredo extended the amnesty program of Geisel, freeing most of the remaining political prisoners. But the civil opposition wanted a complete unrestricted and general amnesty. This came, finally, in 1979, with the government restoring the political rights of all those affected by emergency measures. Despite critics who opposed the granting of amnesty also for the military who had committed acts of repression and torture, the so-called Law of Amnesty represented a major advance in the democratization process and was considered an important achievement of the government. It made possible the return of traditional political leaders, including people who were active members of the Goulart government.

The government's original strategy was to create two parties, with the idea that the military would be able to maintain its power base not only in the period of military rule but also in the period of free civilian elections. But, the ARENA from its inception had little popular support. Its parliamentary majority was only made possible thanks to manipulated changes in the electoral rules that benefited the ruling party and the systematic suppression of political opposition. The opposition seemed able to come to power if there were free and direct elections. Consequently, military leaders decided to support a multiparty solution, hoping to split the opposition into several minor parties – and that's what happened. Several opposition parties were created, but the MDB (unified opposition bloc) survived as the Brazilian Democratic Movement Party (PMDB). Among the various associations created was the Workers' Party (*Partido dos Trabalhadores*, or PT), consisting of the new authentic union leadership under the command of Lula, and including left-wing intellectuals and segments of the urban middle class. The PT was unusual in that it possessed a coherent leadership, ideology, and organization. The other parties, among which was the PMDB, were more fronts than opposition parties organically structured. The ARENA remained unified, but changed its name to the Brazilian Democratic Party (PDS). The extreme right-wing groups were opposed to all these changes and the entire *abertura* process, but would be gradually overcome by the moderates, who managed to complete the transition process.[82]

---

[82] In 1980, there was an attempt to create a climate of terror that culminated in the premature explosion of a bomb in a car at the Riocentro during a popular show. A

Castelo Branco, the first president of the military regime, took power when the country was in deep recession and faced rising inflation. The official analysis of the crisis was provided in the so-called Economic Action Plan of the Government, or PAEG,[83] which identified serious distortions in the economic structure and pointed to a distributive conflict as the main cause of recession and inflation. The distributive conflict occurred because of existing distortions in the productive sector, and excessive pressure on aggregate demand exerted by high public deficits financed by expansion in the money supply, excessive expansion of credit to the private sector, and higher wage demands. The three components created pressure on demand, which when not resolved, manifested itself as a distributive conflict that caused structurally uncontrollable inflation. In the view of those responsible for the economic policy of the new government, economic recovery required the reduction of the public debt, control of private-sector credit, and imposition of limits on wage increases. These technicians also indicated that distortions in the pricing structure of the economy and other problems resulted from inadequate fiscal structure and the rudimentary nature of the financial system. It was claimed that the modernization of these sectors was necessary to restore growth.

With this diagnosis, the government unilaterally put in place a program of stabilization and reforms. Given the authoritarian structure of the government, it could carry out reform with little opposition. The government was very successful in the fiscal area, creating new taxes and instituting an indexation in the economy. The indexation was initially deployed in the correction of tax arrears, increasing fiscal efficiency even with high inflation. This procedure was also used for indexing the federal debt, enabling, for the first time, the sale of medium- and long-term government securities. Indexing in fact explains the formation of a relatively sophisticated capital market in Brazil from the 1970s onward, even though inflation never completely disappeared. If this was a positive aspect of the creation of the monetary correction program, the experience of the 1980s and 1990s show that fighting inflation would be virtually impossible as long as indexing existed. With the changes made in the fiscal area, the deficit was sharply reduced and was now funded primarily

---

captain and a sergeant in the army were involved, and although the government would not arrest anyone, the radical nature of such acts eventually forced the military to crack down on extremist elements.

[83] Celso L. Martone, "Análise do Plano de Ação Econômica do Governo, PAEG (1964–1966)," in *Planejamento no Brasil*, ed. Betty Mindlin Lafer (São Paulo: Perspectiva, 1987), 60–90.

by the placement of public debt, unlike the previous practice of financing through monetization.[84]

There were also several changes in the workplace. Among them, one of the most important was a new wage law because of its immediate impact on the wage growth and income distribution. Before this legislation was passed, salaries had been adjusted annually for the real inflation of the period. The new legislation would correct the wages according to a formula that took into account not only past inflation, but also inflation estimated to occur for the next twelve months.[85] Since future inflation was traditionally underestimated, the new legislation caused systematic wage loss, with negative distributional effects. This deliberate reduction in real wages, the so-called wage squeeze, restricted aggregate demand and the cost of manpower to the private sector. The legislation introduced in a highly repressive regime (which included the control of union activities), caused significant reduction in real wages, and was one of the principal causes for the success of the stabilization program. The real annual average minimum salary, for example, indexed at 100 in 1964, fell to 82 in 1977 (see Graph 3.16). Such a wage repression would have been impossible to implement in a democratic regime with free unions.

Along with fiscal and monetary control, the government promoted an extended correction of prices of goods and public services, including abolishing rent controls. This limited the effects of monetary and fiscal control and the wage squeeze on the rate of inflation. But there was an undeniable success in controlling inflation, as can be seen in the change in consumer prices in the city of Rio de Janeiro, which had reached

---

[84] André Lara Resende, "Estabilização e reforma," in *A ordem no progresso*, ed. Marcelo de Paiva Abreu (Rio de Janeiro: Editora Campus, 1992), 213–232; Mario Henrique Simonsen and Roberto Campos, *A nova economia brasileira* (Rio de Janeiro: José Olympio, 1979); Celso Furtado, *Um projeto para o Brasil* (Rio de Janeiro: Saga, 1968b); Celso Furtado, *Análise do modelo Brasileiro* (Rio de Janeiro: Civilização Brasileira, 1975); Albert Fishlow, "Algumas reflexões sobre a política econômica brasileira após 1964," *Estudos Cebrap* 6 (Janeiro–Março 1974), 5–66; Mario Henrique Simonsen, *Inflação, gradualismo x tratamento de choque* (Rio de Janeiro: Apec, 1970); Albert Fishlow, "A distribuição de renda no Brasil," in *A controvérsia sobre a distribuição de renda e desenvolvimento*, ed. R. Tolipan and A. C. Tinelli (Rio de Janeiro: Zahar, 1975); Paul Singer, *A crise do "Milagre"* (Rio de Janeiro: Paz e Terra, 1977); Antonio Delfim Netto, "Análise do comportamento recente da economia brasileira: diagnóstico" (São Paulo: mimeo, 1967); and Regis Bonelli and Pedro Malan, "Os Limites do Possível: Notas sobre balanço de bagamentos e indústria nos Anos 70," *Pesquisa e Planejamento Econômico* 6,2 (Agosto 1976), 353–406.

[85] Simonsen, *Inflação: Gradualismo x Tratamento de Choque*, 26–27.

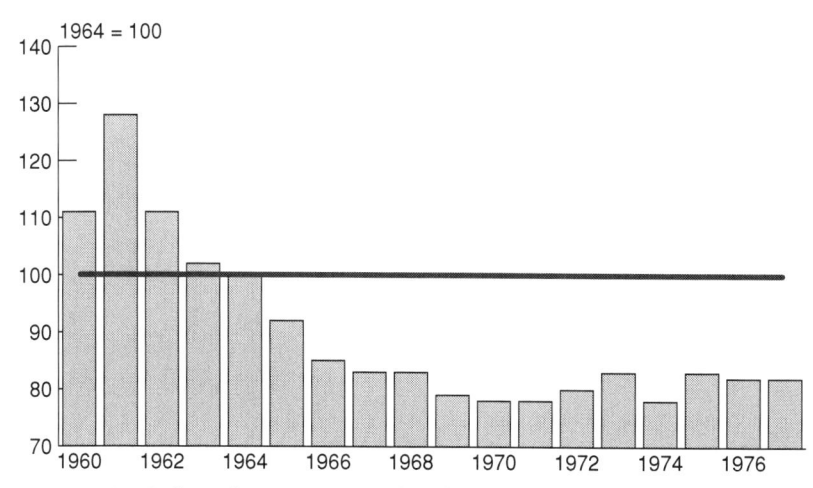

GRAPH 3.16. Index of Minimum Real Salary, 1960–1977. *Source:* Ipeadata, Table "Salário mínimo real"

91 percent in 1964, decreased to 30 percent in 1967. The policies of restricting credit caused a 4.7 percent drop in industrial production in 1965. However, the gross national product (GNP) grew, due to the excellent performance of agriculture that year, and in the following year there was a general recovery as the GNP grew by 6.7 percent despite the temporary decline in agricultural output.

Among the most profound structural changes in the Brazilian economy during the military period, was the creation of a national credit market. In 1964, when the military seized power, the economic authorities had identified the limitations in this sector, which needed to be resolved in order to implement the ambitious program of stabilization and growth that they wanted to develop. The government lacked effective management tools for an appropriate monetary and credit policy. The legal framework was outdated, the functions of a central bank were dispersed among various agencies that were not always in coordination,[86] and, despite rising inflation, the "usury laws" limited the interest rates that could be charged. Savers had limited options for financial investments and rarely had income above inflation. The new government launched a major reform in the existing very inadequate system. It created the Central Bank, giving it the functions of monetary policy coordination and supervision of the

---

[86] Before the creation of the Banco Central the role of monetary authority was carried out by the SUMOC division of the Banco do Brasil and by the National Treasury.

financial system. Furthermore, it completely reorganized the financial market and created a capital market, which had been virtually nonexistent until then in the country. Through the complete reorganization of the financial system and with the institution of monetary correction, there surged a market for medium- and long-term credit and the foundation of the market for public debt. In the same period, there was a new scheme for financing mortgages, with the creation of the National Housing Bank (*Banco Nacional da Habitação*, or BNH) and its agents in the financial sector. The funds for housing were generated through a national system of forced savings. Until 1963, dismissed employees were compensated by payment of one month's salary for each year of service. After ten years of employment the employer was required to double this compensation. This tended to limit the mobility of labor. This system was abolished in 1966 and replaced by the Guarantee Fund for Length of Service (*Fundo de Garantia do Tempo de Serviço*, or FGTS) with funding by a payroll tax of 8 percent paid by the employers. The fund was to be used as a type of unemployment insurance for any workers fired – under the now much-looser forms of labor tenure being enacted – or could be used as a reserve fund for the worker for retirement or housing purchases. Most of the monies collected went to the national housing bank BNH to promote a major expansion of home construction.[87] These funds became crucial in developing urban housing as the cities of Brazil massively expanded in this period and represented the main source of funding for the construction of housing and sanitation.[88]

Furthermore, the indexing was extended to the financial sector, which started to operate with real interest rates. Based on past inflation, the government promoted the monthly index of restatement, which corrected the assets and liabilities indexed. Thus government securities and assets and long-term liabilities were protected from inflation, allowing real interest rates to function.

In 1967, when General Costa e Silva took office, the economy showed signs of recession because of the wage squeeze and the restrictive measures to curb inflation that had been taken at the end of the Castelo Branco government. Industry, for example, which in 1966 presented the extraordinary growth of 11.7 percent, in the following year slowed to

---

[87] James Malloy, *The Politics of Social Security in Brazil* (Pittsburgh, PA: University of Pittsburgh Press, 1979), 125–126.
[88] Francisco Vidal Luna and Herbert S. Klein, *Brazil since 1980* (New York: Cambridge University Press, 2006), Chapter 3.

just 2.2 percent.[89] But the authoritarian regime needed political legitimacy, and the only way to get it was though economic growth. This need became the fundamental objective of the government of Costa e Silva and his successor, General Médici. It was the most repressive period of military rule, extending from 1967 to 1973. It was also the time of the "economic miracle," so called because of high growth rates. Costa e Silva appointed Antonio Delfim Netto as head of the Treasury, and the new minister directed all his efforts to increase growth. Benefiting from the stabilization and reforms undertaken by the previous government, he established new incentives and subsidies and took advantage of the massive overcapacity in the productive sector and the favorable conditions in international markets to give a major boost to this effort. The government immediately carried out a frankly expansionary economic policy, but at the same time implemented a complex system of price controls. It also created an extensive system of subsidies for certain areas of the economy, especially for agriculture and for exports.

In establishing direct incentives for agriculture, the government created a sophisticated scheme of subsidized credit, which enabled agriculture to achieve rapid rates of growth. The reasoning behind this new policy was quite clearly related to industrial growth. Agricultural subsidies were granted to reduce the cost of food, an important component of price indices and therefore the cost of labor. Thus began a complex process of agro-industrial integration, with agriculture representing a significant market for domestic industry and an increasingly important part of Brazilian exports.

To avoid the traditional external strangulation in the export sector, the government introduced mechanisms to encourage the export of manufactured goods, which hitherto had little weight in Brazilian exports. In addition to credit, subsidies, and abundant tax incentives, exports now relied on a realistic and relatively stable exchange rate thanks to a system of periodic mini-devaluations linked to the differential between internal and external inflation, which provided protection to exporters against large swings between the local and international prices.

In the 1960s and 1970s, significant changes occurred in the stock market as well. The stock exchanges were reorganized, and there now emerged investment banks and brokerage firms. There was also established sophisticated new regulation in this area, which included the

---

[89] Ipeadata. IBGE/SCN: PIB da indústria de transformação, valor adicionado, valor real anual.

creation of the Securities and Exchange Commission, or CVM, founded in 1976 with functions similar to the Securities and Exchange Commission in the United States.[90] In the same year there was also approved a new Corporate Law code that was designed to better meet the needs of the capital market, especially as concerned the rights of minority shareholders. The administration also created tax incentives for businesses and investors that operated in the stock market. But this action, except for a short-term bubble, was of little importance in mobilizing resources to meet the capital needs of companies in Brazil. At this time there were relatively few publicly traded corporations, and even those that existed were accustomed to offer some of their shares without voting rights. The typical private company had its capital owned or controlled by a family or by a limited group of shareholders who owned a majority of shares entitled to vote. Only with the privatization of the state enterprises in the 1990s was there an increase in the number of firms that had shared control, professional management, expanded rights for minority shareholders, and with a concern with corporate governance.

In this period in Brazil, the public participated little in the stock market – either on an individual basis or in mutual funds or pensions. Private pension funds appeared in 1977, but few private companies were interested in creating them or in providing supplementary retirement plans to employees. Only the state and some multinational companies created supplementary retirement plans. But by the end of the military era these private pension funds would become increasingly important as investors in the local capital market, taking significant holdings in the capital of several public and private companies.

The federal government, besides conceding credit, incentives, and subsidies to stimulate and direct private investment to priority areas, began to act more intensely through its public enterprises, especially in the areas of infrastructure. The increasing fiscal resources available through the reforms allowed the government to participate in a decisive way in the new investments required by the expanding economy. Through the control and management of prices, the broad system of incentives and subsidies and direct action by the government, the state began to exercise great control over key decisions in either the public or private economic

---

[90] The CVM has the regulatory function of developing the capital market, monitoring the stock markets and the public companies. Before its creation such functions were performed by the Capital Markets Board of the Central Bank of Brazil (*Diretoria de Mercado de Capitais do Banco Central do Brasil*).

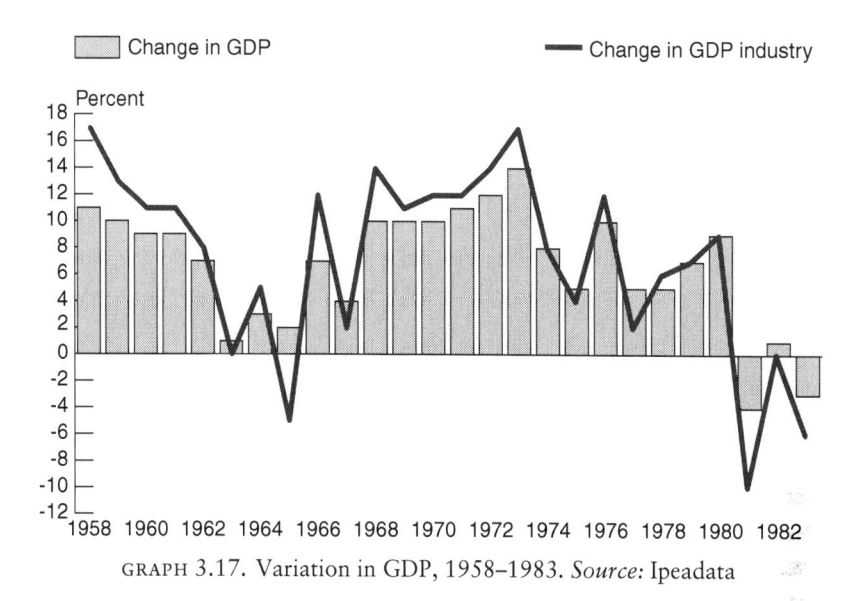

GRAPH 3.17. Variation in GDP, 1958–1983. *Source:* Ipeadata

sectors. In Brazil, few private projects were initiated without the approval of some government institution in order to obtain credit, import licenses, or get tax subsidies. Moreover, few products escaped the price controls. Finally, the state was the major producer of electricity, steel, minerals, fuels, fertilizers, and chemicals, among other inputs; controlled port services, telecommunications, and railways; and exercised a key role in the credit system.

In the industrial sector, the production of durable consumer goods grew strongly, through the increase of the consumer market (particularly as a result of the growing middle class) and by creating a new system of consumer credit, which allowed for the sale of a wide range of products, including cars. Although the expansion of employment entailed rapid increase in the number of employees, maintenance of the wage squeeze and the repression of trade unions meant that wages remained low. The real value of the minimum wage decreased by 34 percent between April 1964 and April 1973.[91]

Between 1967 and 1973, GDP grew at an average annual rate of 10 percent, and industry exhibited an even higher rate of growth (see Graph 3.17 and Appendix Table A.3).[92] The economy was modernized,

[91] Ipeadata. Salário mínimo real, mensal, valor real em R$. Ver também gráfico 3.18.
[92] Ipeadata. IBGE/SCN: PIB, variação real anual, e PIB da indústria de transformação, valor adicionado, valor real anual.

198   *The Economic and Social History of Brazil since 1889*

and given the rapid growth there was significant incorporation of new workers into the formal labor market and the consolidation of a middle segment of consumers. Besides the success of the economic policy adopted domestically, Brazil benefited from a period of strong international growth, when during this period most Latin American countries grew at very high rates.

There are two fundamental criticisms of the economic policies followed by the government at that time. The first is that growth was accompanied by a process of concentration of income that occurred for several reasons, particularly because of the restrictive wage policy that prevented the productivity gains of the economy being transferred to the workers, which reinforced the profound inequality existing in the distribution of income in Brazilian society. The government challenged such arguments, claiming that the increase in concentration that occurred was a transient phenomenon caused by the concentration process.[93]

The process of increasing foreign debt represented the other downside of the growth policy adopted by the military regime in that period. Brazilian economic crises were typically generated in the external sector. At the beginning of the Costa e Silva government, the country was vulnerable to such a crisis of this kind because of its low level of reserves. This explains why the government greatly stimulated exports and opened the country to foreign capital in the form of direct investment and foreign loans. Because of their lower cost and longer terms, there was a great effort made to attract these private funds from abroad. This policy fundamentally

---

[93] During this period, there was extensive debate about the concentration of income. The government claimed that the high degree of inequality in income distribution was a transitory phenomenon, caused by the growth process. Economists, in turn, had different opinions. Some argued that there were structural reasons for this distorted distribution and that it would not be eliminated by growth. Others attributed the blame for the concentration of income to the policy adopted by the government wage squeeze. On this theme, see Carlos G. Langoni, *Distribuição de renda e desenvolvimento econômico no Brasil* (Rio de Janeiro: Expressão e Cultura, 1973); Albert Fishlow, "Brazilian Size Distribution of Income," *American Economic Review* 62,1–2 (March 1972), 391–402; Edmar L. Bacha and Lance Taylor, "Brazilian Income Distribution in the 1960s: 'Facts', Model Results and the Controversy," in *Models of Growth and Distribution for Brazil*, ed. Lance Taylor et al. (New York: Oxford University Press, 1980); Lauro R. A. Ramos and José Guilherme Almeida Reis, "Distribuição da renda: aspectos teóricos e o debate no Brasil," in *Distribuição de renda no Brasil*, ed. José Marcio Camargo and Fabio Giambiagi (Rio de Janeiro: Paz e Terra, 2000), 21–45. Baer shows that between 1960 and 1970, the 40 percent poorest part of the population gained 11.2 percent in income, while the 40 percent richest group increased theirs by 27.4 percent; in 1970 the poorest group saw their income fall by 9 percent, while the richest ones increased theirs by 36.3 percent. Baer, *A economia brasileira*, 98.

changed the structure of the Brazilian external debt. Until then, this debt had been based on official sources of credit that were obtained at fixed interest rates. A new type of debt (which included the funding of state industries) was based on international private bank credit with floating and relatively high interest rates compared to those charged by international agencies. The increase in foreign debt and its floating interest rates meant that the country would become more vulnerable to future changes in the international financial market. And already in the decade of the 1970s, despite the rapid growth of the advanced economies, there were signs of deterioration in that scenario, with rising inflation that even affected the richest countries, and resulting fluctuations in their currencies. The first oil shock (1973) was a clear sign of the next crisis, which manifested itself in the 1980s.

The "economic miracle" occurred in the most reactionary period of the military regimes. At a time when the opposition and the press were muzzled and trade unions controlled, the government's only goal was to show growth at any cost. It did not admit criticism, even unbiased ones, pointing to errors in its economic policy. Even the academic debate was silenced and kept out of the media by the regime. The authoritarianism permeated all levels of government, at a time when it promoted a wide range of investments in the productive sector (with incentives and subsidies to the private sector), when it manipulated the main sources of long and short credit, controlled prices and wages, and managed the exchange rate. These policies increased distortions in the economy, and the society became more unjust because of an economic policy that increased the concentration of wealth. The authoritarianism of economic policy is evident in the handling of the inflation index in 1973. As an annual inflation rate of 12 percent had been predicted for that year, the government simply announced at the end of the year that the inflation rate was 12.6 percent, without showing any relation with the actual variation in prices that year. Subsequent studies have estimated that the inflation rate for that year was 22.5 percent.[94]

---

[94] There occurred an intense debate for and against the model of growth adopted in the period of the "economic miracle." Some of the principal works produced in this period are Delfim Netto, "Análise do comportamento recente da economia brasileira: diagnóstico"; Simonsen, *Inflação, gradualismo x tratamento de choque*; Furtado, *Análise do modelo brasileiro*; Bonelli and Malan, "Os limites do possível: notas sobre balanço de pagamento e indústria nos anos 70," 355–406; Maria da Conceição Tavares and José Serra, "Mais além da estagnação," in *Da substituição de importações ao capitalismo financeiro*, ed. Maria da Conceição Tavares (Rio de Janeiro: Zahar, 1972),

Billions of U.S. dollars

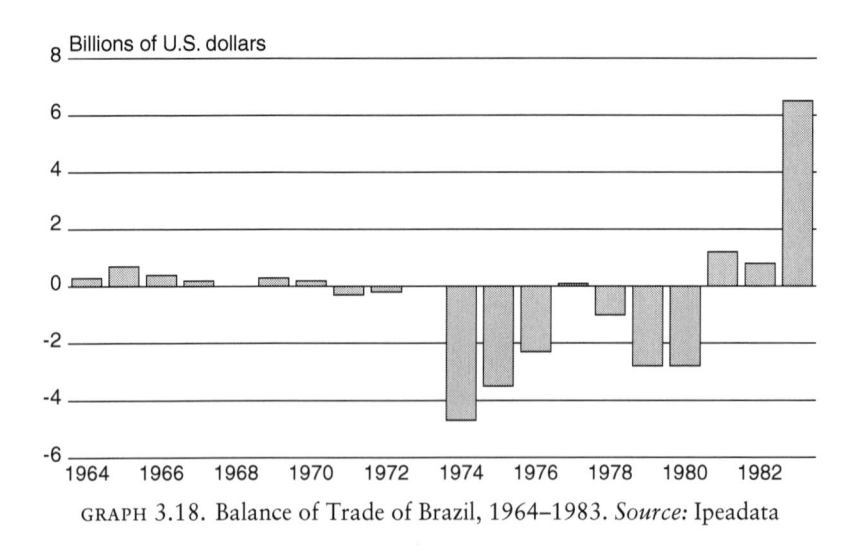

GRAPH 3.18. Balance of Trade of Brazil, 1964–1983. *Source:* Ipeadata

In 1974 the moderate wing of the military represented by General Geisel came to power. Their basic purpose was to open the political system, and to legitimize that opening, they needed to obtain high rates of economic growth. Recessive stabilization plans would not be politically acceptable and would compromise the basic goal of his government defined as a "slow gradual and safe opening." The oil shock of 1973 had greatly affected the country since it imported 73 percent of its petroleum needs. The trade balance had been relatively stable until 1973, but in the following year it showed a deficit of just under U.S.$5 billion, with exports of U.S.$8 billion. Obviously, a deficit was exceptional, considering the size of the Brazilian foreign trade, and was explained by the importation of about U.S.$3 billion in oil and oil products, generating a deficit of more than 6 percent of GDP in the current account. Meanwhile, inflation peaked at 30 percent annually, clearly having resumed its upward trend (see Graph 3.18 and Appendix Table A.2).

153–207; Maria da Conceição Tavares, "Sistema financeiro e o ciclo de expansão recente," in *Desenvolvimento capitalista no Brasil: ensaios sobre a crise*, Vol. 2, ed. Luiz Belluzzo and Renata Coutinho (São Paulo: Brasiliense, 1982), 107–138; Luiz Aranha Correa do Lago, "A retomada do crescimento e as distorções do 'milagre': 1967–1973," in *A ordem no progresso*, ed. Marcelo de Paiva Abreu (Rio de Janeiro: Editora Campus, 1992), 233–294; Antonio Barros de Castro and Francisco Eduardo Pires de Souza, *A economia brasileira em marcha forçada* (Rio de Janeiro: Paz e Terra, 1988).

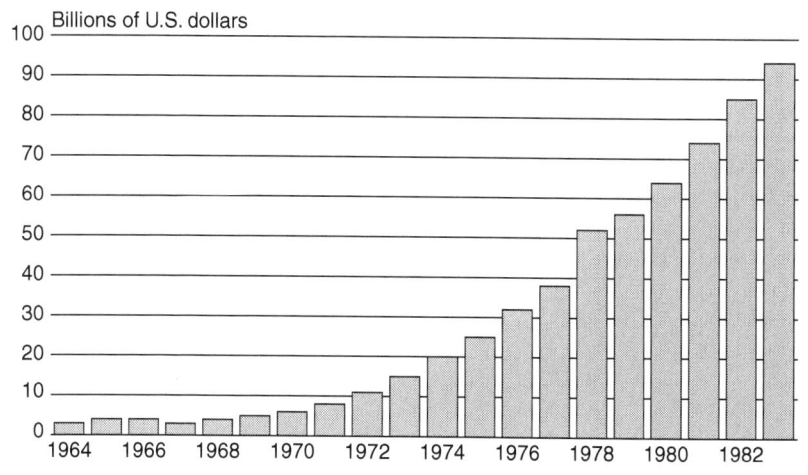

GRAPH 3.19. Foreign Debt of Brazil, 1964–1983. *Source:* Ipeadata, Table "Dívida externa anual"

Most countries affected by the oil crisis adopted recessionary programs, seeking to constrain domestic demand and adjust the economy to the new situation of expensive energy. These importing countries also had to transfer a considerable part of their income to oil-exporting countries. The Brazilian government followed an alternative path, stimulating the economy and developing an ambitious investment program aimed at increasing the domestic supply of capital goods and basic consumer items, thus reducing dependence on imports. The abundance of foreign capital from the recycling of resources generated by oil-exporting countries made it possible for Brazil to follow that path through international borrowing. This was, however, at the cost of an increasing internal and external debt, accelerating inflation and depleting the financial capacity of the state through the administration of a generalized system of subsidies (see Graph 3.19 and Appendix Table A.2).

The Second National Development Plan (II PND), which had established these investment programs, led to major advances in Brazil's production base, resulting in the creation of a complex sector producing capital goods and basic inputs. This allowed Brazil not only to replace imports, but also export part of its manufacturing output. Although the international economic scene showed worrying signs, the PND II projected an optimistic growth trend. Some industries such as pulp and paper showed excellent growth, becoming important export items. In other cases, there were delays in implementation of projects or errors of judgment as to the future conduct of the national and international economies. Typical of these fiascos were an expensive and inefficient nuclear program, the Steel Railway, which was a new railroad line to carry iron ore to the ports and the large steel plant (Açominas). With critical opinion and the opposition muzzled, there was no effective way to challenge the viability of these projects.[95]

In agriculture it sought to modernize a conservative agriculture without changing the structure of landownership and labor relations. The new government saw in agriculture a major source of inflationary pressure because of its deficiencies in supplying the domestic market. Improving the supply and reducing the costs of food were essential to curb urban wage pressures. In an underdeveloped country like Brazil, with low average wages and poorly distributed income, food was a basic component of the cost of living and therefore had a strong impact on the formation of real wages.

The modernization of agriculture occurred with highly concentrated landownership, the legacy of the colonial latifundia system.[96] Compared to most Latin American countries, Brazil had never had a genuine process of agrarian reform or the free distribution of land for economic exploitation. In the countryside the land traditionally represented power and a reserve value. Ownership and economic exploitation were not usually associated. Until the middle of the last century unproductive latifundia and archaic work relations dominated. In the 1950s and 1960s the deficient structure of agriculture was identified as a major constraint to sustainable development of the country, since it restricted the expansion of productive forces and allowed the survival of a conservative and outdated power structure. The concentration of land, besides being politically conservative and socially harmful, hindered the modernization of agriculture

---

[95] On the Geisel period, see Castro and Souza, *A economia brasileira em marcha forçada*; Dionísio Dias Carneiro, "Crise e esperança: 1974–1980," in *A ordem do progresso*, ed. Marcelo de Paiva Abreu (Rio de Janeiro: Editora Campus, 1992), 295–322; Rogério Werneck, *Empresas estatais e política macroeconômica* (Rio de Janeiro: Campus, 1987); Pedro Cezar Dutra Fonseca and Sergio Marley Modesto Monteiro, "O Estado e suas razões: o II PND," *Revista de Economia Política* 28,1 (109) (Janeiro–Março 2007), 28–46; and João P. dos Reis Velloso, "A fantasia política: a nova alternativa de interpretação do II PND," *Revista de Economia Política* 18,2 (70) (1998), 133–144; Castro and Souza, *A economia brasileira em marcha forçada*, 74.

[96] On this theme, see Ruy Cirne Lima, *Pequena História Territorial do Brasil. Sesmarias e Terras Devolutas* (São Paulo: Secretaria do Estado da Cultura, 1990).

which proved incapable of providing an adequate stable and cheap supply of food for the internal market. From 1950 until the military coup of 1964, the proposed solution to the problem was land reform.[97]

The military governments, however, ended the debate on land reform and began to encourage instead the modernization of agriculture through subsidies, price support, and new government credit. The goal was to have plenty of food at low cost, to free rural labor for urban industry, and to open up international markets for agricultural production, using it to generate the foreign exchange needed for growth. But for all the modernization proposed, the government maintained the concentration of landownership and did not challenge the power of the conservative rural elites.

The military support for agricultural modernization included a number of activities. First, was the provision of abundant and subsidized credit. In 1965, the creation of the National Rural Credit (SNCR) provided substantial funding to farmers and represented the government's main instrument in promoting agriculture. Beyond offering credit, it implemented a policy of guaranteed minimum prices and the formation of buffer stocks, which were used to avoid large fluctuations in prices for producers and consumers. Before planting, the government fixed minimum prices for key products, especially those for the domestic market. It funded the production and marketing through the Federal Government Acquisitions Program (AGF) and the Federal Government Loans Program (EGF). An important institution created by the government was the Brazilian Agricultural Research Corporation (Embrapa). Founded in 1973, it played and continues to play a key role in the modernization of Brazilian agriculture.

---

[97] On the debates concerning the factors that influenced the evolution of Brazilian agriculture see José Pastore, Guilherme L. Silva Dias, and Manoel C. Castro, "Condicionantes da produtividade da pesquisa agrícola no Brasil," *Estudos Econômicos* 6,3 (1976), 147–181; Charles Mueller and George Martine, "Modernização agropecuária, emprego agrícola e êxodo rural no Brasil – a década de 1980," *Revista de Economia Política* 17,3 (Julho–Setembro 1997), 85–104; Rodolfo Hoffmann, "Evolução da distribuição da posse de terra no Brasil no período 1960–80," *Reforma Agrária* 12,6 (Novembro–Dezembro 1982), 17–34; Carlos Nayro Coelho, "70 anos de política agrícola no Brasil, 1931–2001," *Revista de Política Agrícola* 10,3 (Julho–Setembro 2001), 695–726; Affonso Celso Pastore, "A resposta da produção agrícola aos preços no Brasil" (PhD thesis, Economics, USP, 1969); Alberto Passos Guimarães, *Quatro séculos de latifúndio* (Rio de Janeiro: Paz e Terra, 1977); and Ruy Muller Paiva, "Reflexões sobre as tendências da produção, da produtividade e dos preços do setor agrícola no Brasil," in *Agricultura subdesenvolvida*, ed. F. Sá (Petrópolis: Vozes, 1968), 167–261.

The rural credit system was based on public resources, through the "Account Movement" of the Bank of Brazil or transfers from the Central Bank, and also from "Liabilities," which corresponded to a proportion of deposits commercial banks had to apply in loans for agriculture. The operation of the Account Movement, which represented an automatic discount of the Bank of Brazil, gave to this bank a power of currency emission, and represented an effective increase in the money supply.[98] The subsidy in credit came from the setting of interest rates in nominal terms, usually below inflation. During the 1970s, the volume of credit multiplied by four, having its best year in 1979. The abundance and negative cost of government credit to the producer funded the modernization of agriculture in terms of equipment and supplies. In the 1970s, an industrial complex in Brazil tied to agriculture was established that supplied machinery, implements, fertilizers, and pesticides. In fact the demand generated by agricultural modernization was an important factor in the rapid industrial development of that period. Between 1960 and 1980, cultivated lands almost doubled from 25 million to 47 million hectares, and this was accompanied by increased mechanization. In the same period, the number of hectares per tractor declined from 410 to just 99. The average consumption of fertilizers per hectare rose from 8.3 kilos in 1964 to 27.8 in 1970 and to 88 in 1980.[99]

Thus the government promoted three key proagricultural policies: subsidized credit, minimum prices, and the buying of buffer stocks. The agricultural products market was highly regulated, particularly for the domestic market; national production was protected by tariffs and prior import authorizations, which made the market virtually immune to foreign competition. Thus the government both guaranteed income to producers and consumer price stability. It also helped the producer by controlling the

---

[98] With the creation of the Central Bank the Bank of Brazil should have lost the function of monetary authority. But in the Central Bank's early stages, when it had no operational structure, the Bank of Brazil held various operational functions on behalf of the Central Bank. The Account Movement was created to account for the financial relationship between the Bank of Brazil, the National Treasury, and the Central Bank and, although transient, was only abolished in 1986. Interestingly, while the Bank of Brazil held powers of the Monetary Authority, the Central Bank of Brazil had an Agricultural Credit Board, which gave it a role as a Development Bank.

[99] There are a good series of data on agriculture in the sites of the following institutions: Ministério da Agricultura, available at www.agricultura.gov.br; IBGE (*Estatísticas do século XX*, available at www.ibge.gov.br); Banco Central, available at www.bcb.gov.br/?RELRURAL; and Ipeadata (Temas: Produção, available at http://ipeadata.gov.br/epeaweb.dll/epeadata?523053171).

price of inputs. Even the products destined for foreign markets experienced strong government intervention. Besides controlling the exchange rate (a variable essential for exportable items), the government established norms for exports, in many cases carried out by the action of important public bodies such as the Institute of Sugar and Alcohol (IAA) and the Brazilian Coffee Institute (IBC).[100] In the case of sugar and alcohol, the government operated a complex system that controlled the production per plant, granted subsidies to compensate for regional differences in productivity, and determined export quotas. Wheat was under another system of complex control by the federal government, which was responsible for internal and external purchases of wheat and regulated its supply for the flour mills of the country, also through a quota system. As the domestic producers of wheat were not competitive, the government controlled imports, bought wheat at prices that reflected the high costs of domestic production, and sold the final product to consumers through subsidies, to avoid the impact that the sale of such an important item would have on the indices of consumer prices.[101] These support policies stimulated the modernization of agriculture in terms of machinery, implements, fertilizers, and pesticides, but created distortions in resource allocation and discouraged potentially greater increases in productivity.

In addition to the incentives for the credit and the minimum price policy, the federal government, under the leadership of *Embrapa (Empresa Brasileira de Pesquisa Agropecuária)*, implemented a major research program crucial to the ability of Brazilian agriculture to modernize itself. With a focus on agribusiness, the goal was to provide solutions for the development of agriculture through the generation, adaptation, and transfer of scientific and technological knowledge.[102] In retrospect, the

---

[100] The two institutes were closed at the beginning of the decade of the 1990s.
[101] On the transformations that then occurred, see Guilherme Leite da Silva Dias and Cicely Moutinho Amaral, "Mudanças estruturais na agricultura brasileira, 1980–1998," in *Uma década de transição*, ed. Renato Baumann (Rio de Janeiro: Campus/Cepal, 2000), 223–253; Guilherme Delgado, "Expansão e modernização do setor agropecuário no pós-guerra: um estudo da reflexão agrária," *Estudos Avançados USP* 15,43 (Setembro–Dezembro 2001), 157–172; Eliseu Alves, *Dilema da política agrícola brasileira: produtividade ou expansão da área agricultável* (Brasília: Embrapa, 1983); Fernando B. Homem de Melo, *Agricultura de exportação e o problema da produção de alimentos*, Texto para Discussão 30 (São Paulo: FEA-USP, 1979); and Fernando Homem de Melo, "Composição da produção no processo de expansão da fronteira agrícola brasileira," *Revista de Economia Política* 5,1 (Janeiro–Março 1985), 86–111.
[102] José Garcia Gasques, José Eustáquio, R. V. Filho, and Zander Navarro, eds., *Desempenho e crescimento do agronegócio no Brasil*, Texto para Discussão 1009 (Brasília: IPEA, Fevereiro 2004b); and Eliseu Alves, *A Embrapa e a pesquisa agropecuária*

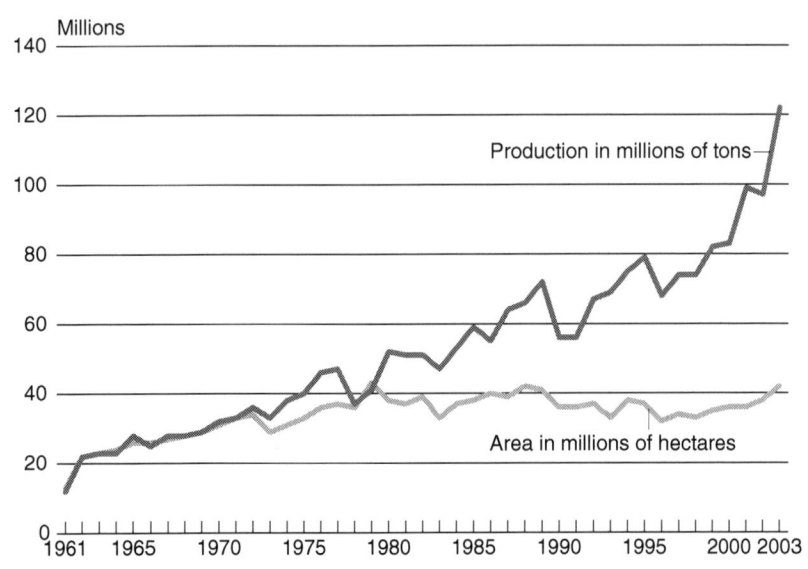

GRAPH 3.20. Grain Production in Brazil, 1961–2003 (wheat, cotton, peanuts, rice, beans, corn, and soybeans). *Source:* Ipeadata

performance of Brazilian agriculture in the period from 1960 to 1980 can be considered reasonably favorable, as it represented the first leap into modernity, with increased acreage as well as increased yield per hectare. The production of grains went from 20 million tons in 1960 to 52 million in 1980. At the same time as there was a duplication of the cultivated area (19 to 38 million hectares), there was also an increase in productivity, making possible a 2.6 multiplication in the volume of crops produced (see Graph 3.20).

Soybeans stood out among the new grains that were part of the new agricultural modernization. Cultivation of soybeans was introduced in the late 1950s and had already reached the level of 15 million tons output in 1980, when it was exceeded only by corn. Among other items that began to be exported on a large scale at that time were processed oranges. There was a remarkable increase in orange production in Brazil and the export

no Brasil (Brasília: Embrapa, 1980). With 37 research centers and a presence in all states of Brazil, Embrapa has as its objective not only applied research but also the dissemination of that research throughout Brazilian agriculture. The introduction of new seeds in various segments, increasing the productive capacity of the *cerrado*, and increased livestock productivity are examples of results from the research at Embrapa and the institution's ability to teach new technology to farmers and ranchers in Brazil.

of processed orange juice to the international market. Sugar cane also had strong growth, especially after the implementation of the Alcohol Program, a program for replacement of gasoline by that of renewable ethanol fuel.

Even a traditional crop like wheat was transformed by strong government incentives. Thanks to government support the Brazilian harvest of this cereal, usually supplemented by imports, greatly increased in volume and productivity. In the mid-1980s, national production finally managed to meet most of the domestic consumption for the first time in modern history. However, other commodities did not show such positive results. The corn and rice harvests almost doubled in this period, but with little increase in productivity. The production of beans and cassava, essential items in the national diet, not only did not increase in productivity, but output did not increase in volume.

At the end of the Geisel government, the country had already undergone profound transformations in its economy, but remained vulnerable in financial terms. State support had completed the process of import substitution, creating a fully integrated Brazilian industrial structure, with a new and important sector of capital goods. Brazil now had one of the largest and most integrated industrial complexes in the developing world. However, during this period, Brazil suffered the impact of rising oil prices, the acceleration in international interest rates, and the slow growth of world exports. At the time, the world economies were in the process of adjusting to the new reality of expensive energy and therefore reduced their imports. The Brazilian approach of maintaining the level of economic activity (which was defined by an annual growth rate exceeding 6 percent during that period) produced high deficits in the Current Account Balance that were financed by international resources that were still abundant. The result was a dramatic increase in foreign debt, which multiplied by four, rising from 17 percent to 27 percent of GDP. The international interest rates exceeded 10 percent in 1979 and continued to rise for years to come, affecting most of the Brazilian international debt, which was based on floating interest rates. For this reason, the annual service on the external debt, which was less than U.S.$1 billion in 1973, reached U.S.$5 billion in 1979 and doubled again in 1981. In this last year, the interest payments of foreign debt accounted for half the value of all exports. This set the stage for a Brazilian foreign debt crisis in the context of an international financial market crisis. Moreover, the deterioration of public accounts and the internal price shock caused by high oil prices resulted in higher prices even in rich countries. In Brazil inflation

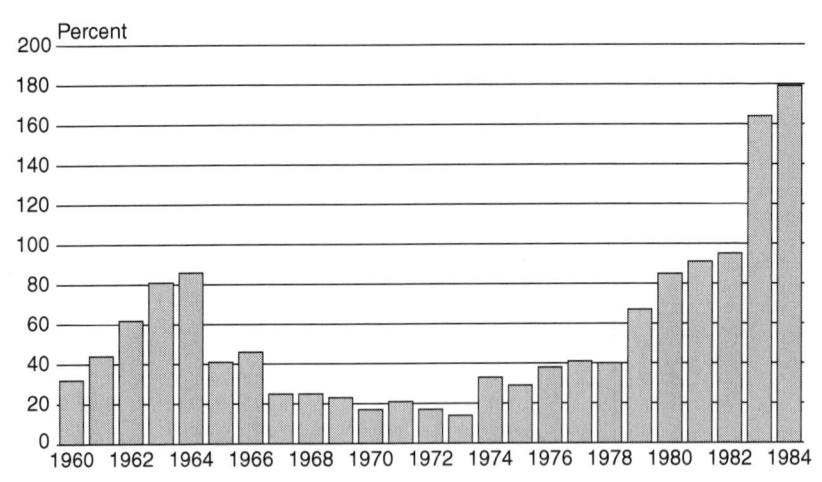

GRAPH 3.21. Annual Variation in the Cost of Living in the City of São Paulo, 1960–1984. *Source:* Ipeadata

resumed its upward trend, rising past 50 percent per annum in 1979 (see Graph 3.21).

The financial sector developed during the military period became extensive, sophisticated, and largely integrated with the international market, despite the persistence of inflation and the external turmoil that periodically affected Brazil. The consolidation of the financial market played a key role in economic performance during the "economic miracle," but suffered severely because of internal imbalances and subsequently suffered deeply the effects of the second oil shock and the "debt crisis" that plagued the international financial market. From the mid-1960s, with the new legislation in place, there developed a tendency to specialize and target market entities, in the tradition of the U.S. financial system. In a few years there appeared a large number of institutions, from investment banks and credit societies to financial and real estate brokerage firms. The process enabled the rapid expansion of the Brazilian financial market, especially the nonbanking segment of that market. Between 1965 and 1973, total financial assets increased from 24 percent to 43 percent of GDP, and lending to the private sector showed a similar increase, exceeding 50 percent in that last year. Conversely, monetary assets, which in 1965 represented 86 percent of all financial assets, was now reduced to 43 percent of all such assets over the same period, despite having increased greatly in absolute terms. This drop in participation was due to the exponential growth of the market for nonfinancial assets, which represented only 4 percent of GDP in 1965 and had risen to 25 percent in 1973. The monetary correction enabled the consolidation of this type of market, and some segments played a crucial role in the rapid growth of the economy. In housing and sanitation, the FGTS, as well as the deposits in savings accounts and real estate bonds, together had assets in 1973 that accounted for 16 percent of total nonmonetary assets. Another important segment was the financing of consumer durables, operated by the credit and finance companies, whose sources were the bills of exchange, which accounted for one-quarter of nonmonetary assets. Another component of such assets was the federal public debt, expressed in Re-adjustable Treasury Bonds (ORTN) certificates, which were issued with a monetary correction clause postfixed, and the National Treasury Bills (LTN), which when created in 1970 had a fixed rate and were more suitable as an instrument of monetary policy. The public debt market was now very important, enabling the financing of budget deficits and the activity of the Central Bank in the money market. The banks were big buyers of these assets, to incorporate them into their own portfolios and made compulsory deposits due on demand deposits – compulsory deposits that, in general, could be made in the form of public debt.[103]

Although the restructuring of the sector was meant to create a market for long-term credit, the results were weak. Investment banks could not establish the necessary mechanisms for long-term loans to become feasible. Only the public sector, through the BNDE and other development banks and institutions, performed these operations, using public or compulsory funds. Until the 1980s, the Central Bank was very active as an agent of development, operating with public funds or transfers of funding from international organizations. The reorganization that then occurred resulted in the transfer of the monetary authority from the Bank of Brazil to the Central Bank, while the activities of the latter, related to the development of industry and the federal public debt, were transferred to the Treasury.

At that time, international credit operations gained importance, and usually were less expensive and provided longer repayment terms. Multinationals and the largest national companies were the main beneficiaries because of their direct access to international banks. The smaller domestic companies depended on the domestic banking system to transfer these resources. The banks obtained these resources in the international

---

[103] Francisco Vidal Luna and Thomaz de Aquino Nogueira Neto, *Correção monetária e mercado de capitais: a experiência brasileira* (São Paulo: Bovespa, 1978).

market and offered credit to the local market, usually at higher cost and with shorter loan terms. These international funds, increasingly sought after by the private and public sectors, account for an important part of the growing foreign debt. Paradoxical as it may seem, this process of external debt also increased the internal debt. The government, on one hand, had a monopoly on foreign exchange reserves and increased its reserves with the dollars received in these transactions. On the other hand, placing the public debt internally was used to sterilize the monetary expansion generated by the purchase of dollars from the private or state enterprises. As the public debt cost more than the yield on reserves, its accumulation represented a cost to the Central Bank or the Treasury. Despite its cost, the accumulation of reserves through domestic borrowing was defended by the economic authorities who claimed that the accumulation of reserves in that period increased the external credibility of the country, offering better credit conditions in international markets.

As previously noted, during the Geisel government, when the first oil crisis occurred, Brazil implemented an ambitious program of investment in basic infrastructure and import substitution industries, which led to huge deficits in current accounts. To stimulate the search for external financial resources, it greatly increased the domestic interest rates. As the state was the main investor, it also became the largest receiver of resources from abroad. Already the private sector, despite the more favorable credit conditions abroad, gradually reduced its liabilities in foreign currency, decreased its investments, and avoided taking on a currency risk in a period of strong external imbalance.

Simultaneously, the state enterprises were forced to accept real declines in rates and prices charged to the public, a policy forced on them by the government in order to contain inflationary pressures, and this reduced their capacity to generate their own resources for investments. This policy of controlling prices for state enterprises forced these public corporations to seek outside funds to finance their investments. The government used the good credit ratings of these state enterprises to obtain external financial resources from abroad. This policy of suppressing the rates and prices that these corporations could charge internally was actually a subsidy to the private sector, and ended up indebting the state by worsening public accounts and increasing the foreign debt of the public sector.

Moreover, there was a mechanism that allowed the transfer of private external debt to the account of the public sector. To encourage the taking of foreign credit by the private sector, the government created a kind of hedge that protected private borrowers from currency risk. The debtors in foreign currency (financial entities and the nonfinancial ones) at any moment could deposit with the Central Bank the value of their foreign debt in national currency. Thus, the private debtor could anticipate the payment owed to foreign creditors in local currency, thus transferring to the Central Bank the responsibility for paying their external debt in foreign currencies. While these operations were in the international market, the borrower assumed responsibility in Brazil in national currency, at the exchange rate on the day of settlement. When the private borrowers saw the risk of sharp devaluation of national currency, they preferred to make the prepayment of their debt through a deposit with the Central Bank. Thus the private sector transferred the currency risk to the Central Bank, especially in periods of great turbulence in the external sector. This was a major instrument of transfer of debt, originally private, into public-sector debt.

Beyond the question of debt, the government needed to decide which index to use in the economy. When inflation reached very high levels, disparity in thousands of prices in the economy increased. With inflation exceeding 30 percent per month, companies or sectors whose prices were lagging could suffer greatly from the correction of its liabilities by an index that did not correspond to the real changes in the selling prices of their goods or their profits. These companies and segments could not afford to correct their liabilities by the restatement that only reflected a rate based on an average change of prices. Slowly, over the course of the 1980s and 1990s, the government assumed part of the obligations for indexing in many areas of the economy. BNDES, which used funds from compulsory savings, limited the index to the percentage of 20 percent, regardless of the rate of indexation for the period. The housing sector, which used funds from the FGTS or from savings accounts, began to correct at below-inflation rates for loans for private home ownership, resulting in losses assumed by the public sector. Agriculture received credit at negative rates. In the long run, part of the indexing of the private sector was taken over by the public sector. Some studies showed that the government operated with a negative spread, because it paid its debt at total monetary correction and high interest, while it managed an extensive system of credit at rates below cost.

By limiting the correction of the outstanding balance of loans in different sectors of the economy, the government was in effect exhausting resources available for new financing, as eventually happened in the housing segment. For several years, it was possible to develop an ambitious program of housing and sanitation. But limiting the correction of the benefits paid by borrowers reduced the return flow of funds, preventing the development of new ventures, especially for low-income families. This lack of public support for housing the poor led to the prevalence of the construction of precarious individual family homes lacking infrastructure and dependent on personal savings for the costs of construction. This deterioration in financial conditions for housing and sanitation is probably one of the causes for the rapid spread of *favelas* all over Brazil.

With rising inflation, consumer credit was dramatically reduced. Individuals who purchased goods that were financed wanted to know how much they would pay for the loan. They feared the lack of income (usually wages) to afford the cost of credit in a system with variable interest rates postfixed. But the market for fixed-rate bonds that would finance these operations were limited to periods of 90 days, there being no fixed supply of credit for six or twelve months. This imbalance between the supply of funds and borrowers preferences considerably reduced borrower loans in the consumer credit market. Brazil became a country where even the purchase of cars was done with one's own resources or short-term credit. And there was never a leasing market. Even the mortgage market, created to finance the construction of housing and sanitation, operated with scarce resources, suffered losses in monetary correction, and thus never created a broad market that could meet the needs of home buyers or resellers. Purchases were usually financed by the buyers' own resources. Moreover, there was no mortgage market that would allow refinancing of housing credit.[104]

In 1979, when Figueiredo assumed the presidency, the country was already extremely vulnerable in terms of internal and international debt, with rising inflation and weak public finances, as it was about to face the second oil shock. During this period, contrary to what occurred with the first oil crisis of 1973, the international markets drastically reduced their supply of resources to debtor countries, which began to have trouble renewing their external loans. Initially, the new Brazilian government formulated an austerity plan, directed by Mario Henrique Simonsen, Minister of Finance. However, the lack of immediate results (particularly as regards the control of inflation) and the political difficulties related to the advancement of democratization made the Figueiredo government

---

[104] The mortgage market in the form that existed in the United States, open to any real estate transaction with a large market and refinancing transactions, has never existed in Brazil, although the mortgage market has grown significantly in recent years, explaining in part the real estate boom that has occurred in Brazil.

abandon the austerity plan. The military then brought back Delfim Netto. In December 1979, Delfim Netto promoted a heterodox policy: carrying out a currency devaluation of 30 percent and, as a way to fight inflation, immediately prefixed the currency devaluation and the index for 1980 (respectively at 45 percent and 40 percent). There was rapid and considerable growth, but inflation soon reached the level of 100 percent, the deficit in current accounts exceeded 5 percent of GDP, and reserves declined by U.S.$3 billion.

Therefore, in the early 1980s, the government was forced to make another radical change in economic policy, following the traditional method of reducing domestic consumption as a way of resolving the crisis in the balance of payments. The second oil shock and rising interest rates in the international market dramatically changed the external conditions affecting the debtor countries. This became clear in the Mexican debt crisis of 1982, with most peripheral countries showing deterioration of external accounts and even rich countries suffering serious consequences. There was recession in most economies, reduced trade between countries, and reduced credit in international financial markets, particularly for indebted countries. The major international banks had problems with their assets, since most of them had significant amounts of credit granted to nations that now were struggling to meet their financial commitments. It was the beginning of the "debt crisis" that would last the entire decade and affect almost all Latin American countries, which were forced to restructure their foreign debt. This broke the long trajectory of growth that these countries had experienced during most of the second half of the twentieth century.

The International Monetary Fund (IMF) began to take a key role in the adjustment process of the most indebted nations. Those who received aid from the IMF were forced to restructure their debt with private banks and had to accept recessive adjustment programs. The logic behind these programs was the same for all countries and was based on the principle that external crises had been stimulated by excessive domestic spending, which caused a deficit in current accounts and in external debt. The idea was to make adjustments in the balance of payments by reducing domestic consumption, in particular reducing public spending. The key variable was called "financing needs of the public sector." The debtor countries needed trade surplus to pay the interest on foreign debt and, if possible, pay off part of the principal. To achieve this plan, it was necessary to drastically reduce domestic consumption through recessionary measures implemented by means of restrictive monetary policy (controlling credit expansion, especially for the public sector, and increasing the interest rate), cuts in public spending, and decreasing consumer demand by controlling wages and increasing taxes on disposable income. Also there should be a balance between income and expenditures in public accounts by cutting spending, especially by the elimination of subsidies and incentives of all kinds. Finally, to stimulate exports, it would be necessary to promote severe devaluation of the exchange. The idea was that recession and devaluation would generate a large trade surplus, allowing the country to reduce in whole or in part its international debts.

In late 1980, after the disastrous heterodox experience (fixing the exchange rate and using monetary correction), Brazil, even without resorting to the IMF, tried to adjust the economy through a drastic restrictive policy designed to reduce domestic demand, balance the external accounts, and contain inflation. It reduced bank lending, forced real interest rates to be used, and restricted public investment. Numerous subsidies were eliminated and tougher legislation was used to correct salaries, further reducing the real value of wages. These measures provoked a deep recession, with GDP falling by 4.3 percent. This was the first negative growth rate of this type in the post-1945 period. The trade balance was again positive, showing a surplus of more than U.S.$1 billion, but the balance of payments was still being strongly affected by interest payments of U.S.$10 billion, an excessive amount when one considers that the country exported only U.S.$23 billion. In 1982, the debt service consumed U.S.$12 billion, and in the global recession and slowdown in import capacity of most countries, exports shrank to U.S.$20 billion. The current account deficit reached 6 percent of GDP, and Brazil's net reserves were exhausted. Thus the country could be characterized as insolvent in external terms.

In August 1982, the turbulence in the international financial markets generated by the Mexican crisis clearly exposed the seriousness of the situation. The international banks closed their doors to Brazil, and demanded that the country sign a formal agreement with the IMF so that Brazilian performance could be monitored by that institution. The agreement was signed on November 20, five days after the important elections of that year. Although the government denied that it was having negotiations with the IMF and tried to hide the truth, it was evident that there was a crisis, and the opposition won an exceptional victory in the election, taking command of almost all major states. In February 1983, the country signed an agreement with creditor banks, but the economic situation continued to worsen, since the absence of reserves made Brazil delay external payments. Moreover, it was very difficult to honor agreements with the IMF, which required deeper adjustments in the economy, although the country was already in deep recession. High inflation and indexing made it almost impossible to meet the demands of the IMF regarding the goals of inflation and public deficit. A series of letters of intent (seven in two years) led to the wearing down of the relationship between the government authorities and the IMF. The government was forced to deepen the recession, including enacting more restrictive salary legislation. In February 1983, there was another devaluation of 30 percent, and in that year the national domestic product declined by 2.9 percent. However, thanks to the devaluation and the reduction of domestic consumption, the trade surplus reached U.S.$6 billion and the deficit in current accounts decreased to 3.5 percent of GDP. The strong domestic adjustment combined with favorable international conditions helped Brazil attain the external goals agreed to with the IMF. The global economic recovery with the fall in oil prices and declining international interest rates were factors that contributed to the adjustment in the balance of payments. The favorable external results were repeated in 1984, and GDP grew by 5.4 percent. Inflation, however, reached a new level, exceeding 200 percent in that year.[105]

This whole process of adjustment had serious consequences for the internal economic structure. Inflation continued rising, reaching unbearable levels that would have destroyed most economies. But in Brazil, from the time of indexation, which began in the early 1960s, the economy could coexist with relatively high levels of inflation, at levels of inflation that would have been disastrous for economies that did not use such a procedure, thanks to its indexation of prices. But even with indexing, when inflation reached very high levels, for example, above 100 percent per year there were serious distributional conflicts created and the efficiency of the economy was reduced even while the indexation mechanisms still permitted the full functioning of the economy, including the financial market. It is easy to imagine that not all economic agents possess equal

---

[105] On the crisis and the process of adjustment see Carneiro and Modiano, "Ajuste externo e desequilíbrio interno: 1980–1984," 323–346; Mario Henrique Simonsen, "Inflação brasileira: lições e perspectivas," *Revista Brasileira de Economia* 5,4 (Outubro–Dezembro 1985), 15–31; Winston Fritsch, "A crise cambial de 1982–83 no Brasil: origens e respostas," in *A América Latina e a crise internacional*, ed. C. A. Plastino and R. Bouzas (Rio de Janeiro: Graal, 1988); Rogério Werneck, "Poupança estatal, dívida externa e crise financeira do setor público," *Pesquisa e Planejamento Econômico* 16,3 (Dezembro 1986), 551–574.

bargaining power or information to protect themselves from inflation, particularly in its phases of acceleration. Usually wages were the prices with the worst indexing, creating a permanent conflict between employers and employees. It should be made clear from the Brazilian experience, that although workers lose with high levels of inflation, when the government introduced more efficient mechanisms of salary adjustments, the conflict between capital and labor usually caused new acceleration of inflation. Various plans have also demonstrated that there would be an explosion in demand when there was a sharp drop in inflation, when the so-called inflation tax[106] was eliminated even temporarily. In an attempt to curb inflation, wages were adjusted so inefficiently that it caused additional losses in real income when inflation accelerated. When inflation temporarily stopped with each new plan, workers gained, since at least temporarily there occurred an explosion in demand because of the greater stability of real salaries. Looking to halt the inflationary spiral the government constrained the adjustment allowed to public service prices to consumers, causing serious problems for companies offering these services and the further deterioration of public accounts. The Brazilian public sector, having difficulty obtaining financing in the international market, began to compete with the private sector for obtaining credit in the domestic market. This resulted in domestic interest rates rising further and it become ever more costly to service the internal debt.

While the adjustment successfully addressed Brazil's international economic problems, it provoked an internal crisis. With rising interest rates and the deterioration of public accounts, productive investment was

---

[106] The inflation "tax" was not actually a tax, but was the cost to everyone of the high inflation rate. When people retain currency or leave it in demand deposits at commercial banks without positive interest and there is high inflation, the value of deposits and the value of the currency erode, causing loss of value to the owner of the cash or bank deposit. This loss is called the "inflation tax." The government gains even as the owners lose money, and banks earn the portion that depositors lose. That is, they earn their share of the inflationary tax. When inflation disappears there is an increase in the demand for money, paper currency, or demand deposits, because there is stability in the value of the currency. In the case of Brazil, there was high inflation and the banks earned this inflation tax, which the government eventually forced them to lend to farmers at subsidized interest rates. These were called "liabilities." It was a way to transfer some of the loss of the owners of the money, which were appropriated by the banks and could then be passed on to the farmers. The existence of the inflation tax also explains the huge expansion of banking agencies to capture demand deposits. As there was no profit to be made in this expansion, the inflation tax ended up paying for this extension of the banking system. But when inflation ended, many banks failed because they had generated huge costs that could no longer be covered by an inflation tax.

significantly decreased. It is worth remembering that at the time most of the foreign debt was the responsibility of the public sector. To meet the obligations of this foreign debt, the country began to generate significant trade surplus. This, however, was produced by the private sector. The public sector needed to buy foreign currency to honor international commitments or increase reserves. As this purchase was made by increasing the money supply, to sterilize this effect the government sold bonds increasing its level of indebtedness. Furthermore, it should be recalled that domestic borrowing was done with short-term and high-interest loans. As the domestic debt service grew, the government tried to cut spending, usually by cutting investments.[107]

Another important aspect of the crisis of the 1980s was inflation. Typically, policies that reduced domestic consumption proved effective in containing inflationary pressures. However, the example of Brazil seemed to indicate that there was a component of price inertia and that conventional methods did not work in an economy with such a high degree of indexation. In the first half of the 1980s, there were proposals for an alternative antiinflationary policy.[108] These studies formed the backdrop to the Cruzado Plan, launched in 1986.

Along with profound economic changes that occurred in this period, the military would also undertake important social changes. The regimes that followed the Vargas period extended Vargas's policies and struggled with the relations he had made with the new popular urban classes. Clearly the rise of a radicalized labor movement was one of the key factors bringing the military into the central government. Equally the military were clearly challenged by the rise of various populist civilian leaders who wanted to emulate Vargas and his ability to generate popular support. But however fearful the military were of the political institutions developed by Vargas, they were committed to his vision of a modern industrial state and in doing so had to resolve a host of social questions both in response to its policies of squeezing wages and in order to obtain support from the growing middle classes.

The period of military rule was thus an era of unusually profound social changes. Many of these changes were induced by the processes of industrialization and the allied growth of an urban society, processes that

[107] Werneck, "Poupança estatal, dívida externa e crise financeira do setor público."
[108] See Pérsio Arida and André Lara Resende, "Inertial Inflation and Monetary Reform in Brazil," in *Inflation and Indexation: Argentina, Brazil and Israel*, ed. J. Williamson (Cambridge, MA: MIT Press, 1985); Francisco L. Lopes, *O choque heterodoxo: combate à inflação e reforma monetária* (Rio de Janeiro: Campus, 1986).

preceded the military rule but that were intensified in this period. Others were provoked by policies carried out by the military and still others were exogenous to the change in political regime. The most profound change in this period related to government policies designed to deal with the social aspects related to massive industrialization, as well as the consequences of the industrialization process. The rapid industrialization of this period had positive and negative aspects. It generated probably the most open and rapid period of social mobility in the nation's history as a new industrial and managerial elite emerged out of a rural and poorly educated population. But it also led to a massive internal migration from poor to rich zones of the country and the consequent growth of metropolitan areas, and the lack of housing in these ever-expanding centers would lead to the rise of the squatter settlements in all the major cities. There was also a major increase in the pace of primary and secondary education as the military sought to gain the support of the emerging middle class. The military also promoted the expansion of university and technical education. Finally, the government compensated for its wage squeeze policies with the active expansion of the social welfare system, which included major advances in health delivery and the significant expansion of a national pension system. It even engaged in a massive program of public housing and sanitation through its National Housing Bank. In fact this period of military rule has been defined as the time when Brazil finally established the foundation of a modern welfare state, though this system was based on authoritarian and technocratic models that would be transformed in the postmilitary era.[109]

But partially independent of the actions of the military government, there also occurred fundamental changes in the demographic structure of the Brazilian population. Initially, fertility and mortality remained at traditionally high levels by world standards with resulting life expectancy at very low levels. Life expectancy as late as the 1950s was close to levels of the late nineteenth and early twentieth centuries. This would all change in the twenty-one years of the military regime – some of this change was due to government policies, especially as related to health, while

[109] Sônia Draibe defined this period as marking the establishment of a welfare state in Brazil because of the universalization of services and the creation of active government institutions in all areas defined by a modern welfare state. Though this model would be profoundly reformed in the postmilitary period, the basic structure was elaborated in the decades of the 1960s and 1970s. Sônia Miriam Draibe, "O Welfare State in Brazil: Caracteristicas e Perspectivas," *Caderno de Pesquisa* 8 (Campinas: UNICAMP, NEPP, 1993), 19–21.

other changes were influenced by developments outside Brazil. These exogenous influences were especially profound in the area of fertility as Brazilian women significantly altered their views on the norms of fertility and family size for the first time in national history.

Not all of these social changes began in this period, or were clearly defined by the time the military regimes ended. But all of them would lead to long-term institutional and even cultural change in the following decades. In the military era mortality and fertility would reach historic levels never before experienced. The former continued its dramatic decline as infant mortality finally began to drop at an ever-faster pace, while the total natural growth rate of the population reached unprecedented heights as fertility declined far more slowly and more and more women survived to their fertile years. Even literacy began to change as the nation finally became predominantly literate by the census of 1960. By the end of the military era Brazil would quickly pass through a demographic transition in which fertility was declining so dramatically that it would profoundly influence the age structure of the nation as well as its capacity for population growth. In turn, this had an impact on everything from family structure to employment. Mortality rates now began to decline at an ever-more rapid pace, and with it life expectancy began to climb toward European and North American levels. Finally, in this period Brazil became a predominantly urban and industrial society. Not only would urban centers grow dramatically, but for the first time the rural area would begin to experience negative growth rates. This along with the beginnings of modernization in agriculture led to massive internal migration, to the cities as well as across state boundaries. For all that change, Brazil was still marked by an ever-increasing inequality in terms of class and color, which was well reflected in increasing regional disparities. While most regions saw significant advances in wealth, health, and education, the northeast fell further behind the other major regions. More and more the advanced regions of Brazil were attaining the standard of life of the advanced industrial countries of the world, while the northeast remained at levels experienced by underdeveloped countries in Africa and Asia. If anything, this was a period when regional differences were most marked in the history of the nation.

Government policies toward creating a major industrial base were at the heart of the military government. Holding wages constant, closing the market to foreign products, and investing in basic infrastructure, the state encouraged national capital to invest in industrial activities. The result was an extraordinary rapid economic growth that had been accelerating even before the arrival of the military regime. Per capita income had doubled from 2,110 *reais* (in 2006 currency) in 1940 to 4,490 *reais* in 1960. It then increased at an even faster pace to 11,040 *reais* in 1980. In 1960 agriculture still accounted for 18 percent of national GDP and by 1980 it had fallen to 11 percent. In turn, industry had climbed from 33 percent to 44 percent of the GDP, its highest level in the twentieth century.[110] At the same time there was a major increase in jobs in the service and manufacturing sectors. From 1960 to 1980 the number of men working in the primary sector remained constant at 11 million, while the secondary sector rose from 2.4 million to 9 million workers and the tertiary sector from 5.2 million to 11.4 million.[111]

All this rapid growth and shift in the base of the economy had a profound impact on social mobility. The change in occupation and classes between generations profoundly changed in this period. Whereas mobility had been largely circular before 1960 due to the relatively fixed number of elite positions, it would become largely structural in this period of massive industrial and urban growth. That is, there was a major increase in new managerial and other high-status positions and these were filled by persons whose parents had been low-status individuals in terms of occupation. It was argued at the time that Brazil had probably the world's highest levels of elite leaders with low-status parents of any major industrial country.[112] The relative stagnation of the economy in the post-1980 period would mean that the nation would quickly return to more standard circular mobility for the rest of the century with each class gaining and losing members at roughly the same rate.[113] Moreover, once these

---

[110] Adalberto Cardoso, "Transições da Escola para o Trabalho no Brasil: Persistência da Desigualdade e Frustração de Expectativas," *DADOS, Revista de Ciências Sociais* 51,3 (2008), 573.

[111] Carlos Antonio Costa Ribeiro, *Estrutura de classe e mobilidade social no Brasil* (Bauru, SP: Educ, 2007), 310, Table 6.

[112] Pastore estimated that as of 1973, more than half (58 percent) of all sons had changed their status from their fathers' occupations. He then estimated that of these changes, 57 percent were due to the expansion of new jobs (structural) and 43 percent to circular mobility, which is the normal movement up and down without being related to any increase in jobs. José Pastore, *Inequality and Social Mobility in Brazil* (Madison: University of Wisconsin Press, 1982), 33.

[113] This model of circular and structure mobility is the predominant model used in the literature. Recently, newer studies have begun to use more complex occupational distributions than previously and have replaced this model with a new methodology that is called "social fluidity," which measures total mobility (intra- and intergenerational) and seeks to measure immobility in a more refined way. But these new measures confirm that after 1982 immobility returned to the upper levels of the occupational structure,

upper-level positions were filled, it was possible to maintain them through growth of the elite, rather than from continued recruitment from below, which further restricted mobility. Thus despite the early period of very rapid mobility during the boom years, especially pronounced for those whose parents were from a rural background, the total mobility in the military period was no more rapid than in other advanced industrial countries of the world. As late as 1973 some 71 percent of the workers had parents who came from the rural area, which meant that the majority of workers came from poor and poorly educated families.[114] But this ratio quickly declined in the following decades. Surprisingly women had more mobility than men, in relation to parents' and child's occupation (intergenerational) but did less well than men in changing their status from first to last job in one's own lifetime (intrageneration).[115] Not surprisingly whites did better than nonwhites in terms of both types of mobility, though this discrimination seems to have declined over time.[116] Thus while mobility was impressive in this period, at least in the upper levels of the occupational structure, the majority of workers found themselves locked into lower-status positions with relatively lower mobility in later

which had previously seen the most mobility. See Ribeiro, *Estrutura de classe e mobilidade social*, 199. Using this new methodology, Ribeiro also suggests that while elite and middle-rank mobility was high for those with rural backgrounds in this period, overall mobility in Brazil was about average for an advanced industrial country throughout this period. This is because the mobility of urban workers to middle- and upper-class occupations was either very low or just average by advanced country standards. Ribeiro, *Estrutura de classe e mobilidade social*, 251, 253, and 255, 258, Tables 18–19.

[114] Ribeiro, *Estrutura de classe e mobilidade social*, 77. As Ribeiro notes, given the characteristics of the poor distribution of income and land in the rural area, "the great majority of sons of rural workers who experienced social mobility in the 20th century, principally those whose fathers were workers [rather than landowners] until the decade of the 1960s, can be defined by their lack of social and economic resources. This lack certainly limited their chances of upward mobility." Ribeiro, *Estrutura de classe e mobilidade social*, 79.

[115] Using an alternative set of occupational categories Maria Scalon estimates that women had far more mobility than men. She finds in the 1988 PNAD survey that a third of the mobility of men was structural and a surprising 46 percent of female mobility was structural – with total mobility for men being 65 percent and for women 76 percent in this period. She also shows that intrageneration mobility – that is between a person's first and last jobs – is less mobile than the intergeneration mobility between parents and children occupations. Maria Celi Scalon, *Mobilidade social no Brasil, padrões e tendências* (Rio de Janeiro: Rena, IUPERJ-UCAM, 1999), 85, 102. On the findings about intra- and intergenerational mobility and sex, also based on this same 1988 PNAD survey, see Felícia Picanço, "O Brasil que sobe e desce: Uma análise da mobilidade sociooccupacional e realização de êxito no mercado de trabalho urbano," *DADOS – Revista de Ciências Sociais* 50,2 (2007), 403, 405, Tables 1 and 5.

[116] Picanço, "O Brasil que sobe e desce," 404, 406, Tables 4 and 6.

years due to their poor starting position in terms of human capital. Using wages rather than occupations, a recent study found that Brazil had a higher than average immobility of wages between fathers and sons. It also found that the greatest mobility occurred at the bottom of the wage scale, largely as a result of universal primary education, which lessened the impact of fathers' wages. This favored nonwhite rates of mobility. But at the top of the wage scale (the top quintile), immobility was more pronounced, with race reversed. Here the probability of a white maintaining his father's level of income was 50 percent compared to sons of rich black fathers whose probability was only 25 percent.[117]

But there were also changes in other areas that would come to influence mobility. The one area where major change occurred in this period as a result of government action was in education and scientific research. Although there had been slow but steady progress in the development of primary and secondary education before 1964, it was the military regime that gave a great impulse to these two areas of activity. In 1960 only 73 percent of the children ages five to nine attended primary school, but this figure rose to 89 percent by 1968. Though comparable figures are unavailable for later years, by 1985 some 79 percent of children aged 5 to 14 years of age were in primary school.[118] Moreover, secondary and university education enrollments were growing faster than the national population in the period from 1960 to 1980.[119]

It was in the secondary school system that the most dramatic changes occurred. While the primary school system had been on a long trajectory of growth, which was simply stimulated by continuing investments, there was an expansion and substantial change in secondary education. Between 1963 and 1984, the number of secondary school teachers doubled from approximately 121,000 to 215,000 and enrollments increased from 1.7 million to three million students. But the big change was the role the government now played in this secondary market. In 1963 some 60 percent of the secondary students were enrolled in private secondary schools, but by 1984 this was reversed and now 65 percent of the students were enrolled in public schools.[120] These approximately 3 million

---

[117] Sérgio Guimarães Ferreira and Fernando A. Veloso, "Intergenerational Mobility of Wages in Brazil," *Brazilian Review of Econometrics* 26,2 (November 2006), 181–211.
[118] Ribeiro, *Estrutura de classe e mobilidade social*, 309, Table 4.
[119] Simon Schwartzman, *A Space for Science – The Development of the Scientific Community in Brazil* (College Station: Pennsylvania State University Press, 1991), 220, Table 10.
[120] These numbers come from AEB (1964), 341–342, and AEB (1986), 174–175.

secondary school students now made up 22 percent of all children ages 15 to 19, up from just 12 percent of this age group enrolled in 1972.[121]

This was also a period when the government invested heavily in science and technology for the first time in its history. The leading scholar of the history of science in Brazil has declared this period was one of the Great Leap Forward.[122] The government's National Development Bank (BNDES) in 1964 established a 10-year Fund for Technology with U.S.$100 million. Then in 1974 the small national research council was expanded and more adequately funded and became the CNPq – the National Council for Scientific and Technical Development. Soon the military government was investing heavily in advanced research as well as in basic infrastructure and industrial development, all in the name of a nationalist program. But at the same time, scientists at the University of São Paulo and a growing number of newer centers pushed for a solution modeled on the U.S. National Science Foundation, which would play such a crucial role in post–World War II America in making the nation a world premier center for science and technology. Starting as early as 1953 the government had established a fund for scholarships for students training primarily in the sciences. This program was run by CAPES, which had been founded in 1951.[123] By the 1960s several hundred Brazilian scientists had been trained abroad, especially in the United States and England, and on their return they formed a powerful interest group pressing for the creation of modern laboratories and other crucial research tools to allow Brazil to compete in this new postwar world of modern science. In 1968 came a new University Reform Law that essentially established the North American system of departments, and three levels of degrees, from undergraduate to masters and doctorates. Recently founded federal universities in Minas Gerais and in Brasília were developed along this model and new public-supported federal universities were soon established in all the states. Also the state of São Paulo founded a new state university in the city of Campinas two years earlier, with a great representation of foreign scholars, which became known as UNICAMP and quickly competed with the University of São Paulo as the nation's premier university. It was designed from the beginning to be an advanced research center, especially in physics, and several Brazilian scientists working at Bell Labs and U.S. universities returned to work at the new university.[124] The government

---

[121] Ribeiro, *Estrutura de classe e mobilidade social*, 309, Table 4.
[122] Schwartzman, *A Space for Science*, Chapter 9.
[123] Campanha Nacional de Aperfeiçoamento de Pessoal de Nível Superior. On the history of this institution see http://www.capes.gov.br/sobre-a-capes/historia-e-missao.
[124] Schwartzman, *A Space for Science*, Chapter 9.

also created an airplane and computer industry and a nuclear research program inside and outside the university. All this effort lead to Brazil becoming a significant player in world science and along with India was one of the few from the less developed world that could compete.

It was the expansion of the secondary schools especially that began to lead to a slow expansion of university students. By 1984 there were 68 universities in Brazil, 35 federal ones, 10 state universities, 2 municipal ones, and 20 private institutions and the university student population had expanded from 142,000 in 1964 to 1.3 million in 1984, with women slightly outnumbering men.[125] Within this group, graduate programs doubled their student enrollments to the 40,000 level by the mid-1980s.[126] The percentage of youths 20 to 24 years of age who were in tertiary educational institutions – universities and technical schools – rose from just 2 percent of all such youths in 1965 to 12 percent in 1985.[127]

All of this increasing in schooling also had a profound impact on literacy. As of 1940 only 38.4 percent of the population was literate and this had increased only to 42.7 percent of the population in 1950. By 1970 literates were two-thirds of the population and by 1980 they represented 74 percent of the nation.[128] It was only in the census of 1960 that for the first time literate men and women represented the majority of the population. In 1950 men 10 years of age and older had become a majority literate for the first time, but in that year women were still at only 44 percent literate. In 1960, the key transition year, literate women now accounted for 57 percent of the female population 10 years of age and older and men had risen to 64 percent of that male age group.[129] But it would take until the early 1980s for women to become as literate as men, largely as a result of a major increase of women attending school. This slow decline of bias against women in education can be seen in an examination of the illiterate population by age from the census of 1970. Not only were older persons more illiterate than younger ones, but in the older age cohorts there were more illiterate women than men,

---

[125] Carlos Benedito Martins, "O ensino superior brasileiro nos anos 90," *São Paulo em Perspectiva* 14,1 (2000), 42–43, 48, Tables 1 and 4; and for the breakdown by sex see AEB (1984), 251, Table 2.6.
[126] Schwartzman, *A Space for Science*, 220, Table 10.
[127] Ribeiro, *Estrutura de classe e mobilidade social*, 309, Tables 4–5.
[128] IBGE, *Estatísticas do Século XX*, Table "População1981aeb-002," available at http://www.ibge.gov.br/seculoxx/arquivos_xls/populacao.shtm.
[129] IBGE, *Estatísticas do Século XX*, Table "pop_1965aeb-06.2," available at http://www.ibge.gov.br/seculoxx/arquivos_xls/populacao.shtm.

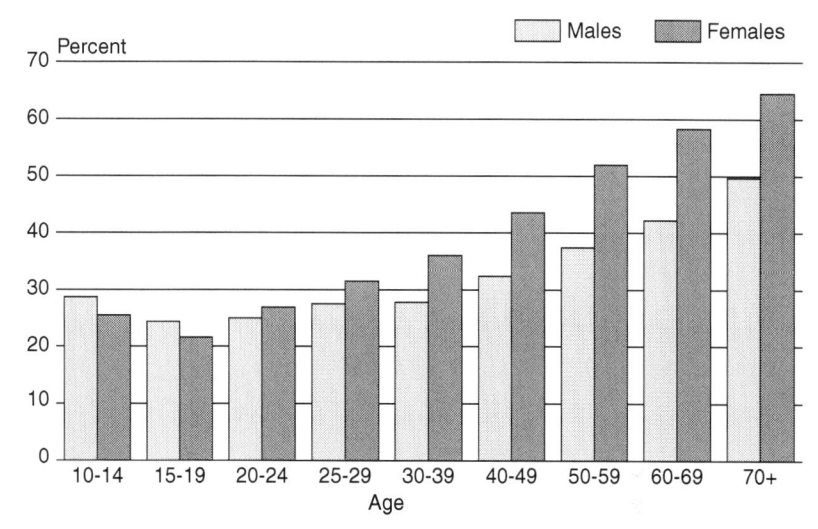

Formative Democracies and the Military Interregnum 225

GRAPH 3.22. Illiterates by Age and Sex in 1970. *Source:* IBGE, *Estatísticas do Século XX*, Table "educacaomc1978aeb-01"

reflecting historical biases in educational opportunities for women (see Graph 3.22).

Aside from earlier sex discrimination in literacy, there was also discrimination by color. While by 1982 women were even more literate than men, the ratio of illiterates among blacks and browns was still quite high compared to Asians and whites (see Graph 3.23), and it would take another thirty years and the arrival of universal primary education to begin to reduce this disadvantage and the comparable disadvantage of urban and rural residence.[130]

---

[130] By the census of 2010, the gap between whites and Afro-Brazilians was still the same, but the ratio of illiterates for both groups had declined dramatically:

Percentage Illiterates among Persons Five Years of Age and Older by Color and Sex in the Census of 2010

	Men	Women
TOTAL	11.5%	10.4%
White	7.4%	7.0%
Brown	15.1%	13.3%
Black	15.4%	14.6%
Asian	10.8%	9.2%
Amerindian	25.4%	27.1%

Source: http://www.sidra.ibge.gov.br/bda/tabela/listabl.asp?c=3176&z=cd&o=7.

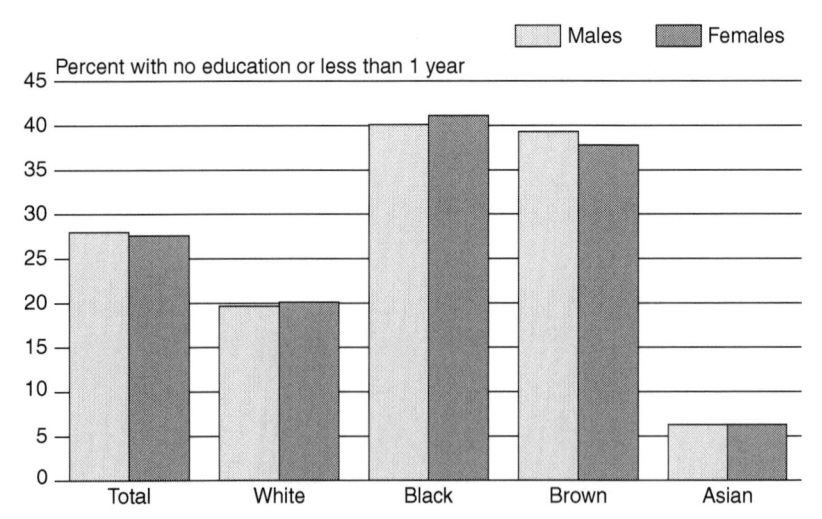

226   *The Economic and Social History of Brazil since 1889*

GRAPH 3.23. Illiterates by Color and Sex in 1982. *Source* IBGE, *Estatísticas do Século XX*, Table "educacaom1983aeb_215"

Other major sociodemographic developments in this period were the massive internal migration and the major increase in urbanization. This pull factor of increasing urban employment and better living conditions in the cities was matched by the major push factor of an increasing mechanization of Brazilian agriculture. The substantial increase in new rural credit provided by the military regime led to a revolution in agricultural technology, if not of land tenure – which remained stable throughout this period. Such mechanization reduced labor needs in the countryside, so that an ever-increasing output of agricultural products was being produced by an ever-declining number of workers.[131]

One of the largest of such population movements was the migration of poor northeasterners to the farms and factories of the major southern states. This movement involved millions of Brazilians and would remake the settlement patterns of the nation in profound ways. Examining the leading coffee-exporting and immigrant-importing states in this period (see Graph 3.24) we can see that the three states of São Paulo, Rio de

---

[131] A useful survey of this vast movement and its changing patterns and numbers is found in Fausto Brito, "Final de século: a transição para um novo padrão migratório?" Paper presented at the *XII Encontro Nacional de Estudos Populacionais, ABEP* (2000); and Fausto Brito, Ricardo Alexandrino Garcia, and Renata G. Vieira de Souza, "As tendências recentes das migrações interestaduais e o padrão migratório." Paper presented at the *XIV Encontro Nacional de Estudos Populacionais, ABEP* (2004).

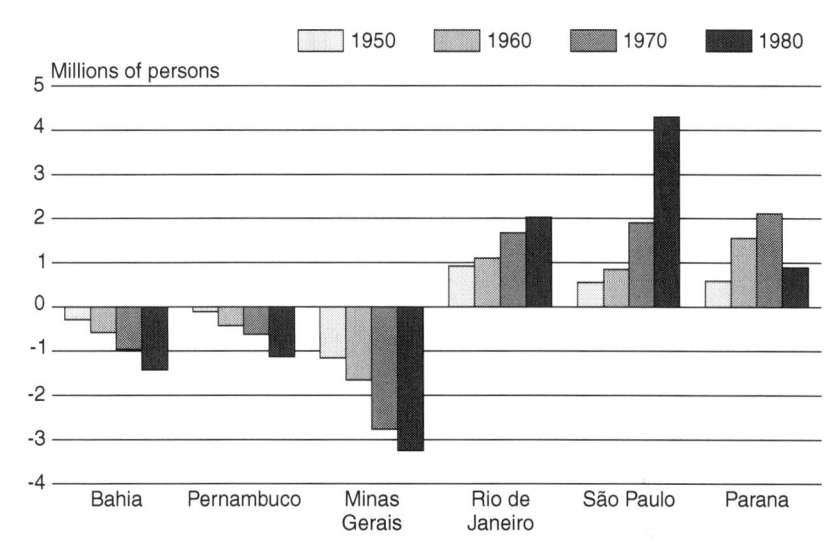

Formative Democracies and the Military Interregnum 227

GRAPH 3.24. Major States Experiencing Internal Migration by Decade, 1950–1980. *Source:* IBGE, *Estatísticas do Século XX*, Table "População1982aeb-035"

Janeiro, and Paraná between them absorbed two million native-born immigrants in 1950 and steadily increased their intake to 7.2 million in 1980. In turn, the leading out migration states of Bahia, Pernambuco, and Minas Gerais between them lost 1.5 million residents in 1950, with out-migration increasing in each decade and reaching 5.8 million by 1980. Beside these north to south migrations, there was a major movement of southerners from Rio Grande do Sul to new agricultural lands opening up in the far north and west, such that the northern and center west regions steadily gained population in this period.

The period from 1940 to 1980 also marked the transformation of Brazil into an urban society. By 1970 the urban population finally passed that of the rural population in Brazilian history for the first time. Since 1970 there has been a relative and then absolute decline of the rural population at the same time as the urban population has grown at impressive rates, even by world standards. This urban growth was so rapid that the urban population went from just half of the national population in 1970 to more than three-quarters of that population in 1980 (see Graph 3.25).

Much of this urban growth initially occurred in just two major cities, São Paulo and Rio de Janeiro, which grew very rapidly in this period. But there was also increasing growth in secondary cities and the capitals of

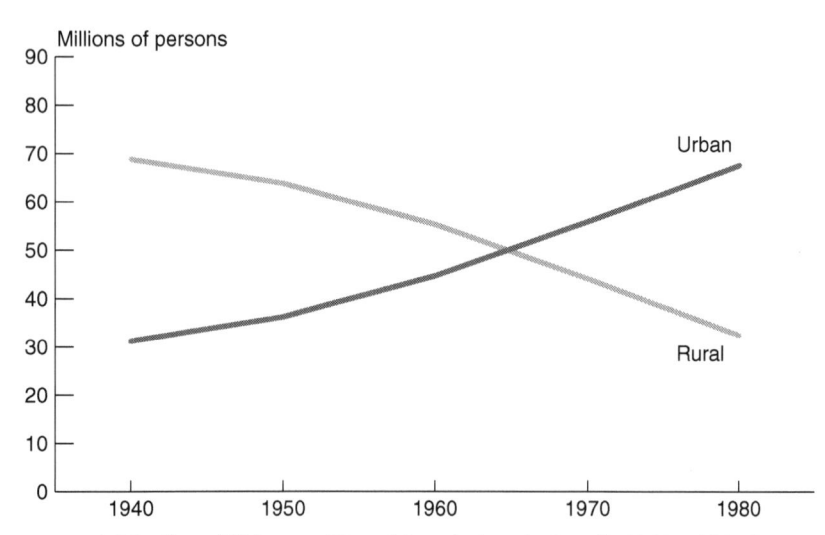

GRAPH 3.25. Size of Urban and Rural Populations in Brazil, 1940–1980. *Source:* IBGE, *Estatísticas do Século XX*, Table "População1983aeb-005"

all the provinces. Cities of 50,000 or more persons numbered just 32 in 1950 and they contained only 8.4 million persons. By 1960 their numbers almost doubled, to 68 cities and now housed 15.9 million persons. By 1980 there were 201 cities with more than 50,000 persons and they accounted for 47 million persons; and by the census of 2010 these cities numbered 433, accounted for 98.8 million persons,[132] and contained 52 percent of the national population, up from 49 percent in 2000.[133] But the growth of the primer cities was also impressive. In 1960 São Paulo reached seven million and was now the principal city of the nation, and Rio de Janeiro followed with five million. In 1960 São Paulo had finally passed Rio de Janeiro in size and by 1980 it was a world metropolis of 8.6 million persons and was still growing quite rapidly (see Graph 3.26). But the share of urban population accounted for by these two cities was also on the decline as such cities as Salvador, Belo Horizonte, Recife, and Porto Alegre now grew to more than a million in population

---

[132] IBGE, Censo 2010, Table 1294 – "Número de cidades e População nas cidades nos Censos Demográficos por tamanho da população," available at http://www.sidra.ibge.gov.br/cd/cd2010sp.asp?o=5&i=P.

[133] IBGE, Censo 2010, "Tabela 1.21 – Número de cidades e população nos Censos Demográficos, segundo as Grandes Regiões e as classes de tamanho da população das cidades – 1960/2010."

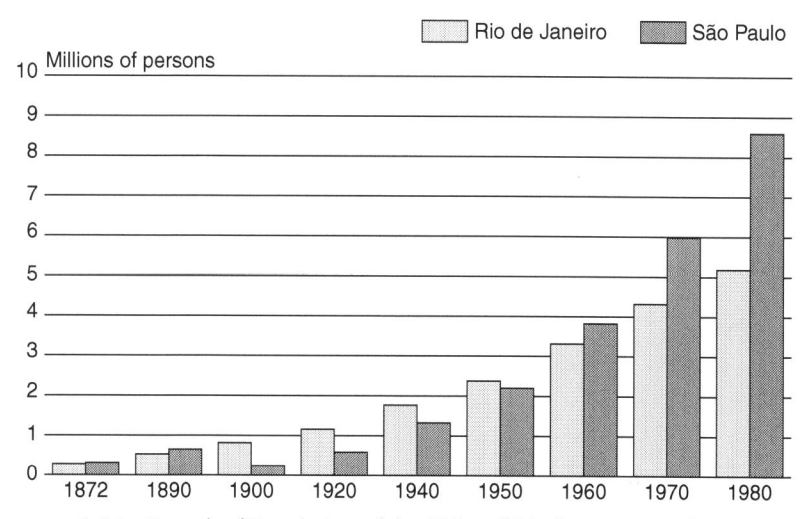

GRAPH 3.26. Growth of Population of the Cities of Rio de Janeiro and São Paulo, 1872–1980. Source: IBGE – Censo 2010, Table 1.6, "População nos Censos Demográficos, segundo os municípios das capitais – 1872/2010"

by 1980.[134] In 1950 the metropolitan centers of Rio de Janeiro and São Paulo accounted for 56 percent of the population of all the capital cities of the states. But this concentration steady declined, going to just 47 percent of the population of state capitals in 1980, and would fall to a third of their total population by the census of 2010.[135] All this suggests that urbanization in this period was occurring throughout the nation as more and more capital and noncapital cities were growing rapidly, and these two primer cities would experience declining growth rates and loss of their relative importance within the total urban population in the following decades. Thus Brazil in this period was not experiencing the overconcentration in one or two giant urban centers – so-called megapolis – that marked many other Latin American nations at this time.

All this urban growth came at a social cost. Given the declining investments in housing, sanitation, and electricity in these centers due to government fiscal retrenchment, the growing metropolitan areas were incapable of housing all the new immigrants. The result was the expansion of the so-called *favelas*, which were illegal squatter housing settlements on

[134] IBGE, Censo 2010, "Tabela 1.21 – Número de cidades e população... 1960/2010."
[135] IBGE, Censo 2010, "Tabela 1.6 – População nos Censos Demográficos, segundo os municípios das capitais – 1872/2010," available at http://www.ibge.gov.br/home/estatistica/populacao/censo2010/sinopse/sinopse_tab_brasil_zip.shtm.

unused land. Although *favelas* had existed long before the arrival of the military regime, the rapid urban growth of the 1960s and 1970s meant that they became a far more urgent problem. As these *favelas* grew in size and numbers and invaded ever more prestigious areas, such as the Zona Sur in metropolitan Rio de Janeiro, the military government and its supports initially followed a policy of destruction and removal, destroying these settlements and forcing *favelados* to move to distant public housing in the outskirts of the metropolitan region. But the eventual collapse of the state housing bank and the inability to stop *favela* growth through removal slowly forced the government to change its position. Even as thousands were removed in the 1960s and early 1970s, more *favelas* were established and the number of their residents continued to grow. By the late 1970s and early 1980s even the military regime came to realize that the cities would have to integrate these settlements because removal was no longer a viable policy.[136] This process would be greatly aided by the return to democratic government and especially after the 1988 constitution returned urban planning to the cities. These newer accommodating policies would be aided by a major slowing in the growth of the major cities.[137] Thus from the early 1980s onward began a long and slow process of turning *favelas* into barrios – or normal city neighborhoods – with such infrastructure as schools, clinics, roads, electricity, and sanitation. There was also a systematic attempt to rehouse all those houses built on precarious foundations to prevent the systematic mudslides that had bedeviled these communities for years and caused multiple deaths annually. It would take large public national and international funding to finally make a dent in this whole system, but after some thirty years cities like São Paulo had integrated most of these former slums, and Rio was slowly accomplishing this task as well.[138]

---

[136] A good survey of the evolution of this removal program is found in Alejandro Portes, "Housing Policy, Urban Poverty, and the State: The Favelas of Rio de Janeiro: 1972–1976," *Latin American Research Review* 14,2 (1979), 3–24. The standard study of the *favelados* in this period is by Janice Perlman, *The Myth of Marginality: Urban Poverty and Politics in Rio de Janeiro* (Berkeley: University of California Press, 1980).

[137] Thus from 5.5 percent growth in the period from 1960 to 1970, the growth of the São Paulo metropolitan area declined to 4.4 percent in the decade from 1970 to 1980 and to 1.9 percent in the decade of the 1980s. The same occurred in the metropolitan area of Rio de Janeiro, which declined from 3.6 percent in the earliest period to just 1 percent in the 1980s. See Marcelo Lopes de Souza, "Metropolitan Deconcentration, Socio-political Fragmentation and Extended Suburbanisation: Brazilian Urbanisation in the 1980s and 1990s," *Geoforum* 32,4 (2001), 438, Table 1.

[138] On the Rio program, see Ayse Pamuk and Paulo Fernando A. Cavallieri, "Alleviating Urban Poverty in a Global City: New Trends in Upgrading Rio-de-Janeiro's Favelas,"

Along with the change from rural to urban residence, Brazilians in this period also profoundly changed their attitude toward fertility for the first time in the nation's history. Like most of the rest of the world after 1960, Brazil went through what demographers have called the demographic transition.[139] The long, slow decline in mortality that began in most of the world at the end of the nineteenth century, accelerated especially after World War II with the introduction of antibiotics. The most profound change would first come in the decline of infant mortality, which would be followed progressively by a shift from epidemic diseases to generative diseases as being the primary causes of death in the national population.[140] This evermore rapid decline in mortality without an initially corresponding change in very high fertility meant an explosive growth of national population. It was in this military period that Brazil experienced the highest rates of population growth in its history.

But at the same time, it was during this period that the first massive changes in fertility began. The decline of fertility, which had begun in the premilitary period in the more advanced urban centers of the country, now quickly spread far and wide even into the most rural areas with the introduction of the birth control pill, sterilization, and other contraceptive methods in the decade of the 1960s. This rapid decline in fertility can be seen in the fall of the total fertility rate (a period measure of the average number of children born to women in the age group 14 to 49 at a given point in time) for all of Brazil. Whereas Brazilian women were still averaging more than six children per woman in their fertile years from the 1940s to the 1960s, this number dropped to 5.8 children in 1970. By the end of the 1970s women were having almost four children fewer than they did just twenty years before. This total fertility rate consistently declined in the following years, reaching just under three children per woman 14 to 49 years of age in 1991 and 2.4 children by 2000. By the end of the first decade of the twenty-first century, Brazilian fertility was reaching the 2.1 children level needed for replacing the current population.

Habitat International 22,4 (1998), 449–462; and Adauto Lucio Cardoso, "O Programa Favela-Bairro-Uma Avaliação." Habitação e meio ambiente: assentamentos urbanos precários. IPT-Instituto de Pesquisas Tecnológicas; Programa Tecnologia de habitação (São Paulo: Habitare, 2002).

[139] The classic study on this demographic revolution is Jean-Claude Chesnais, *The Demographic Transition, Stages, Patterns and Economic Implications* (Oxford: Clarendon Press, 1991).

[140] For a survey of this epidemiological change see Pedro Reginaldo Prata, "A Transição Epidemiológica no Brasil, " *Cadernos de Saúde Pública* 8,2 (Abril–Junho 1992), 168–175.

This decline in births was directly related to increasing use of some form of contraceptives by Brazilian women. By the decade of the 1980s, approximately 70 percent of women married or living in consensual unions used some form of birth control.[141] Of those women using contraception, 44 percent carried out sterilization, a figure slightly below the norm for a less developed country like Brazil, and 41 percent were using the birth control pill, with a mixture of other contraceptive practices accounting for the rest.[142] Although illegal abortions were relatively high in Brazil by world standards, they were normal for Latin America. Moreover, their trend differed from that of fertility. Initially, the abortion rate remained steady and increased somewhat at the end of the decade of the 1990s, but they have since slowly declined as more women and men used modern contraceptive methods.[143] The rate and trend of abortions show that it had little impact on the trend in the fertility decline. It was thus use of anticontraception methods of all types that drove the decline in fertility.

This fertility decline occurred not through delayed marriage and ever later childbearing, as was the pattern in the advanced industrial nations, but in the decline of births at older ages. Age at first birth and age at marriage held steady and remained low throughout this period, so that

---

[141] Elza Berquó, "Brasil, um Caso Exemplar-anticoncepção e parto cirúrgicos – à espera de uma ação exemplar, " *Estudos feministas* 1,2 (2008), 368. The figure was 43 percent for all women when nonpartnered women are included.

[142] Berquó, "Brasil, um Caso Exemplar-anticoncepção," 369, 371, Tables 1 and 3.

[143] Greice Menezes and Estela M. L. Aquino, "Pesquisa sobre o aborto no Brasil: avanços e desafios para o campo da saúde coletiva," *Cadernos de Saúde Pública* 25,2 (Suppl. 2) (2009), 193–204; Susheela Singh and Gilda Sedgh, "The Relationship of Abortion to Trends in Contraception and Fertility in Brazil, Colombia and Mexico," *International Family Planning Perspectives* 23,1 (March 1997), 7, 9, Tables 1 and 3; and for the latest data on world and regional rates see Gilda Sedgh, Stanley Henshaw, Susheela Singh, Elisabeth Åhman, and Iqbal H. Shah, "Induced Abortion: Estimated Rates and Trends Worldwide," *Lancet* 370 (October 13, 2007), 1338–1345. The first complete national survey on abortions carried out in Brazil was done in 2010 and found that 15 percent of women ages 18 to 39 had had an abortion, a relatively low rate compared to other Latin American countries. Like all other studies, it found that abortions were higher for poorer, less educated, and nonwhites than for other groups, and thus there were marked regional differences in these rates between the northeast and southern regions. Interestingly, there were no differences in mortality rates by religion of the mother. Debora Diniz and Marcelo Medeiros, "Aborto no Brasil: uma pesquisa domiciliar com técnica de urna," *Ciência & Saúde Coletiva* 15,1 (2010), 959–966. On regional variations in abortion rates, see Leila Adesse and Mário F. G. Monteiro, "Magnitude do aborto no Brasil: aspectos epidemiológicos e sócio-culturais," available at http://www.aads.org.br/wp/wp-content/uploads/2011/06/factsh_mag.pdf.

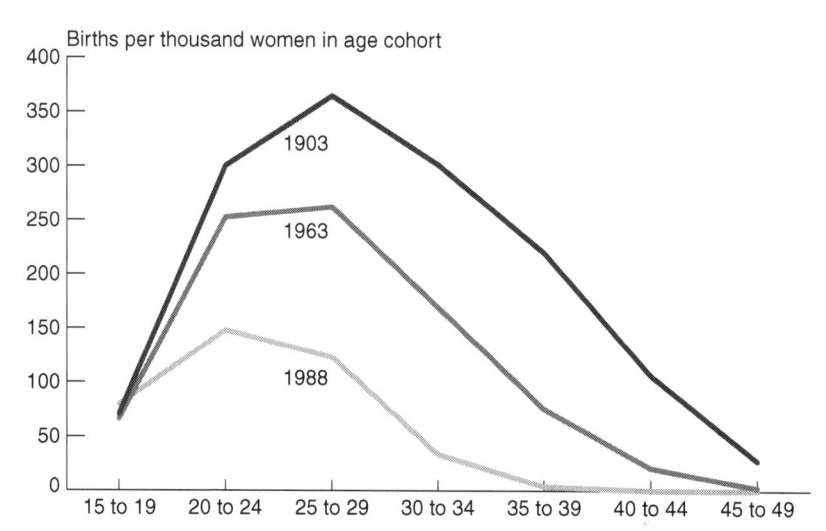

GRAPH 3.27. Distribution of Births by Age of Mothers in 1903, 1963, and 1988. *Source:* Horta, Carvalho, and Farias 2000, "Recomposicao da fecundidade por geração para Brasil Anais XII ABEP 2000"

women were having children quite early but terminating their reproduction much earlier than in previous periods. Although total births in each age group declined, the faster decline at older ages meant that the ratio of mothers aged 20 to 24, who were the second most important group in 1903, moved to first place by 1963 (see Graph 3.27). Moreover, even the relative share of the youngest group of mothers kept increasing over time. In 1980 mothers aged 15 to 19 years of age giving birth accounted for 9 percent of all births, and they increased their share to 14 percent in 1991 and then to 20 percent in 2000.[144]

As could be expected, fertility control began in the richer southeastern and southern states. But toward the end of the transition, fertility declined at a much faster pace among the poorest and least educated women and in the most backward regions of the north and northeast.[145] As late as the 1970s the northern region had close to a natural fertility schedule of

---

[144] Elza Berquó and Suzana Cavenagh, "Increasing Adolescent and Youth Fertility in Brazil: A New Trend or a One-Time Event?" Paper presented at the Annual Meeting of the Population Association of America (2005), 4. Available at http://www.abep.nepo.unicamp.br/docs/PopPobreza/BerquoelzaeCavenaghiSuzana.pdf.

[145] Elza Berquó and Suzana Cavenagh, "Mapeamento sócio-econômico e demográfico dos regimes de fecundidade no Brasil e sua variação entre 1991 e 2000." Trabalho apresentado no *XIV Encontro Nacional de Estudos Populacionais, ABEP* (CaxambuMG – Brasil, Setembro 20–24, 2004).

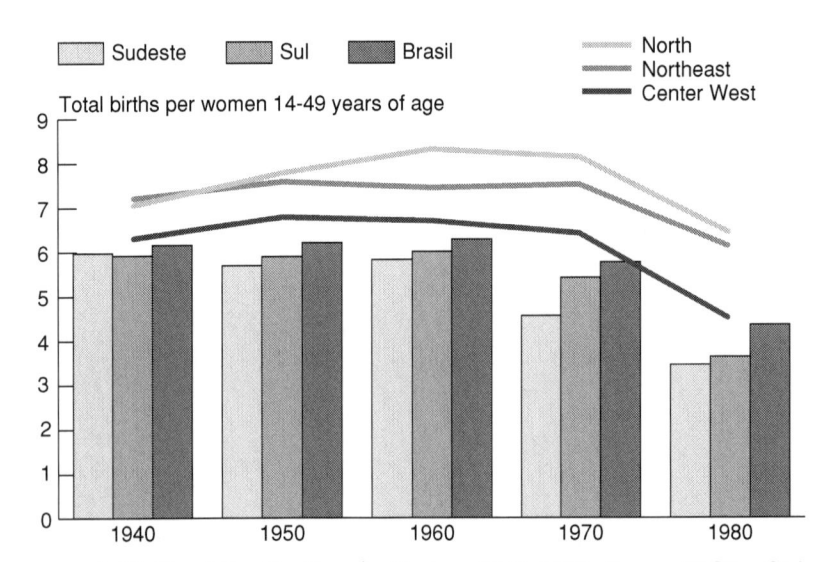

234   *The Economic and Social History of Brazil since 1889*

GRAPH 3.28. Total Fertility Rate by Region, 1940–1980. *Source:* IBGE – Série: POP263 – Taxa de fecundidade tota. Available at http://seriesestatisticas.ibge.gov.br/series.aspx?vcodigo=POP263&sv=36&t=taxa-de-fecundidade-total

more than eight children per women 14 to 49 years of age. By then the difference had increased to 3.6 children between the high fertility states of the northern region and the low fertility states of the southeast – the two extremes in the country. But by the 1980s even the northern women began to enter more systematically into fertility control, which meant that the gap between high and low fertility regions was now slowly closing (see Graph 3.28).

The fact that fewer children were being born by the decade of the 1970s began to influence the age pyramids of the population. Compared to the age distribution in 1980 (see Graph 3.29) the age pyramid of 1991 began to show a more limited base in the younger years (see Graph 3.30) all of which would have a profound impact on the age distribution of the Brazilian population for the next century.

This sudden drop in the total fertility finally expressed itself in terms of age distribution in the census of 1980. For the first time in some 40 years the ratio of persons 0 to 14 dropped significantly as fewer children were being born (see Graph 3.31).

While fertility remained high until the 1970s, mortality continued its slow but steady decline in this same period. Much of this decline had to do with the improvement in public health and the expansion of welfare

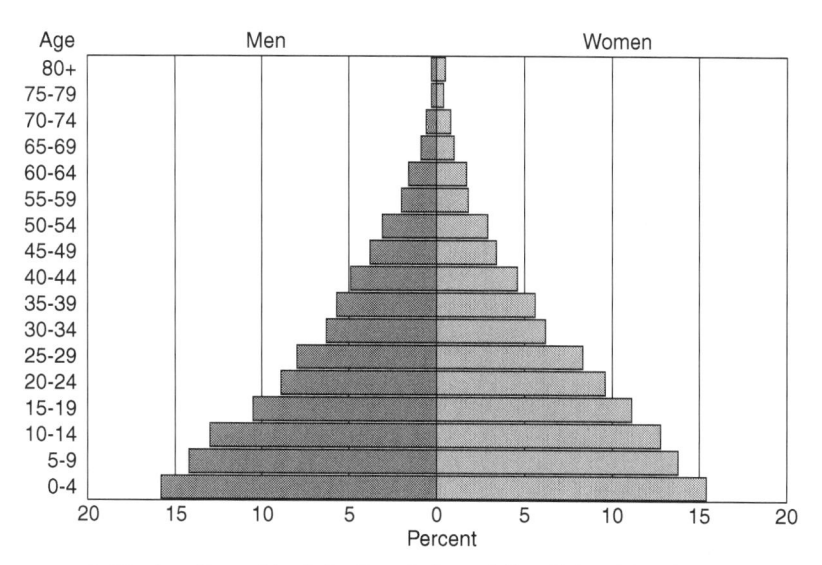

Formative Democracies and the Military Interregnum 235

GRAPH 3.29. Age Pyramid of the Population of Brazil in 1980. *Source:* IBGE, *Estatística do Século XX*, Table "População1983aeb-045"

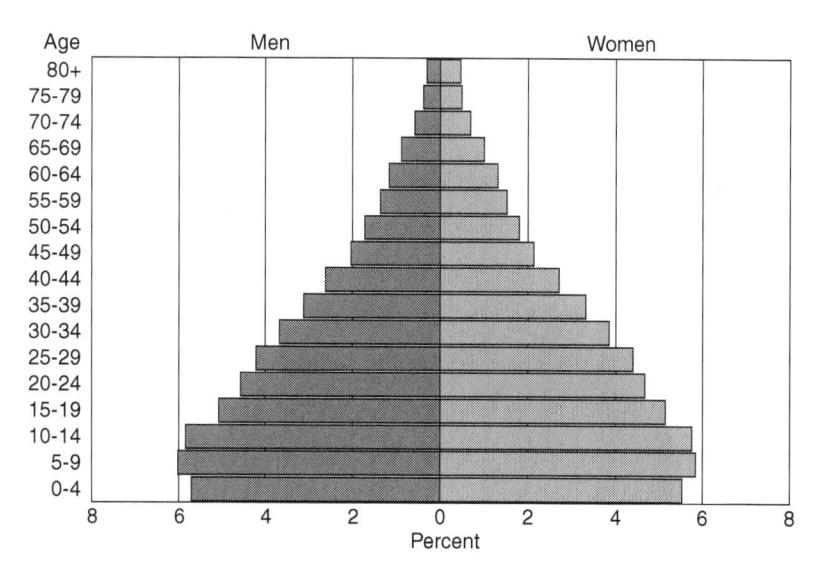

GRAPH 3.30. Age Pyramid of the Population in 1991. *Source:* IBGE: DATA-SUS Table 200. Available at http://www.sidra.ibge.gov.br/cd/cd2000cgp.asp?o=22&i=P

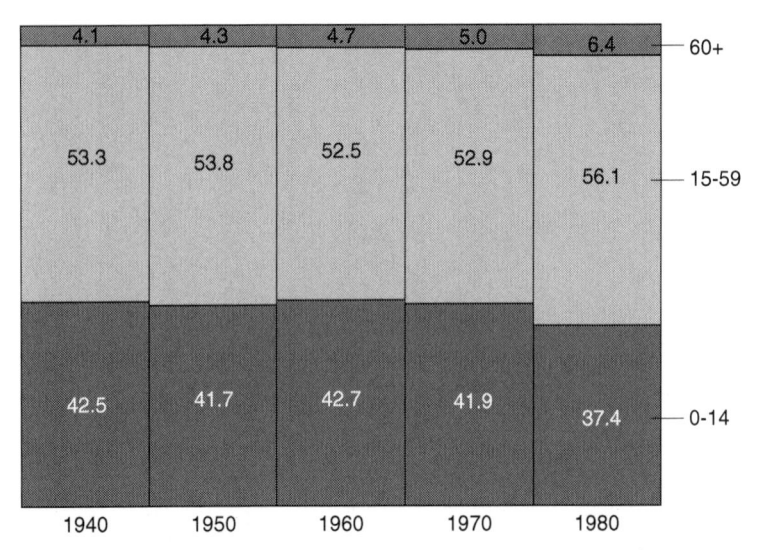

1940	1950	1960	1970	1980	
4.1	4.3	4.7	5.0	6.4	60+
53.3	53.8	52.5	52.9	56.1	15-59
42.5	41.7	42.7	41.9	37.4	0-14

GRAPH 3.31. Relative Share of Various Age Categories, Brazil, 1940–1980. *Source:* IBGE, *Estatística do Século XX*, Table "População1982aeb-038"

institutions by the military government, which sought to satisfy middle-class demands and prevent worker agitation. There were major changes in public health. In 1967 a unified National Social Security Institute (*Instituto Nacional de Previdência Social*, or INPS) was established. INPS not only dealt with pensions, but initially also covered health insurance. But when a Ministry of Social Security was established in 1974 there was a clear demarcation between pensions and health, with the latter now under National Social Security Healthcare Institute (*Instituto Nacional de Assistência Médica e Previdência Social*, or INAMPS).[146] A host of other institutional changes led to a major expansion of a public health system. Between 1970 and 1980 hospital admission went from 6 million to 13 million – the latter figure being the norm until today.[147] Finally,

---

[146] Mauricio C. Coutinho and Cláudio Salm, "Social Welfare," in *Social Change in Brazil 1945–1985: The Incomplete Transformation*, ed. Edmar L. Bacha and Herbert S. Klein (Albuquerque: University of New Mexico Press, 1989), 233–262. On the history of these reforms see Herbert S. Klein and Francisco Vidal Luna, "Mudanças Sociais no Período Militar (1964–1985)," in *Cinquenta Anos: A ditadura que mudou o Brasil*, ed. Daniel Aarão, Marcelo Ridenti, and Rodrigo Patto Sá Motta (Rio de Janeiro: Zahar Editora, forthcoming 2014).

[147] Jairnilson Paim, Claudia Travassos, Celia Almeida, Ligia Bahia, and James Macinko, "The Brazilian Health System: History, Advances, and Challenges," *The Lancet* 377,9779 (2011), 1782.

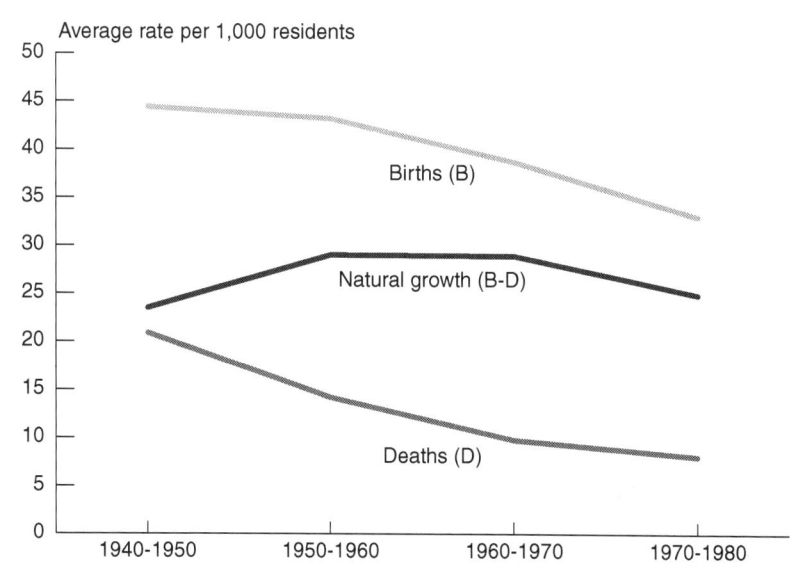

GRAPH 3.32. Components of Growth of the Brazilian Population, 1940–1980.
Source: IBGE, *Estatística do Século XX*, Table "População1981aeb-037"

in the 1960s came state national and internationally supported programs of infant and child immunization.[148] All of this growth in public health had a direct impact on mortality. Already the crude death rate was at 15 deaths per thousand residents, which given the rather steady nature of births and age structure meant that the overall death rate was low. While that rate would change little in the next decade, it began to decline at a more rapid pace in the next few years and was down to 8 deaths per thousand births by the early 1980s (see Graph 3.32).

This decline was driven mostly by the steady decline in infant mortality, which fell by half from 135 deaths of infants to 1,000 live births in 1950/55 to just 63 deaths per thousand live births in 1980/85 (see Graph 3.33). The impact of this decline can be seen in the slow decline of infant and children deaths (0–14 years of age) as a share of total Brazilian deaths. This began in the late 1970s – with infant and child deaths going from more than half of all deaths recorded, to just a third of such deaths

---

[148] The 1970s and early 1980s were also a period of active debate developed among academics and doctors about the nature of the health care system, which would have a profound effect on the creation of SUS and the decentralization reforms of health carried out in the postmilitary period. See Hésio Cordeiro, "Instituto de Medicina Social e a luta pela reforma sanitária: contribuição à história do SUS," *Physis* 14,2 (2004), 343–362.

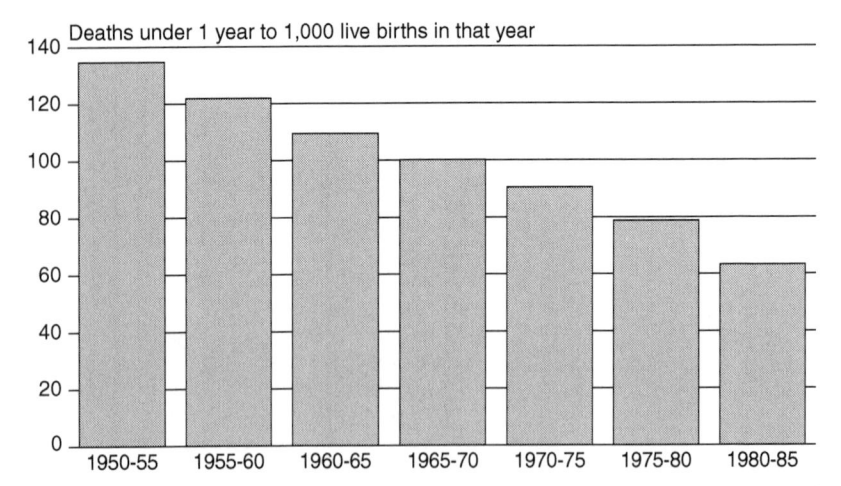

140 Deaths under 1 year to 1,000 live births in that year

| 1950-55 | 1955-60 | 1960-65 | 1965-70 | 1970-75 | 1975-80 | 1980-85 |

GRAPH 3.33. Infant Mortality 1950/1955 to 1980/1985. *Source:* CELADE, Brasil Indices de Crecimento Demográfico. Available at http://www.eclac.org/celade/proyecciones/basedatos_BD.htm

by the early 1980s. At the same time there was a rapid increase in the share of total deaths accounted by aged deaths (those more than 65 years of age), which now took an ever-greater share of total deaths (see Graph 3.34).

Although the overall rates of infant mortality had declined in this period, well more than half of these deaths were still postneonatal – that is occurring 28 days to 364 days after the birth.[149] This ratio did not fall below the neonatal (less than 28 days) rate until 1987,[150] and was a reflection of the fact that socioeconomic factors, rather than genetic or gestational problems, were the key influence on infant mortality until the end of the twentieth century. This meant that most of these infant deaths in this period to 1980 were due to nutritional problems after birth and were a direct result of poor sanitation and nutrition. Equally, while infant mortality declined everywhere, the variation between regions was still quite pronounced and the overall rate was still high even by Latin

---

[149] Antônio Prates Caldeira, Elisabeth França, Ignez Helena Oliva Perpétuo, and Eugênio Marcos Andrade Goulart, "Evolução da mortalidade infantil por causas evitáveis, Belo Horizonte, 1984–1998," *Revista de Saúde Pública* 39,1 (2005), 68.

[150] Maria da Conceição Nascimento Costa, Eduardo Luiz Andrade Mota, Jairnilson Silva Paim, Lígia Maria Vieira da Silva, Maria da Glória Teixeira, and Carlos Maurício Cardeal Mendes, "Mortalidade infantil no Brasil em períodos recentes de crise econômica," *Revista de Saúde Pública* 37,6 (2003), 702.

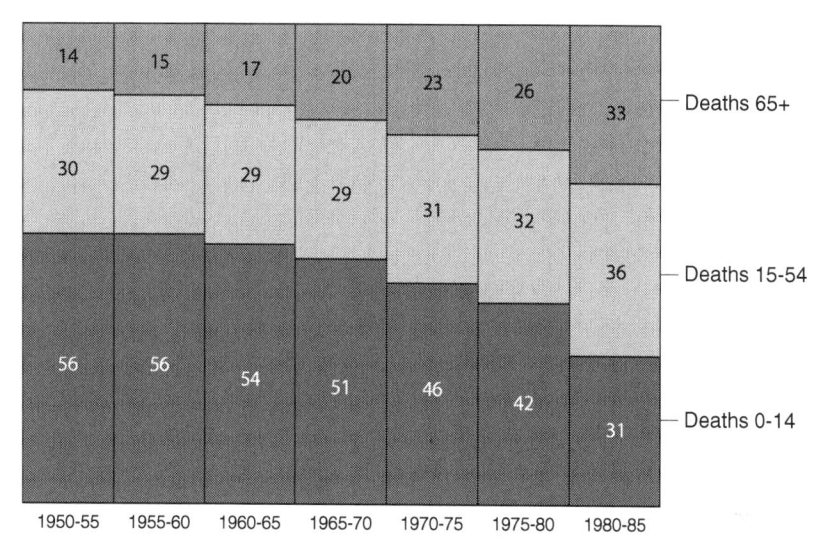

GRAPH 3.34. Share of Total Mortality by Age Group, 1950/1955 to 1980/1985. *Source:* CELADE, Brasil Indices de Crecimento Demográfico. Available at http://www.eclac.org/celade/proyecciones/basedatos_BD.htm

American standards.[151] The northeast had almost twice the rate of infant mortality as the south and southeastern states in 1980. The difference was greater in this year than in 1950, reflecting the fact that the decline in the more economically advanced regions was faster than in the poorer northern states (see Graph 3.35).

The schedule of total deaths as late as 1949/1951 still reflected a traditional society where death from infectious diseases was the major killer for most of the population. In this year the biggest killer was tuberculosis, which accounted for 15 percent of all deaths of all ages. Next came adult diarrhea at 10 percent of deaths followed by heart disease at just 9 percent of all deaths and well below this were cancers at just 5 percent of all deaths. Taken together all the major infectious diseases (tuberculosis, diarrhea, pneumonia, and syphilis) accounted for 37 percent of all deaths for all ages, while the two modern deadly killers in advanced industrial

---

[151] Brazil in 1980–1985 had an infant mortality rate almost twice the rate of Uruguay and even above the average infant mortality rate for Latin America. CELADE, *Boletín Demográfico*, 34,74 (Julio 2004), 24, Table 6. Maternal mortality was also quite high in this period, see Arnaldo Augusto Franco de Siqueira, Ana Cristina d'Andretta Tanaka, Renato Martins Santana, and Pedro Augusto Marcondes de Almeida, "Mortalidade materna no Brasil, 1980," *Revista de Saúde Pública* 18 (1984), 448–465.

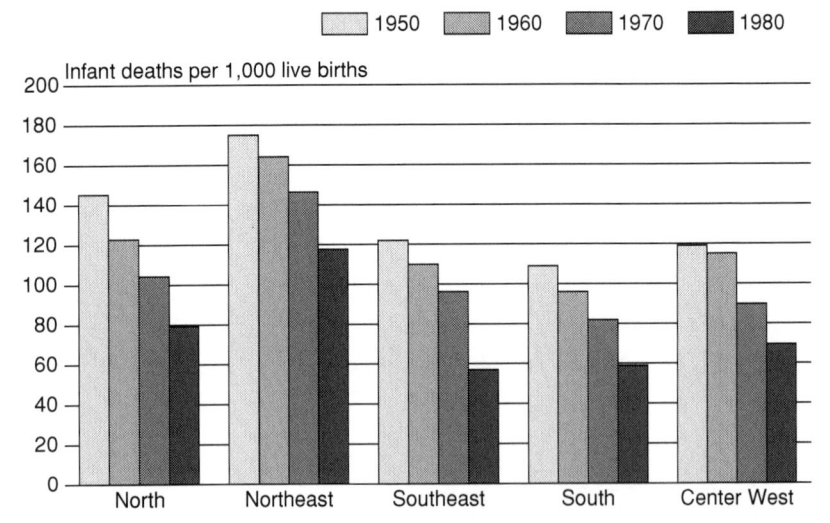

240   The Economic and Social History of Brazil since 1889

☐ 1950   ☐ 1960   ■ 1970   ■ 1980

Infant deaths per 1,000 live births

[Bar chart showing infant mortality by region: North, Northeast, Southeast, South, Center West]

GRAPH 3.35. Infant Mortality by Region, 1950–1980. *Source:* IBGE Série: CD100 – Taxa de mortalidade infantil. Available at http://seriesestatisticas.ibge .gov.br/series.aspx?vcodigo=CD100&sv=46&t=taxa-de-mortalidade-infantil

societies, cancer and heart disease, accounted for only 14 percent of all deaths.[152]

Nevertheless, despite continued inequalities and very high rates of deaths in childhood and of the impact of infectious diseases, life expectancy did significantly advance in this period as child and adult mortality continued to decline. Men and women experienced this increase in life expectancy, with men adding 11.1 years in the thirty year period between 1950 and 1980 and women an even more impressive 14.1 years (see Graph 3.36). While overall rates of life expectancy were changing for all Brazilians, the sharp regional contrasts that reflected class and race differences in access to resources meant that the northern regions had much lower rates than the southern and western states of the federation. The classic pattern of a nation divided between an advanced and retarded region, what one economist called "Belindia," is quite evident in the life expectancy by region available even for as late as 1980. That is, one area of the country was more like Belgium in its vital statistics while another part was similar to India.[153] Though this sharp variation would

[152] IBGE, *Estatísticas do Século XX*, Table "pop_1956aeb-042," available at http://www.ibge.gov.br/seculoxx/arquivos_xls/populacao.shtm.
[153] See Edmar L. Bacha and Herbert S. Klein, ed., *Social Change in Brazil 1945–1985: The Incomplete Transformation* (Albuquerque: University of New Mexico Press, 1989), 3.

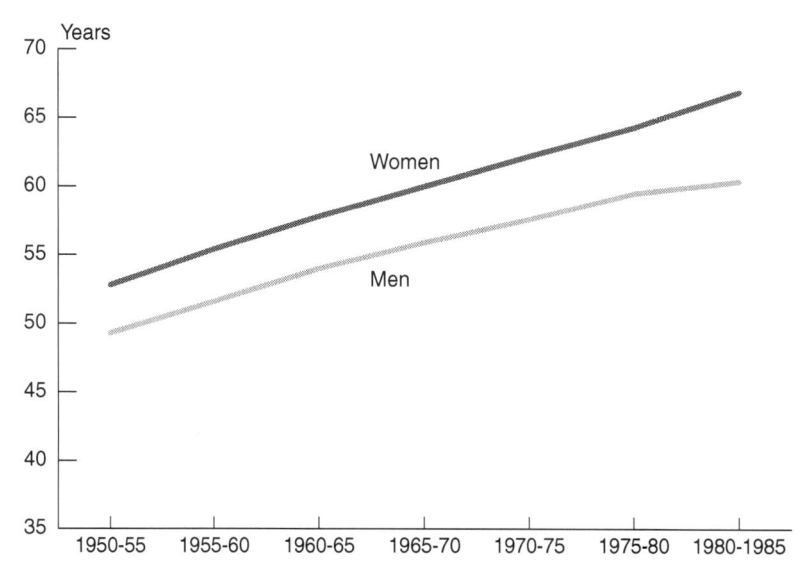

GRAPH 3.36. Life Expectancy at Birth in Brazil, 1950/1955 to 1980/1985. *Source:* CELADE, Brasil Indices de Crecimento Demográfico. Available at http://www.eclac.org/celade/proyecciones/basedatos_BD.htm

slowly change over the next half century, in 1980 it was still very much in evidence.[154] Thus the difference in life expectancy from the worst region to the best region was a startling 7.9 years for men and 7.9 years for women (see Graph 3.37). This regional difference reflected class differences that even within regions clearly marked differential life experiences for Brazilians. In this same year the difference in life expectancy for those with one minimum salary and those who received five minimum salaries or more was a startling 14.8 years.[155]

Although birth rates started to seriously decline by 1970 and the pace continued at a more rapid rate for all regions after that date, the impact of declining mortality rates meant that far more women were surviving to fertile years, and in the period from 1950 to 1960 Brazilian growth peaked at a natural growth rate of 3 percent per annum, then among the highest in the world (see Graph 3.38). At this rate the Brazilian population of 51 million would have duplicated itself in 17.3 years. But that figure

---
[154] A good survey of the regional differences in this period can be found in Charles H. Wood and José Alberto Magno de Carvalho, *The Demography of Inequality in Brazil* (Cambridge: Cambridge University Press, 1988).
[155] IBGE, *Estatísticas do Século XX*, Table "População1981aeb-043.1," available at http://www.ibge.gov.br/seculoxx/arquivos_xls/populacao.shtm.

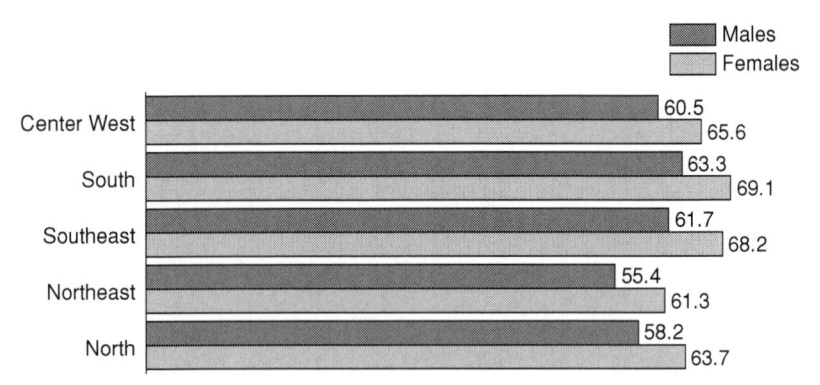

242 The Economic and Social History of Brazil since 1889

■ Males
□ Females

Center West: 60.5 / 65.6
South: 63.3 / 69.1
Southeast: 61.7 / 68.2
Northeast: 55.4 / 61.3
North: 58.2 / 63.7

GRAPH 3.37. Life Expectancy at Birth by Region and Sex in 1980. *Source:* Oliveira and Albuquerque 2005, "A mortalidade no Brasil no período 1980–2004," Tables 2–3, pp. 8–9

of 102 million was reached a decade later than 1967 because of the progressive decline of the natural growth rate.

The rapidly changing rate of natural growth in this period was related to changes in the crude rates of mortality and fertility, with international migration no longer playing a significant role. Initially, in this period of exceptional natural growth mortality declined faster than fertility from 1940 to 1960. But from 1960 to 1980 it was fertility that fell faster than mortality and the result was that the growth rate fell

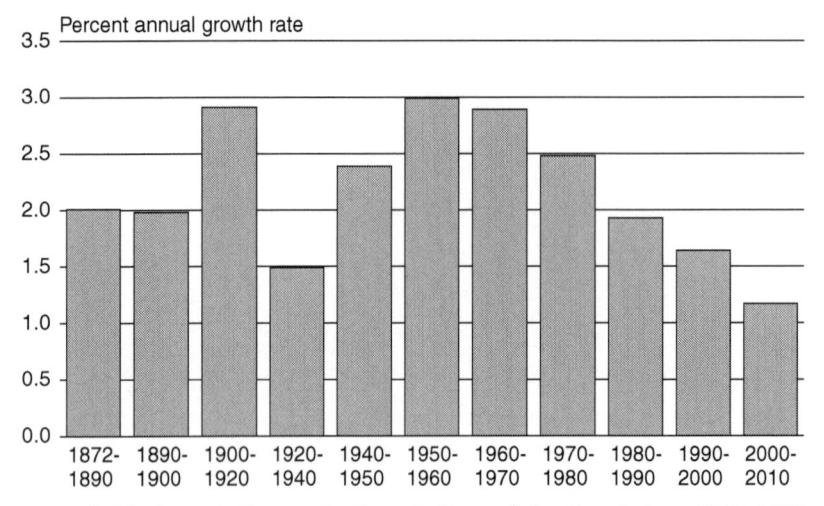

GRAPH 3.38. Annual Geometric Growth Rate of the Population, 1872–2010. *Source:* IBGE, Sinopse do Censo Demográfico 2010 (Rio de Janeiro, 2011), Table 2

significantly in the decade from 1970 to 1980, a fall that would continue in the next period as the crude birth rate continued its steady decline while the crude death rate changed more slowly after 1980 (see Appendix Table A.11).

Along with its expansion of public health initiatives, the government also began a major effort to modernize and stabilize the pension system in this post-Vargas period. Just before the arrival of the military government, the Goulart presidency had created the first national social security plan in 1964 called the *Lei Orgânica da Previdência Social*. This last civilian government had also made the first serious gesture to insure rural workers with the creation of the *Fundo de Assistência ao Trabalhador Rural* (FUNRURAL) in 1961, but could not advance this new reform. Significant reform, however, would come in all pension areas after the seizure of power by the military in April 1964. The conservative first labor minister and his chief of cabinet under the new military regime were well-known social insurance experts.[156] In 1966 the individual IAPs and CAPs were finally replaced by the INPS, which placed the entire system on a sounder financial basis and expanded the coverage to an ever-larger ratio of the national population. By 1968, two years after its founding, INPS, which was supposed to cover employees and self-employed workers, was insuring 7.8 million persons.[157] In the 1970s INPS systematically expanded its coverage of the workforce even further, in 1971 it extended coverage to rural workers (making FUNRURAL an effective institution for the first time), and in 1972 it incorporated those working in domestic service. Inscription of insured workers now grew rapidly and by 1980 INPS had tripled the number of insured participants to 24 million Brazilians, three times the number originally insured in its first full year of operation.[158] Along with insuring pensions of various kinds, INPS and FUNRURAL also began providing health benefits through INAMPS and in 1974 through the new Ministry of Welfare and Social Insurance (*Ministério da Previdência e Assistência Social*), which incorporated all these various insurance, pension, and health delivery plans under one ministry until the end of the military era.

As can be seen from this review of the social changes in this period, the regimes that followed the Vargas period both extended Vargas policies and struggled with the relations he had made with the new popular

---

[156] Malloy, *The Politics of Social Security*, 124–125.
[157] IBGE, *Estatísticas do Século XX* (2003), Table "Prev_social19693aeb_02."
[158] IBGE, *Estatísticas do Século XX* (2003), Table "Prev_social1983aeb_01."

urban classes. Even the military regimes, however fearful they were of the political institutions developed by Vargas, were fully committed to his vision of an industrial modern state and had to adjust their policies to this new vision, which led them to support the establishment of a modern welfare system. Equally the democratic leaders who emerged at the end of this period were intent on extending Vargas's political coalitions, furthering his economic plans in a more systematic and prolabor way, and expanding the welfare state that the military had most fully developed.

In economic terms this was the period in which a modern banking and credit system was created, a coherent industrial policy was implemented, and the country was opened up to foreign investment, especially in the industrial sector. Though much of this "pump priming" would lead to long-term deficits and the growing impact of price inflation, there is little question that the government created an industrial base that was fundamental in making Brazil the leading industrial power in Latin America. The period also represented an important step in the consolidation of a domestic market, spurred by the industrialization process and the government-induced programs that created increasing scales of production in order to satisfy that market, particularly for the manufacture of consumer durables. Thus was created a mass market, and a middle class firmly established itself in Brazil with the active support of the military, clearly seen by them as a counterweight to the laboring classes.

This early postwar period also saw increasing changes in the social area. Health care now became far more available throughout the country as the nation began to experience changes that were leading to a modern demographic structure. Degenerative diseases were becoming the leading cause of death, deaths from infectious diseases were declining in importance, and infant mortality rates were reaching ever-lower levels at a faster pace. In this period the educational system was expanded to the majority of school age children, and Brazil for the first time had a majority of its population who were literate. The differences in access to education by sex were slowly disappearing and a new system of industrial education was able to supply a well-educated labor force for industry. In their need for popular support, the military regimes greatly expanded secondary and tertiary education. Along with the "massification" of secondary education, new science-based universities were established. Moreover, this was the greatest period of interregional migrations, and population densities shifted as the southeast became a Mecca for poor northeasterners. The building of Brasilia also began a new direction of internal migration as the center west and north now attracted migrants from all over Brazil.

Even agriculture was beginning to change in this period with the need to supply food to the growing urban population and the need to replace coffee as the single most important agricultural export. Mechanization, the growing use of fertilizers, and the modernization of the cattle industry were now increasing productivity in agriculture as never before in Brazilian history.

The long and bitter struggle to return to democratic government and remove the military from power was essential in creating new political alliances and attitudes, which, in turn, was fundamental in establishing a modern democratic state after 1984. This long conflict would eventually create a new set of political parties and a more moderate political atmosphere better related to the realities of Brazilian economic and political structures. A new industrial elite now successfully challenged the old planter oligarchy and a powerful labor force was more committed to bettering working conditions than to revolutionary activities. The repression of the military years also forced the economic and political elite to reconsider basic human rights and democratic institutions as fundamental to any new political system that would emerge in the postmilitary period.

4

Consolidation of Democracy since 1985

In the 1982 direct elections for governors, the opposition parties won a major victory, especially the PMDB (Brazilian Democratic Movement Party), which came to power in some of the most important states. Along with the loss of political support, the increasing economic crisis undermined the military government, and protests were expanding. The most relevant of these movements would be a huge mobilization of civil society and opposition parties by the "Elections Now" (or *Diretas Já*) movement. A bill to change the constitution and establish the direct election for the presidency was presented in Congress. There were large rallies, culminating in a huge demonstration in the city of São Paulo, bringing together more than a million people.

Although the last military regime rejected these demands and kept indirect elections, the electoral result was a surprise to the military. The Brazilian Democratic Party (PDS), which constituted the civilian political base of military rule, split when choosing its candidate. The official candidate was Colonel Mário Andreazza, a minister under Figueiredo. But there also emerged a civilian candidate, Paulo Maluf, a politician who had ascended to power in São Paulo under the protection of the military regime, having been mayor of the capital and governor of the state. Although not having official support, Maluf was able to launch himself as the candidate of the government party. Although the indirect election was decided by an electoral college that the government electors controlled, the split in the PDS made possible the victory of the opposition candidate Tancredo Neves, governor of Minas Gerais, known for his moderation and political skill. Jose Sarney, a traditional government party man, who

Consolidation of Democracy since 1985   247

had opposed the candidacy of Maluf, was the vice president on the opposition ticket.[1]

Thus the civilian opposition arrived to the government ahead of the schedule set by the military, disrupting the long-planned transition that began with Geisel, had continued in the six years of the Figueiredo government, and should have been completed in another six years of a final military presidency. Some hard-line officers expressed dissatisfaction with the results and threatened to overturn the election and the possession of the civilian president. But the transition still brought surprises. On March 14, 1985, one day before his inauguration as president, Tancredo Neves became ill and died a month later. Vice President José Sarney then assumed the presidency of the republic, and became the first civilian president since 1964.

Sarney's presidency represented an historical irony, since it brought to power a traditional government politician who had been president of the party that upheld the military regime and not one of the leaders of the opposition to military rule. But Sarney understood the unusual situation and decided to rule with the parliamentary base of the former opposition, centered on the PMDB. He took possession in a moment of political tension when the legitimacy of his possession was questioned, and he was forced to run a country in deep economic crisis, a crisis that was aggravated on his mandate. But his presidency represented an advance in the democratic process, accelerating the long transition started in the Geisel period.[2]

The return to democracy also opened up the nation to a host of new movements and ideas. In the long struggle against the Cold War dictatorships in Latin America, there emerged a series of new ideas and new

---

[1] José Sarney had been president of Arena, the party that anticipated the PDS. He was, therefore, a politician with close ties to the military regime. Sarney was part of a group of politicians who abandoned the PDS and formed the Partido da Frente Liberal (PFL). The PFL joined with the PMDB, the principal party of the opposition, to launch the candidacy of Tancredo Neves and Sarney was indicated by the PFL to be part of the electoral team as vice president.

[2] Tancredo's illness created a constitutional problem, because there was no certainty as to whether the vice president would take over when the president was unable to take power. The alternative would be the temporary possession of the presidency by the president of the Chamber of Deputies who would call new elections in case the president could not assume office, but this created the risk of a setback in the democratic process with the possibility of a new military coup. But the legitimacy of the mandate of Sarney was frequently questioned.

political positions that would become dominant themes in the post-1980 period. The failure of armed struggle by the far left, combined with the major campaign of torture and assassinations carried out by the military regimes, led to a basic reevaluation of the importance of what came to be called "human rights." This involved a new commitment on the Left to the need for democratic institutions, the rule of law, and a host of basic rights that had been considered of no great importance by the traditional radical and revolutionary movements. But the combination of the failure of armed revolt, and the need to obtain international support for prodemocratic groups created a new set of goals and ideals on which the Center and Left movements could finally agree, and that even attracted interest on the Right.

Among the new ideas that emerged were not only a need to protect minorities, be they ethnic or sexual, but also for the first time there arose a mass movement concerned with what became known as the "*meio ambiente*" – or the environment. In the decade of the 1970s and 1980s there emerged a major environmental movement in Brazil, the first in Latin America.[3] Given the importance of the Amazon and Atlantic forests and rivers to world climate conditions there was also a corresponding buildup of international concern to the ever-greater expansion of farming, ranching, and lumbering that was leading to massive deforestation and to unrestrained Brazilian investments in road and dam constructions that was supported by international lending agencies. The grassroots movement in Brazil, the emergence of international nongovernmental organizations (NGOs) concerned with the environment, and the rise of a new middle class in Brazil now aware of the increasing degradation of urban life due to pollution, all combined in the last three decades of the twentieth century to create a power green movement in Brazil.

The first formal ecological defense group in Brazil was founded in June 1971 in Rio Grande do Sul.[4] It was the first ecological association founded in Latin America. Other local groups soon followed in other

---

[3] On the impact of these recent and earlier policies, see Warren Dean, *With Broadaxe and Firebrand: The Destruction of the Brazilian Atlantic Forest* (Berkeley: University of California Press, 1995). For a good survey of this question in Latin America, see Shawn W. Miller, *An Environmental History of Latin America* (Cambridge: Cambridge University Press, 2007), and his earlier study on colonial deforestation, *Fruitless Trees: Portuguese Conservation and Brazil's Colonial Timber* (Stanford, CA: Stanford University Press, 2000).

[4] This was the Gaucho Association for the Protection of the Natural Environment (*Associação Gaucha de Proteção ao Ambiente Natural*, or AGAPAN).

regions and education campaigns began to raise awareness of conservation issues. The first indication of the impact of national and international concerns about deforestation and degradation of soil and water resources of the country occurred in the presidency of General Geisel. In 1974 he established the Special Secretariat of the Environment (*Secretaria Especial de Meio Ambiente*) because of insistence of international aid organizations on the necessities of a formal government agency that could produce environmental impact studies before international loans could be approved.

Between the oil crises of 1973–1974 and 1978–1979 and the slow return toward democracy, the ecological movement began to expand from its elite origins and become a more political and militant movement in Brazil. One of the more impressive such movements was led by the rubber collection workers of the northeastern state of Pará under Chico Mendes who organized systematic opposition to deforestation in the mid- to late 1970s and became a symbol to the ecological movement internationally.[5] By the late 1970s and early 1980s state ecological associations had been founded, the first of many national ecological journals was produced, and a major national discussion had emerged on the need to protect the Amazon. The increasing strength of this movement was shown with the creation in 1985 of a new pressure group intent on influencing the constitutional assembly writing the new democratic constitution, the so-called Inter-State Organization of Ecologists for the Constituent Assembly. This highly political organization promoted green candidates for the constitutional assembly and demanded a say on ecology for the new constitution.[6] Its success was evident in the new Constitution of 1988, in which the environment appeared in 18 different acts and the government for the first

---

[5] Margaret E. Keck, "Social Equity and Environmental Politics in Brazil: Lessons from the Rubber Tappers of Acre," *Comparative Politics* 27,4 (Julho 1995), 409–424.

[6] For the early history of this movement see Eduardo J. Viola, "The Ecologist Movement in Brazil (1974–1986): From Environmentalism to Ecopolitics," *International Journal of Urban and Regional Research* 12,2 (June 1988), 211–228; and Onil Banerjee, Alexander J. Macpherson, and Janaki Alavalapati, "Toward a Policy of Sustainable Forest Management in Brazil: A Historical Analysis," *The Journal of Environment & Development* 18,2 (June 2009), 130–153; and Wilson José Ferreira de Oliveira, "Gênese e redefinições do militantismo ambientalista no Brasil," *DADOS Revista de Ciências Sociais* 51,3 (2008), 751–777. On the evolution of policies and institutions at the state level, see Barry Ames and Margaret E. Keck, "The Politics of Sustainable Development: Environmental Policy Making in Four Brazilian States," *Journal of Interamerican Studies and World Affairs* 39,4 (Winter 1997–1998), 1–40.

time systematically committed itself to the defense of the environment.[7] Not only did the movement slowly influence the major opposition parties and push for "green" candidates, but it also led to the foundation of a formal Partido Verde (or Green Party) in early 1986. By 2010 the party led by Marina Silva obtained 20 percent of the national vote in the presidential election of that year, coming in third after the PT and PMDB.

Aside from its formal political involvement and educational campaigns, the ecology movement has had an impact on state and federal laws designed to protect the environment. One of its earliest achievements was the establishment in 1985 of a new Ministry of the Environment and Urban Development in the first democratic government. In 1989 was created the Brazilian Institute for the Environment and Renewable Natural Resources (IBAMA) which by the Constitution of 1988 was given control over all national forests. Slowly these government agencies have begun to have an impact on preserving forest and wetlands and establishing systematic legislation to protect the environment. But enforcement has varied from government to government in the past twenty-five years, and in 2012 there was even an attempt to emasculate the important and well-regarded 1965 forestry law – which was eventually opposed by the Dilma administration.[8]

Brazilian and international environment groups have also systematically pressured the big international lending agencies to change their lending policies to the Brazilian government. This became evident in the late 1970s when the Word Bank began to give its first loans for work in the Amazon region. The most controversial of which was a major investment in colonization in the Northwest Amazon called the POLONOROESTE project. Although some attempt to control ecological conditions was written into the grant, this was largely unsuccessful and the bank was roundly

---

[7] Vladimir Passos de Freitas, "A constituição federal e a efetividade das normas ambientais" (PhD thesis Faculdade de Direito da Universidade Federal do Paraná, 1999); and Antonio Herman De Vasconcellos E. Benjamin, "O Meio Ambiente na Constituição Federal de 1988," *Informativo Jurídico da Biblioteca Ministro Oscar Saraiva* 19,1 (Janeiro–Junho 2008), 37–80. On regular law changes related to conservation issues, see Carlos José Saldanha Machado, "Mudanças conceituais na administração pública do meio ambiente," *Ciência e Cultura* 55,4 (2003), 24–26.

[8] Under pressure from the green movement, President Dilma was forced to veto 12 items of the code and modify another 32 provisions. See the reports in *O Estado de São Paulo* and *O Globo*, available at http://www.estadao.com.br/noticias/vidae,dilma-veta-12-pontos-e-faz-32-modificacoes-no-codigo-florestal,877923,0.htm and http://veja.abril.com.br/noticia/brasil/dilma-veta-12-itens-do-codigo-florestal.

criticized for its investment by national and international NGOs, thus forcing the bank to temporarily suspend its support in the mid-1980s and change its environmental guidelines.[9] Meanwhile the bank published two critical reports in the late 1980s showing how Brazilian tax laws fostered ecological degradation and the extent of Amazonian deforestation.[10] At the same time the bank was becoming increasingly greener. By 1987 the bank had established a central Environment Department, as well as Environment Divisions for the areas of the world, which was raised to the level of a vice presidency in 1992.[11]

As a response to the two world oil shocks, the Brazilian government also began to actively concern itself with alternative fuel sources, especially as Brazil was then still a major importer of foreign oil. In 1975 as a result of the oil shock of the previous year the government established PROACOOL to use sugar as an alternative fuel. It subsidized the production of sugar and ruled that 24 percent of all gasoline contain ethanol and required PETROBRAS, the government oil agency, to distribute ethanol products throughout the country. The government expanded the program after the second oil crisis in 1976, and by 2005 Brazil was producing four million gallons of ethanol about the same as was being produced from corn in the United States. All told ethanol now accounted for 40 percent of fuel consumption in Brazil compared to only 3 percent in the U.S. fuels market. Moreover, the more efficient Brazilian program allowed it to produce the same amount of bio-fuel as the United States on half the amount of land. By the crop year of 2004/05, Brazil was not only the world's largest sugar cane producer by far, but also its leading ethanol producer, accounting for 37 percent of world production.[12] But

---

[9] On the problems related to ecology on all these joint World Bank and Brazilian government Amazonian projects, see Sérgio Margulis, "O Desempenho ambiental do Governo Brasileiro e do Banco Mundial em Projetos Co-financiados pelo Banco," Textos Para Discussão No. 194 (Brasília: IPEA, 1999).

[10] See the two papers by Hans Binswanger, "Brazilian Policies That Encourage Deforestation," Environment Department Paper No. 16 (Washington, DC: World Bank, 1988); and Dennis J. Mahar, *Government Policies and Deforestation in the Brazilian Amazon* (Washington, DC: World Bank, 1989).

[11] John Redwood II, *World Bank Approaches to the Brazilian Amazon: The Bumpy Road toward Sustainable Development*, LCR Sustainable Development Working Paper No. 13 (Washington DC: World Bank, November 2002).

[12] Marcus Renato S. Xavier, "The Brazilian Sugarcane Ethanol Experience" (Washington, DC: Competitive Enterprise Institute, February 17, 2007); and J. Martines-Filho, H. L. Burnquist, and C. E. F. Vian, "Bioenergy and the Rise of Sugarcane-based Ethanol in Brazil," *Choices* 21,2 (2006), 91–96.

even this development has led to much debate among ecologists as to its positive and negative environmental impacts.[13]

Despite the developing power of the green movement and increasing government action, there is still a continuation of illegal logging and ranching in the Amazon, and other natural habitats with a decrease in biodiversity and native fauna and flora.[14] Moreover, the rate of deforestation has not decreased in recent decades, and Brazil's environmental efforts have produced far fewer results than other areas of the world. The United Nations in its 2011 survey of world forests estimated that Brazil contained 520 million hectares of forests which represented 13 percent of the total world forests. In the decade from 1990 to 2000 Brazil lost on average 2.9 million hectares of forest per annum, which represented 35 percent of the total world forest loss in that decade. But in the decade from 2000 to 2010 Brazil lost another 2.6 million hectares per annum, which now accounted for 51 percent of total world forest destruction.[15] There are also serious and long-term problems of sanitation, air quality, potable water, and substandard housing in many urban centers, which Brazil is only slowly resolving. Nevertheless, there is a powerful green movement that continues to undertake systematic campaigns to improve conditions in the country, especially from an evermore reluctant PT

---

[13] Luiz A. Martinelli and Solange Filoso, "Expansion of Sugarcane Ethanol Production in Brazil: Environmental and Social Challenges," *Atmospheric Environment* 18,4 (2008), 885–898.

[14] On the difficulties of controlling deforestation, see Sérgio Margulis, *Causes of Deforestation of the Brazilian Amazon*, World Bank Working Papers No. 22 (Washington, DC: World Bank, 2004). Also see Stephen G. Bunker, *Underdeveloping the Amazon: Extraction, Unequal Exchange, and the Failure of the Modern State* (Urbana: University of Illinois Press, 1985); Michael Goulding, Nigel J. H. Smith, and Dennis J. Mahar, *Floods of Fortune: Ecology and Economy along the Amazon* (New York: Columbia University Press, 1996). On the subtropical Atlantic coast forests of Brazil known as the Mata Atlantica and their precarious survival, see Milton Cezar Ribeiro, Jean Paul Metzger, Alexandre Camargo Martensen, Flávio Jorge Ponzoni, and Márcia Makiko Hirota, "The Brazilian Atlantic Forest: How Much Is Left, and How Is the Remaining Forest Distributed? Implications for Conservation," *Biological Conservation* 142 (2009), 1141–1153. To date, most of the native bird loss in Brazil has occurred in the Mata Atlântica zone. See Miguel Angelo Marini and Federico Innecco Garcia, "Bird Conservation in Brazil," *Conservation Biology* 19,3 (June 2005), 665–671. But it is evident that mammals are being seriously affected by increasing deforestation in the Amazon. See William F. Laurance, Heraldo L. Vasconcelos, and Thomas E. Lovejoy, "Forest Loss and Fragmentation in the Amazon: Implications for Wildlife Conservation," *Oryx* 34,1 (2000), 39–45; and William F. Laurance et al., "The Fate of Amazonian Forest Fragments: A 32-Year Investigation," *Biological Conservation* 144 (2011), 56–67.

[15] FAO, *State of the World's Forests 2011* (Rome: Food and Agriculture Organization of the United Nations, 2011), 110–118, Table 2.

series of governments, which have stressed growth over environmental protection. All these national and international movements have led to a massive amount of scientific research on sustainable resources, reforestation, and the protection of the fragile Amazon, which has made the Brazilian environment one of the most studied in the world.[16]

The democratic government was also forced to change the legal structure that was inherited from the military regime, based as it was on centralization and authoritarianism. The main question was to approve a new constitution, which returned to democratic principles. The new constitution, though highly advanced in terms of political and social rights, has been widely criticized since its approval in 1988.[17] The constitution is very extensive and detailed, reflecting the clash of many segments of society, free from the shackles of dictatorship, but without one group or vision dominating.[18] For example, there was a trend of strengthening fiscal decentralization, and states and municipalities increased their share in fiscal revenue relative to the federal government, but without taking corresponding responsibility. In addition, there were created additional commitments to public spending making the execution of the budget and establishing a fiscal balance more difficult. Several public monopolies were enshrined in the constitution under pressure from nationalist groups or as reflections of corporate interests. On the other hand, the Constitution of 1988 was considered one of the most advanced in terms

---

[16] On the relation between deforestation and global warming, see the latest essay by P. M. Fearnside and W. F. Laurance, "Tropical Deforestation and Greenhouse Gas Emissions," *Ecological Applications* 14,4 (2004), 982–986. On sustainable activities, see among the more general studies Daniel C. Nepstad, Claudia M. Stickler, Britaldo Soares-Filho, and Frank Merry, "Interactions among Amazon Land Use, Forests and Climate: Prospects for a Near-term Forest Tipping Point," *Philosophical Transactions of the Royal Society B* 363 (2008), 1737–1746; Daniel C. Nepstad et al., "The End of Deforestation in the Brazilian Amazon," *Science* 326 (December 2009), 1350–1351; Britaldo Silveira Soares-Filho et al., "Modelling Conservation in the Amazon Basin," *Nature* 440,23 (March 2006), 520–523; Luiz A. Martinelli, Rosamond Naylor, Peter M. Vitousek, and Paulo Moutinho, "Agriculture in Brazil: Impacts, Costs, and Opportunities for a Sustainable Future," *Current Opinion in Environmental Sustainability* 2 (2010), 431–438.

[17] The PT – the Workers Party – did not approve the new constitution. In an interview, President Lula justified his opposition to the new constitution: "The PT came to Congress with a draft constitution ready and finished that, if approved, would certainly have made it much more difficult to govern than today. As an opposition party that had never come to power, we had magical solutions to all the country's ills. Maybe we did not realize that, in such a short time, we could come to power. And then we would have had the responsibility to put into practice all that we proposed." São Paulo, interview of Luis Ignacio Lula da Silva, *Jornal a Folha de São Paulo*, 5 de outubro de 2008.

[18] Since 1988 there have been 70 amendments to the federal constitution.

of political and social rights. The extension of voting rights to illiterates and the reduction of the minimum voting age represented major policy innovations. The constitution provided for a presidency to be decided by a majority of voters in two rounds of elections if necessary, with a four-year term without reelection.

The party structure became more complex during the period of President Sarney, with the proliferation of new parties. The PMDB, which was the largest opposition party to the military regime, lost some of its members with the creation of the Brazilian Social Democracy Party (PSDB), which assumed a position of center-left, and would eventually reach the presidency with the election of Fernando Henrique Cardoso. The old PDS, which upheld the military regime, also split, with the formation of the Liberal Front Party (PFL), which became the main center-right group. Finally, the PT experienced very rapid growth and soon became the main opposition party. It identified itself with union issues and had significant representation of the middle class. Over the years, it also became an important representative of government employees. Another party of the Left created in that period was the Democratic Labor Party (PDT), which resurrected the old Brazilian Labor Party of Vargas and was led by Leonel Brizola, one of the politicians most feared by the military regime, who at the end of the military period had been elected governor of the state of Rio de Janeiro. Numerous other parties of the Left and Right were created in this postmilitary period, often emerging from dissenting elements in preexisting parties.[19]

One of the characteristics of the party system in Brazil is its weakness in terms of party loyalty, with frequent changes of parties even by politicians active in the legislative assembly or the executive branch. These parties also did not always have a programmatic or ideological coherence. Some analysts felt that the weakness of political parties strengthened governance, with party fragmentation and fluid identities permitting the executive to form the parliamentary basis needed for government stability.[20] Another feature of the Brazilian party system is the creation of parties

---

[19] Lourdes Sola, ed., *O Estado e a transição: política e economia na Nova República* (São Paulo: Vértice, 1988); Maria do Carmo Campello de Souza, "A Nova República sob a espada de Dâmocles," in *Democratizando o Brasil*, ed. Alfred Stepan (Rio de Janeiro: Paz e Terra, 1985), 568–591; Alfred Stepan, "As prerrogativas militares nos regimes pósautoritários," in *Democratizando o Brasil*, ed. Alfred Stepan (Rio de Janeiro: Paz e Terra, 1985), 521–562; Rachel Meneguello, *Partidos e governos no Brasil contemporâneo (1985–1997)* (Rio de Janeiro: Paz e Terra, 1998); and Margaret E. Keck, *The Workers' Party and Democratization in Brazil* (New Haven, CT: Yale University Press, 1992).

[20] The crisis of the so-called *mensalão* (monthly payments by the government to opposition deputies for their support) in the first Lula administration showed the difficulties of

or the use of small local parties to support the rise of political leaders who find no room in the more traditional associations. The election of the successor of Sarney was an example of this process.

But beyond the questions of political transition and the natural instability that continued for two decades after the dictatorship, the economic crisis deepened and inflation became explosive under the new civilian rule. The previous government had signed several letters of intent with the International Monetary Fund (IMF) that promoted a recessive economic policy. With the new government this led to an impasse. The IMF insisted that the new administration accept the compromises agreed to by the previous military government and that it sign a new letter of intent adopting these recessive policies. But this was impossible for the new administration, for two reasons. The opposition fiercely criticized such policies and the new administration could not make commitments to the IMF. The end of military rule and democratic openness made it difficult to maintain recessive measures and the wage squeeze. Furthermore, the previous government had obtained a major surplus in the balance of trade of U.S.$12 billion in 1985. This favorable trade balance was another argument against a new agreement with the IMF. But the overall situation was critical, because the external debt totaled U.S.$105 billion and interest due that year was close to U.S.$11 billion. The public accounts were in poor condition and the federal government and the states had difficulties in honoring their commitments. Monthly inflation was now above 10 percent.[21]

Typically, policies that reduced domestic consumption were capable of containing inflationary pressures. However, the high level of indexation existing in Brazil suggested that the traditional recessive methods were not sufficient to control the inflation in the country. Faced with such evidence, in the first half of the 1980s, there were new ideas proposed about alternative antiinflationary policies. In January 1986, less than a year after the inauguration of Sarney, inflation reached a new level of 16 percent per month.[22] The unions rightly pushed for more frequent adjustments than the semester correction still in force, proposing adjustments in

---

governing with a fragmented power structure and lacking the means necessary to co-opt such opposition parties.

[21] In March 1985, when Sarney assumed power, the monthly inflation was Cost of Living for São Paulo-FIP: 12 percent; General Indice of Prices-FGV: 10 percent; and Indice National of Consumer Prices-FIBGE: 12 percent.

[22] In January 1986, monthly inflation reached the following levels: Cost of Living for São Paulo-FIP: 19 percent; General Indice of Prices-FGV: 16 percent; and Indice National of Consumer Proces-FIBGE: 14 percent.

wages quarterly or monthly. More realistic salary corrections, quarterly or monthly, no matter how justified they were to prevent further deterioration of real wages, probably would cause a further acceleration of inflation, with unforeseeable consequences in a period of political transition and given a still fragile democracy. If in the authoritarian period restrictive stabilization and wage squeeze policies could be adopted, the new democratic civilian regime could not disregard the potential political and social opposition that would arise with the implementation of such a new recessive program, which in any case would have had doubtful results. These facts led to the implementation of monetary reform of February 28, 1986, known as the Cruzado Plan, which changed the system of national currency, froze all prices, including exchange rates, and eliminated indexing.[23]

The plan was an instant success. There was a dramatic reduction of inflation and strong popular support for the price freeze. As with other plans of the same type that would later be introduced in Brazil, there was a marked increase in demand, with growth in output and employment. The sharp decline in inflation had positive effects on income and consumption of the poorest population, since they had had less capacity to protect themselves from high and increasing inflation. There was also exceptional monetary expansion with the end of the so-called inflation tax, which had affected the retention of currency and demand deposits, and also by the monetary illusion caused by the dramatic fall of the nominal interest rate. But frozen prices encouraged speculation in commodities. Since it was believed that the price freeze could not be maintained indefinitely there were anticipated purchases of stocks of goods, with buyers taking advantage of low interest rates then in force. High interest rates could have reduced demand and prevented the speculative retention of stock. Domestic demand grew vigorously, pressuring productive capacity, causing lack of supplies, shortages of goods, and disregard for price controls. At the same time, the increase in domestic consumption generated a trade deficit. While the monthly trade surplus exceeded U.S.$1 billion in early 1986, by October of that year it was in deficit. In July, there had already occurred

---

[23] Conversion in the form of salaries for the new currency was 8 percent increase in real wages and 15 percent for those receiving minimum wage, increasing the pressure on consumption. An explanation of the rules for converting wages is available at Eduardo Modiano, "A ópera dos três cruzados: 1985–1989," in *A ordem do progresso*, ed. Marcelo de Paiva Abreu (Rio de Janeiro: Editora Campus, 1992), 347–386; and Francisco Vidal Luna, "O Programa de Estabilização e os Salários," *Revista de Economia Política* 6,3 (Julho–Setembro 1986), 129–131.

the first attempt to reduce demand, but the measures taken were very mild and did not resolve the situation. In October, given the deterioration of the trade balance, the government decided to carry out a small change in the exchange rate and announced that further devaluations could occur.

After the general elections of November 1986, came new measures to curb demand and improve the public accounts, with the authorization to increase various prices, including public tariffs. The effects of these measures were immediate: inflation, which had remained relatively low during 1986, jumped to 7 percent per month in December and 12 percent per month in January. At the start of 1987, the Cruzado Plan was over. Brazil, in the face of external difficulties, and with the closing of the international financial market for Latin American countries, was forced to suspend foreign debt service and to enforce a moratorium.[24]

In the short run, the Cruzado Plan had positive effects in terms of income distribution, particularly by reducing the inflation tax and increasing employment. There was also expanded social spending. However, the return of inflation, the end of international loans and investments and the deterioration of public accounts, led to a failure to sustain the social progress achieved. GDP, which grew during the first two years of the Sarney government, showed only modest growth in the next three years.

In the Sarney government, when inflation reached uncontrollable levels two other plans were tried with similar characteristics. Although these two plans had succeeded in assimilating the experience of the Cruzado Plan, they were less successful and had no popular support.[25] The results

---

[24] There is an extensive bibliography on the Plano Cruzado, which represented a theoretical innovation in the policies to combat inertial inflation. On this experience, see Modiano, "A ópera dos três cruzados: 1985–1989"; João Sayad, *Planos Cruzado e Real: acertos e desacertos. Seminários Dimac* (Rio de Janeiro: IPEA, Setembro 30, 2000); Maria Silva Bastos Marques, "O Plano Cruzado: teoria e prática," *Revista de Economia Política* 8,3 (Julho–Setembro 1983), 101–130; Luiz Carlos Bresser Pereira, "Inflação inercial e o Plano Cruzado," *Revista de Economia Política* 6,3 (Julho–Setembro 1986), 9–24; Edmar L. Bacha, "Moeda, inércia e conflito: reflexões sobre políticas de estabilização no Brasil," *Pesquisa e Planejamento Econômico* 18,1 (1988), 1–16; J. M. Rego, *Inflação inercial, teoria sobre inflação e o Plano Cruzado* (Rio de Janeiro: Paz e Terra, 1986). Innumerable articles of the Plano Cruzado are found in *Revista de Economia Politica* 6,3 (Julho–Setembro 1986), 121–151.

[25] Modiano, "A ópera dos três cruzados: 1985–1989"; Ricardo Carneiro, *Desenvolvimento em crise. A economia brasileira no último quarto do século XX* (São Paulo: Editora UNESP, 2002); José Pedro Macarini, "A política econômica do Governo Sarney: os Planos Cruzado (1986) e Bresser (1987)," Texto para Discussão No. 157 (Campinas: IE/UNICAMP, Março 2009); Luiz Carlos Bresser Pereira, "Heterodoxia e Ortodoxia no Plano Bresser," *Revista Conjuntura Econômica* 47,2 (Fevereiro 1993), 52–54.

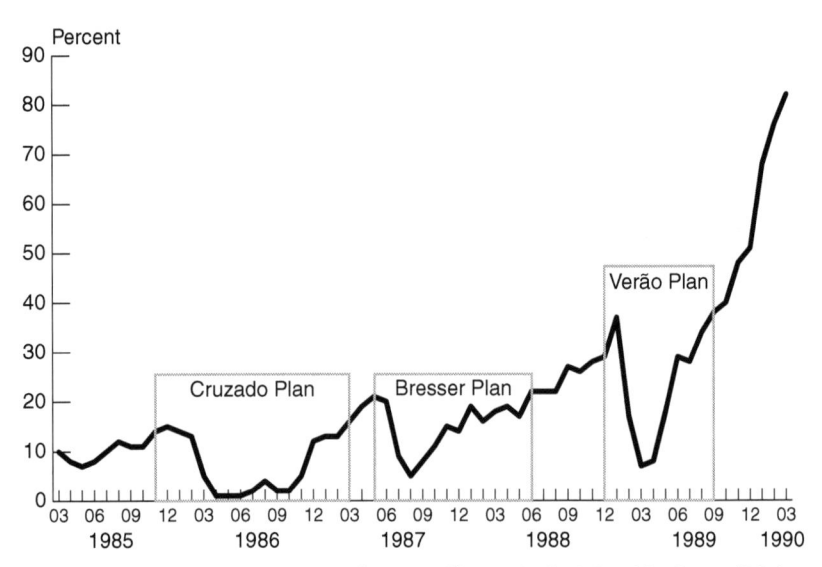

GRAPH 4.1. Sarney Government – Average Change in the Monthly Cost of Living, IPCA, 1985–1990. *Source:* Ipeadata

were similar: inflation was temporarily reduced, and when it returned it did so at even higher levels. The merit of these two plans was to delay or avoid hyperinflation. Although the country had experienced long periods of extremely high inflation, there was no lack of economic activity. A new plan was launched as soon as inflation returned, reintroducing indexation mechanisms that allowed relatively normal functioning of the economy, including the broad financial markets. The local currency was never replaced by another form of payment or the dollar. The dollar was used as reference and served for large transactions in some markets, such as real estate. Since there were exchange controls, there formed a significant parallel market whose premium at times exceeded 100 percent. But the dollar served mainly as a store of value, not as a means of payment. But high inflation deteriorated general economic conditions and hampered growth.

Inflation fluctuated at the whim of the plans, and worked as a spring. After an abrupt reduction, it quickly returned to a new higher level, reaching monthly rates of 80 percent at the end of the Sarney government (see Graph 4.1). Although President Sarney had completed his mandate before the conclusion of negotiations of the foreign debt, there was a recovery in the trade balance with a surplus of U.S.$20 billion in 1988 and U.S.$16 billion the next year.[26] In both years, even the current account showed a positive balance. Throughout his tenure, the amount of external debt remained relatively stable at around U.S.$115 billion, and the presidency ended with reserves of about U.S.$10 billion. In the 1980s, the country accumulated a trade surplus of U.S.$86 billion, but paid U.S.$94 billion in foreign debt interest. However the government postponed all reforms of an increasingly dysfunctional tax system.[27]

It is often said that this was a "lost decade." From the political point of view there were huge democratic advances. But from the economic perspective, the 1980s disrupted the long growth cycle of the first seven decades of the century. During those seven decades, Brazil grew at an average rate of 5.25 percent.[28] In the 1980s, the economy had accumulated overall growth of just more than 30 percent versus 130 percent in the previous decade (see Graph 4.2). Brazil was not the only developing country to experience poor economic performance in those ten years. At that time, few countries in the region managed to balance their external accounts and regain their ability to grow (see Table 4.1). Besides the internal problems faced by Brazil, particularly the acceleration of inflation, the high internal and external indebtedness, as well as the fiscal difficulties faced by the state, the international financial market conditions contributed to the low growth of the country during the 1980s. In general, the so-called debt crisis of the 1980s affected all indebted countries. Even central core countries suffered by the need for adjustment in this period.[29] It should be recalled that Brazil only concluded its negotiations on its external debt in 1994.

---

[26] Although the discussion about the renegotiation of the external debt had begun in the late 1980s, it was completed only in 1994, following the Brady Plan model, which allowed the renegotiation of external debt in many countries. Brazil renegotiated a total of U.S.$55 billion of debt, and by 2006 this renegotiated debt was effectively paid off. *Dívida Pública Mobiliária Reestruturada.* Tesouro Nacional, available at http://www.stn.fazenda.gov.br/divida_publica/downloads/div_r_bib.pdf.

[27] The difficulties to control public expenditures, as well as the experience of high inflation, forced the federal government to promote complex tax changes that completely distorted Brazilian taxes, creating an irrational, inefficient, and regressive system. The modernization of the tax system that had been promoted in the early 1960s during the early years of the military regime lost its functionality.

[28] Ipeadata. PIB – var. real anual – (% a.a.).

[29] The United States, e.g., had a negative growth of GDP in 1980 (–0.3 percent) and 1982 (–2.0 percent) and a high inflation in the years 1980 (13.5 percent) and 1981 (10.3 percent).

260 *The Economic and Social History of Brazil since 1889*

TABLE 4.1. *Annual Change in GDP of the Principal Latin American Countries, 1980–1989 (%)*

	1980	1981	1982	1983	1984	1985	1986	1987	1988	1989	1980–1989
Argentina	4	–6	–5	4	2	–8	8	3	–3	–8	–8
Brazil	9	–4	1	–3	5	8	8	4	0	3	33
Chile	8	5	–10	–4	8	7	6	7	7	11	51
Colombia	4	2	1	2	3	3	6	5	4	3	40
Dominica	8	4	2	5	1	–2	4	10	2	4	44
Ecuador	4	3	–1	–3	4	3	4	–2	8	1	25
Mexico	9	9	–1	–4	4	3	–4	2	1	4	24
Paraguay	15	9	–4	–3	3	4	0	4	6	6	46
Peru	3	7	–1	–12	5	3	10	8	–9	–12	0
Uruguay	6	2	–10	–10	–1	2	9	8	2	1	5
Venezuela	–4	0	–2	–4	1	0	7	4	6	–9	–3

Source: http://data.worldbank.org/indicator/NY.GDP.MKTP.KD.ZG.

Like all other sectors of the economy, agriculture was affected by the crisis of the 1980s. The need for internal and external adjustments led to the adoption of recessionary policies, reenforced by agreements with the IMF. The provision of rural credit, based on large government subsidies and the use of funds derived from deposits, underwent dramatic reduction. Inflation made demand deposits scarce, and changed the basis

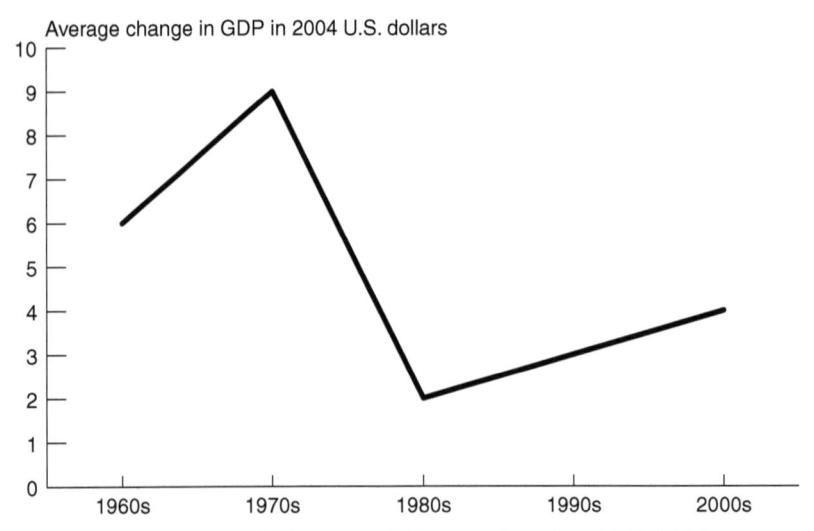

GRAPH 4.2. Variation of Average GDP per Decade, 1960–2000. *Source:* Ipeadata – GAG_PIBCAP

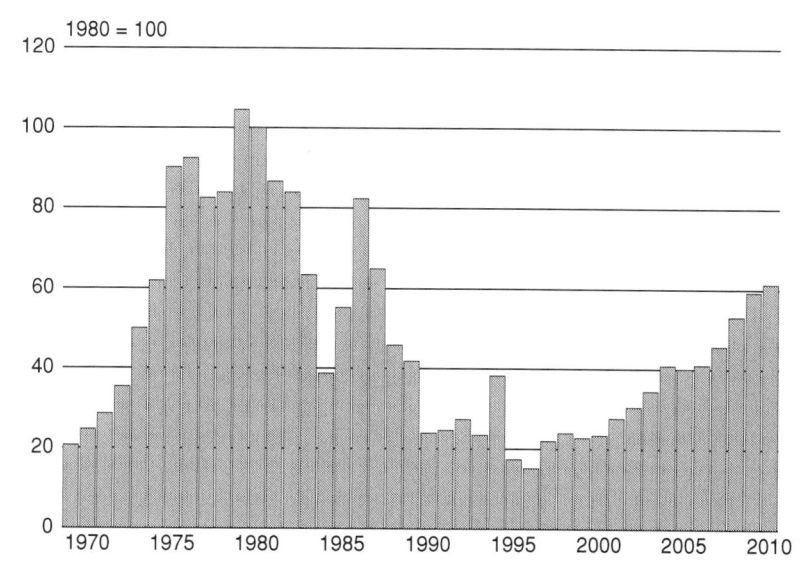

GRAPH 4.3. Evolution of Rural Credit in Constant Prices, 1969–2010. *Source:* Banco Central do Brasil, *Anúario Estatístico do Crédito Rural* 2010.

on which to fix the liability that banks were required to spend on rural credit. At the same time the need to control the public accounts restricted grants. In 1984, credit available for agriculture represented just 39 percent of the volume available in 1980, and in 1990 this fell to just 24 percent of the 1980 amount (see Graph 4.3).[30] Moreover, from the mid-1980s rural loans were adjusted for indexation: the cost of borrowing thus became positive and gradually rose following the other market rates. Finally, the need to control inflation led the government to manipulate the price of various products in the domestic market, especially foods that had great weight in the indices of cost of living. These measures had a negative impact on producers and had little impact on inflation, the same way as the succession of recessionary policies and heterodox plans were generally ineffective in curbing inflation. All these measures and changes increased the uncertainty and caused additional prejudice to agriculture.

Although government-provided credit declined, the oil crisis and the deterioration of external accounts that culminated in the 1987 moratorium provided a new role for agriculture to expand exports and to assist

[30] *Anuário Estatístico de Crédito Rural de 2010* (Brasília: Banco Central do Brasil, 2010); Banco do Brasil, Diretoria de Agronegócios, "Evolução histórica do crédito rural," *Revista de Política Agrícola* 12,4 (Outubro–Dezembro 2004), 10–17.

in replacing oil imports with ethanol. As there was a direct government intervention in agricultural activities, it created different policies for agricultural products oriented toward the external market (such as coffee, sugar, soybeans, orange juice, peanuts, cocoa, cotton, and tobacco) and another for products destined only for the internal market (such as rice, potatoes, beans, maize, cassava, tomatos, and onions). The latter group could count on protection from foreign competition through tariffs and quotas. The control of domestic prices occurred through minimum price policies, subsidies, and the management of buffer stocks. The supply of credit was essential in the decision of planting and maintenance of stocks by farmers. International prices and the exchange rate only slightly influenced the structure of prices of domestic agricultural goods. However, the exchange rate and international prices were the key variables in the decisions of farmers involved with products intended for export. Some of these products, like coffee and sugar, suffered greater government interference, which operated through public entities such as the Institute of Sugar and Alcohol and the Brazilian Coffee Institute.

But even the controls on the internal market were soon threatened by the growing budget deficit. The wheat market was one of the most regulated agricultural activities since 1967, when public control of production, imports, processing, and marketing of the product was adopted. But the cost of the policy of subsidizing consumption and protecting producer's income were heavy charges against the public accounts. With the economic deterioration and the fiscal crisis, pressures increased internally and internationally from the World Bank and the IMF to abolish such subsidies. The importance of wheat in the basic diet and the potential political impact of the adoption of a free market led to the delay in implementing changes. But in 1987 subsidies were eliminated and in 1990 the free market for all stages of production and marketing of wheat was introduced. In 1987, national production reached 6.2 million tons, meeting 90 percent of domestic demand, but by 1995 it fell to 1.5 million tons, accounting for only 17 percent of the market.[31] Besides the impact that the elimination of subsidies had on producers, the removal of consumer subsidies affected domestic consumption of wheat, which remained almost stable at about six million tons per year throughout the 1980s.[32]

---

[31] The production of wheat only returned to the levels of 1887–1888 after the harvest of 2003–2004, with a great increase in productivity. See www.conab.gov.br/conabweb/download/safra/TrigoSerieHist.xls.

[32] Célio Alberto Cole, "A cadeia produtiva do trigo no Brasil: contribuição para geração de emprego e renda" (MA thesis, Porto Alegre: Iepe-UFRGS, 1998); J. F. Fernandes

With the oil crisis, the government implemented an ambitious Ethanol Program, aimed at boosting domestic production of ethanol for use as automotive fuel. Launched in 1975, the program accelerated after 1979, especially after the second oil shock. Besides the addition of alcohol in gasoline sold in the country (20–25 percent of content), the production of cars that worked exclusively with hydrated ethanol was encouraged. The first alcohol cars launched in the market were merely adapted to gasoline vehicles, but from the early 1980s came new efficient engines, especially developed for the use of ethanol. Thanks to heavy government subsidies, the product became advantageous for consumers, who spent heavily to buy cars running on ethanol: 95 percent of cars manufactured in Brazil in 1984 were alcohol-powered engine only.

During that decade, the program was much criticized for the fiscal costs and prioritization of cane sugar at the expense of other crops, especially those geared to domestic consumption. The sugar cane for ethanol production was planted in the best soils in the country with extremely efficient and mechanized cultivation. There also developed a national technology of processing of sugar cane, which became comparable to the best in the world. However, with the subsequent decline in international oil prices, the program become ever more costly for the government, and alcohol could no longer compete with gasoline prices. In 1985, the Alcohol Program began facing a crisis, with the progressive decline in sales of cars with alcohol-consuming motors, and in the mid-1990s, sales virtually ceased.[33] But the ethanol gasoline mixture was never abandoned. The novelty in this sector would be the development of flex-fuel engines in 2003, which allowed car owners to consume either petroleum or alcohol. This facilitates the decision-making process of the car buyer and the uncertainty about the future behavior of the price relationship between the two fuels, and by 2008 such flex-fuel engine cars accounted for 91.5 percent of the 2.3 million cars produced that year in Brazil.[34]

Filho, "A política brasileira de fomento à produção de trigo, 1930–1990," in *Anais do XXXIII Congresso Brasileiro de Economia Rural* (Brasília: Sober, 1995), 1:443–474; Roque Silvestre Annes Tomasini and Ivo Ambrosi, "Aspectos econômicos da cultura do trigo," *Cadernos de Ciência e Tecnologia* 15,2 (Brasília) (Maio–Agosto 1998), 59–84.

[33] On Pró-alcohol see Fernando B. Homem de Melo and Eduardo Giannetti, *Proálcool, energia e transportes* (São Paulo: Fipe/Pioneira, 1981); Fernando B. Homem de Melo, *O problema alimentar no Brasil* (Rio de Janeiro: Paz e Terra, 1983); José Cláudio Bittencourt Lopes, "O Proálcool: uma avaliação" (MA thesis, Universidade Federal de Viçosa, 1992).

[34] Alcohol is less efficient than gasoline in terms of energy and can cost up to 70 percent of the price of gasoline. On the current importance of flex cars, see Fernando Lagares

The 1980s were turbulent years for agriculture as a result of prolonged economic crisis facing the country in traditional credit sources and the basic shift toward new credit arrangements that began in this period. In this decade, the sector had an average annual growth of 3 percent, which was above average GDP growth in that period. However, it was an uneven performance, with positive growth years alternating with periods of zero or negative growth, and showing better results in exports compared to the production of food staples for domestic consumption. If we consider the economic instability of the time, and the elimination of support policies for the agricultural sector, particularly the end of abundant and subsidized credit, the sector performed better than expected.

The emergence of alternative financing for the sector, involving other segments of agribusiness, was essential to explain this performance and its positive trend in terms of modernization and productivity. Suppliers of inputs and equipment began to directly finance farmers, and there was a greater financial and operational integration in the production and marketing chain, that is in the processing industries, and in the distribution channels, both wholesale and retail (including grocery chains), and particularly with the creation of "trading companies." New sources of funds of these producers or third parties were used to finance production in agriculture. The integration among producer, supplier, and customer, which began in the 1980s with the sudden withdrawal of government credit, in the following decade would become the primary source of rural credit and remains today the basis of the financing of Brazilian agribusiness.

Along with this important change in the sources of credit, the government support for agricultural research was crucial in creating this agricultural revolution. The activities of *Embrapa* and other research centers, such as the Campinas Agronomy Institute, are among the main factors that explain the relative dynamism of agriculture, even during the crisis that affected Brazil for more than twenty years. In the last three decades there has been a continuing increase in productivity in all crops and the gradual expansion of agriculture through the introduction of new seed varieties, compatible with the soils and climatic conditions of the country. In the 1980s began the exploration of the vast *cerrado* region in central Brazil, where various crops (particularly soybeans) have adapted well to land previously considered unsuitable for commercial agriculture. Today these new areas represent the main grain-producing regions of the

Távora, *História e economia dos biocombustíveis no Brasil*, Textos para Discussão No. 89 (Brasília: Centro de Estudos da Consultoria do Senado, Abril 2011), 26.

country and one of the most important in the world, where a modern and highly productive agriculture is practiced.

From the mid-1980s there also developed extended internal discussions about the need to liberalize agricultural markets and to reduce the level of government intervention. The liberalization of agricultural products and their inputs affected multiple interests, both public and private actors, directly involved in the process. Because of the difficulties faced by the country in international credit markets and the need for balancing public accounts, the economic authorities sought to reduce expenditures in the agricultural sector, reducing public funding sources and the multiplicity of subsidies directly linked to the sector. The government also had major pressure coming from the IMF and the World Bank to liberalize this sector and open it to international competition. External agreements and loans from those entities imposed stringent conditions with respect to these so-called conditionalities.

Between the government budget crises, international pressure and, finally, the maturation of the rural sector in the 1980s, there began an opening of the agricultural market. Once started, the process could not be reversed and this openness to the world market would be enhanced by liberalization policies that swept the country during the 1990s. The government progressively reduced agricultural subsidies. As of 1987, the total awarded was U.S.$5.3 billion, two years later, these subsidies declined to just U.S.$1 billion. This volume included more than U.S.$2 billion support for wheat; another U.S.$1.5 billion allocated for the purchase of products (AGF – Government Acquisitions Program) and the creation of buffer stocks; sugar and ethanol received U.S.$1 billion; and rural credit U.S.$700 million (see Graph 4.4). These values represent the actual subsidies and not the total resources mobilized for these agricultural support policies, which involved much higher figures. But after that date, most of these government funds were no longer made available to this sector.[35]

With the end of subsidies came the equally important end of any agricultural protective tariffs. In 1988 the government announced major tariff reductions, and then in 1990 it abolished all restrictions on imports of agricultural products. The following year the reform was completed with the reduction and simplifying of all tariffs. The average tariff fell from 32 percent to 14 percent, the maximum rate went from 105 percent to 35 percent, and when the system had been completely installed, the

---

[35] José Graziano da Silva, *A nova dinâmica da agricultura brasileira* (Campinas: Instituto de Economia da Unicamp, 1996).

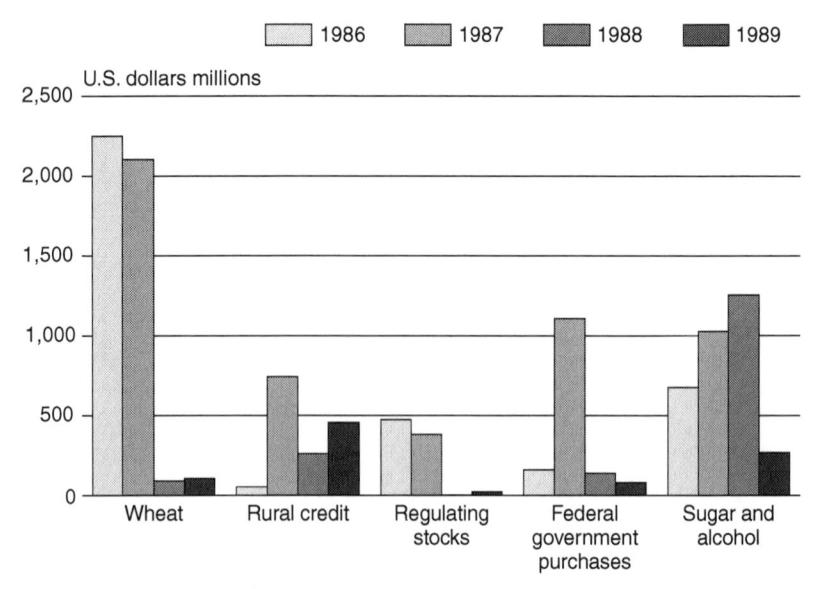

GRAPH 4.4. Estimates of Government Agricultural Subsidies, 1986–1989. *Source:* Silva 1996, p. 116

majority of products began to be taxed at only 10 percent. The extreme case was cotton, with zero tariffs, showing the government's intention to support the textile industry. The new tariff structure also included fertilizer and other agricultural inputs: for such inputs produced locally there was only a tariff of 10 percent on foreign products, all other such agricultural imports could be imported free of any tariff. Industrial machinery, equipment, and tractors were the most protected, and even then, import tariffs were decreased to 20 percent. Between 1991 and 1992 were also eliminated the licenses needed to import and export agricultural products and taxes on exports of various agricultural products. Even the sugar and alcohol sectors, whose exports were regulated by a complex quota system, began operating in the free market.

The policy of guaranteed minimum prices and the operation of buffer stocks also would be recast. Until the 1980s, most of the cotton, rice, beans, corn, and soybean harvests were funded by the EGF (Federal Government Loan Program) and acquired by AGF[36] (see

---

[36] EGF was the Federal Government Loans Program and AGF was the Federal Government Acquisitions Program. The operation was initially a loan to the farmer by EGF, who then had the option to sell his product to the AGF at a minimum price.

Consolidation of Democracy since 1985

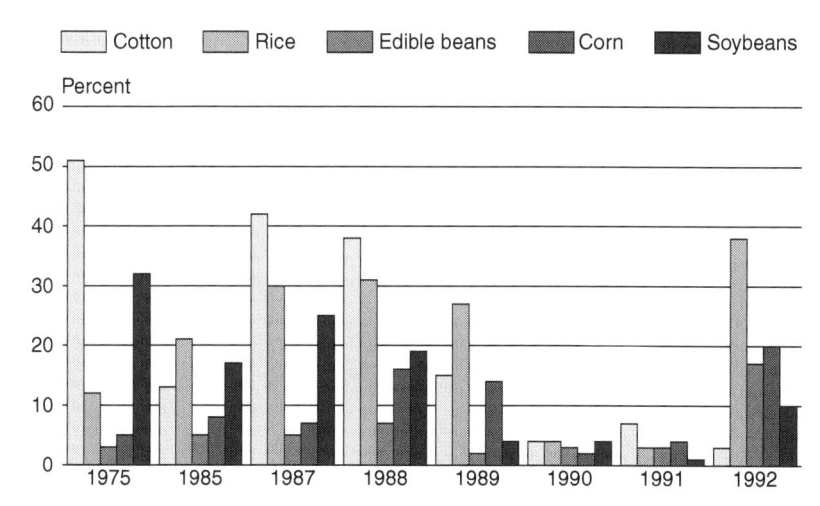

GRAPH 4.5a. Government Storage Loans as Percentage of Production of Major Crops, 1975–1992. *Source:* World Bank, 1944, p. 48

Graphs 4.5a and 4.5b). With the crops it purchased, the government formed buffer stocks that were made available only when the need arose to intervene in the market. Initially, however, there were no clearly defined rules to guide such interventions. The creation of stocks without a clear policy on sales generated market uncertainty. Only in 1988, with the

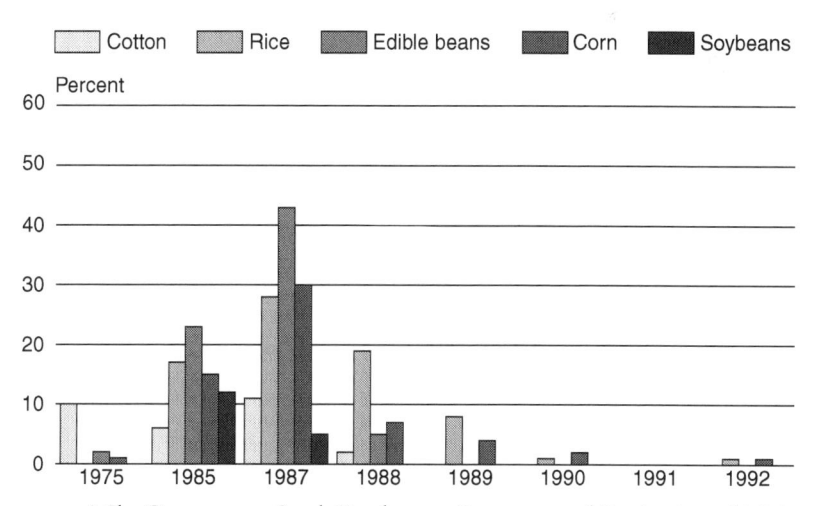

GRAPH 4.5b. Government Stock Purchase as Percentage of Production of Major Crops, 1975–1992. *Source:* World Bank, 1944, p. 48

fixing of pricing for inventory liquidation, was there defined a clear rule to guide these interventions. For each product there was calculated a moving average price, and when the market price exceeded the average by 15 percent, the government was forced to sell stocks. In 1993, to reduce the costs involved with the EGF the government transferred to the private sector the part of EGF's obligation of delivering grains and other products from the stocks and also by establishing new stock liquidation prices. When the liquidation price exceeded the market one, the producer had the right to sell the product on the market and the government paid the difference between the value obtained and the liquidation price. Thus the government avoided direct purchases and the burden of managing and regulating the stocks. Aside from the fiscal and monetary benefits arising from the limitation on purchase of such stocks, it reduced the costs of managing such stocks, which had been done inefficiently by the government.

Rural production, traditionally protected from foreign competition, now felt the impact of competition, amidst successive international crises: the first Mexican crisis, after which came the Asian crisis, then the Russian crisis, and finally the crisis of the Brazilian foreign debt. The government was forced to reduce the level of economic activity and maintain high interest rates. Nevertheless, despite the stability of prices for production, agriculture in general did not suffer in this crisis period. The competition caused by the opening of the economy brought benefits to agriculture in terms of the decline in the cost of equipment and supplies. This is evident in the favorable relationship between the Index of Prices Received (IPR), which represented the evolution of average prices received by producers, and the Index of Prices Paid (IPP), which represented the evolution of average prices paid by producers for basic inputs. In addition to the relation between prices and costs, there was continuous improvement in agricultural productivity. To introduce the topic we use the concept of total factor productivity, which represents the ratio between total agricultural production and total agricultural consumption of materials and machineries. According to a study of the federal government's Institute of Applied Economic Research (IPEA),[37] the increased productivity of Brazilian agriculture exceeded the increase of the total factor productivity of American agriculture, which reached an annual average of 1.6 percent

---

[37] José Garcia Gasques et al., *Condicionantes da produtividade da agropecuária brasileira*, Texto para Discussão No. 1017 (Brasília: IPEA, 2004a), 22.

between 1990 and 1999, against 3.3 percent for Brazilian agriculture in this same period.[38]

Given this growth of agriculture in the beginnings of the liberalization process, there would be less opposition for these changes than would occur with industry. The fact that the rural area suffered less may help explain why there was so little opposition to this opening of the Brazilian economy. The deregulation of the economy would receive a major boost with the presidential election of 1989, which was the first by direct vote since 1960. It occurred during a major economic crisis, with inflation reaching around 50 percent per month, thus characterizing the economy as one experiencing hyperinflation. Because of this crisis, Sarney, at the end of his term, had little political or popular support. The left parties threw themselves into the election with two major candidates, Brizola and Lula, candidates who frightened the elite and middle class. In opinion polls one or the other appeared as favorites, surpassing extremely prestigious candidates of the major central parties: Ulysses Guimarães for the PMDB, Mario Covas for the PSDB, and Aureliano Chaves of the PFL. During the year, there suddenly emerged the name of a young politician who was governor of Alagoas, a small and poor northeastern state, who launched his candidacy for the unknown National Reconstruction Party (PRN). It is thought that he launched his candidacy in order to become a candidate for vice president on the ticket of a major party. But like Quadros thirty years before, he emerged as a popular figure on a moralizing conservative populist platform. He proposed ending government

---

[38] For a survey of the changes that occurred in agriculture during the 1990s, see José Garcia Gasques et al., *Desempenho e crescimento do agronegócio no Brasil*, Texto para Discussão No. 1009 (Brasília: IPEA, Fevereiro 2004b); Guilherme Leite da Silva Dias and Cicely Moutinho Amaral, "Mudanças estruturais na agricultura brasileira, 1980–1998," in *Uma década de transição*, ed. Renato Baumann (Rio de Janeiro: Campus/ Cepal, 2000), 223–254; Gervazio Castro de Rezende, *A política de preços mínimos e o desenvolvimento agrícola da região Centro-Oeste*, Texto para Discussão No. 870 (Brasília: IPEA, 2002); José Garcia Gasques and Humberto Francisco Silva Spolador, *Taxas de juros e políticas de apoio interno à agricultura*, Texto para Discussão No. 952 (Brasília: IPEA, 2003); Junia Cristina P. R. da Conceição, *A política dos preços mínimos e a política alimentar*, Texto para Discussão No. 993 (Brasília: IPEA, 2003); José Garcia Gasques and Carlos Monteiro Villa Verde, *Gastos públicos na agricultura: evolução e mudança*, Texto para Discussão No. 948 (Brasília: IPEA, 2003); Roberto Rodrigues and Ivan Wedekin, "Uma estratégia para o agronegócio brasileiro," in *O novo governo e os desafios do desenvolvimento*, ed. Antonio Dias Leite and João Paulo Reis Velloso (Rio de Janeiro: Fórum Nacional, 2002), 549–570; José Eli da Veiga, "O Brasil rural ainda não encontrou seu eixo de desenvolvimento," *Estudos Avançados USP* 43 (Setembro–Dezembro 2001), 101–119; and José Graziano da Silva, "Velhos e novos mitos do rural brasileiro," *Estudos Avançados USP* 43 (Setembro–Dezembro 2001), 37–50.

corruption and attacked the so-called *marajas* (or *maharajas*), that is civil servants with high wages. When the surveys indicated his growing popularity, conservative groups began to see him as potential candidate who could defeat Lula and Brizola. In the first round of elections, Fernando Collor de Mello won 29 percent of the votes, followed by Lula with 16 percent, and Brizola with 15 percent. Candidates of major parties like the PMDB, PSDB, PFL, and PDS were soundly defeated. In the second round, Collor, after a brutal antileftist campaign, beat Lula for the presidency.

Collor initiated his government with a very unorthodox and authoritarian economic shock, including the freezing of bank accounts. The justification given for this extraordinary measure was the need to reduce the huge liquidity in the market – since in an inflationary economy, all investments, including public debt, were very short term, with almost daily liquidity. The stabilization program, despite its intensity, showed few results. Inflation had been reduced from 21 percent per month in February 1991 to 8 percent in March 1991, but reached 26 percent per month in January 1992 and remained at that level throughout the year. The intensity of the shock affected the level of activity, evidenced by the change in GDP, which rose 1 percent in 1991 and the following year was negative at 0.5 percent. The manufacturing industry performed poorly, being down 4 percent in 1992, and in the external sector the issue of the external debt remained unsolved.

Collor also inaugurated the liberal discourse in Brazil known as the Washington Consensus and took the first steps to open the market to international competition, promote foreign investment, privatize the economy, and eliminate state monopolies in the production of goods and services. Considering that his political base was a small party and that he won as an alternative to the leftist candidates, Collor had not assumed any political commitments during the campaign, and felt free to make such radical changes in the economy. The structure of protection in the industrial sector, which had remained almost unchanged for forty years, would change after 1990. The severe import controls that justified high tariffs and the "Law of National Similarity" (requiring proof that the imported article could not be supplied by a Brazilian producer) had been an important part of that system. There was even a list (called Annex C) of 1,300 products whose importation was banned. Of course, there were some exceptions to allowing the importation of capital goods. In the late 1980s, there were also some minor changes in this scheme, but the system kept essentially the basic structure that guaranteed full protection against foreign competition.

The Collor government profoundly changed the system and made liberal reforms in all sectors of the economy. Opening the market to foreign competition and globalization were central to the program of the new government. In the external area, the reforms were quick and very intense. Custom tariffs were drastically reduced, the prohibitions in Annex C were abolished and numerous bureaucratic restrictions on importers, as well as most of the controls on imports, were eliminated. The program of tariff reductions began in the capital goods and raw materials inputs sectors and was extended to consumer goods. In three years, Brazil was opened up fully to foreign competition.[39]

The liberal ideology of the Washington Consensus was well developed in the rest of Latin America when it finally managed to penetrate into Brazil. The delay was largely due to the existence of a large and sophisticated industrial structure in the country, far superior to existing businesses in other Latin American countries. The strong presence of a state productive sector and of a strong private-business sector with interests that overlapped with the public bureaucracy, made possible a vast and complex industry that survived the crisis of the 1980s. However, the overwhelming force of the ideology that now swept the continent, which arose when the state faced a deep fiscal crisis, weakened the powerful opposition that opposed economic liberalization and privatization.

The new liberalism attacked the model of import substitution on several fronts. It was argued that by relying on foreign technology, the

---

[39] Regis Bonelli and Armando Castelar Pinheiro, "Abertura e crescimento econômico no Brasil," in *Brasil Globalizado*, ed. Octavio de Barros and Fabio Giambiagi (Rio de Janeiro: Campus, 2008), 89–124; José Luiz Rossi Jr. and Pedro Cavalcanti Ferreira, *Evolução da produtividade industrial brasileira e a abertura comercial*, Texto para Discussão No. 651 (Rio de Janeiro: IPEA, 1999); André Averbug, "Abertura e Integração Comercial Brasileira na Década de 90," in *A Economia Brasileira nos Anos 90*, ed. Fabio Giambiagi and Maurício Mesquita Moreira (Rio de Janeiro: BNDES, 1999), 43–84; Maurício Mesquita Moreira, "Estrangeiros em uma Econômica Aberta: Impactos Recentes sobre a Produtividade, a Concentração e o Comércio Exterior," in *A economia brasileira nos Anos 90*, ed. Fabio Giambiagi and Maurício Mesquita Moreira (Rio de Janeiro: BNDES, 1999), 333–374; C. R. Albuquerque, "A liberalização comercial brasileira recente: uma leitura a partir das matrizes de relações intersetoriais de 1985, 90 e 95" (MA thesis, Belo Horizonte, CEDEPLAR/UFMG, 1999); R. Fonseca, M. C. Carvalho Jr., and H. Pourchet, "A orientação externa da indústria de transformação brasileira após a Liberação Comercial," Texto para Discussão No. 135 (Rio de Janeiro: IPEA, Abril 1998), 22–38; Marcio de Oliveira Júnior, *A Liberação Comercial Brasileira e os Coeficientes de Importação – 1990/95*, Texto para Discussão No. 703 (Rio de Janeiro: IPEA, Fevereiro 2000); Lia Valls Pereira, *Brazil Trade Liberalization Program*. UNCTAD, available at http://www.unctad.info/upload/TAB/docs/TechCooperation/brazil_study.pdf.

process of import substitution favored capital- and technology-intensive industries, factors scarce in Brazil. Thus incentives and subsidies were granted to promote an industrialization that absorbed little labor. The generalized protection did not stimulate productivity and competitiveness that would expand industrial exports. The strong protection generated a cost structure incompatible with the reality of the international market. The protection and isolation discouraged productivity, technological improvement, economies of scale, and the reduction of costs. In some sectors, such as in automotives, products were offered that were totally outdated in relation to the international market. The position of the new government can be summarized in the phrase of President Collor: "Brazil does not produce cars, it produces carts."

The alternative approach seemed promising. It was hoped that the opening to the world market would promote productive integration between international and domestic industry, and would lead to technological improvement and increased productivity and economies of scale. The increase in productivity would reduce costs and the resulting benefits would be passed on to the consumer. Integrating production with the international market would increase the penetration of foreign products in the Brazilian market, and this would also include primary materials and components used in manufacturing. At the same time, it would increase the proportion to be exported by industry. This view represents the basis of industrial policy that has prevailed since then.

Although his limited commitment to traditional parties allowed Collar relative freedom to make radical economic changes, it also encouraged his political isolation and an authoritarian style of governing. The continuing deterioration of the economy, and the obvious evidence of major government corruption despite the anticorruption theme of his electoral campaign, led to the impeachment of the president. The anti-Collor campaign provoked massive protests; impeachment, however, took place according to constitutional rules and without institutional crisis – a key indicator of the maturation of Brazil's young democracy.

In December 1992, with the impeachment of Collor, his constitutional successor, Vice President Itamar Franco assumed office. For the second time in two consecutive terms, the vice president succeeded a president. Itamar, a senator from the Minas Gerais wing of the PMDB, had abandoned the party to join the Collor candidacy. When he assumed the presidency, there was a broad agreement made among the parties to support the government, to ensure good governance and to avoid an institutional crisis. A conservative nationalist politician, Itamar took on an economy in deep crisis, with rampant inflation, and already in the early process of liberalization. In May 1993, Fernando Henrique Cardoso, the PSDB senator and then chancellor, took over the Ministry of Finance. In December of that year, under the direction of Cardoso, there was adopted what became known as the Real Plan, named for the new currency that was established. This proved to be the most successful modern plan ever enacted to stabilize the economy and stem the inflationary process that had persisted for nearly half a century. The new regime extended the measures of economic liberalization, including privatization of state enterprises, as was the case of the National Steel Company, one of the symbols of state capitalism that was created in the first Vargas government. Ironically, Itamar, a staunch nationalist and supporter of public monopolies, and Cardoso, a respected left-wing intellectual and one of the proponents of dependency theory,[40] eventually promoted privatization and liberalization of the national economy.

As Minister of Finance, the success of the Real Plan made it possible for Cardoso to succeed President Itamar Franco in the 1994 election, in opposition to Lula, again the candidate of the PT. Cardoso and the PSDB represented social democracy in Brazil, but were pragmatically allied with the PFL, the center-right party, which indicated the candidate for vice president. Cardoso was elected in the first round, with 54 percent of the votes; Lula got 27 percent, and Brizola only 3 percent.

Once elected, Cardoso sought to consolidate the economic stabilization plan and implement a comprehensive program of reforms, which represented a break with the statist model that had begun with Vargas and was further emphasized during the military period. This dismantling of the interventionist state, a process that had begun during the Collor administration and continued modestly with the Itamar administration, now became a full-fledged and coherent program in the administration of Fernando Henrique Cardoso. The Brazilian state ceased to be an active agent in the national productive structure and was transformed into the regulator state, responsible only for typical state activities, such as

---

[40] Among the studies of Cardoso on this theme, see Fernando Henrique Cardoso and Enzo Faletto, *Dependência e Desenvolvimento na América Latina – Ensaios de interpretação sociológica* (Rio de Janeiro: Zahar, 1970). According to the Theory of Dependence formulated by the authors, the analysis of the historical process of developing the periphery in the international capitalist order explains the dynamics of the relationship between social classes in the domestic nations of the periphery.

security, justice, education, and health. The activity of producing goods now fell to the private sector. Cardoso also sought to implement an ambitious program of state reform.[41]

Despite strong opposition from the leftist parties,[42] the government managed to form a parliamentary majority, which enabled Cardoso to implement many of his desired reforms, several of which required constitutional amendments. In the economic arena, reforms were aimed at improving the market economy and reducing state intervention. Thus were abolished state monopolies of oil, electricity, telecommunications, and coastal shipping. Moreover, Cardoso sought to carry out a broad program of reforms in social security[43] and in the public administration. Although these ideas were developed out of long and complex discussions, several reforms could not be enacted. These included reforms in the areas of labor, fiscal reform, and the judicial system, which were unable to be enacted during the Cardoso administration. These reforms represented major changes in the legal structure of the country that were strongly opposed by entrenched interests and large segments of society along with the PT, which positioned itself against all reforms.

In 1997 a constitutional amendment was passed allowing reelection for all heads of executive power, allowing Cardoso to run for a second term. He won the election in the first round of voting, with 53 percent of the votes, against 32 percent for Lula. In his second term, Cardoso

---

[41] Although ambitious, the plan to reform the state had partial results, even despite strong opposition to changes in the structure of the functioning of the state. Even innovative actions like the regulatory agencies, successfully deployed during the administration of Fernando Henrique Cardoso, were subsequently distorted by the appointment of politicians to purely executive technical positions. On the reform of the state, see Valeriano Mendes Ferreira Costa, "A dinâmica Institucional da Reforma do Estado: um balanço do período FHC," in *O Estado Numa Era de Reformas: os Anos FHC* (Brasília: MP, SEGES, 2002), Part 2, 9–56.

[42] The PT, which later would elect two presidents, Lula and Dilma, represented the greatest opposition to all the reforms implemented by the government of Fernando Henrique Cardoso.

[43] During the Cardoso administration, despite strong opposition, political progress was made in welfare reform, with the approval of the Constitutional Amendment of December 20, 1998. One of the most important changes was the so-called pension time, which takes into account the age and time of the taxpayer's contribution to social welfare, overturning the right to retirement for length of service. The legislation also changed the legal rules for civil servants. But the reforms were still incomplete and would require further amendments. Maria Ines Nassif, "Previdência Social," in *A Era FHC. Um Balanço*, ed. Bolivar Lamounier and Rubens Figueiredo (São Paulo: Cultura Associados, 2002), 569–598; Fabio Giambiagi and Lavinia Barros de Castro, "Previdência Social: Diagnósticos e propostas de reforma," *Revista do BNDES* 10,19 (Junho 2003), 265–292.

continued his reform attempts, but difficulties in the international arena led to a restrictive economic policy, with low growth rates and large increases in unemployment.

In the economic area, the main achievement of the governments of Itamar Franco and Fernando Henrique Cardoso was undeniably the Real Plan, which halted a chronic inflationary process that had existed since the 1950s and had become explosive. It was not until May 1993, when Fernando Henrique Cardoso became Minister of Finance that a full-fledged plan could be enacted, and by that time inflation was 30 percent per month and rising. The Real Plan took place in three distinct phases. The first, announced in December 1993, consisted of a set of fiscal measures to increase tax collections. Those responsible for the plan understood the necessity of ensuring the need to balance state finances before the implementation of new monetary reform could be carried out. By eliminating inflation, the government would lose the inflation tax. This meant that the supposedly balanced budget in a high-inflation regime could become a deficit fiscal situation once inflation had been eliminated. The first stage of the plan sought to create a balanced budget even with price stability. The measures necessary for this equilibrium were established in February 1994.

The second phase occurred in March 1994 when the monthly inflation rate reached 42 percent. This phase was the major innovation of the Real Plan and consisted in introducing an indexed currency. The lack of synchronization in price adjustments represented a major problem faced by previous plans. Even in an environment of high inflation, there were differences in the correction of prices in general. At the time of a new plan, there were products whose prices had been fixed the day before and others perhaps with corrections made much earlier, for market or contract reasons. When a new monetary reform plan was implemented, the products whose price correction occurred long ago were caught with their prices out of date and sought to correct them after the currency reform and therefore represented a pressure on prices in the new currency. The Real Plan launched the Real Unit of Value (URV), whose daily oscillations would take into account the average of three price indices. There were rules and obligations for the conversion of wages, rents, and public tariffs in URVs. The other prices could be kept in the old currency or be freely set in URVs, and their value was governed by a contract that could be negotiated between the parties. It was intended to introduce in most prices a voluntary process of negotiation, but there was a need to establish clear rules on some segments of the economy, as in the conversion of wages made by the actual average wage received in the previous four months.

The URV was only a unit of value, for traditional currency continued to circulate. Inflation remained high and accelerating, but its effects occurred in the old currency. The risk would be inflation in URV. In July 1994, after four months of transition, the URV became the new currency and was named the *real*, with parity of one *real* equivalent to a dollar. The stability achieved with the Real Plan was based on an exchange-rate anchor, the overvaluation of the *real* and the general openness of the economy. These were the foundations of the program. The Real Plan, unlike previous plans, had the possibility of using an exchange-rate variable, without the need to freeze prices. Since the early 1990s, a reversal occurred in the international finance markets and now there existed an abundance of resources. Furthermore, Brazil had renegotiated its foreign debt, which would allow it to return to international financial markets and enjoy excellent credit conditions, with high liquidity and low interest rates compared to the previous decade. This allowed it to deploy an exchange anchor, impossible to achieve in previous plans. The exchange rate could fluctuate freely in appreciating the *real*, but if it fell against the dollar, the Central Bank would intervene in the market. This meant that the Central Bank guaranteed a minimum price for the *real*. At the same time, in the domestic market real interest rates were extremely high, which attracted foreign funds, generating an abundance of U.S. dollars, which put pressure on the valorization of the domestic currency.[44]

The deepening of the process of trade liberalization, another basic element of the Real Plan, also had a great impact on the Brazilian economy, one of the most closed of the world until the late 1980s. Beginning in the late 1980s changes occurred in the tariff structure that reduced average tariffs on imports from 51 percent to 31 percent. In the early 1990s, in the Collor period, there were further reductions in tariffs, to an

---

[44] After years of fighting inflation by orthodox and unorthodox methods, the Real Plan has achieved effective results, and inflation has remained controlled for almost 20 years. The extensive bibliography on the subject includes Sayad, *Planos Cruzado e Real: acertos e desacertos*; Luiz Filgueiras, *História do Plano Real* (São Paulo: Boitempo, 2000); Aloízio Mercadante, ed., *O Brasil pós-Real: a política econômica em debate* (Campinas: UNICAMP, 1997); Fabio Giambiagi and Maurício Mesquita Moreira, *A economia brasileira nos anos 90* (Rio de Janeiro: BNDES, 1990); Maria da Conceição Tavares, *Destruição não-criadora* (Rio de Janeiro: Record, 1990); Gustavo Franco, *O Plano Real e outros ensaios* (Rio de Janeiro: Francisco Alves, 1995); Gustavo Franco, *O Desafio Brasileiro: ensaios sobre desenvolvimento, globalização e moeda* (São Paulo: Editora 34, 1999).

average rate of 15 percent by 1993. The computer industry was one of the most protected in the country, yet the Brazilian manufacturers never reached international standards, and the result was a significant technological backwardness in various productive sectors that, because of the tariff wall, had no access to new computer technologies available on the international market. In 1992 this protection of the computer market was finally eliminated. A year earlier, the Mercosul treaty (or the Southern Common Market) established a regional market among Argentina, Brazil, Paraguay, and Uruguay, which led to further tariff reductions. The emergence of Mercosul created, without a doubt, an important free trade zone and brought about a great development of inter-American trade in the continent. However, due to domestic economic problems in member countries, Mercosul suffered periodic major setbacks. Thus, Mercosul, despite its growing importance, lives in a constant state of negotiation and adjustment, even though trade has benefited by its existence.[45]

The rapid opening of the economy, its exposure to international competition at the same time in which an overvalued currency was maintained, had a positive effect on price stability. Goods imported or Brazilian commodities with international prices had their prices controlled by the competition. This helped the initial phase of the plan and may have been the price to be paid for stability. The idea was for Brazil to expose itself to international competition in order to have a modernizing impact on the economy, especially on its domestic industry. The rapid opening and the overvaluation of the exchange rate acted in the same direction, exposing domestic production to a significant foreign competition. The foreign companies entered Brazil in the process of globalization of production and of international capital flows. The result was a sharp increase in the degree of internationalization of national production, an intense reduction in integration of the Brazilian industry, and increased productivity, with greater intensity in the use of foreign technology. There was also an increase in the foreign ownership and control of Brazilian enterprises. The continuity of such a policy was only made possible thanks to the huge influx of foreign capital to fund the trade deficit and current account transaction.

---

[45] The frequent external instability of the Mercosul countries and fluctuations in their exchange rates caused numerous conflicts between its members and generated constant negotiations, including the establishment of import and export quotas. In 2012, e.g., opposition to the impeachment of President Lugos of Paraguay led to the exclusion of the country from the Mercosul and at the same time there was approved Venezuela's entry into the organization, a process that involved negotiations since 2005.

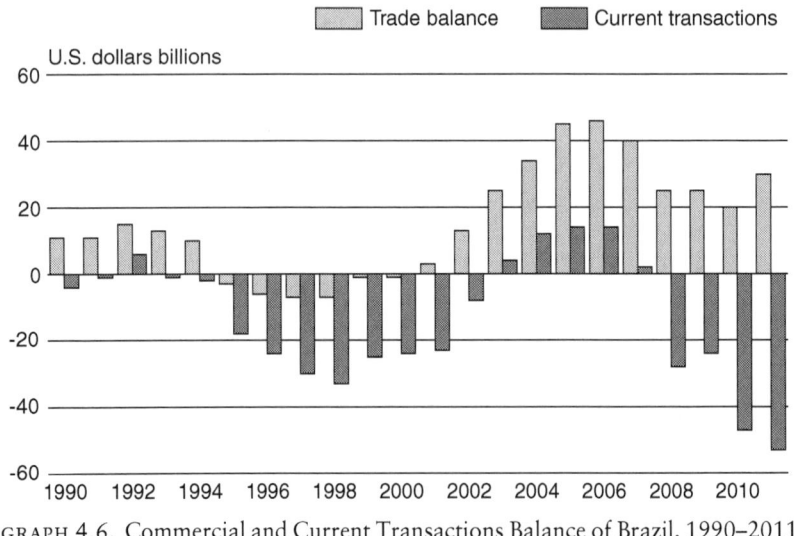

GRAPH 4.6. Commercial and Current Transactions Balance of Brazil, 1990–2011
Source: Ipeadata-Balança Comercial (FOB); Transações correntes

As with all other plans, there was an explosion of demand as much due to the immediate elimination of the inflation tax as to the reduction of prices of national and imported goods. There was also a question of monetary illusion. Although interest rates were set high in real terms, the sudden disappearance of inflation again created the illusion of falling income from small savings, stimulating spending. The stabilization also stimulated the expansion of credit, whether consumer or business. The level of activity accelerated and the GDP, which had grown by 4.9 percent in 1993, would grow by 5.3 percent in 1994. The price for all this expansion of demand and spending was a reversal in the balance of trade. The trade surplus, which had been maintained above the U.S.$10 billion level between 1987 and 1994, now turned negative in November of that year, reaching a monthly deficit of U.S.$1 billion between February and March 1995 (see Graph 4.6). The exchange, which began with parity between the *real* and the dollar declined in March to R$0.83 to the dollar, because of the strong inflow of foreign capital into the country, particularly short-term capital, which was encouraged by the policy of appreciation of the *real* and high interest rates in the country, which created major profits in the arbitrage of the interest rates.

In this context of expansion and market opening and increasing dependence on external resources, came the Mexican crisis in December 1994.

While government authorities guaranteed that the Brazilian situation was different, capital flight caused a reduction of U.S.$10 billion in reserves between November 1994 and March 1995. In response to this crisis, the government took a series of drastic measures. It increased interest rates to more than 60 percent per year, which represented a real rate of more than 40 percent. There was a significant increase in reserve requirements of banks and credit was constrained for consumers. It increased taxes on many imported consumer goods and imposed quotas on car imports. The exchange-rate regime was changed to allow for the gradual devaluation of the *real*, though it remained overvalued. In the state finances, there were strong budgetary cuts.

All these measures greatly restricted liquidity and had a severe impact on economic activities, causing a process of dramatic adjustments. Many companies went bankrupt, and even large national banks were affected, some of which had faced problems since the establishment of the Real Plan. To avoid a systemic crisis in the financial sector, the government created the Program of Incentives to the Restructuring and Strengthening of National Financial System (*Proer*), and the Central Bank could intervene in troubled financial institutions. The program was one of the key measures to strengthen the Brazilian financial sector and one that prevented the successive Asian, Russian, Brazilian crises and the U.S. real estate market collapse from affecting the financial sector. These crises were absorbed by the Brazilian economy without serious disturbances in this economic sector. Openness and market consolidation, with the entrance of many foreign banks into the country, also was of great help in maintaining the stability of this financial sector.

With the Mexican crisis, industrial production, which until March 1995 had been growing at relatively high rates, fell to levels lower than those observed in 1994. In the same period, the hours worked declined by 10 percent, and the actual real interest rates, as we have seen, exceeded 40 percent per year. Government and private companies suffered with interest rates so high. In 1994, the public sector managed to generate an operating surplus, but in 1995 it began to show a growing deficit, and in 1998, this deficit reached 7.4 percent of GDP. This policy, however, had positive effects on external accounts. The reserves increased as a result of the foreign capital that entered the country, for investment and for short-term gains, in order to take advantage of high domestic interest rates. Thanks to these capital inflows, the *real* was still overvalued, playing a key role in maintaining domestic prices.

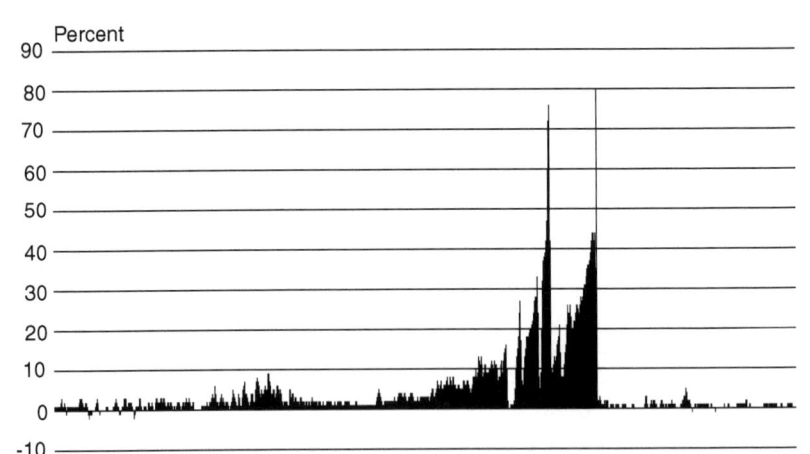

GRAPH 4.7. Monthly Variation in General Price Index (FGV), 1944–2012. Source: Ipeadata

The Real Plan was a success: inflation was finally contained (see Graph 4.7 and Appendix Table A.3). However, despite the widespread criticism about the negative impact of an open economy and an overvalued currency, this strategy was maintained and defended by the economic authorities. Multinationals and larger domestic companies began to use the international credit market. Many firms closed and others were sold to foreign or stronger national groups. Still others were able to modernize and face the new competitive structure, using the weak dollar to invest and import the equipment they needed. In this period, because of the exchange rate, even business segments in which Brazil was extremely competitive (e.g., in cellulose) lost market. The economic policy stifled exports and encouraged imports. The trade deficit increased, reaching U.S.$8 billion in 1998, the same year the deficit in current transactions reached 4 percent of GDP.

Despite Brazil's continuing external vulnerability, the government decided to stimulate the economy. With the recovery in reserves (which were between U.S.$55 billion and U.S.$60 billion), the government decreased interest rates and eliminated credit constraints. This allowed a modest economic recovery, which was soon reflected in the trade balance. There was also a slight improvement in the unemployment rate. But in July 1997 came the Asian crisis, which hit all developing countries. There was again a flight of capital and reserves fell from U.S.$63 billion in August 1997 to U.S.$52 billion in November of that year. The government's reaction was the same: the interest rates were raised and a new fiscal program was adopted. The interest rate, which had gradually fallen to 20 percent a year, rose in November 1997 to 42 percent – a very high rate considering that the variation in domestic prices was only 5 percent that year. Furthermore, the *real* continued to be overvalued, which since the establishment of the plan had declined by only 10 percent when the cost of living had varied by an order of 75 percent. It was an inappropriate rate given the turbulent period. However, the government insisted on maintaining this foreign exchange policy, regardless of the cost entailed in terms of falling production, rising unemployment, deterioration in public accounts, and increasing difficulties in the external sector.

The privatization process carried out by the government of Fernando Henrique Cardoso deserves some consideration. Brazilian industrialization had been largely based on state investments not only for infrastructure but also for the production in industries such as steel, oil and oil products, electricity, telecommunications, and the aviation industry. Privatization began in 1981 when a commission was created to privatize industries, but this commission would have little practical effect until the end of that decade. The few privatizations undertaken were of state enterprises that were bankrupt; moreover, foreign investors were not involved in these purchases given the unattractive nature of these privatized firms and the external constraints on foreign capital investment then operating in Brazil. However, privatization became a priority in the 1990s, after new legislation was passed in March 1990. The National Bank of Economic and Social Development, or the BNDES, which had participated in some of the first privatizations, played an important role in the process. The privatization program developed during the entire decade was considered one of the largest in the world.

The amount obtained from the sale of state enterprises between 1990 and 2002 reached the extraordinary sum of U.S.$87 billion. Also buyers took over more than U.S.$18 billion of debts of the privatized companies. In general terms, then, the total came to U.S.$105 billion, with almost half of the sales occurring between 1997 and 1998. The Cardoso government encouraged the participation of foreign investors, who accounted for more than 50 percent of the purchases. Electricity and telecommunications accounted for almost 30 percent of sales; metallurgy and mining 8 percent; oil and gas, about 6 percent; and the financial sector by 5 percent (see Graph 4.8). The privatizations involved some emblematic companies such as Cia Siderurgica Nacional, founded by Vargas in

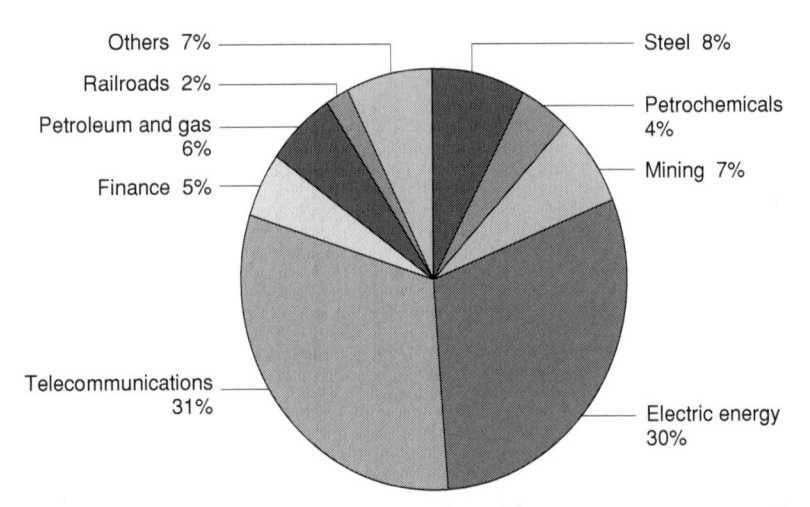

282   *The Economic and Social History of Brazil since 1889*

GRAPH 4.8. Industrial Source of Funds Collected for Privatization. *Source:* Pinheiro 2002

1940, and the Vale do Rio Doce, one of the largest mining companies in the world. The monopoly on oil exploration and communications was broken, with huge political repercussions.[46]

Along with national and foreign capital there was a significant participation of pension funds in the privatization process. Created in the late 1970s, these funds gained in importance in the mid-1990s. Given that much of this pension money belonged to state enterprises, there was much criticism about their major participation in the privatization process. The privatized state enterprises were being acquired in part by pension funds controlled by other nonprivatized public companies, such as Petrobrás, the Banco do Brasil, the Central Bank, and the *Caixa Econômica Federal*. But despite the criticism about the privatization program, the process occurred during a period of great fiscal difficulty and external vulnerability, and the income obtained from these privatizations was crucial to the balancing of public accounts.[47]

---

[46] Licínio Velasco Jr., *Privatização: mitos e falsas percepções* (Rio de Janeiro: BNDES, 1999); Armando Castelar Pinheiro, *A experiência brasileira de privatização: o que vem a seguir*, Texto para Discussão No. 87 (Rio de Janeiro: IPEA, 2002).

[47] The privatization has been very successful in some segments, such as steel. The situation of the national industrial park required heavy investments, but was easily mobilized by the private sector. Telecommunications were also successfully privatized, since the rapid technological change that occurred in the sector also required huge investments, which did not justify the maintenance of government control. Once privatized this sector has been modernized and expanded rapidly, with massive investment by the

Despite the abundant resources raised by the state with the privatization program, there was still a deterioration of public finances primarily because of the maintenance of the high interest rates used to attract foreign capital. It was a policy that threatened the future of the country and prevented any kind of recovery. It also created increasing difficulties in the external accounts. It was a vicious cycle that needed to be changed in an orderly manner to avoid a speculative crisis. But the Asian crisis delayed its solution.

The Russian crisis, which occurred in the second half of 1998, was another blow to the country. The increased international instability and the reaction of the Brazilian authorities remained the same: they raised interest rates and taxes and reduced government spending, reproducing the actions already taken since the Real Plan. Since 1998, thanks to reduced government spending, there had occurred a small primary surplus – although the government's operating deficit corresponded to about 7 percent of GDP. However, the set of measures that were now announced with this new international crisis were not enough to calm markets, since Brazil was considered very vulnerable in relation to its economic fundamentals. The country had accumulated an enormous debt, the servicing of which required U.S.$15 billion annually, or the equivalent of one-third of Brazilian exports. Debt due to the maintenance of an exchange rate was clearly inadequate. Moreover, in 1998, the current account deficit reached 4.3 percent of GDP. All international indicators of vulnerability showed that the country was in critical condition. The reserves, reaching a maximum of U.S.$70 billion in 1998, fell rapidly. In October of that year they decreased by 40 percent (see Graphs 4.9a and 4.9b and Appendix Table A.2); however, the *real* was still priced at U.S.$1.18 and was seriously overvalued. Financial openness promoted by the government, which allowed for the relative mobility of capital and a cheap dollar, facilitated massive external flight of the country's resources.

The worsening crisis in Brazil led to emergency aid from the IMF and developed countries. For the size of the country and size of the debt, it

---

private sector. The privatization had a positive impact on the economy and consumers. In the electricity sector, privatization has been problematic. The regulation that was necessary (and had been adequately established for telecommunications) did not follow properly the privatization process, creating future vulnerability, because there were no investments made that needed to occur to meet the growing demand for energy. In 2001, when the Brazilian economy seemed to head for a slow but consistent growth, the lack of investment in infrastructure led to energy shortages and rationing, especially in manufacturing.

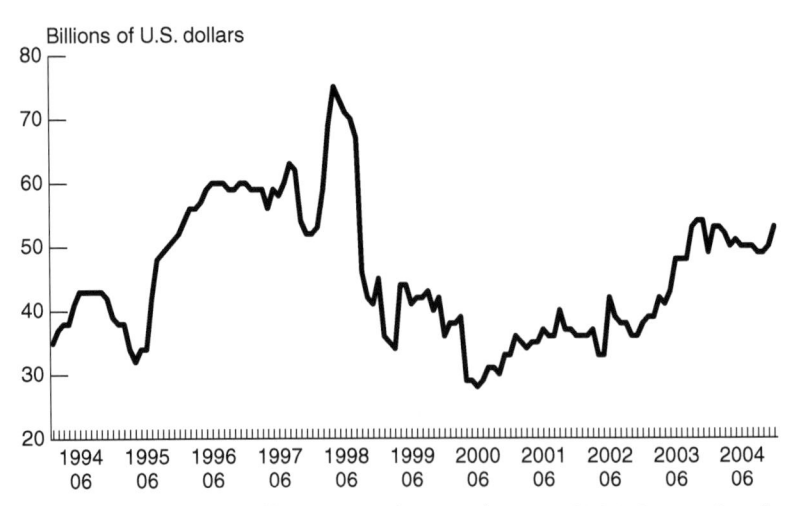

GRAPH 4.9a. Brazilian Dollar Reserves by Month, 1994–2004. *Source:* Ipeadata

was feared that the deterioration of external conditions in Brazil would magnify the crisis in other emerging countries. This explains the rapidity of the agreement made in December 1998, which gave the country a credit of U.S.$41.5 billion. The signed document as always involved compromises on the behavior of several important indicators, such as the public deficit, the need for a positive balance in current accounts, and the approval of fiscal measures that were then under discussion in Congress. Moreover, as a measure of adjustment to the crisis, the

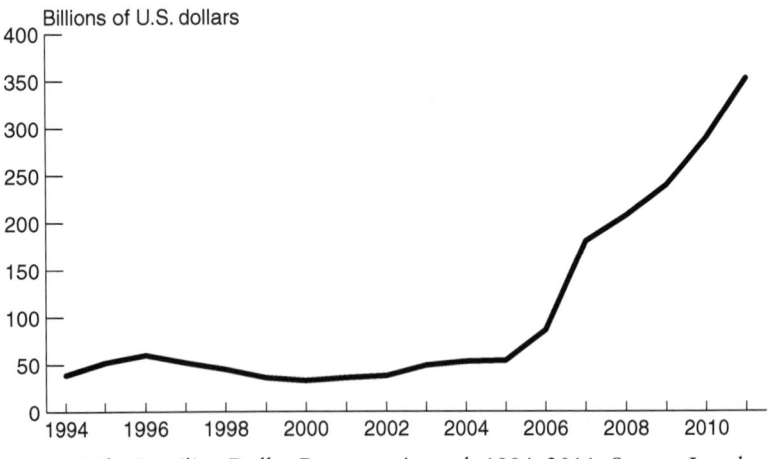

GRAPH 4.9b. Brazilian Dollar Reserves, Annual, 1994–2011. *Source:* Ipeadata

federal government launched the Stabilization Fiscal Plan. The government listed the measures already implemented: constitutional and legal reforms of the economic order, which allowed the privatization of public enterprises; fiscal adjustment agreements with the states; and reorganization and privatization of state banks, improving mechanisms of control of the indebtedness of states, municipalities, and the state enterprises. But since these measures were not sufficient, the government committed itself to reforms in social security, public and private, to tax reform, reform of labor legislation, and the creation of the Fiscal Responsibility Law.[48] In response to the strong deterioration in the public finances,[49] the Fiscal Stabilization Plan enumerated several actions to be performed and indicated the relationship between public debt and GDP as the main indicator of long-term solvency of the public sector. In this way, considering the imbalances that were projected for the next year, the Action Plan accompanying the program sought to enable the generation of primary surpluses to stabilize the ratio of consolidated net debt of the public sector and the GDP.[50] For 1999 there was projected a primary surplus of 1.8 percent.[51] There was also established a set of goals for generating a primary surplus that would be maintained by subsequent administrations.

Besides the difficulties in administering its federal budget, the central government had limited powers to control the spending and the financial imbalances of the states and municipalities. Since the 1980s federal authorities sought to control the debt of subnational entities, however, with little success. State and municipal budgets ran deficits, became

---

[48] Although the federal government failed to achieve full success in the measures announced, much was achieved. These successes involved the regulation of administrative reform, the reform of social welfare (public and private), the creation of a Fiscal Responsibility Law, tax reform, restructuring of the Federal Tax administration (Receita Federal), a Multi-Year Plan and Budget of the Union, and deregulation of the fuel sector. The government also wanted to enact labor reform, but faced strong opposition from the PT. In other areas, such as tax reform, although it was not really a reform, it took advantage of ordinary legislation to expand federal revenue. In the welfare area, despite strong opposition, the government obtained significant results. About the Plan Fiscal Stabilization see http://www.fazenda.gov.br/portugues/ajuste/respef.asp.

[49] The sharp rise in interest rates throughout the period after the establishment of the Real Plan explains much of the fiscal deterioration. But from the standpoint of the debt and revenue, the government of Fernando Henrique Cardoso made major progress. It identified several "skeletons" not previously computed in the public accounts. Also its massive sale of public enterprises offset potential future liabilities of these companies and limited the potential bloodletting that future deficits of such public enterprises might entail.

[50] Available at http://www.fazenda.gov.br/portugues/ajuste/respef.asp.

[51] The goal of 1999 was attained.

indebted to the banking system, and, through the placement of government securities freely traded on the market, created hidden liabilities, particularly with suppliers. Some states had commercial banks and most of them were insolvent. Within this process of restructuring public-sector debt, a law was passed in 1995 that limited spending by personnel of the public administration.[52] In August 1996 there was created the Incentive Program for the Reduction of State Public Sector in Banking Activities (*Proes*). In 1997, during the Asian crisis, there was a major monetary and fiscal adjustment of the federal government, making the financial situation of state and local governments untenable and leading the federal government to assume the debts of the states and municipalities.[53] The states and municipalities signed a contract with the federal government that assumed their debts, which reached R$132 billion. To pay for the servicing of the debt that had been transferred to the federal government, the subnational entities had to pay a percentage of their annual revenues to the federal government.[54] But it was necessary to create rules that maintained fiscal balance over the long run, and this was done through the adoption of the Fiscal Responsibility Law, which represents one of the most innovative and important instruments of public governance in Brazil, in terms of providing government transparency and accountability, applying practices that only exist in a few countries with a tradition of good fiscal practice.[55]

---

[52] Lei Complementar No. 82 of 27 March 1995. In a general way this law fixed the limit to 60 percent of current liquid income.

[53] Programa de Apoio à Reestruturação Fiscal e Financeira, instituted by Law 9496/1997.

[54] Cristiane Kerches da Silva Leite, *Federalismo, processo decisório e ordenamento fiscal: a criação da Lei de Responsabilidade Fiscal*, Texto para Discussão No. 1593 (Brasília: IPEA, 2011); Fernando Álvares Correia Dias, *O Refinanciamento dos Governos Subnacionais e o ajuste fiscal 1999/2003*, Texto para Discussão No. 17 (Brasília: Consultoria Legislativa do Senado Federal, 2004). This funding, which has been kept fully up to date by subnational entities, has generated a strong criticism of the way they were originally signed. While states and municipalities pay about 13 percent of their current net revenue, the outstanding balance, corrected by IGPM plus 6 percent or 9 percent, in most cases tends to grow. The cost of this debt has been much higher than the cost of funding the Federal Treasury. The IGPM index, which is an average rate (consumer, construction, and wholesale), has great influence on the fluctuation of the exchange and has no relation to government revenues, which is more in step with the consumer price index. Moreover, currently 6 percent or 9 percent real interest is unrealistic, given that the nominal rate, the primary, is approximately 8 percent.

[55] "Another point that also we are very proud of having passed the National Congress, is the Fiscal Responsibility Law, which has exactly the pair of factors – transparency and accountability – as two basic elements. It was a law inspired by European experiences, and those of New Zealand, and the United States, but that has much

In 1998, there was zero growth, unemployment was growing, and instability and loss of reserves continued despite the fiscal reforms and the agreement with the IMF. Now the international financial markets experienced the "Brazilian Crisis" moment. The government systematically refused to promote a change of exchange-rate policy, which could have been done in times of greater tranquility. In January 1999 it was forced to make this change in the midst of a major external crisis. It let the exchange rate float freely, and immediately the *real* fell by more than 60 percent against the dollar. The country abandoned the exchange anchor. An appropriate measure at the time of the establishment of the Real Plan, the persistence of the overvalued currency constrained the country's growth, increased unemployment, and led to a deterioration of public finances and a major increase in the foreign debt, all of which ultimately left the country economically vulnerable. In March 1999 inflation targeting in Brazil was implemented using the Consumer Price Index (IPCA).

Thus, there were several distinct phases in the economic policies of the Cardoso administration. In the first period, the need was to consolidate the Real Plan, giving top priority to price stability. The anchor currency, or peg, was the basic element in the process of price controls, which suffered from competition from imported products. The overvaluation of the *real* led to a deteriorating trade balance, but the high interest rates attracted speculative capital that helped in closing the external accounts. The privatization of public companies, acquired by international groups, was another important element in addressing the external area. These high interest rates also undermined the public accounts. The successive external crises faced by the government prevented the continuation of this process, and gradually there were deployed the bases that guided the final years of that government and also represented the foundation of

to do with our history of institutional change, the desire to increase transparency and create mechanisms to have a responsible administration of public resources." Prounancement of the Minister Ministro Martus Tavares, "Forum Internacional sobre Responsabilidade e Transparência no Setor Público," Brasília, Dezembro 5, 2001, available at http://www.bndes.gov.br/SiteBNDES/export/sites/default/bndes_pt/Galerias/Arquivos/bf_bancos/e0001733.pdf. Also see José Serra and José Roberto Afonso, "Mais prática do que discurso," *Valor Econômico* (Maio 5, 2010), available at http://www.joserobertoafonso.com.br/index.php?option=com_content&view=article&id=1187:mais-pratica-que-discursos-valor-&catid=36:assuntos-fiscais&itemid=37; José Roberto Afonso, Guilherme L. N. P. de Carvalho, and Kleber Pacheco de Castro, "Desempenho comparado dos principais governos brasileiros depois de dez anos da LRF," *Revista Técnica dos Tribunais de Contas* (Belo Horizonte) 1,0 (Setembro 2010), 13–48, available at http://www.joserobertoafonso.com.br/attachments/article/1429/ATRICON-10AnosLRF.pdf.

the Lula government's economic policy: inflation targeting, goals set for the primary budget surplus, and a free-floating exchange rate.[56] In the case of the free-floating exchange, it would be more precise to speak of a "dirty float" since the government has never failed to intervene, either through measures to attract or discourage the inflow of dollars, or by direct intervention in the exchange market, buying or selling currencies to avoid periods of high market volatility.

After the recovery from the crisis of 1999 there was a relative return of confidence in the economy because of the measures already implemented, particularly the establishment of the primary surplus targets. But when growth began again there was an internal crisis due to the lack of electricity, which was caused by several factors. There was a severe drought that emptied the hydroelectric reservoirs, but there were also failures in planning for development in the energy sector. This energy crisis led to major electricity rationing in all segments of the economy. The power crisis had an impact on the growth of GDP, which fell to 1.31 percent in 2001, after having risen to 4.31 percent in 2000.

At the end of his second term, the political prestige of Cardoso was very low. Although he made important reforms in the federal administration and consolidated economic stability in his second term, successive external and internal crises disrupted growth. Lula was set to launch a presidential candidacy. It was his fourth attempt, and this time he won. As usual, he started ahead in the polls on voting intentions. However, it was believed that the support of Cardoso and his political allies would lead to the victory of the alternative candidate. But the general exhaustion of the second Cardoso government as well as a split between the PSDB and PFL (a coalition that had permitted the two previous electoral victories) opened the way for Lula. There was also a significant change in the electoral program of the PT, and for the first time the party coalition agreed to accept as vice president a right-of-center candidate from the Partido Liberal. The party also abandoned the traditional values of PT, and Lula appeared as a candidate who would continue the Cardoso reforms, maintain macroeconomic stability, and accept the maintenance agreement with the IMF. There would be no breach of contracts or

---

[56] Gesner de Oliveira and Frederico Turolla, "Política Econômica do segundo governo FHC: mudança em condições adversas," *Tempo Social* (São Paulo) 15,2 (Novembro 2003), available at http://www.scielo.br/scielo.php?script=sci_arttext&pid=S0103-20702003000200008.

discontinuity in economic policy. Instead Lula and his party stressed their commitment to social issues. The official candidate was José Serra, Minister of Planning and Health in the Cardoso government. A respected and very well-prepared politician, Serra was unable to provide a platform to distinguish himself from the Cardoso government, which was now far less popular than it had been in the first administration. In the first round, Lula had 46 percent of the vote against 23 percent for Serra. In the second, he won with 61 percent.[57]

Although Lula and the PT criticized the government of Fernando Henrique Cardoso, saying that they had received a "terrible legacy," there would be perfect continuity in the economic policy of the two governments. The Lula administration took advantage of the price stability achieved with the Real Plan and the relative calm in international financial markets, which would only be broken by the crisis that would occur in 2008. Although at times, particularly in Lula's second term, there was suggestion of a development project or implementation of a new industrial policy, economic stability was undoubtedly the priority of the government. Growth was higher in the Lula period than in the Cardoso period, but less than it could have been if we consider the favorable international market conditions or if we compare the performance of Brazil with other countries in the group classified as BRICS.[58] In the opinion of many economists, Brazil lost the opportunity to grow faster because of its economic policy and the inability to increase public investment and encourage private investment.

Upon assuming power in January 2003, Lula faced an instability generated from the time of the uncertainty over the presidential election. Although during the electoral debates he made a formal declaration that he would maintain the same economic policy of his predecessor, including maintaining the agreement with the IMF, economic conditions since 2002 had deteriorated, with increased capital flight, sharp devaluation of the *real*, accelerating inflation, and monetary tightening. When he

---

[57] The political friction of the Cardoso government at the end of its mandate can be judged by the level of its popularity, which reached only 26 percent of public opinion which thought it was "good." When he took office his rating was 70 percent "excellent and good." Franco ended up his term with 40 percent "excellent and good," benefiting from the initial phase of the Real Plan and its positive impact on inflation, which helped in the election of Cardoso, his finance minister and the person responsible for the implementation of the plan.
[58] BRICS is represented by Brazil, Russia, India, China, and South Africa.

took office Lula honored his prior declarations, and to demonstrate his and his party's commitment to monetary stability and fiscal measures he intensified the contractionary fiscal and monetary policies of his predecessor. This calmed the local and international markets and the economy returned quickly to economic stability.[59]

After obtaining that stability, the economic policy of the Lula government followed the general guidelines established at the end of the Fernando Henrique Cardoso period, with a "dirty" floating exchange rate, generating a primary surplus in public accounts and meeting inflation targets. However, it is possible to identify a slightly different general orientation evolving over eight years of the Lula government, and showing some differences between his two terms. At first, there was greater rigor with inflation targets, even compromising growth. In the second term, he preserved the overall direction of economic policy, including inflation targeting, but now there was a greater concern with growth through the so-called Growth Acceleration Program and some scattered industrial policy measures. Unfortunately, neither was the Growth Acceleration Program a coherent plan of development nor were the specific measures of industrial policy a systematic program to promote national production. All such attempts at encouraging industry would be impaired by the maintenance of an overvalued national currency, which basically prejudiced competition from domestic producers.[60] Although it represented a breakthrough in concern about growth, the Accelerated Development Program, which sought to broaden the pattern of investments in the Brazilian economy, was insufficient to ensure sustainable growth. It had little impact in changing the structure of national investments and

---

[59] "Lula surfed on a very favorable sea thanks to the surfboard provided by his predecessor, Fernando Henrique Cardoso, which allowed him to surf the waves of the international economy in such a way that he obtained spectacular success at home and abroad. Remember that Lula, in his first year in office (2003), faced difficulties in the economy that he even caused, by threatening a complete 'break' with the past before realizing his error. After that he started to follow the gospel practiced by FHC, no longer trapped by his earlier threats and thus was able to ride the good waves of the international sea." Roberto Macedo, "Dilma e suas circunstâncias," *Jornal O Estado de São Paulo* (São Paulo), Julho 19, 2012, A2.

[60] The overvalued *real*, while it undermined local production that was losing competitiveness, exercised a key role in controlling inflation. The government sought to prevent further appreciation of the *real* by buying dollars, increasing reserves from U.S.$39 billion at the beginning of the Lula government to U.S.$352 billion in December 2012. The attractiveness of the Brazilian economy has stimulated capital inflows not only in the form of foreign direct investments, but also by the maintenance of extraordinarily high interest rates that attracted speculative capital flows into the country.

Consolidation of Democracy since 1985   291

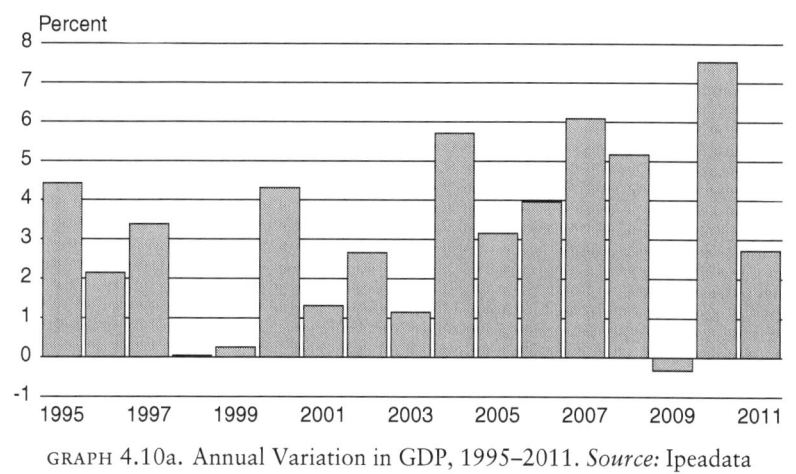

GRAPH 4.10a. Annual Variation in GDP, 1995–2011. *Source:* Ipeadata

Brazil did not grow at the same rate as the other BRICs (Graphs 4.10a and 4.10b).

There is one fundamental difference between the two governments. One had to deal with a succession of crises and create basic policies, and the second functioned with basic structural reforms enacted and a calm economic scene. In the Cardoso period the government was required to cope with rapid inflation and implement a program of stability at the expense of growth, the debt, and the restructuring of the public sector.

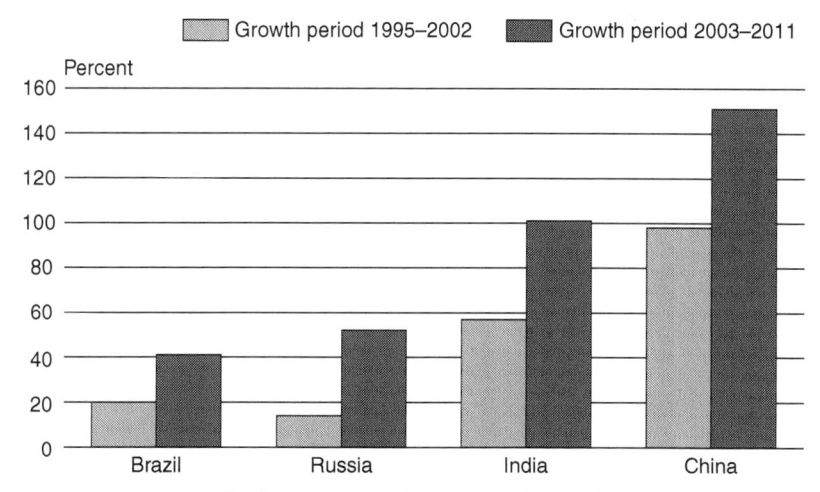

GRAPH 4.10b. Growth of BRICs (Brazil, Russia, India, and China), 1995–2011. *Source:* Ipeadata

He needed as well to consolidate unsecured liabilities, and though he offered a list of reforms, these were not enough to change the structure of the Brazilian state. Moreover, his government suffered the effects of successive international crises. At the end of his government, he left the bases of a coherent economic policy, with the targets for a primary surplus, a floating exchange rate, and goals related to inflation. Lula's government accepted this new configuration of state and economic policy and for a long time there was tranquility in the external sector until he had to face the crisis of the Great Recession, which started in 2008. The strength of the economy; the stability of the banking system, guaranteed by the reforms made during the Cardoso period;[61] the strength of the so-called fundamentals of the economy; and the economic policies adopted all prevented the deepening world crisis from having a significant impact on the national economy.

The Fiscal Responsibility Law and the implementation of the goals set for obtaining a primary budget surplus have usually been achieved by revenue growth as a proportion of GDP and not by reduction in current expenditures. Thus government expenditures show real growth in the last ten years. But the maintenance of high interest rates, the allocation of a large proportion of the budget to payments of interest on the public debt, elevated current expenditures, and other forms of transfers restrict the ability of the central government to invest in the national economy (see Graphs 4.11 and 4.12).

Given the chronic inflation that has affected Brazil for more than half a century, price stability has been the crux of recent economic policy. Since the final years of the second Cardoso government there has been a policy of inflation targeting, with the government establishing a tight band of variation permitted for price inflation, with the center point in this range being the desired rate that would be permitted. This range for inflation is fixed by the Central Bank, which orients its monetary policy to achieve the targeted central value and prevents prices from exceeding the upper and lower bands. From the second term of the Lula government, conflicts arose between the economists and political leaders pressing for growth and opposed to the policies adopted by the Central Bank. But the power of the monetary authorities prevailed and inflation has been kept

---

[61] The banking system was reorganized during the Fernando Henrique Cardoso government through *Proer* – Incentive Program for the Restructuring and Strengthening the National Financial System – and the *Proes* – Sanitation Program of the State Banks.

Consolidation of Democracy since 1985 293

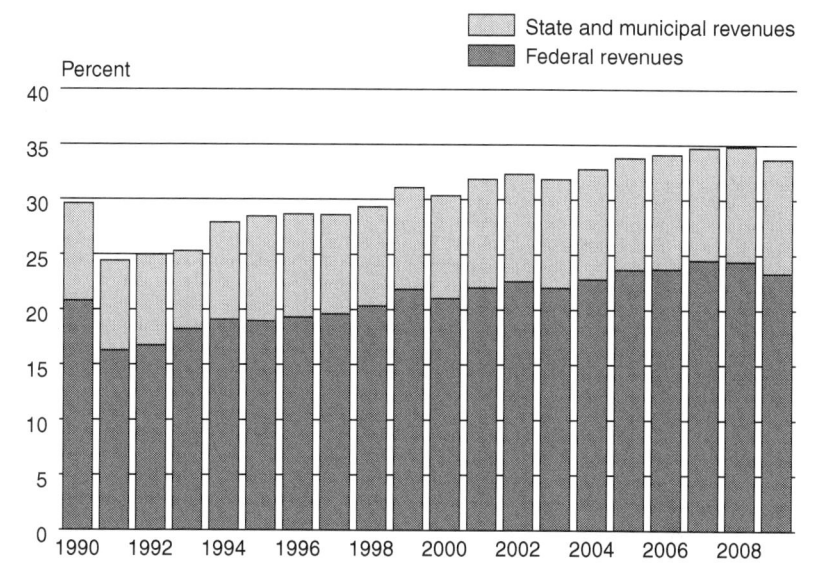

GRAPH 4.11. Government Revenues (federal and local) as a Percentage of GDP, 1990–2009. *Source:* Ipeadata

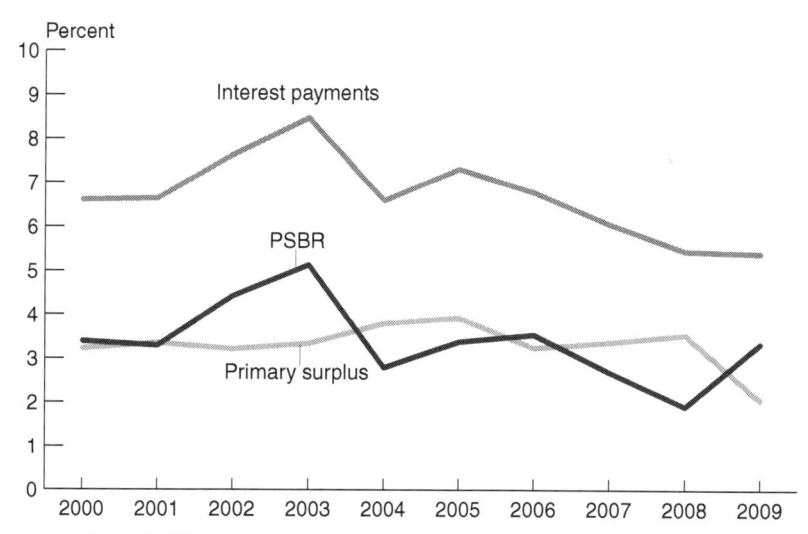

GRAPH 4.12. Public-Sector Borrowing Requirements (PSBR), Primary Surplus and Interest Payments, as a Percentage of GDP, 2000–2009. *Source:* Tesouro Nacional – Estatísticas

relatively controlled. The cost is low growth, and inflation still remains at a relatively high level, which is incompatible with current interest rates.[62]

But this policy resulted in Brazil having at the time the highest interest rates in the world, and although there was widespread criticism of the permanence of such rates, there was no consensus among economists about the causes. Only in the year 2012, due to poor economic performance, did the monetary authority begin a process of significant reduction in real interest rates. The results are still unpredictable in terms of inflation and the inflow of risk capital for the country. The high reserves allow such movement, which could reduce the net inflow of foreign funds that entered the country to take advantage of the differences in internal and external interest rates.

The floating exchange rate, as has been said, represented one of the three pillars of economic policy implemented at the end of the Cardoso government. After a period of turbulence in the years 2002 and 2003,[63] the *real* showed a persistent trend of recovery, with harmful effects on domestic production. The high domestic interest rates, abundance of external resources, and positive view of the international financial community about Brazil and its main economic fundamentals have attracted risk capital to take advantage of differentials in interest rates. But it also attracted capital for investment expansion, deployment, and purchase of companies in Brazil, through foreign direct investments. Furthermore, in recent years, due to new demand from China, there was an extraordinary increase in commodity prices, benefiting Brazilian exports of agricultural and mineral products, but dramatically reducing the participation of manufactured goods in exports. The deepening of the external crisis, particularly in Europe; the reduction of interest rates in Brazil; and

---

[62] On this theme, see André Lara Rezende, "Em plena crise: uma tentativa de recomposição analítica," *Estudos Avançados* (Universidade de São Paulo) 65 (2009), 73–87; Edmar L. Bacha, "Além da Tríade: há como reduzir os juros?" Texto para Discussão No. 17 (Rio de Janeiro: Instituto de Estudos de Política Econômica, Setembro 2010). Available at http://iepecdg.com.br/uploads/texto/TPD17_Bacha.pdf.
[63] Added to this internal crisis was the negative reaction of international markets when it appeared that there was a possibility of electing the candidate of the PT, Luiz Inacio Lula da Silva, to the presidency. These preoccupations about the possible election of Lula increased the volatility of the economy in the second semester of 2002 and had an effect on the exchange rate, which went from R$2.36 per dollar in April to R$3.53 in December of the same year. In the same period the basic interest rates went from 18 percent per annum to 25 percent per annum.

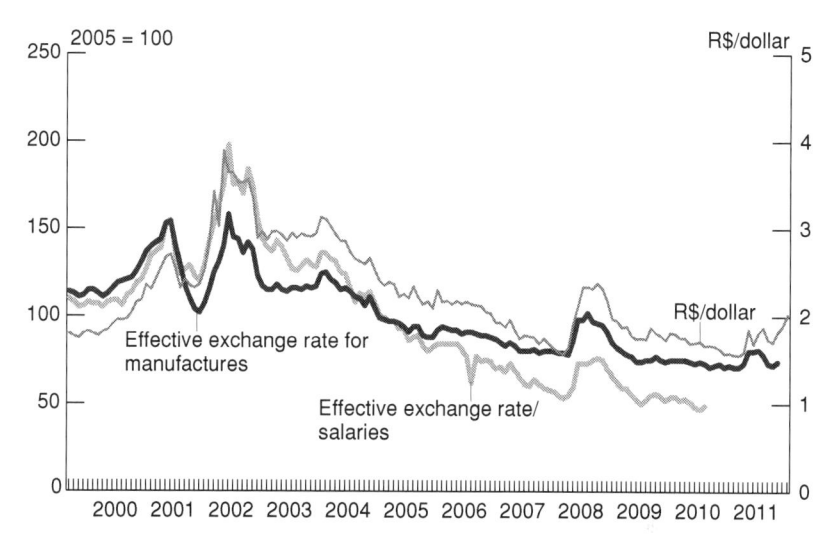

GRAPH 4.13. Exchange Rate, and Effective Exchange, 2000–2012 (effective rate and effective exchange rate). *Source:* Ipeadata

measures taken to discourage the entry of short-term capital promoted a significant devaluation of the *real* between mid-2011 and mid-2012, on the order of 30 percent (Graphs 4.13 and 4.14).

The importance of the international economic environment for Brazilian development is an aspect that should be emphasized. As seen throughout this work, external vulnerability accompanied the economic history of the country throughout the twentieth century. External shocks created acute internal crises. The international debt, and shortage of reserves, generated an ongoing external instability and resulted in exchange and import controls, which represented for decades the most relevant aspect of Brazilian economic policy. Moreover, the servicing of the external debt accounted for a significant proportion of exports.

But this has changed in recent years. The successful negotiation of the foreign debt in the mid-1990s, along with the success in eliminating chronic inflation, long-term political stability, continuity of economic policy for more than 15 years, as well as the potential of Brazilian agriculture and industry and its large domestic market, turned Brazil into one of the preferred destinations of foreign investors. These now introduced capital into the country in the form of foreign direct investments, or through short-term capital driven by differential interest rates. The flow of foreign capital into Brazil resulted in a major accumulation of reserves, which

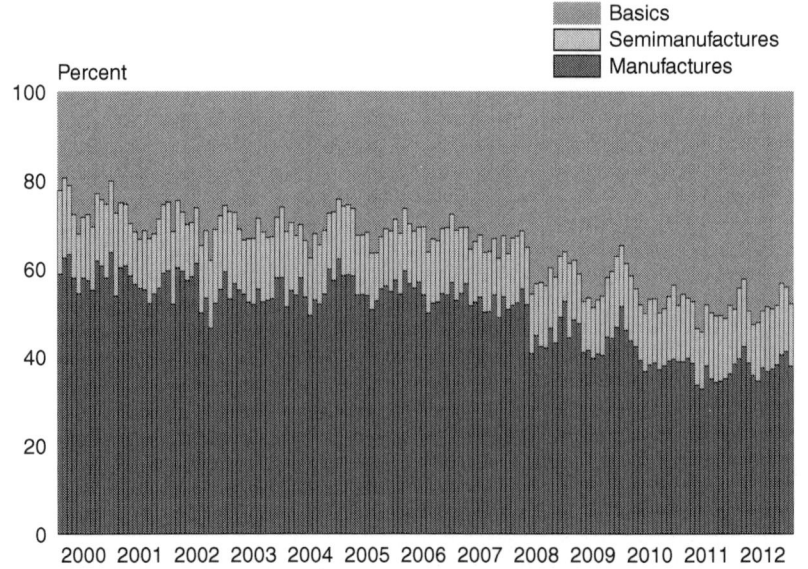

GRAPH 4.14. Participation in Brazilian Exports, 2000–2012. Source: Ipeadata

reached U.S.$372 billion in May 2012, which represented 124 percent of the total debt of the country and was one of the largest such reserves in the world.[64] That is, the excess reserves in relation to the indebtedness represented 4 percent of GDP. The excellent indicators of external solvency, coupled with the elimination of chronic inflation that plagued the country for half a century and the maintenance of relative fiscal equilibrium, largely the result of the Fiscal Responsibility Law and the targets established by the state relating to the primary surplus (fiscal income of the state before paying down debt), represent key economic achievements and increased the attractiveness of Brazil to foreign investments (Table 4.2).

At the end of his mandate, Lula obtained the highest levels of popularity achieved by any president at the end of his term (an 87 percent

[64] Miguel Bueno and Marcelo Dias Carcalholo, "Inserção externa e vulnerabilidade da econômica brasileira no governo Lula," in Os anos Lula: contribuições para um balanço crítico 2003–2010, ed. J. P. A. Magalhães (Rio de Janeiro: Garamond, 2010), 109–132; and Adhemar S. Mineiro, "Desenvolvimento e inserção externa: Algumas considerações sobre o período 2003–2009 no Brasil," in Os anos Lula: contribuições para um balanço crítico 2003–2010, ed. J. P. A. Magalhães (Rio de Janeiro: Garamond, 2010), 133–160.

TABLE 4.2. *Indicators of External Debt, 2007–2011 (U.S.$ million)*

	2007	2008	2009	2010	2011
Debt Service	52,028	37,638	43,561	46,348	52,596
Total Debt	193,219	198,340	198,192	256,804	298,204
Total Public-Sector Debt	85,956	84,160	95,502	103,940	102,441
International Reserves	180,334	193,783	238,520	288,575	352,012
Total Liquid Debt	11,948	27,683	61,771	−50,628	−72,868
Exports (goods and services)	184,603	228,393	180,723	233,736	294,473
GDP	1,366,544	1,650,897	1,625,636	2,143,921	2,482,070
Indicators					
Debt Service/Exports of Goods and Services (%)	28.2	16.5	24.1	19.8	17.9
Debt Service/GDP (%)	3.8	2.3	2.7	2.2	2.1
Interest/Exports of Goods and Services (%)	8.3	6.8	7.7	5.8	5.3
Total Debt/GDP (%)	14.1	12.0	12.2	12.0	12.0
Total Public-Sector Debt/Total Debt (%)	44.5	42.4	48.2	40.5	34.4
Total Liquid Debt/GDP (%)	−0.9	−1.7	−3.8	−2.4	−2.9
International Reserves/Total Debt (%)	93.3	97.7	120.3	112.4	118.0
Total Debt/Exports of Goods and Services (ratio)	1.0	0.9	1.1	1.1	1.0
Total Liquid Debt/Exports of Goods and Services (ratio)	−0.1	−0.1	−0.3	−0.2	−0.2
Reserves/Debt Service (ratio)	3.5	5.1	5.5	6.2	6.7
Reserves/Interest (rate)	11.8	12.4	17.1	21.4	22.8

Source: Banco Central do Brasil, http://www.bcb.gov.br/?INDECO.

positive rating).[65] Despite the political scandals that marked his administration, and that of the PT and other allied parties participating in the

---

[65] According to the survey of Ibope, paid for by the CNI – Confederação Nacional da Indústria, available at http://igepri.org/news/2010/12/popularidade-de-lula-e-recorde/. On the government of Lula, see Joseph LeRoy Love and Werner Baer, eds. *Brazil*

government, the charisma of Lula, along with his social policies, such as the *Bolsa Família*, the increase in the minimum wage, and particularly the good performance of the economy, maintained high levels of popularity for Lula throughout his second term. His popularity was fundamental in electing Dilma Rousseff to the presidency, since she was little known when President Lula decided to launch her candidacy for the office. President Rousseff, or Dilma, had actively participated in organizations that have opted for armed struggle against the military regime of the seventies. After being arrested and serving her time, she joined the PDT of Rio Grande do Sul, where she held various positions in state government. In the first term of President Lula she took over the Ministry of Mines and Energy, and in 2005 when there occurred the so-called *mensalão* scandal (or monthly bribes for votes of national legislators), she replaced Lula's Chief of Staff and potential replacement who had been implicated in the scandal.[66] Although unknown by the public at large, her candidacy for president was launched by Lula, who bet that his own charisma was sufficient to elect his successor. This did occur. José Serra, who then held the office of governor of São Paulo, was again the candidate of the opposition. The election was decided in the runoff by 56 percent for Dilma to 44 percent of the votes for Serra.

Although successfully riding out the 2008 crisis, the country has had difficulty getting back to an appropriate level of growth. This is demonstrated by the reduced growth in GDP in the two last two years: just 2.73 percent in 2011 and barely 0.9 percent in 2012.[67] The new administration has significantly changed the conduct of economic policy, focusing on growth, with a strong reduction in interest rates, tax relief for various sectors, and activities and relative abandonment of the floating exchange rate, maintaining a relative constant of 2 *reais* per dollar until

---

under Lula: Economy, Politics, and Society under the Worker-President (New York: Palgrave/Macmillan, 2009); Marilena de Paula, ed., *"Nunca antes na História desse país"... ? Um Balanço das Políticas do Governo Lula* (Rio de Janeiro: Fundação Heinrich Böll, 2011).

[66] In 2012, after 10 years, the Federal Supreme Court (STF) ruled on the so-called *mensalão* scandal, which involved the leadership of the PT and some of its ministers, including the Chief of Staff and President of the PT, José Dirceu. The Supreme Court held that there was a conspiracy to divert public resources and corrupt leaders of various allied parties in order to obtain their support of policies of the Lula government. Whatever the eventual outcome of appeals from this conviction, the importance of the accused guaranteed that this trial represented a milestone in the country's institutional consolidation.

[67] Preliminary estimate given by IBGE, and available at http://www.ibge.gov.br/home/presidencia/noticias/noticia_visualiza.php?id_noticia=2205&id_pagina=1.

recently.[68] But there are structural issues that hinder growth, such as low investment, poor infrastructure, and a complex and irrational tax structure that hinders investment and exports.[69]

Moreover, since 2010 there has been considerable debate about whether Brazil was in the process of deindustrialization and affected by the so-called Dutch disease. In the Netherlands in the 1960s, with the sharp rise in gas prices, there was a marked increase in revenues from exports of the Netherlands, overvaluing the local currency and undermining the competitiveness of other Dutch products. It was thought that this was happening in Brazil, with the strong appreciation of the *real*, due partly to high commodity exports, the increase in international prices, and the Brazilian competitiveness in agricultural and mining production, which, in turn, would reduce the competitiveness of other sectors, particularly the manufacturing industry, which had no conditions to compete. The proportion of manufactures in GDP and in exports has declined and the percentage of manufactured goods in the percentage of imports increased (see Graph 4.15). There is no doubt that this is occurring. The question is how much of the competitiveness of Brazilian industry should be credited to an overvalued exchange rate and how much to the productivity of national industry. Regardless of extreme positions taken and the impact and importance of each of the causes that explain the loss of competitiveness of Brazilian industry, the truth is that national industry has grown less than other sectors of the national economy, and there has been a decline in its participation in national production and a growth in the imported component of national industrial output. As we have seen, from mid-2011 to mid-2012, there was a real devaluation of around 30 percent in the *real* – which solves part of the exchange problem. This slow devaluation is increasing in the recent period. This should have a positive impact on industry, but perhaps the industrial problem is more serious and is really due to low productivity of Brazilian industry. If the cause is primarily foreign exchange, the industry will recover in the medium

---

[68] The former Minister of Finance, Mailson da Nobrega, said in September 2012 that the Dilma government ended with the three pillars of the economic policies of Fernando Henrique Cardoso and Lula, with the Central Bank having no more inflation targets. Instead its targets are the interest and exchange rates. He said the Central Bank operates an informal band, which gives its policies the characteristics of a fixed and not floating exchange. *Jornal O Estado de São Paulo*, Setembro 24, 2012, B4.

[69] Since the economic stability achieved in 1994 with the Real Plan, the average GDP growth has only been 3.1 percent. According to Pastore, Brazil is unable to grow beyond 4 percent per year, "Estrevista com Affonso Celso Pastore," *O Estado de São Paulo*, Julho 8, 2012, B4.

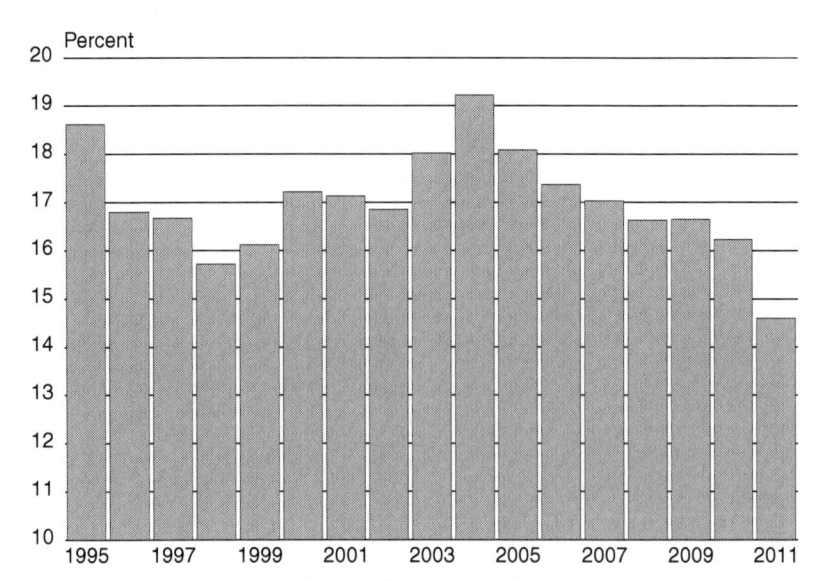

300   The Economic and Social History of Brazil since 1889

GRAPH 4.15. Participation of Manufacturing in the GDP, 1995–2011. *Source:* Ipeadata

term, but if the cause is primarily one of low productivity, only active government economic policies of the medium and long term may change this picture.[70]

Unlike industry, agriculture has shown exceptional performance for many years. Agriculture represents about 5 percent of GDP, but it is a central component of a large agribusiness complex, which is estimated at approximately 22 percent of GDP.[71] The agribusiness can compete so successfully in the international market due to high crop yields and the sophisticated processing of raw materials. The continental size of

---

[70] Affonso Celso Pastore, Maria Pinotti, and Leonardo Porto de Almeida, "Cambio e crescimento: o que podemos aprender?," in *Brasil Globalizado*, ed. Fabio Giambiagi and Octávio de Barros (Rio de Janeiro: Elsevier, 2008), 268–298; Octavio de Barros and Robson Rodrigues Pereira, "Desmitificando a tese da desindutrialização: reestrutração da indústria brasileira em uma época de transformações globais," in *Brasil Globalizado*, ed. Fabio Giambiagi and Octávio de Barros (Rio de Janeiro: Elsevier, 2008), 299–330; Marcos S. Jank et al., "Exportações: existe uma 'doença brasileira'?," in *Brasil Globalizado*, ed. Fabio Giambiagi and Octávio de Barros (Rio de Janeiro: Elsevier, 2008), 331–352; Wilson Cano and Ana Lúcia Gonçalves da Silva, "Política Industrial do Governo Lula," in *Os anos Lula: contribuições para um balanço crítico 2003–2010*, ed. J. P. A. Magalhães (Rio de Janeiro: Garamond, 2010), 181–208.

[71] According to the Centro de Estudos Avançados em Economia aplicada – Esalq/USP the agrobusiness had a participation of 22.74 percent of the GNP in 2010. Available at http://www.cepea.esalq.usp.br/pib/.

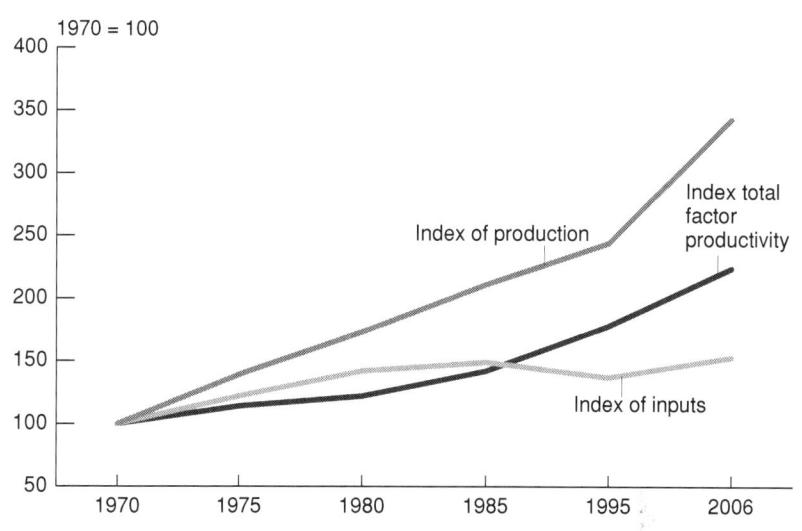

GRAPH 4.16. Agriculture: Index of Production, Inputs, and Total Factor Productivity, 1970–2006. *Source:* Gasques et al. 2010, p. 31

the country and the gradual improvement in its productivity rates put it in a leadership position in Latin America and among the first nations in world agriculture. In the crop year 2010–2011 production of cereals reached 162.8 million tons, using 49.9 million hectares. Output and planted area have been growing systematically over several decades, but what marks the Brazilian agriculture in the last thirty years is the extraordinary increase in productivity, which in previous decades had remained stagnant (Table 4.3 and Graph 4.16).[72] Despite the impressive development of production and agricultural productivity, landownership remains highly concentrated, with the Gini index at the level of 0.85 since 1975.[73]

The high productivity of the agricultural sector and the persistence of high prices of general commodities, including agricultural ones, meant that Brazilian agribusiness accounted for much of Brazil's exports and balance of payments (see Graph 4.17). In the 12 months ending in September 2011, agribusiness exports totaled U.S.$90.3 billion and imports of

---

[72] José Garcia Gasques, Eliana T. Bastos, Mirian R. P. Bacchi, and Constanza Valdes, "Produtividade total dos fatores e transformações da agricultura brasileira: análise dos dados dos censos agropecuários," in *A agricultura brasileira: desempenho, desafios e perspectivas*, ed. José G. Gasques, José E. R. Vieira Filho, and Zander Navarro (Brasília: IPEA, 2010), 19–44.

[73] In the agrarian census of 1975, 1980, 1985, 1995, and 2006, the same Gini index of 0.85 was produced. Rodolfo Hoffmann and Marlon Gomes Ney, *Evolução recente da*

TABLE 4.3. *Principal Characteristics of Agriculture in the Agropastoral Census of 2006*

	1920	1940	1950	1960	1970	1975	1980	1985	1995	2006
Agricultural Establishments	648,153	1,904,589	2,064,642	3,337,769	4,924,019	4,993,252	5,159,851	5,801,809	4,859,865	5,175,489
Total Area (hectares)	175,104,675	197,720,247	232,211,106	249,862,142	294,145,466	323,896,082	364,854,421	374,924,929	353,611,239	329,941,393
Crop Areas (há)	6,642,057	18,835,430	19,095,057	28,712,209	33,983,796	42,207,566	57,723,959	62,810,423	50,104,483	59,846,618
% of Area in Crops	0.04	0.10	0.08	0.11	0.12	0.13	0.16	0.17	0.14	0.18
Total Persons Employed	6,312,323	10,159,545	10,996,834	15,633,985	17,582,089	20,345,692	21,163,735	23,394,919	17,930,890	16,567,574
Total Tractors	1,706	3,380	8,372	61,345	165,870	323,113	545,205	665,280	799,742	820,673
Average Crop Area per Tractor	3,893	5,573	2,281	468	205	131	106	94	63	73
Number of Animals	34,271,324	34,392,419	46,891,208	56,041,307	78,562,250	101,673,753	118,085,872	128,041,757	153,058,275	171,613,337
Pastures of Animals	2.6		2.3	2.2	2.0	1.6	1.5	1.4	1.2	0.9
Average Return per Hectare										
Rice	1,562		1,287	1,275	1,222	1,333	1,416	1,737	2,711	3,921
Beans	1,078		525	398	372	410	397	377	507	718
Corn	2,040		1,254	1,074	1,197	1,335	1,521	1,476	2,442	3,606
Wheat	641		706		926	679	914	1,519	1,701	1,737
Soybeans					862	1,542	1,639	1,773	2,334	2,602
Sugar Cane	33,736		26,861	34,196	39,970	42,979	53,618	60,525	62,086	68,876
Cotton Seed	878		378	438	849	923	1,121	1,063	1,333	2,986

Source: Gasques et al. 2010, "Produtividade total dos fatores e transformações da agricultura brasileira: análise dos dados Agropecuários," pp. 22–25.

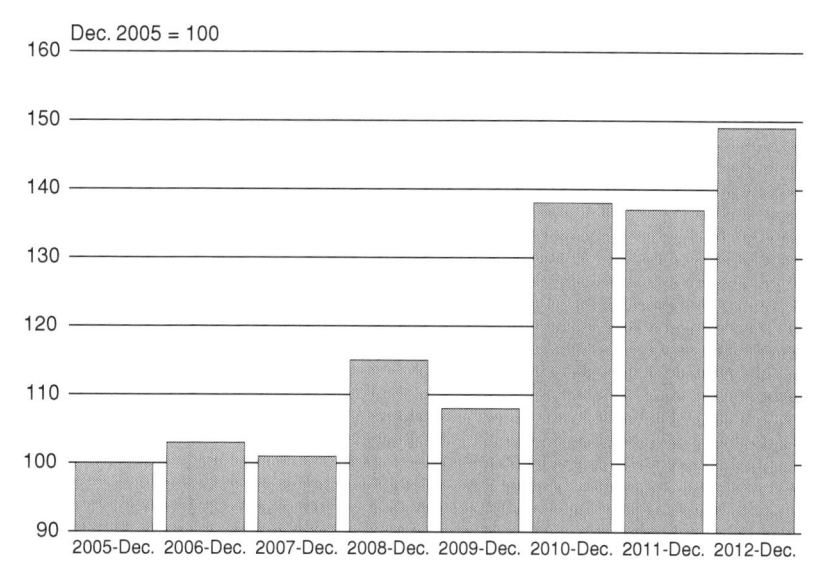

GRAPH 4.17. Index of Agro-Pastoral Commodity Prices – IC-Br, 2005–2012.
Source: Banco Central do Brasil

agribusiness were only U.S.$16.6 billion, allowing for a positive trade balance of agribusiness of U.S.$73.6 billion.[74] In that same period, Brazil generated a trade surplus of U.S.$30.5 billion, which meant that agribusiness covered the external deficits of other economic sectors.

When analyzing the overall performance of the Brazilian economy from stabilization achieved with the Real Plan to today, it is evident that there were general advances in the Brazilian economy. But there are still major issues hindering growth. Although it has remained within the ranges set by the monetary authorities, inflation remains high by the standards of major international countries, including the G20 of which Brazil is a part. Also there are still sectors with indexation, which means that inflation has not been fully controlled. Finally, inflation controls compromise growth by keeping the interest rates high. Internal imbalances persist, such as the low educational level of the population, poor infrastructure, and low productivity in various sectors of the economy. Moreover, the country has been unable to resume the pace of investments

---

estrutura fundiária e propriedade rural no Brasil (Brasília: Ministério do Desenvolvimento Agrário, 2010), 20.

[74] Portal Brasil, available at http://www.brasil.gov.br/noticias/arquivos/2011/10/11/exportacoes-do-agronegocio-brasileiro-cresce-24-8-em-12-meses-e-soma-us-90-3-bi.

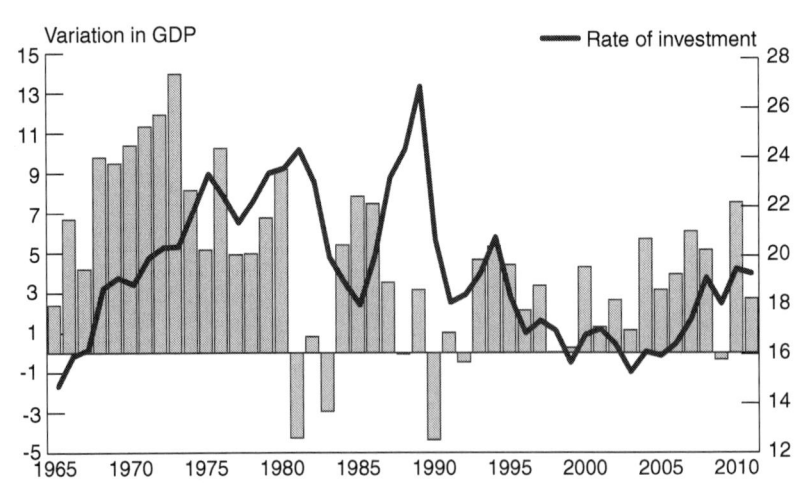

GRAPH 4.18. Rate of Investment and Variation in the GDP, 1965–2010. *Source:* Ipeadata

that marked the 1970s and that led to rapid growth. In the last ten years, when signs of growth have appeared, imbalances in the market, the emergence of inflationary signals, and high interest rates have quashed these developments.

If in the first 80 years of the twentieth century there was an average growth of 5.7 percent, in the last 31 years the rate has fallen to just an average annual 2.6 percent. Just considering the last 10 years, the performance is not much better, resulting in an average annual growth of just 3.6 percent (Graph 4.18). In the same period the BRICs grew at an average rate of 6.1 percent. Moreover, in recent years growth was based on internal consumption. This was done by the expansion of employment, real increase in the minimum wage, and policies of income transfers and strong credit expansion. But there are evident signs of exhaustion of this growth cycle.[75] The future seems to require greater investments and productivity improvements. The infrastructure is poor, and national industry finds it difficult to compete with foreign companies not only because of the

---

[75] The strong expansion of consumer credit and housing has increased the level of indebtedness of Brazilian families significantly. Previously the consumer credit market was small because of such restrictions as high credit costs, very limited time periods for repayment, and the near absence of credit for home purchases. Recent studies show the current level of household debt has generated an overcommitment of income to service the debt of households, reaching 30 percent of income in December 2012. Available at http://www.infomoney.com.br/emprestimos-dividas-e-inadimplencia/noticia/2403899-.

exchange-rate issue, but also because of the low standard of competitiveness. According to a recent study, Brazil should invest between 5 percent and 7 percent of GDP in infrastructure in order to boost economic growth and approach the standard of Korea and other industrialized countries of East Asia. However, the proportion of investment has been only 2 percent of GDP.[76]

In 2013 expectations about the Brazilian economy became even more pessimistic, partly for internal causes and partly because of external causes. Internally, there was widespread criticism of the conduct of economic policy, as the government has shown less concern with the fiscal balance than with increasing its intervention in the economy. Low growth and strong inflationary pressures have generated a disorderly response from the economic authorities. Despite incentives and subsidies given to different sectors, growth is timid and inflation is high, particularly in services and in market prices in general. In mid-2013, for example, the services had an annual growth of 8.48 percent in prices, while administered prices increased by only 1.31 percent, due to the control exercised by the government. But more worrying is the performance of the external sector. Throughout this study we have shown how the succession of external crises affected Brazil and the unusual tranquility of this sector in the last ten years. Since 2000 Brazil has accumulated significant balances on its trade balance. But the accumulated deficit in the first half of 2013 is worrying. Furthermore, there has been an increase every year in the negative balance of the current account. The external instability generated by the strong U.S. recovery has led to an appreciation of the dollar against most international currencies. But the effect in Brazil has been extremely strong, because of the internal conditions of the country, with

---

[76] According to the author, "[T]he country faces essentially two types of restrictions on investment in infrastructure, both the result of 'state failures.'" Perhaps the most important concerns the legal and regulatory framework in the country, which establishes rules for specific sectors and their implementation. The vagueness of the rules and the delay in decision making, including conflicts of interpretation of legislation, adversely affect investments. Conversely, this experience demonstrates the importance of a clear definition of a legal framework; a regulatory regime and governing institutions that combine transparency and stability of rules; technical competence; and agility in decision making. In transport (roads, rail, ports, waterways, and airports), particularly, there is an aggravating factor: the complementarity of public and private investment implies that the quality of institutions charged with implementing public investment has a direct impact on private investment. Therein lies possibly another "failed state" that would explain the lack of private investment. Cláudio R. Frischtak, "O investimento em infra-estrutura no Brasil: Histórico recente e perspectivas," *Pesquisa e Planejamento Econômico* 38,2 (Agosto 2008), 307–348.

its low growth, inflationary pressures, and deterioration in its external accounts. Thus in the first eight months of 2013 there was a devaluation of 15 percent in the *real*, despite the intervention of policy makers to contain the devaluation of the national currency.

The recent economic performance and changes were accompanied by important changes in the social area. Undeniably the end of inflation, with its inflation tax that especially burdened the poor, is one of the key factors explaining the exceptional social performance that the country has experienced in recent years. Domestic demand exploded in the Real Plan, particularly for consumer goods destined to lower-income groups. But the obvious process of social mobility that began to affect all classes was not only due to the Real Plan. Employment has grown significantly, and today Brazil shows indicators of unemployment well below the previous normal levels attained in Brazilian society.[77] Moreover, in recent years, formal employment has grown at the expense of the informal labor market. Increasing shares of workers now have broad social benefits and pension plans. Since the government of Fernando Henrique Cardoso, there occurred a persistent real appreciation of the minimum wage, which continued during the Lula government. From July 1994, when the Real Plan was implemented, to December 2011, there has occurred a net increase in real wages of 123 percent, which clearly has had an impact on income distribution in Brazil (see Graphs 4.19 and 4.20).[78] Finally, the Cardoso government established several income transfer programs, which were consolidated into one program by the Lula government and today benefits an important part of the national population. The *Bolsa Escola* and *Bolsa Alimentação* (school and food grants) of the Cardoso government were focused on poor families with children. The *Bolsa Escola* benefited low-income families with children ages 6 to 15 years and *Bolsa Alimentação* served families with children up to seven years. The structure

---

[77] According to the survey of IBGE in the principal metropolitan regions of the country between March 2003 and December 2011, the proportion of the population employed in the official labor market – with a legal registration, went from 69 percent to 77 percent. For the current EAP data see Ipeadata.

[78] According to a study of the Fundação Getúlio Vargas, in the decade from 2001 to 2010 the richest 10 percent had an increase in income of only 10.3 percent, while the poorest 50 percent showed an increase in income of close to 67.9 percent. Thus the distance of average incomes of both extracts decreased from 18.2 (December 2000) to 9.76 (December 2010). According to the study, "There is in Brazilian history, statistically documented since 1960, nothing similar to the reduction of income inequality observed since 2001" (46). Marcelo Cortes Neri, ed., *Desigualdade de Renda na Década* (Rio de Janeiro: Fundação Getúlio Vargas, Centro de Políticas Sociais, 2011).

Consolidation of Democracy since 1985 307

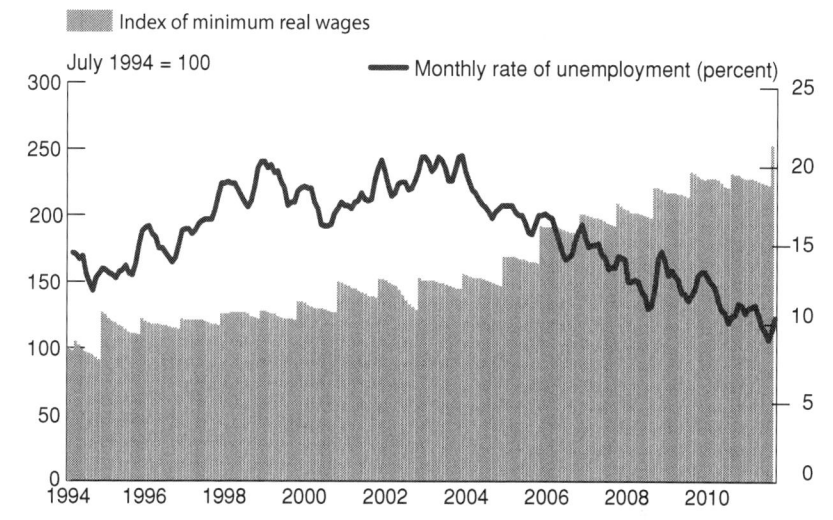

GRAPH 4.19. Rate of Unemployment and Minimum Real Wage, 1994–2012.
Source: Ipeadata and IBGE, Pesquisa Mensal Emprego.

of the two programs was relatively similar, with direct payments to beneficiaries, by magnetic ATM cards.[79] In the Lula government there was a change in income transfer programs, with the launching of *Bolsa Família* (family grant),[80] unifying all income transfer programs and changing the profile of the beneficiaries, which now depends on the average household income, as well as the number and age of children. Currently there are 13 million families benefiting,[81] and the *Bolsa Família* is one of the most popular programs enacted by the Lula government.[82]

---

[79] Sonia Rocha, "Impacto sobre a pobreza dos novos programas federais de transferência de renda," n.d. Available at http://www.anpec.org.br/encontro2004/artigos/A04A137.pdf.

[80] Then, on assuming the government in 2003, Lula launched with great acclaim the Zero Hunger Program (Programa Fome Zero), but given the difficulties in its implementation, it was also incorporated into the *Bolsa Família* program.

[81] Ministério do Desenvolvimento Social, available at http://www.mds.gov.br/bolsafamilia. In addition to the income criteria, there are conditionalities in the area of education (as a minimum frequency of school attendance) and in health, including taking the children to health clinics for monitoring and participating in vaccination campaigns. Marcelo Medeiros, Tatiana Britto, and Fábio Soares, *Programas focalizados de Transferência de Renda no Brasil: Contribuições para o Debate*, Texto para Discussão No. 1283 (Brasília: IPEA, 2007), 8.

[82] For an analysis of these programs see Rocha, "Impacto sobre a pobreza dos novos programas federais." Several scholars argue that the preference of government programs for the *Bolsa Família* (Family Grant Program), in relation to the other continuous benefits,

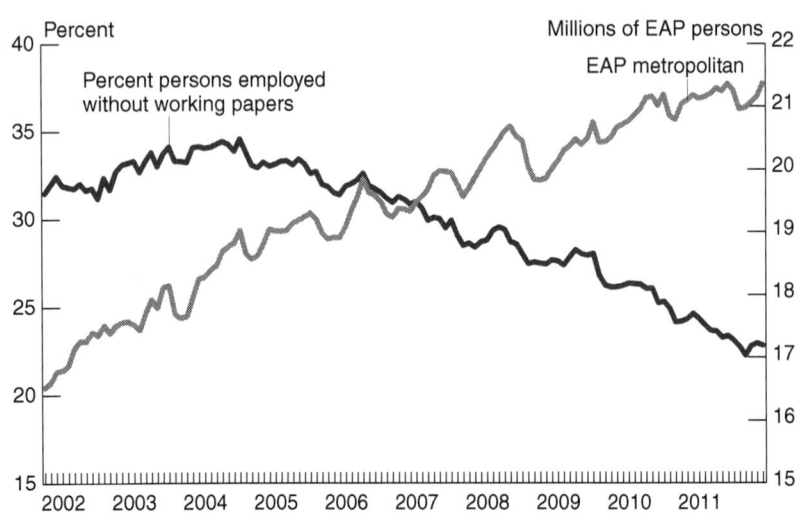

GRAPH 4.20. Economically Active Population in Metropolitan Regions, 2002–2012. *Source:* IBGE, Pesquisa Mensal Emprego

The results of these policies can be seen in the profound social changes that have occurred in Brazil in the last two decades of the twentieth century and the first decade of the twenty-first century. Many of the trends evident in the period from 1945 to 1980 accelerated. The most significant changes were those affecting poverty, population growth, health, and education. The result of these developments, especially since the return of democratic governments, has been to create an evermore uniform society as regional, class, and color differences decline and a more coherent nation emerges. Slowly over these recent thirty years all the states and regions of the country followed the patterns of the most advanced states of southern and southeastern regions, often at a faster pace than the advanced regions. Thus the spread between the advanced and more backward regions progressively declined as even the northeastern states reached levels of income, education, fertility, and mortality ever closer to the advanced regions. The distinction of the country into a sharply divided traditional poor backward north and a contrasting advanced industrial and modern south, no longer held true for the nation. Class,

such as the monthly transfer of income to people with severe disabilities of any age and seniors more than 65, is because the political effect is greater with the *Bolsa Família*. Medeiros et al., *Programas focalizados de Transferência de Renda no Brasil*, 9–10.

race, and region still defined important inequalities in Brazil in the late twentieth and early twenty-first century, but they were no longer so far apart geographically as to define two different societies. Industrialization, urbanization, and modernization of agriculture everywhere have all reduced the differences between regions and thus slowed the massive movements of Brazilians across regions. This 30-year period marked the peak of interregional migrations in the first 20 years and their systematic decline in the past decade as such push factors as regional variation in resources has declined and opportunities for a better life have become more equal among the regions.

Along with the progressive movement of all regions to a national norm, there also has been a tremendous amount of individual social and economic mobility. In the 1970s and early 1980s with massive industrialization had come very rapid upward mobility for the educated elite. Then democratic government policies of redistribution of income and the progressive expansion of education, health, and social services in the next three decades have, along with general economic growth, progressively reduced the informal labor market, and have led to a massive movement of poor into the working and lower-middle classes. Especially since the late 1990s there has been a major expansion in what Brazilians have come to call classes B and C, which grew at the expense of the poorest class (D). Malnutrition has been eliminated, the stark contrast between urban and rural life reduced, education in the primary grades now incorporates all children, and illiteracy is slowly disappearing from all age groups. Brazil now matriculates almost all children into primary schooling such that illiteracy has virtually disappeared among persons under 15 years of age. Finally, almost all Brazilians now have access to public health and consequently the death rates from all types of diseases have fallen.

Initially, all this rapid growth and expansion led to a more stable and in some ways more rigid society. Mobility now is more circular than structural as the industrial and urban sectors have matured and are no longer expanding at the same rate. The rural population is now more stable and is not sending as large a contingent to the urban workforce as had been the case in the earlier period. Also there has been more universal access to primary and secondary education for all classes. Thus the early high levels of structural mobility noted in the 1970s and especially in the early 1980s have declined significantly. Mobility obviously continues, but is now more circular in nature with descending movement becoming more important. In fact Brazil seems to be a bit less mobile than comparable and advanced industrial societies.[83] Moreover, mass secondary education has paradoxically led to a decline in the quality of this education. Initially, more persons had moved up than moved down the class ladder, especially at the top. But there has been relatively slow growth in the wealthiest class since then and, in turn, new educational barriers have emerged that slow mobility into that class and prevent higher levels of downward mobility. This barrier is defined by restricted access to the elite public university education, which is denied to the majority of graduates of public secondary schools because of the low quality of these public high schools. Only high-cost private secondary education permits easy access to public universities. The rise of a major private university system that is open to public school graduates has led to a two-tier tertiary education system that, in turn, shunts graduates to different levels of the labor market, as private university graduates receive fewer skills than public university graduates.

The recent creation of subsidized tuition for low-income students to attend private tertiary faculties (the *Prouni* program established in 2004) has brought more students into the university system, but without an increase in the quality of these private for-profit faculties. Brazil has created an unusual system of higher education by world standards in which for-profit private universities dominate higher education in terms of matriculation. Already by 1970, 51 percent of all students in higher education were in private universities, and by 2011, this figure had risen to 74 percent despite the major growth of federal, state, and municipal universities since the late 1970s.[84] As scholars have noted, this leaves Brazil with one of the highest levels of university privatization in the world, which even the United States does not come close to achieving. These for-profit universities have little interest in research and low standards of admission.[85] Despite this reliance on the market, Brazil still has one of the lowest ratios of young adults matriculated in higher education even within Latin America.

---

[83] See José Pastore, *Inequality and Social Mobility in Brazil* (Madison: University of Wisconsin Press, 1982); Carlos Antonio Costa Ribeiro, *Estrutura de classe e mobilidade social no Brasil* (Baru, SP: Educ, 2007), Chapters 3 and 5; and Maria Celi Scalon, *Mobilidade social no Brasil: padrões e tendências* (Rio de Janeiro: Revan, 1999).
[84] José Marcelino de Rezende Pinto, "O accesso à educação superior no brasil," *Educação Social* (Campinas) 25,88 (Outubro 2004), 731, Table 2; and MEC, INEP, *Censo da educação superior 2010* (Outubro 2011), 8, Table 2.
[85] Pinto, "O accesso à educação superior," 732, Table 3.

While regional differences within the country have systematically declined, Brazil remains a traditional capitalist society and one that grew out of slavery. Thus class and race still define inequalities in access to the resources that the society offers.[86] Moreover, new blockages have been introduced that obstruct upward mobility to the top while there is major mobility at the bottom and middle sectors. Because of these rigidities and inequalities in the educational system, income inequality in Brazil, while declining, has still remained at extraordinarily high levels by world standards and class and race nationally still divide the society. Thus all indices of health and well-being still show strong class differences, a pattern common to most capitalist societies. The more extreme of these differences in health have been moderated quite significantly in this period as government services have slowly and steadily expanded to cover all the national population. In this, Brazil has achieved universal access to immunization, prenatal care, and medical treatment. But a very extensive private health care system also guarantees that some have more access to resources than others, and upward and downward mobility is still influenced by color and by level and quality of education.

Although the patterns of mobility have slowed in the recent period, there have been long-term changes in the population that have profoundly altered the nature of Brazilian society. This is especially the case of fertility, in which the change was abrupt and affected all regions and all groups in society whatever their class or color. It was only in the decades of the 1970s and 1980s that a true demographic transition occurred, with births finally declining faster than deaths. In a pattern somewhat different than what has occurred in other advanced industrial societies, fertility control initially did not occur through later marriage and delayed fertility by women, but primarily through reducing fertility in the later ages and moving the modal fecundity to a younger age. This pattern which began in the 1970s accelerated as all forms of contraception from sterilization and use of birth control pills were becoming standard practice among women. Although the peak age of fertility was 25 to 29 for Brazilian women in most of the twentieth century, with the fertility revolution the modal age of birth initially shifted downward to women 20 to 24 years of age, and then very rapidly declined in all the later ages (see Graph 4.21). This

---

[86] See, e.g., Carlos Hasenblad and Nelos do Valle Silva, eds., *Origens e Destinos: Desigualidades sociais ao longo da vida* (Rio de Janeiro: Topbooks, 2003); and the older study by Charles H. Wood and José Alberto Magno de Carvalho, *The Demography of Inequality in Brazil* (Cambridge: Cambridge University Press, 1988).

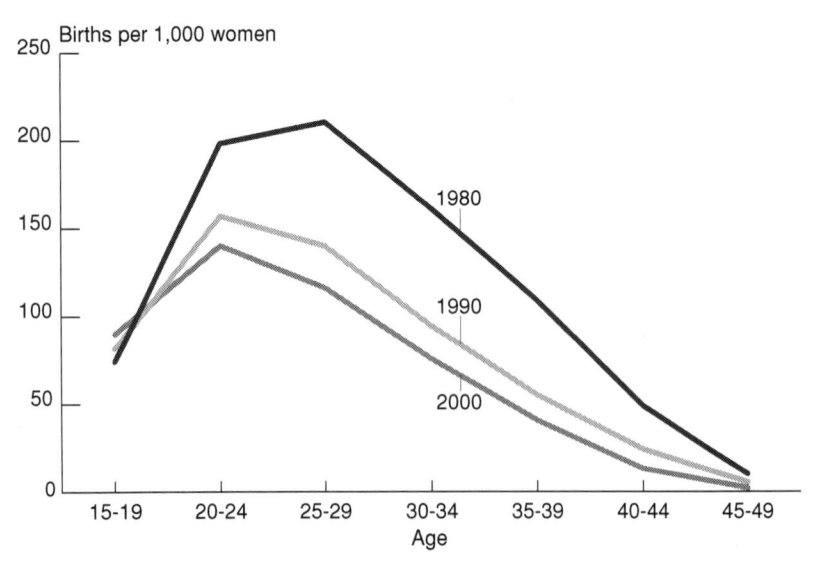

GRAPH 4.21. Birth Rates by Age of Mother, 1980–2000. *Source:* IBGE, *Projeção da população do Brasil por sexo e idade, 1980–2050, Revisão 2008*, Table 11

pattern of concentration of births at the earliest ages has continued to be the norm for Brazilian women despite the continued massive entrance of women into education and the labor market.[87] Between 1991 and 2000 the age of Brazilian mothers at first birth initially declined further from 23.1 years to 22.3 years of age.[88] This compares to 25 years of age for U.S. mothers at first birth and to 30 years of age for women at first birth in the United Kingdom and Sweden in the same period.[89]

---

[87] While women seemed to have achieved equality fairly early in advanced education, there seems to have been little change in the past decade. Thus as early as 1999 women represented 55.6 percent of all university students at all levels, which was almost identical to the 55.4 percent figure for 2010. But they were still a minority in the elite institutions. Thus, e.g., only 44 percent of the students enrolled in the elite state universities in São Paulo were women in both years, even as the total of matriculated students almost doubled from 79,000 to 152,000 in the same period. The same ratio of 44 to 45 percent was found in the federal universities in the state; again that more than doubled their students in this period from 6,754 to 22,683. INEP, *Sinopse Estatística do Ensino Superior Graduação – 1999*, Table 4.4; and *Censo da Educação Superior 2010*, Table 5.4, both available at http://portal.inep.gov.br/superior-censosuperior-sinopse.

[88] IBGE, *Perfil das Mães* Comunicação Social, Maio 6, 2005, available at http://www.ibge. gov.br/home/presidencia/noticias/noticia_impressao.php?id_noticia=357.

[89] OECD, "Data for Chart SF2.3.A: Mean age of women at the birth of the first child, 2009," available at http://www.oecd.org/document/4/0,3746,en_2649_37419_ 37836996_1_1_1_37419,00.html. Of 30 countries in this OECD database, only Mexico with an average age of 21 years came close to the Brazilian rate.

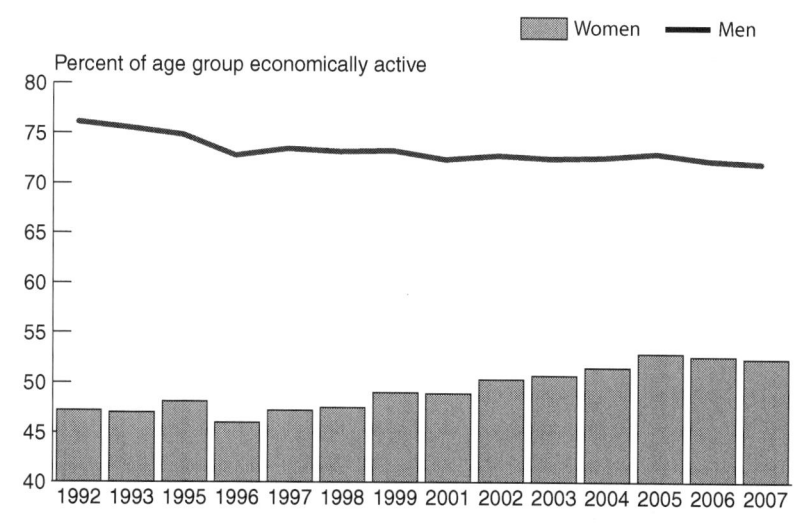

GRAPH 4.22. Percentage of Economically Active Population by Sex, 1992–2007. *Source:* IBGE, Série: FDT212 – Taxa de atividade, por sexo – População de 10 anos ou mais de idade

But it was clear that this trend of births concentrated in the 20 to 24 age group would slowly change. One indicator of this was that the median age of marriage between 1980 and 2010 has been steadily rising. In the earlier period the median age of women marrying was 20 to 24 years of age whereas by 2010 it had risen to 25 to 29 years of age. In the short period from 2003 to 2010 the median age of marriage for women rose an impressive two years of age, signifying a long-term rise in this index.[90] Although marital fertility is no longer the single predicator of overall fertility, given that 36 percent of persons who were living together lived in free unions by 2010,[91] it can be assumed that all women, married formally or not, are being influenced by the changes in their education and their participation in the job market. It is evident that women have steadily increased their participation in the workforce (see Graph 4.22),[92]

---

[90] IBGE, Tabelas Série: RC63 & RC46 Casamento – por faixa etária de mulheres, available at http://seriesestatisticas.ibge.gov.br/lista_tema.aspx?op=0&no=10.

[91] IBGE *Censo Demográfico 2010 – Resultados Preliminares da Amostra*, Table 3.3, "Pessoas de 10 anos ou mais de idade, que viviam em união conjugal, por natureza da união conjugal, segundo as Grandes Regiões e as Unidades da Federação – 2010," available at http://www.ibge.gov.br/home/estatistica/populacao/censo2010/resultados_preliminares_amostra/default_resultados_preliminares_amostra.shtm.

[92] The labor force participation rate of Brazilian women in 2007 (52.4 percent women employed to women aged 10 to 60 years of age) was not that different from the

and their added years of schooling compared to men suggests that they are also entering in professional and tertiary education in large numbers. The evolution of these rates in Europe and the United States shows these potential trends. In the 17 countries of the European Union the median age of all mothers had reached 30 years of age by 2005 and was still rising in the following years. In the United States it was 28 years.[93] These new trends have also finally appeared in Brazil as can be seen in the birth data for 2003 and 2011. As of 2003 the peak age group producing children was still 20- to 24-year-old women but in the PNAD national household survey of 2011 the primary age group was now 25 to 29 years of age. Moreover, the percentage of children born to women less than 20 years of age declined in this same period and those born to those more than 30 years of age increased, finally showing the same trends that are evident in the advanced industrial societies of the world (see Graph 4.23).[94]

Although there now seems to be a definite shift to older ages for fertility, there is no indication that the low fertility rates overall will change anytime soon. The postdemographic transition decline in fertility has affected and will continue to affect all regions and all classes until well into the twenty-first century. This decline is now universal and the use of modern contraceptives is on the increase everywhere.[95] Although the

---

original 16 European Union countries EAP rate of 57.8 percent in 2007 for women employed to all women aged 15 to 64 years of age. EUROSTAT, "Employment rate by gender, age group 15–64," available at http://epp.eurostat.ec.europa.eu/tgm/table.do?tab=table&init=1&plugin=1&language=en&pcode=tsiem010.

[93] The European data and the United States data will be found at EUROSTAT, Table "Mean age of women at childbirth," updated December 19, 2011 and available at http://epp.eurostat.ec.europa.eu/tgm/table.do?tab=table&init=1&plugin=1&language=en&pcode=tps00017.

[94] This is not the conclusion reached by the IBGE in its population projections. It estimated women ages 20 to 24 will still be the primary category of mothers until the mid-twenty-first century. But this is a questionable assumption given other data available. See IBGE, *Projeção da população do Brasil por sexo e idade, 1980–2050, Revisão 2008* (Rio de Janeiro: IBGE, 2008), n.p., Table 11. However, recent research has shown that the more education and the higher the occupation the more delay there is in childbearing among Brazilian women, and also sees the increase of the modal rate among southern region women ages 25 to 29 as a long-term trend. See Cláudio Santiago Dias Júnior, "Comportamento reprodutivo: Uma análise a partir do grupo ocupacional das mulheres" (PhD thesis, Belo Horizonte: CEDELAR/UFMG, Março 2007), Chapter 1.

[95] A detailed study of the data in the PNAD household surveys from 1986 and 2006 shows that the use of contraceptives among women ages 14 to 49 increased from 66 percent to 81 percent and that at the later date 77 percent were using modern methods compared to only half who did so 30 years earlier. Moreover, there was a definite decline of sterilizations and rise of the use of the pill – almost equal among these women. There was also a major increase in condom use, from 2 percent to 12 percent in this same

Consolidation of Democracy since 1985   315

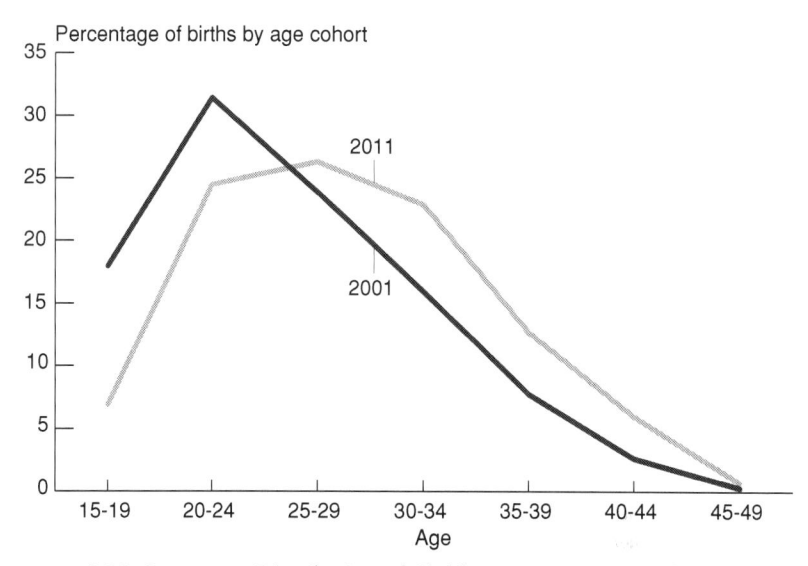

GRAPH 4.23. Percentage Distribution of Children Born in 2001 and 2011 by Age of Mothers (PNAD 2001, 2011). *Source:* IBGE, PNAD, Table 1934. Available at http://www.sidra.ibge.gov.br/pnad/pnadpb.asp

northern regions initially experienced this fertility decline at a slower pace than the southern regions, the spread between regions has declined significantly. Thus the peak year of difference between the northeast and southeastern region was reached in 1980 when the spread between the two regions was 2.9 children. In the next two decades, however, fertility declined faster in the northeast than in the southeast, such that the difference between the two regions was just 0.4 children in 2010 (see Graph 4.24). Thus it can be said that in terms of fertility Brazil has essentially moved toward one basic pattern of low fertility, which is now the norm throughout the country. There are lingering racial and class influences, with black and mulatto women having higher rates than whites and with those with lower incomes and education consistently having more children than those with higher incomes and education, but even here the range is far more limited than in previous periods.[96]

period. Flávia Alfenas Amorim, "Mudanças recentes no uso de métodos contraceptivos no Brasil: a questão da esterilização voluntária" (MA thesis, Rio de Janeiro: IBGE, Escola Nacional de Ciências Estatísticas – ENCE, 2009), 86, Table 4.

[96] See the data for the TFR by income and education for 1991 and 2000 in Elza Berquó and Suzana Cavenaghi, "Mapeamento sócio-econômico e demográfico dos regimes de fecundidade no Brasil e sua variação entre 1991 e 2000." Paper presented at *XIV*

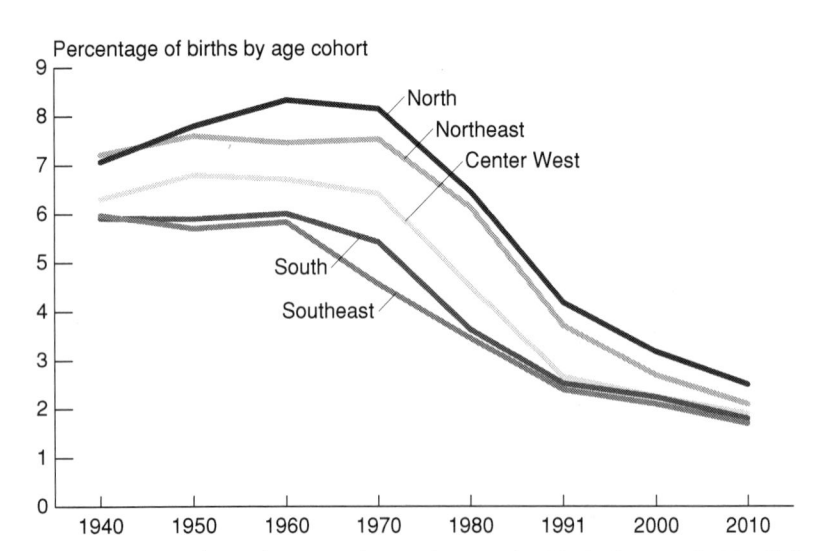

GRAPH 4.24. Total Fertility Rate by Region, 1940–2010. *Source:* IBGE, Série: POP263 – Taxa de fecundidade total and Censo 2010, Res Amsotra, Nup, fec e migracao (2010), Table 7

Although different scholars offer different estimates of fertility rates, all indicate long-term decline.[97] The official government estimate is that the total fertility rate fell below replacement in 2005, and is currently at 1.75 children per woman in the 14 to 49 age category.[98] Because that fertility rate is expect to continue to decline and to remain at a very low rate until mid-century, the latest Brazilian census bureau (IBGE, the national statistical agency of Brazil) projections show that growth will continue to decline and that in 2039 Brazil's actual resident population will start to decline (see Graph 4.25).

Encontro Nacional de Estudos Populacionais ABEP (2004), 9–10, Tables 3–4. As for color differences, the analysis of the 2011 PNAD survey shows that Pretas and Pardas had a total fertility rate of 2.15 children, compared to a rate of just 1.63 children per white woman ages 14 to 49. The overall rate for Brazil was 1.95 children. IBGE, *Síntese de indicadores sociais. Uma análise das condições de vida da população brasileira,* 2012, Estudios e Pesquisas No. 29 (Rio de Janeiro, 2012), Table 1.5, "Taxa de fecundidade total, por cor ou raça das mulheres, segundo as Grandes Regiões – 2011."

[97] For just those from the United Nations, CEDEPLAR along with IBGE, which all differ as to rate but not as to trend, see Dias Júnior, "Comportamento reprodutivo: Uma análise a partir do grupo ocupacional das mulheres," Março 13, Table 1.

[98] IBGE, *Projeção da população do Brasil por sexo e idade...2008,* Table 11.

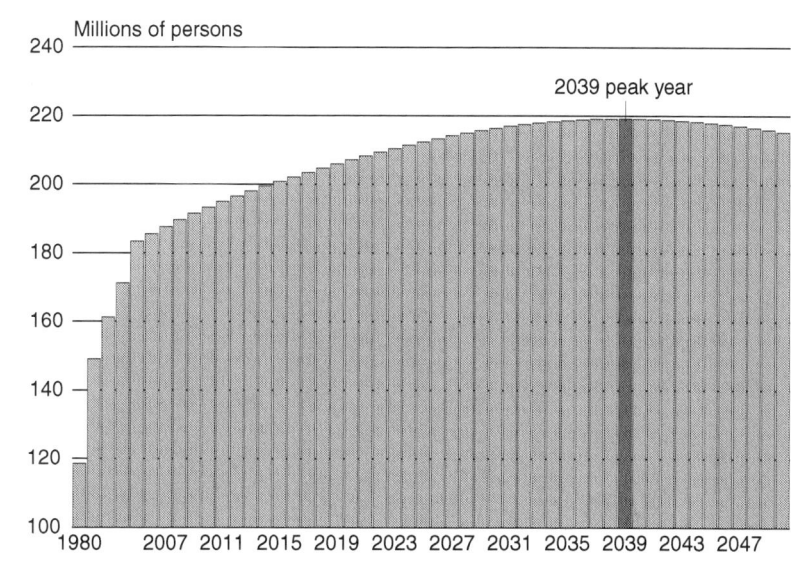

GRAPH 4.25. Projected Growth of the Brazilian Population, 1980–2050 (based on 2008 IBGE projections). Source: IBGE, *Projeção da população do Brasil por sexo e idade, 1980–2050, Revisão 2008*, Table 8

Along with fertility, mortality has also shown a long-term downward trend since the early 1980s, but at a slower pace (see Graph 4.26). From the late nineteenth century, the urban campaigns for vaccination, purified drinking water, and sanitation improvements have led to a slow but steady decline in mortality rates beginning early in the century. This was the case for all of Latin America, and there was an especially pronounced secular decline in mortality between 1930 and 1950.[99] In Brazil, the crude death rate by the 1940s was in the low 20s per thousand resident population and, in turn, this rate dropped to just 14 deaths per thousand population in the next decade and to just 6 per thousand population by 1980,[100] and this rate held steady into the twenty-first century.

Although infant mortality was extraordinarily high for most of this period, even it began to decline, going from more than 200 deaths per thousand live births in the 1940s to just over 100 deaths per thousand

---

[99] Eduardo E. Arriaga and Kingsley Davis, "The Pattern of Mortality Change in Latin America," *Demography* 6,3 (1969), 226.
[100] Elza Berquó, "Demographic Evolution of the Brazilian Population in the Twentieth Century," in *Population Change in Brazil: Contemporary Perspectives*, ed. David Joseph Hogan (Campinas: UNICAMP, 2001), 15, Table 3.

Births and deaths per 1,000 residents

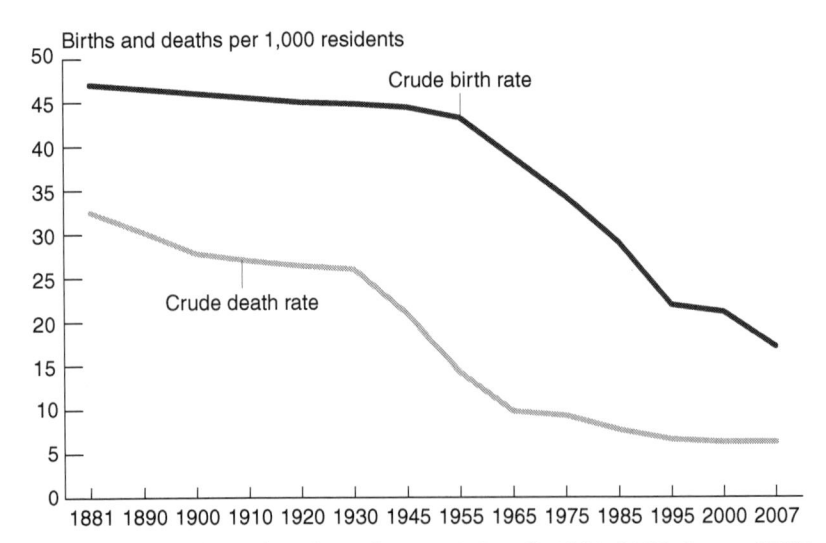

GRAPH 4.26. Crude Birth and Death Rates in Brazil, 1881–2007. *Source:* IBGE, Série: CD109 – Taxas brutas de natalidade e de mortalidade, and for 2010 DATA-SUS Table A.10 Taxa bruta de mortalidade. Available at http://tabnet.datasus.gov.br/cgi/idb2011/matriz.htm#demog

live births – still a very high figure – in 1970.[101] It then dropped to 50 deaths by 1990 and to 33 deaths by 2001, and most recently stood at 18 deaths per thousand live births in 2008, a very impressive decline, but with a rate that unfortunately was still high by western European and Asian standards.[102] The government estimates that it will take until 2050 for Brazil to reach the current European and North American rate of 6 deaths per thousand live births.[103]

There have also been significant changes in the composition of the infant mortality rate. As late as 1983/85 post neonatal deaths (from 28 to 364 days after birth), which were those deaths most influenced by social and economic conditions, still accounted for more than half of all infant deaths, with a very broad spread from 66 percent of all infant deaths

---

[101] The only available infant mortality rates are for urban populations, and these were clearly well below the national averages. In 1941 the urban infant mortality rate was 202 deaths per thousand live births, and in 1970 it was 109 deaths per thousand live births. See Elza S. Berquó and Candido Procopio F de Camargo, eds., *La population du Brésil* (Paris: UN/CICRED, 1974), 52, Table 26.
[102] For the 1990 to 2001 figures, see IBGE, "Indicadores demográficos," available at http://www.ibge.gov.br/.
[103] IBGE, *Projeção da população do Brasil por sexo e idade, 1980–2050, Revisão 2008*, Table 17.

in the northeast to just 48 percent of such deaths in the southeast. But like all other demographic aspects the level and the regional variations declined. By 2003/2005 such deaths accounted for just over a third of all deaths in the country and the spread between the northeast and the southeast was between 36.1 percent and 31.2 percent of deaths.[104] In turn, in this period perinatal deaths went from less than half to two-thirds of all infant deaths, a rate identical to that of the United States.[105] Even if the level of infant mortality is still high, the composition of that rate is now similar to most advanced industrial countries with most infant deaths related to problems in the gestation period. There has also been a dramatic decline in maternal mortality. In 1990 some 143 mothers died for every 100,000 live births. By 2008 such deaths had declined to less than half that rate, or 66 deaths. Surprisingly, while Brazil's level of infant mortality placed it about the middle of the region's countries, its maternal mortality of 2008 meant that it had one of the lowest such rates in the region.[106]

Along with a declining national trend in these various types of mortality related to children and mothers, there has also been a systematic decline in regional mortality, and thus class differences as well since region is often a proxy for class and color. All regions saw a decline in infant and child mortality, but what is especially impressive is that the spread in both indices between the worst region (the northeast) and the best (the south) declined dramatically in the past decade. Thus in 1997, the northeast had 33 more infant deaths per thousand live births than the south; this difference fell to less than eight deaths in 2010. In turn, in regard to child mortality (deaths of children under five to thousand live births) the difference between the northeast and the south fell

---

[104] Elisabeth França and Sônia Lansky, "Mortalidade infantil neonatal no Brasil: situação, tendências e perspectivas." Texto elaborado por solicitação da RIPSA para o Informe de Situação e Tendências: Demografia e Saúde, 2008 [Textos de Apoio, 3] (2008), 4, Table 1.
[105] The pre-28 days in the United States in 2001 was 67 percent and for Brazil in the pre-28-day period 66 percent of all deaths. For the U.S. data, see Kenneth D. Kochanek and Joyce A. Martin, *Supplemental Analyses of Recent Trends in Infant Mortality*, available at http://www.cdc.gov/nchs/products/pubs/pubd/hestats/infantmort/infantmort.htm; for the Brazilian data see REDE Interagencial de Informação para a Saúde, *Indicadores básicos para a saúde no Brasil: conceitos e aplicações*, 2nd ed. (Brasília: Organização Pan-Americana da Saúde, 2008), 83 (hereafter referred to as RIPSA).
[106] CEPAL, *Anuario estadístico de América Latina y el Caribe, 2010*, 58, Table 1.4.1, "Indicadores seleccionados de salud," and 59, Table 1.4.2, "Tasa de mortalidad infantil, por quinquenios, por sexo."

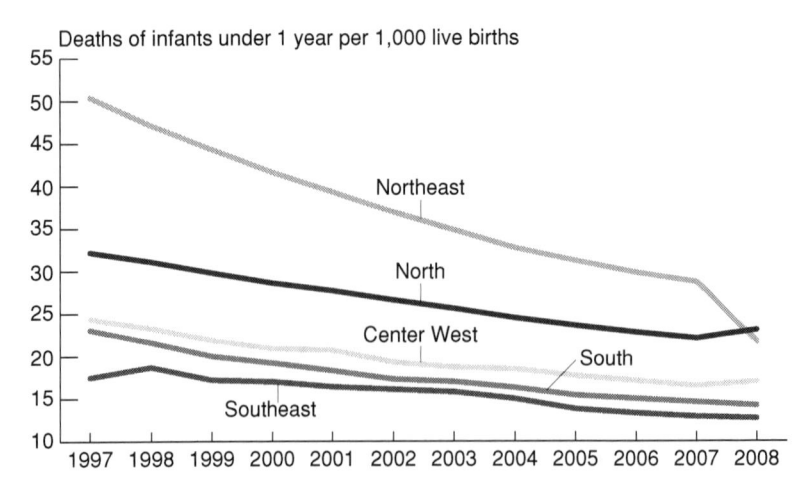

320   The Economic and Social History of Brazil since 1889

Deaths of infants under 1 year per 1,000 live births

GRAPH 4.27a. Infant Mortality Rates by Region, 1997–2008. *Source:* DATASUS "C.1 Taxa de mortalidade infantil." Available at http://tabnet.datasus.gov.br/cgi/idb2010/c01b.htm

from 29 child deaths in 2000 to just a difference of nine child deaths in 2010 (see Graphs 4.27a and 4.27b). One of the dreaded killers of children in the developing world, acute diarrhea, was one of the major diseases to experience a very rapid decline in all regions of Brazil in this period, going from 11 percent of infant and child deaths in 1991 for all regions

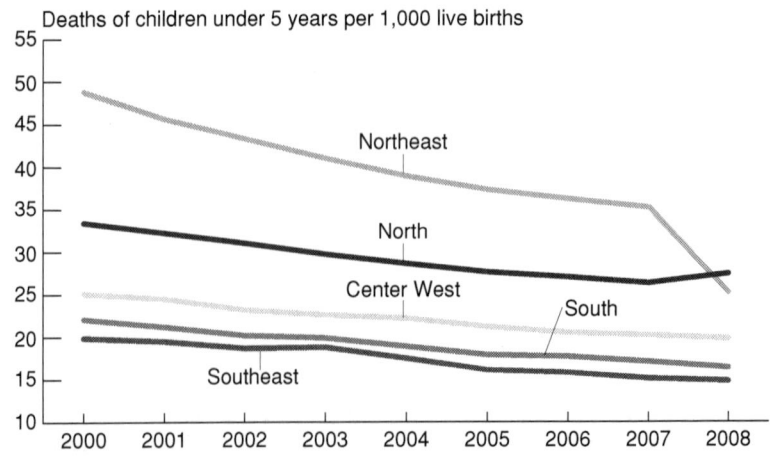

Deaths of children under 5 years per 1,000 live births

GRAPH 4.27b. Child Mortality Rates by Region, 2000–2008. *Source:* DATASUS "C.16 Taxa de mortalidade na infância." Available at http://tabnet.datasus.gov.br/cgi/idb2011/c01.htm

to just 4 percent of all deaths for children under five years of age in 2004.[107]

Adult mortality followed more slowly the changes occurring in infant and child mortality in this period, a pattern typical in all countries. Average life expectancy for men and women rose significantly for both sexes from 1980 to 2010 largely due to the decline in infant and child mortality. In the former year men had a life expectancy at birth of some 59.6 years and women 66.0 years. Thirty years later these rates had risen an impressive 10 years for men and 11 years for women reaching 69.7 for men and 77.3 years for women.[108] But Brazil remains far behind the advanced countries of Europe. The difference in 2007 was some seven years less than the average life expectancy for women and 10 years less than for men living in the original 16 European Union countries.[109]

As was the norm for most of the past century, life expectancy for women exceeded that for men. In 2010, the difference in potential average life at birth between the sexes was 7.6 years, which is a rate at the high end of differentiation by advanced world standards and should decline over time.[110] This difference in life expectancy between men and women is clearly revealed in the low survival of men into the older age categories. Starting in their late 20s, more women survive than men and this difference becomes more pronounced as age increases with the sex ratio dropping to 85 men per 100 women by 65 years of age (see Graph 4.29).

Along with improvement in life expectancy at birth, there occurred a slow decline in adult mortality due primarily to major improvements in

---

[107] The spread between the northeast and the southeast is still significant, with the percentage in the former being 6.2 percent of the child deaths and in the latter just 1.9 percent of such deaths. RIPSA, *Indicadores básicos para a saúde no Brasil: conceitos e aplicações*, 125–127. It is worth noting, however, that deaths of children from acute respiratory infections declined quite dramatically in all regions from 10 percent of all child deaths in 1991 to just 6 percent of all deaths. In this case the northeast actually had a lower percentage of such deaths (5 percent) than did the southeastern region. RIPSA, *Indicadores básicos para a saúde no Brasil: conceitos e aplicações*, 129.

[108] IBGE, *Projeção da população do Brasil por sexo e idade, 1980–2050, Revisão 2008*, Table 11.

[109] EUROSTAT, Table "Life expectancy at birth by gender," updated December 16, 2011 and available at http://epp.eurostat.ec.europa.eu/tgm/table.do?tab=table&init=1&plugin=1&language=en&pcode=tps00025.

[110] In the United States, e.g., the difference between men and women dropped from 6.4 years in 1949/1951 and steadily declined to just five years of difference in 2007. *Statistical abstract of the USA 2011*, 74, Table 104, "Selected Life Table Values."

the delivery of health services. For the population over 60 years of age, for example, average life expectancy increased some five years for these older women in the period from 1980/85 to 2007, and more than four years for men older than 60 – giving a total of 22.6 years more of life for older women and 19.4 for these older men.[111] In turn, these rates were just two years less than those for 60-year-old women and three years less than for 60-year- old men in the 16 original European Union countries.[112] Most of this improvement in life expectancy for all age groups was due to the decline of mortality from infectious diseases.[113] Whereas infectious diseases were the prime killers at mid-century, by the end of the twentieth century they had been replaced by degenerative diseases.[114] With this rise of heart disease and cancer as primary causes of death at the end of the century, and with infectious diseases no longer a significant element among the major killers, Brazil finally fell in line with the pattern common to the advanced industrial countries of the world since the beginning of the twentieth century. Thus in 2004 the major causes of death were heart disease (32 percent of all deaths), and cancer (13 percent of all deaths), with nondisease-related deaths (accidents, killings, etc.) being the second-largest cause of death accounting for 14 percent of the total deaths. Infectious diseases had fallen to just 5 percent of all deaths. The spread in infectious disease deaths went from 7 percent in the north to 4 percent in the south, but the leading causes of death were the same in all regions.[115]

This change in mortality, especially the rather abrupt decline of deaths of infants and children, also was reflected in changes in the age participation in total deaths. Whereas those less than age 15 made up an extraordinary 56 percent of deaths at the middle of the twentieth

---

[111] For the 1950–1955 estimates see CELADE, *Boletín Demográfico* 67 (Enero 2001), and for 2007 see the male and female tables provided at IBGE, Table "Brasil: Tábua Completa de Mortalidade...2007," op. cit.

[112] EUROSTAT, Table "Life expectancy at birth by gender," updated December 16, 2011 and available at http://epp.eurostat.ec.europa.eu/tgm/table.do?tab=table&init=1&plugin=1&language=en&pcode=tps00025.

[113] E.g., infectious diseases accounted for only 5 percent of the deaths in the state of São Paulo (and 7 percent of deaths among infants and children) in 2001. SEADE, *Anuário Estatístico do Estado de São Paulo – 2001*, Quadro 25, available at http://www.seade.gov.br.

[114] Some 30 percent of the deaths in São Paulo state in 2001 were due to heart disease – the biggest killer, followed by cancers, which accounted for another 15 percent. SEADE, *Anuário Estatístico do Estado de São Paulo – 2001*, Quadro 25.

[115] RIPSA, *Indicadores básicos para a saúde no Brasil*, 115.

Consolidation of Democracy since 1985 323

century, they represented only 16 percent of all persons who died by the first decade of the twenty-first century.[116]

All of these trends in births and deaths had a direct impact on the natural growth rate of the national population. Although mortality was on the decline from the end of the nineteenth century and was declining more rapidly from the middle decades of the twentieth century, fertility initially did not follow this trend. The total of births actually increased slightly until the mid-1960s due to declining rates of mortality and morbidity among young women. As occurred in many countries in Latin America in this period, as health improved, sterility rates for women declined and far higher numbers of women survived into their child-bearing years, with these improvements in health initially leading to a higher volume of births. The result of this combination of continuing high fertility and declining mortality led to a process of very rapid population growth in Brazil in the late twentieth century. In the period from 1960 to 1970 the Brazilian population grew at the quite impressive rate of 3 percent per annum.[117] Because of this the Brazilian population, which stood at 52 million in 1950, doubled to 104 million in 1974, just 24 years later. If the high 3 percent rate of the period from 1960 to 1970 had continued, the 1974 population would have doubled again to 208 million by 1983. But by the 1970s the natural growth rate had started to decline and dropped to 2.5 percent and then fell again to just 1.9 percent in the 1980s, reaching 1.0 percent by the first decade of the twenty-first century.[118] Because of this decline in growth the population had only reached 191 million persons by the census of 2010.[119]

The consequence of this earlier rapid growth meant that initially the average age of the Brazilian population was falling to historic lows. In 1950 the median age of the population was 18 years of age, and by

---

[116] CELADE, "Estimaciones y Proyecciones de Población, 1950–2050, Brasil, Populación Total, Indicadores del crecimiento demográfico estimados y proyectados por quinquenios, 1950–2050," available at http://www.eclac.cl/celade/proyecciones/intentoBD-2002.htm.

[117] Rates of growth calculated from mid-year population estimates of IBGE, available at Ipeadata: População residente – 1º de julho – Anual – Pessoa – IBGE Outras/Pop – DEPIS_POP.

[118] IBGE: *Censo Demográfico 2010 Sinopse do Censo e Resultados Preliminares do Universo* (Rio de Janeiro, 2011), Table "Taxa média geométrica de crescimento anual 1940/2010 Brasil."

[119] IBGE: *Censo Demográfico 2010 Sinopse do Censo e Resultados Preliminares do Universo*, Table "População e taxa média geometrica de crescimento annual Brasil 1872/2010."

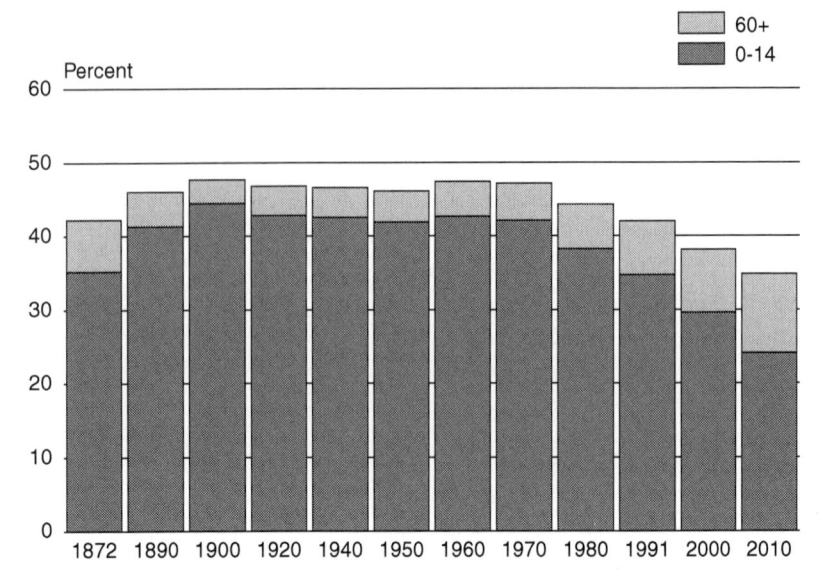

GRAPH 4.28. Relative Share of Youths and Aged in Total Population, 1872–2010. *Source:* Série: IBGE, POP22 – "População por grupos de idade (população presente e residente"

1965 at the height of the mid-century fertility boom, it dropped a full year to just 17 years of age.[120] But the declining fertility and mortality would progressively increase the median age of the population. By the census of 1991 the median age of the population had risen to 26.5 years and rose again to 32.1 years in the census of 2010.[121] This not only meant that the share of the younger population was declining, but also that declining mortality and longer life expectancy meant that the share of the elderly population 60 years of age and older was increasing (see Graph 4.28). The ratio of the population more than 64 years of age is projected to pass the ratio of children 0 to 14 years of age by 2050.[122]

The changes in mortality and fertility affected the age breakdown of the Brazilian population in all age categories. All this becomes apparent for the first time in the age pyramid constructed for the 2010 census, which looks more and more like that of the jar-shaped pyramids of the

---

[120] Calculated from tables presented in CELADE, *Boletín Demográfico* 66 (Julio 2000).
[121] IBGE, *Censo Demográfico 2010 Características da população e dos domicílios, Resultados do universo,* Table 5, "Idade média em anos, total... 1991/2010," n.p.
[122] IBGE, *Projeção da população do Brasil por sexo e idade 1980–2050, Revisão 2008,* Table 14, "Projeção da população, segundo os grupos de idade – Brasil – 1980/2050."

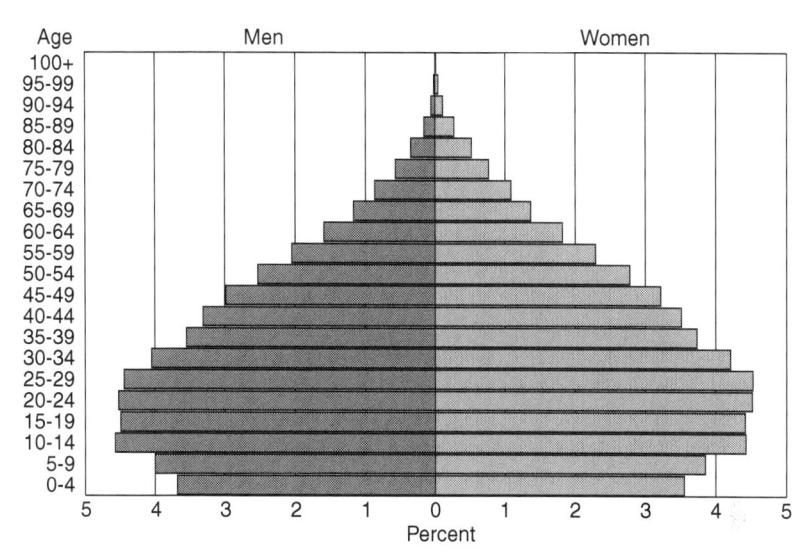

GRAPH 4.29. Age Pyramid of the Brazilian Population in 2010. *Source:* IBGE, *Censo Demográfico 2010 Características da população e dos domicílios, Resultados do universo*, Table 1.1.1 "População residente... segundo os grupos de idade – Brasil – 2010" (n.p.)

advanced industrial world, especially evident in the birth cohorts less than 25 years of age (see Graph 4.29). Not only has the average age of the population risen, but the ratio of workers to children and adults is projected to increase for another 30 years;[123] this ratio will eventually decline leading to what demographers call a higher dependency ratio, which is the number of nonworkers to workers in the population. At the moment this ratio is still low by the standards of the advanced countries in Europe and Asia, but it will present problems in the future. Since Brazil has been expanding its welfare system for most of the past half century, it will mean that the finances of the welfare system will become more difficult as the ratio of workers to total population declines. This is the current theme in the advanced world, and will become a major theme in Brazil in the future.

Along with influencing the changing age structure of the national population, the evolution of birth and death rates since the middle of the twentieth century has also had a major impact on internal migration. Although there has recently been convergence of regions to a national

[123] IBGE, *Projeção da população do Brasil por sexo e idade 1980–2050*, Table 14.

norm in births and deaths, this has been a most recent development. For the period from the 1950s to the 1990s, the continued high fertility in the northern states and their sharply different wages and living standards created the classic push factors to get a massive internal emigration movement developing. At the same time, the industrialization of the south and its tremendous economic expansion created a demand for labor and a wage differential that attracted large numbers of unskilled and semiskilled workers from other regions.[124] Thus a perfect combination of push-and-pull factors set off a massive movement of population. By the census of 1980 it was estimated that 46 million Brazilians out of the 119 million resided in a municipality other than the one they were born in – or some 39 percent of the total population.[125] While there was a major amount of intrastate and rural to urban movement, there was also a massive migration across state and regional boundaries, with the long-distance flow in this period mostly of northeasterners coming to Rio de Janeiro and São Paulo. In 1980, for example, there resided in the state of São Paulo some 6 million persons who were born in another state, of whom 1 million were born in Bahia, 702,000 who were born in Pernambuco, another 295,000 came from Ceara, and 272,000 from Alagoas. In turn, Rio de Janeiro had 2.5 million migrants living in the state, with 295,000 from Paraiba and another 239,000 from Pernambuco. Interestingly, the sex ratio of the nonnatives residing in São Paulo was 102 males per 100 females, whereas the migrants to Rio had a sex ratio of 89 men to 100 women.[126] Traditionally female migration was predominant given the large service sector in urban centers available to women, which seems to be the case with Rio. In turn, males seem to have had more job opportunities in São Paulo as the sex ratio would suggest.

In the early period of the migration the city of São Paulo grew at an extraordinary pace. Between 1940 and 1970 the São Paulo metropolitan area grew at 5.6 percent per annum, the fastest growth rate of any metropolitan region in the country. In the next decade São Paulo fell

---

[124] As late as 1987, the average family income per capita in the southeast was twice as much as in the northeastern region. Lena Lavinas, Eduardo Henrique Garcia, and Marcelo Rubens do Amaral, *Desigualdades Regionais: Indicadores Socioeconômicos nos Anos 90*, Texto para Discussão No. 460 (Rio de Janeiro: IPEA, Fevereiro 1997), 12, Table 2, "Evolução da Renda Familiar per capita Urbana- Ufs e Regiões (reais de 1995)."
[125] IBGE, *IX Recenseamento Geral do Brasil 1980*, Vol. 1, Tomo 4, No. 1, "Dados gerais-migração-instrução-fecundidade-mortalidade" (Rio de Janeiro, 1983), Table 2.4.
[126] Data generated from IBGE, *IX Recenseamento Geral do Brasil 1980*, Vol. 1, Tomo 4, No 1, 71–84, Table 2.10, "Brasileiros natos, por naturalidade e sexo, segundo as regioes e as unidades da federação."

behind such fast-growing cities as Belo Horizonte and its annual growth rate declined to just 1.9 percent in the period from 1980 to 1991.[127] These declining rates reflected declining migration in the twenty-first century. By the census of 2010 only 21 percent of the residents of the state of São Paulo were born in another state, and the figure for the state of Rio de Janeiro was 14 percent. Moreover, in the 10 years between the census of 2000 and that of 2010 the number of migrants is estimated to have dropped from 11.3 to 9.9 million persons.[128] The states that still had 30 to 40 percent of their population coming from other states were Rondônia, Roraima, Amapá, and Tocantins in the north, and Matto Grosso and the Federal District (Brasília) in the center west.[129] These were the states or districts that were now attracting a large number of immigrants from the northeast and the southeastern regions, largely to new farming frontiers.[130]

Even the backward Northeast has seen a slow but steady convergence of wages and opportunities in jobs, education, and health between the poorest and richest zones, which proved one of the key factors in slowing this overall migration in the past decade.[131] But while this internal

---

[127] George Martine, *A redistribuição espacial da população brasileira durante a década de 80*, Texto para Discussão No. 329 (Brasília: IPEA, Janeiro 1994), 30, Table 10.

[128] IBGE, *Censo Demográfico 2010, Nupcialidade, fecundidade e migração, Resultados da amostra* (Rio de Janeiro, 2010), n.p., Table 17. It was estimated in the PNAD survey of 2011 that 40 percent of the Brazilian population resided in a municipio other than their municipio of birth – which captures inter- and intrastate and regional mobility. IBGE, *Pesquisa Nacional por Amostra de Domicílios, Síntese de indicadores 2011* (Rio de Janeiro, 2012), Table 2.5.

[129] IBGE, *Censo Demográfico 2010 – Resultados Preliminares da Amostra*, Table 2.2, "População residente, por naturalidade em relação ao município e à Unidade da Federação, segundo as Grandes Regiões e as Unidades da Federação – 2010," available at http://www.ibge.gov.br/home/estatistica/populacao/censo2010/resultados_preliminares_amostra/default_resultados_preliminares_amostra.shtm.

[130] This was also the result of the latest PNAD survey of 2006. It was determined that 5.9 million Brazilians were interstate migrants, and they were by and large better educated and younger than the nonmigrating Brazilians. Sex and color were not determinants as migrations were no different from nonmigrants in these variables. Most of the migration was now interregional, with only São Paulo still attracting interregional migrants (northeasterners) on a significant scale, and even São Paulo, in turn, was exporting population to other regions. See Adolfo Sachsida, Paulo Furtado de Castro, Mario Jorge Cardoso de Mendonça, and Pedro H. Albuquerque, *Perfil do migrante brasileiro*, Texto para Discussão No. 1410 (Rio de Janeiro: IPEA, Julho 2009), 10–11.

[131] On convergence of wages, see Cézar Santos and Pedro Cavalcanti Ferreira, "Migração e distribuição regional de renda no Brasil," *Pesquisa e Planejamento Econômico* 37,3 (Dezembro 2007), 405–426; Ricardo Paes de Barros, Samuel Franco, and Rosane Mendonça, *Discriminação e segmentação no mercado de trabalho e desigualdade de*

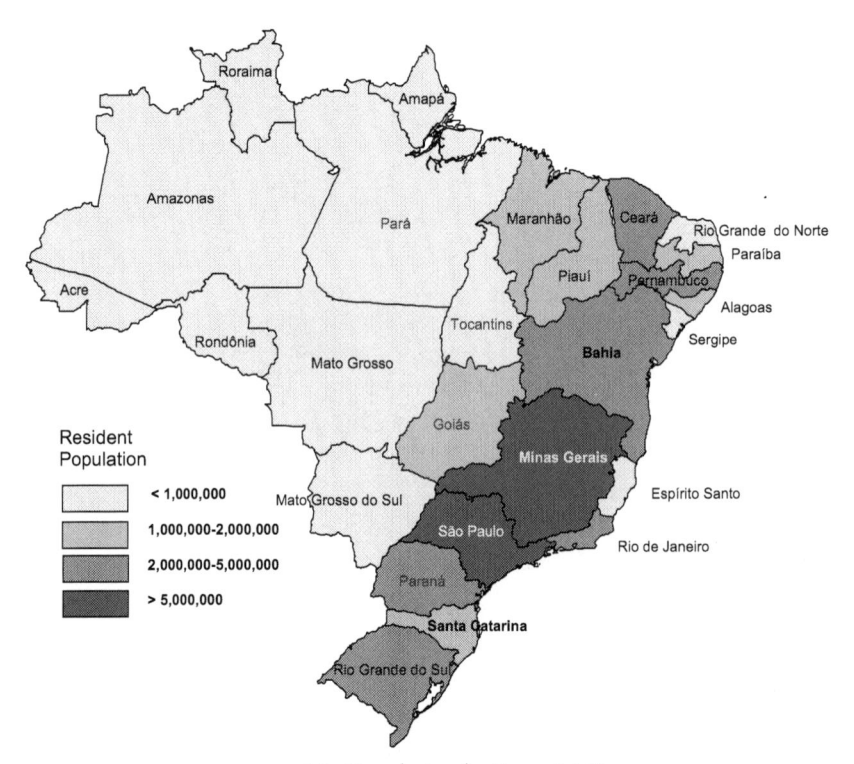

328   *The Economic and Social History of Brazil since 1889*

MAP 4.1. Population by State, 1950

migration has slowed, its impact is lasting. There has been over this sixty-year period a major redistribution of the national population, which has essentially moved a large share of the population into the formerly sparsely populated regions of the far north and center west regions and made the states of the southeast region the biggest in the nation. This can be seen in the change in the distribution of populations by states between 1950 and 2010 (see Maps 4.1 and 4.2).

But interstate and interregional migration was not the only migration occurring in Brazil in this time. The period also saw the massive movement of rural workers to urban centers even within regions. Between 1950 and

renda no Brasil, Texto para Discussão No. 1288 (Rio de Janeiro: IPEA, Julho 2007); and Rodolfo Hoffmann, "Transferências de renda e a redução da desigualdade no Brasil e cinco regiões entre 1997 e 2004," *Econômica* 8,1 (2006), 55–81. On the debate over regional convergence, see André Braz Golgher, Lízia de Figueiredo, and Roberto Santolin, "Migration and Economic Growth in Brazil: Empirical Applications Based on the Solow-Swan Model," *The Developing Economies* 49,2 (June 2011), 148–170.

Consolidation of Democracy since 1985 329

MAP 4.2. Population by State, 2010

1980 it was the rural areas of the southeastern and southern regions that provided the majority of rural to urban migrants with this movement decelerating in the 1990s. Then in the 1980s and 1990s the biggest movements were from rural northeast to its urban centers. It is estimated that 27 million rural workers migrated to urban centers between 1960 and 1980. Because of this rural to urban migration the rural population of Brazil has been slowly and steadily declining. The rural population that had grown throughout the twentieth century reached 41 million persons in 1970, or 44 percent of the total population. But in the next decade it declined to 38.5 million persons (and 32 percent of the national population) and then to 33.8 million by the late 1990s, or just 22 percent of the national population.[132] By the census of 2010 they numbered

---

[132] Ana Amélia Camarano and Ricardo Abramovay, *Êxodo rural, envelhecimento e masculinização no Brasil: panorama dos últimos 50 anos*, Texto para Discussão No. 621 (Rio de Janeiro: IPEA, Janeiro 1999), 3, Table 2.

only 29.8 million and now represented only 16 percent of the national population.[133]

It is estimated that 40 percent of the rural population migrated to cities in the 1970s and 33 percent left in the following decade. In the early 1990s another 5.5 million rural persons migrated – representing 28 percent of the rural population at that time. Given that the majority of the migrants from the 1970s on were women, this had a major impact on moving the rural population from a sex ratio of 91 males per 100 females in 1950 to 109 males to 100 females by the mid-1990s. In this, Brazil was no different from the great rural to urban migrations in nineteenth- and twentieth-century Europe and Latin America where women were the primary migrants. Equally, as the migration became evermore massive the peak ages of migration went from 30 to 39 years of age for men and women in the 1950s to 20 to 24 years of age for men and an even younger 15 to 19 years of age for women in the 1990s.[134] The two biggest regions of rural to urban migration were the northeast, which had an estimated 21.6 million rural residents migrate to cities in the period 1950 to 1995, and the southeastern region where the figure for the same period was 18.6 million. It would appear that in the twenty-first century this process has now slowed if not totally stabilized. All the regions have become predominantly urban by 2010, from a ratio of 73.1 percent in the northeast to 92.9 percent in the southeast,[135] and there seems to be finally a stability to the rural population. In the census of 2000 it was estimated that there were only three million persons who were rural migrants, of which two-thirds had carried out a rural to urban migration over short or long distances and a quarter of whom migrated to other rural areas.[136]

There seems to be general agreement that this rural migration in whatever direction, either to the city or to expanding agricultural frontiers, had an impact on the reduction in rural poverty in general. Though all studies show that the better educated and younger persons migrated, there was

---

[133] IBGE, *Resultados do Universo do Censo Demográfico 2010*, Table 1.1.1, "População residente, por situação do domicílio e sexo, segundo os grupos de idade – Brasil – 2010." Available at http://www.ibge.gov.br/home/estatistica/populacao/censo2010/caracteristicas_da_populacao/caracteristicas_da_populacao_tab_brasil_zip_xls.shtm.

[134] Camarano and Abramovay, *Êxodo rural, envelhecimento e masculinização no brasil*, 4–5.

[135] IBGE, *Sinopse do Censo Demográfico 2010* (Rio de Janeiro, 2011), Table 7, "Grau de urbanização, segundo as Grandes Regiões – 1991/2010."

[136] André Braz Golgher, "The Selectivity of Migration in Brazil: Implications for Rural Poverty," Taller Nacional sobre "Migración interna y desarrollo en Brasil: diagnóstico, perspectivas y políticas," April 30, 2007, Brasília.

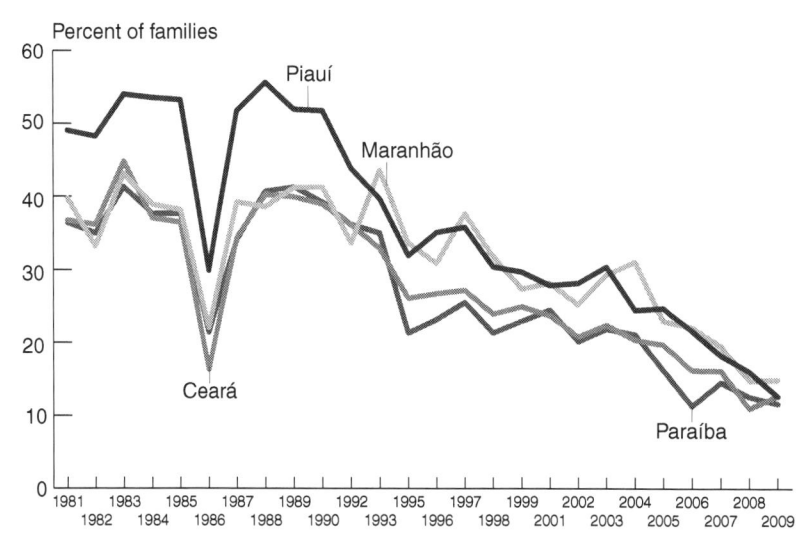

GRAPH 4.30. Evolution of the Percentage of Extremely Poor Households in the States in 1981 with Rates over 30 Percent. *Source:* Ipeadata, Table "Pobreza – proporção de domicílios extremamente pobres"

a reduction in poverty in those migration origin areas. For those who remained behind there were income transfers from the migrants and their own wages increased due to scarcity of local labor. Moreover, all this was occurring as agriculture was modernizing everywhere and the government was initiating major transfers of funds through programs such as *Bolsa Família* and PRONAF, which subsidized small farm agriculture, all of which also had an impact on reducing rural poverty.[137] This decline can be seen by analyzing the changes in the worst states in 1981, those with households suffering extreme poverty of 30 percent or more of all households,[138] and seeing their current status in 2009 (see Graph 4.30). Extreme poverty in these regions declined dramatically and the spread between the worst and the best has slowly disappeared.

[137] On the debate over the impact of migration on rural poverty, see the two essays by André Braz Golgher, *Diagnóstico do processo migratório no Brasil: comparação entre não-migrantes e migrantes* (Belo Horizonte: UFMG/CEDEPLAR, 2006); and "The Selectivity of Migration in Brazil: Implications for Rural Poverty." For a discussion of the work and impact of the program to support small farmers, see Carlos E. Guanziroli, "PRONAF dez anos depois: resultados e perspectivas para o desenvolvimento rural," *Revista de Economia e Sociologia Rural* 45,2 (Brasília) (Abril–Junho 2007), 301–328.

[138] According to IPEA, *extreme poverty* is defined as "an estimate of the value of a basket of food with the minimum calories required to adequately supply a person, based on recommendations of the FAO and WHO."

Between the Plan Real of 1997 with its control over inflation, the increase in the minimum wage, the systematic growth of income transfer programs, and finally the progressive incorporation of the overwhelming majority of workers into the formal labor sector there has been a massive change in the profile of poverty in the past decade.[139] It was estimated that as of 2011 of the 54 million civilian employees (excluding those in the military and public service), 71 percent had formal work papers.[140] As late as 2000 when there were 40 million workers in the civilian labor force, those with formal work papers had represented just 59 percent of such workers.[141]

All of these developments have influenced the major decline of poverty in Brazil. The most dramatic decline has been among the extremely poor, especially in the most recent period, and although the percentage of simple poor families also declined, this was at a slower pace (see Graph 4.31). Most impressive has been the change in the period of the two Lula governments. In this period the *Bolsa Família* (family grant) was but one of several major income-transfer programs that included the rural pension program and the BFC program, or Continuous Cash Benefits, established in 1995, which guaranteed monthly pensions for all retired persons with incomes below the minimum wage. All these nonwage incomes were going to 52 percent of all Brazilian households by 2005.[142] It has been

---

[139] A recent careful review of the changes in extreme poverty in Bahia and the whole northeastern region shows that there was an abrupt fall in this indice between 1996 and 1997 at the time of the implementation of the Plan Real and again between 2003 and 2006 with the expansion of conditional cash transfers under Lula, with a corresponding significant fall in the Gini index of inequality. Rafael Guerreiro Osorio and Pedro H. G. Ferreira de Souza, *Evolução da pobreza extrema e da desigualdade de renda na Bahia: 1995 a 2009*, Textos para Discussão No. 1696 (Brasilia: IPEA, Janeiro, 2012).

[140] That is "com carteira de trabalho assinada"... Censo Demográfico 2010 – Resultados Preliminares da Amostra, Table 6.2, "Pessoas de 10 anos ou mais de idade, ocupadas na semana de referência, por posição na ocupação e categoria do emprego no trabalho principal, segundo as Grandes Regiões e as Unidades da Federação – 2010," available at http://www.ibge.gov.br/home/estatistica/populacao/censo2010/ resultados_preliminares_amostra/default_resultados_preliminares_amostra. For a survey of the changing relative weights of the formal and informal sector since the 1970s see Fernando Augusto Mansor de Mattos, *Emprego público no Brasil: aspectos históricos, inserção no mercado de trabalho nacional e evolução recente*, Textos para Discussão No. 1582 (Brasilia: IPEA, Fevereiro 2011).

[141] IBGE, SIDRA, Table 2031, "Pessoas de 10 anos ou mais de idade ocupadas na semana de referência por posição na ocupação e categoria do emprego no trabalho principal," available at http://www.sidra.ibge.gov.br/bda/tabela/listabl.asp?z=cd&o=13& i=P&c=2031.

[142] Ricardo Paes de Barros, Mirela de Carvalho, and Samuel Franco, "O papel das Transferências Públicas na queda recente da desigualdade de Renda Brasileira," in *Brasil: A*

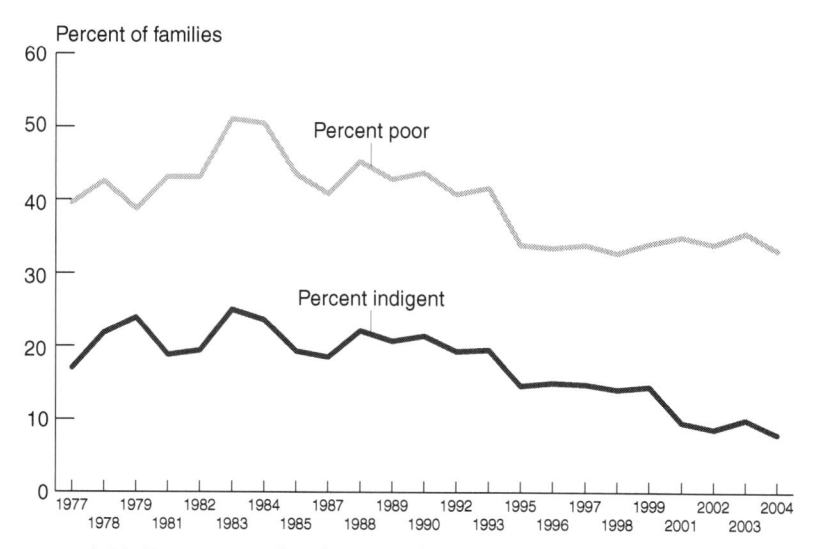

GRAPH 4.31. Percentage of Indigent and Poor Families in Brazil, 1977–2004. Source: Henriques, Desigualidade e Pobreza (2000), p. 24, Table 1 and Rocha "Alguns aspectos..." (2006), p. 16, Table 1

argued by most recent economists that these government income transfers have had a major impact in reducing rural poverty and extreme poverty everywhere and were behind the dramatic fall in inequality that began in 2001.[143] This combined with the greater incorporation of workers

nova agenda social, ed. Edmar Lisboa Bacha and Simon Schwartzman (Rio de Janeiro: LTC, 2011), 41. These authors emphasize the causal importance of the *Bolsa Família* and the BFC cash transfers.

[143] For the evolution of these recent programs, see André Portela Souza, "Políticas de distribuição de renda no Brasil e o Bolsa Família," in *Brasil: A nova agenda social*, ed. Edmar Lisboa Bacha and Simon Schwartzman (Rio de Janeiro: LTC, 2011), 166–186. There have been a large number of studies attempting to explain the fall of extreme poverty and of the Gini index of inequality. Most argue that nonlabor income through public transfers is as crucial as universal education and the value of the minimum wage (upon which so much of the income and pension schemes are based) in explaining this decline. See, e.g., Ricardo Paes de Barros, Mirela de Carvalho, Samuel Franco, and Rosane Mendonça, "Markets, the State and the Dynamics of Inequality: Brazil's Case Study," in *Declining Inequality in Latin America: A Decade of Progress?*, ed. Luis Felipe Lopez-Calva and Nora Lustig (Washington, DC: Brookings Institution Press, 2010), 134–174; Barros et al., "O papel das Transferências Públicas na queda recente desigualdade de Renda Brasileira," 41–85; Sergei Soares, "Análise de bem-estar e decomposição por fatores da queda na desigualdade entre 1995 e 2004," *Econômica* 8,1 (2006), 83–115; and Rodolfo Hoffmann, "Transferências de renda e a redução da desigualdade no Brasil," 55–81. Hoffmann has stressed that there is an obviously regional variation in this impact, which was far greater in the northeast and other

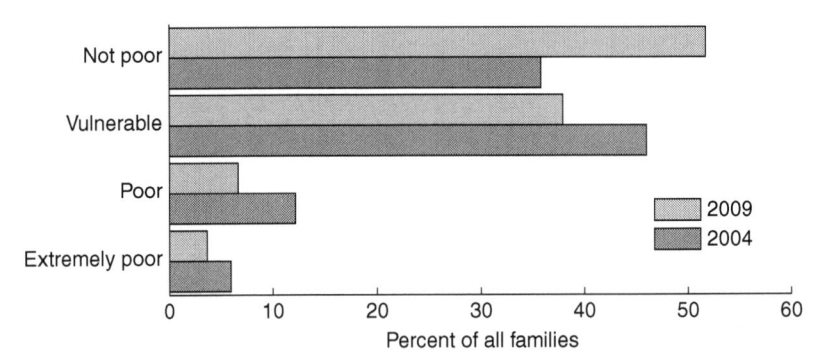

GRAPH 4.32. Reduction of Poverty for Brazilian Families, 2004 and 2009. *Source:* Osorio et al. 2011, p. 17, Table 2

into the formal market and the consequent impact of the raising of the minimum wage has led to the massive decline of extreme poverty and the virtual elimination of malnutrition and hunger in Brazil. Extreme poverty by 2008 accounted for only 8.8 percent of all families, down from 17.4 percent of all families as late as 2004. It is estimated that more than 15.9 million families had moved out of poverty (i.e., those living in extreme poverty, as well as the poor and those earning above the minimum wage but were considered vulnerable) in the period from 2004 to 2009. This resulted in the percentage of nonpoor families climbing from 35.8 percent of all families in 2004 to 51.5 percent of the 56.8 million families five years later (see Graph 4.32).[144]

Much of this social change has come about through increasing income and the evolution of a more diversified market as a result of general economic growth. But a major share of change in health, education, and welfare is due to the state and its activities. Brazil, like all the other major nations in the world, began to implement a modern welfare state from the 1930s onward. But the expansion of the welfare state had taken decades to create and Brazil has only slowly and laboriously begun to provide the basic social services that a modern industrial society takes for granted in the twenty-first century. The provision of unemployment

---

very poor regions than in the rest of the country. For one of the few opponents to this emphasis on the impact of government income transfers on poverty reduction, see Emerson Marinho and Jair Araujo, "Pobreza e o sistema de seguridade social rural no Brasil," *Revista Brasileira de Economia* 64,2 (2010), 161–74.

[144] Rafael Guerreiro Osorio, Pedro H. G. F. de Souza, Sergei S. D. Soares, and Luis Felipe Batista de Oliveira, *Perfil da pobreza no Brasil e sua evolucão no período 2004–2009*. Texto para Discussão No. 1647 (Brasilia: IPEA, Agosto 2011), 17, Table 2.

insurance, pensions, workmen's compensation, and health care are only now being addressed nationally in the past quarter century. As was the case with most of the countries in the Western Hemisphere, the first formal pension plans began with small groups of workers in well-defined industries in the 1920s and 1930s. These were coordinated under Vargas into industry-wide pension systems under the title of "Institutos." In turn, these industry-wide institutes became training centers for a new group of professional technocrats, who would expand the pension system under the military regimes.[145] In 1988, with the full return of democracy to Brazil, social welfare became an active area of government discussion, which resulted in major sections of the Constitution of 1988 being written in response to social welfare considerations. Not only was health declared a universal right in the constitution, but so, too, was an integrated system of social insurance and social assistance. Now all federal government workers and all private workers were put into one social security system. Financing of the system was put on a more solid tax base, and the value of pensions was now pegged to inflation. Finally, pension rights were now made universal for all women and men in the rural areas, whether registered workers or not, and regardless of whether they had paid into any previous pension schemes. At the beginning of the 1990s these reforms were finally enacted into an organic social security law. The assistance and insurance programs were reorganized into a new National Social Security Institute – INSS, or *Instituto Nacional do Seguro Socia* – which replaced the *Instituto Nacional de Previdência Social*, or INPS; *Fundo de Assistência ao Trabalhador Rural*, or FUNRURAL; and other separate sectors of social assistance, and also involved the transfer of all health activities to a separate Ministry of Health.[146]

In this, Brazil essentially deviated from most of the liberalizing pension reforms carried out in Latin America beginning with Chile in the 1980s and expanding to many Latin American countries in the 1990s. Unlike many other nations, Brazil did not privatize its pension scheme but instead solidified and rationalized its pay as you go system, though it did open

---

[145] Kaizô Iwakami Beltrão, Sonoe Sugahara Pinheiro, and Francisco Eduardo Barreto de Oliveira, *Population and Social Security in Brazil: An Analysis with Emphasis on Constitutional Changes*, Texto para Discussão No. 862 (Rio de Janeiro: IPEA, 2002), 2–3; Celso Barroso Leite, "Da lei Elói Chaves ao Sinpas," in *Um século de previdência social: balanço e perspectivas no Brasil e no mundo*, ed. Celso Barroso Leite (Rio de Janeiro: Zahar, 1983), 39–44; and James Malloy, *The Politics of Social Security in Brazil* (Pittsburgh, PA: University of Pittsburgh Press, 1979), 124–125.

[146] Beltrão et al., *Population and Social Security in Brazil*, 5–6.

the door for supplementary private insurance plans.[147] By 2004 it was estimated that some 42 million Brazilian workers (aged 16 to 59) were contributing to the INSS and state and municipal pension systems, and some 22 million persons were beneficiaries, although roughly 27 million active workers were still not covered.[148] By 2009 it was estimated that a significant 59.3 percent of the economically active population was now covered by some pension plan.[149]

The new commitment to universal pensions for rural workers has had a profound impact on reducing indigence and poverty among the older populations and especially those situated in the rural area.[150] Although these rural pensions were originally quite small – with some 85 percent of the rural population receiving below the minimum wage in 1985 – they have progressively become evermore important. In the Constitution of 1988, the basic pension for rural retirees was raised to the minimum wage.[151] It is estimated that such pensions for rural workers has not only reduced rural poverty but has also significantly reduced inequality in rural Brazil.[152] Brazil is among the most advanced countries in the developing world in reducing levels of poverty among its rural population.[153]

---

[147] For the comparative differences from other regional reforms, see Florencia Antía and Arnaldo Provasi, "Multi-pillared Social Insurance Systems: The Post-reform Picture in Chile, Uruguay and Brazil," *International Social Security Review* 64,1 (2011), 53–71; and Fabio M. Betranou and Rafael Rofman, "Providing Social Security in a Context of Change: Experience and Challenges in Latin America," *International Social Security Review* 55,1 (2002), 67–82.

[148] *Informe de Previdência Social* 16,5 (Maio 2004), 1, 18. This growth in the number of beneficiaries was quite fast. Beginning in 1995, only 15.7 million people were benefiting from the system, and by 2003 this number had risen 40 percent, to 21.7 million beneficiaries. *Informe da Previdência Social* 16,2 (Fevereiro 2004), 1.

[149] This was up from 53.8 percent in 2002. IPEA, *Políticas sociais: acompanhamento e análise*, Vol. 19 (2011), 18, Table 1, "Evolução da cobertura previdenciária – 2002–2009."

[150] In 1999, approximately 79 percent of Brazilians 60 years of age and older were receiving pensions. Helmut Schwarzer and Ana Carolina Querino, *Benefícios sociais e pobreza: Programas não contributivos da seguridade social brasileira*, Texto para Discussão No. 929 (Brasília: IPEA, 2002), 7.

[151] Kaizô Iwakami Beltrão and Sonoe Sugahara Pinheiro, *Brazilian Population and the Social Security System: Reform Alternatives*, Texto para Discussão No. 929 (Rio de Janeiro: IPEA, 2005), 6.

[152] It is estimated that in 2002 the Gini index for income distribution, excluding pensions, would have been 0.56, falling to 0.52, when pensions are included. Beltrão and Pinheiro, *Brazilian Population and the Social Security System*, 12.

[153] Approximately 35 percent of the persons who received a pension in 2003, with residence declared, lived in the rural area, a much higher proportion than the actual total population. *Informe da Previdência Social* 16,2 (Fevereiro 2004), 1. The unusual form

Thus, for the first time, being elderly and of rural residence are no longer automatically correlated with poverty in Brazil.

Most of the elimination of extreme poverty and the incorporation of many more persons into the economy has been the result of the control over inflation and of the government provision of conditional cash transfers. The government adopted this new redistributive system of financial support in the first Fernando Henrique Cardoso administration with the establishment of the Program to Eradicate Child Labor (*Programa de Erradicação do Trabalho Infantil*, or PETI) – which it eventually expanded in 2001 into a more complete *Bolsa Escola*, a national program designed to eliminate child employment and encourage school attendance through payment of a conditional cash payment from the state to poor families with school age children if they maintained these children in school.[154] In the same year there was added a *Bolsa Alimentação* to encourage prenatal care for pregnant women, and finally all these cash transfer programs were incorporated into a more complete *Bolsa Família*, in 2003. There was also a rationalization of the distribution of these resources through a modern census of all participants (or *Cadastro Único*) and the use of the *Caixa Econômica Federal* to pay all recipients. This and all previous programs were means tested in the sense that they were designed for families that gained less than the minimum wage or some other line of poverty defined by the government. Also these transfers required the same previous counterpart activities from the families to keep their children in school and/or carry out systematic prenatal care. By 2008 some 11.3 million families were receiving this income, which represented a cost to the government of 0.37 percent of GDP.[155] That these income transfers had a powerful impact on reducing indigence and poverty in Brazil is now recognized by all observers and by the Brazil public, which granted Lula the highest ratings of popularity of any American president. But it also had a major impact on getting children into schools and expectant mothers into clinics in their first trimester of pregnancy.

---

adopted by Brazil in the provision of retirement for the rural elderly, even by Latin American standards, can be seen in CELADE, *Los adultos mayores en América Latina y el Caribe datos e indicadores* (Boletín Informativo, Edición Especial; Santiago de Chile, 2002), Graphs 8, 9, 16, 18.

[154] Schwarzer and Carolina Querino, *Benefícios sociais e pobreza*.
[155] A history of all the local and subsequent conditional cash transfer programs is found in Sergei Soares and Natália Sátyro, *O programa bolsa família: desenho institucional, impactos e possibilidades futures*, Texto para Discussão No. 1424 (Brasília: IPEA, Outubro 2009).

There is little question that this has been the single most dramatic change that has affected Brazilian society in the twenty-first century.

Like pensions, modern public health programs began in the 1920s associated with differing professional and worker pension *caixas* and institutes, which in the postwar period became evermore tied to the national pension schemes of the INSS. By the 1970s there was elaborated a new model, much influenced by the British Beveridge plan of 1942, which sought to universalize health care for all citizens. First came the provision of emergency care for persons not covered by health plans under social security. Then in the Constitution of 1988 it was declared a right of all citizens to have health care provided by the government. Article 198 of the constitution called for the establishment of a Unified Health System (*Sistema Único de Saúde*, or SUS) that would cover all citizens no matter what their formal work status was and, in turn, would decentralize the health system, from the federal government to the states and municipalities that it was felt could best determine local needs, though funding would come primarily from the federal government. In the 1990s most of the SUS reforms were instituted, including new funding from local and regional as well as federal government sources.[156] There was also a concentrated effort to establish basic health clinics to provide primary care to all citizens, and in 1994 these primary care clinics were integrated into a Family Health Program (*Programa de Saúde da Família*, or PSF) under SUS. Coverage in the smaller towns and rural areas was highly successful and rapid, though these primary clinics have been slower to evolve in the larger cities.[157] By the end of the twentieth century, the SUS employed close to half a million health professionals and was responsible for more than 5,000 hospitals containing 430,000 beds, and maintained some 63,000 ambulatory care centers in all parts

---

[156] A detailed history of this complex evolution toward a universal system is found in Otávio Azevedo Mercadante et al., "Evolução das Politicas e do Sistema de Saúde no Brasil," in *Caminhos da Saúde Pública no Brasil*, ed. Jacobo Finkelman (Rio de Janeiro: Fiocruz, 2002), 235–313.

[157] In 2009, more than 80 percent of the population in municipalities of less than 20,000 persons were covered, while in large cities with more than half a million persons such clinics covered only 30 percent of the population. IPEA, *Políticas sociais: acompanhamento e análise*, Vol. 19 (2011), 95. For a history of the evolution of primary care clinics, see Allan Claudius Queiroz Barbosa, Júnia Marçal Rodrigues, and Luis Fernando Rolim Sampaio, "De Programa a Estratégia: A Saúde da Família no Brasil em Perspectiva. Um comparativo da década de 2000." Paper presented at *Anais do XIV Seminário sobre a Economia Mineira*, 2010.

of the country.[158] The number of hospital beds has remained stable since then, and in 2009 there were 2.3 beds per thousand population, a reasonable rate by Latin American and world standards.[159] Popular usage of the system has increased over time. By 2009 the national average was 2.7 medical consultations per inhabitant at the SUS,[160] and 90 percent of the women who gave birth in Brazil in 2009 had four or more prenatal medical consultations and only 2 percent had none.[161] By this date the country contained 352,000 doctors (62 percent of whom were men), or 1.8 doctors per thousand inhabitants, which was also a reasonable rate by world standards.[162]

But Brazil still has not completely resolved all questions about financing its health care system.[163] SUS and its organizations mostly cater to poorer elements in the population, while private plans and hospitals cater to mostly middle- and upper-class clients. Moreover, it only devotes 29 percent of its financing to primary care facilities and the rest

---

[158] Paulo Eduardo M. Elias and Amelia Cohn, "Health Reform in Brazil: Lessons to Consider," *American Journal of Public Health* 93,1 (January 2003), 46.

[159] In the first decade of the twenty-first century WHO estimated that Brazil had 2.4 beds per thousand inhabitations, while all lower middle-income nations averaged 2.2 beds per thousand population and most Latin American countries were below the Brazilian rate. As an example of a well-functioning national health system, Canada had 3.4 beds per thousand inhabitants, which was well below the average for the richest countries of 5.9 beds. World Health Organization, *World Health Statistics 2011* (Geneva, Switzerland: World Health Organization, 2012), Table 6, "Health workforce, infrastructure and essential medicines," 116–125.

[160] DATASUS, Table F.1, "Número de consultas médicas (SUS) por habitante...por Região, Período: 2009," available at http://tabnet.datasus.gov.br/cgi/deftohtm.exe?idb2010/f01.def.

[161] DATASUS, Table F.6, "Cobertura de consultas de pré-natal Proporção de nascidos vivos (%) por Região e Número de consultas, Período: 2009," available at http://tabnet.datasus.gov.br/cgi/tabcgi.exe?idb2010/f06.def.

[162] This is a relatively good ratio by world standards. On average from 2000 to 2010, Canada had 1.9 doctors per thousand inhabitations with the majority of Latin American countries having less than 1.5 doctors and only Uruguay, Argentina, and Cuba exceeding this rate with the latter being an outlier with a very high ratio of 6.4 doctors per thousand inhabitants. Lower middle-income countries averaged 1.0 doctor and upper middle-income countries averaged just 2.2 doctors per thousand inhabitants. World Health Organization, *World Health Statistics 2011*, Table 6. On the Brazil numbers see DATASUS, Table E.1, "Número de profissionais de saúde por habitante...Região, Período: 2009," available at http://tabnet.datasus.gov.br/cgi/deftohtm.exe?idb2010/e01.def.

[163] See, e.g., Jairnilson Paim, Claudia Travassos, Celia Almeida, Ligia Bahia, and James Macinko, "The Brazilian Health System: History, Advances, and Challenges," *The Lancet* 377,9779 (2011), 1778–1797.

to intermediate and advanced centers.[164] Along with a state health system, the 1988 constitution permitted the use of supplementary private health insurance plans in Brazil, though the ideal was for the use of non-profit providers. Quickly some 40 million persons signed up for these plans, which represented about a quarter of the population, a ratio that has remained stable until the present day. Despite its minority status in Brazil, this system of private health insurance is the second largest such private medical insurance market in the world today.[165] All told this multitiered and private and public health care system is still evolving, but there is little question that Brazil now has in place a decentralized health care system that is providing at least basic service to the entire population.

What is unquestionable as well is that years of schooling and literacy are highly correlated with the well-being of the population. The more literate and better educated the population, the better are its health and living standards. Thus the fact that all economic groups, even those families listed as extremely poor, had levels of school attendance of children ages 7 to 14 at the 99 percent level in 2009,[166] suggests that living standards for all groups will improve in the future. Along with the delivery of health care, it is education that has made the most advances since 1980. By the census of 2010, some 90 percent of the population 15 years of age is now literate, a rate that has had a secular trend upward throughout the twentieth and twenty-first centuries (see Graph 4.33). The evolution of literacy can well be seen in the breakdown of literates by age. While literacy is more than 90 percent in the earlier ages, by the cohort of the late twenties it drops below that rate for men, and for women the drop occurs by the early thirties. Women are more literate than men at every age group until the mid-fifties cohort. Then the historic bias against educating women shows up when the relationship of literates by sex changes to one in which in every age group above the 50 to 54 age cohort, women are less literate than men.

---

[164] DATASUS, Table E.21, "Gasto do Ministério da Saúde com atenção à saúde per capita (em reais correntes), por componente, segundo ano Brasil: 2004–2009," available at http://tabnet.datasus.gov.br/cgi/idb2010/e21.htm.

[165] Mônica Viegas Andrade and Ana Carolina Maia, "Demanda por planos de saúde no Brasil," ANPEC, *Anais do XXXIV Encontro Nacional de Economia* 106 (2006), 3. In 2009, some 65 percent of the 430,000 hospital beds in the country were private and only 153,000 beds were available in public hospitals. DATASUS, Table E.2, "Número de leitos hospitalares por habitante – AMS/IBGE . . . por Região, Período: 2009," available at http://tabnet.datasus.gov.br/cgi/tabcgi.exe?idb2010/e02.def.

[166] Osorio et al., *Perfil da pobreza*, 28.

Consolidation of Democracy since 1985   341

Percent of total population

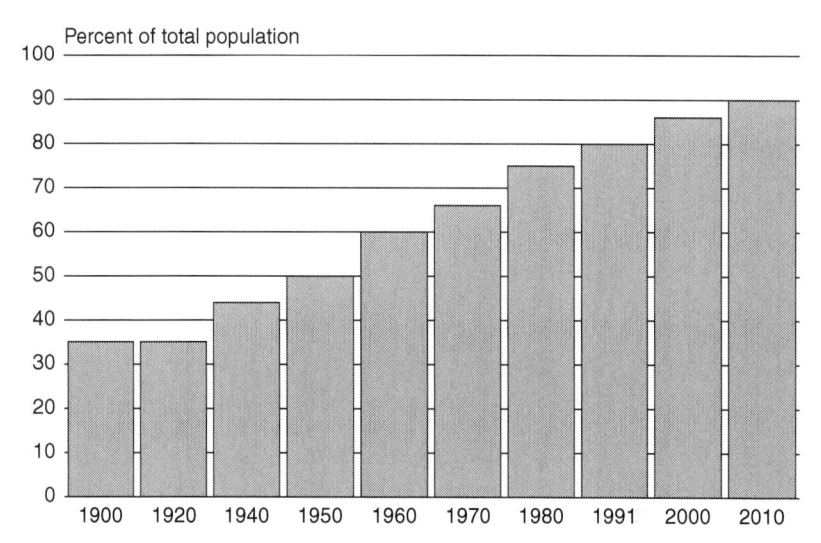

[Bar chart showing literacy rate percentages for years: 1900 (~35), 1920 (~35), 1940 (~45), 1950 (~50), 1960 (~60), 1970 (~65), 1980 (~75), 1991 (~80), 2000 (~85), 2010 (~90)]

GRAPH 4.33. Literacy Rate of Brazilian Population 15 Years of Age and Older, 1900–2010. *Source:* Souza 1999, p. 7, Table 1; and IBGE, *Censo Demográfico 2010 Características da população e dos domicílios, Resultados do universo,* Gráfico 31 for 2000 and 2010

Along with matriculating more than 98.5 percent of all children 7 to 14 years of age in schools, Brazil has now guaranteed that there is no distinction whatsoever in matriculation for this age group for any region in the country – all are at this level. Even for 15 to 17 year olds some 84 percent are in school, again with virtually no variation by region.[167] Also with each passing year the average number of years of schooling of the population is increasing, reaching 7.3 years by 2011. In years of schooling as in literacy, women have systematically outpaced men in the recent period. In just the past 15 years two years of schooling have been

---

[167] The latest PNAD 2011 survey gives the following rates by region:

Rate of Schooling by Age Cohort by Region, 2011

Age Group	BRASIL	Norte	Nordeste	Sudeste	Sul	Centro-Oeste
6–14	98.2	96.5	98.1	98.7	98.3	98.3
7–14	98.5	97.4	98.2	98.9	98.8	99.0
15–17	83.7	83.2	83.1	84.7	82.2	85.2
18–24	28.9	32.6	29.3	27.0	29.1	32.2
25 +	4.5	6.7	5.0	3.8	4.3	5.6

Source: PNAD 2011, Table 3.7.

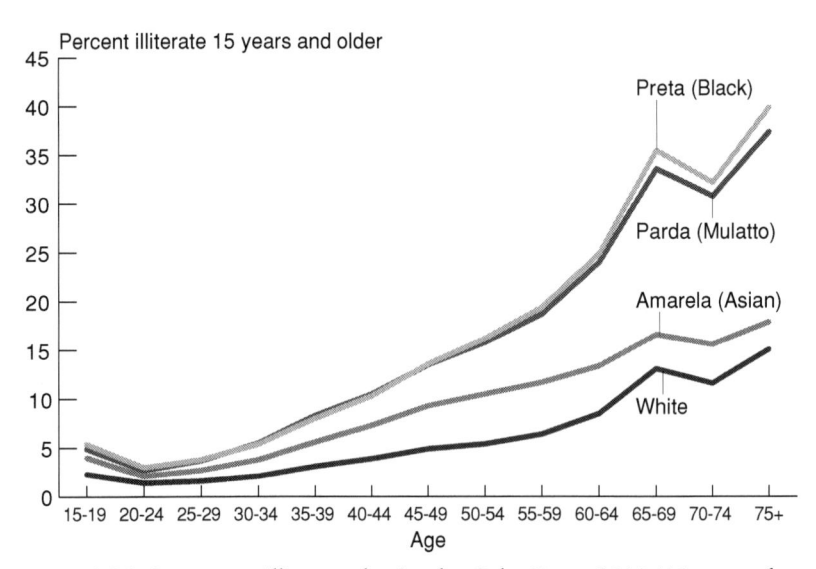

GRAPH 4.34. Percentage Illiterates by Age by Color/Race, 2010 (15 years of age and older). *Source:* IBGE, SIDRA, Censo 2010, Table 3176. Available at http://www.sidra.ibge.gov.br/bda/tabela/listabl.asp?c=3176&z=cd&o=5

added for both sexes, but the gap between men and women remains constant.[168]

While bias against women no longer exists, class and color are still apparently important markers of inequality in terms of education. Nevertheless, even here the differences in literacy between mulattoes and whites – the two major color groups – is quite small in the earlier ages, and only increases with each succeeding age cohort, which reflects older traditional disadvantages that are quickly disappearing (see Graph 4.34). For the population 10 to 14 years of age in the census of 2010, the literacy rate for whites was 98 percent; for the blacks and browns it was 95 percent; and even the Indians were at 82 percent literacy.[169] Thus like bias against women, the universalization of primary education, and to a lesser

---

[168] Marcelo Medeiros Coelho de Souza, *O analfabetismo no Brasil sob o enfoque demográfico*, Texto para Discussão No. 639 (Brasília: IPEA, April 1999), 7, Table 1.

[169] IBGE, *Censo Demográfico 2010 Características da população e dos domicílios, Resultados do universo*, Table 1.3.3, "Tabela 1.3.3 – Pessoas de 5 anos ou mais de idade, por cor ou raça e sexo, segundo a condição de alfabetização e os grupos de idade – Brasil – 2010," n.p.

extent of secondary education, has profoundly reduced the differences in literacy by color as well.[170]

Nevertheless, the quality of education is still subject to major deficiencies. It was estimated that 22 percent of the primary students were still not of the correct age, and that this was highly varied by region, from 40 percent of primary students in the northeast to only 16 percent in the southeastern region.[171] Fortunately, however, the rate of abandonment of students at the primary level is quite low, going from 5 percent in the northeast to 1.5 percent in the southeastern region and this rate, in turn, has been steadily falling in the past decade. Equally the number of primary school students who failed has been slowly falling with the rate varying from 13 percent in the northeast to 8 percent in the southeast.[172] Also given that the years of schooling has steadily increased in the last several decades, functional illiteracy, which is defined as those persons having three years of school or less, has also declined.[173]

All these profound social changes have been driven by changes in culture and ideology, and in turn, they have had an impact on the structure of Brazilian society. Not only has Brazil become less Catholic in the past 60 years, but it has also become less religious as the pattern of marriages suggests. From 1950 to the census of 2010 the number of marriages performed only by priests has declined from 30 percent of all unions to just 3 percent of such marriages. Marriages before a civil and a religious authority peaked at 65 percent in 1970 and has declined to just 43 percent by 2010. The big change has been the rise of consensual unions from just

---

[170] Given their late start in education, I have left out the Indian populations from this analysis. Moreover, this small difference in literacy at the younger ages does not show the entire issue of years of schooling and color and the inequalities by color and race that may exist at the higher levels of education. Unfortunately, years of schooling by color is a variable that is currently unavailable from the standard government sources.

[171] IBGE, Tabela Série: M16 – Distorção idade/série – Ensino Fundamental de 8 e 9 anos (série nova), available at http://seriesestatisticas.ibge.gov.br/series.aspx?vcodigo=M16&sv=57&t=distorcao-idadeserie-ensino-fundamental-de-8-e-9-anos-serie-nova.

[172] IBGE Série: M101 – Aprovação, reprovação e abandono – Ensino Fundamental (série nova), available at http://seriesestatisticas.ibge.gov.br/series.aspx?vcodigo=M101&sv=57&t=aprovacao-reprovacao-e-abandono-ensino-fundamental-serie-nova.

[173] For the definition of *functional illiteracy*, see IBGE, Série: PD384 – Taxa de analfabetismo functional, available at http://seriesestatisticas.ibge.gov.br/series.aspx?vcodigo=PD384&sv=8&t=taxa-de-analfabetismo-funcional. It is estimated that the average years of schooling now is 7.3 years.

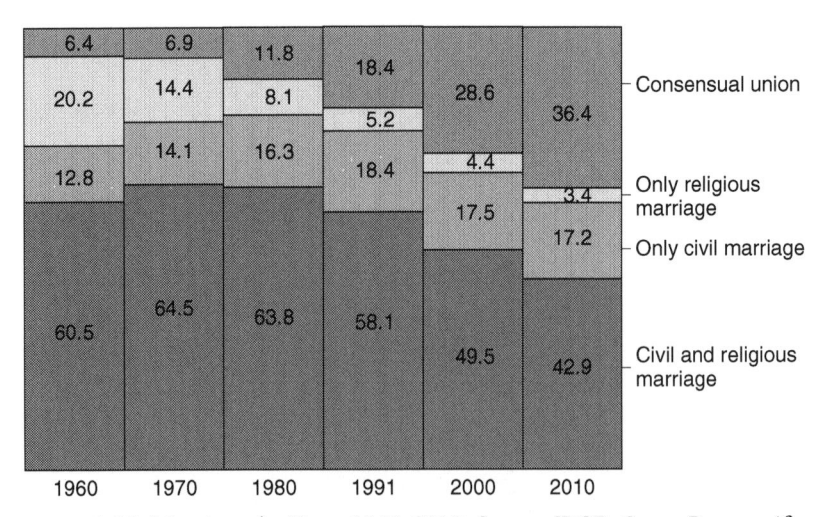

344 *The Economic and Social History of Brazil since 1889*

GRAPH 4.35. Marriages by Type, 1960–2010. *Source:* IBGE, *Censo Demográfico 2010 – Resultados Preliminares da Amostra* and IBGE, Tendências demográficas no período de 1950/2000, Grafico 8

6 percent in 1950 to 35 percent of all couples in the census of 2010 (see Graph 4.35).[174]

There have also been slow changes in household type in this period with the significant growth of unipersonal or single-person households and the female-headed households with and without children, at the expense of the traditional dual-partner household (see Graph 4.36). In 1981 unipersonal households represented just 5.8 percent of all households, but doubled their share to 12.2 percent of all households by the census of 2010. Single female–headed households with and without children rose significantly. They represented just a quarter of all households as late as 1992 and rose to 35 percent of all households in the latest PNAD survey of 2011.[175] In turn, nuclear families with children declined from 59.4 percent to just 47.3 percent of such households in the 2009 PNAD survey, as the society began to slowly deemphasize the standard

---

[174] The numbers of the census are reenforced by the data provided in the latest National Household (PNAD) survey of 2011. IBGE, *Pesquisa Nacional por Amostra de Domicílios... 2011*, Table 1.7
[175] IBGE, *Pesquisa Nacional por Amostra de Domicílios... 2011*, Table 5.1. The tabulations for the 1992 and subsequent PNAD surveys is available from the Instituto de Estudos do Trabalho e Sociedade (IETS) at http://www.iets.org.br/rubrique.php3?id_rubrique=94.

Consolidation of Democracy since 1985   345

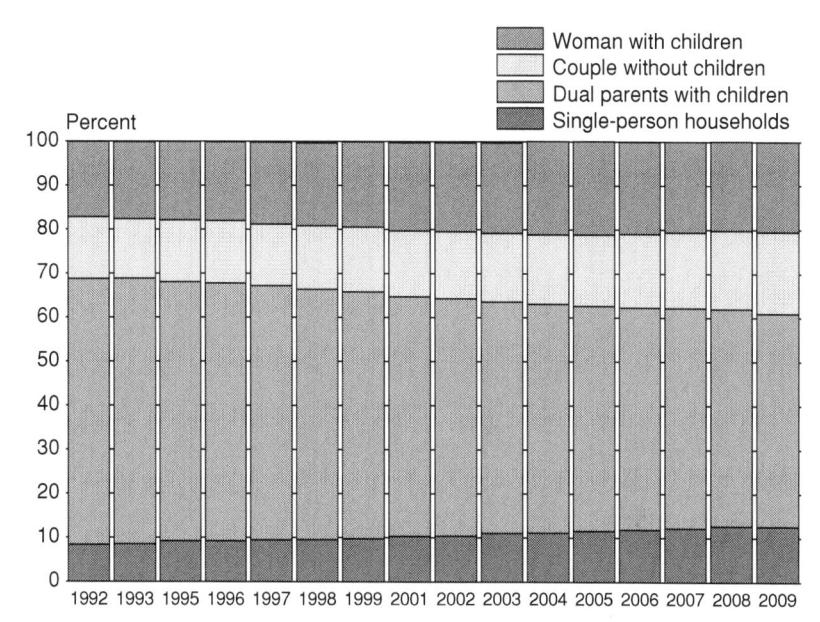

GRAPH 4.36. Heads of Families by Type, 1992–2009. Source: IBGE, Estatísticas históricas do Brasil, Tables FED 303 and 304. Available at http://seriesestatisticas.ibge.gov.br/lista_tema.aspx?op=0&no=6

nuclear family model.[176] Given the recent availability of legal divorce, there has also been a steady increase of households headed by women. That divorce and separation is the origin of most female-headed households with children in Brazil can be seen in the PNAD survey of 2011, in which 53 percent of such female-headed households have children older than 16 years of age.[177] This evolution of marriage and household patterns has occurred in all regions, though it would appear that marriages made in solely religious settings and consensual unions are now more prevalent in the north and northeast than other regions. But everywhere consensual unions and civil-religious marriages make up three-quarters

---

[176] IBGE, SIDRA, Table 1211, "Domicílios particulares permanentes e Moradores em domicílios particulares permanentes, por espécie de unidade doméstica," available at http://www.sidra.ibge.gov.br/bda/tabela/listabl.asp?z=t&c=1211. For the 1997 and 2007 data see Elisa Hijino de Oliveira, "Arranjos unipessoais no brasil 1997–2007: uma análise sócio-demográfica e de gênero das pessoas que moram sozinhas" (MA thesis, Rio de Janeiro: IBGE, Escola Nacional de Ciências Estatísticas, 2009), 42, Table 1.

[177] IBGE, Síntese de indicadores sociais...2012, Graph 2.11, "Proporção de arrranjos familiares monoparentais com filhos, por sexo da pessoa de referência, segundo os grupos de idade dos filhos – Brasil – 2011."

of the total of marriages, and in all areas unipersonal and female-headed households are increasing. In these household arrangements Brazil seems to be following the patterns of the advanced industrial world.

But surprisingly, single mothers heading a household with children grew far less in this same period. In 1992 they accounted for 15.1 percent of all households and increased only to 17.4 percent of households in the PNAD 2009 survey.[178] Though the international literature stresses the negative economic conditions of female as opposed to dual-parent households with children, this seems to be less the case in the context of Brazil. Though studies are few and the available data are limited (it would appear that female-headed households with children are only slightly poorer than the norm), the difference is not extreme. Thus in the 2010 census 16.5 percent of dual-parent households had an income of two or more minimum salaries, while 14.6 percent of female-headed households with children were in this category. Conversely, the ratio of such households with less than one minimum salary differed little between the two types of households.[179] Women who headed Brazilian families (with or without children) tended to be better educated than male heads, though they did slightly worse in terms of employment.[180]

As these marriage patterns clearly show, there has been a loss of control by the Roman Catholic Church of the marriage market where it now participates in only 46 percent of all unions in any capacity, but it also is another indication of its loss of members within Brazilian society. At one point Brazil was the largest Catholic country in the world, but this is changing with the rise of the Protestant evangelical movement, which has had a profound impact in the past quarter century, and the increase of nonbelievers. Whereas as late as 1970 Roman Catholics represented 92 percent of the population, by 2000 this number had dropped to 74 percent, and Protestants now made up 15 percent of the total, with

---

[178] IBGE, *Síntese de indicadores sociais. Uma análise das condições de vida da população brasileira 2010* (Rio de Janeiro, 2012), Table 4.1, "Arranjos familiares residentes em domicílios particulares, total e respectiva distribuição percentual, por tipo, segundo as Grandes Regiões, as Unidades da Federação e as Regiões Metropolitanas – 2009."

[179] IBGE, *Censo Demográfico 2010 Famílias e domicílios Resultados da Amostra* (Rio de Janeiro, 2010), Table 1.1.4, "Famílias únicas e conviventes principais residentes em domicílios particulares, por classes de rendimento nominal mensal familiar per capita, segundo a situação do domicílio e o tipo de composição familiar – Brasil – 2010."

[180] Data for persons 15 years of age who headed households in the PNAD survey shows the following results:

Consolidation of Democracy since 1985   347

evangelicals being the fastest-growing group now accounting for 10 percent of the total population. Another 7 percent of the population declared formally that they had no religion, up from less than half a percent in 1950.[181] By the latest available estimate of 2009, Roman Catholics were

Characteristics of the Heads of Household by Sex, Brazil 2009

		Women 2009[a]	Men 2009[a]
Illiterates (%)		13.0	12.3
Schooling (%)		7.1	6.9
	1st grade incomplete	50.2	52.4
	1st grade complete	9.3	9.7
	2nd grade incomplete	4.7	4.6
	2nd grade complete	22.1	21.6
	Superior incomplete or more	13.7	11.8
Race (%)	White	49.0	49.5
	Black or mulatto	51.0	50.5
Age (%)	15–24	7.3	5.6
	25–49	47.0	56.4
	50+	45.7	38.1
Situation in labor market (%)			
	Employed	53.4	81.5
	Unemployed	5.4	2.6
	Inactive	41.2	15.9
		467	1062
Position in occupation			
	Employed with working papers	33.2	38.6
	Military	0.0	0.4
	Public functionary	11.1	5.9
	Employed without papers	26.9	15.7
	Self-employed	19.9	28.6
	Employer	3.2	7.2
	Self-consumption	4.3	3.0
	No income	1.3	0.5

Source: IETS based on PNAD surveys.
Notes: Grades 1 and 2 are for Ensino Fundamental 1 & 2 (years 1–4 and 5–8).
[a] Estimates including missing northern region rural families.

[181] IBGE, SIDA, Table 2470, "Pessoas de 10 anos ou mais de idade por estado civil, condição de convivência, sexo e religião," available at http://www.sidra.ibge.gov.br/bda/tabela/listabl.asp?z=cd&o=17&i=P&c=2470. The data for religion in earlier censuses is found in IBGE, *Tendências demográficas no período de 1950/2000*, Graph 5, available at http://www.ibge.gov.br/home/estatistica/populacao/censo2000/tendencias_demograficas/comentarios.pdf.

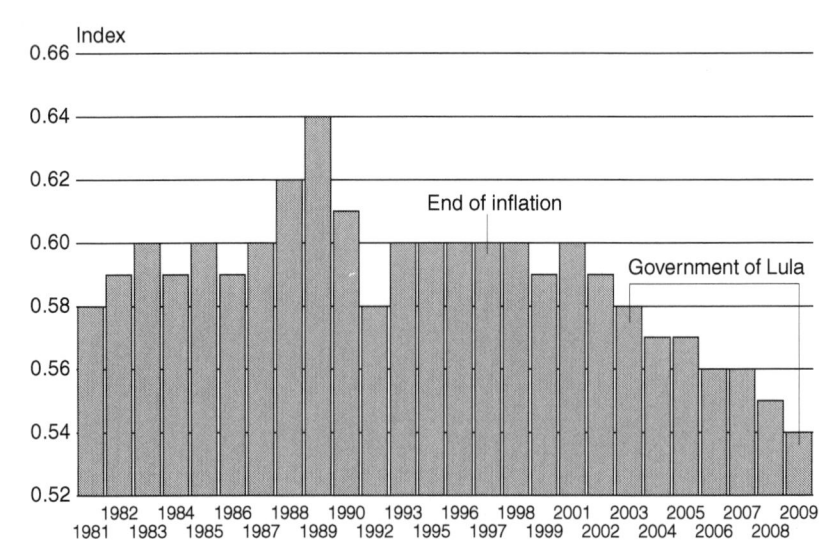

348   *The Economic and Social History of Brazil since 1889*

GRAPH 4.37. Gini Index of Inequality in Brazil, 1981–2009. *Source:* Ipeadata Tabela Renda – desigualdade – coeficiente de Gini

now 68 percent of the population, while Protestants were up to 20 percent and those without religions were fairly stable at 7 percent with other religions slowly increasing their share of the total.[182]

Reducing indigence and poverty, increasing literacy, and providing universal health care combined with incorporation of the majority of workers into the formal labor market have all had an important impact in lowering the Gini index of inequality. It is only with the end of inflation in the Cardoso period and the maturation of social welfare programs in the Lula administration that there was finally an historic break in the rigidity of income distribution. The Gini index, the ratio demonstrating the level of inequality of income in the country, finally is showing signs of major decline (see Graph 4.37).[183] But for all the improvement, Brazil still

---

[182] Marcelo Côrtes Neri, ed., *Novo Mapa das Religiões* (Rio de Janeiro: Fundação Getúlio Vargas, Centro de Políticas Sociais, 2011), 8.

[183] A recent major study of the decline of inequality by region in Brazil, which showed a striking convergence of regions toward a national norm, concluded that "since the early 1980s, per capita real incomes grew faster in non-metropolitan areas, which were propelled by a booming labor market which accounted for over 60% of the growth. On the other hand, about two-thirds of the income growth in metropolitan areas was caused by the expansion of Social Security benefits. Between 1981 and 2009, the decrease in inequality between metropolitan and nonmetropolitan areas accounted for 51% of the total decrease in income inequality; between 1995 and 2009 by 20%. Had this

remains one of the most unequal societies in the world. While regional, class, and color differences have declined and the country moves toward a more national pattern of education and health, class divides remain strong and continue to define differences in income, well-being, and mobility. Recent studies have shown that children of elite, white, educated families have very low levels of downward mobility compared to all other groups in society. This compares to elite black families, which have far less ability to pass on their elite status to their sons. Equally, there is less upward mobility in the poorer and more colored regions of the country than in the richer and whiter ones.[184]

The average income by race and color was markedly different for whites and Asians compared to all other groups in society, with mulattoes, the second-largest race/color group in the nation having an average income 45 percent less than the white income, and 43 percent less than the Asian income.[185] Moreover, rates of change in income have differed by color as well. Whites and Asians moved up faster than blacks and mulattoes. Although many blacks and mulattoes made it out of poverty in the recent five-year period, moving out of the lower classes to the middle- and upper-managerial positions and classes is a much slower process. Moreover, once reaching such higher levels, maintaining their status intergenerationally is more difficult for blacks and mulattoes than for whites.

Class is also still a major marker of social as well as income inequality. For those with less income and less education, life expectancy is below the national norms and morbidity is higher. Life chances are more reduced and mobility is limited. Even in the physical distribution of resources, class and residence continue to play a major role. Despite all the movement out of extreme poverty, there remain major deficits in living condition by class. While color television ownership is almost universal,[186]

---

convergence not occurred, per capita income inequality in 2009 would be 10% higher than observed." Pedro Herculano Guimarães Ferreira de Souza and Rafael Guerreiro Osorio, *A redução das disparidades regionais e a queda da desigualdade nacional de renda (1981–2009)*, Texto para Discussão No. 1648 (Brasília: IPEA, Agosto 2011), 1.

[184] Sérgio Guimarães Ferreira and Fernando A. Veloso, "Intergenerational Mobility and Education in Brazil," *Brazilian Review of Econometrics* 26,2 (November 2006), 183.

[185] IBGE, *Censo Demográfico 2010 Características da população e dos domicílios, Resultados do universo*, Table 1.8.8.

[186] In 2009 some 95 percent of Brazilian households had color televisions. IBGE, Série: PD282 – Domicílios particulares permanentes, por posse de televisão, available at http://seriesestatisticas.ibge.gov.br/series.aspx?vcodigo=PD282&sv=14&t=domicilios-particulares-permanentes-por-posse-de-televisao.

access to modern sanitation is far more limited. Only 79 percent of urban houses had either a septic tank or were connected to a modern system of collection, but very few municipalities actually treated their sewage and converted it into viable water products.[187] Thus as late as 2010, there were 265 hospitalizations per hundred thousand residents for fecal-water related diseases.[188]

Although access to primary education is now universal and little difference exists by sex, color, or income in completion rates for primary education (*escola fundamental*), secondary education does show marked differences by income and to a lesser extent by race. As of 2003 only families with a per capita income of one to two minimum salaries or above had half or more of youths ages 18 to 24 graduating secondary school (*escola média*), and in turn, only those homes with a per capita income of two or more minimum salaries had more than half these youths able to go to university. Only 32 percent of all persons ages 18 to 24 had access to a university, and the rates by color were markedly different. Some 40 percent of white youths and only 19 percent of Afro-Brazilian ones (*preto*, or black and *pardo* or mulatto combined) were able to attend university, though even here income was highly correlated with rates of access for both groups.[189] These differences, more pronounced in earlier periods, can be seen in the relationship between color and years of schooling completed. Here there remained a very important difference between whites and colored until the last couple of years. Given that whites started with a greater lead and continued to add years of schooling, it took until the end of the first decade of the twenty-first century before pardos and pretos were able to increase their years of schooling faster than whites and thus reduce the differences between the two groups (see Graph 4.38).

The return of democracy brought with it a set of political and social values and institutional changes that have created a well-founded democratic state in Brazil. The new democratic governments quickly set about

---

[187] IBGE, Série: IU28 – Acesso ao esgotamento sanitário – área urbana, available at http://seriesestatisticas.ibge.gov.br/series.aspx?vcodigo=IU28&t=acesso-ao-esgotamento-sanitario-area-urbana. For the rural areas, the rate was only 25 percent of all homes that had either option.

[188] IBGE, Série: AM38 – Doenças relacionadas ao saneamento ambiental inadequado (DRSAI), available at http://seriesestatisticas.ibge.gov.br/series.aspx?vcodigo=AM38&sv=95&t=doencas-relacionadas-ao-saneamento-ambiental-inadequado-drsai.

[189] Cibele Yahn de Andrade and J. Norberto W. Dachs, "Acesso à educação por faixas etárias segundo renda e raça/cor," *Cadernos de Pesquisa* 37,131 (Maio–Agosto 2007), 409, 411, Tables 3–4.

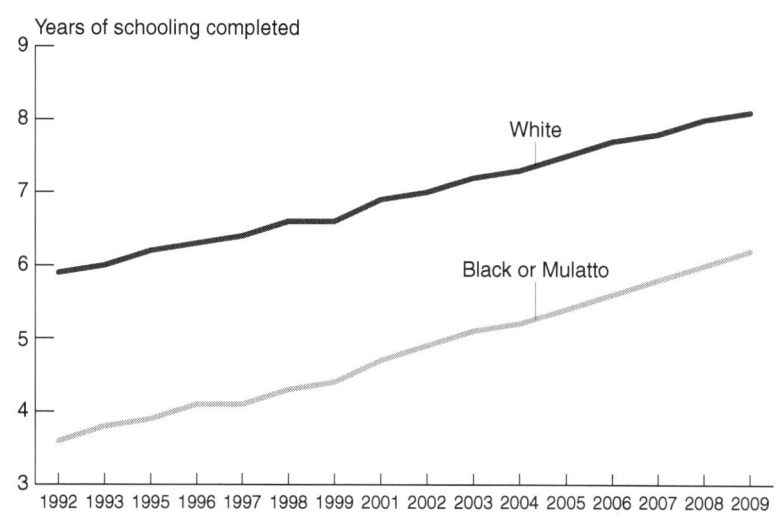

GRAPH 4.38. Average Years of Schooling by Color for Persons 25 Years of Age and Older, 1992–2009. *Source:* IBGE, tabela Série: IU36

dismantling the more repressive institutions created by the military. They began a long process of decentralization and increasing popular participation in government and committed themselves to democratic stabilization and human rights protections. All of these ideas and values were enshrined in the new Constitution of 1988, which then became a fundamental charter for the implantation of a well-established modern democratic welfare state.

But the new postmilitary regimes inherited a far less stable economic situation. The costs of forced industrialization were fully manifesting themselves in an endless inflation that could not be controlled. Reform programs, whether orthodox or heterodox, which involve monetary reforms, price controls, or the freezing of prices, were unable to contain the high and growing chronic inflation that plagued Brazil for several decades. The high inflation created numerous distortions in the economy and represented a heavy burden for the population subject to what has been called an inflation tax, particularly the poor who had fewer resources to protect their income from the corrosion generated by inflation.

Two major developments occurred in the 1990s that finally brought the economic situation under control, but that resulted in fundamental changes in industrial policy and activity. The first was the opening up of the Brazilian economy, which began under Collor and was fully supported by the Cardoso government. As the Brazilian economy had already reached a high level of complexity and vertical integration, the opening and the accelerated process of globalization of the Brazilian economy led to dramatic changes in the economy, particularly in the industrial sector. Survival required companies to increase productivity and resulted in an extensive process of business concentration and an increase in foreign participation in the economy.

The second major change was the Plan Real, which finally controlled the runaway inflation that the country had experienced since the late 1940s. The end of the inflation tax created greater stability in the income of the population, especially of the poor, and greatly expanded the demand for consumer goods. The price stability achieved by the Real Plan was accompanied by a long process of the appreciation of the new *real* currency. The open and globalized economy suffered the adverse effects of an overvalued exchange rate, which created an additional burden for national industry in its competition with the outside world. If in the first years after the Real Plan, the overvalued *real* represented one of the anchors of the plan, the continuation of that policy has been identified as one of the factors that explain the poor performance of Brazilian industry in recent years. Finally, it should be emphasized that the stability achieved and maintained in the last ten years and the continuity of economic policy since the Real Plan have been of crucial importance to the stability of the national economy. This stability allowed the expansion of the formal labor market, the real increase in salaries, the maintenance and expansion of important welfare policies, and the vast expansion of consumer credit with everything from home mortgages to car loans being made available for the first time. All these changes were felt in the decline of the high levels of income inequality.

Finally, in the late 1970s and early 1980s, Brazil completed its demographic transition, which led to an extraordinary and rapid decline in fertility and a consequent slowing of population growth to new historic lows. At the same time, child and infant mortality also declined rapidly, such that Brazil now found itself among the healthier states of Latin America. Life expectancy rose systematically from census to census and the mortality schedule looked ever more like an advanced First World country, with cancer and heart diseases now being the biggest killers and infectious diseases declining in importance.

The new and stronger federal regime now was firmly committed to expanding health and pension benefits to all citizens. The result was an increasingly decentralized health system, the incorporation of evermore workers into the social security system through the formal labor market, and the provision of pensions not only for the elderly but even those outside of such coverage who were now pensioned with conditional cash transfers. So effective have these governmental programs become, that by the second decade of the twenty-first century extreme poverty and hunger had been virtually eliminated for the first time in Brazil's history. All this occurred with an explosive expansion of the working and middle-income classes. For the first time in modern history, the Gini index of inequality has finally begun to decline in this most unequal of societies.

That inefficiencies and blockages exist in these government programs cannot be denied. But their impact in general has been quite positive, and Brazil now finds itself with an overwhelmingly literate and educated population fully integrated into a market economy. The country is now significantly urbanized, with rates quite comparable to other major advanced states. Equally regional disparities in health education and wealth are progressively disappearing, and the country is moving toward a more uniform general pattern for all regions.

Finally, a quiet but profound revolution has occurred in agriculture, which became the new engine of growth for the post-1980 regimes. Brazilian agriculture today is as efficient and modern as those of any other advanced country, and today Brazil ranks with the United States, Canada, Argentina, and Australia as one of the greatest of the world's agricultural producers. It is the world's most efficient and largest sugar producer, one of the world's major suppliers of everything from orange juice to chickens, and is expanding rapidly in all areas of the nation. This agricultural revolution was behind the explosive growth of the new western region, which is now equal in almost all social and economic indices to the most advanced regions of the south and southeast. It also revalued the Cerrado area, which extends well into the northeastern region and is now the heartland of national agriculture.

It is the power of its agriculture and its modern mining sector that has made Brazil a major world player and one of the key nations in the so-called BRIC societies that have emerged as a counterweight to the old economic blocks. Even in a few select manufacturing industries, such as aircraft manufacturing, Brazil has become an internationally important presence, while its industries dominate the mercosur region.

With the transition from middle-class to working-class parties in free and efficient election after election, and with the military now completely controlled, Brazil can be considered a model democracy. Clearly there remain fundamental problems that still require profound reforms. These include the need to reform the tax system, to restructure the parties, and to change the distorted form of representation of the Chamber of Deputies left over from the military era. There is also the need to totally reform the highly inefficient judiciary and complete the overhaul of the pension system. Severe problems exist in infrastructure from ports and airports to road and railroads, as well as the electricity-producing sector. There also remain the needs to increase public-sector efficiency and private-sector productivity. But one can only marvel at the crucial changes that have occurred since 1980 and the extraordinary unity in which the nation finds itself as a society that feels that the future may have finally arrived.

APPENDIX

TABLE A.1. Basic Data on the Coffee Economy of Brazil, 1870–1990

Year	Brazil Exports (£ millions)	Brazil Exports (U.S.$ millions)	World Exports (U.S.$ millions)	Brazil Exports (millions of sacks)	NY Price Rio 7	NY Price Santos 4	World Production	Brazil Production	São Paulo Production	Parana Production	World Stocks	Brazilian Stocks	World Consumption	Trees in Production Brazil	Trees in Production São Paulo
1870	6.0		93	3.5	16.3		7.2	3.8					6.9		
1871	7.8		112	3.9	15.9		6.0	2.3					7.1		
1872	7.2		137	3.8	18.4		7.5	3.5					7.2		
1873	12.0		156	3.1	20.0		6.4	2.8					7.4		
1874	12.0		166	3.3	21.1		8.0	3.9					7.6		
1875	13.5		162	3.6	19.0		7.6	3.4					7.7		
1876	13.4		163	3.5	18.0		7.8	3.6					7.9		
1877	11.8		170	3.7	19.7		7.3	3.5					8.1		
1878	11.3		166	4.4	16.5		9.2	4.9					8.4		
1879	12.8		138	3.8	14.9		8.6	4.1					8.9		
1880	11.2		129	3.1	15.1		9.8	5.6	1.2				9.3		
1881	11.6		125	3.9	10.6		9.7	5.5	1.5				9.8		
1882	9.6		120	5.4	8.8		10.3	6.7	2.0				10.3		
1883	10.8		122	6.0	9.3		9.2	5.1	1.9		5.2		10.7		
1884	11.7		116	5.8	9.3		11.1	6.2	2.1		5.4		11.2		
1885	13.1		103	5.8	8.1		9.8	5.6	1.7		5.1		11.2		
1886	9.7		117	5.8	11.4		10.3	6.1	2.6		4.0		11.1		
1887	21.5		145	4.7	14.6		7.0	3.0	1.1		4.1		9.1		
1888	10.9		129	3.4	14.0		11.1	6.8	2.6		2.3		10.3		
1889	19.0		186	5.6	14.7		7.6	4.3	1.9		3.6		10.5		
1890	17.9		199	5.1	17.9		9.0	5.4	2.9		2.4		9.8	416,667	200,000
1891	17.6		187	5.4	16.7		11.7	7.4	3.7		1.9		10.8	461,117	221,336
1892	22.0		255	7.1	14.3		11.0	6.2	3.2		2.9		11.0	510,310	244,949

(*continued*)

TABLE A.1 (continued)

Year	Brazil Exports (£ millions)	Brazil Exports (U.S.$ millions)	World Exports (U.S.$ millions)	Brazil Exports (millions of sacks)	NY Price Rio 7	NY Price Santos 4	World Production	Brazil Production	São Paulo Production	Parana Production	World Stocks	Brazilian Stocks	World Consumption	Trees in Production Brazil	Trees in Production São Paulo
1893	21.7		202	5.3	17.2	16.6	8.7	4.3	1.7		3.1		10.6	564,751	271,081
1894	20.9		205	5.6	16.5	15.6	11.2	6.7	4.0		2.2		11.2	625,500	300,000
1895	22.4		218	6.7	15.9	13.0	10.1	5.5	3.1		3.1		11.1	712,765	342,127
1896	19.7		191	6.7	12.3	7.4	13.5	8.7	5.1		2.6		12.2	812,853	390,170
1897	16.5		174	9.5	7.9	6.4	15.4	10.5	6.2		4.0		14.6	926,997	444,958
1898	13.8		129	9.3	6.3	6.1	13.1	8.8	5.6		5.4	1.3	13.5	1,057,169	507,441
1899	14.5		124	9.8	6.0	9.0	13.9	9.0	5.7		6.2	2.6	15.0	1,205,620	578,697
1900	18.9		123	9.2	8.2	6.0	18.1	13.9	8.9		5.8	3.7	14.3	1,374,917	659,960
1901	24.0		170	14.8	6.5	5.5	19.3	15.1	10.2		6.9	4.1	15.5	1,389,720	667,066
1902	20.3		146	13.2	5.9	5.4	18.5	13.6	8.4		11.3	3.6	16.0	1,404,683	674,248
1903	19.1		155	12.9	5.6	7.3	16.7	11.2	6.4		11.9	4.7	16.1	1,419,808	681,508
1904	20.0		144	10.0	7.8	7.1	15.6	11.2	7.4		12.4	9.4	16.2	1,435,095	688,845
1905	21.4		163	10.8	8.3	7.9	16.0	11.7	7.0		11.3	9.7	16.7	1,438,353	690,409
1906	27.6		194	14.0	8.1	6.4	25.2	20.6	15.4		9.6	9.6	17.5	1,441,619	691,977
1907	28.6		199	15.7	6.6	6.4	15.6	11.6	7.2		16.4	8.7	18.1	1,444,892	693,548
1908	23.0		165	12.7	6.3	7.5	18.8	14.0	9.5		16.4	7.5	19.3	1,448,173	695,123
1909	33.5		212	16.9	7.8	8.5	20.2	15.6	12.1		14.1	14.8	19.0	1,451,461	696,701
1910	26.7		163	9.7	9.5	13.3	16.2	11.5	8.5		12.8	12.6	18.1	1,451,460	696,701
1911	40.4		238	11.3	13.4	14.8	19.0	14.0	10.6		13.7	11.1	18.4	1,451,460	696,701
1912	46.6		294	12.1	14.6	13.2	19.0	13.5	9.5		11.1	11.9	17.9	1,502,021	720,970
1913	40.8		318	13.3	11.1	11.5	18.7	13.8	10.1		10.3	9.4	19.3	1,505,044	722,421
1914	27.0		242	11.3	8.2	9.6	20.5	15.2	9.2		11.3	8.6	22.2	1,532,175	735,444
1915	32.2		294	17.1	7.5	10.6	21.6	15.8	11.7		7.5	9.5	20.7	1,573,804	755,426
1916	29.3		249	13.0	9.4		19.2	14.0	9.9		7.3	6.1	15.4	1,648,450	791,256

Year														
1917	23.1		203	10.6	9.0	10.2	21.1	15.6	12.2		7.8	6.3	14.9	1,737,894	834,189
1918	19.0		190	7.4	9.9	12.7	18.1	11.9	7.3		8.8	6.6	15.9	1,725,740	828,355
1919	66.1		576	13.0	17.8	24.8	15.8	9.7	4.2		10.0	6.1	18.5	1,708,419	823,943
1920	40.5		467	11.5	11.5	18.6	23.9	16.8	10.2		6.9	1.3	18.5	1,780,856	843,593
1921	27.1		282	12.4	7.3	10.0	21.9	15.2	8.2		8.6	3.9	19.8	1,832,359	871,897
1922	39.5		348	12.7	10.1	14.1	20.1	12.5	7.0		8.6	4.2	19.1	1,883,724	899,239
1923	44.2		394	14.5	11.4	14.5	25.7	17.3	10.4		5.3	0.8	22.0	1,956,917	949,149
1924	65.7		525	14.2	17.3	21.0	24.8	17.0	9.2		9.6	1.4	20.5	2,021,343	951,288
1925	74.0		630	13.5	20.3	24.3	27.1	17.9	10.1		6.8	2.1	21.7	2,099,643	966,143
1926	69.6		647	13.8	18.0	22.1	26.9	18.4	9.9		7.3	4.1	21.3	2,253,181	1,047,496
1927	62.7		589	15.1	14.6	18.5	39.5	29.6	18.0		7.7	5.6	23.5	2,381,604	1,123,233
1928	69.7		676	13.9	16.4	23.0	26.6	16.1	8.8		18.2	16.4	22.2	2,482,584	1,152,521
1929	67.3		644	14.3	15.8	21.9	41.4	30.8	19.5		14.3	13.9	23.6	2,587,846	1,188,058
1930	41.2		446	15.3	8.6	12.9	30.9	19.2	10.1		31.4	24.4	25.2	2,697,571	1,265,152
1931	34.1		373	17.9	6.1	8.7	43.0	31.0	18.7		28.7	24.9	23.7	2,811,948	1,438,916
1932	26.2		272	11.9	8.0	10.7	35.8	22.6	15.0		31.7	29.6	22.9	2,978,400	1,475,000
1933	26.2		275	15.5	7.8	9.0	44.5	32.4	21.9		23.1	25.4	24.5	2,846,311	1,384,520
1934	21.5		293	14.1	9.8	11.1	33.8	21.0	11.7		27.1	26.7	22.7	2,899,094	1,420,556
1935	17.4		272	15.4	7.1	8.9	38.1	23.8	13.5		24.1	15.2	25.9	2,788,991	1,366,605
1936	17.8		281	14.5	7.4	9.8	44.1	29.3	17.8		28.9	7.0	24.9	2,800,623	1,372,305
1937	17.9		297	12.1	8.9	11.0	41.0	26.4	15.9		3.5	9.3	25.5	2,760,207	1,352,501
1938	16.2		274	17.1	5.2	7.6	40.3	26.2	15.6		23.3	3.7	26.7	2,696,769	1,321,417
1939	14.9		266	16.4	5.4	7.3	36.8	22.1	12.4		23.0	5.3	26.7	2,593,653	1,270,890
1940		96	185	12.0	5.4	7.1	32.1	19.5	10.2	0.9	23.5	7.6	28.6	2,532,471	1,240,911
1941		122	204	11.1	7.9	11.1	32.8	18.9	9.3	0.8	17.4	9.7	27.9	2,576,417	1,262,445

(*continued*)

TABLE A.1 (continued)

Year	Brazil Exports (£ millions)	Brazil Exports (U.S.$ millions)	World Exports (U.S.$ millions)	Brazil Exports (millions of sacks)	NY Price Rio 7	NY Price Santos 4	World Production	Brazil Production	São Paulo Production	Parana Production	World Stocks	Brazilian Stocks	World Consumption	Trees in Production Brazil	Trees in Production São Paulo
1942	106	267	7.3	9.4	13.4	31.3	16.8	8.5	0.6	14.7	12.5	25.7	2,588,323	1,268,278
1943	151	344	11.1	9.4	13.4	29.5	15.5	5.9	0.2	18.7	15.4	24.7	2,039,674	1,002,192
1944	209	415	13.6	9.4	13.4	27.0	12.4	4.7	0.6	17.9	15.2	20.4	2,078,287	1,000,587
1945	229	464	14.2	9.4	13.4	31.1	16.1	6.1	0.7	17.5	10.4	24.9	2,099,096	1,007,986
1946	350	669	15.5	12.4	23.1	35.6	17.5	8.9	1.1	16.4	8.2	27.1	2,078,538	1,004,168
1947	414	911	14.8	14.2	26.7	34.6	17.2	6.5	1.6	17.1	7.0	25.6	2,105,352	995,464
1948	491	1,065	17.5	14.5	22.3	40.5	20.7	11.2	1.9	13.3	4.5	27.9	2,147,326	1,015,763
1949	632	1,230	19.4	18.7	31.7	37.6	20.0	7.4	2.3	10.8	3.8	30.5	2,241,348	1,070,125
1950	865	1,727	14.8	37.7	50.5	38.2	20.6	8.1	4.0	9.3	3.2	30.7	2,313,278	1,079,091
1951	1,059	2,125	16.4	45.7	54.2	38.5	18.9	6.3	2.8	7.7	3.4	31.0	2,376,340	1,086,365
1952	1,045	2,177	15.8	48.9	54.0	41.5	20.2	7.2	5.0	6.5	2.1	31.6	2,451,900	1,109,580
1953	1,090	2,415	15.6	51.1	58.0	44.0	19.3	6.2	3.2	6.0	3.2	32.7	2,431,049	1,166,200
1954	948	2,599	10.9	63.0	78.9	42.2	18.8	7.3	1.3	6.5	4.0	29.2	2,410,375	1,185,800
1955	844	2,326	13.7	43.4	57.1	50.4	26.5	9.3	6.3	11.2	2.7	38.3	2,389,876	1,205,100
1956	1,030	2,599	16.8	44.5	58.1	45.4	17.1	6.0	2.2	16.5	7.8	36.2	2,369,552	1,230,100
1957	846	2,376	14.3	44.2	56.9	55.0	26.3	9.5	4.7	15.0	5.4	37.3	2,349,401	1,255,000
1958	688	2,119	12.9	40.5	48.3	61.7	31.7	10.7	8.6	23.9	13.4	39.0	2,329,422	1,279,700
1959	733	2,008	17.5	33.4	36.9	78.9	44.1	15.6	20.7	36.9	24.0	42.4	2,309,612	1,321,600
1960	713	1,930	16.8	34.1	36.6	65.8	29.8	8.2	14.3	59.5	44.3	42.9	2,289,970	1,240,800
1961	710	1,876	17.0		36.2	72.0	35.9	11.3	21.4	65.9	52.0	46.1	2,270,496	1,168,500
1962	643	1,862	16.4		34.1	67.4	28.7	5.2	18.0	74.9	57.3	46.9	2,251,187	960,900
1963	748	1,959	19.5		34.1	71.0	23.2	10.1	9.5	81.3	62.6	51.1	2,232,043	757,100
1964	760	2,449	15.0		46.7	50.6	18.1	1.8	3.6	78.0	59.7	41.9	2,213,061	750,200
1965	707	2,234	13.5		44.8	81.6	37.8	11.2	20.4	72.2	57.7	50.0	2,194,241	772,100
1966	774	2,269	17.0		40.8	60.6	17.5	6.2	7.7	86.8	70.8	49.0	2,175,581	694,000

1967	733	2,407	17.3	39.8	68.6	23.4	8.5	12.9	82.2	66.8	55.7	2,157,079	631,800
1968	797	2,394	19.0	37.4	61.1	16.8	4.6	8.3	80.2	64.8	53.6	2,138,735	632,730
1969	846	3,099	19.6	41.0	66.4	15.2	6.1	12.3	71.0	54.9	55.0	2,152,997	653,000
1970	982	2,882	17.1	55.8	58.3	11.0	4.4	1.6	64.5	45.7	51.7	2,058,301	637,000
1971	822	3,294	18.4	44.7	71.8	24.6	9.8	12.8	53.8	31.6	58.7	2,030,864	630,000
1972	1,057	4,496	19.2	52.5	76.6	24.5	9.4	9.7	53.8	31.8	61.2	2,048,219	631,900
1973	1,344	4,282	19.8	69.3	62.5	14.3	7.0	4.1	55.1	31.8	60.6	2,045,480	640,000
1974	980	4,192	13.3	73.3	81.7	27.5	9.8	11.5	40.3	20.8	55.4	2,086,362	657,190
1975	934	9,057	14.6	82.6	73.5	22.8	7.0	11.7	49.5	28.2	59.6	2,059,990	678,000
1976	2,398	7,259	15.6	149.5	61.2	9.0	1.9	0.0	44.8	29.9	56.3	1,952,940	551,600
1977	2,625	10,303	10.1	308.0	69.6	17.1	7.6	1.8	29.6	12.5	48.7	2,043,782	613,500
1978	2,394	12,199	12.6	165.5	74.5	19.1	8.3	4.6	32.7	14.0	64.6	2,179,928	726,200
1979	2,326	10,929	12.0	147.2	81.9	20.9	8.4	2.0	30.5	14.6	62.1	2,309,855	698,110
1980	2,771	6,696	15.1	102.9	86.3	17.4	6.0	3.0	32.7	16.5	59.8	2,590,696	730,000
1981	1,754	8,018	16.0	179.6	98.2	33.7	11.0	8.3	34.6	9.3	65.3	2,649,601	746,660
1982	2,108	9,719	17.1	143.7	84.5	16.2	5.5	1.6	52.4	20.0	65.1	2,681,970	818,366
1983	2,339	10,997	17.8	142.8	88.7	30.4	7.4	5.9	52.0	13.9	68.2	2,855,704	784,470
1984	2,851	1,445	19.4	149.7	93.6	21.8	6.5	4.0	54.9	16.7	72.0	2,869,078	653,805
1985	2,621	15,267	19.2	151.8	96.5	32.6	8.9	5.4	48.3	11.1	69.8	2,928,884	658,394
1986	2,327	10,329	9.9	231.2	79.6	13.9	1.6	2.0	45.2	16.4	66.0	3,109,879	635,117
1987	2,169	10,499	18.3	106.4	103.1	38.0	12.7	10.0	42.6	14.5	66.7	3,380,385	711,358
1988	2,222	9,660	17.1	121.8	93.6	25.0	4.4	2.3	64.0	31.0	69.1	3,424,823	674,531
1989	1,781	6,800	18.3	98.8	97.1	26.0	4.7	4.6	65.2	28.6	78.1	3,482,408	618,589
1990	1,284	6,488	17.0	999.0	99.7	31.0	6.0	3.0	56.8	26.9	78.4		

Sources: IBGE, *Estatísticas Históricas Retrospectivas*; Delfim Netto 1981, pp. 346–348; and Bacha and Greenhill 1992, Tables 1.1–1.2, 1.6, 1.8, 2.12–2.13.

TABLE A.2. *Economic Indicators for the External Sector, 1870–2011*

Year	Exports (₤ 000)	Imports (₤ 000)	Exports (U.S.$ millions)	Imports (U.S.$ millions)	Balance of Payments (U.S.$ millions)	Terms of Exchange (2006 = 100)	External Debt (₤ millions)	Total External Debt (U.S.$ millions)	International Reserves (US$ millions)
1870	15,453	13,195				96	13		
1871	15,439	14,925				98	16		
1872	19,089	15,045				90	15		
1873	22,392	16,516				119	15		
1874	20,620	16,609				133	15		
1875	22,392	17,995				124	19		
1876	20,820	19,522				148	19		
1877	20,573	16,504				141	19		
1878	19,063	16,728				132	18		
1879	19,508	15,631				131	17		
1880	19,789	15,454				161	17		
1881	21,249	16,529				144	16		
1882	19,138	16,621				116	15		
1883	17,378	16,782				92	19		
1884	19,493	18,187				110	18		
1885	19,504	15,381				110	18		
1886	15,110	15,306				103	24		
1887	32,205	16,120				119	23		
1888	21,714	19,724				167	30		
1889	28,552	24,002	139	117		164	31		
1890	26,382	24,019	128	117		159	31		

1891	27,136	25,565	132	124	150	31
1892	30,854	26,302	150	128	153	30
1893	32,007	26,215	156	127	182	33
1894	30,491	27,145	148	132	166	33
1895	32,586	29,212	158	142	160	40
1896	28,333	27,880	138	136	140	40
1897	25,883	22,990	126	112	110	40
1898	25,019	23,536	122	115	105	40
1899	25,545	22,563	124	110	102	42
1900	33,163	21,409	161	104	103	44
1901	40,622	21,377	198	89	93	60
1902	36,437	23,279	177	97	93	60
1903	36,833	24,208	179	102	95	68
1904	39,430	25,915	192	109	116	70
1905	44,643	29,830	217	126	120	78
1906	53,059	33,204	258	139	110	88
1907	54,177	40,528	263	170	99	91
1908	44,155	35,491	215	149	96	112
1909	63,724	37,139	310	156	121	114
1910	63,092	47,872	307	201	145	128
1911	66,839	52,822	325	221	144	132
1912	74,649	63,425	363	261	146	132
1913	65,451	67,166	319	274	111	144
1914	46,803	35,473	229	146	91	161
1915	53,951	30,088	257	115	76	162
1916	56,462	40,369	269	148	76	162

(*continued*)

TABLE A.2 (continued)

Year	Exports (₤ 000)	Imports (₤ 000)	Exports (U.S.$ millions)	Imports (U.S.$ millions)	Balance of Payments (U.S.$ millions)	Terms of Exchange (2006 = 100)	External Debt (₤ millions)	Total External Debt (U.S.$ millions)	International Reserves (US$ millions)
1917	63,031	44,510	300	159		60	159		
1918	61,168	52,817	292	194		57	154		
1919	117,388	71,867	581	280		83	152		
1920	82,346	88,369	408	382		60	150		
1921	45,411	46,033	224	201		45	169		
1922	61,317	43,609	366	232		62	185		
1923	68,562	47,441	337	208		83	183		
1924	86,737	62,502	423	283		111	182		
1925	102,875	84,443	497	359		121	183		
1926	94,254	79,876	458	340		117	210		
1927	88,689	79,634	431	335		99	234		
1928	97,426	90,669	474	389		113	255		
1929	94,831	86,653	460	368		111	252		
1930	65,746	53,619	319	226	-116	73	266		
1931	49,544	28,756	244	117	16	70	276		
1932	36,630	21,744	179	93	36	84	268		
1933	35,790	28,132	217	148	-12	73	266		
1934	35,240	25,467	293	185	-12	80	264		
1935	33,012	27,431	270	197	23	72	259		
1936	39,069	30,066	321	196	-51	82	253		

1937	42,530		347				
1938	35,945	40,608	294				
1939	37,298	35,916	300				
1940		31,801	273				
1941			370	279	0	78	243
1942			401	247	75	57	243
1943			467	218	−1	59	243
1944			575	227	4	54	241
1945			655	253	60	63	240	863
1946			985	210	150	76	232	959
1947			1,152	275	253	75	226	929
1948			1,180	360	157	79	187	883
1949			1,096	389	62	83	173	875
1950			1,355	584	96	79	160	821
1951			1,769	1,056	136	86	154	584
1952			1,418	973	−67	83	146	482
1953			1,539	957	33	83	116	421
1954			1,562	942	−30	138	107	372
1955			1,423	1,725	−81	124		442
1956			1,482	1,720	−27	113		2,736	608
1957			1,392	1,145	−40	117		2,491	474
1958			1,243	1,415	11	148		2,870	465
1959			1,282	1,104	12	120		3,160	366
1960			1,269	1,075	183	121		3,738	345
1961			1,403	1,285	−161	119		3,291	470
1962			1,214	1,177	−30	115		3,533	285

(continued)

363

TABLE A.2 (*continued*)

Year	Exports (₦ 000)	Imports (₦ 000)	Exports (U.S.$ millions)	Imports (U.S.$ millions)	Balance of Payments (U.S.$ millions)	Terms of Exchange (2006 = 100)	External Debt (₦ millions)	Total External Debt (U.S.$ millions)	International Reserves (US$ millions)
1963			1,406	1,294	−37	96		3,612	215
1964			1,430	1,086	−2	118		3,294	244
1965			1,595	941	218	119		3,823	483
1966			1,741	1,303	−9	109		3,771	421
1967			1,654	1,441	−262	107		3,440	198
1968			1,881	1,855	97	102		4,092	257
1969			2,311	1,993	531	106		4,635	656
1970			2,739	2,507	534	117		6,240	1,187
1971			2,904	3,247	537	110		8,284	1,723
1972			3,991	4,232	2,538	111		11,464	4,183
1973			6,199	6,192	2,380	124		14,857	6,416
1974			7,951	12,641	−1,041	103		20,032	5,269
1975			8,670	12,210	−1,064	98		25,115	4,040
1976			10,128	12,383	2,688	110		32,145	6,544
1977			12,120	12,023	714	128		37,951	7,256
1978			12,659	13,683	4,262	110		52,187	11,895
1979			15,244	18,084	−3,215	102		55,803	9,689
1980			20,132	22,955	−3,472	82		64,259	6,913
1981			23,293	22,091	625	72		73,963	7,507
1982			20,175	19,395	−4,542	70		85,487	3,994
1983			21,899	15,429	−24	70		93,745	4,563
1984			27,005	13,916	7,027	74		102,127	11,995

1985	25,639	13,153	−457	71	105,171	11,608
1986	22,349	14,044	−3,836	90	111,203	6,760
1987	26,224	15,051	1,015	80	121,188	7,458
1988	33,789	14,605	1,249	86	113,511	9,140
1989	34,383	18,263	886	82	115,506	9,679
1990	31,414	20,661	481	75	123,439	9,973
1991	31,620	21,040	−369	79	123,910	9,406
1992	35,793	20,554	14,670	80	135,949	23,754
1993	38,555	25,256	8,709	81	145,726	32,211
1994	43,545	33,079	7,215	93	148,295	38,806
1995	46,506	49,972	12,919	103	159,256	51,840
1996	47,747	53,346	8,666	103	179,935	60,110
1997	52,994	59,747	−7,907	109	199,998	52,173
1998	51,140	57,714	−7,970	107	241,644	44,556
1999	48,011	49,210	−7,822	93	241,468	36,342
2000	55,086	55,783	−2,262	96	236,156	33,011
2001	58,223	55,572	3,307	96	226,067	35,866
2002	60,362	47,240	302	95	227,689	37,823
2003	73,084	48,290	8,496	93	235,414	49,296
2004	96,475	62,835	2,244	94	220,182	52,935
2005	118,308	73,606	4,319	95	187,987	53,799
2006	137,807	91,351	30,569	100	199,372	85,839
2007	160,649	120,617	87,484	102	240,495	180,334
2008	197,942	173,107	2,969	106	262,910	206,806
2009	152,995	127,705	46,651	103	277,563	239,054
2010	201,915	181,768	49,101	120	351,941	288,575
2011	256,040	226,233	58,637	129	402,385	352,012

Source: Ipeadata.

TABLE A.3. *Economic Indicators for the Internal Sector, 1870–2011*

Year	Government Budget Surplus/Income (%)	M1 (% year)	Exchange Rate Pence/*mil réis*	GDP	GDP Agriculture	GDP Industry	Investment as % of GDP	GDP per Capita (U.S.$)	GDP per Capita (U.S.$ – preços 2011)	Cost of Living (%)	Inflation (IGP-DI)
1870	-49%	1	22.1							4	
1871	-4%	4	24.0							-6	
1872	1%	-1	25.0							0	
1873	-10%	0	26.1							4	
1874	-18%	-2	25.8							0	
1875	-20%	-6	27.2							-6	
1876	-26%	4	25.3							12	
1877	-37%	3	24.6							15	
1878	-39%	12	22.9							-4	
1879	-62%	6	21.4							-1	
1880	-25%	-1	22.1							0	
1881	-8%	-1	21.9							2	
1882	-7%	-2	21.2							4	
1883	-18%	-3	21.6							0	
1884	-16%	5	20.7							-10	
1885	-30%	2	18.6							15	
1886	-21%	-6	18.7							-20	
1887	-4%	1	22.4							-4	
1888	2%	2	25.3							-6	
1889	-16%	7	26.4							10	
1890	-13%	99	22.6							8	
1891	4%	51	14.9							28	
1892	-23%	-11	12.0							44	
1893	-16%	2	11.6							7	
1894	-41%	7	10.1							-3	
1895	-12%	2	9.9							-5	
1896	-7%	2	9.1							28	

1897	−25%	8	7.7	14.4	21.0	2.7	4.2		18
1898	−106%	3	7.2	−0.5	−4.3	3.5	6.0		6
1899	8%	−5	7.4	1.9	1.9	2.6	6.5		−2
1900	−41%	−16	9.5	1.4	0.6	5.0	8.1	0.034	0.79	−13
1901	−10%	−5	11.4	3.3	3.1	2.4	10.1	0.039	0.87	−18
1902	13%	−2	12.0	12.7	18.3	5.4	9.9	0.042	0.84	−8
1903	13%	−1	12.0	0.8	−7.4	8.8	13.6	0.043	0.84	2
1904	−5%	10	12.2	−3.2	−1.4	0.0	12.7	0.046	0.82	6
1905	7%	−4	15.7	10.3	6.1	21.6	11.2	0.043	0.82	−11
1906	2%	8	16.2	2.6	−3.9	4.4	12.3	0.073	0.90	22
1907	3%	15	15.2	5.8	2.7	9.0	14.0	0.068	0.88	−5
1908	−16%	−4	15.2	6.9	4.5	10.7	15.5	0.063	0.82	2
1909	−15%	15	15.2	2.9	4.3	0.9	20.3	0.064	0.88	−5
1910	−19%	15	16.2	−1.3	1.0	−8.7	9.6	0.073	0.87	−7
1911	−21%	13	16.1	0.3	4.1	12.9	5.9	0.074	0.90	12
1912	−28%	2	16.2	0.9	−2.8	11.4	7.8	0.083	0.93	8
1913	−17%	−10	16.1	9.4	11.9	8.7	7.0	0.074	0.93	−2
1914	−81%	−9	14.8	−2.0	−7.4	−1.1	5.5	0.058	0.89	−6
1915	−70%	11	12.6	7.9	3.0	14.8	9.7	0.053	0.87	42
1916	−44%	24	12.1	12.5	19.0	5.2	10.2	0.060	0.86	6
1917	−49%	18	12.8	1.9	4.1	−1.8	15.3	0.075	0.92	21
1918	−40%	31	13.0	7.8	0.5	18.8	12.6	0.078	0.88	19
1919	−49%	6	14.2	8.6	3.9	13.3	7.7	0.094	0.93	32
1920	−33%	−1	14.6	1.4	1.0	−1.1	9.0	0.101	1.02	10
1921	−33%	41	8.4	0.0	−3.2	1.1	9.6	0.052	1.03	−16
1922	−47%	23	7.2	5.2	3.2	2.4	9.1	0.060	1.09	−4
1923	−12%	12	5.4	10.8	10.8	10.8	11.2	0.064	1.16	35
1924	−6%	10	6.0	11.5	18.4	7.0	9.3	0.076	1.16	23
1925	−1%	−12	6.2	1.1	0.3	−2.2	11.0	0.099	1.14	8
1926	−11%	2	7.2						1.19	−10
1927	2%	15	5.9					0.087	1.30	2
1928	9%	14	6.0					0.105	1.43	0
1929	7%	−6	5.9					0.101	1.42	5

(continued)

TABLE A.3 (continued)

Year	Government Budget Surplus/Income (%)	M1 (% year)	Exchange Rate Pence/mil réis	GDP	GDP Agriculture	GDP Industry	Investment as % of GDP	GDP per Capita (U.S.$)	GDP per Capita (U.S.$ – preços 2011)	Cost of Living (%)	Inflation (IGP-DI)
1930	−50%	−15	4.9	−2.1	1.2	−6.7	8.8	0.079	1.38	−18	
1931	−17%	16	3.8	−3.3	−6.3	1.2	6.9	0.043	1.31		
1932	−63%	17	5.0	4.3	6.0	1.4	6.6	0.046	1.35		
1933	−15%	−1	4.6	8.9	12.0	11.7	7.9	0.054	1.45		
1934	−21%	13	4.0	9.2	6.2	11.1	9.6	0.056	1.56		
1935	−5%	5	4.1	3.0	−2.5	11.9	11.8	0.048	1.59		
1936	−3%	11	4.1	12.1	9.5	17.2	12.1	0.054	1.75		
1937	−20%	11	4.2	4.6	0.1	5.4	12.9	0.066	1.81		
1938	−22%	21	4.2	4.5	4.2	3.7	13.6	0.063	1.86		
1939	−14%	−4	3.4	2.5	−2.3	9.3	13.1	0.065	1.87		
1940	−15%	2		−1.0	−1.8	−2.7	13.8		1.82		
1941	−20%	27		4.9	6.3	6.4	11.8	0.066	1.87		
1942	−31%	23		−2.7	−4.4	1.4	11.3	0.073	1.79		
1943	−9%	53		8.5	7.3	13.5	9.4	0.091	1.90		
1944	−1%	25		7.6	2.4	10.7	8.9	0.118	2.00		11%
1945	−11%	19		3.2	−2.2	5.5	9.1	0.137	2.02		24%
1946	−23%	10		11.6	8.4	18.5	11.0	0.175	2.20		2%
1947	3%	−2		2.4	0.7	3.3	14.9	0.199	2.20		7%
1948	0%	8		9.7	6.9	12.3	12.7	0.225	2.35		12%
1949	−16%	18		7.7	4.5	11.0	13.0	0.256	2.46		13%
1950	−22%	31		6.8	1.5	12.7	12.8	0.290	2.56		12%
1951	10%	16		4.9	0.7	5.3	15.4	0.349	2.61		11%
1952	7%	15		7.3	9.1	5.6	14.8	0.398	2.72		22%
1953	−8%	19		4.7	0.2	9.3	15.1	0.218	2.77		25%
1954	−6%	24		7.8	7.9	9.3	15.8	0.192	2.90		12%
1955	−14%	16		8.8	7.7	11.1	13.5	0.190	3.06		26%
1956	−44%	22		2.9	−2.4	5.5	14.5	0.236	3.05		5%
1957	−38%	32		7.7	9.3	5.4	15.0	0.263	3.19		

368

1958	−26%	23	10.8	2.0	16.8	17.0	0.185	3.42	26%
1959	−17%	43	9.8	5.3	12.9	18.0	0.225	3.65	38%
1960	−14%	39	9.4	4.9	10.6	15.7	0.244	3.87	31%
1961	−32%	52	8.6	7.6	11.1	13.1	0.239	4.08	50%
1962	−42%	64	6.6	0.5	8.1	15.5	0.261	4.22	54%
1963	−34%	65	0.6	1.0	−0.2	17.0	0.304	4.12	82%
1964	−38%	82	3.4	1.3	5.0	15.0	0.265	4.14	86%
1965	−23%	79	2.4	12.1	−4.7	14.7	0.277	4.12	36%
1966	−2%	14	6.7	−1.7	11.7	15.9	0.339	4.27	37%
1967	−11%	46	4.2	5.7	2.2	16.2	0.362	4.33	24%
1968	2%	39	9.8	1.4	14.2	18.7	0.384	4.63	25%
1969	5%	33	9.5	6.0	11.2	19.1	0.410	4.93	19%
1970	6%	33	10.4	5.6	11.9	18.8	0.454	5.30	19%
1971	3%	31	11.3	10.2	11.9	19.9	0.511	5.75	19%
1972	3%	38	11.9	4.0	14.0	20.3	0.595	6.27	16%
1973	4%	47	14.0	0.1	16.6	20.4	0.830	6.97	16%
1974	5%	34	8.2	1.3	7.8	21.8	1.067	7.35	34%
1975	−3%	44	5.2	6.6	3.8	23.3	1.222	7.54	30%
1976	2%	38	10.3	2.4	12.1	22.4	1.413	8.12	47%
1977	2%	38	4.9	12.1	2.3	21.3	1.589	8.32	38%
1978	0%	41	5.0	−2.7	6.1	22.3	1.762	8.53	42%
1979	4%	73	6.8	4.7	6.9	23.4	1.902	8.89	79%
1980	3%	77	9.2	9.6	9.1	23.6	2.001	9.52	111%
1981	4%	88	−4.3	8.0	−10.4	24.3	2.125	8.91	95%
1982	3%	66	0.8	−0.2	−0.2	23.0	2.183	8.77	102%
1983	6%	98	−2.9	−0.5	−5.8	19.9	1.491	8.32	212%
1984	7%	202	5.4	2.6	6.2	18.9	1.447	8.57	228%
1985	3%	304	7.8	9.6	8.4	18.0	1.586	9.04	243%
1986	3%	307	7.5	−8.0	11.3	20.0	1.889	9.52	61%
1987	5%	127	3.5	15.0	1.0	23.2	2.042	9.66	432%
1988	1%	570	−0.1	0.8	−3.4	24.3	2.179	9.47	1118%

(*continued*)

TABLE A.3 (continued)

Year	Government Budget Surplus/Income (%)	M1 (% year)	Exchange Rate Pence/mil réis	GDP	GDP Agriculture	GDP Industry	Investment as % of GDP	GDP per Capita (U.S.$)	GDP per Capita (U.S.$ – preços 2011)	Cost of Living (%)	Inflation (IGP-DI)
1989	-6%	1,384		3.2	2.8	2.9	26.9	2.868	9.58		2013%
1990	0%	2,336		-4.3	-3.7	-9.5	20.7	3.172	9.01		1217%
1991	0%	331		1.0	1.4	0.1	18.1	2.735	8.95		497%
1992	4%	867		-0.5	5.4	-4.2	18.4	2.577	8.76		1167%
1993	9%	2,129		4.7	1.0	9.3	19.3	2.846	9.02		2851%
1994	3%	2,586		5.3	7.4	8.1	20.7	3.492	9.36		908%
1995	3%	25		4.4	5.7	4.9	18.3	4.840	9.62		15%
1996	3%	5		2.2	3.0	0.1	16.9	5.205	9.68		9%
1997	6%	59		3.4	0.8	2.5	17.4	5.319	9.85		7%
1998	2%	7		0.0	3.4	-4.8	17.0	5.076	9.71		2%
1999	3%	24		0.3	6.5	-1.9	15.7	3.478	9.59		20%
2000	5%	19		4.3	2.7	5.7	16.8	3.763	9.86		10%
2001	1%	13		1.3	6.1	0.7	17.0	3.187	9.84		10%
2002	7%	29		2.7	6.6	2.4	16.4	2.870	9.96		28%
2003	5%	2		1.1	5.8	1.9	15.3	3.090	9.94		7%
2004	3%	17		5.7	2.3	8.5	16.1	3.664	10.37		12%
2005	5%	13		3.2	0.3	1.2	15.9	4.808	10.56		1%
2006	1%	20		4.0	4.8	1.0	16.4	5.868	10.85		4%
2007	2%	33		6.1	4.8	5.6	17.4	7.281	11.38		8%
2008	-3%	-3		5.2	6.3	3.0	19.1	8.717	11.85		9%
2009	7%	12		-0.3	-3.1	-8.7	18.1	8.469	11.69		-1%
2010		13		7.5	6.3	10.1	19.5	11.083	12.46		11%
2011		1		2.7	3.9	0.1	19.3	12.689	12.69		5%

Sources: Ministério da Fazenda, Secretaria do Tesouro Nacional, and Ipeadata.

TABLE A.4. *Principal Agricultural Exports, 1821–1939 (in £000)*

Year	Coffee	Sugar	Cacao	Yerba Mate	Tobacco	Ginned Cotton	Rubber	Leather & Skins	Subtotal	Total Exports
1821	704	1,096	31		191	921		596	3,539	4,324
1822	789	741	18		118	991		654	3,311	4,030
1823	878	1,779	16		103	941		460	4,177	4,358
1824	704	904	25		156	902		394	3,085	3,851
1825	623	1,058	36		102	1,421		583	3,823	4,622
1826	690	984	33		37	363		642	2,749	3,319
1827	774	1,365	28		67	584		504	3,323	3,662
1828	659	1,989	6		103	683	1	381	3,824	4,142
1829	705	1,282	6		71	579	3	590	3,239	3,441
1830	663	1,228	2		40	684	6	510	3,134	3,348
1831	964	852	4	10	69	774	7	440	3,119	3,373
1832	1,832	1,383	14	16	145	555	6	445	4,400	4,677
1833	1,383	828	14	20	88	483	10	278	3,102	3,263
1834	2,775	1,039	13	23	169	812	8	321	5,167	5,632
1835	2,435	1,092	13	17	69	468	15	454	4,563	5,328
1836	2,555	1,891	24	39	83	534	15	540	5,683	6,776
1837	2,237	1,182	26	34	74	477	17	615	4,663	5,476
1838	2,197	1,064	56	30	58	312	18	93	3,825	4,129
1839	2,494	1,033	62	25	100	358	15	323	4,425	4,863
1840	2,657	1,434	54	30	87	525	30	397	5,218	5,688
1841	2,300	1,536	50	37	84	506	34	350	4,889	5,384
1842	2,311	1,057	59	34	115	407	26	372	4,366	4,936
1843	1,909	1,117	41	35	85	386	11	408	3,990	4,584

(*continued*)

TABLE A.4 (continued)

Year	Coffee	Sugar	Cacao	Yerba Mate	Tobacco	Ginned Cotton	Rubber	Leather & Skins	Subtotal	Total Exports
1844	1,933	1,109	47	34	83	392	8	500	4,106	4,708
1845	1,838	1,504	37	40	105	344	16	553	4,437	4,941
1846	2,259	1,681	57	38	103	309	22	610	5,079	5,685
1847	2,465	1,659	61	45	105	354	29	624	5,342	5,885
1848	2,936	1,648	55	69	87	419	26	457	5,697	6,760
1849	2,242	1,655	60	75	93	364	27	411	4,927	5,865
1850	2,462	1,610	70	70	114	622	40	394	5,382	5,932
1851	3,906	1,890	70	68	204	682	125	540	7,485	8,121
1852	3,997	1,638	67	108	218	520	105	547	7,200	8,083
1853	3,874	2,084	56	63	134	582	161	556	7,510	8,418
1854	4,207	1,879	93	101	249	580	424	693	8,226	9,121
1855	5,581	1,920	48	99	233	539	326	669	9,415	10,439
1856	5,512	2,171	71	204	238	647	262	735	9,840	10,831
1857	6,211	2,967	169	303	395	802	183	1,087	12,117	13,150
1858	4,824	2,518	184	230	263	738	138	784	9,679	10,669
1859	5,340	2,947	141	186	325	588	201	764	10,492	11,372
1860	6,289	1,624	134	221	420	672	357	993	10,710	11,793
1861	8,564	1,172	159	168	256	503	313	977	12,112	13,241
1862	6,257	2,449	135	150	520	829	260	925	11,525	12,857
1863	6,201	2,051	150	166	680	1,843	359	795	12,245	13,424
1864	6,144	2,230	128	171	399	3,385	419	902	13,778	14,892
1865	7,151	1,816	131	98	325	3,519	404	806	14,250	15,733

1866	6,377	2,003	125	154	542	4,889	482	799	15,371	16,370
1867	7,044	1,280	143	187	427	3,379	590	953	14,003	15,786
1868	7,818	2,070	153	292	480	2,996	711	927	15,447	17,326
1869	6,409	942	99	189	384	2,498	555	916	11,992	14,351
1870	6,039	2,294	165	242	554	3,452	556	958	14,260	15,453
1871	7,766	1,660	143	344	583	2,224	926	1,001	14,647	15,439
1872	7,172	2,814	190	403	681	4,649	1,050	1,178	18,137	19,089
1873	12,013	2,891	157	348	712	2,816	1,049	1,551	21,537	22,392
1874	11,976	1,918	148	253	584	2,625	1,149	1,259	19,912	20,620
1875	13,512	2,484	256	245	643	2,138	1,102	1,351	21,731	22,392
1876	13,414	1,593	311	279	868	1,236	1,147	1,348	20,196	20,820
1877	11,752	3,158	362	251	723	1,270	1,161	1,059	19,736	20,573
1878	11,299	2,748	285	338	708	703	1,201	713	17,995	19,063
1879	12,813	2,085	298	260	686	947	1,082	847	19,018	19,508
1880	11,237	2,789	288	224	682	462	1,090	799	17,571	19,789
1881	11,604	2,386	336	249	695	471	1,091	761	17,593	21,249
1882	9,553	3,324	384	246	722	881	1,095	720	16,925	19,138
1883	10,817	2,049	391	93	432	1,090	1,251	385	16,508	17,378
1884	11,681	3,514	357	80	428	1,144	849	395	18,448	19,493
1885	13,140	1,957	391	59	481	943	916	442	18,329	19,504
1886	9,671	1,091	239	171	546	502	886	587	13,693	15,110
1887	21,501	2,250	449	424	827	1,805	2,160	752	30,168	32,205
1888	10,857	2,118	404	388	634	976	4,024	983	20,384	21,714
1889	18,983	1,582	385	442	721	767	2,788	1,183	26,851	28,552
1890	17,850	1,636	249	398	547	635	2,550	959	24,824	26,382

(*continued*)

TABLE A.4 *(continued)*

Year	Coffee	Sugar	Cacao	Yerba Mate	Tobacco	Ginned Cotton	Rubber	Leather & Skins	Subtotal	Total Exports
1891	17,561	2,674	365	274	381	1,095	2,686	757	25,793	27,136
1892	22,028	2,423	276	226	270	547	3,012	659	29,441	30,854
1893	21,712	1,946	470	168	611	1,906	3,403	487	30,703	32,007
1894	20,884	2,038	341	410	290	1,208	3,554	477	29,202	30,491
1895	22,385	1,833	320	425	389	477	5,055	526	31,410	32,586
1896	19,663	1,686	263	374	330	355	3,774	630	27,075	28,333
1897	16,506	1,235	360	460	909	599	4,232	635	24,936	25,883
1898	13,830	1,450	553	443	1,118	314	5,325	707	23,740	25,019
1899	14,459	642	589	475	688	147	6,126	1,091	24,217	25,545
1900	18,889	1,431	732	676	1,310	1,147	6,499	1,018	31,702	33,163
1901	23,979	1,551	847	936	1,655	451	8,627	1,069	39,115	40,622
1902	20,327	936	1,022	1,084	1,206	1,204	7,294	1,529	34,602	36,437
1903	19,076	199	1,012	677	949	1,324	9,734	1,821	34,792	36,833
1904	19,958	93	1,096	971	839	826	11,220	2,385	37,388	39,430
1905	21,421	406	1,040	1,247	825	1,158	14,416	1,852	42,365	44,643
1906	27,616	606	1,386	1,857	932	1,657	14,056	2,476	50,586	53,059
1907	28,559	136	2,013	1,610	1,284	1,735	13,690	2,379	51,406	54,177
1908	23,039	306	1,977	1,650	841	206	11,785	2,021	41,825	44,155
1909	33,475	671	1,599	1,658	1,329	592	18,926	2,792	61,042	63,724
1910	26,696	679	1,383	1,959	1,607	893	24,646	2,428	60,291	63,092
1911	40,401	409	1,641	1,983	965	979	15,057	2,447	63,882	66,839
1912	46,558	56	1,531	2,103	1,434	1,037	16,095	2,770	71,584	74,649
1913	40,779	66	1,594	2,372	1,652	2,308	10,375	3,378	62,524	65,451

1914	27,000	373	1,901	1,668	1,553	1,864	7,063	2,432	43,854	46,803
1915	32,191	756	2,894	1,862	1,179	287	7,040	4,032	50,241	53,951
1916	29,281	1,306	2,500	1,885	1,551	120	7,496	5,042	49,181	56,462
1917	23,054	3,860	2,536	1,818	1,296	793	7,484	5,190	46,031	63,031
1918	19,041	5,459	2,158	2,151	2,263	524	3,998	4,592	40,186	61,168
1919	66,081	3,106	5,025	2,829	3,887	1,978	5,686	7,970	96,562	117,388
1920	40,456	4,973	3,038	2,376	1,974	3,792	2,742	5,156	64,507	82,346
1921	27,067	2,507	1,263	1,153	1,464	1,220	954	1,978	37,606	45,411
1922	39,549	3,030	1,795	1,409	1,265	2,725	1,282	2,762	53,817	61,317
1923	44,182	2,951	1,937	1,146	1,212	2,477	1,688	3,370	58,963	68,562
1924	65,747	680	2,204	1,975	1,679	875	1,778	3,126	78,064	86,737
1925	74,032	55	2,624	2,864	2,349	3,307	5,058	3,791	94,080	102,875
1926	69,582	226	2,949	3,323	1,959	1,181	3,359	3,481	86,060	94,254
1927	62,689	636	4,560	2,677	1,718	1,023	2,799	4,386	80,488	88,689
1928	69,701	571	3,656	2,821	1,709	893	1,448	6,768	87,567	97,426
1929	67,307	222	2,577	2,613	1,628	3,783	1,501	4,148	83,779	94,831
1930	41,179	577	2,040	2,139	1,676	1,920	764	3,204	53,499	65,746
1931	34,104	62	1,396	1,348	956	826	375	2,338	41,405	49,544
1932	26,238	295	1,656	1,274	585	25	155	1,388	31,616	36,630
1933	26,168	174	1,340	807	379	369	263	1,396	30,896	35,790
1934	21,541	148	1,337	735	518	4,666	342	1,364	30,651	35,240
1935	17,373	361	1,302	543	514	5,223	292	1,243	26,851	33,012
1936	17,786	342	2,077	511	529	7,455	543	1,667	30,910	39,069
1937	17,887	2	1,924	552	732	8,018	630	2,551	32,296	42,530
1938	16,192	20	1,502	419	603	6,559	329	1,474	27,098	35,945
1939	14,892	156	1,494	420	643	7,645	377	1,633	27,260	37,298

Source: IBGE, Estatísticas históricas do Brasil, Vol. 3.

TABLE A.5. *Principal Agricultural Exports, 1953–2010 (in U.S.$000)*

Year	Coffee	Sugar	Cacao	Yerba Mate	Tobacco	Ginned Cotton	Rubber	Leather and Skins	Soybeans	Soybean Meal	Beef	Chicken	Orange Juice
1953	1,088,270	22,411	75,223	7,246	16,468	101,756	1,667	14,668	3,304		545		
1954	948,077	12,380	135,606	12,832	18,386	223,116	1,825	11,351	3,003				
1955	843,937	46,911	90,907	13,567	18,464	131,365	1,616	10,123	5,756		453		
1956	1,029,782	1,604	67,207	15,103	20,433	85,944	1,190	10,488	4,097		3,241		
1957	845,531	45,871	69,693	14,144	17,627	44,207	1,867	10,407	1,809		8,851		
1958	687,515	57,367	89,415	15,096	15,375	24,768	1,219	10,534	3,690		11,433		
1959	733,040	42,771	59,447	12,650	15,543	35,541	1,894	18,493	4,890		9,158		
1960	712,714	57,815	69,181	8,983	18,735	45,586	2,958	14,300			3,203		
1961	710,386	65,611	45,923	9,484	26,864	109,682	5,308	12,611	6,872		7,082		
1962	642,671	39,495	24,227	7,476	23,831	112,166	5,208	10,224	8,376		5,236		84
1963	748,284	72,412	35,030	7,664	24,239	114,241	1,500	9,042	3,107	3,969	5,143		2,167
1964	759,703	33,134	34,816	7,776	28,535	108,259	2,632	11,719		2,852	11,115		1,437
1965	706,587	56,727	27,689	6,940	26,359	95,651	5,007	23,913	7,343	7,225	20,942		1,884
1966	763,983	80,535	50,731	6,876	22,329	111,004	3,797	30,323	13,028	13,489	10,338		4,737
1967	704,725	80,426	59,161	4,984	20,486	90,844	3,888	25,557	29,243	10,023	3,959		6,693
1968	774,474	101,577	46,098	4,890	18,938	130,817	3,036	23,262	6,291	18,160	14,494		11,631
1969	812,955	115,045	105,490	4,910	26,715	196,008	3,706	44,498	29,249	22,001	31,682		10,910
1970	939,266	726,657	77,679	4,784	31,591	154,435	4,421	41,084	27,084	40,654	68,686		14,736
1971	772,479	152,951	61,681	5,662	36,953	137,140	4,406	31,722	24,309	78,070	98,707		35,859
1972	989,218	403,548	59,156	3,226	47,132	188,702	3,804	63,771	127,928	145,920	169,211		41,499
1973	1,244,272	558,686	88,522	3,475	59,160	218,068	3,882	56,311	494,153	418,636	148,547		63,622
1974	864,313	1,321,932	210,002	7,522	99,637	90,934	1,784	49,822	586,271	301,539	29,532		59,170
1975	854,513	1,099,773	220,369	9,955	143,374	97,794	1,749	53,196	684,901	463,746	8,530	3,290	82,213
1976	2,172,687	306,537	218,757	12,025	163,544	6,957	2,075	93,335	788,538	791,746	16,021	19,565	100,882
1977	2,298,942	462,704	435,467	13,370	189,079	40,894	1,476	95,258	709,606	1,145,709	39,560	31,572	177,040
1978	1,946,509	350,064	453,813	14,810	242,562	52,759	1,442	99,721	169,886	1,047,725	17,155	46,872	332,638
1979	1,917,618	363,809	486,873	17,470	291,199	499	498	164,986	179,506	1,136,933	8,041	81,148	281,452
1980	2,486,055	1,288,253	291,688	37,422	289,596	11,226	91	100,644	393,930	1,449,013	18,399	206,690	338,714

Year												
1981	1,516,646	1,061,732	241,618	28,276	362,223	41,497	107	—	403,672	2,136,176	123,568	354,291	659,206
1982	1,857,526	580,007	215,978	15,041	470,882	61,769	76	—	123,457	1,619,165	188,287	285,475	574,972
1983	2,095,526	526,803	283,773	17,633	465,991	188,510	13	—	308,571	1,793,219	210,318	242,212	607,931
1984	2,564,136	586,293	249,035	15,649	460,480	41,556	140	122,100	454,116	1,460,179	213,910	263,538	1,414,981
1985	2,369,178	367,954	360,796	14,088	449,764	76,754	19	113,035	762,683	1,174,857	262,683	242,873	748,927
1986	2,005,902	381,406	273,322	17,007	404,249	16,756	15	91,035	241,897	1,253,440	164,749	224,235	678,453
1987	1,959,196	324,616	265,587	19,562	415,587	160,179	7	158,543	570,277	1,449,966	207,665	215,909	830,671
1988	2,008,945	345,119	215,495	34,595	522,785	31,287		311,500	728,356	2,020,917	374,313	235,028	1,144,556
1989	1,560,391	306,198	134,324	22,298	569,378	157,741		170,219	1,153,709	2,136,528	137,716	323,769	—
1990	1,105,788	525,860	127,785	22,344	623,607	127,938		248,106	910,016	1,610,450	100,253	387,036	1,468,568
1991	1,382,064	398,087	88,452	26,552	818,362	147,724		272,386	448,168	1,369,415	178,439	424,639	900,521
1992	970,366	599,421	83,513	30,717	981,604	28,976		386,870	808,566	1,886,000	283,312	542,275	1,047,125
1993	1,064,898	786,675	97,640	35,444	900,782	3,772		394,886	946,466	2,121,000	—	313,125	827,578
1994	2,218,689	992,205	107,835	34,362	1,030,708	4,496		459,764	1,315,979	2,808,000	268,090	585,248	987,734
1995	1,969,847	1,919,460	25,041	39,695	1,174,961	91,543		574,269	770,425	3,028,000	180,780	627,518	1,108,371
1996	1,718,579	1,611,494	46,557	39,773	1,515,392	2,419		677,809	1,017,918	3,440,000	194,305	835,720	—
1997	2,746,213	1,773,984	7,865	34,608	1,664,806	361		740,058	2,452,427	3,277,000	196,296	867,863	1,006,661
1998	2,332,080	1,943,434	9,273	34,077	1,558,990	4,245		671,189	2,178,475	2,577,000	276,595	733,743	1,266,424
1999	2,230,111	1,910,693	4,758	30,174	961,237	4,588		594,483	1,593,293	2,175,000	443,835	872,620	1,239,034
2000	1,559,125	1,199,111	2,004	28,170	841,321	—		744,721	2,187,879	2,007,000	786,300	828,747	943,745
2001	1,207,574	2,279,060	3,785	27,720	944,316	—		863,192	2,725,508	2,571,000	1,022,500	1,333,800	837,704
2002	1,195,000	2,093,644	7,000	21,100	1,008,169	—		930,239	3,031,984	2,977,000	1,107,300	1,392,816	1,050,836
2003	1,302,292	2,140,022	3,074	16,040	1,090,219	—		1,036,098	4,290,443	3,835,000	1,509,700	1,798,953	1,111,272
2004	1,749,810	2,640,229	1,875	18,050	1,425,763	—		1,241,190	5,394,907	4,653,000	2,457,300	2,594,883	1,149,389
2005	2,516,093	3,918,850	1,783	25,750	1,706,520	449,600		1,320,783	5,345,047	4,132,000	3,032,800	3,508,548	1,104,734
2006	2,928,193	6,167,015	830	32,500	1,751,784	337,300		1,810,021	5,663,424	3,618,000	3,800,000	3,203,414	1,610,935
2007	3,378,038	5,100,530	1,709	36,030	2,262,374	543,600		2,165,938	6,709,381	4,613,000	4,500,000	4,217,500	2,291,106
2008	4,131,465	5,483,037	1,581	45,847	2,752,032	727,700		1,854,923	10,952,197	7,035,000	5,500,000	5,821,900	1,872,168
2009	3,761,267	8,377,828	936	42,746	3,046,032	664,700		1,144,136	11,424,283	5,816,000	4,950,000	4,817,900	1,597,827
2010	5,181,628	12,761,731	1,052	—	2,762,246	821,600		1,729,790	11,043,000	6,071,000	3,861,100	5,789,500	1,913,405

Sources: IBGE, *Estatísticas históricas do Brasil*; Ipeadata, Ministério do Desenvolvimento, Indústria e Comércio Exterior (aliceweb.desenvolvimento.gov.br); CEPLAC (www.ceplac.gov.br); and AFIC (www.afic.com.br).

TABLE A.6. *Brazilian Exports by Type of Product, 1964–2011 (in U.S.$ millions FOB)*

	Basics	Semimanufactured	Manufactured	Total
1964	1,221	115	89	1,430
1965	1,301	154	130	1,595
1966	1,444	141	152	1,741
1967	1,302	147	196	1,654
1968	1,492	178	202	1,881
1969	1,796	211	284	2,311
1970	2,049	249	416	2,738
1971	1,988	241	581	2,904
1972	2,649	399	898	3,991
1973	4,030	574	1,434	6,199
1974	4,577	917	2,147	7,951
1975	5,027	849	2,585	8,670
1976	6,129	842	2,776	10,128
1977	6,959	1,044	3,840	12,120
1978	5,978	1,421	5,083	12,659
1979	6,553	1,887	6,645	15,244
1980	8,488	2,349	9,028	20,132
1981	8,920	2,116	11,884	23,293
1982	8,238	1,433	10,253	20,175
1983	8,535	1,782	11,276	21,899
1984	8,706	2,872	15,132	27,005
1985	8,538	2,758	14,063	25,639
1986	7,280	2,491	12,404	22,349
1987	8,022	3,175	14,839	26,224
1988	9,411	4,892	19,187	33,789
1989	9,549	5,807	18,634	34,383
1990	8,746	5,108	17,011	31,414
1991	8,737	4,691	17,757	31,620
1992	8,830	5,750	20,754	35,793
1993	9,366	5,445	23,437	38,555
1994	11,058	6,893	24,959	43,545
1995	10,969	9,146	25,565	46,506
1996	11,900	8,613	26,413	47,747
1997	14,474	8,478	29,194	52,994
1998	12,977	8,120	29,387	51,140
1999	11,828	7,982	27,329	48,011
2000	12,562	8,499	32,528	55,086
2001	15,342	8,244	32,901	58,223
2002	16,952	8,964	33,001	60,362
2003	21,179	10,943	39,654	73,084
2004	28,518	13,431	52,948	96,475
2005	34,721	15,961	65,144	118,308
2006	40,285	19,523	75,018	137,807
2007	51,596	21,800	83,943	160,649
2008	73,028	27,073	92,682	197,942
2009	61,957	20,499	67,349	152,995
2010	90,005	28,207	79,563	201,915
2011	122,457	36,026	92,929	256,040

Source: Ministério do Desenvolvimento, Indústria e Comércio Exterior, Secretaria de Comércio Exterior – SECEX.

TABLE A.7. *Value of Industrial Production by States, 1907–1938*
(in contos de réis*)*

Years	Contos de réis			Contos réis of 1914 (1)		
	Brazil	São Paulo	Others	Brazil	São Paulo	Others
1907	741,536	118,087	623,449	–	–	–
1914	956,557	293,663	662,894	956,557	293,663	662,894
1915	1,215,820	379,336	836,484	1,215,820	379,336	836,484
1916	1,571,698	496,025	1,074,973	1,347,170	425,164	921,405
1917	2,424,193	778,166	1,646,027	1,887,540	605,900	1,281,639
1918	2,370,000	770,445	1,600,155	1,644,490	534,594	1,110,312
1919	2,989,176	986,110	2,003,066	2,005,894	661,732	1,344,163
1920	2,948,531	987,758	1,960,773	1,800,899	603,301	1,197,598
1921	3,020,631	1,023,994	1,996,637	1,791,304	607,252	1,184,052
1922	3,840,031	1,320,971	2,519,060	2,083,421	716,697	1,366,724
1923	5,895,551	2,051,652	3,843,899	2,905,054	1,010,959	1,894,095
1924	4,411,835	1,557,378	2,854,457	1,859,534	656,416	1,203,118
1925	4,326,070	1,544,407	2,781,663	1,710,307	610,580	1,099,727
1926	4,822,046	1,745,581	3,076,465	1,849,055	669,358	1,179,697
1927	5,566,663	2,037,399	3,529,264	2,079,852	761,226	1,318,626
1928	7,149,210	2,652,357	4,496,853	2,710,853	1,005,726	1,705,126
1929	6,723,442	2,521,291	4,202,151	2,568,506	963,190	1,605,316
1930	5,906,826	2,244,594	3,662,232	2,479,408	942,175	1,537,233
1931	5,806,406	2,229,660	3,576,746	2,530,997	971,903	1,559,094
1932	5,561,939	2,219,214	3,342,725	2,414,118	963,233	1,450,885
1933	5,953,045	2,339,547	3,613,498	2,606,054	1,024,179	1,581,875
1934	6,805,743	2,708,686	4,097,057	2,765,680	1,100,741	1,664,939
1935	8,438,728	3,392,369	5,046,359	3,248,114	1,305,742	1,942,372
1936	9,653,085	3,928,806	5,724,279	3,238,864	1,318,218	1,920,646
1937	11,234,610	4,617,425	6,617,185	3,603,554	1,481,061	2,122,493
1938	12,000,000	5,000,000	7,000,000	3,589,443	1,495,601	2,093,842

Source: *Anuário Estatístico do Brasil* (1939–1940), Apêndice Quadros Retrospectivos, p. 1318.

TABLE A.8. *Annual Indices of Industrial Production by Class and Type of Product, 1971–2000 (1991 = 100)*

	1971	1972	1973	1974	1975	1976	1977	1978	1979	1980
General Industries	–	–	–	–	72.11	80.69	82.42	87.48	93.57	102.17
Mineral Extraction	–	–	–	–	37.91	38.95	37.60	40.42	45.29	51.10
Manufacturing	49.58	56.51	65.88	71.00	73.71	82.65	84.53	89.69	95.84	104.57
Nonmetallic Minerals	46.75	53.31	62.00	71.17	77.58	87.20	93.43	98.65	104.45	112.53
Metallurgy	52.80	59.29	65.34	68.23	74.50	81.66	87.05	91.80	99.34	111.74
Mechanical	57.57	69.05	88.75	99.08	114.08	124.57	116.21	118.16	127.21	145.63
Electrical and Communication Materials	34.48	42.10	53.86	59.38	59.67	70.22	70.41	82.36	88.71	99.62
Transport Materials	54.58	66.87	85.32	101.40	101.92	110.93	110.60	122.11	130.27	136.14
Wood	–	–	–	–	–	–	–	–	–	–
Furniture	–	–	–	–	–	–	–	–	–	–
Paper and Cardboard	40.16	43.17	47.22	49.24	41.95	50.73	51.96	57.79	65.41	72.74
Rubber	39.42	44.55	54.50	64.42	67.47	74.93	73.42	78.99	84.69	92.61
Leather and Skins	–	–	–	–	–	–	–	–	–	–
Chemicals	39.95	46.73	57.64	60.74	62.26	72.31	75.96	81.77	89.42	93.97
Pharmaceuticals	–	–	–	–	81.21	91.90	77.03	78.12	82.44	92.06
Perfume, Soap, and Candles	28.04	30.61	32.61	36.36	37.70	43.44	42.00	46.79	53.84	58.71
Plastic Materials	34.05	40.29	51.67	63.64	66.90	80.75	80.99	88.55	94.34	107.96
Textiles	79.46	82.45	88.13	85.08	87.06	91.31	93.19	99.27	107.69	114.70
Clothes, Shoes, and Cloths	83.35	87.53	99.90	101.99	109.31	120.74	120.04	129.24	135.88	150.38
Food Products	48.82	56.73	62.19	65.58	65.50	73.87	78.76	77.90	77.59	84.10
Drinks	30.37	31.82	37.49	40.61	42.84	48.51	54.79	58.67	61.39	62.64
Tobacco	37.33	39.56	42.09	47.48	51.23	55.94	60.55	64.03	68.85	66.19

	1981	1982	1983	1984	1985	1986	1987	1988	1989	1990
General Industry	91.77	91.80	87.05	93.23	101.14	112.20	113.18	109.51	112.71	102.68
Mineral Extraction	49.96	53.43	61.68	80.48	89.82	93.13	92.43	92.78	96.45	99.09
Manufacturing	93.72	93.56	88.08	93.52	101.32	112.77	113.84	109.96	113.12	102.41
Nonmetallic Minerals	106.74	103.71	86.81	86.67	93.57	109.70	112.26	107.57	111.68	99.36
Metallurgy	92.74	89.36	87.03	99.02	106.27	118.96	119.47	115.59	121.39	106.07
Mechanical	117.16	96.95	84.00	99.76	110.08	134.28	139.70	127.68	134.04	111.44
Electrical and Communication Materials	84.32	86.67	77.09	78.63	93.60	114.74	112.18	107.20	113.28	107.04
Transport Materials	105.00	101.90	95.11	99.47	111.14	125.06	112.36	122.57	119.12	100.23
Wood	–	–	–	–	–	–	–	–	–	–
Furniture	–	–	–	–	–	–	–	–	–	–
Paper and Cardboard	67.73	72.62	73.84	78.90	84.02	92.81	96.18	94.66	99.98	93.73
Rubber	78.71	74.00	76.82	82.78	89.82	101.99	105.68	107.94	105.90	101.26
Leather and Skins	–	–	–	–	–	–	–	–	–	–
Chemicals	91.78	99.25	97.76	107.11	113.79	115.45	121.83	118.16	117.81	108.30
Pharmaceuticals	94.43	95.10	87.69	95.46	100.46	123.41	126.34	108.43	113.50	102.48
Perfume, Soap, and Candles	59.50	61.62	62.42	61.73	71.57	85.88	96.40	88.84	99.08	93.45
Plastic Materials	85.83	93.65	84.11	87.72	97.80	118.93	113.94	105.71	118.78	100.24
Textiles	98.95	103.92	92.89	89.53	101.63	115.37	114.68	107.67	108.20	97.25
Clothes, Shoes, and Cloths	149.45	153.96	133.84	136.80	145.55	156.11	141.11	131.55	133.99	115.23
Food Products	85.93	87.04	89.87	89.26	89.45	89.77	95.89	93.62	94.81	96.54
Drinks	57.90	56.53	53.68	53.40	59.29	73.03	70.53	72.22	82.84	84.73
Tobacco	68.62	71.53	70.30	72.62	81.13	87.18	89.01	89.87	94.47	93.19

(*continued*)

TABLE A.8 (continued)

	1991	1992	1993	1994	1995	1996	1997	1998	1999	2000
General Industry	100.00	96.27	103.50	111.37	113.41	115.37	119.85	117.42	116.66	124.28
Mineral Extraction	100.00	100.77	101.40	106.20	109.69	120.39	129.09	145.16	158.35	177.25
Manufacturing	100.00	95.92	103.66	111.77	113.70	114.98	119.13	115.25	113.39	120.13
Nonmetallic Minerals	100.00	92.32	96.85	99.82	103.91	110.48	118.63	118.20	114.51	116.57
Metallurgy	100.00	99.36	107.02	117.91	115.81	117.66	124.72	119.96	118.66	127.72
Mechanical	100.00	90.52	106.23	128.61	122.77	107.05	114.74	110.12	102.22	120.67
Electrical and Communication Materials	100.00	87.35	99.80	118.73	136.06	142.48	139.95	126.18	111.76	125.11
Transport Materials	100.00	97.84	118.16	134.04	139.47	139.00	153.84	132.02	125.22	148.71
Wood	100.00	98.80	105.55	102.80	99.35	101.45	105.38	98.88	105.79	109.04
Furniture	100.00	88.44	106.48	107.72	114.42	130.13	128.17	117.70	115.13	124.04
Paper and Cardboard	100.00	97.99	102.73	105.59	106.04	109.16	112.28	112.66	119.72	124.60
Rubber	100.00	99.92	109.17	113.56	113.21	112.66	117.33	108.36	113.38	126.72
Leather and Skins	100.00	96.89	107.09	102.48	85.37	83.72	82.33	71.16	68.61	63.08
Chemicals	100.00	99.54	103.81	110.69	110.15	115.67	121.54	126.38	127.53	129.65
Pharmaceuticals	100.00	88.75	99.73	97.28	114.93	105.08	117.02	121.72	121.22	118.80
Perfume, Soap, and Candles	100.00	99.40	103.82	106.37	112.01	116.60	122.64	126.53	135.63	139.15
Plastic Materials	100.00	88.66	95.50	99.44	109.14	121.50	125.87	122.81	115.10	112.05
Textiles	100.00	95.49	95.06	98.67	92.99	87.61	81.89	76.30	77.94	82.62
Clothes, Shoes, and Cloths	100.00	92.35	102.11	99.96	93.09	90.75	84.69	80.77	78.08	82.57
Food Products	100.00	99.92	100.47	102.71	110.62	116.46	117.62	119.18	122.94	119.81
Drinks	100.00	83.35	90.59	100.03	117.19	113.29	112.93	110.46	110.44	114.59
Tobacco	100.00	117.72	122.91	104.74	99.39	111.80	136.67	105.61	98.09	90.45

Source: IBGE, *Estatísticas do século XX*, Table "7_25u_ind1971_00."

TABLE A.9. Distribution of the Population by State and Region in the Demographic Censuses of Brazil, 1872–2010

Region and State	1872	1890	1900	1920	1940	1950	1960	1970	1980	1991	2000	2010
Brazil	9,930,478	14,333,915	17,438,434	30,635,605	41,236,315	51,944,397	70,992,343	94,508,583	121,150,573	146,917,459	169,590,693	190,755,799
Norte	332,847	476,370	695,112	1,439,052	1,627,608	2,048,696	2,930,005	4,188,313	6,767,249	10,257,266	12,893,561	15,864,454
Rondônia	–	–	–	–	–	36,935	70,783	116,620	503,125	1,130,874	1,377,792	1,562,409
Acre	–	–	–	92,379	79,768	114,755	160,208	218,006	306,893	417,165	557,226	733,559
Amazonas	57,610	147,915	249,756	363,166	438,008	514,099	721,215	960,934	1,449,135	2,102,901	2,813,085	3,483,985
Roraima	–	–	–	–	–	18,116	29,489	41,638	82,018	215,950	324,152	450,479
Pará	275,237	328,455	445,356	983,507	944,644	1,123,273	1,550,935	2,197,072	3,507,312	5,181,570	6,189,550	7,581,051
Amapá	–	–	–	–	–	37,477	68,889	116,480	180,078	288,690	475,843	669,526
Tocantins	–	–	–	–	165,188	204,041	328,486	537,563	738,688	920,116	1,155,913	1,383,445
Nordeste	4,638,560	6,002,047	6,749,507	11,245,921	14,434,080	17,973,413	22,428,873	28,675,110	35,419,156	42,470,225	47,693,253	53,081,950
Maranhão	359,040	430,854	499,308	874,337	1,235,169	1,583,248	2,492,139	3,037,135	4,097,231	4,929,029	5,642,960	6,574,789
Piauí	202,222	267,609	334,328	609,003	817,601	1,045,696	1,263,368	1,734,894	2,188,150	2,581,215	2,841,202	3,118,360
Ceará	721,686	805,687	849,127	1,319,228	2,091,032	2,695,450	3,337,856	4,491,590	5,380,432	6,362,620	7,418,476	8,452,381
Rio Grande do Norte	233,979	268,273	274,317	537,135	768,018	967,921	1,157,258	1,611,606	1,933,126	2,414,121	2,771,538	3,168,027
Paraíba	376,226	457,232	490,784	961,106	1,422,282	1,713,259	2,018,023	2,445,419	2,810,032	3,200,677	3,439,344	3,766,528
Pernambuco	841,539	1,030,224	1,178,150	2,154,835	2,688,240	3,395,766	4,138,289	5,253,901	6,244,275	7,122,548	7,911,937	8,796,448
Alagoas	348,009	511,440	649,273	978,748	951,300	1,093,137	1,271,062	1,606,174	2,011,875	2,512,991	2,819,172	3,120,494
Sergipe	176,243	310,926	356,264	477,064	542,326	644,361	760,273	911,251	1,156,642	1,491,867	1,781,714	2,068,017
Bahia	1,379,616	1,919,802	2,117,956	3,334,465	3,918,112	4,834,575	5,990,605	7,583,140	9,597,393	11,855,157	13,066,910	14,016,906
Sudeste	4,016,922	6,104,384	7,824,011	13,654,934	18,345,831	22,548,494	31,062,978	40,331,969	52,580,527	62,660,700	72,297,351	80,364,410
Minas Gerais	2,039,735	3,184,099	3,594,471	5,888,174	6,763,368	7,782,188	9,960,040	11,645,095	13,651,852	15,731,961	17,866,402	19,597,330
Espírito Santo	82,137	135,997	209,783	457,328	790,149	957,238	1,418,348	1,617,857	2,063,679	2,598,505	3,094,390	3,514,952
Rio de Janeiro	1,057,696	1,399,535	1,737,478	2,717,244	3,611,998	4,674,645	6,709,891	9,110,324	11,489,797	12,783,761	14,367,083	15,989,929
São Paulo	837,354	1,384,753	2,282,279	4,592,188	7,180,316	9,134,423	12,974,699	17,958,693	25,375,199	31,546,473	36,969,476	41,262,199
Sul	721,337	1,430,715	1,796,495	3,537,167	5,735,305	7,840,870	11,892,107	16,683,551	19,380,126	22,117,026	25,089,783	27,386,891
Paraná	126,722	249,491	327,136	685,711	1,236,276	2,115,547	4,296,375	6,997,682	7,749,752	8,443,299	9,558,454	10,444,526
Santa Catarina	159,802	283,769	320,289	668,743	1,178,340	1,560,502	2,146,909	2,930,411	3,687,652	4,538,248	5,349,580	6,248,436
Rio Grande do Sul	434,813	897,455	1,149,070	2,182,713	3,320,689	4,164,821	5,448,823	6,755,458	7,942,722	9,135,479	10,181,749	10,693,929
Centro-Oeste	220,812	320,399	373,309	758,531	1,093,491	1,532,924	2,678,380	4,629,640	7,003,515	9,412,242	11,616,745	14,058,094
Mato Grosso do Sul	–	–	–	–	–	238,640	309,395	579,652	1,401,151	1,778,741	2,074,877	2,449,024
Mato Grosso	60,417	92,827	118,025	246,612	193,625	212,649	330,610	612,887	1,169,812	2,022,524	2,502,260	3,035,122
Goiás	160,395	227,572	255,284	511,919	661,226	1,010,880	1,626,376	2,460,007	3,229,219	4,012,562	4,996,439	6,003,788
Districto Federal	–	–	–	–	–	–	141,742	546,015	1,203,333	1,598,415	2,043,169	2,570,160

Source: IBGE, Censo Demográfico, 2010, Sinopse, available at http://www.sidra.ibge.gov.br/cd/cd2010sp.asp?o=5&i=P.

383

TABLE A.10. *Origin of Brazilian Transoceanic Immigrants, 1820–1972*

Year	Portuguese	Italians	Spaniards	Germans	Japanese	Others	TOTAL
1820	–	–	–	–	–	1,682	1,682
1821	–	–	–	–	–	–	–
1822	–	–	–	–	–	–	–
1823	–	–	–	–	–	–	–
1824	–	–	–	–	–	126	126
1825	–	–	–	–	–	909	909
1826	–	–	–	–	–	828	828
1827	–	–	–	–	–	1,088	1,088
1828	–	–	–	1,261	–	799	2,060
1829	–	–	–	723	–	1,689	2,412
1830	–	–	–	–	–	–	–
1831	–	–	–	–	–	–	–
1832	–	–	–	–	–	–	–
1833	–	–	–	–	–	–	–
1834	–	–	–	–	–	–	–
1835	–	–	–	–	–	–	–
1836	–	180	–	–	–	1,000	1,180
1837	–	–	–	207	–	277	484
1838	–	–	–	–	–	396	396
1839	141	–	–	–	–	248	389
1840	206	–	–	63	–	–	269
1841	159	–	10	191	–	195	555
1842	48	–	–	332	–	188	568
1843	–	–	–	–	–	694	694
1844	–	–	–	–	–	–	–
1845	–	–	–	53	–	–	53
1846	–	–	–	–	–	435	435
1847	78	5	–	1,500	–	767	2,350
1848	–	–	–	–	–	28	28
1849	–	–	–	–	–	40	40
1850	178	–	122	643	–	1,129	2,072
1851	53	–	5	400	–	3,967	4,425
1852	231	2	17	1,221	–	1,260	2,731
1853	8,329	22	–	2,214	–	370	10,935
1854	7,384	–	–	846	–	959	9,189
1855	9,839	–	–	532	–	1,427	11,798
1856	9,159	–	37	1,822	–	2,990	14,008
1857	9,340	–	–	2,639	–	2,265	14,244
1858	9,327	–	–	2,333	–	6,869	18,529
1859	9,342	–	–	3,165	–	7,607	20,114
1860	5,914	–	–	3,748	–	6,112	15,774
1861	6,460	–	–	2,211	–	4,332	13,003

Appendix 385

Year	Portuguese	Italians	Spaniards	Germans	Japanese	Others	TOTAL
1862	5,625	431	–	4,037	–	4,202	14,295
1863	4,420	–	–	367	–	2,855	7,642
1864	5,097	2,092	83	234	–	2,072	9,578
1865	3,784	500	–	275	–	1,893	6,452
1866	4,724	–	–	360	–	2,615	7,699
1867	4,822	–	–	1,128	–	4,952	10,902
1868	4,425	841	218	3,779	–	2,052	11,315
1869	6,347	1,052	332	375	–	3,421	11,527
1870	4,458	7	38	6	–	649	5,158
1871	8,124	1,626	510	296	–	1,875	12,431
1872	12,918	1,808	727	1,103	–	2,663	19,219
1873	1,310	–	–	1,082	–	12,350	14,742
1874	6,644	5	–	1,435	–	12,248	20,332
1875	3,692	1,171	39	1,308	–	8,380	14,590
1876	7,421	6,820	763	3,530	–	12,213	30,747
1877	7,965	13,582	23	2,310	–	5,588	29,468
1878	6,236	11,836	929	1,535	–	3,920	24,456
1879	8,841	10,245	911	2,022	–	764	22,783
1880	12,101	12,936	1,275	2,385	–	1,658	30,355
1881	3,144	2,705	2,677	1,851	–	1,171	11,548
1882	10,621	12,428	3,961	1,804	–	775	29,589
1883	12,509	15,724	2,660	2,348	–	774	34,015
1884	8,683	10,502	710	1,719	–	1,960	23,574
1885	7,611	21,765	952	2,848	–	1,548	34,724
1886	6,287	20,430	1,617	2,114	–	2,202	32,650
1887	10,205	40,157	1,766	1,147	–	1,657	54,932
1888	18,289	104,353	4,736	782	–	3,910	132,070
1889	15,240	36,124	9,712	1,903	–	2,186	65,165
1890	25,174	31,275	12,008	4,812	–	33,550	106,819
1891	32,349	132,326	22,146	5,285	–	23,133	215,239
1892	17,797	55,049	10,471	800	–	1,789	85,906
1893	28,986	58,552	38,998	1,368	–	4,685	132,589
1894	17,041	34,872	5,986	790	–	1,493	60,182
1895	36,055	97,344	17,641	973	–	12,818	164,831
1896	22,299	96,505	24,154	1,070	–	13,395	157,423
1897	13,558	104,510	19,466	930	–	6,402	144,866
1898	15,105	49,086	8,024	535	–	4,112	76,862
1899	10,989	30,846	5,399	521	–	5,855	53,610
1900	8,250	19,671	4,834	217	–	4,835	37,807
1901	11,261	59,869	212	166	–	11,608	83,116
1902	11,606	32,111	3,588	265	–	2,902	50,472
1903	11,378	12,970	4,466	1,231	–	2,896	32,941
1904	17,318	12,857	10,046	797	–	3,688	44,706

(*continued*)

TABLE A.10 *(continued)*

Year	Portuguese	Italians	Spaniards	Germans	Japanese	Others	TOTAL
1905	20,181	17,360	25,329	650	–	4,968	68,488
1906	21,706	20,777	24,441	1,333	–	4,075	72,332
1907	25,681	18,238	9,235	845	–	3,920	57,919
1908	37,628	13,873	14,862	2,931	830	20,412	90,536
1909	30,577	13,668	16,219	5,413	31	18,182	84,090
1910	30,857	14,163	20,843	3,902	948	16,038	86,751
1911	47,493	22,914	27,141	4,251	28	31,748	133,575
1912	76,530	31,785	35,492	5,733	2,909	25,438	177,887
1913	76,701	30,886	41,064	8,004	7,122	26,556	190,333
1914	27,935	15,542	18,945	2,811	3,675	10,324	79,232
1915	15,118	5,779	5,895	169	65	3,307	30,333
1916	11,981	5,340	10,306	364	165	3,089	31,245
1917	6,817	5,478	11,113	201	3,899	2,769	30,277
1918	7,981	1,050	4,225	1	5,599	937	19,793
1919	17,068	5,231	6,627	466	3,022	3,613	36,027
1920	33,883	10,005	9,136	4,120	1,013	10,885	69,042
1921	19,981	10,779	9,523	7,915	840	9,438	58,476
1922	28,622	11,277	8,869	5,038	1,225	9,976	65,007
1923	31,866	15,839	10,140	8,254	895	17,555	84,549
1924	23,267	13,844	7,238	22,168	2,673	26,862	96,052
1925	21,508	9,846	10,062	7,175	6,330	27,626	82,547
1926	38,791	11,977	8,892	7,674	8,407	42,945	118,686
1927	31,236	12,487	9,070	4,878	9,084	31,219	97,974
1928	33,882	5,493	4,436	4,228	11,169	18,920	78,128
1929	38,879	5,288	4,565	4,351	16,648	26,455	96,186
1930	18,740	4,253	3,218	4,180	14,076	18,143	62,610
1931	8,152	2,914	1,784	2,621	5,632	6,362	27,465
1932	8,499	2,155	1,447	2,273	11,678	5,442	31,494
1933	10,695	1,920	1,693	2,180	24,494	5,099	46,081
1934	8,732	2,507	1,429	3,629	21,930	7,800	46,027
1935	9,327	2,127	1,206	2,423	9,611	4,891	29,585
1936	4,626	462	355	1,226	3,306	2,798	12,773
1937	11,417	2,946	1,150	4,642	4,557	9,965	34,677
1938	7,435	1,882	290	2,348	2,524	4,909	19,388
1939	15,120	1,004	174	1,975	1,414	2,981	22,668
1940	11,737	411	409	1,155	1,268	3,469	18,449
1941	5,777	89	125	453	1,548	1,946	9,938
1942	1,317	3	37	9	–	1,059	2,425
1943	146	1	9	2	–	1,150	1,308
1944	419	3	30	–	–	1,141	1,593
1945	1,414	180	74	22	–	1,478	3,168
1946	6,342	1,059	203	174	6	5,255	13,039

Year	Portuguese	Italians	Spaniards	Germans	Japanese	Others	TOTAL
1947	8,921	3,284	653	561	1	5,333	18,753
1948	2,751	4,437	965	2,308	1	11,106	21,568
1949	6,780	6,352	2,197	2,123	4	6,388	23,844
1950	14,739	7,342	3,808	2,725	33	6,845	35,492
1951	28,731	8,285	9,636	2,858	106	12,978	62,594
1952	40,561	15,254	14,082	2,326	261	12,236	84,720
1953	30,675	16,379	17,010	2,149	1,255	12,602	80,070
1954	30,062	13,408	11,338	1,952	3,119	12,369	72,248
1955	21,264	8,945	10,738	1,122	4,051	9,046	55,166
1956	16,803	6,069	7,921	844	4,912	8,257	44,806
1957	19,471	7,197	7,680	952	6,147	12,166	53,613
1958	21,928	4,819	5,768	825	6,586	9,913	49,839
1959	17,345	4,233	6,712	890	7,123	8,217	44,520
1960	13,105	3,431	7,662	842	7,746	7,721	40,507
1961	15,819	2,493	9,813	703	6,824	7,937	43,589
1962	13,713	1,900	4,968	651	3,257	6,649	31,138
1963	11,585	867	2,436	601	2,124	6,246	23,859
1964	4,249	476	616	323	1,138	3,193	9,995
1965	3,262	642	550	365	903	4,116	9,838
1966	2,708	643	469	377	937	3,041	8,175
1967	3,838	747	572	550	1,070	4,575	11,352
1968	3,917	738	743	723	597	5,803	12,521
1969	1,933	477	568	524	496	2,615	6,613
1970	1,773	357	546	535	435	3,241	6,887
1971	807	254	281	354	260	4,422	6,378
1972	493	193	122	161	–	1,354	2,323
	1,790,194	1,629,249	717,424	260,478	248,007	955,904	5,601,256

Note: We have included Austrians with Germans.

Sources: 1872–1972, from Levy 1974, "O Papel da Migracao Internacional na evolucao da populacao brasileira (1872 a 1972)," Table 1, pp. 71–73; 1820–1871 from Directoria Geral de Estatistica, Boletim Commemorativo da Exposicao Nacional de 1908, pp. 82–85.

TABLE A.11. *Estimate of Brazilian Population Change, 1980–2050, IBGE Projections of 2008*

Years	Population	Average Geometric Rate of Growth (%)	Crude Birth Rates (per 1,000 inhabitants)	Crude Death Rates (per 1,000 inhabitants)
1980	118,562,549		32.13	8.57
1981	121,381,328	2.350	31.85	8.42
1982	124,250,840	2.337	31.54	8.24
1983	127,140,354	2.299	30.73	8.05
1984	130,082,524	2.288	30.94	7.87
1985	132,999,282	2.217	28.99	7.68
1986	135,814,249	2.094	28.08	7.49
1987	138,585,894	2.020	27.16	7.34
1988	141,312,997	1.949	26.36	7.20
1989	143,997,246	1.882	25.56	7.08
1990	146,592,579	1.786	24.21	6.95
1991	149,094,266	1.692	23.42	6.83
1992	151,546,843	1.632	22.79	6.74
1993	153,985,576	1.596	22.55	6.67
1994	156,430,949	1.576	22.23	6.60
1995	158,874,963	1.550	21.93	6.55
1996	161,323,169	1.529	21.72	6.51
1997	163,779,827	1.511	21.49	6.47
1998	166,252,088	1.498	21.37	6.42
1999	168,753,552	1.493	21.30	6.38
2000	171,279,882	1.486	21.13	6.34
2001	173,808,010	1.465	20.84	6.33
2002	176,303,919	1.426	20.33	6.32
2003	178,741,412	1.373	19.76	6.30
2004	181,105,601	1.314	19.12	6.29
2005	183,383,216	1.250	18.45	6.28
2006	185,564,212	1.182	17.75	6.27
2007	187,641,714	1.113	17.06	6.27
2008	189,612,814	1.045	16.38	6.27
2009	191,480,630	0.980	15.77	6.27
2010	193,252,604	0.921	15.20	6.27
2011	194,932,685	0.866	14.68	6.29
2012	196,526,293	0.814	14.22	6.32
2013	198,043,320	0.769	13.82	6.34
2014	199,492,433	0.729	13.48	6.37
2015	200,881,685	0.694	13.19	6.41
2016	202,219,061	0.664	12.96	6.46
2017	203,510,422	0.637	12.76	6.52

Appendix

Years	Population	Average Geometric Rate of Growth (%)	Crude Birth Rates (per 1,000 inhabitants)	Crude Death Rates (per 1,000 inhabitants)
2018	204,759,993	0.612	12.59	6.59
2019	205,970,182	0.589	12.43	6.65
2020	207,143,243	0.568	12.29	6.71
2021	208,280,241	0.547	12.16	6.79
2022	209,380,331	0.527	12.03	6.86
2023	210,441,362	0.505	11.89	6.94
2024	211,459,352	0.483	11.73	7.03
2025	212,430,049	0.458	11.57	7.11
2026	213,348,475	0.431	11.39	7.22
2027	214,209,414	0.403	11.20	7.32
2028	215,008,982	0.373	11.01	7.44
2029	215,743,582	0.341	10.80	7.55
2030	216,410,030	0.308	10.59	7.68
2031	217,004,993	0.275	10.38	7.81
2032	217,526,053	0.24	10.18	7.95
2033	217,972,789	0.205	9.98	8.10
2034	218,345,419	0.171	9.79	8.25
2035	218,644,711	0.137	9.61	8.41
2036	218,870,898	0.103	9.44	8.58
2037	219,024,784	0.07	9.29	8.75
2038	219,108,650	0.038	9.15	8.93
2039	219,124,700	0.007	9.02	9.10
2040	219,075,130	−0.023	8.91	9.28
2041	218,960,969	−0.052	8.81	9.47
2042	218,783,084	−0.081	8.71	9.67
2043	218,543,546	−0.11	8.62	9.86
2044	218,244,527	−0.137	8.54	10.05
2045	217,888,409	−0.163	8.47	10.23
2046	217,476,404	−0.189	8.39	10.42
2047	217,009,177	−0.215	8.32	10.60
2048	216,488,045	−0.24	8.25	10.78
2049	215,913,883	−0.266	8.17	10.96
2050	215,287,463	−0.291	8.10	11.13

Notes: Projection of the Brazilian population for July 1, 2050 (revision 2008) on the basis of five-year age cohorts in July 1, 1980, with a total fertility rate limit = 1.5 children; without international migration and the official mortality 1980–2000 IBGE/CELADE; 2001–2050 PROJEÇÃO IBGE.

Source: IBGE, Projeção da População do Brasil por Sexo e Idade para o Período 1980–2050 – Revisão 2008; available at ftp://ftp.ibge.gov.br/Estimativas_Projecoes_Populacao/Revisao_2008_Projecoes_1980_2050/.

TABLE A.12. *Religion of the Brazilian Population, 1872–2010*

Year	Roman Catholic	Protestant	Spiritist	Nonreligious	Unknown or Other Religions	Total Population
1872	9,902,712	–	–	–	27,766	9,930,478
1890	14,179,615	143,743	–	7,257	3,300	14,333,915
1940	39,177,880	1,074,857	463,400	189,304	330,874	41,236,315
1950	48,558,854	1,741,430	824,553	412,042	407,518	51,944,397
1960	65,329,520	2,824,775	977,561	388,126	1,472,361	70,992,343
1970	85,472,022	4,814,728	1,178,293	715,056	2,328,484	94,508,583
1980	105,861,113	7,885,846	1,538,230	2,252,782	3,612,602	121,150,573
1991	122,366,692	13,189,284	2,292,819	7,542,246	1,526,418	146,917,459
2000	124,980,132	26,184,941	2,262,401	12,876,356	3,286,863	169,590,693
2010	123,280,172	42,275,440	3,848,876	15,335,510	6,015,801	190,755,799

Sources: For data from 1872 to 2000, IBGE, Table "POP60 População por religião," available at http://seriesestatisticas.ibge.gov.br/lista_tema.aspx?op=0&no=10, and for census 2010 Table 2094, "População residente por cor ou raça e religião," available at http://www.sidra.ibge.gov.br/cd/cd2010CGP.asp?o=13&i=P.

TABLE A.13. *Number of Students Enrolled in Higher Education by Type of Institution, 1960–2010*

		MATRICULATIONS				
			PUBLIC			PRIVATE
Total	TOTAL	Total	Federal	State	Municipal	Private
1960	93,000	52,000				41,000
1970	425,478	210,613				214,865
1975	1,072,548	410,225	248,849	107,111	54,265	662,323
1980	1,377,286	492,232	316,715	109,252	66,265	885,054
1985	1,367,609	556,680	326,522	146,816	83,342	810,929
1990	1,540,080	578,625	308,867	194,417	75,341	961,455
1995	1,759,703	700,540	367,531	239,215	93,794	1,059,163
2000	2,694,245	887,026	482,750	332,104	72,172	1,807,219
2001	3,036,113	944,584	504,797	360,537	79,250	2,091,529
2002	3,520,627	1,085,977	543,598	437,927	104,452	2,434,650
2003	3,936,933	1,176,174	583,633	465,978	126,563	2,760,759
2004	4,223,344	1,214,317	592,705	489,529	132,083	3,009,027
2005	4,567,798	1,246,704	595,327	514,726	136,651	3,321,094
2006	4,883,852	1,251,365	607,180	502,826	141,359	3,632,487
2007	5,250,147	1,335,177	641,094	550,089	143,994	3,914,970
2008	5,808,017	1,552,953	698,319	710,175	144,459	4,255,064
2009	5,954,021	1,523,864	839,397	566,204	118,263	4,430,157
2010	6,379,299	1,643,298	938,656	601,112	103,530	4,736,001

Sources: For years up to 2000, see Pinto 2004, "O acesso à educação superior no Brasil," Table 2, p. 731; for years 2001–2010, see MEC, INEP, *Censo da Educação Superior 2010* (Outubro 2011), Table 2, p. 8.

Bibliography

Government Publications

Anuário Estatístico do Brasil (Rio de Janeiro: IBGE, various years).
Anuário Estatístico de Crédito Rural de 1999 (Brasília: Banco Central do Brasil, 1999).
Banco do Brasil, Diretoria de Agronegócios, "Evolução histórica do crédito rural," *Revista de Politica Agricola* XII.4 (Outubro–Dezembro 2004), 10–17.
Banco Central. Available at www.bcb.gov.br/?RELRURAL.
Banco Central do Brasil. Available at http://www.bcb.gov.br/?INDECO.
―――. *Anuário Estatístico de Crédito Rural de 2010* (Brasília: Banco Central do Brasil, 2010).
CELADE. *Los adultos mayores en América Latina y el Caribe datos e indicadores* (Boletín Informativo, Edición Especial; Santiago de Chile, 2002).
―――. *Boletín Demográfico*, various years.
―――. "Estimaciones y Proyecciones de Población, 1950–2050, Brasil, Población Total, Indicadores del crecimiento demográfico estimados y proyectados por quinquenios, 1950–2050." Available at http://www.eclac.cl/celade/proyecciones/intentoBD-2002.htm.
CENSO 1872: Quadros do Império. As reproduced and recalculated by NEPO/UNICAMP.
CEPAL. Anuario estadístico de América Latina y el Caribe, various years.
Comissão Mista Brasil-EEUU. Brasileiros e Americanos Estudam Problemas do Brasil. As soluções indicadas pela Comissão Mista Brasil-EEUU. Um capítulo da história econômica do nosso país (Rio de Janeiro: CPDOC/FGV). Available at http://www.centrocelsofurtado.org.br/arquivos/image/201109231638540.MD2_0_277_1.pdf.
DATASUS. Available at http://www2.datasus.gov.br/DATASUS/.
Directoria General de Estatistica. *Recenseamento do Brazil realizado em 1 de Setembro de 1920* (Rio de Janeiro: Typ. da Estatistica, 1922).

———. *Sexo, raça e estado civil, nacionalidade, filiação culto e analfabetismo da população recenseada em 31 em Dezembro de 1890* (Rio de Janeiro: Officina da Estatística, 1898).
Discourse of the Assuming the Presidency of Janio Quadros. Available at http://brasilrepublicano.com.br/fontes/30.pdf.
Dívida Pública Mobiliária Reestruturada. Tesouro Nacional. Available at http://www.stn.fazenda.gov.br/divida_publica/downloads/div_r_bib.pdf.
EUROSTAT. "Employment rate by gender, age group 15–64." Available at http://epp.eurostat.ec.europa.eu/tgm/table.do?tab=table&init=1&plugin=1&language=en&pcode=tsiem010.
———. Table "Life expectancy at birth by gender." Updated December 16, 2011 and available at http://epp.eurostat.ec.europa.eu/tgm/table.do?tab=table&init=1&plugin=1&language=en&pcode=tps00025.
———. Table "Mean age of women at childbirth." Updated December 19, 2011 and available at http://epp.eurostat.ec.europa.eu/tgm/table.do?tab=table&init=1&plugin=1&language=en&pcode=tps00017.
FAO. *State of the World's Forests 2011* (Rome: Food and Agriculture Organization of the United Nations, 2011).
Fundação Getúlio Vargas, *Conjuntura Econômica* 25,9 (Rio de Janeiro, Setembro, 1991).
IBGE. *Pesquisa Nacional por Amostra de Domicílios, Síntese de indicadores 2011* (Rio de Janeiro: IBGE, 2012).
———. *Síntese de indicadores sociais. Uma análise das condições de vida da população brasileira, 2010* (Rio de Janeiro: IBGE, 2012).
———. *Censo Demográfico 2010 Características da população e dos domicílios, Resultados do universo* (Rio de Janeiro: IBGE, 2011).
———. *Censo Demográfico 2010 Sinopse do Censo e Resultados Preliminares do Universo* (Rio de Janeiro: IBGE, 2011).
———. *Sinopse do Censo Demográfico 2010* (Rio de Janeiro: IBGE, 2011).
———. *Censo Demográfico 2010 Famílias e domicílios Resultados da Amostra* (Rio de Janeiro: IBGE, 2010).
———. *Censo Demográfico 2010, Nupcialidade, fecundidade e migração Resultados da amostra* (Rio de Janeiro: IBGE, 2010).
———. *Censo Demográfico 2010 – Resultados Preliminares da Amostra* (Rio de Janeiro: IBGE, 2010).
———. *Pesquisa Nacional por Amostra de Domicílios, PNAD 2008* (Rio de Janeiro: IBGE, 2008).
———. *Projeção da população do Brasil por sexo e idade 1980–2050, Revisão 2008* (Rio de Janeiro: IBGE, 2008).
———. *Perfil das Mães* Comunicação Social, Maio 6, 2005. Available at http://www.ibge.gov.br/home/presidencia/noticias/noticia_impressao.php?id_noticia=357.
———. *Estatísticas do século XX* (Rio de Janeiro: IBGE, 2003).
———. *Censo Demográfico 2000: Resultados Do Universo, Características Da População e Dos Domicílios* (Rio de Janeiro: Instituto Brasileiro de Geografia e Estatística, 2001).

———. *Estatísticas históricas do Brasil, Séries Estatísticas Retrospectivas*, Vol. 3, *Séries Econômicas, Demográficas e Sociais de 1550 a 1988* (2nd ed. rev. and updated, 1990).

———. *IX Recenseamento Geral do Brasil 1980* (Rio de Janeiro: IBGE, 1983).

———. *Sinopse Preliminar do Censo Demográfico, IX Recenseamento geral – 1980* (Rio de Janeiro: IBGE, 1981).

———. *Recenseamento Geral do Brasil de 1950* (Rio de Janeiro: IBGE, 1953).

———. *Recenseamento Geral do Brasil, 1. de Setembro de 1940 (Rio de Janeiro: IBGE, 1950–1952), various volumes.*

———. *Recenseamento Geral do Brasil, 1. de Setembro de 1940: Sinopse do Censo Demográfico, Dados Gerais* (Rio de Janeiro: Serviço Gráfico do Instituto Brasileiro de Geografia e Estatistica, 1946).

———. *Anuário Estatístico do Brasil (1939–1940)* (Rio de Janeiro: IBGE, 1941).

———. *Estatísticas do Século XX*. Available at http://www.ibge.gov.br/seculoxx/ arquivos_xls/populacao.shtm.

INEP. *Sinopse Estatística do Ensino Superior Graduação – 1999*, and *Censo da Educação Superior 2010*. Both available at http://portal.inep.gov.br/ superior-censosuperior-sinopse.

Infomoney: Pesquisa sobre endividamento das famílias.

Informe de Previdência Social, various years and issues.

IPEA. *Políticas sociais: acompanhamento e análise*, Vol. 19 (2011).

Ipeadata. Available at http://www.Ipeadata.gov.br/.

MEC, INEP. *Censo da educação superior 2010* (Outubro 2011).

Ministério da Agricultura. Available at www.agricultura.gov.br.

Ministério da Agricultura, Indústria e Comércio. *Indústria assucareira no Brazil* (Rio de Janeiro: Directoria Geral de Estatística, 1919).

Ministério do Desenvolvimento Social. Available at http://www.mds.gov.br/ bolsafamilia.

OECD. "Data for Chart SF2.3.A: Mean age of women at the birth of the first child, 2009." Available at http://www.oecd.org/document/4/0,3746,en_ 2649_37419_37836996_1_1_1_37419,00.html.

Prounancement of the Minister Ministro Martus Tavares. "Forum Internacional sobre Responsabilidade e Transparência no Setor Público," Brasília, December 5, 2001. Available at http://www.bndes.gov.br/SiteBNDES/export/sites/ default/bndes_pt/Galerias/Arquivos/bf_bancos/e0001733.pdf.

Recenseamento do…1920. IV, Part 1 (população), Table 1, "População brasileira e estrangeira dos estados, 1872, 1890, 1900, 1920," lxiii.

REDE Interagencial de Informação para a Saúde. *Indicadores básicos para a saúde no Brasil: conceitos e aplicações*, 2nd ed. (Brasília: Organização Pan-Americana da Saúde, 2008). *Relatório apresentado ao Presidente dos Estados Unidos do Brazil pelo Ministério de Estado dos Negócios da Fazenda no anno de 1900* (Rio de Janeiro: Imprensa Nacional).

Relatório do Ministério da Fazenda de 1949 (Rio de Janeiro, 1949).

Relatório do Ministério dos Negócios do Império 1871 Apresentado Em Maio De 1872.

São Paulo, Censo Agrícola de 1905. Available in digital format from the Núcleo de Estudos de População (NEPO), of the Universidade de Campinas.
SEADE. Anuário Estatístico do Estado de São Paulo, various years.
Statistics of Railways in the United States (Washington, DC: Government Printing Office, 1894). Available at http://archive.org/stream/sixthannualrepo00govegoog#page/n6/mode/2up.
Tesouro Nacional. Available at http://www.tesouro.fazenda.gov.br/estatistica/index.asp.
World Bank. *Management of Agriculture, Rural Development and Natural Resources.* 2 vols. (Washington, DC: World Bank, 1994).
World Health Organization. *World Health Statistics 2011* (Geneva, Switzerland: World Health Organization, 2012).

Books and Articles

Abranches, Sérgio H. "Governo, empresa estatal e política siderúrgica: 1930–1975," in *As origens da crise: Estado autoritário e planejamento no Brasil,* ed. Olavo Brasil de Lima Jr. and Sérgio H. Abranches (São Paulo: IUPERJ/Vértice, 1987), 158–193.
Abreu, Marcelo de Paiva. "Os Funding Loans Brasileiros, 1898–1931," *Pesquisa e Planejamento Econômico* 32,3 (December 2002), 515–540.
———. "Inflação, estagnação e ruptura: 1961–1964," in *A ordem do Progresso,* ed. Marcelo de Paiva Abreu (Rio de Janeiro: Editora Campus, 1992a), 197–212.
———. "Crise, crescimento e modernização autoritária, 1930–1945," in *A ordem do Progresso,* ed. Marcelo de Paiva Abreu (Rio de Janeiro: Editora Campus, 1992b), 73–104.
———. "A dívida externa do Brasil, 1824–1931," *Estudos Econômicos* 15,2 (1985), 168–189.
Adesse, Leila, and Mário F. G. Monteiro. "Magnitude do aborto no Brasil: aspectos epidemiológicos e sócio-culturais." Available at http://www.aads.org.br/wp/wp-content/uploads/2011/06/factsh_mag.pdf.
Afonso, José Roberto, Guilherme L. N. P. de Carvalho, and Kleber Pacheco de Castro. "Desempenho comparado dos principais governos brasileiros depois de dez anos da LRF," *Revista Técnica dos Tribunais de Contas* (Belo Horizonte) I,0 (Setembro 2010), 13–48. Available at http://www.joserobertoafonso.com.br/attachments/article/1429/ATRICON-10AnosLRF.pdf.
Albuquerque, C. R. "A liberalização comercial brasileira recente: uma leitura a partir das matrizes de relações intersetoriais de 1985, 90 e 95." MA thesis, Belo Horizonte, CEDEPLAR/UFMG, 1999.
Almeida, Paulo Roberto de. *Formação da diplomacia econômica no Brasil: as relações econômicas internacionais do Império* (São Paulo: Editora Senac-Funag, 2001).
Alves, Eliseu. *Dilema da política agrícola brasileira: produtividade ou expansão da área agricultável* (Brasília: Embrapa, 1983).
———. *A Embrapa e a pesquisa agropecuária no Brasil* (Brasília: Embrapa, 1980).

Bibliography 395

Alves, Maria Helena Moreira. *Estado e oposição no Brasil, 1964–1984* (Petrópolis: Vozes, 1984).
Alvim, Zuleika. *Brava Gente!: Os Italianos em São Paulo 1870–1920* (São Paulo: Brasiliense, 1986).
Amed, Fernando José, and Plínio J. L. C. Negreiros. *História dos Tributos no Brasil* (São Paulo: Sinafresp, 2000).
Ames, Barry, and Margaret E. Keck. "The Politics of Sustainable Development: Environmental Policy Making in Four Brazilian States," *Journal of Interamerican Studies and World Affairs* 39,4 (Winter 1997–1998), 1–40.
Amorim, Flávia Alfenas. "Mudanças recentes no uso de métodos contraceptivos no Brasil: a questão da esterilização voluntária." MA thesis, Rio de Janeiro: IBGE, Escola Nacional De Ciências Estatísticas – ENCE, 2009.
Andrade, Cibele Yahn de, and J. Norberto W. Dachs. "Acesso à educação por faixas etárias segundo renda e raça/cor," *Cadernos de Pesquisa* 37,131 (Maio–Agosto 2007), 399–422.
Andrade, Eli Iôla Gurgel. "Estado e previdência no Brasil: uma breve história," in *A previdência social no Brasil*, ed. Rosa María Marques et al. (São Paulo: Editora Fundação Perseu Abramo, 2003).
Andrade, Mônica Viegas, and Ana Carolina Maia. "Demanda por planos de saúde no Brasil," ANPEC, *Anais do XXXIV Encontro Nacional de Economia* 106 (2006).
Antía, Florencia, and Arnaldo Provasi. "Multi-pillared Social Insurance Systems: The Post-reform Picture in Chile, Uruguay and Brazil," *International Social Security Review* 64,1 (2011), 53–71.
Antunes, Ricardo, and Arnaldo Gonçalves. *Por um novo sindicalismo* (São Paulo: Editora Brasiliense, 1980).
Araújo, Gisele Silva. "Tradição Liberal, positivismo e pedagogia. A síntese derrotada de Rui Barbosa," *Perspectivas* (São Paulo) 37 (Janeiro–Junho 2010), 113–144.
Arida, Pérsio, and André Lara Resende. "Inertial Inflation and Monetary Reform in Brazil," in *Inflation and Indexation: Argentina, Brazil and Israel*, ed. J. Williamson (Cambridge, MA: MIT Press, 1985), 27–45.
Arriaga, Eduardo E. *New Life Tables for Latin American Populations in the Nineteenth and Twentieth Centuries*. Population Monograph Series, No. 3 (Berkeley: University of California, 1968).
Arriaga, Eduardo E., and Kingsley Davis. "The Pattern of Mortality Change in Latin America," *Demography* 6,3 (1969), 223–242.
Averbug, André. "Abertura e Integração Comercial Brasileira na Década de 90," in *A Economia Brasileira nos Anos 90*, ed. Fabio Giambiagi and Maurício Mesquita Moreira (Rio de Janeiro: BNDES, 1999), 43–84.
Bacha, Edmar L. "Além da Tríade: há como reduzir os juros?" Texto para Discussão No. 17 (Rio de Janeiro: Instituto de Estudos de Política Econômica, Setembro 2010). Available at http://iepecdg.com.br/uploads/texto/TPD17_Bacha.pdf.
_____. "Moeda, inércia e conflito: reflexões sobre políticas de estabilização no Brasil," *Pesquisa e Planejamento Econômico* 18,1 (1988), 1–16.

Bacha, Edmar L., and Robert Greenhill. *150 anos de café*. 2nd ed., rev. ed. (Rio de Janeiro: Marcelino Martins & E. Johnston Exportadores, 1992).
Bacha, Edmar L., and Herbert S. Klein, ed. *Social Change in Brazil 1945–1985: The Incomplete Transformation* (Albuquerque: University of New Mexico Press, 1989).
Bacha, Edmar L., and Simon Schwartzman, eds. *Brasil: A nova agenda social* (Rio de Janeiro: LTC, 2011).
Bacha, Edmar L., and Lance Taylor. "Brazilian Income Distribution in the 1960s: 'Facts,' Model Results and the Controversy," in *Models of Growth and Distribution for Brazil*, ed. Lance Taylor et al. (New York: Oxford University Press, 1980), 296–342.
Baer, Werner. *A economia brasileira* (São Paulo: Nobel, 2002).
Bahia, Luiz Bias, and Edson Paulo Domingues. *Estrutura de inovações na indústria automobilística brasileira*. Texto para Discussão No. 1472 (Brasília: IPEA, 2010).
Baleeiro, Aliomar, and Barbosa Lima Sobrinho. *Constituições Brasileiras: 1946* (Brasília: Senado Federal e Ministério de Ciência e Tecnologia, 2001).
Banerjee, Onil, Alexander J. Macpherson, and Janaki Alavalapati. "Toward a Policy of Sustainable Forest Management in Brazil: A Historical Analysis," *The Journal of Environment & Development* 18,2 (June 2009), 130–153.
Barbosa, Allan Claudius Queiroz, Júnia Marçal Rodrigues, and Luis Fernando Rolim Sampaio. "De Programa a Estratégia: A Saúde da Família no Brasil em Perspectiva. Um comparativo da década de 2000." Paper presented at *Anais do XIV Seminário sobre a Economia Mineira*, 2010.
Barbosa, Rui. *Finanças e política da República. Discursos e escritos* (Rio de Janeiro: Cia. Impressora, 1892).
Barros, Octavio de, and Robson Rodrigues Pereira. "Desmitificando a tese da desindutrialização: reestrutração da indústria brasileira em uma época de transformações globais," in *Brasil Globalizado*, ed. Octavio de Barros and Fabio Giambiagi (Rio de Janeiro: Elsevier/Campus, 2008), 299–330.
Barros, Ricardo Paes de, Mirela de Carvalho, and Samuel Franco. "O papel das Transferências Públicas na queda recente da desigualdade de Renda Brasileira," in *Brasil: A nova agenda social*, ed. Edmar Lisboa Bacha and Simon Schwartzman (Rio de Janeiro: LTC, 2011), 41–85.
Barros, Ricardo Paes de, Samuel Franco, and Rosane Mendonça. *Discriminação e segmentação no mercado de trabalho e desigualdade de renda no Brasil*. Texto para Discussão No. 1288 (Rio de Janeiro: IPEA, Julho 2007).
Barros, Ricardo Paes de, Mirela de Carvalho, Samuel Franco, and Rosane Mendonça. "Markets, the State and the Dynamics of Inequality: Brazil's Case Study," in *Declining Inequality in Latin America: A Decade of Progress?*, ed. Luis Felipe Lopez-Calva and Nora Lustig (Washington, DC: Brookings Institution Press, 2010), 134–174.
Bassanezi, Maria, Sílvia C. Beozzo, and Priscila M. S. Bergamo Francisco, eds., *Estado de São Paulo: estatística agrícola e zootécnica, 1904–1905* (Campinas: NEPO/UNICAMP, 2003).
Bastos, Pedro Paulo Zahluth, and Pedro Cezar Dutra, eds. *A Era Vargas. Desenvolvimento, economia e sociedade* (São Paulo: Editora UNESP, 2012).

———. "Desenvolvimento incoerente? Comentários sobre o projeto do segundo governo Vargas e as ideias econômicas de Horário Lafer (1948-1952)," *Economia* (Brasília) 6,3 (Dezembro 2005), 191-222. Available at http://www.anpec.org.br/revista/vol6/vol6n3p191_222.pdf.

Batalha, Claudio. *O movimento Operário na Primeira República* (Rio de Janeiro: Jorge Zahar Editor, 2000).

Bello, José Maria. *História da República* (São Paulo: Cia Editora Nacional, 1976).

Beltrão, Kaizô Iwakami, and Sonoe Sugahara Pinheiro. *Brazilian Population and the Social Security System: Reform Alternatives.* Texto para Discussão No. 929 (Rio de Janeiro: IPEA, 2005).

Beltrão, Kaizô Iwakami, Sonoe Sugahara Pinheiro, and Francisco Eduardo Barreto de Oliveira. *Population and Social Security in Brazil: An Analysis with Emphasis on Constitutional Changes.* Texto para Discussão No. 862 (Rio de Janeiro: IPEA, 2002).

Benevides, Maria Victoria de Mesquita. *O governo Kubitschek. Desenvolvimento Econômico e Estabilidade Política* (Rio de Janeiro: n.p., 1977).

Benjamin, Antonio Herman De Vasconcellos E. "O Meio Ambiente na Constituição Federal de 1988," *Informativo Jurídico da Biblioteca Ministro Oscar Saraiva* 19,1 (Janeiro–Junho 2008), 37-80.

Berquó, Elza. "Brasil, um Caso Exemplar-anticoncepção e parto cirúrgicos – à espera de uma ação exemplar," *Estudos feministas* 1,2 (2008), 366-381.

———. "Demographic Evolution of the Brazilian Population during the Twentieth Century," in *Population Change in Brazil: Contemporary Perspectives*, ed. David Joseph Hogan (Campinas: UNICAMP, 2001), 13-33.

Berquó, Elza, and Candido Procopio F de Camargo, eds. *La population du Brésil* (Paris: UN/CICRED, 1974).

Berquó, Elza, and Suzana Cavenagh. "Increasing Adolescent and Youth Fertility in Brazil: A New Trend or a One-Time Event?" Paper presented at the Annual Meeting of the Population Association of America (2005), 4. Available at http://www.abep.nepo.unicamp.br/docs/PopPobreza/BerquoelzaeCavenaghiSuzana.pdf.

———. "Mapeamento sócio-econômico e demográfico dos regimes de fecundidade no Brasil e sua variação entre 1991 e 2000." Paper presented at *XIV Encontro Nacional de Estudos Populacionais, ABEP* (Caxambu, MG – Brasil, Setembro 20-24, 2004).

Betranou, Fabio M., and Rafael Rofman. "Providing Social Security in a Context of Change: Experience and Challenges in Latin America," *International Social Security Review* 55,1 (2002), 67-82.

Binswanger, Hans. "Brazilian Policies That Encourage Deforestation." Environment Department Paper No. 16 (Washington, DC: World Bank, 1988).

Bojunga, Claudio. *JK: o artista do impossível* (Rio de Janeiro: Objetiva, 2001).

Bonelli, Regis, and Pedro Malan. "Os limites do possível: notas sobre balanço de pagamento e indústria nos anos 70," *Pesquisa e Planejamento Econômico* 6,2 (1976), 355-406.

Bonelli, Regis, and Armando Castelar Pinheiro. "Abertura e crescimento econômico no Brasil," in *Globalizado*, ed. Octavio de Barros and Fabio Giambiagi (Rio de Janeiro: Campus, 2008), 89-124.

Bourn, Richard. *Getúlio Vargas of Brazil, 1883–1954: Sphinx of the Pampas* (London: Knight, 1974).
Brito, Fausto. "Final de século: a transição para um novo padrão migratório?" Paper presented at the *XII Encontro Nacional de Estudos Populacionais, ABEP* (2000).
Brito, Fausto, Ricardo Alexandrino Garcia, and Renata G. Vieira de Souza. "As tendências recentes das migrações interestaduais e o padrão migratório." Paper presented at the *XIV Encontro Nacional de Estudos Populacionais, ABEP* (2004).
Britto, Marcelo, Tatiana Medeiros, and Fábio Soares. *Programas focalizados de Transferência de Renda no Brasil: Contribuições para o Debate*. Texto para Discussão No. 1283 (Brasília: IPEA, 2007).
Buarque de Holanda, Sérgio, ed. "O Brasil Monárquico," in *História Geral da Civilização Brasileira*, II:5 (Rio de Janeiro: Bertrand Brasil, 1997).
Bueno, Miguel, and Marcelo Dias Carcalholo. "Inserção externa e vulnerabilidade da econômica brasileira no governo Lula," in *Os anos Lula – contribuições para um balanço crítico 2003–2010*, ed. J. P. A. Magalhães (Rio de Janeiro: Editora Garamond, 2010), 109–132.
Bunker, Stephen G. *Underdeveloping the Amazon: Extraction, Unequal Exchange, and the Failure of the Modern State* (Urbana: University of Illinois Press, 1985).
Caldeira, Antônio Prates, Elizabeth França, Ignez Helena Oliva Perpetuo, and Eugênio Marcos Andrade. "Evolução da mortalidade infantil por causas evitáveis, Belo Horizonte, 1984–1998," *Revista de Saúde Pública* 39,1 (2005), 67–74.
Calógeras, João Pandiá. *A política monetária do Brasil* (São Paulo: Cia Editora Nacional, 1960).
Camarano, Ana Amélia, and Ricardo Abramovay. *Êxodo rural, envelhecimento e masculinização no brasil: panorama dos últimos 50 anos*. Texto para Discussão No. 621 (Rio de Janeiro: IPEA, Janeiro 1999).
Campos, André Luiz Vieira de. *Políticas internacionais de saúde na era Vargas: O Serviço Especial de Saúde Pública, 1942–1960* (Rio de Janeiro: Editora Fiocruz, 2006).
Canabrava, Alice P. *O algodão no Brasil, 1861–1875* (São Paulo: T. A. Queiróz Editor, 1984).
———. "A grande Lavoura," in *História da civilização brasileira*, II:4, ed. Sérgio Buarque de Holanda (São Paulo: Difusão Europeia do Livro, 1971), 85–140.
Cano, Wilson. *Raízes da Concentração Industrial em São Paulo* (São Paulo: Difel, 1977).
Cano, Wilson, and Ana Lúcia Gonçalves da Silva. "Política Indústrial do Governo Lula," in *Os anos Lula: contribuições para um balanço crítico 2003–2010* (Rio de Janeiro: Garamond, 2010), 181–208.
Caputo, Ana Cláudia, and Hildete Pereira de Melo. "A industrialização brasileira nos anos de 1950: Uma análise da Instrução 111 da Sumoc," *Estudos Econômicos* 39,3 (Julho–Setembro 2009), 513–538.
Cardoso, Adalberto. "Transições da Escola para o Trabalho no Brasil: Persistência da Desigualdade e Frustração de Expectativas," *DADOS, Revista de Ciências Sociais* 51,3 (2008), 569–616.

Bibliography

Cardoso, Adauto Lucio. "O Programa Favela-Bairro-Uma Avaliação." Habitação e meio ambiente: assentamentos urbanos precários. IPT-Instituto de Pesquisas Tecnológicas; Programa Tecnologia de habitação (São Paulo: Habitare, 2002).

Cardoso, Fernando Henrique. "Dos Governos Militares a Prudente – Campos Sales," in *História Geral da Civilização Brasileira*, III:1, ed. Boris Fausto (Rio de Janeiro: Ed. Bertrand Brasil, 1989), 15–50.

———. *Mudanças Sociais na América Latina* (São Paulo: Difusão Européia do Livro, 1969).

Cardoso, Fernando Henrique, and Enzo Faletto. *Dependência e Desenvolvimento na América Latina – Ensaios de interpretação sociológica* (Rio de Janeiro: Zahar, 1970).

Cardoso de Mello, João Manoel. *O capitalismo tardio* (São Paulo: Brasiliense, 1982).

Carli, Gileno de. *O açúcar na formação econômica do Brasil* (Rio de Janeiro: Annuário Açucareiro, 1937).

Carneiro, Dionísio Dias. "Crise e esperança: 1974–1980," in *A ordem do Progresso*, ed. Marcelo de Paiva Abreu (Rio de Janeiro: Editora Campus, 1992), 295–322.

Carneiro, Dionísio Dias, and Eduardo Modiano. "Ajuste externo e desequilíbrio interno: 1980–1984," in *A ordem do Progresso*, ed. Marcelo de Paiva Abreu (Rio de Janeiro: Editora Campus, 1992), 323–346.

Carneiro, Ricardo. *Desenvolvimento em crise. A economia brasileira no último quarto do século XX* (São Paulo: Editora UNESP, 2002).

Carone, Edgard. *A segunda República* (São Paulo: Difusão Européia do Livro, 1973).

Castro, Antonio Barros de, and Francisco Eduardo Pires de Souza. *A economia brasileira em marcha forçada* (Rio de Janeiro: Paz e Terra, 1985).

CELADE. *Boletín demográfico* 34,74 (Julio 2004).

Centro de Estudos Avançados em Economia aplicada – Esalq/USP the agrobusiness had a participation of 22.74% of the GNP in 2010. Available at http://www.cepea.esalq.usp.br/pib/.

Chesnais, Jean-Claude. *The Demographic Transition, Stages, Patterns and Economic Implications* (Oxford: Clarendon Press, 1991).

CNI – Confederação Nacional da Indústria. "Pesquisa sobre popularidade do Presidente Lula." Available at http://igepri.org/news/2010/12/popularidade-de-lula-e-recorde/.

Coelho, Alexandre Bragança. "A cultura do Algodão e a questão da integração entre preços internos e externos." MA thesis, Universidade de São Paulo, 2002.

Coelho, Carlos Nayro. "70 anos de política agrícola no Brasil, 1931–2001," *Revista de Política Agrícola* 10,3 (Julho–Setembro 2001), 695–726.

Cohn, Amélia. *Previdência social e processo político no Brasil* (São Paulo: Editora Moderna, 1981).

Cole, Célio Alberto. "A cadeia produtiva do trigo no Brasil: contribuição para geração de emprego e renda." MA thesis, Porto Alegre: Iepe-UFRGS, 1998.

Committee on Population and Demography. *Levels and Recent Trends in Fertility and Mortality in Brazil*. Report No. 21 (Washington, DC: National Academy Press, 1983), 15.

Conceição, Junia Cristina P. R. da. *A política dos preços mínimos e a política alimentar*. Texto para Discussão No. 993 (Brasília: IPEA, 2003).
Conjuntura Econômica, Fundação Getúlio Vargas. Available at http://www.docpro.com.br/BibliotecaVirtual/Conjuntura/Pesquisalivre.html.
Corazza, Gentil. *O Banco Central do Brasil – Evolução Histórica e Institucional*. Available at http://www.net.fee.com.br/sitefee/download/jornadas/1/s3a4.pdf.
Cordeiro, Hésio. "Instituto de Medicina Social e a luta pela reforma sanitária: contribuição à história do SUS," *Physis* 14,2 (2004), 343–362.
Costa, Maria da Conceição Nascimento, Eduardo Luiz Andrade Mota, Jairnilson Silva Paim, Lígia Maria Vieira da Silva, Maria da Glória Teixeira, and Carlos Maurício Cardeal Mendes. "Mortalidade infantil no Brasil em períodos recentes de crise econômica," *Revista de Saúde Pública* 37,6 (2003), 699–706.
Costa, Valeriano Mendes Ferreira. "A dinâmica Institucional da Reforma do Estado: um balanço do período FHC," in *O Estado Numa Era de Reformas: os Anos FHC* (Brasília: 2002), Part 2, 9–56.
Coutinho, Mauricio C., and Cláudio Salm. "Social Welfare," in *Social Change in Brazil 1945–1985: The Incomplete Transformation*, ed. Edmar L. Bach and Herbert S. Klein (Albuquerque: University of New Mexico Press, 1989), 233–262.
Couto, Ronaldo Costa. *Juscelino Kubitschek* (Brasília, Edições Senado: Camara Federal, 2011).
D'Araujo, Maria Celina. *O segundo governo Vargas 1951–1954: democracia, partidos e crise política*. 2nd ed. (São Paulo: Ática, 1992), 156–167. Available at http://www.cpdoc.fgv.br.
Davatz, Thomaz. *Memórias de um colono no Brasil (1850)* (Belo Horizonte, Itatiaia; São Paulo: Ed. Universidade de São Paulo, 1980).
Dean, Warren. *With Broadaxe and Firebrand: The Destruction of the Brazilian Atlantic Forest* (Berkeley: University of California Press, 1995).
———. *Rio Claro: A Brazilian Plantation System, 1820–1920* (Stanford, CA: Stanford University Press, 1976).
———. *The Industrialization of São Paulo* (Austin: University of Texas Press, 1969).
Deerr, Noel. *The History of Sugar* (London: Chapman and Hall, 1949).
Delfim Netto, Antonio. *O problema do café no Brasil* (São Paulo: IPE-USP, 1981).
———. "Análise do comportamento recente da economia brasileira: diagnóstico" (São Paulo: mimeo, 1967).
Delgado, Guilherme. "Expansão e modernização do setor agropecuário no pós-guerra: um estudo da reflexão agrária," *Estudos Avançados USP* 15,43 (Setembro–Dezembro 2001), 157–172.
Delgado, Lucila de Almeida Neves. "O governo João Goulart e o golpe de 1964: memória, história e historiografia," *Tempo* (Niterói) 14,18 (Junho 2010), 123–143.
Dias, Fernando Álvares Correia. *O Refinanciamento dos Governos Subnacionais e o ajuste fiscal 1999/2003*. Texto para Discussão No. 17 (Brasília: Consultoria Legislativa do Senado Federal, 2004).

Dias Júnior, Cláudio Santiago. "Comportamento reprodutivo: Uma análise a partir do grupo ocupacional das mulheres." PhD thesis, Belo Horizonte: CEDELAR/UFMG, March 2007.
Dias, Guilherme Leite da Silva, and Cicely Moitinho Amaral. *Mudanças estruturais na agricultura brasileira, 1980-1998* (Naciones Unidas, CEPAL, Red de Desarrollo Agropecuario, Unidadde Desarrollo Agrícola, División de Desarrollo Productivoy Empresarial, 2001).
Diniz, Debora, and Marcelo Medeiros. "Aborto no Brasil: uma pesquisa domiciliar com técnica de urna," *Ciência & Saúde Coletiva* 15,1 (2010), 959-966.
Diniz, Eli. "O Estado novo: estutura de poder e relações de classe," in *História Geral da Civilização Brasileira*, ed. Boris Fausto (São Paulo: Difel, 1981). Tomo 3: O Brasil Republicano. Vol. 3: *Sociedade e política (1930-1964)*, 77-119.
Draibe, Sônia Miriam. "O Welfare State in Brazil: Caracteristicas e Perspectivas," *Caderno de Pesquisa* 8 (Campinas: UNICAMP, NEPP, 1993).
———. *Rumos e Metamorfoses. Estado e Industrialização no Brasil: 1930-1960* (Rio de Janeiro: Paz e Terra, 1985).
Dulles, John W. F. *Vargas of Brazil: A Political Biography* (Austin: Universitiy of Texas Press, 1967).
Dutra, Pedro Cezar. *Vargas: o Capitalismo em Construção* (São Paulo: Brasiliense, 1986).
Eisenberg, Peter. *The Sugar Industry in Pernambuco: Modernization without Change, 1840-1910* (Berkeley: University of California Press, 1974).
Elias, Paulo Eduardo M., and Amelia Cohn. "Health Reform in Brazil: Lessons to Consider," *American Journal of Public Health* 93,1 (January 2003), 46.
Faleiros, Rogério Naques. *Fronteiras do Café* (São Paulo: Fapesp-Edusc, 2010).
Faria, Lina. *Saúde e Política: a Fundação Rockefeller e seus parceiros em São Paulo* (Rio de Janeiro: Editora Fiocruz, 2007).
Faoro, Raymundo. *Os donos do Poder. Formação do Patronato político brasileiro*. 2 vols. (Porto Alegre: Ed. Globo; São Paulo: Ed. Universidade São Paulo, 1975).
Fausto, Boris. "Populismo in the Past and Its Resurgence." Paper presented at the Conference in Honor of Boris Fausto, Stanford, CA, May 21, 2010.
———. *Trabalho urbano e conflito social* (São Paulo: DIFEL, 1997).
———. *A revolução de 1930* (São Paulo: Brasiliense, 1975).
Fearnside, P. M., and W. F. Laurance. "Tropical Deforestation and Greenhouse Gas Emissions," *Ecological Applications* 14,4 (2004), 982-986.
Fernandes, Eduardo, Bruna Almeida Guimarães, and Ramalho Romulo Matheus. *Principais Empresas e Grupos Brasileiros no Setor de Fertilizantes*. Available at http://funcex.org.br/material/redemercosul bibliografia/ biblioteca/ESTUDOS BRASIL/BRA 160.PDF.
Fernandes Filho, J. F. "A política brasileira de fomento à produção de trigo, 1930-1990," in *Anais do XXXIII Congresso Brasileiro de Economia Rural*, Vol. 1 (Brasília: Sober, 1995), 443-474.

Ferraro, Alceu Ravanello. "Analfabetismo e níveis de letramento no Brasil: o que dizem os censos? *Revista Educação & Sociedade* (Campinas) 23,81 (Dezembro 2002), 21–47. Available at http://www.scielo.br/pdf/es/v23n81/13930.pdf.

Ferreira, Jorge. "1946–1964: A experiência democrática no Brasil," *Revista Tempo* 28 (Junho 2010), 11–18. Available at http://www.historia.uff.br/tempo/site/?cat=57.

———. "O nome e as coisas: o populismo na política brasileira," in *O populismo e sua história*, ed. Jorge Ferreira (Rio de Janeiro: E. Civilização Brasileira, 2000), 59–124.

Ferreira, Jorge, and Lucília de Almeida Neves (Rio de Janeiro: Civilização Brasileira, 2003), 2:241–285.

Ferreira, Sérgio Guimarães, and Fernando A. Veloso. "Intergenerational Mobility of Wages in Brazil," *Brazilian Review of Econometrics* 26,2 (November 2006), 181–211.

Filgueiras, Luiz. *História do Plano Real* (São Paulo: Boitempo, 2000).

Filomeno, Felipe Amin. "A crise Baring e a crise do Encilhamento nos quadros da economia-mundo capitalista," *Economia e Sociedade* 19,1 (Abril 2010), 135–171.

Fishlow, Albert. "Origens e conseqüências da substituição de importações no Brasil," in *Formação Econômica do Brasil. A experiência da industrialização*, ed. Flavio Rabelo Versiani and José Roberto Mendonça de Barros (São Paulo: Saraiva, 1977), 7–41.

———. "A distribuição de renda no Brasil," in *A controvérsia sobre a distribuição de renda e desenvolvimento*, ed. R. Tolipan and A. C. Tinelli (Rio de Janeiro: Zahar, 1975), 159–189.

———. "Algumas reflexões sobre a política brasileira após 1964," *Estudos Cebrap* 6 (Janeiro–Março 1974), 5–66.

———. "Brazilian Size Distribution of Income," *American Economic Review* 62,1–2 (March 1972), 391–402.

Fonseca, Cristina M. Oliveira. *Saúde no Governo Vargas (1930–1945): dualidade institucional de um bem público* (Rio de Janeiro: Editora Fiocruz, 2007).

Fonseca, Pedro Cezar Dutra. *Vargas: o capitalismo em construção (1906–1954)* (São Paulo: Brasiliense, 1989).

Fonseca, Pedro Cezar Dutra, and Sergio Marley Modesto Monteiro. "O Estado e suas razões: o II PND," *Revista de Economia Política* 28,1 (109) (Janeiro–Março 2007), 28–46.

Fonseca, R., M. C. Carvalho Jr., and H. Pourchet. *A orientação externa da indústria de transformação brasileira após a liberalização comercial.* Texto para Discussão No. 135 (Rio de Janeiro: IPEA, Abril 1998).

Fontanari, Rodrigo. "O problema do financiamento: uma análise histórica sobre o crédito no complexo cafeeiro paulista. Casa Branca (1874–1914)." MA thesis, Franca, UNESP, 2011.

França, Elisabeth, and Sônia Lansky. "Mortalidade infantil neonatal no Brasil: situação, tendências e perspectivas." Texto elaborado por solicitação da RIPSA para o Informe de Situação e Tendências: Demografia e Saúde [Textos de Apoio 3] (2008): 83–112.

Franco, Gustavo. *O Desafio Brasileiro: ensaios sobre desenvolvimento, globalização e moeda* (São Paulo: Editora 34, 1999).
_____. *O Plano Real e outros ensaios* (Rio de Janeiro: Francisco Alves, 1995).
_____. "A Primeira década republicana," in *A ordem do Progresso*, ed. Marcelo de Paiva Abreu (Rio de Janeiro: Editora Campus, 1992), 11–30.
_____. "Reforma Monetária e instabilidade durante a transição republicana." MA thesis, Economics, Rio de Janeiro: PUC/Rio, 1982.
Frank, Zephyr, and Aldo Musacchio. "Overview of the Rubber Market, 1870–1930" (posted in 2010). Available at http://eh.net/encyclopedia/article/frank.international.rubber.market.
Freitas, Vladimir Passos de. "A constituição federal e a efetividade das normas ambientais." PhD thesis, Faculdade de Direito da Universidade Federal do Paraná, 1999.
French, John D. "Proclamando Leis, metendo o pau e lutando por direitos," in *Direitos e Justiças no Brasil, Ensaios de História Social*, ed. Silva Hunold Lara and Joseli M. N. Mendonça (Campinas: Ed. UNICAMP, 2006), 379–416.
_____. *The Brazilian Workers' ABC: Class Conflict and Alliances in Modern São Paulo* (Chapel Hill: University of North Carolina Press, 1992).
Frischtak, Cláudio R. "O investimento em infra-estrutura no Brasil: Histórico recente e perspectivas," *Pesquisa e Planejamento Econômico* 38,2 (Agosto 2008), 307–348.
Fritsch, Wilton. "Apogeu e crise na primeira república: 1900–1930," in *A ordem do Progresso*, ed. Marcelo de Paiva Abreu (Rio de Janeiro: Campus, 1992), 31–72.
_____. "A crise cambial de 1982–83 no Brasil: origens e respostas," in *A América Latina e a crise internacional*, ed. C. A. Plastino and R. Bouzas (Rio de Janeiro: Graal, 1988), 105–143.
Fritscher, André Martínez, Aldo Musacchio, and Martina Viareng. "The Great Leap Forward: The Political Economy of Education in Brazil, 1889–1930." Working Papers No. 10–075 (Cambridge, MA: Harvard Business School, 2010).
Furtado, Celso. *Análise do modelo brasileiro* (Rio de Janeiro: Civilização Brasileira, 1972).
_____. *Formação Econômica do Brasil* (São Paulo: Cia Editora Nacional, 1968a).
_____. *Um projeto para o Brasil* (Rio de Janeiro: Saga, 1968b).
Gaspari, Elio. *A ditadura encurralada* (São Paulo: Companhia das Letras, 2004).
_____. *A ditadura derrotada* (São Paulo: Companhia das Letras, 2003).
_____. *A ditadura envergonhada* (São Paulo: Companhia das Letras, 2002a).
_____. *A ditadura escancarada* (São Paulo: Companhia das Letras, 2002b).
Gasques, José Garcia, José Eustáquio, R. V. Filho, and Zander Navarro, eds. *Agricultura brasileira: desempenho, desafios e perspectivas* (Brasília: IPEA, 2010).
_____, et al. *Condicionantes da produtividade da agropecuária brasileira*. Texto para Discussão No. 1017 (Brasília: IPEA, 2004a).
_____, et al. *Desempenho e crescimento do agronegócio no Brasil*. Texto para Discussão No. 1009 (Brasília: IPEA, Fevereiro 2004b).

Gasques, José Garcia, and Humberto Francisco Silva Spolador. *Taxas de juros e políticas de apoio interno à agricultura*. Texto para Discussão No. 952 (Brasília: IPEA, 2003).
Gasques, José Garcia, and Carlos Monteiro Villa Verde. *Gastos públicos na agricultura: evolução e mudança*. Texto para Discussão No. 948 (Brasília: IPEA, 2003).
Gasques, José Garcia, Eliana T. Bastos, Mirian R. P. Bacchi, and Constanza Valdes. "Produtividade total dos fatores e transformações da agricultura brasileira: análise dos dados dos censos agropecuários," in *A agricultura brasileira: desempenho, desafios e perspectivas*, ed. José G. Gasques, José E. R. Vieira Filho, and Zander Navarro (Brasília: IPEA, 2010), 19–44.
Giambiagi, Fabio, and Lavinia Barros de Castro. "Previdência Social: Diagnósticos e propostas de reforma," *Revista do BNDES* 10,19 (Junho 2003), 265–292.
Giambiagi, Fabio, and Maurício Mesquita Moreira. *A economia brasileira nos anos 90* (Rio de Janeiro: BNDES, 1990).
Giannotti, Vito. *Historia das lutas dos trabalhadores no Brasil* (Rio de Janeiro: Mauad X, 2007).
Goldsmith, Raymond W. *Brasil 1850–1984. Desenvolvimento Financeiro Sob um Século de Inflação* (São Paulo: Editora Harper & Row do Brasil, 1986).
Golgher, André Braz. "The Selectivity of Migration in Brazil: Implications for Rural Poverty," Taller Nacional sobre "Migración interna y desarrollo en Brasil: diagnóstico, perspectivas y políticas," Abril 30, 2007, Brasília.
_____. *Diagnóstico do processo migratório no Brasil: comparação entre não-migrantes e migrantes* (Belo Horizonte: UFMG/CEDEPLAR, 2006).
Golgher, André Braz, Lízia de Figueiredo, and Roberto Santolin. "Migration and Economic Growth in Brazil: Empirical Applications Based on the Solow-Swan Model," *The Developing Economies* 49,2 (June 2011), 148–170.
Gomes, Angela de Castro. "O populismo e as ciências sociais no Brasil: notas sobre a trajetória de um conceito," in *O populismo e sua história*, ed. Jorge Ferreira (Rio de Janeiro: Civilização Brasileira, 2000), 17–57.
_____. *A invenção do Trabalhismo* (São Paulo: Vértice, 1988).
Goulding, Michael, Nigel J. H. Smith, and Dennis J. Mahar. *Floods of Fortune: Ecology and Economy along the Amazon* (New York: Columbia University Press, 1996).
Graham, Richard. *Patronage and Politics in Nineteenth-Century Brazil* (Stanford, CA: Stanford University Press, 1990).
_____. *Britain and the Onset of Modernization in Brazil 1850–1914* (London: Cambridge University Press, 1968).
Grandin, Greg. *Fordlandia: The Rise and Fall of Henry Ford's Forgotten Jungle City* (New York: Metropolitan Books, 2009).
Guanziroli, Carlos E. "PRONAF dez anos depois: resultados e perspectivas para o desenvolvimento rural," *Revista de Economia e Sociologia Rural* 45,2 (Brasília) (Abril–Junho 2007), 301–328.
Guimarães, Alberto Passos. *Quatro séculos de latifúndio* (Rio de Janeiro: Paz e Terra, 1977).

Haber, Stephen H. "Business Enterprise and the Great Depression in Brazil: A Study of Profits and Losses in Textile Manufacturing," *The Business History Review* 66,2 (Summer 1992), 335–363.
Haguenauer, L., R. Markwald, and H. Pourchet. *Estimativas do valor da produção industrial e elaboração de coeficientes de exportação e importação da indústria brasileira (1985–96)*. Texto para Discussão No. 563 (Rio de Janeiro: IPEA, Julho 1998).
Hanley, Anne G. *Native Capital: Financial Institutions and Economic Development in São Paulo, Brazil, 1850–1920* (Stanford, CA: Stanford University Press, 2005).
Hasenblad, Carlos, and Nelos do Valle Silva, eds. *Origens e Destinos: Desigualdades sociais ao longo da vida* (Rio de Janeiro: Topbooks, 2003).
Henriques, Affonso. *Ascensão e Queda de Getúlio Vargas*. 2 vols. (Rio de Janeiro and São Paulo: Distribuidora Record, s/d).
Hoffmann, Rodolfo, "Transferências de renda e a redução da desigualdade no Brasil e cinco regiões entre 1997 e 2004," *Econômica* 8,1 (2006), 55–81.
_____. "Evolução da distribuição da posse de terra no Brasil no período 1960–80,"*Reforma Agrária* 12,6 (Novembro–Dezembro 1982), 17–34.
Hoffmann, Rodolfo, and Marlon Gomes Ney. *Evolução recente da estrutura fundiária e propriedade rural no Brasil* (Brasília: Ministério do Desenvolvimento Agrário, 2010). Available at http://www.nead.gov.br/portal/nead/publicacoes/download_orig_file?
Holloway, Thomas H. *Immigrants on the Land: Coffee and Society in São Paulo, 1886–1934* (Chapel Hill: University of North Carolina Press, 1980).
Homem de Melo, Fernando B. "Composição da produção no processo de expansão da fronteira agrícola brasileira," *Revista de Economia Política* 5,1 (Janeiro–Março 1985), 86–111.
_____. *O problema alimentar no Brasil* (Rio de Janeiro: Paz e Terra, 1983).
_____. *Agricultura de exportação e o problema da produção de alimentos*. Texto para Discussão No. 30 (São Paulo: FEA-USP, 1979).
Homem de Melo, Fernando B., and Eduardo Giannetti. *Proálcool, energia e transportes* (São Paulo: Fipe/Pioneira, 1981).
Horta, Cláudia Júlia Guimarães, José Alberto Magno de Carvalho, and Luís Armando de Medeiros Frias. "Recomposição da fecundidade por geração para Brasil e regiões: atualização e revisão." Paper presented at Anais do ABEP 2000.
Jank, Marcos S., et al. "Exportações: existe uma 'doença brasileira'?" in *Brasil Globalizado*, ed. Fabio Giambiagi and Octávio de Barros (Rio de Janeiro: Campus, 2008), 331–352.
Kalmanovitz, Salomón. "Las conseqüências econômicas de la Independencia en América Latina," in *Institucionalidade y desarrollo econômico en América Latina*, ed. Luis Bértola and Pablo Gerchunoff (Santiago de Chile: Cepal, 2012), 62–63.
Keck, Margaret E. "The Politics of Sustainable Development: Environmental Policy Making in Four Brazilian States," *Journal of Interamerican Studies and World Affairs* 39,4 (Winter 1997–1998), 1–40.

———. "Social Equity and Environmental Politics in Brazil: Lessons from the Rubber Tappers of Acre," *Comparative Politics* 27,4 (July 1995), 409–424.
———. *The Workers' Party and Democratization in Brazil* (New Haven, CT: Yale University Press, 1992).
Klein, Herbert S. *The Atlantic Slave Trade*. 2nd ed., rev. ed. (New York and Cambridge: Cambridge University Press, 2010).
———. "A Participação politíca no Brasil do século XIX: Os votantes de São Paulo em 1880," *Dados. Revista de Ciências Sociais* (Rio de Janeiro) 38,3 (1995), 527–544.
———. "The Supply of Mules to Central Brazil: The Sorocaba Market, 1825–1880," *Agricultural History* 64,4 (Fall 1990), 1–25.
Klein, Herbert S., and Francisco Vidal Luna. "Mudanças Sociais no Período Militar (1964–1985)," in *Cinquenta Anos A ditadura que mudou o Brasil*, ed. Daniel Aarão, Marcelo Ridenti, and Rodrigo Patto Sá Motta (Rio de Janeiro: Zahar Editora, forthcoming 2014).
Kochanek, Kenneth D., and Joyce A. Martin. *Supplemental Analyses of Recent Trends in Infant Mortality*. [NIH, CDC]. Available at http://www.cdc.gov/nchs/products/pubs/pubd/hestats/infantmort/infantmort.htm.
Kubitschek de Oliveira, Juscelino. *Juscelino Kubitschek I (depoimento de 1974)*, DPDOC, 1979, and Juscelino Kubitschek I (depoimento de 1976), DPDOC, 1979.
Lafer, Betty Mindlin, ed. *Planejamento no Brasil* (Sao Paulo: Perspectiva, 1987).
Lafer, Celso. "O planejamento no Brasil: Observações sobre o Plano de Metas," in *Planejamento Econômico no Brasil*, ed. Betty Mindlin (São Paulo: Perspectiva, 1973), 29–49.
Lago, Luiz Aranha Correa do. "A retomada do crescimento e as distorções do 'milagre': 1967–1973," in *A ordem do Progresso*, ed. Marcelo de Paiva Abreu (Rio de Janeiro: Editora Campus, 1992), 233–294.
Lamounier, Bolivar. "O 'Brasil autoritário' revisitado: o impacto das eleições sobre a ditadura," in *Democratizando o Brasil*, ed. Alfred Stepan (Rio de Janeiro: Paz e Terra, 1985), 83–134.
Langoni, Carlos G. *Distribuição de renda e desenvolvimento econômico no Brasil* (Rio de Janeiro: Expressão e Cultura, 1973).
Lattes, Zulma Recchini de, and Alfredo E. Lattes. *La Población de Argentina* (Buenos Aires: C.I.C.R.E.D. Series, 1974).
Laurance, William F., et al. "The Fate of Amazonian Forest Fragments: A 32-Year Investigation," *Biological Conservation* 144 (2011), 56–67.
Laurance, William F., Heraldo L. Vasconcelos, and Thomas E. Lovejoy. "Forest Loss and Fragmentation in the Amazon: Implications for Wildlife Conservation," *Oryx* 34,1 (2000), 39–45.
Lavinas, Lena, Eduardo Henrique Garcia, and Marcelo Rubens do Amaral. *Desigualdades Regionais: Indicadores Socioeconômicos nos Anos 90*. Texto para Discussão No. 460 (Rio de Janeiro: Fevereiro 1997).
Leite, Celso Barroso. "Da lei Elói Chaves ao Sinpas," in *Um século de previdência social: balanço e perspectivas no Brasil e no mundo*, ed. Celso Barroso Leite (Rio de Janeiro: Zahar, 1983), 39–44.

Leite, Cristiane Kerches da Silva. *Federalismo, processo decisório e ordenamento fiscal: a criação da Lei de Responsabilidade Fiscal.* Texto para Discussão No. 1593 (Brasília: IPEA, 2011).

Leopoldi, Maria Antonieta Parahyba. "A economia política do primeiro governo Vargas (1930–1945): a política econômica em tempos de turbulência," in *O tempo do nacional-estadismo: doinício da década de 1930 ao apogeu do Estado Novo*, 2 vols., ed.

Lessa, Carlos. *Quinze anos de política econômica* (São Paulo: Brasiliense/ UNICAMP, 1975).

Lessa, Carlos, and José Luiz Fiori. "Houve uma política nacional-populista," *Encontro Nacional da ANPEC* (São Paulo: ANPEC, 1984).

Levine, Robert M., *Father of the Poor? Vargas and His Era* (New York: Cambridge University Press, 1998).

Levy, Maria Bábara. *A indústria do Rio de Janeiro através de suas sociedades anonimas* (Rio de Janeiro: Prefeitura do Município do Rio de Janeiro, 1994).

Levy, Maria Stella Ferreira. "O Papel da Migração Internacional na evolução da população brasileira (1872 a 1972)," *Revista de Saúde Publica* 8 (Suppl.) (1974), 71–73, Table 1.

Lima, José Luiz. "*Estado e desenvolvimento do setor elétrico no Brasil: das origens à criação da Eletrobrás.*" MA thesis, São Paulo, Faculdade de Economia e Administração, USP, 1983.

Lima, Ruy Cirne. *Pequena História Territorial do Brasil. Sesmarias e Terras Devolutas* (São Paulo: Secretaria do Estado da Cultura, 1990).

Limoncic, Flávio. "The Brazilian Automotive Industry in International Context: From European to American Crisis," Michigan, "New Perspectives on Latin American and US Noon Lectures Series," January 2009, 8 pp.

Linz, Juan J. "The Future of an Authoritarian Situation or the Institutionalization of an Authoritarian Regime: The Case of Brazil," in *Authoritarian Brazil*, ed. Alfred Stepan (New Haven, CT: Yale University Press, 1976), 233–254.

Loewenstein, Karl. *Brazil under Vargas* (New York: The Macmillian Company, 1942).

Lopes, Francisco L. *O choque heterodoxo: combate à inflação e reforma monetária* (Rio de Janeiro: Campus, 1986).

Lopes, José Cláudio Bittencourt. "O Proálcool: uma avaliação." MA thesis, Universidade Federal de Viçosa, 1992.

Lopes de Souza, Marcelo. "Metropolitan Deconcentration, Socio-political Fragmentation and Extended Suburbanisation: Brazilian Urbanisation in the 1980s and 1990s," *Geoforum* 32,4 (2001), 437–447.

Lourenço Filho, Manoel Bergström. *Tendências da educação brasileira.* 2nd ed. (Brasília: Inep/MEC, 2002).

Love, Joseph LeRoy. *The Revolt of the Whip* (Stanford, CA: Stanford University Press, 2012).

―――. *São Paulo in the Brazilian Federation, 1889–1937* (Stanford, CA: Stanford University Press, 1980).

Love, Joseph LeRoy, and Werner Baer, eds. *Brazil under Lula: Economy, Politics, and Society under the Worker-President* (New York: Palgrave/Macmillan, 2009).

Luna, Francisco Vidal. "O Programa de Estabilização e os Salários," *Revista de Economia Política* 6,3 (Julho–Setembro 1986), 129–131.
Luna, Francisco Vidal, and Herbert S. Klein. *Brazil since 1980* (New York: Cambridge University Press, 2006).
Luna, Francisco Vidal, and Thomaz de Aquino Nogueira Neto. *Correção monetária e mercado de capitais: a experiência brasileira* (São Paulo: Bovespa, 1978).
Luna, Francisco Vidal, Herbert S. Klein, and William R. Summerhill. "A agricultura paulista em 1905," *Estudos Econômicos* (São Paulo), forthcoming.
Lupu, Noam, and Susan C. Stokes. "The Social Bases of Political Parties in Argentina, 1912–2003," *Latin American Research Review* 44,1 (2009), 58–87.
Luz, Nícia Vilela. *A luta pela industrialização do Brasil* (São Paulo: Editora Alfa Omega, 1978).
Macarini, José Pedro. "A política econômica do Governo Sarney: os Planos Cruzado (1986) e Bresser (1987)." Texto para Discussão No. 157 (Campinas: IE/UNICAMP, March 2009).
Macedo, Roberto. "Dilma e suas circunstâncias," *Jornal O Estado de São Paulo* (São Paulo) (Julho 19, 2012).
_____. "Plano Trienal de Desenvolvimento Econômico e Social," in *Planejamento no Brasil*, ed. Betty Mindlin (São Paulo: Perspectiva, 2001), 51–68.
Machado, Carlos José Saldanha. "Mudanças conceituais na administração pública do meio ambiente," *Ciência e Cultura* 55,4 (2003), 24–26.
Maddison, Angus. *The World Economy: A Millennial Perspective* (Geneva, Switzerland: OCDE, 2001).
Mahar, Dennis J. *Government Policies and Deforestation in the Brazilian Amazon* (Washington, DC: World Bank, 1989).
Maia, Rosane de Almeida. "Estado e Industrialização no Brasil: Estudo dos Incentivos ao setor privado, nos quadros do Programa de Metas do Governo Kubitschek." MA thesis, São Paulo, FEA-USP, 1986.
Malloy, James. *The Politics of Social Security in Brazil* (Pittsburgh, PA: University of Pittsburgh Press, 1979).
Marcondes, Renato Leite. "O Financiamento Hipotecário da Cafeicultura no Vale do Paraíba Paulista (1865–87)," *Revista Brasileira de Economia* 56,1 (Janeiro–Março 2002), 147–170.
Margulis, Sergio. "Causes of Deforestation of the Brazilian Amazon." World Bank Working Papers No. 22 (Washington, DC: World Bank, 2004).
_____. "O Desempenho ambiental do Governo Brasileiro e do Banco Mundial em Projetos Co-financiados pelo Banco." Textos para Discussão No. 194 (Brasilia: IPEA, 1999).
Marichal, Carlos, and Steven Topik. "The State and Economic Growth in Latin America: Brazil and Mexico, Nineteenth and Early Twentieth Centuries," in *Nation, State and the Economy in History*, ed. Alice Teichova and Herbert Matis (Cambridge: Cambridge University Press, 2002), 349–372.
Marinho, Emerson, and Jair Araujo. "Pobreza e o sistema de seguridade social rural no Brasil," *Revista Brasileira de Economia* 64,2 (2010), 161–174.
Marini, Miguel Angelo, and Federico Innecco Garcia. "Bird Conservation in Brazil," *Conservation Biology* 19,3 (June 2005), 665–671.

Marques, Maria Silva Bastos. "O Plano Cruzado: teoria e prática," *Revista de Economia Política* 8,3 (Julho–Setembro 1983), 101–130.

Martine, George. *A redistribuição espacial da população brasileira durante a década de 80*. Texto para Discussão No. 329 (Brasília: IPEA, Janeiro 1994).

Martinelli, Luiz A., and Solange Filoso. "Expansion of Sugarcane Ethanol Production in Brazil: Environmental and Social Challenges," *Atmospheric Environment* 18,4 (2008), 885–898.

Martinelli, Luiz A., Rosamond Naylor, Peter M. Vitousek, and Paulo Moutinho. "Agriculture in Brazil: Impacts, Costs, and Opportunities for a Sustainable Future," *Current Opinion in Environmental Sustainability* 2 (2010), 431–438.

Martines-Filho, J., H. L. Burnquist, and C. E. F. Vian. "Bioenergy and the Rise of Sugarcane-based Eethanol in Brazil," *Choices* 21,2 (2006), 91–96.

Martínez Fritscher, André, Aldo Musacchio, and Martina Viareng. "The Great Leap Forward: The Political Economy of Education in Brazil, 1889–1930," Working Papers No. 10–075 (Cambridge, MA: Harvard Business School, 2010), 2. Available at http://www.hbs.edu/research/pdf/10-075.pdf.

Martins, Carlos Benedito. "O ensino superior brasileiro nos anos 90," *São Paulo em Perspectiva* 14,1 (2000), 41–60.

Martone, Celso. "Análise do Plano de Ação Econômica do Governo, PAEG (1964–1966)," in *Planejamento no Brasil*, ed. Betty Mindlin (São Paulo: Perspectiva, 2001), 69–90.

Matos, Odilon Nogueira de. *Café e ferrovias: a evolução ferroviária de São Paulo e o desenvolvimento da cultura cafeeira* (São Paulo: Alfa-Omega, 1974).

Matos, Raquel Silvério, and Ana Fávia Machado. "Diferencial de rendimento por cor e sexo no Brasil (1987–2001)," *Econômica* (RJ) 8,1 (Junho 2006), 5–27.

Mattoon Jr., Robert H. "Railroads, Coffee, and the Growth of Big Business in Sao Paulo, Brazil," *The Hispanic American Historical Review* 57,2 (May 1977), 273–295.

Mattos, Fernando Augusto Mansor de. *Emprego público no Brasil: aspectos históricos, inserção no mercado de trabalho nacional e evolução recente*. Textos para Discussão No. 1582 (Brasília: IPEA, Fevereiro 2011).

Medeiros, Marcelo, Tatiana Britto, and Fábio Soares. *Programas focalizados de Transferência de Renda no Brasil*. Texto para Discussão No. 1283 (Brasília: IPEA, Junho 2007).

Mello, Pedro Carvalho de. "The Economics of Labor in Brazilian Coffee Plantations, 1850–1888." PhD thesis, Department of Economics, University of Chicago, 1977.

Meneguello, Rachel. *Partidos e governos no Brasil contemporâneo (1985–1997)* (Rio de Janeiro: Paz e Terra, 1998).

Menezes, Greice, and Estela M. L. Aquino. "Pesquisa sobre o aborto no Brasil: avanços e desafios para o campo da saúde coletiva," *Cadernos de Saúde Pública* 25 (Suppl. 2) (2009), 193–204.

Mercadante, Aloízio, ed., *O Brasil pós-Real: a política econômica em debate* (Campinas: UNICAMP, 1997).

Mercadante, Otávio Azevedo, et al. "Evolução das Políticas e do Sistema de Saúde no Brasil," in *Caminhos da Saúde Pública no Brasil*, ed. Jacobo Finkelman (Rio de Janeiro: Fiocruz, 2002), 235–313.

Merrick, Thomas, and Douglas Graham. "População e desenvolvimento no Brasil: Uma perspectiva histórica," in *Economia Brasileira: Uma Visão Histórica*, ed. Paulo Nauhaus (Rio de Janeiro: Editora Campus, 1980), 45–88.

_____. *Population and Economic Development in Brazil, 1800 to the Present* (Baltimore, MD: Johns Hopkins University Press, 1979).

Miller, Shawn W. *An Environmental History of Latin America* (Cambridge: Cambridge University Press, 2007).

_____. *Fruitless Trees: Portuguese Conservation and Brazil's Colonial Timber* (Stanford, CA: Stanford University Press, 2000).

Milliet, Sérgio. *Roteiro do Café e outros ensaios* (São Paulo: Hucitec, 1982).

Mineiro, Adhemar S. "Desenvolvimento e inserção externa: Algumas considerações sobre o período 2003–2009 no Brasil," in *Os anos Lula: contribuições para um balanço crítico 2003–2010*, ed. J. P. A. Magalhães (Rio de Janeiro: Garamond, 2010), 133–160.

Modiano, Eduardo. "A ópera dos três cruzados: 1985–1989," in *A ordem do Progresso*, ed. Marcelo de Paiva Abreu (Rio de Janeiro: Editora Campus, 1992), 347–386.

Monbeig, Pierre. *Pioneiros e Fazendeiros de São Paulo* (São Paulo: Hucitec-Polis, 1984).

Monteiro, Sérgio. "Política econômica e credibilidade: uma análise dos governos Jânio Quadros e João Goulart." Available at http://www8.ufrgs.br/ppge/pcientifica/1999_13.pdf.

Moreira, Maurício Mesquita. "Estrangeiros em uma Econômica Aberta: Impactos recentes sobre a produtividade, a concentração e o comércio exterior," in *A Economia Brasileira nos Anos 90*, ed. Fabio Giambiagi and Maurício Mesquita Moreira (Rio de Janeiro: BNDES, 1999), 333–374.

Mortara, Giorgio. "The Development and Structure of Brazil's Population," *Population Studies* 8,2 (November 1954), 121–139.

Motta, José Flavio. "Escravos daqui, dali e de mais além: o tráfico interno de escravos em Constituição (Piracicaba), 1861–1880," *Revista Brasileira de História* 26,52 (2006), 15–47.

Motta, José Flavio, and Renato L. Marcondes. "O comércio de escravos no Vale do Paraíba paulista: Guaratinguetá e Silveiras na década de 1870," *Estudos Econômicos* 30,2 (Abril–Junho 2000), 267–299.

Moura, Gerson. *O alinhamento sem recompensa: a política externa do governo Dutra* (Rio de Janeiro: Fundação Getúlio Vargas. Centro de Documentação de História Contemporânea, 1990). Available at http://bibliotecadigital.fgv.br/dspace/bitstream/handle/10438/6613/792.pdf?sequence=1.

Mueller, Charles, and George Martine. "Modernização agropecuária, emprego agrícola e êxodo rural no Brasil – a década de 1980," *Revista de Economia Política* 17,3 (Julho–Setembro 1997), 85–104.

Murilo de Carvalho, José. *A construção da Ordem: a elite política imperial; Teatro das sombras: a política imperial* (Rio de Janeiro: Civilização Brasileira, 2003).

Nassif, Maria Ines. "Previdência Social," in *A Era FHC. Um Balanço*, ed. Bolivar Lamounier and Rubens Figueiredo (São Paulo: Cultura Associados, 2002), 569–598.

Nepstad, Daniel C., Claudia M. Stickler, Britaldo Soares-Filho, and Frank Merry. "The End of Deforestation in the Brazilian Amazon," *Science* 326 (December 2009), 1350-1351.

―――, et al. "Interactions among Amazon Land Use, Forests and Climate: Prospects for a Near-term Forest Tipping Point," *Philosophical Transactions of the Royal Society B* 363 (2008), 1737-1746.

Neri, Marcelo Côrtes, ed. *Novo Mapa das Religiões* (Rio de Janeiro: Fundação Getúlio Vargas, Centro de Políticas Sociais, 2011a).

―――, ed. *Desigualdade de Renda na Década* (Rio de Janeiro: Fundação Getúlio Vargas, Centro de Políticas Sociais, 2011b).

Neto, Lira. *Getúlio 1882-1830. Dos anos de formação à conquista do poder* (São Paulo: Cia. das Letras, 2012).

―――. *Castelo: a marcha para a ditadura* (São Paulo: Contexto, 2004).

Nicol, Robert N. V. C. "A agricultura e a Industrialização no Brasil (1850/1930)." PhD thesis, Economics, Universidade de São Paulo, FFLCH-USP, 1974.

Oberacker Jr., Carlos H. "A colonização baseada no regime de pequena propriedade agrícola," in *História Geral da Civilização Brasileira*, II:3, ed. Sérgio Buarque de Holanda (São Paulo: Difusão Europeia do Livro, 1969), 220-245.

Oliveira, Elisa Hijino de. "Arranjos unipessoais no brasil 1997-2007: uma análise sócio-demográfica e de gênero das pessoas que moram sozinhas." MA thesis, Rio de Janeiro: IBGE, Escola Nacional de Ciências Estatísticas, 2009.

Oliveira, Francisco Eduardo Barreto de, Kaizô Iwakami Beltrão, and Antonio Carlos de Albuquerque David. *Dívida da União com a Previdência Social: uma perspectiva histórica*, Texto para Discussão No. 638 (Rio de Janeiro: IPEA, 1999).

Oliveira, Gesner de, and Frederico Turolla. "Política Econômica do segundo governo FHC: mudança em condições adversas," *Tempo Social* (São Paulo) 15,2 (Novembro 2003), 195-217. Available at http://www.scielo.br/scielo.php?script=sci_arttext&pid=S0103-20702003000200008.

Oliveira, Juarez de Castro, and Fernando Roberto P. de C. e Albuquerque. "A mortalidade no Brasil no período 1980-2004: desafios e oportunidades para os próximos anos," Rio de Janeiro: IBGE, Diretoria de Pesquisas, Coordenação de População e Indicadores Sociais, December 2005.

Oliveira Júnior, Marcio de. *A Liberação Comercial Brasileira e os Coeficientes de Importação – 1990/95*. Texto para Discussão No. 703 (Rio de Janeiro: IPEA, Fevereiro 2000).

Oliveira, Wilson José Ferreira de. "Gênese e redefinições do militantismo ambientalista no Brasil," *DADOS Revista de Ciências Sociais* 51,3 (2008), 751-777.

Orenstein, Luiz, and Antonio Claudio Sochaczewski. "Democracia com Desenvolvimento: 1956-1961," in *A ordem do Progresso*, ed. Marcelo de Paiva Abreu (Rio de Janeiro: Editora Campus, 1992), 171-212.

Osorio, Rafael Guerreiro, and Pedro H. G. Ferreira de Souza. *Evolução da pobreza extrema e da desigualdade de renda na Bahia: 1995 a 2009*. Textos para Discussão No. 1696 (Brasília: IPEA, Janeiro 2012).

Osorio, Rafael Guerreiro, Pedro H. G. F. de Souza, Sergei S. D. Soares, and Luis Felipe Batista de Oliveira. *Perfil da pobreza no Brasil e sua evolução no período 2004-2009*. Texto para Discussão No. 1647 (Brasília: IPEA, Agosto 2011).

Paes de Barros, Ricardo, Ricardo Henriques, and Rosane Mendonça. "Desigualdade e Pobreza no Brasil. Retrato de uma estabilidade inaceitável." *Revista Brasileira de Ciências Sociais* 15,42 (February 2000), 123–142.

Paim, Jairnilson, Claudia Travassos, Celia Almeida, Ligia Bahia, and James Macinko. "The Brazilian Health System: History, Advances, and Challenges," *The Lancet* 377,9779 (2011), 1778–1797.

Paiva, Ruy Muller. "Reflexões sobre as tendências da produção, da produtividade e dos preços do setor agrícola no Brasil," in *Agricultura subdesenvolvida*, ed. F. Sá (Petrópolis: Vozes, 1968), 167–261.

Palloni, Alberto. "Fertility and Mortality Decline in Latin America," *Annals of the American Academy of Political and Social Science* 510 (Julho 1990): 126–144.

Pamuk, Ayse, and Paulo Fernando A. Cavallieri. "Alleviating Urban Poverty in a Global City: New Trends in Upgrading Rio-de-Janeiro's Favelas." *Habitat International* 22,4 (1998), 449–462.

Pastore, Affonso Celso. "A resposta da produção agrícola aos preços no Brasil." PhD thesis, Economics, USP, 1969.

Pastore, Affonso Celso, Maria Pinotti, and Leonardo Porto de Almeida. "Cambio e crescimento: o que podemos aprender?" in *Brasil Globalizado*, ed. Fabio Giambiagi and Octávio de Barros (Rio de Janeiro: Elsevier, 2008), 268–298.

Pastore, José. *Inequality and Social Mobility in Brazil* (Madison: University of Wisconsin Press, 1982).

Pastore, José, Guilherme L. Silva Dias, and Manoel C. Castro. "Condicionantes da produtividade da pesquisa agrícola no Brasil," *Estudos Econômicos* 6,3 (1976), 147–181.

Paula, Marilena de, ed. *"Nunca antes na História desse país"...? Um Balanço das Políticas do Governo Lula* (Rio de Janeiro: Fundação Heinrich Böll, 2011).

Peláez, Carlos Manuel. *História da Industrialização Brasileira. Crítica à Teoria Estruturalista no Brasil* (Rio de Janeiro: Apec, 1972).

Peláez, Carlos Manuel, and Wilson Suzigan. *História Monetária do Brasil* (Brasília: Universidade de Brasília, 1981).

Pereira, Lia Valls. *Brazil Trade Liberalization Program*. UNCTAD. Available at http://www.unctad.info/upload/TAB/docs/TechCooperation/brazil_study.pdf.

Pereira, Luiz Carlos Bresser. "Heterodoxia e Ortodoxia no Plano Bresser," *Revista Conjuntura Econômica* (Feverero 1993), 52–54.

———. "Inflação inercial e o Plano Cruzado," *Revista de Economia Política* 6,3 (Julho–Setembro 1986), 9–24.

Perissinotto, Renato Monseff. *Estado e Capital Cafeeiro em São Paulo (1889–1930)* (São Paulo: Fapesp; Campinas: UNICAMP, 1999).

Perlman, Janice. *The Myth of Marginality: Urban Poverty and Politics in Rio de Janeiro* (Berkeley: University of California Press, 1980).

Petrone, Maria Thereza Schorer. "Imigração assalariada," in *História Geral da Civilização Brasileira*, ed. Sérgio Buarque de Holanda, Tomo 2, Vol. 3 (São Paulo: Difel, 1985), 274–296.

Picanço, Felícia. "O Brasil que sobe e desce: Uma análise da mobilidade socioocupacional e realização de êxito no mercado de trabalho urbano," *DADOS – Revista de Ciências Sociais* 50,2 (2007), 393–433.

Pinheiro, Armando Castelar. *A experiência brasileira de privatização: o que vem a seguir.* Texto para Discussão No. 87 (Rio de Janeiro: IPEA, 2002).

Pinho Neto, Demosthenes Madureira de. "A Estratégia brasileira em perspectiva internacional," in *O BNDES e o Plano de Metas* (Rio de Janeiro: BNDES, Junho 1996). Available at http://www.bndes.gov.br/SiteBNDES/export/sites/default/bndes_pt/Galerias/Arquivos/conhecimento/livro/plametas.pdf.

Pinto, Adolpho Augusto. *História da viação pública de São Paulo* (São Paulo: Governo do Estado de São Paulo, 1977).

Pinto, José Marcelino de Rezende. "O acesso à educação superior no Brasil." *Educação Social* 25,88 (Outubro 2004), 727–752.

Portes, Alejandro. "Housing Policy, Urban Poverty, and the State: The Favelas of Rio de Janeiro, 1972–1976," *Latin American Research Review* 14,2 (1979), 3–24.

Prado, Junior Caio. *História Econômica do Brasil* (São Paulo: Brasiliense, 1972).

Prado, Maria Lígia Coelho. *A democracia ilustrada. O Partido Democrático de São Paulo, 1926–1934* (São Paulo: Ática, 1986).

Prado, Maria Lígia Coelho, and Maria Helena Rolim Capelato. "A borracha na economia brasileira na primeira república," in *História geral da civilização brasileira*, ed. Boris Fausto, Tomo III, Vol. 1 (Rio de Janeiro: Bertrand Brasil, 1989), 285–307.

Prata, Pedro Reginaldo. "A Transição Epidemiológica no Brasil," *Cadernos de Saúde Pública* 8,2 (Abril–Junho 1992), 168–175.

Prebisch, Raúl. "O desenvolvimento econômico da América Latina e seus principais problemas," *Revista Brasileira de Economia* 3 (1949), 49–111.

Queiroz, Maria Isaura Pereira de. *O mandonismo local na vida política brasileira* (São Paulo: Alfa-Omega, 1976).

Quine, Maria Sophia. *Italy's Social Revolution: Charity and Welfare from Liberalism to Fascism* (New York: Palgrave, 2002).

Ramos, Lauro R. A., and José Guilherme Almeida Reis. "Distribuição da renda: aspectos teóricos e o debate no Brasil," in *Distribuição de renda no Brasil*, ed. José Marcio Camargo and Fabio Giambiagi (Rio de Janeiro: Paz e Terra, 2000), 21–45.

Redwood II, John. *World Bank Approaches to the Brazilian Amazon: The Bumpy Road toward Sustainable Development.* LCR Sustainable Development Working Paper No. 13 (Washington, DC: World Bank, November 2002).

Rego, J. M. *Inflação inercial, teoria sobre inflação e o Plano Cruzado* (Rio de Janeiro: Paz e Terra, 1986).

Resende, André Lara. "Em plena crise: uma tentativa de recomposição analítica," *Estudos Avançados* (Universidade de São Paulo) 65 (2009), 73–87.

———. "Estabilização e reforma," in *A ordem do Progresso*, ed. Marcelo de Paiva Abreu (Rio de Janeiro: Editora Campus, 1992), 213–232.

Rezende, Gervazio Castro de. *A política de preços mínimos e o desenvolvimento agrícola da região Centro-Oeste.* Texto para Discussão No. 870 (Brasília: IPEA, 2002).

Ribeiro, Carlos Antonio Costa. *Estrutura de classe e mobilidade social no Brasil* (Bauru, SP: Educ, 2007).

Ribeiro, Milton, Cezar Jean Paul Metzger, Alexandre Camargo Martensen, Flávio Jorge Ponzoni, and Márcia Makiko Hirota. "The Brazilian Atlantic Forest: How Much Is Left, and How Is the Remaining Forest Distributed? Implications for Conservation," *Biological Conservation* 142 (2009), 1141–1153.

Rocha, Sonia. "Alguns aspectos relativos à evolução 2003–2004 da pobreza e da indigência no Brasil," Janeiro 2006. Available at http://www.iets.org.br/biblioteca/Alguns_aspectos_relativos_a_evolucao_2003-2004.pdf.

———. "Impacto sobre a pobreza dos novos programas federais de transferência de renda," n.d. Available at http://www.anpec.org.br/encontro2004/artigos/A04A137.pdf.

Rodrigues, Roberto, and Ivan Wedekin. "Uma estratégia para o agronegócio brasileiro," in *O novo governo e os desafios do desenvolvimento*, ed. Antonio Dias Leite and João Paulo Reis Velloso (Rio de Janeiro: Fórum Nacional, 2002), 549–570.

Rossi Jr., José Luiz, and Pedro Cavalcanti Ferreira. *Evolução da produtividade industrial brasileira e a abertura comercial*. Texto para Discussão No. 651 (Rio de Janeiro: IPEA, 1999).

Sachsida, Adolfo, Paulo Furtado de Castro, Mario Jorge Cardoso de Mendonça, and Pedro H. Albuquerque. *Perfil do migrante brasileiro*. Texto para Discussão No. 1410 (Rio de Janeiro: IPEA, Julho 2009).

Saes, Flávio A. M. "A controvérsia sobre a Industrialização na Primeira República," *Estudos Avançados* 3,7 (Setembro–Dezembro 1989), 20–39.

———. *A grande empresa de serviços públicos* (São Paulo: Hucitec, 1986).

———. *As ferrovias de São Paulo, 1870–1940* (São Paulo: Hucitec-INL-MEC, 1981).

Sánchez-Albornoz, Nicolás. "The Population of Latin America, 1850–1930," in *The Cambridge History of Latin America*, Vol. IV, ed. Leslie Bethell (Cambridge: Cambridge University Press, 1986), 121–152.

Santos, Cézar, and Pedro Cavalcanti Ferreira. "Migração e distribuição regional de renda no Brasil," *Pesquisa e Planejamento Econômico* 37,3 (December 2007), 405–426.

Saretta, Fausto. "O Governo Dutra na Transição Capitalista no Brasil," in *História Econômica do Brasil Contemporâneo*, ed. Tamáz Szrecsányi and Wilson Suzigan (São Paulo: Edusp/Hucitec/Imprensa Oficial SP, 1996), 99–120.

Sayad, João. *Planos Cruzado e Real: acertos e desacertos*. Seminários Dimac (Rio de Janeiro: IPEA, Setembro 30, 2000).

Scalon, Maria Celi. *Mobilidade social no Brasil, padrões e tendências* (Rio de Janeiro: Revan, 1999).

Schmitter, Philippe C. "The 'Portugalization' of Brazil," in *Authoritarian Brazil*, ed. Alfred Stepan (New Haven, CT: Yale University Press, 1976), 179–232.

Schulz, John. *The Financial Crisis of Abolition* (New Haven, CT, and London: Yale University Press, 2008).

Schwarcz, Lilia Moritz. *As Barbas do Imperador. D. Pedro II, um monarca nos trópicos* (São Paulo: Cia. das Letras, 1999).

Schwartzman, Simon. *A Space for Science – The Development of the Scientific Community in Brazil* (College Station: Pennsylvania State University Press, 1991).

Schwartzman, Simon, Helena M. B. Bomeny, and Vanda M. R. Costa. *Nos tempo de Capanema* (São Paulo: Editora da Universidade de São Paulo and Ed. Paz e Terra, 1984).
Schwarzer, Helmut, and Ana Carolina Querino. *Benefícios sociais e pobreza: Programas não contributivos da seguridade social brasileira.* Texto para Discussão No. 929 (Brasília: IPEA, 2002).
Sedgh, Gilda, Stanley Henshaw, Susheela Singh, Elisabeth Åhman, and Iqbal H Shah. "Induced Abortion: Estimated Rates and Trends Worldwide," *Lancet* 370 (October 13, 2007), 1338–1345.
Senado Federal. *A Abolição no Parlamento: 65 anos de luta, 1823–1888* (Brasília: Subsecretaria de Arquivo, 1988).
Serra, José, and José Roberto Afonso. "Mais prática do que discurso," *Valor Econômico* (Maio 5, 2010). Available at http://www.joserobertoafonso.com .br/index.php?option=com_content&view=article&id=1187:mais-pratica-que-discursos-valor-&catid=36:assuntos-fiscais&itemid=37.
Silber, Simão. "Análise da política econômica e do comportamento da economia brasileira durante o período 1929/1939," in *Formação Econômica do Brasil. A experiência da industrialização*, ed. Flavio Rabelo Versiani and José Roberto Mendonça de Barros (São Paulo: Saraiva, 1977), 173–207.
――――. "Política econômica. Defesa no nivel de renda e industrialização no período 1929–1939." MA thesis, São Paulo, FEAUSP, 1973.
Silva, Ana Rosa Cloclet da. "Tráfico interprovincial de escravos e seus impactos na concentração da população da província de São Paulo: século XIX," *VIII Encontro da ABEP, Associação Nacional de Estudos Populacionais, 1992.*
Silva, André Luis Corrêa da. "'João Ferrador na República de São Bernardo': O impacto do 'novo' movimento sindical do ABC Paulista no processo de transição democrática (1977–1980)." MA thesis, Porto Alegre, Universidade Federal do Rio Grande do Sul, 2006.
Silva, Iliane Jesuina da. "Estado e agricultura no primeiro governo Vargas (1930–1945)." PhD thesis, Campinas, Universidade Estadual de Campinas, 2010.
Silva, José Graziano da. "Velhos e novos mitos do rural brasileiro," *Estudos Avançados USP* 43 (Setembro–Dezembro 2001), 37–50.
――――. *A nova dinâmica da agricultura brasileira* (Campinas: Instituto de Economia da UNICAMP, 1996).
Silva, Sérgio. *Expansão cafeeira e origens da indústria no Brasil* (São Paulo: Alfa-Omega, 1995).
Simonsen, Mario Henrique. "Inflação brasileira: lições e perspectivas," *Revista Brasileira de Economia* 5,4 (Outubro–Dezembro 1985), 15–31.
――――. *Inflação, gradualismo x tratamento de choque* (Rio de Janeiro: Apec, 1970).
Simonsen, Mario Henrique, and Roberto Campos. *A nova economia brasileira* (Rio de Janeiro: José Olympio, 1979).
Singer, Paul. *A crise do "Milagre"* (Rio de Janeiro: Paz e Terra, 1977).
Singh, Susheela, and Gilda Sedgh. "The Relationship of Abortion to Trends in Contraception and Fertility in Brazil, Colombia and Mexico," *International Family Planning Perspectives* 23,1 (March 1997), 4–14.

Siqueira, Arnaldo Augusto Franco de, Ana Cristina d'Andretta Tanaka, Renato Martins Santana, and Pedro Augusto Marcondes de Almeida. "Mortalidade materna no Brasil, 1980," *Revista de Saúde Pública* 18 (1984), 448–465.
Skidmore, Thomas E. *The Politics of Military Rule in Brazil, 1964–85* (New York: Oxford University Press, 1988).
_____. "Politics and Economic Policy Making in Authoritarian Brazil, 1937–1971," in *Authoritarian Brazil*, ed. Alfred Stepan (New Haven, CT: Yale University Press, 1976), 3–46.
_____. *Politics in Brazil, 1930–1964: An Experiment in Democracy* (New York: Oxford University Press, 1967).
Soares, Sergei. "Análise de bem-estar e decomposição por fatores da queda na desigualdade entre 1995 e 2004," *Econômica* 8,1 (2006), 83–115.
Soares, Sergei, and Natália Sátyro. *O programa bolsa família: desenho institucional, impactos e possibilidades futuras*. Texto para Discussão No. 1424 (Brasília: IPEA, Outubro 2009).
Soares-Filho, Britaldo Silveira, et al. "Modelling Conservation in the Amazon Basin," *Nature* 440,23 (March 2006), 520–523.
Sochaczewski, Antonio Claudio. *O desenvolvimento econômico e financeiro do Brasil, 1952–1968* (São Paulo: Trajetória Cultural, 1993).
Sola, Lourdes, ed. *O Estado e a transição: política e economia na Nova República* (São Paulo: Vértice, 1988).
_____. "O Golpe de 37 e o Estado Novo," in *Brasil em Perspectiva*, ed. Carlos Guilherme Motta (São Paulo: Difusão Européia do Livro, 1969), 257–284.
Sorj, Bila, and Adriana Fontes. "Children in Female Household Headship in Brazil: Are They More Vulnerable?" Paper presented at the XXVI IUSSP International Population Conference 2009. Available at http://iussp2009.princeton.edu/papers/90368.
Sorj, Bila, Adriana Fontes, and Danielle Carusi Machado. "Políticas e práticas de conciliação entre família e trabalho no Brasil," *Cadernos de pesquisa* 37,132 (2007), 573–594.
Souza, André Portela. "Politicas de distribuição de renda no Brasil e o Bolsa Família," in *Brasil: A nova agenda social*, ed. Edmar Lisboa Bacha and Simon Schwartzman (Rio de Janeiro: LTC, 2011), 166–186.
Souza, Marcelo Medeiros Coelho de. *O analfabetismo no Brasil sob o enfoque demográfico*. Texto para Discussão No. 639 (Brasília: IPEA, April 1999).
Souza, Maria do Carmo Campello de. "A Nova República sob a espada de Dâmocles," in *Democratizando o Brasil*, ed. Alfred Stepan (Rio de Janeiro: Paz e Terra, 1985), 568–591.
Souza, Pedro Herculano Guimarães Ferreira de, and Rafael Guerreiro Osorio. *A redução das disparidades regionais e a queda da desigualdade nacional de renda (1981–2009)*. Texto para Discussão No. 1648 (Brasília: IPEA, Agosto 2011).
Spalding, Rose J. "Welfare Policymaking: Theoretical Implications of a Mexican Case Study," *Comparative Politics* 12,4 (July 1980), 419–438.
Stefani, Célia Regina Baider. "O sistema ferroviário paulista: um estudo sobre a evolução do transporte de transporte de passageiros sobre trilhos." MA thesis, FFLCH-USP, São Paulo, 2007.

Stein, Stanley J. *The Brazilian Cotton Manufacture: Textile Enterprise in an Underdeveloped Area, 1850-1950* (Cambridge, MA: Harvard University Press, 1957a).

———. *Vassouras, a Brazilian Coffee County, 1850-1900* (Cambridge, MA: Harvard University Press, 1957b).

Stepan, Alfred. "As prerrogativas militares nos regimes pós-autoritários: Brasil, Argentina, Uruguai e Espanha," in *Democratizando o Brasil*, ed. Alfred Stepan (Rio de Janeiro: Paz e Terra, 1985), 521-572.

———, ed. *Authoritarian Brazil: Origins, Policies and Future* (New Haven, CT: Yale University Press, 1973).

Summerhill, William R. *Order against Progress: Government, Foreign Investment, and Railroads in Brazil, 1854-1913* (Stanford, CA: Stanford University Press, 2003).

Suzigan, Wilson. *Indústria Brasileira. Origens e Desenvolvimento* (São Paulo: Brasiliense, 1986).

Sweigart, Joseph Earl. "Financing and Marketing Brazilian Export Agriculture: The Coffee Factors of Rio De Janeiro, 1850-1888." PhD thesis, University of Texas at Austin, 1980.

Szmrecsányi, Tamáz. "O Desenvolvimento da Produção Agropecuária (1930-1970)," in *História da civilização brasileira III. O Brasil Républicano, 4. Economia e cultura (1930-1964)*, ed. Boris Fausto (Rio de Janeiro: Beltrand Brasil, 1995), 107-207.

Tavares, Maria da Conceição. *Destruição não-criadora* (Rio de Janeiro: Record, 1990).

———. "Sistema financeiro e o ciclo de expansão recente," in *Desenvolvimento capitalista no Brasil: ensaios sobre a crise*, Vol. 2, ed. Luís Belluzzo and Renata Coutinho (São Paulo: Brasiliense, 1982), 107-138.

———. "Auge e Declínio do processo de substituição de importações no Brasil," in *Da substituição de importações ao capitalismo financeiro*, ed. Maria da Conceição Tavares (Rio de Janeiro: Zahar, 1973), 27-115.

Tavares, Maria da Conceição, and José Serra. "Mais além da estagnação," in *Da substituição de importações ao capitalismo financeiro*, ed. Maria da Conceição Tavares (Rio de Janeiro: Zahar, 1972), 155-207.

Távora, Fernando Lagares. "História e economia dos biocombustíveis no Brasil," Textos para Discussão No. 89 (Brasília: Centro de Estudos da Consultoria do Senado, Abril 2011).

Teodoro, Rodrigo da Silva. "O crédito no mundo dos senhores do café. Franca 1885-1914." MA thesis, Campinas, Instituto de Economia, UNICAMP, 2006.

Tomasini, Roque Silvestre Annes, and Ivo Ambrosi. "Aspectos econômicos da cultura do trigo," *Cadernos de Ciência e Tecnologia* (Brasilia) 15,2 (Maio-Agosto 1998), 59-84.

Topik, Steven. *The Political Economy of the Brazilian State, 1889-1930* (Austin: University of Texas Press, 1987).

———. "State Enterprise in a Liberal Regime: The Banco do Brasil, 1905-1930," *Journal of Interamerican Studies and World Affairs* (Special Issue) 22,4 (November 1980), 401-422.

_____. "The Evolution of the Economy Role of the Brazilian State, 1889–1930," *Latin American Studies* 11,2 (November 1979), 325–342.
Triner, Gail D. *Mining and the State in Brazilian Development* (London: Pickering & Chatto, 2011).
_____. *Banking and Economic Development: Brazil, 1889–1930* (New York: Palgrave, 2000).
Triner, Gail D., and K. Wandschneider. "The Baring Crisis and the Brazilian Encilhamento, 1889–1891: An Early Example of Contagion among Emerging Capital Markets," *Financial History Review* 12,2 (2005), 199–225.
Vargas, Getúlio. *A Nova política do Brasil: O Estado Novo (10 de novembro de 1937 a 15 de julho de 1938)* (Rio de Janeiro: José Olympio, 1944).
Veiga, José Eli da. "O Brasil rural ainda não encontrou seu eixo de desenvolvimento," *Estudos Avançados USP* 43 (Setembro–Dezembro 2001), 101–119.
Velasco Jr., Licínio. *Privatização: mitos e falsas percepções* (Rio de Janeiro: BNDES).
Velloso, João P. dos Reis. "A fantasia política: a nova alternativa de interpretação do II PND," *Revista de Economia Política* 18,2 (70) (1998), 133–144.
Versiani, Flávio Rabelo, and Maria Tereza R. O. Versiani. "A industrialização brasileira antes de 1930: uma contribuição," in *Formação Econômica do Brasil. A experiência da industrialização*, ed. Flavio Rabelo Versiani and José Roberto Mendonça de Barros (São Paulo: Saraiva, 1977), 121–142.
Vianna, Sérgio Besserman. "Duas Tentativas de Estabilização: 1951–1954," in *A ordem do Progresso*, ed. Marcelo de Paiva Abreu (Rio de Janeiro: Editora Campus, 1992a), 123–150.
_____. "Política econômica externa e industrialização: 1946–1951," in *A ordem do Progresso*, ed. Marcelo de Paiva Abreu (Rio de Janeiro: Editora Campus, 1992b), 105–122.
_____. "A Política Econômica no Segundo Governo Vargas (1951–1954)." MA thesis, Rio de Janeiro, PUC/RJ, 1987.
Vieira, Dorival Teixeira. *Evolução do Sistema Monetário Brasileira* (São Paulo: IPE-USP, 1981).
Vilardo, Franceschina. "A burguesia cafeeira paulista e a política econômica na Primeira República." MA thesis, Campinas, Departamento de Ciências Sociais, UNICAMP, 1986.
Villa, Marco Antonio. *A História das Constituições Brasileiras* (São Paulo: Editora Leya, 2011).
Villela, Annibal Villanova, and Wilson Suzigan. *Política do governo e crescimento da econômica brasileira – 1889–1945* (Brasília: IPEA, 2001).
Viola, Eduardo J. "The Ecologist Movement in Brazil (1974–1986): From Environmentalism to Ecopolitics," *International Journal of Urban and Regional Research* 12,2 (June 1988), 211–228.
Wahrlich, Beatriz M. de Souza. *Reforma administrativa da era de Vargas* (Rio de Janeiro: Fundação Getúlio Vargas, 1983).
Weffort, Francisco. *O populismo na política brasileira* (Rio de Janeiro: Paz e terra S/A, 1980).
Weidnmier, Marc D. "The Baring Crises and the Great Latin American Meltdowns of the 1890s." Available at http://emlab.berkeley.edu/~webfac/eichengreen/e211_fa06/Mitchener.pdf.

Weinstein, Barbara. *For Social Peace in Brazil: Industrialists and the Remaking of the Working Class in São Paulo, 1920–1964* (Chapel Hill: University of North Carolina Press, 1996).

———. "The Industrialists, the State, and the Issues of Worker Training and Social Services in Brazil, 1930–50," *Hispanic American Historical Review* 70,3 (August 1990), 379–404.

———. *The Amazon Rubber Boom, 1850–1920* (Stanford, CA: Stanford University Press, 1983).

Werneck, Rogério. *Empresas estatais e política macroeconômica* (Rio de Janeiro: Campus, 1987).

———. "Poupança estatal, dívida externa e crise financeira do setor público," *Pesquisa e Planejamento Econômico* 16,3 (December 1986), 551–574.

Wirth, John D. *The Politics of Brazilian Development 1930–1954* (Stanford, CA: Stanford University Press, 1970).

Wood, Charles H. and José Alberto Magno de Carvalho. *The Demography of Inequality in Brazil* (Cambridge: Cambridge University Press, 1988).

Xavier, Marcus Renato S. "The Brazilian Sugarcane Ethanol Experience" (Washington, DC: Competitive Enterprise Institute, February 17, 2007).

Index

ABC district, 189n80
abertura ("opening"), 187
abortion rates, 2010, 232n143
Accelerated Development Program, 290–291
Account Movement, 204n98
Açominas steel plant, 202
adult diarrhea, 239–240
Afro-Brazilians, 24, 134–135, 350
AGAPAN (*Associação Gaucha de Proteção ao Ambiente Natural*; Gaucho Association for the Protection of the Natural Environment), 248n4
age distribution, military period, 234
age pyramid, military period, 234
age structure, 323–325
AGF (Federal Government Loans Program), 203, 265, 266n36, 268
Agricultural Portfolio Loan and Industrial Bank of Brazil, 113
agricultural research, 203, 205–206, 205n102, 264–265
agriculture sector
  expansion of, impact of, 60–61
  internal market, 57–59
  international market, 59–60
  in Juscelino period, 161, 170–171, 172–173
  mechanization, 152, 204, 226, 245, 263
  modernization in military period, 202–207
  in Old Republic, 60–61, 73–74, 81
  as percentage of GDP, 1948, 114
  as predominant activity, 73–74, 73n145
  relationship with industry, Old Republic (1889–1930), 73–74
  in Sarney period, 260–262, 264–265
  structural reform of, 95
  and Target Plan, 161
  and technology, 59–60, 152, 204, 226, 245, 263
  temporary/permanent crop increase, 121n84
  in twenty-first century, 300–304, 353
  in Vargas first period, 112–121, 121n84, 125
    doctrine of national security, 185–186
    exports, 112–113, 115–116
    family farms, 123–124
    land distribution, 120–123
    machinery use, 124–125
    productivity lack, 119–120
    total output, growth in, 116–118
    workforce, 114–115
AI-1 decree, 183, 185, 186, 188
Alcohol Program, 207
Aliança Nacional Libertadora, 88
Aliança Renovadora Nacional (ARENA; Renovating National Alliance), 185, 190
alternative fuels, 251–252
Amado, Jorge, 56–57
Amapá, 327
Amazon region, ecological issues, 250–251
Andreazza, Mário, 246
Annex C, 270, 271

421

anonymous societies, state control over, 37n81
antibiotics, 136–137
ARENA (Aliança Renovadora Nacional; Renovating National Alliance), 185, 190
Argentina
  bank collapses in, 38–39, 38n84
  doctors compared with world standards, 339n162
  life expectancy in, 5n1
  literacy in, 26n57
  Mercosul membership, 277
  urbanization in, 29
Asians, 130–131, 134, 225, 349
assassinations, 248
Associação Gaucha de Proteção ao Ambiente Natural (AGAPAN; Gaucho Association for the Protection of the Natural Environment), 248n4
Association to Aid Colonization and Immigration (*Associação Auxiliadora de Colonização e Imigração*), 9
authoritarianism, 86, 87–88
automotive industry, 161, 163
aviation industry, privatization of, 281

Baer, Werner, 93–94, 93n28
Bahia, 56–57, 227, 326
balance of payments, 34n71
  effect of exchange rate fluctuations, 17
  effect of industrialization post–World War II on, 149n15
  effect of wage labor on, 17
Banco do Brasil. See Bank of Brazil
Banco Nacional de Desenvolvimento Econômico. See National Economic Development Bank (*Banco Nacional de Desenvolvimento Econômico*; BNDES)
Banco Nacional da Habitação (BNH; National Housing Bank), 194, 218
bandeirantes (raiders), 2
Bank of Brazil (*Banco do Brasil*), 92–93, 96
  Account Movement of, 204
  discounts for active commercial banks, 167n59
  financial relationship with Central Bank of Brazil, 204n98
  modernization of, 157
  multiple functions of, 167–168, 167n61
  during Old Republic, 96n37
  and privatization of pension funds, 282
  Banking Cash Mobilization, 167n59
  Banking Mobilization Fund, 167
Barbosa, Rui, 36, 36n76, 36n79, 37
Baring Brothers Bank, 38–39, 38n84
Barros, Ademar de, 151n19
beans, 207
Belém, population statistics for, 27–28
Belindia, 240
Bello, José Maria, 85n7
Belo Horizonte, 28, 228–229
Bernardes, Artur, 83, 83n1, 84
BFCs (Continuous Cash Benefits), 332
birth rates
  Old Republic, 5, 22, 80
  Vargas first period, 138
  See also fertility rates
blacks (*pretos*), 24, 315, 349. *See also* race inequalities
BNDES. *See* National Economic Development Bank (*Banco Nacional de Desenvolvimento Econômico*)
BNH (*Banco Nacional da Habitação*; National Housing Bank), 194, 218
Boards of Labor Conciliation, 102
Bolsa Alimentação (food grants), 306–307, 337
Bolsa Escola (school grants), 306–307, 337
Bolsa Família (Family Grant Program), 298, 307–308, 307n82, 331, 332
bond issuance, 9n12
Brasília
  construction of, 160, 163n50
  interstate migration to, 327
  universities in, 223
Braudel, Fernand, 99–100
Brazilian Agricultural Research Corporation (Embrapa), 203, 205–206, 205n102
Brazilian Coffee Institute (IBC), 205, 262
Brazilian Democratic Movement Party (PMDB), 190, 246, 254, 269, 270
Brazilian Democratic Party (PDS), 190, 246–247, 254, 270
Brazilian Institute for the Environment and Renewable Natural Resources (IBAMA), 250
Brazilian Labor Party (*Partido Trabalhista Brasileiro*; PTB), 145, 288

Index

Brazilian Social Democracy Party (PSDB), 254, 269, 270, 273, 288
Bretton Woods conferences, 148
BRICs, 289, 290–291, 304–305, 353
Brizola, Leonel, 254, 269, 270, 273
Broad Front, 185n77
bubonic plague, 104
budget deficits
 and crisis of 1980s, 262
 in Kubitschek period, 166–168
 in military period, 209
 in republican period, 39–40, 40n87, 41
buffer stocks, 203, 204, 262, 265

Cacao Institute of Bahia, 57n113
cacao production, 56–57, 59, 116
Cachoeira, 11–12
Cadastro Único (census of cash transfer recipients), 337
Caixa de Aposentadoria e Pensões (CAPS), 103–104, 243
Caixa Econômica Federal, 282
Calógeras, João Pandiá, 34n68
Campanha Nacional de Aperfeiçoamento de Pessoal de Nível Superior (CAPES; National Campaign for Improving Personnel in Higher Education), 157–158, 223
Campinas Agronomy Institute, 223–224
Canada, health care in, 339n159, 339n162
cancer, 239–240, 322, 352
Canudos conflict, 33n66
Capanema, Gustavo, 99
CAPES (*Campanha Nacional de Aperfeiçoamento de Pessoal de Nível Superior*; National Campaign for Improving Personnel in Higher Education), 157–158, 223
capital flight, 79
CAPS (*Caixa de Aposentadoria e Pensões*), 103–104, 243
captaincies, 1
Cardoso, Fernando Henrique
 elected president, 273
 reelected president, 274–275
Cardoso period, 70–71, 70n135
 economy, 275–279, 291–292
 capital flight, 278–279
 crisis, effects on international markets, 283–285
 economic stimulation, 280–281
 monetary illusion, 278
 phases in economic policy, 287–288
 privatization, 281–283
 Real Plan, 273, 275–276
 response to international crisis, 283–285
 state and local governments, 285–286
 electrical energy crisis, 288
 income transfers, 306
 industry, 279
 popularity of, 289n57
 and Real Plan, 273, 275–276
 reelected president, 274–275
 reforms, 273–275
 economic, 274
 electoral, 274–275
 legal, 274
 social, 274, 274n43
 trade liberalization, 276–277
Carter, Jimmy, 187
cassava, 207
Castelo Branco, 183
 election as president, 184, 191–194
Castelo Branco period
 correction of goods/public service prices, 192–193
 economic policy, 191–192
 economic policy, criticism of, 198–199
 national credit market, 193–194
 workplace changes, 192
cattle industry, 245
Ceará, 177–178, 326
censorship, 183–184
centesimal system, 178n66
Central Bank of Brazil
 financial relationship with Bank of Brazil, 204n98
 interest and exchange rates as targets of, 299n68
 and privatization of pension funds, 282
 and rural credit system, 204
centralization
 in military period, 83, 86, 104, 105, 183–184
 in monarchy, 21–22
CEPAL, 62n120
cereal production, 59n114
Cerrado region, geographic extent of, 121n85
Chagas, Carlos, 104–105
Chaves, Aureliano, 269
child labor, 337

child mortality
    decline in, 352
    regional differences, 321n107
Chile, 29, 335
cholera epidemic, 104
Cia Siderurgica Nacional, 281–282
class inequalities, 4–5
    in education attainment, 310
    in life expectancy, 240–241
    in Lula period, 311, 349–350
    in military period, 219
climate change, 16
Clube Militar (Brazil), 21
CNPq (*Conselho Nacional de Pesquisa*;
    National Research Council), 157,
    223
coffee *fazendas*, 71, 72
coffee industry
    coffee valuation program, 48–49,
        48n101
    consumption, worldwide, 13
    crisis in, 41–51
    exports, 53–55
    government intervention, 44–49, 262
    in Kubitschek period, 173–174
    in Old Republic, 44–49, 78, 79
    opposition to Instruction 70 of SUMOC,
        154n29
    permanent defense plan for, 48–49
    prices, 16n29, 41–51
        cycles in, 1857–1906, 16–17
        influences on, 14–17
        during World War II, 146n8
        post World War II, 147n12
    and structural reform, 95
    tax on, 90, 90n17
    valorization scheme for, 42–44, 47
    in Vargas first period, 89–92
coffee merchants (*comissários*), 48
coffee production
    change in regional base of, 13–14
    in colonial era, 2–3
    expansion of, 6, 7–8
    labor issues, 7–11
    overproduction, 41–44, 44n94, 51
    transition to wage labor, 6, 8–10, 17–18
    transport issues, 11–13
    as worldwide leader, 59
coffee valuation program, 48–49, 48n101
Cold War, 151, 183, 186–187
Collor de Mello, Fernando
    economics of, 270–271

election of, 269–270
    impeachment of, 272
    industry sector, 271–272
    Washington Consensus, 270–271
colonial period
    captaincies, 1
    capital moved to Rio de Janeiro, 2
    education, 4
    fertility rates, 4
    mining industry, 2
    mortality/life expectancy, 4, 5–6
    phases of settlement, 2
    as settler colony, 1
    social stratification, 4–5
    See also coffee production; population
        growth; sugar industry
colonos, 10–11, 70–71, 70n135,
    71n135
    in Old Republic (1889–1930), 10–11
color, definitions of, 25n52. *See also* race
    inequalities
communists, 87
Conselho Nacional de Pesquisa (CNPq;
    National Research Council), 157,
    223
consumer goods industry, 110
Consumer Price Index (IPCA), 287
consumption tax (1899), 68n128
Continuous Cash Benefits (BFCs), 332
contraceptives, 232, 311, 314–315,
    314n95
corn, 57, 59, 121, 172
coronels (*coronéis*; local landlords),
    56–57
Corporation Law (1890), 37n81
corporations, rise of, 37
Cosipa steel mill (in São Paulo), 164–165
Costa e Silva, 185–186, 194–199
    economic miracle, 195, 199
    economy, 194–197
    industrialization, 197–198
cotton industry
    expansion of, 63, 115–116
    exports, 115
    exports, fall between 1951/1952,
        153n26
    in Old Republic, 52, 53–55, 57–58
    percentage of worldwide output, 59
    variations in market for, 115–116,
        115n80
cotton seed oil, 115
Council of Industrial Development, 157

Covas, Mario, 269
credit expansion, 304
Cruz, Oswaldo, 104
Cruzado Plan, 217, 256–257
cruzeiro, exchange rate of, 93n27
Cuba, medical care in, 339n162
Currency Board (*Caixa de Estabilização*), 44–45, 46–47, 48, 89
currency crisis, 1935, 97n41
currency devaluation, 18, 37–38, 37n83, 41
currency-issuing banks, 36n78
CVM (Securities and Exchange Commission), 196n90

Dean, Warren, 71–72, 72n139
debt
  1889, federal government of Brazil, 40n86
  1980s crisis, 213–214, 217, 255–259
  Collar government, 276
  Mexican crisis, 1982, 213
  military period, 198–199, 207–208, 210–211
  republican period, 39–41
  Russian crisis, 1998, 283
  Sarney government, 258–259
decentralization
  of economy, 79
  fiscal, 253
  of government, 73, 351
  of health care system, 104–105, 338, 340, 352
deforestation, 249, 252–253
deindustrialization, 299–300
Delfim Netto, Antonio, 195, 213
Democratic Brazilian Movement (*Movimento Democrático Brasileiro*; MDB), 190
Democratic Labor Party (PDT), 254, 298
Democratic Party of São Paulo (Partido Democrático de São Paulo), 84–85
Deodoro da Fonseca, Marechal, 21, 32–33
Department of Health, 105
dependency theory, 273, 273n40
deregulation of economy, 269
diamond exports, decline in, 51
diamond mining, 2
dirty floating exchange rate, 288, 290
divorce, 345
DKW (Vemag Brazil), 169

DNER, 166
DNSP (National Public Health Department), 104–105
doctors, Brazil compared with world standards, 339n162
doctrine of national security, 185–186
durable consumer goods, 197–198, 209, 244
Dutch Disease, 299–300
Dutra, Gaspar, election of, 145
Dutra period
  economy, 143–144, 146–148, 149–150
  industrial sector, 148
  international transformations, influence on, 148–149
  political concerns, 144–146, 150–151

Economic Action Plan of the Government (PAEG), 191
Economic Betterment Fund (*Fundo de Reaparelhamento Econômico*), 152, 157
economic miracle, 195, 199
economic policy
  in Cardoso period, 275–279, 291–292
  in Dutra period, 143–144, 146–148, 149–150
  in Itamar Franco period, 273
  in Kubitschek period, 158, 159
  in Lula period, 289–296
  in military period, 194–197, 200–201, 207–212, 244
  in Old Republic, 33–37, 41, 44n96
  Real Plan, 273, 275–276
economy
  crisis of 1913, 78
  crisis of 1920, 79
  crisis of 1929, 79
  decentralization of, 79
  deregulation of, 269
  foreign reserves, 153n27
  opening of, 351–352
  Real Plan, 273, 275–276, 285n49, 306, 352
  World War II effect on, 125–126, 141
  See also exchange rate; exports; foreign investment; imports
education
  at creation of independent nation, 27
  decrease of regional disparities in, 353
  increase in state investments in, 26n56

education (cont.)
  in Lula period, 309, 310, 340–343, 350
  in monarchy and early republican era, 25–27, 80
  rate of schooling by age and region, 2011, 26n56
  in Vargas first period, 99–101, 126, 128–134
    industrial and commercial education, 100–101
    religious education in public schools, 99
    tertiary education in public schools, 99–100
  in Vargas second period, 157–158
  See also universities
EGF (Federal Government Loans Program), 203, 266–267, 266n36
Eisenberg, Peter, 52n103
Eisenhower administration, 155
Elections Now (*Diretas Já*) movement, 246
electrical/communications equipment, 169–170
electricity sector
  foreign vs. domestic owned companies, 110
  hydroelectric power, 108–109
  privatization of, 274, 281, 282–283, 282n47
Eletrobrás, 157, 157n35
Elói Chaves law, 103
Embrapa (*Empresa Brasileira de Pesquisa Agropecuária*; Brazilian Agricultural Research Corporation), 203, 205–206, 205n102
Encilhamento (market bubble), 37–38, 37n83, 63
enterprise vs. establishment, 110n72
environmental protection, 248–253
Escola Superior de Guerra (ESG; Superior War College), 185–186
Espírito Santo, internal migration to, 30
establishment vs. enterprise, 110n72
Estado Novo, creation of, 88. See also Vargas, Getúlio, first period
Estrada de Ferro D. Pedro II (railroad), 11–12
ethanol, 251–252, 261–262, 263
Ethanol Program, 263
exchange confiscation, 154n29

exchange rate
  and Central Bank of Brazil, 299n68
  of *cruzeiro*, 93n27
  devaluation, 39
  dirty floating exchange rate, 288, 290
  fixed, 45, 46, 147, 153
  floating, 287–288, 292, 294, 298
  fluctuations in, 17, 34n71
  free market in, 154
  rates, 2002, 294n63
  two tier, 148
Executive Commission for Rural Economic-Recovery of Cocoa Farming (CEPLAC), 57n113
Executives Group (*Grupos Executivos*), 169
Eximbank, 152
exports
  agriculture, Vargas first period, 112–113, 115–116
  cacao, 116
  coffee industry, 53–55
  cotton industry, 115, 153n26
  cycle of, correlation to factory investments, Old Republic, 63
  diamond exports decline, 51
  export houses, 35n74
  gold exports decline, 51
  iron ore, 174
  in Kubitschek period, 174
  licenses for, 266
  primary export model, Depression era, 92n23
  quota system for, 266
  sugar industry, 116
  textile industry, 115
  tobacco, 116
  Vargas first period, 92n23, 125–126
  wood, 174
  yerba mate, 116

Family Health Program (*Programa de Saúde da Família*; PSF), 338
fascists (*integralistas*), 87, 88n15
favelas, 229–230
fazendas, 71, 72
FDI (foreign direct investment), 295–296
Federal district, industry sector in, 107, 109
Federal Electricity Foundation, 157
Federal Government Acquisitions Program (AGF), 203, 266–268

Federal Government Loans Program
 (EGF), 203, 265, 266n36, 267
federalist movement, 32, 32n64
Federal Railroad system (Rede Ferroviária
 Federal), 165
fertility rates
 in colonial era, 4, 5
 decline in, 352
 in Lula period, 311–316
 in military period, 218, 219, 231–234
 in Old Republic, 5, 22
 in Vargas, first period, 126, 138–139
fertilizers, 171, 204, 205
FGTS (Fundo de Garantia do Tempo de
 Serviço; Guarantee Fund for Length
 of Service), 194, 209, 211
Figueiredo, João Baptista, 189–190,
 212–217
 amnesty program, 190
 party system, 190
financing needs of the public sector (NFSP),
 213–214
Fiscal Responsibility Law, 285, 292
fish, imported, 175
fixed exchange rate, 45, 46, 147, 153
flex-fuel engines, 263
floating exchange rate, 287–288, 292, 294,
 298
 dirty, 288, 290
floating interest rate, 199, 207–208
Fonseca, Floriano da, 33
Fonseca, Pedro Cezar Dutra, 113n74
Ford, Henry, 56
foreign direct investment (FDI), 295–296
foreign investment
 in Brazil, 60n117
 in Collor period, 270
 in Juscelino period, 168
 in Lula period, 296
 in military period, 244
 and Mixed Brazil–United States
  Commission, 152
 in republican period, 38
 in Vargas second period, 155
foreign reserves, 153n27
Foreign Trade Portfolio (Cacex), 167
forests, and deforestation, 249, 252–253
Four Points Program, 152n23
Franco, Gustavo H. B., 34n71, 289n57
Franco, Itamar, 272–273
Fund for Technology, 223

Fundo de Assistência ao Trabalhador
 Rural (FUNRURAL; National Road
 Fund), 166n55, 243, 335
Fundo de Garantia do Tempo de Serviço
 (FGTS; Guarantee Fund for Length
 of Service), 194, 209, 211
Fundo de Reaparelhamento Econômico
 (Economic Betterment Fund), 152,
 157
Furnas, hydroelectric plant at, 165
Furtado, Celso, 40n87, 61n119, 62n120,
 91–92

Gaucho Association for the Protection of
 the Natural Environment
 (Associação Gaucha de Proteção ao
 Ambiente Natural; AGAPAN),
 248n4
GDP
 agriculture, 1929, 73–74
 agriculture, 1948, 114
 agriculture, twenty-first century, 300
 during Collor administration, 270–271,
 278, 279, 280
 electric power crisis effect on, 288
 in empire, 75
 in Figueiredo administration, 214, 215
 and Financial Stabilization Plan, 285
 income transfers as percentage of, 337
 infrastructure as percentage of, 305
 in Juscelino administration, 176–178
 and manufactures, 299
 during military period, 197, 208–209
 in Old Republic, 75–76
 and operating deficit, 1998, 283
 recent growth in, 298
 and trade deficit, 279, 280
 in Vargas first period, 93–94, 106–112,
 113
Geisel, Ernest, assumption to power,
 186–190, 200–202
Geisel period
 ecological issues, 249
 economy, 200–201, 207–212
 first oil shock of 1973, 187, 200–201
 manufacturing, 201–202
 move toward democracy, 187–188
 municipal elections, 188
 "opening" (abertura), 187
 repression, 187–188
 trade union movement, 188–189

gender differences
  in education attainment, 134, 350
  in employment, 134
  heads of households, 2009, 346–347, 346n180
  in labor force participation, 313–314, 313n92
  in life expectancy, 240, 321–322
  in literacy, 130–134, 224–225, 225n130
  in university attendance, 312n87
General Inspectorship of Hygiene, 104
GINI index of inequality, 348, 352–353
globalization, 271, 277, 351–352
Goiás state, mining in, 2
gold exports, decline in, 51
gold mining, 2
gold reserves, 49–51, 79
gold standard, 18
Goulart, João
  assumes presidency, 181–182
  and economic crisis, 182
  election as vice president, 180
  military coup overthrows, 182
  relationship with military, 158n41
  and social security, 243
  Triennial Plan of, 182
Great Britain, 125, 147
Great Depression, 79, 81, 85, 86, 125, 126
Great Leap Forward, 223
Great Recession of 2008, 292
Growth Acceleration Program, 290
Guanabara, 176–177, 184, 184n76
Guarantee Fund for Length of Service (*Fundo de Garantia do Tempo de Serviço*; FGTS), 194, 209, 211
guarantee minimum Prices (PGPM), 266–267
Guevara, Che, 180
Guimarães, Ulysses, 269

Haber, Stephen H., 93–94, 93n28
heads of households
  dual parent vs. female, 346
  by sex, 2009, 346–347, 346n180
health care
  access to, 338n157, 352–353
  beds compared with world standards, 339n159
  decrease of regional disparities, 353
  immunization, 236–237, 311

private health insurance, 340
vaccination campaigns, 22–24, 104, 317
health policy
  in Lula period, 338–340
  military interregnum, 234–237
  in Vargas first period, 104–105
heart disease, 239–240, 322, 352
Hermes da Fonseca, Marechal, 77
highway system. *See* transport system
Hospedaria dos Imigrantes, 9
household debt, 2012, 304n75
Household Survey (PNAD; 2011), 344–345
housing
  favelas, 229–230
  funding for, 194, 211–212
  during military interregnum, 229–230
  mortgage financing, 194, 212
  public housing, 218, 230
  See also sanitation
human rights, post-1980, 247–248, 351
hunger, 333–334
Hydroelectric Company of São Francisco, 98
hydroelectric power, 108–109
hyperinflation, 258, 269

IAA (Institute of Sugar and Alcohol), 205, 262
IAPS (Institutes), 103, 141, 243
IBC (Brazilian Coffee Institute), 205, 262
IGP-M index, 286n54
illiterates, voting rights for, 80, 181–182, 182n71, 254. *See also* literacy rates
IMF (International Monetary Fund), 213–214, 255, 260, 262, 265, 283–284
immigration, 10n15
  effect on color composition of population, 24–25
  effect on population growth, 24
  and industrialization of São Paulo, 72
  in Old Republic, 9–10, 25
  in Vargas first period (1930–1945), 126–128
immunization, 236–237, 311
impeachment, of Collor, 272
Imperial Council of Public Hygiene, 104
imports
  change in distribution of, 97n40
  in Kubitschek government, 174–175

licenses for, 153–154, 154n28, 197, 266
textile industry, 65n126, 66
import substitution, 96–98, 97n42, 158–159, 271–272
Incentive Program for the Reduction of State Public Sector in Banking Activities (*Proes*), 286n54
income disparities, decrease, 2001–10, 306n78
indexation
  in military period, 215
  by National Economic Development Bank, 211
  and rural loans, 261
  under Sarney administration, 255, 258, 261
Index of Prices Paid by Rural Producers (IPP), 268
Index of Prices Received by Rural Producers (IPR), 268
Indians, 2, 29
industry sector
  automotive industry, 161, 163
  aviation industry privatization, 281
  in Collor period, 271–272
  consumer goods industry, 110
  development in, 37–38, 61–68
  in Dutra period, 148
  electricity generation companies, 108–109, 110
  in Federal District, 107
  firm size, 110
  five-year plan for, 98n43
  foreign-born industrialists, 72–73
  foreign vs. domestic capital investment in, 109
  in Kubitschek period, 159, 164, 169–170
  livestock industry, 57, 60
  mining industry, 2
  in Old Republic, 61–73, 79
  participation in GDP, by state, 113
  privatization of, 282–283, 282n47
  processed food industry, 109–110
  rubber industry, 55–56, 169–170
  steel industry, 98n45
  structural reform and, 95–96, 98–99
  textile industry, 110
  theory of adverse shocks, 62n120, 65n125
  in Vargas first period, 88, 106–112, 125

workforce, 110–112
  See also agriculture sector; coffee industry; cotton industry; textile industry
infant mortality
  decline in, 352
  in Lula period, 317–321
  in military period, 231, 237–239
  recent, 318n101
  in Vargas first period, 126, 136–137
infectious disease, 136–137, 239–240, 322, 352
inflation
  hyperinflation, 258, 269
  in Lula period, 292–294
  in military period, 215–216, 217
  in postmilitary regimes, 351
  in Sarney period, 255–259
inflation tax, 216n106, 256, 278
infrastructure, restrictions on investment in, 305n76
INPS (*Instituto Nacional de Previdência Social*; National Social Security Institute), 236, 243
Institute of Sugar and Alcohol (IAA), 205, 262
Institutes (IAPS), 103, 141, 243
institutional authoritarianism, 87
Instituto Nacional de Assistência Médica e Previdência Social (INAMPS; National Social Security Healthcare Institute), 236
Instituto Nacional de Previdência Social (INPS; National Social Security Institute), 236, 243
Instituto Osvaldo Cruz, 100
integralistas (fascists), 87, 88n15
interest rates
  and Central Bank of Brazil, 299n68
  fixed, 199
  in Lula period, 294
  rise after establishment of Real Plan, 285n49
internal markets, 113n74
internal migration, 29–30
  education and age of migrants, 327n130
  in Lula period, 325–331
  to Paraná, 226–227
  to Rio de Janeiro, 30, 226–227, 326
  in Vargas first period, 126–127

International Bank of Reconstruction and Development, 152
international finance markets
  closed to Latin America, 257
  retraction in relation to Brazil, 38
International Monetary Fund (IMF), 213–214, 255, 260, 262, 265, 283–284
International Organization of Coffee, 174
Inter-State Organization of Ecologists for the Constituent Assembly, 249–250
interventor system, 87, 87n12
IPCA (Consumer Price Index), 287
IPEA, 268–269, 331n138
IPP (Index of Prices Paid by Rural Producers), 268
IPR (Index of Prices Received by Rural Producers), 268
iron ore exports, 174

Jango, 181n70
Joint Brazil–United States, 152n23
judicial system, 145–146, 274
Junta Militar, 186

Korean War, 151, 153–154, 173–174
Kubitschek, Juscelino
  election of, 158
  relationship with the military, 158n39, 159–160, 159n45
Kubitschek period
  agriculture sector, 161, 170–171, 172–173
  automotive industry, 161, 163
  coffee sector, 173–174
  construction of Brasilia, 163
  economy, 158, 159
  employment, 176
  energy, 160
  exports, 174
  financing of, 163–164, 166–168
  GDP, disparities in, 176–178
  imports, 174–175
  import substitution, 158–159
  industrialization, 159, 164, 169–170
  landownership, 171–172
  military, role of, 159–160
  new administrative structures, 168–169
  opening to foreign capital, 164
  political stability, 159–160
  public-sector expansion in economic activity, 164–166

Target Plan (*See* Target Plan [*Plano de Metas*])
technical personnel, 161
transport system, 160–161

Labor Day (May 1), 102
labor force participation, women, 2007, 313–314, 313n92
labor issues
  Catholic Church involvement in, 181, 189
  and coffee production, 7–11
  labor movement in Rio de Janeiro, 76–77
  labor movement in São Paulo, 76–77
  in Old Republic, 76–77, 79–80
  strikes in Brazil, 76–77
  trade union movement in Geisel period, 188–189
  unicidade sindical policy, 102, 102n53
  in Vargas first period, 101–102
  in Vargas second period, 155–156
  See also wage labor, transition to
Labor Justice system, 102
labor reserve army, 171
Lacerda, 156–157, 185n77
latifundia system, 202
Latin America, health care in, 339n159, 339n162
Law of Amnesty, 190
Law of Free Birth (Brazil), 9, 18–19
Law of National Similarity, 270
Lei Áurea (abolition of slavery), 19
Lei Orgânica da Previdência Social, 243
Levi Straus, Claude, 99–100
liabilities, 204
Liberal Front Party (PFL), 254
lieutenants, 86n8
life expectancy, 5n1
  class differences in, 240–241
  in colonial era, 4
  gender differences in, 240, 321–322
  increase in, 352
  in Lula period, 321–322
  in Old Republic, 5
  race differences in, 240–241
  in Vargas first period, 126, 137–138
  See also mortality rates
Lisbon Declaration, 185n77
literacy programs, influence on electoral equilibrium, 182n71

literacy rates
  by color and sex, 2010, 225n130
  late nineteenth/early twentieth century, 25–26
  in Vargas first period, 126, 130–134
livestock industry, 57, 60
Lloyd Brasileiro, 165–166
loan of last resort, 167n59
Luís, Washington, 85, 89
Luiz Inacio Lula da Silva (Lula)
  economic policy, 289–296
    inflation, 292–294
    interest rates, 294
    and international crisis, 295–296
    Real Plan, 306
  election of, 288–289
  popularity of, 296–298
  social policy, 305–350
    class inequalities, 311, 349–350
    education, 309, 310, 340–343, 350
    fertility rates, 311–316
    household type, 344–346
    income distribution, 348–349
    infant mortality, 317–321
    interregional migration, 325–331
    life expectancy, 321–322
    mobility, 309–311
    mortality, 317–323
    pensions, 334–337
    poverty, 331–334
    public health, 338–340
    race inequalities, 311, 348–349, 350
    religion, 343–344, 346–348
    transfer programs, 306–307, 337–338
  as union president, 189

malnutrition, 333–334
Maluf, Paulo, 246
marajas (maharajas), 269–270
Maranhão, 177–178
marriage, 343–346, 348
Masonry, 20
Matarazzo, Francisco, 72n139
maternal mortality, 126
Mato Grosso state, 2, 327
MDB (*Movimento Democrático Brasileiro*; Democratic Brazilian Movement), 190
Médici, Emílio Garrastazu, 186
meio ambiente (environment) movement, 248–253
Mendes, Chico, 249

mensalão scandal (monthly bribes for votes of national legislators), 254–255, 254n20, 298, 298n66
merchant marine, 165–166
Mercosul treaty (Southern Common Market), 277, 277n45
mestizos (*caboclos*), 2
metalists, 34
migration. *See* internal migration; immigration
military period
  agriculture modernization in, 202–207
    beans, 207
    cassava, 207
    concentration of land, 202–203
    corn, 206, 207
    mechanization, 226
    National Rural Credit (SNCR), 203–204
    processed oranges, 206–207
    proagricultural policies, 203–205
    research program, 205
    rice, 207
    soybeans, 206
    sugar and alcohol, 205, 207
    wheat, 205, 207
  Castelo Branco presidency, 184, 191–194
    correction of goods and public service prices, 192–193
    economic policy, 191–192
    economic policy, criticism of, 198–199
    national credit market, 193–194
    workplace changes, 192
  corruption in military, 186
  Costa e Silva presidency, 185–186, 194–199
    economic miracle, 195, 199
    economy, 194–197
    industrialization, 197–198
  debt crisis of 1980s, 213–214, 217
    domestic adjustment/favorable international conditions effect on, 214–217
    IMF agreement, 214
    indexing, 215
    inflation, 215–216, 217
    internal economic structure, 215–217
    recession, 214
  economy, 244

military period (*cont.*)
  Emílio Garrastazu Médici presidency, 186
  Ernesto Geisel period, 186–190, 200–202
    ecological issues, 249
    economy, 200–201, 207–212
    first oil shock of 1973, 187, 200–201
    manufacturing, 201–202
    move toward democracy, 187–188
    municipal elections, 188
    "opening" (*abertura*), 187
    repression, 187–188
    trade union movement, 188–189
  governance under, 183
  internal divisions among military, 183–184
  João Baptista Figueiredo period, 189–190, 212–217
    amnesty program, 190
    party system, 190
  political repression, 183
  relationship with United States, 186–187
  social changes, 217–245
    contraception use, 232
    education, primary and secondary, 222–223
    education, university, 223–224
    fertility rates, 218, 219, 231–234
    housing, 229–230
    industrialization effect on, 217–218, 219
    infant mortality, 231, 237–239
    internal migration, 219, 226–227
    life expectancy, 218, 219, 240–241
    literacy, 219, 224–225
    manufacturing jobs, 220
    mortality rates, 218, 219, 231, 234–237, 239–240
    natural growth rate, 241–243
    pension system, 243
    per capita income, 220
    PIB, 220
    public health system, 234–237
    race and class inequality, 219
    science and technology, 223–224
    service-sector jobs, 220
    social mobility, 220–222
    urbanization, 219, 227–230
  state governor elections, 184–185
mil réis, devaluation of, 18

Minas Gerais
  agricultural machinery use, 124–125
  foreign vs. domestic capital investment in industry sector, 109
  governor elections in, 184
  industrial growth in, 107
  internal migration to, 30
  livestock industry in, 60
  mining in, 2
  out-migration, 227
  universities in, 223
  Usiminas steel mill in, 164–165
Mineiros, manifesto of, 1943, 144n2
mineral resource sector
  exports, 174
  structural reform and, 95
minimum voting age, 254
minimum wage, 102, 156, 197, 304, 306, 333–334, 336
mining industry
  diamond mining, 2
  gold mining, 2
Ministry of Education and Health, 105
Ministry of the Environment and Urban Development, 250
Ministry of Health, 105
Ministry of Labor, 102
Ministry of Social Security, 236
Ministry of Welfare and Social Insurance (*Ministério da Previdência e Assistência Social*), 243
Mixed Brazil–United States Commission (CMBEU), 152–153
mobility
  circular, 220n112
  gender differences in, 221n115
  in Lula period, 309–311
  in military period, 220–222
  social fluidity measure, 220–221, 220n113
  structural, 220n112
moderator power, 159–160, 159n45
monarchical regime, 21
monarchy
  evaluation of, 21–22
  overthrowing of, 21
monetary scarcity, during empire, 33–34, 34n68
Monetary Stabilization Program (EMP), 166n57
Morais, Prudente de, 33, 33n65

mortality rates
  child mortality, 321n107, 352
  in colonial era, 4, 5–6
  decrease in, 352
  effect of sanitation on, 80
  in Lula period, 317–323
  maternal, 126
  in military period, 218, 219, 231, 234–237, 239–240
  in Old Republic, 5, 22, 80
  in Vargas first period, 126
  See also infant mortality; life expectancy
mortgage financing, 194
mothers, average age of, 314n94
Movimento Democrático Brasileiro (MDB; Democratic Brazilian Movement), 190
mulattos (pardos), 24, 131, 315, 349
  See also race inequalities
mule transport, 12
multinational companies, 164, 168, 196, 209, 280
Murtinho, Joaquim, 42, 42n91

National Campaign for Improving Personnel in Higher Education (Campanha Nacional de Aperfeiçoamento de Pessoal de Nível Superior; CAPES), 157–158, 223
National Coffee Council, 90
National Democratic Union (União Democrática Nacional; UDN), 144–145, 151n19, 156–157, 184
National Department of Coffee, 90
National Economic Development Bank (Banco Nacional de Desenvolvimento Econômico; BNDES)
  creation of, 152
  and foreign loans, 169
  indexation by, 211
  and industrial expansion, 160
  and privatization, 281
  technology fund, 223
  and Vargas government, 157
National Health and Social Medicine Assistance Department, 105
National Highway Fund, 166
National Housing Bank (Banco Nacional da Habitação; BNH), 194, 218

National Information Service (Serviço Nacional de Informações; SNI), 185
National Public Health Department (DNSP), 104–105
National Reconstruction Party (PRN), 269–270
National Research Council (Conselho Nacional de Pesquisa; CNPq), 157, 223
National Road Fund (Fundo de Assistência ao Trabalhador Rural; FUNRURAL), 166n55, 243, 335
National Road Plan, 157
National Rural Credit (SNCR), 203–204
National Salt Company, 98
National Social Security Healthcare Institute (Instituto Nacional de Assistência Médica e Previdência Social; INAMPS), 236, 243
National Social Security Institute (Instituto Nacional de Previdência Social; INPS), 236, 243
National Social Security Institute (Instituto Nacional do Seguro Social; INSS), 335
National Steel Company, 98–99
National Treasury Bills (LTN), 209
Netherlands, 299–300
Neves, Tancredo, 246, 247
NFSP (financing needs of the public sector), 213–214
Nicol, Robert N. V. C., 62n121, 63n122
Nobrega, Mailson da, 299n68
nuclear program, 202, 223–224

oil crisis, 187, 200–201, 251, 261–262, 263
oil and oil products, privatization of, 274, 281
Old Republic (1889–1930)
  agriculture, 60–61, 73–74, 81
  cacao production, 56–57
  coffee market, 44–49, 78, 79
  colonos in, 10–11
  cotton industry, 53–55
  decentralization, 79
  economy, 33–41
  education, 27, 28
  electoral regime in, 83
  evaluation of, 77–81
  fertility/birth rate, 5, 22

434 Index

Old Republic (1889–1930) (cont.)
  first provisional government, 32–33
  free wage labor, 6–7, 9, 17–18
  GDP increase, 75–76
  government structure, 32
  immigration, 9–10, 25
  industrialization, 61–73, 79
  labor relations, 76–77, 79–80
  livestock industry, 60
  mortality/life expectancy, 5
  per capita GDP, 75–76
  per capita income, 21–22
  political activism, 76–77
  political basis of, 82–83
  Politics of Government agreement, 33
  popular protests in, 84–85
  population growth, 24
  rebellions of 1920s, 83–84
  rubber industry, 55–56
  sugar industry, 51–53
  transportation sector, 60–61
  urbanization, 27–29
  youthfulness of population, 24
  See also coffee production; sugar industry
"opening" (abertura), 187

PAEG (Economic Action Plan of the Government), 191
Pará, ecological movement in, 249
Paraguay, and Mercosul, 277, 277n45
Paraiba Valley
  coffee production in, 10–11
  emancipation, effect on, 35
  out-migration, 326
  railroads and, 12
Paraná
  coffee production in, 118n81
  internal migration to, 226–227
Pariba Valley, remuneration for colonos in, 10–11
parliamentary system, 181–182
Partido Democrático de São Paulo (Democratic Party of São Paulo), 84–85
Partido dos Trabalhadores, 190, 250, 252–254, 273–274, 285, 288–289, 294, 297–298. See Workers' Party (Partido dos Trabalhadores; PT)
Partido Liberal (PL), 288

Partido Republicano Paulista (Republican Party of São Paulo), 20
Partido Social Democrático (PSD; Social Democratic Party), 145, 151n19, 184
Partido Trabalhista Brasileiro (PTB; Brazilian Labor Party), 145, 288
Partido Verde (Green Party), 250
PBF (Programa Bolsa Família), 337
PDS (Brazilian Democratic Party), 190, 246–247, 254, 270
PDT (Democratic Labor Party), 254, 298
Pedro II (Brazil), 20n37
pelegos, 145–146
pension funds (caixas de pensões), 102–104, 105
  privatization of, 282
pensions
  beneficiary growth, 336n148
  conditional cash transfers for, 352–353
  in Lula period, 334–337
  in military period, 243
  per capita growth, nineteenth century, 21–22
  per capita income, convergence in, 348–349, 348n183
Permanent Defense of Coffee, 48–49
Permanent Defense of National Production, 48
Pernambuco, 227, 326
Pessoa, João, 85
pesticides, 171, 204, 205
PETI (Programa de Erradicação do Trabalho Infantil; Program to Eradicate Child Labor), 337
Petrobrás
  and alternative fuels, 251
  and privatization of pension funds, 282
  and Testament Letter, 157n35
  and Vargas government, 157
petroleum production, 165n54
PFL (Partido da Frente Liberal), 269, 270, 288
PGPM (guarantee minimum prices), 266–267
pharmaceuticals, 169–170
Piauí, 177–178
Pious IX (pope), 20
Piracicaba, 11

PMDB (Brazilian Democratic Movement Party), 190, 246, 254, 269, 270
PNAD (Household Survey; 2011), 344–345
pneumonia, 239–240
policy of guarantee minimum prices (PGPM), 266–268
Politics of the Governors (Brazil), 33
POLONOROESTE project, 250–251
population growth
 average age, nineteenth century, 24
 decline in, 352
 immigration, effect on, 24
 in nineteenth century, 3–4, 22–24
 Vargas first period, 126
population statistics
 Porto Alegre, 28, 228–229
Portfolio Exchange, 167
Portfolio Rediscount, 167n59
Porto Alegre, population statistics for, 28, 228–229
potato production, 59
poverty, extreme
 fall in extreme, 332n139
 IPEA definition of, 331n138
Prado, Antonio da Silva, 71n138, 72n139
Prestes column, 84, 84n2
Prestes, Julio, 85
Prestes, Luis Carlos, 84n2
price freeze, 256
primary export model, Depression era, 92n23
private health insurance, 340
privatization, 282–283, 282n47
 of aviation industry, 281
 in Cardoso period, 281–283
 of electricity sector, 274, 281, 282–283, 282n47
 of oil and oil products, 274
 of pension funds, 282
 of steel industry, 281
 of telecommunications sector, 274, 281, 282–283, 282n47
PROACOOL, 251
processed food industry, 109–110
Programa Bolsa Família (PBF), 337
Programa de Saúde da Família (PSF; Family Health Program), 338
Program to Eradicate Child Labor (*Programa de Erradicação do Trabalho Infantil*; PETI), 337

Program of Incentives to the Restructuring and Strengthening of National Financial System (*Proer*), 279
PRONAF, 331
Protestants, 346–348
Prouni program, 310
PSD (*Partido Social Democrático*; Social Democratic Party), 145, 151n19, 184
PSDB (Brazilian Social Democracy Party), 254, 269, 270, 273, 288
PSF (*Programa de Saúde da Família*; Family Health Program), 338
PT. See Workers' Party (*Partido dos Trabalhadores*; PT)
PTB (*Partido Trabalhista Brasileiro*; Brazilian Labor Party), 145, 288

Quadros, Janio
 economic policy of, 180–181
 election of, 179–180
 inaugural speech of, 181n68
 relationship with United States, 180
 resignation of, 181

race inequalities
 in education attainment, 350
 in employment, 134
 income distribution, 348–349
 in life expectancy, 240–241
 in literacy, 130–134, 225
 in literacy rates, 130–134, 225n130
 in Lula period, 311, 348–349, 350
 in place of residence, 134–136
railroads
 Estrada de Ferro D. Pedro II, 11–12
 expansion of, 12n24, 60–61, 70
 Federal Railroad system, 165
 in Paraiba Valley, 11
 in Rio de Janeiro, 11–12
 in Rio Grande do Sul, 11
 in São Paulo, 11–13, 70
 social impact of, 13
 Steel Railway, 202
 subsidies, 11–12, 11n19, 13n25
Ramenzoni, Dante, 72n139
Re-adjustable Treasury Bonds (ORTN) certificates, 209
real, consequences of overvaluation of, 290n60

Index

Real Plan, 273, 275–276, 285n49, 306, 352
Real Unit of Value (URV), 275–276
Recife, population statistics for, 27–28, 228–229
Rede Ferroviária Federal (Federal Railroad system), 165
Rediscount Portfolio, 167
regions, definitional issues, 127n90
religion, freedom of, 32
religious education in public schools, 99
repression, 183–184, 187–188, 190
Republican movement, 20–21, 32–34
Republican Party of São Paulo (*Partido Republicano Paulista*), 20
Revolution of 1930, 85n7, 101n52
rice, 59, 121, 172
Rio de Janeiro
  capital moved to during colonial era, 1
  favelas in, 229–230
  growth of service sector, 115
  hydroelectric power in, 108–109
  internal migration to, 30, 226–227, 326
  labor movement in, 76–77
  merger with Guanabara State, 184n76
  population statistics for, 27–28
  railroads and, 11–12
  textile industry in, 63n123
  urbanization of, 227, 228–229
  urban unrest in, 1920s, 84–85
  yellow fever epidemic in, 104
Rio Grande do Sul
  agricultural machinery use, 124–125
  crude birth rates, Vargas first period, 138
  ecological association, 248–249
  Federal Revolt in, 33n66
  foreign vs. domestic capital investment in industry sector, 109
  immigration not related to export economy, 123–124, 123n86
  industrial growth in, 107
  livestock industry in, 60
  out-migration, 227
  railroads and, 11
Rockefeller Foundation, 105
Roman Catholic Church
  labor movement and, 181, 189
  membership loss, 346–348
  and religiosity, 343–344
  republican movement and, 20

Rondônia, 327
Roraima, 327
Rousseff, Dilma, 298
rubber industry, 55–56, 169–170
rural credit, 203–204, 260–261
Russian crisis, 1998, 283

Sales, Campos, 33
  and budget deficit, 40
  and stabilization of coffee market, 41–42
Salvador, population statistics for, 27–28, 228–229
sanitation
  access to, twenty-first century, 349–350
  effect on infant mortality, 237–238
  effect on life expectancy, 5, 137
  effect on mortality, 80
  funding for, 194, 211–212
  program in military period, 218
  sanitation movement, 22–24, 104
  See also housing
Santa Catarina, 123–124, 123n86
Santos, 11, 11n18, 12, 76–77
São Paulo
  agricultural machinery use, 124–125
  agricultural output, 1940, 123
  coffee industry
    coffee planters, influence of, 73
    defense of coffee transferred to, 48–49
    importance in production, 1893–1991, 42n92
    overproduction in, 42, 45–46
    production in, 13–14
  Cosipa steel mill in, 164–165
  cotton production, 116
  crude birth rates, Vargas first period, 138
  foreign vs. domestic capital investment in industry sector, 109
  growth of, 326–327
  hydroelectric power, 108–109
  immigrants in, 9–10, 10n15
  industrialization of, 68–73, 107
    coffee planters' role in, 71–72
    immigrants' role in, 72
    importers' role in, 71
  internal income from agriculture, 114–115
  internal migration to, 30, 226–227, 326, 327n130
  labor movement in, 76–77
  population growth in, 28, 227, 228–229

Index 437

railroads in, 11–13, 70
reaction to interventor system, 87n12
universities in, 99–100, 223–224
urbanization of, 227, 228–229
wage workers in, 70
São Paulo industrial federation (FIESP; *Federação das Indústrias do Estado de São Paulo*), 100
Sarney, José, 247n1
  assumes presidency, 247
  runs for vice presidency, 246–247
Sarney period
  agricultural research, 264–265
  agriculture, 260–262
  Cruzado Plan, 217, 256–257
  environmental movement, 248–253
  inflation and economy, 255–259
  legal structure, 253–254
  party structure, 254–255
  return to democracy, 247
Scalon, Maria Celi, 221n115
Scarpa, Nicholas, 72n139
science
  agricultural research, 203, 205–206, 205n102, 264–265
  in military period, 223–224
  in Vargas second period, 157–158
Second National Development Plan (II PND), 201–202
second oil crisis, 1976, 251
Securities and Exchange Commission (CVM), 196n90
SENAC (*Serviço Nacional de Aprendizagem Comercial*), 100–101
SENAI (*Serviço Nacional de Aprendizagem Industrial*), 100–101
Serra, José, 289
service sector
  military period, 220
  Rio de Janeiro, 115
  Vargas first period, 114–115
Serviço Nacional de Aprendizagem Comercial (SENAC), 100–101
Serviço Nacional de Aprendizagem Industrial (SENAI), 100–101
Serviço Nacional de Informações (SNI; National Information Service), 185
sharecropping, 10–11
Silva, Marina, 250
Silva, Sérgio, 45n98
Simca, 169

Simonsen, Mario Henrique, 212
Simonsen, Roberto, 100
Sistema Único de Saúde (SUS; Unified Health System), 338–339
Skidmore, Thomas, 181n70
slavery, abolition of, 9, 18–19
slaves
  African, 1–2
  Indian, 1–2
  minor children of, 19n34
smallpox vaccination, 104
SNCR (National Rural Credit), 203–204
SNI (*Serviço Nacional de Informações*; National Information Service), 185
Social Democratic Party (*Partido Social Democrático*; PSD), 145, 151n19, 184
social fluidity. *See* mobility
Social Progressive Party (PSP), 151n19
social security, 236, 243
soybeans, 172, 206, 264
Special Secretariat of the Environment (*Secretaria Especial de Meio Ambiente*; SEMA), 249
Stabilization Fiscal Plan, 284–285
steel industry, 98n45, 99
  privatization of, 281
Steel Railway, 202
Stein, Stanley J., 37–38, 37n83, 63n123
stock market speculation, 37
submarine warfare, 78n150
suffrage, female, 32n64
sugar as alternative fuel, 251, 252
sugar industry
  central mill system, 52–53
  decline in international market, 2
  exports, 116
  government interference under Sarney administration, 262
  in military period, 205, 207
  on Old Republic, 51–53
  plantation economy, 1–2
  usinas (sugar factories), 53
Superintendency of Money and Credit (*Superintendência da Moeda e do Crédito*; SUMOC), 96, 96n38
  Instruction 70 of, 154n29, 163–164
Superior War College (*Escola Superior de Guerra*; ESG), 185–186
Suzigan, William, 62–63, 74–75
syphilis, 239–240

438 Index

Target Plan (*Plano de Metas*), 152–153, 158, 159, 160
  agriculture, 161
  automotive industry, 161, 163
  construction of Brasilia, 163
  energy, 160
  financing of, 163–164, 166–168
  new administrative structures, 168–169
  technical personnel, 161
  transport system, 160–161
tariff protection, 74, 96–97, 164
Taubaté Convention, 44, 45
technical personnel, 161
technical schools, 224
technology, 52n103
  and agriculture, 59–60, 152, 204, 226, 245, 263
  in military period, 223–224
technology fund, 223
telecommunications sector
  and price controls, 197
  privatization of, 274, 281, 282n47, 282–283
tenentismo movement, 83n1, 84, 88
terrorism, 190–191, 190n82
Testament Letter, 157n35
textile industry, 37–38, 37n83, 65
  average employment per company, 110, 169–170
  capitalization of, 63n123
  exports, 115
  foreign vs. domestic owned companies, 110
  imports, 65n126, 66
  numbers of workers, 110–112
theory of adverse shocks, 62n120
Theory of Dependence, 273, 273n40
tobacco, 59, 66, 116, 170
Tocantins, 327
Topik, Steven, 44n96, 48–49, 48n101
torture, 183–184, 187–188, 190, 248
trabalhista party, 145
trade
  balance, 38, 147, 200–201, 214, 255, 256–257, 258–259, 280
  deficit, 38, 200–201, 256–257, 277, 280
  liberalization, 276–277
  surplus, 213–215, 217, 256–257, 258–259, 278, 303
trading companies, 264
transport system
  federal road system increase, 161n48

  in Kubitschek period, 160–161
  mule transport, 12
  National Road Fund, 166n55, 243, 335
  in Old Republic, 60–61
  railroads. *See* railroads
Treasury Cashier, 167
Triennial Plan, 182
tuberculosis, 239–240
two-tier exchange rate, 148

UDN (*União Democrática Nacional*; National Democratic Union), 144–145, 151n19, 156–157, 184
unemployment insurance, 194, 334–335
UNICAMP, 223–224
unicidade sindical policy (monopoly of labor union by territorial unit), 102, 102n53
Unified Health System (*Sistema Único de Saúde*; SUS), 338–339
union tax, 102, 102n53, 102n55
United States
  Eisenhower administration, 155
  exports to Brazil, 147
  military regime relationship with, 183
  Mixed Brazil–United States Commission, 152–153
  Quadros relationship with, 180
Universidade de São Paulo (University of São Paulo), 99–100, 223
universities
  in Brasília, 223
  in colonial era, 26–27
  and color differences, 350
  gender difference in attendance, 310, 312n87
  Lula, 310
  in military interregnum, 223–224
  in Minas Gerais state, 223
  in Old Republic, 27
  in postmilitary period, 224
  in Vargas first period, 99–100
  See also education
University of São Paulo (*Universidade de São Paulo*), 99–100, 223
University Reform law (1968), 223
UN Security Council, Brazil seeks permanent seat on, 149n13
urbanization
  in military interregnum, 219
  in Old Republic, 27–29

in Rio de Janeiro, 227, 228–229
in São Paulo, 227, 228–229
in twenty-first century, 353
in Vargas first period, 127–128
Uruguay, 277, 339n162
Usiminas steel mill (in Minas Gerais), 164–165
usinas (sugar factories), 53
U.S. Steel, 99
usury law, 166, 193

vaccination campaigns, 22–24, 104, 317
Vale do Rio Doce Company, 98, 281–282
valorization (price support scheme for coffee), 42–44, 47
Vargas, Getúlio
  election of, 85
  suicide of, 156–157
Vargas, Getúlio, first period
  agriculture, 112–125
  authoritarianism, 86, 87–88
  coffee policy, 89–92
  currency depreciation, 93
  economic growth, 139–141
  education, 99–101
  exports, 92n23, 125–126
  GDP, 93–94
  government control over foreign exchange markets, 92–93
  health policy, 104–105
  immigration, 126–128
  industrialization, 88, 106–112, 125
  industrialization, five-year plan, 98n43
  internal markets, 113n74
  interventor system, 87, 87n12
  labor relations, 101–102
  power base, 114n78
  power structure, 86–87
  race differences in residence, 134–136
  repression, 88
  service-sector growth, 114–115
  social policy, 99–106, 141
  social welfare institutions, 102–104
  structural reform, 94–99
  urbanization, 127–128
Vargas, Getúlio, second period
  army, role of, 151
  economic issues, 151–155, 157
  education, 157–158
  labor relations, 155–156

political crisis, 156–157
science, 157–158
Vemag Brazil (DKW), 169
Venezuela, entry into Mercosul, 277n45
Versiani, Flávio Rabelo, 65n125
Versiani, Maria Tereza R.O., 65n125
Vianna, Sérgio Besserman, 154n28
Volkswagen, 169
voting
  female suffrage, 32n64
  minimum age, 254
  rights for illiterates, 80, 181–182, 182n71

wage, minimum, 102, 156, 197, 304, 306, 333–334, 336
wage labor, transition to, 6–7, 8–9, 10, 17–18, 61, 80
wage squeeze policy, 192, 194–197, 217, 218, 255, 256
Washington Consensus, 270–271
wealth, decrease of regional disparities in, 353
Weffort, Francisco, 86
welfare reform, during Cardoso administration, 274n43
West Paulista
  coffee production in, 10–11
  geographical extent of, 8n9
  remuneration for colonos in, 10–11
wheat, 59, 121, 161, 175, 205, 207, 262
Willys Overland, 169
wood exports, 174
Workers' Party (*Partido dos Trabalhadores*; PT)
  creation of, 190
  and environmental protection, 252–253
  opposition to new constitution, 253n17
  and reform, 252–253, 254, 274, 274n42
  scandals, 297
workmen's compensation, 334–335
World Bank, 250–251, 262, 265
World War II
  effect on Brazilian economy, 125–126, 141
  export market, 99n46

yellow fever epidemic, 104
yerba mate, 116

zona de mata, 7

Printed in Great Britain
by Amazon